Stamps of
British North America

STAMPS OF BRITISH NORTH AMERICA

Fred Jarrett

QUARTERMAN PUBLICATIONS, INC.
Lawrence, Massachusetts

This Quarterman edition is a reproduction of the original edition published in Toronto in 1929 entitled *B.N.A. Book: "Stamps of British North America"* with advertising deleted. A new foreword has been added.

International Standard Book Number: 0–88000–052–X
Library of Congress Catalog Card Number: 74–82308

Printed in the United States of America.

Quarterman Publications, Inc.
5 South Union Street
Lawrence, Massachusetts 01843

HIGHEST AWARD

3rd Canadian Philatelic Exhibition. Montreal, 1925
International Philatelic Exhibition, New York, 1926

Fred Jarrett receiving the Order of Canada

FOREWORD

Fred Jarrett's magnus opus *Stamps of British North America* was originally published in 1929 and represented the most comprehensive work published on Canadian philately at that time.

Incorporating the best of his prior works on the subject, the book represented the result of his enormous philatelic output which began in 1904—the year he first started collecting stamps. Mr. Jarrett first began to gather notes for his books in 1924. His particular emphasis on cancellations, almost totally ignored previously, is one aspect which gives the work its enduring value.

Original editions of the work are difficult to come by and now command prices at auction as high as 25 times the original list price, although remaining unsold copies of the original edition were sold for a low price following Mr. Jarrett's retirement from professional philately soon after its publication.

Mr. Jarrett was an expert speed typist as a teenager and later traveled throughout the world, including the Far East, as a representative for Underwood typewriters. Later, he served as special secretary to Sir Edward Kemp, Minister of Canadian Overseas Military Forces during World War I.

Mr. Jarrett has lectured extensively in Canada and the United States, speaking on both the collecting and the professional aspects of philately—his repertoire of philatelic legend and fact seems inexhaustible.

Now in his 86th year, Fred Jarrett is the oldest living signatory of the "Roll of Distinguished Philatelists," an honor headed by King George V in 1921. He is an Honorary Fellow of the Canadian Philatelic Society of Great Britain and the Royal Philatelic Society of Canada.

Mr. Jarrett was among 66 Canadians named last year to receive the Order of Canada. This represents the first time this award was granted for significant achievement in philately.

In addition to the reproduction of the picture of Mr. Jarrett contained in the original volume, this edition adds a photograph showing Mr. Jarrett receiving the Order of Canada from His Excellency the Right Honorable Jules Leger, C.C., Governor General of Canada at Government House, Ottawa, in April 1974.

I know that this generation of students of Canadian philately will find this republication as useful and informative as it was when it was first published.

Toronto
February 1975

Vincent G. Greene
FRPSL

INDEX TO CONTENTS

A

B

C

I

J

K

L

M

Q

R

S

T

U

V

W

Y

ADDENDA

No.	Type	
		Georgian Coils, CANADA, Feb., 1928. Perf. 8 Vert.
19	A62	1c.
20		2c.

Dates of Issue, Georgian Type A62, A63, Etc.

1c. Oct. 29, 1928.
2c. Oct. 17, 1928.
3c. Dec. 12, 1928.
5c. Dec. 12, 1928.
8c. Dec. 21, 1928.
10c. Dec. 5, 1928.
12c. Jan. 8, 1928.
20c. Jan. 8, 1928.
50c. Jan. 8, 1928.
$1 Jan. 8, 1928

Postage Due, Type A120.

4c. July 3, 1928.
10c. July 3, 1928.

Airmail

5c. Sept. 21, 1928.

Fred Jarrett (1929)

PREFACE

In these pages an attempt has been made to give in concise form the information required by serious collectors of the stamps of British North America.

Where possible credit has been given for information gleaned from writings by other authors. It is unfortunate that due credit cannot be given for much of the data now commonly used by writers on British North America, and which must have been secured in the first instance at considerable expenditure of time and intelligent effort.

An earlier preface gave the names of all who had contributed to the store of information in this book, but as the work progressed the list of those who had rendered genuine co-operation grew until it became almost an index of B.N.A. philatelists throughout the world. To all of you I hereby express sincere appreciation.

Values have been given for all items of philatelic interest. These values are dictated by the operation of the law of supply and demand. Important pieces have been valued in accordance with prices obtained when last sold. All values are based on "good average condition" and discounts should not be applied unless the item in question fails to qualify for that standard. Stamps that may be correctly described as "fine" or "very fine" are worth as much as double catalogue. Stamps that are "thinned," "'slightly torn," "badly centered" or "heavily cancelled" are worth much less than catalogue. A stamp that is obviously damaged has no value in relation to catalogue prices.

Indulgence is asked for any inaccuracies and omissions, which are unavoidable in the earlier editions of a work which attempts to cover a field so large, and of which no one philatelist can ever hope to acquire a full knowledge.

THE AUTHOR.

SANDRINGHAM, NORFOLK.

11th January, 1927.

Dear Sir,

I have laid before the King the copy of your book entitled "Stamps of British North America", which you were good enough to forward with your letter to Lord Stamfordham of December 22nd.

I am desired to convey to you the sincere thanks of the King for this interesting addition to his philatelic library, which His Majesty is graciously pleased to accept.

Yours truly,

A H L [illegible]

F. Jarrett Esq.,
135 Victoria Street,
Toronto.

EARLY POSTAL HISTORY.

In 1755 a monthly packet service was inaugurated between Falmouth in Cornwall, and Boston. A post office was established in Halifax and a small vessel carried the mails between Boston and Halifax. Older Canada, it will be noted, was still a French possession, remaining so until the Battle of the Plains of Abraham, in September, 1759, from which date all of Canada became virtually a British colony, although three years elapsed before the country was assured by treaty to Great Britain.

Steps were then taken to connect the new British colony with its sister colonies by a postal service. Benjamin Franklin, who had been deputy to the Postmaster-General in England for some years, set out for America, and in August, 1763, six months after the treaty of peace in Paris, he had opened the post offices of Quebec, Trois Rivieres and Montreal, appointed a postmaster in charge of the Canadian post offices, and established a monthly service between Montreal and New York. The latter port was in regular communication with Europe by a packet service.

It is interesting to note that the establishment of civil government in Canada did not take place until a year after the establishment of the Government Post Office.

It was not until after the American Revolution that an attempt was made to bridge the gap between Canada and Nova Scotia and New Brunswick. Prior to the revolution a letter from Quebec could follow the route by way of New York and Boston to Halifax, but the independence of the United States made it necessary for mail to be carried over British territory between these widely separated points. In the summer a vessel could carry mail from Quebc down the river and gulf to one of the Maritime ports, from whence it could be carried overland to Halifax by favor of the next traveller making the trip. But in winter there was no alternative for a journey of 627 miles overland by foot, dog team, canoe or sailing vessel as the season dictated.

In 1784 at the instigation of Deputy Postmaster-General Finlay, a French-Canadian named Durand made a trial trip, leaving Quebec January 11th and reaching Halifax six weeks later. The hardships of this journey were what might be expected, but the return trip exceeded them in heart-breaking experiences. The ice had broken up in the St. John River and the Temiscouata Portage (36 miles of precipitous hill and low swamp) was well-nigh impassable. He arrived in Quebec on April 24th—102 days for his return trip. The cost was $764 and the revenue collected was not more than $300.

When in 1788—four years later—the British Post Office inaugurated a packet boat service carrying mail from a British port to Halifax, it was necessary to follow the route pioneered by Durand, and a regular service was established between Quebec and Halifax to connect with the packet. Post offices were opened along the line of the Annapolis valley; in New Brunswick between St. John and Fredericton; and in Lower Canada, on the shores of the St. Lawrence. This line of communication was continued by stage coach until 1876, when the Intercolonial Railway connected Quebec with Halifax.

In the spring and summer of 1784 the United Empire Loyalists settled in Upper Canada, principally in and about Kingston and the Bay of Quinte. Between them and the nearest French settlements lay many miles of trackless forest. For the first five years communication with the outside world depended upon flat-bottomed boats plying more or less regularly between Kingston and Lachine, outside of Montreal. The King's ships served the settlements as far west as Niagara. When navigation closed communication was closed—unless a settler driven by necessity and never by choice, undertook the terrible journey through the virgin forest to Montreal, carrying with him the letters of his neighbors and returning with such letters as he found addressed to them in the Montreal post office. They and their friends abroad remained in complete ignorance of the fate of one another until navigation opened in the following spring.

These conditions could not last long. In 1787 the settlers petitioned the Governor-General for a post road to be opened as far west as Kingston, with post offices along the route. Two years later offices were opened at Lachine, Kingston, and nine intermediate points, including Cornwall and Brockville. A courier was employed to make one trip a year from Montreal to Niagara. Leaving Montreal in January and travelling an average of 18 miles a day, the return trip took three months. This arrangement continued with some slight increases in frequency until 1810, by which time a fortnightly service had been established between Montreal and Kingston and (for the winter months) between Kingston and York.

For the territory along the shores of Lake Ontario between York (Toronto) and the U.S. border, this service was of little use. Settlement in Northern New York had developed rapidly and a fairly frequent mail service was carried on as far west as Buffalo. Settlers in Toronto and west, principally in the Niagara Peninsula, took full advantage of this service. A post office had existed on the Canadian side of the Niagara frontier since 1789, and another at Queenstown, a few miles farther down the river, since 1803. These offices exchanged mails with the U.S. offices on the other side of the river, and practically all correspondence between this part of Canada and Great Britain was carried on through these offices.

As for the Western Provinces of Manitoba, Saskatchewan and Alberta, the Hudson's Bay Company conveyed letters, by courtesy, on their annual trips (brigades) made to the different forts scattered over that great territory.

In 1853 the establishment of a post office at Fort Ripley, Minnesota, by the U.S. Post Office Department, led the settlers at Fort Garry (now Winnipeg) to open an office and to exchange mails monthly. Four years later the U.S. extended their service to Pembina, North Dakota, on the border of the Hudson's Bay Territory, and Fort Garry had the advantage of a shortened route, as well as avoiding the Hudson's Bay Company censorship of mail carried by their couriers and brigades.

The postmaster at Fort Garry having no Canadian postage stamps, made a cash charge to cover postage to Pembina and sold U.S. stamps to prepay the rate from Pembina to destination. Later, stamps were available and the 7½d green is known with the Pembina cancellation—heavy letters 5 mm. high, with single circle.

Prior to the building of the Canadian Pacific Railway (which carried the first trans-continental mail on June 18, 1885, from Montreal to Port Moody) the Royal Canadian North-West Mounted Police took their mail to Bismarck, Dakota, and other mail was sent to Fargo, going thence around to Detroit and into Canada. What might be called "Pony Express" was used in the Canadian West, but it was not an organized service, there were no stamps, and there is no record of any stipulated scale of rates.

The Canadian Government as early as 1858 made an attempt to connect the Western settlements with the Eastern by means of a service entirely through British territory—being apprehensive as to the effect of the intimate relationships naturally developing through the Canadian West being so dependent on the rapidly developing Western United States—and accordingly mails were carried from Collingwood, on the Georgian Bay, to Fort William by steamer and thence to the Red River, connecting with Fort Garry by canoe. In winter the mails were carried by dog sleigh along the north shore of Lake Huron and Lake Superior. Owing to the difficulties of this route and the inferiority of the service the attempt was abandoned after two years.

When in 1870 Manitoba was incorporated as a Province of the Dominion of Canada, the Dominion Government legalized the arrangement with the U.S. for the exchange of mails. The building of a railroad from Pembina to Winnipeg in 1878 enabled mails to go all the way by rail. In 1884 the C.P.R. was completed, establishing an all-Canada service between Manitoba and the Eastern Provinces.

A study of the chapter on British Columbia mail services will show the absolute dependence of that colony or province upon the United States postal service. The extension of the C.P.R. to the Pacific coast gave British Columbia a line of communication with Eastern Canada and Great Britain, through Canadian territory.

Post Offices in Canada.

Year.	Offices.	Letters.	Year.	Offices.	Letters.
1791	11		1856	1,395	7,000,000
1796	12		1857	1,506	8,500,000
1800	26		1858	1,566	9,000,000
1827	101	340,000	1859	1,658	8,500,000
1831	151		1860	1,698	9,000,000
1838	380	1,000,000	1868	3,638	
1848	539	2,000,000	1878	5,378	
1851	601	2,132,000	1888	7,671	
1852	840	3,700,000	1898	9,282	
1853	1,016	4,250,000	1903	10,150	
1854	1,166	5,100,000	1908	11,823	
1855	1,293	6,000,000	1910	12,887	

A SUGGESTED PLAN FOR THE SYSTEMATIC STUDY OF THE VARIOUS STAMPS OF THE PROVINCES AND THE DOMINION OF CANADA

(Adapted from Plan Prepared by Franklyn Meine.)

1. **Information About the Stamp.**
   a. Description of design.
   b. Occasion for issue.
   c. Relation to postal rates.
   d. Date of issue.
   e. Statistics of issue.
   f. Outline of chief types.

2. **Proofs and Essays.**
   a. **Essays.**
      i. Paper.
      ii. Color.
   b. **Die.**
      i. Paper.
      ii. Color.
   c. **Plate.**
      i. Paper.
      ii. Color.

3. **The Normal Stamp.**
   a. **Unused.**
      i. Gum or adhesive.

   b. **Used.**
      i. Covers.
      ii. Bisects.
      iii. Combinations.
      iv. Cancellations—Unique, Special, Boat, Railway, Way, Paid.
      v. Year date.
      vi. Town.
      vii. Colored.
      viii. Pen.

4. **Shade Varieties.**
   a. Normal.
   b. Varieties.
      i. Dates of issue.
   c. Color error.

5. **Perforation.**
   a. Normal. Gauge?
   b. Double, triple.
   c. Perfs. include portion of adjoining stamp.
      i. Horizontal.
      ii. Vertical.
   d. Imperforate.
      i. Two sides.
      ii. One side—natural straight edge.
   e. Center line (or arrow) perf.
   f. Perforations missing.
   g. Discs of paper not punched out.

6. **Watermark.**
   a. **Official Watermark.**
      i. Design.
      ii. Direction, horiz. or vert.
      iii. Measurements.
   b. Stitch watermark.

7. **Paper.**
   a. Normal.
   b. Variations according to fibres in making.
      i. Wood.
      ii. Rag.
      iii. Straw.
      iv. India.
      v. Pelure.

c. Variations according to texture.
   i. Wove.
   ii. Laid—horiz. or vert., close or wide.
   iii. Thick or thin.
   iv. Hard or soft.
   v. Smooth or rough.
d. Color.
e. Ribbed.
   i. Direction, horiz. or vert.
   ii. Nature of ribbing.
f. Shrinkage—variations in size of design.

8. **Printing or Impression Varieties.**
   a. Printing or offset on both sides.
   b. Double printing.
   c. Worn plate.
   d. Moisture of paper.
      i. Dry print.
      ii. Wet print.
   e. Creased paper.
   f. Wiping of plate.
      i. Too little—smudgy impression.
      ii. Unevenly—streaky impression.
   g. Color film over stamp (first prints).
   h. Ink.
      i. Spots and foreign substances.
      ii. Smears.

9. **Plate Varieties.**
   a. Sheet margins.
   b. Spacing and alignment.
   c. Center lines or arrows.
   d. Imprints and plate numbers.
   e. Guide dots and guide lines.
   f. Transfer roll relief varieties.
   g. Short transfers.
   h. Shifted transfers.
   i. Cracked plate.
   j. Plate damages other than cracks—scratches and marks.
   k. Recutting.
      i. Normal, but unusual.
      ii. Errors.
   l. Plate reconstruction—specific plate positions.

10. **Reprints, etc.**
   a. Reprints.
   b. Reissues.
   c. Special printings.
   d. Surcharges.

11. **Counterfeits and Fakes.**
   a. Counterfeits.
   b. Fakes.
      i. Cancellations.
      ii. Perforations.
      iii. Covers.

Stamps as an Investment.

I cannot do better than reprint portions of an article by Chas. J. Phillips, in which he gives sound advice to philatelists who collect with the investment side of the hobby in mind.

"Those of us who take philately seriously and who invest considerably, according to our means, cannot afford to ignore the finanical side of the question, and should have the best possible guide as to their investments.

"Avoid poor condition. This is the chief point of all in forming a collection from an investment point of view. If you collect used stamps, see that they are lightly cancelled. In most countries it is of great importance to obtain dated postmarks to show when particular colors, perforations, watermarks, etc., came into use, and as an investment a specialized collection is much improved by a judicious selection of such stamps.

"Do not be tempted to buy a scarce stamp in poor condition because it is offered to you at a half, third or quarter catalogue. As an investment it pays far better to buy the superb copy at even double catalogue price than the poor one at half catalogue. In unused stamps I consider that well-centred stamps are of more importance than original gum.

"Purchase from reliable firms. This is *most* important. Buy from men who have studied stamps, and who have a good reputation, and then you won't find yourself loaded up with reprints, fakes and mended stamps. You will have to pay a little more, but you won't find your collection full of rubbish when you sell.

"For investment purposes I advise the formation of specialized collections of well defined groups of stamps of one or more countries.

"At this moment I know of two leading American collectors, both of whom have half a million dollars invested in their stamps. They have both bought so judiciously that I should be very glad to purchase either collection at 25% over what it has cost its owner, and quite possibly I could pay much more on a careful valuation.

"I doubt if any of their other investments would show anything like so great an advance in value in the same period. Many collectors that I knew in Great Britain kept a strict account of what they spent on their collections and I quote a few examples, which I know to be authentic and for which I can vouch. I have taken the exchange at $4.60=£.

"Mr. W. Hughes Hughes started his collection in 1859, spent $318.00 on it and sold it in 1896 to Stanley Gibbons, Ltd., for $13,800.00.

"Mr. Theo. Pauwels made a collection, which up to 1871 cost him $1,656.00. He sold this in 1898 to Stanley Gibbons, Ltd., for $18,400.00.

"Mr. M. P. Castle, about 1890 commenced a collection of Australian stamps upon which he told me he spent $25,300.00. In 1904 he sold this to Stanley Gibbons, Ltd., for $46,000.00. After this Mr. Castle turned his attention to forming a magnificent collection of the whole of Europe. Upon this he estimated he spent $75,900.00, and twelve years after he commenced it he sold it, through Mr. G. Hamilton Smith, now the head of Stanley Gibbons, Ltd., to Mr. W. W. Mann, for $127,700.00.

"Mr. F. W. Hunter, a well-known American collector, kept a careful account of the money he spent on his collection which amounted to about $7,360.00. Some years after he sold his stamps at auction through the Scott Stamp and Coin Co., and they realized $25,300.00, a remarkable return on the original investment."

GENERAL NOTES.

Burland:

The Burland Litho. Co. became the British American Bank Note Co. Limited (G. B. Burland, Manager), and printed the "small cents" issue, from 1870.

Examination:

The author does not examine stamps or give opinions except in the case of stamps or covers of considerable value, when such opinion will be photographically identified with the stamp or cover (if genuine) to prevent fraudulent use. The charge is $5.00.

Stamps in Wrong Color.

A stamp that is listed as green sometimes turns up in a blue color. Collectors and dealers offer many plausible explanations when the 1c green King George or the 5c green Registered appear in blue. Such stamps are *not* the result of a printing from a press previously inked for other values of the set which are normally blue. Green is a combination of blue and yellow. Spirits of Salts will dissolve the yellow, leaving the blue. Other chemicals will dissolve the blue, turning a green stamp into a yellow one. Such stamps are valueless except as curiosities.

Single Imperforates:

In cases where stamps printed from the same plate have been issued in perforated and imperforate condition, it is rarely possible to guarantee the genuineness of a single imperforate. In the "small cents" issue of Canada the perforating was so varied that copies of nearly all values may be found with sufficiently wide margins to permit of the perforations being trimmed and the trimmed stamp even then being wide and long enough to cover an ordinary perforated specimen. The author has given the values for imperforates on the basis of pairs and not singles.

Minor Varieties:

There is a commendable tendency on the part of collectors of moderate means to follow the example of wealthier collectors who are able to specialize in and study the earlier and more expensive stamps. Students of later issues must keep the following facts in mind:

1. In the Pence issue but one or two plates were used for each value, and minor varieties may be traced to a specific stamp in the plate. In succeeding issues the number of plates increased, until to-day it is difficult to determine whether a minor variety discovered in one of the current stamps is an accidental flaw existing but one time on one sheet, or the result of a defect in the plate, in which case it would occur in the same stamp in every sheet printed from that plate, and the great number of plates used makes it impossible to definitely trace the variety to any particular plate.

2. The varieties discovered for the Pence and 1859 issues were nearly all true plate varieties and therefore constant, later issues produce many varieties which are the result of careless press work, defects in the paper, dirty plates, etc., and such varieties have no constancy.

3. Stamp printing processes have changed much since the early issues. Notes on minor varieties which apply to the different values in the earlier issues might have no application to stamps of later issues.

Reprints:

Printings from the original plates after the stamp has become obsolete, usually varying in shade of color or variety or paper. (Example: Reprints of the 3s 6d and 1s New Brunswick.)

Centering:

To be in a perfect state the design should have an equal margin within the perforations on all sides.

Reversed Covers:

A term applied to covers or envelopes turned inside out and re-addressed. These are of considerable interest to collectors and have a value beyond the limitations of "catalogue."

Straight Edge:

If the perforations have been cut off the top or side of a stamp it is designated as a "straight edge." When stamps are printed in sheets and afterwards cut into panes, or post office sheets, the stamps on two sides of each pane will of necessity have straight edges. These are called "natural straight edges." In modern Canadian issues 19% of all stamps issued in post office sheets of 100 are "natural straight edges."

Oxidized:

An oxidized stamp is one in which the natural color has turned to a darker shade, as orange changed to brown-orange or brown, vermilion to brown, etc. An immersion in peroxide will usually restore the natural color. After the peroxide bath the stamp should be given a thorough soaking in clear water.

Unauthorized Bisecteds or Provisionals:

Almost any "made to order" cover can be sent through the mail (although we warn philatelists of impending trouble with the P.O. Department if too much zeal is shown), but such items are in no way official and should be bought, if at all, as curiosities.

Original Covers:

Covers are useful in placing beyond argument the dates of use of stamps, in preserving completely the interesting postal markings, in recording postal rates, in fixing the authenticity of bisected and imperforate stamps, and in many other ways. They are the true philatelic minute book of history, for they set down the life of a stamp, from the first day of issue to the last. Every legitimately used stamp has at some time or other been on a cover, wrapper, card or tag, and generally most of the interesting postmark and cancellation falls on the cover. Philatelists need the cover to tell the whole story.

Early issues on cover have already reached high levels. Many common stamps off cover are extremely rare on cover.

The term "original cover" is usually applied to stamps on the envelope, but the word "cover" originates from the use of a sheet of paper folded to contain the letter, in the days when envelopes were not known. The letter and "cover" were usually one and the same, the paper being a double sheet and the writing being folded on the inside. One fold was tucked within the other and the "flap" sealed with a "wafer"—a thin manufactured seal of wax. The term "cover" also includes envelopes.

Envelopes:

The dictionary meaning permits its use in reference to any covering for a letter or message. Machine made coverings in the form which we now know them were unknown until after 1840. S. K. Brewer, a bookseller, of Brighton, England, is credited with the inventive genius which resulted in a cover or envelope being made up ready for an enclosure. The gummed flap improvement made its appearance about 1841. In Canada, previous to 1843, the postal rates were such than the use of an envelope doubled the rate. In 1843 a system of reckoning the charge entirely by weight, on the unit basis of ¼ oz., made the use of envelopes optional. Their use did not become at all general until about 1850.

"Stitch Watermark."

Stitch Watermark.

This occurs where the paper, during manufacture, passed over a portion of the canvas which had been stitched together, the stitches leaving a watermark in the paper. This watermark may be found in the stamps of the Pence, 1859, 1868 and 1870 issues.

Obsolete.

Stamps that are no longer on sale at a post office owing to the fact that they have been superseded by a new issue are said to be obsolete. Many obsolete stamps are available for postage long after they have ceased to be in issue.

Demonetised:

Old issues are often the result of legislation which deprives them of franking power. No Canadian postal issues have been demonetised, and the collector may still mail a letter to his sweetheart franked with a 3c 1868 laid paper catalogued at $15.00. Canadian bill stamps, however, have been demonetised, making it possible to buy a complete sheet, face value $50.00, for as little as $5.00.

Rouletting:

Differing from perforating, when the perforations take small circular cuts out of the paper, rouletting cuts the paper without removing any, the cutting taking the form of:

a. Arc. The cuts are curved. Also termed serrated.
b. Straight. Small sectional cuts end to end, as in Newfoundland 1876-79 issue.
c. Perce en scié. Parallel slanting cuts.

Perforation Gauge:

The spacing of the perforation holes.

Plate Numbers:

Numbers inserted in the margin of plates from which stamps are printed, indicating the order in which the plates for those particular values were made.

Postal Fiscals:

Fiscal or revenue stamps used as postage stamps. The 3rd issue

Bill Stamps (Canada) were occasionally used as postage stamps, either by intention or accident. The 1914 "War Tax" stamps issued for the Inland Revenue Department were used postally.

Offset:
An impression from the face of a moist sheet of stamps found on the back of another sheet that has been laid on the former.

Removing Spots from Stamps:
Candle grease may be removed with blotting paper and hot iron. Chocolate may be removed with borax and cold water. Cold water also removes cream spots. Use boiling water for spots from fruit, tea or coffee. Milk or lemon juice and salt will remove ink spots. Salt and lemon juice removes iron rust. Paint may often be removed with a treatment of turpentine or benzine.

Repaired Stamps:
Collectors should be on guard against mended specimens, some of which have margins added so skilfully that only the most careful examination reveals them.

Original Gum (O.G.):
The gum applied to the stamp when manufactured.

Overprint:
An inscription printed on the face of a stamp which alters the usage of the stamp but not its value. (Example: "War Tax Inland Revenue.")

Surcharge:
The printing on the face of a stamp to give it a new value. (Example: "Two Cents" on 3c Maple Leaf.)

First Day Covers:
The collecting of first day covers is a new branch of philately that has many followers. These covers are the records which settle definitely the dates of introduction of different stamps.

Re-entry:
A re-entry is a constant plate variety showing portions of the design doubled or even trebled, one over the other. It occurs in the same position on every sheet printed from the plate on which the re-entry occurs. It is usually the result of the steel transfer roller being impressed more than once in approximately the same position on the plate from which the stamps are printed.

A second type of re-entry resulted when a faulty portion of the plate was removed by hammering the plate from the back and burnishing the faulty impression off the surface (usually with charcoal) before rocking or rolling in the design in the correct position. In this process it sometimes happened that traces of the original impressions remained and were, of course, reproduced in the printing.

Re-entries may be caused by the slipping of the plate under pressure of the transfer roll when the separate designs are being rocked or rolled into the steel. These may also be correctly called "*shifts.*"

When a line or portion of the design does not print clearly, a "*retouch*" is made on the plate, by cutting the lines of the design deeper at that point.

Guide Dots, Guide Lines:

In the Monthly Report of the Herts Philatelic Society, May, 1910, Mr. Dunbar Heath, of Messrs. Perkins, Bacon & Co., explained the various guide dots and guide lines which have been the object of so much study on the part of philatelists. He states: "The stamps must for purposes of correct perforation be laid down at equal distances apart, some transferers using faint lines for making the spaces on the blank plates, others using dots. Stamp manufacturers sometimes find it advisable to wear large sleeves; they find them useful for laughing into when they see serious argument on the appearance of an unfortunate dot between certain stamps which does not appear between others, and it is sought by the appearance of a dot or line to tell whether a stamp was engravel by the American Bank Note Company or ourselves.

All such birthmarks, as I may call them, are simply evidence of haste, or pressure of work. In every case, the rubbing down or cutting away of the displaced metal, and of the space marks, dots or lines, or whatever they may be, is a more tedious job than the mere rolling in of the stamps, and is what may be called "donkey work," performed by some junior. Theoretically, every mark or trace of a mark between the stamps that might print should be removed before the plate is hardened; but what wonder is it that in the hurry of business "that'll do" is responsible for many dots or dashes being left in that should be absent.

This is the plain explanation of all manner of variations and defects, both with stamps themselves and in the margins—simple pressure of business and urgency preventing sufficient time being given to a tedious and annoying operation. I believe philatelists would readily forgive our operators even if they erred on the side of more variations and dots; but this is not the view of the manufacturer, who aims at a plate without blemish, every T crossed in the same way, every i with the same sized dot, and not a mark to be discovered by the most powerful microscope between each stamp."

U.S. 1847 Stamps Used in Canada.

Previous to the appearance of Canada's first adhesive, Canadian postmasters collected the charges in cash and stamped the letters "PAID" in black, or in red if the amount was to be collected at destination.

Adhesive stamps for the prepayment of postage made their appearance in the United States about four years before the first Canadian stamps. The Act of March 3, 1845, established U.S. rates of postage as follows: "For every single letters . . . . conveyed in the mail, for any distance under three hundred miles, five cents; and for any distance over 300 miles, ten cents; and for a double letter there shall be charged double these rates; and for a treble letter, treble these rates; and for a quadruple letter, quadruple these rates; and for every letter or parcel not exceeding half an ounce in weight shall be deemed a single letter, and every additional weight of half an ounce, shall be charged with an additional single postage. . . . "

Two 5c 1847 stamps or one 10c 1847 stamp will therefore be found on single letters carried over 300 miles and on double letters carried under 300 miles. Since it is over 300 miles from New York city to the Canadian border, Canadian letters to or from New York carried or were charged with 10c in U.S. postage. Letters originating nearer the border would be carried for 5c if the distance to the border via the usual mail route to destination was less than 300 miles.

Letters from Toronto to New York, or Montreal to New York, would require 10c in postage to prepay the rate from the border to New York, in addition to whatever postage was required to prepay the letter from the Canadian city to the border.

Canada, by virtue of an Act of the British Parliament passed 28th July, 1849, assumed control of her own postal affairs and on August 10th, 1850, passed "The Post Office Act." An agreement was drawn up between the Post Office Departments of Canada and the United States regulating the interchange of mails between the two countries, and this was signed on 25th March, 1851, to be passed on to the Canadian postmasters by Order No. 1, dated 2nd Apr., 1851, issued from the Post Office Department, Toronto, relative to letters between Canada and the United States.

Sections 1 and 2 of this order, quoted elsewhere, fix the rate for ordinary letters from Canada to the United States at 6d currency, and from the United States to Canada at 10c, equal to 6d currency. Section 4 states that these rates include "the whole charge." The Lichtenstein collection contains several covers showing "the whole charge" prepaid from cities in Canada to New York by the affixing of the current 10c 1847 U.S. stamp. These cities include Quebec, Montreal, Toronto, and St. John, N.B., the latter dated April 8, 1851.

Section 6 of a notice to postmasters issued from the General Post Office, Montreal, 14th March, 1851 (20 days earlier than the Toronto Order No. 1) states "Letters to and from the United States will be liable to the uniform rate of 3d per half-ounce, between the frontier line and the place of posting or place of destination in Canada; and until further arrangements can be made, this charge on letters from Canada to the United States must be prepaid at the time of posting."

The notice dated 2nd April, 1851, stated that the "whole charge" for ordinary letters to the United States was 6d. Prior to that date, according to the earlier notice, the rate for ordinary letters was 3d "between the frontier line and the place of posting or place of destination in Canada."

This indicates some arrangement in effect prior to 2nd April, 1851, whereby postmasters had to take cognizance of a division of the rate on account of the border between the two countries, part of the charge being for carriage to the border and the other part for carriage to destination beyond the border.

To obviate any delays or difficulties it would follow naturally that important offices on either side of the border would obtain a supply of stamps of the other country, but whether or not these were supplied officially cannot be said.

In the Lichtenstein collection there are two covers, one dated Sept. 23, 1851, from Quebec to a destination in the U.S., and the other from Montreal to New York, dated June, 1851, each bearing a 3d Beaver stamp of Canada and a 5c 1847 of the U.S. Clearly, then, the 3d Beaver prepaid the postage "between the place of posting and the frontier line" and the 5c 1847 prepaid the postage "between the frontier line and destination."

(See notes following.)

As the section partially quoted referred to mail "to and from" it would be expected that letters *from* the United States might be similarly prepaid to the border with United States postage and beyond the border to destination in Canada with Canadian postage, that is, of course, after Canadian stamps were available. The author's collection contains a cover from Boston to Toronto dated Boston, May 27th, Toronto, May 28th, 1852, bearing a 3c U.S. 1851 and a Canada 3d Beaver. The U.S. stamp is cancelled with the black Boston PAID and the 3d Beaver with the Canadian concentric ring cancellation.

An Act of Congress in March, 1851, set the rate for such a letter to Canada at 10c. This letter should have been prepaid with U.S. stamps to this amount. The 3c stamp affixed, however, is in accordance with the U.S. domestic rate of that date. This cover affords an illustration of the continuance of a practice not necessary at the date the letter was sent, i.e., prepaying the domestic rate with U.S. postage and prepaying from border to destination with Canadian postage.

The U.S. postmaster cancelled the U.S. stamp but did not cancel the Canadian stamp. It was in order that this letter should go to the border as a result of the 3c prepaid—the charge from the border to destination was something for the Canadian Post Office to decide, and the fact that the Canadian stamp was cancelled by a Canadian cancellation and the letter marked with "10" in black in and "6d" in black circle indicates that the two stamps were accepted as prepaying the full rate.

A cover, prepaid from Portland, Me., to Montreal, with a pair of 3d Beavers, was sold in April, 1826, by B. L. Drew, Boston. This cover was examined by the author and is undoubtedly genuine. While there was no authorization for using the Beaver stamps to prepay the full rate from the U.S. to a destination in Canada, the necessity may have arisen through the supply of U.S. stamps in the U.S. post office in Portland having been temporarily exhausted, when the P.M. might have collected 5c in cash for the rate to the border and affixed a single 3d Beaver to prepay the rate from the border to the Canadian destination, as in the case of the illustrated cover from Boston. However, the P.M. did not do this, but affixed a pair of 3d Beavers, and these prepaid the rate from office of origin to destination, affording a very rare example of the use of Canadian stamps in the U.S.

These two letters of June and September, 1851, and the third letter of May, 1852, would be in accordance with the regulations outlined in the notice issued April, 1851.

Similar procedure was followed prior to the date of the above notice, but Canada had no stamps previous to April 6th, 1851. Ordinary letters from Canada to the U.S. were usually marked "Canada Paid 10 Cents," but, once again referring to the Lichtenstein collection, we find covers from Canada to the United States as early as March 20th, 1848, the rate being prepaid in full by United States stamps. The following covers were prepaid in this way:

1. Prepaid with the 10c U.S. 1847 Toronto to New York Mar. 20, 1848.

2. Prepaid with pair 5c U.S. 1847 Montreal to New York via "Steam Boat" Lake Champlain.

3. Prepaid with 10c U.S. 1847 Montreal to New York, Feb. 3, 1851.

In the case of the fourth and fifth covers, which each bear a single 5c U.S. 1847, the rate was doubtless paid in cash from point of mailing to border, while the U.S. stamp prepaid the rate from border to destination.

4. Prepaid with 5c U.S. 1847 Montreal to New York, Dec. 14, 1849.

5. Prepaid with 5c U.S. 1847 Montreal to New York, July, 1850.

(In Sept., 1928, Eugene Telfer, of Detroit, added to his collection two covers addressed to Kennedy, Wall street, New York, one from Montreal April 5, 1850, prepaid with a pair of U.S. 5c 1847, and the other from Montreal Feb. 24, 1849, prepaid with a U.S. 10c 1847. Both covers had "4½" written in red ink on the envelope.)

With this substantial evidence we know that a definite working arrangement existed between the P.O. Departments of the two countries whereby Canada prepaid her letters to the United States with United States stamps.

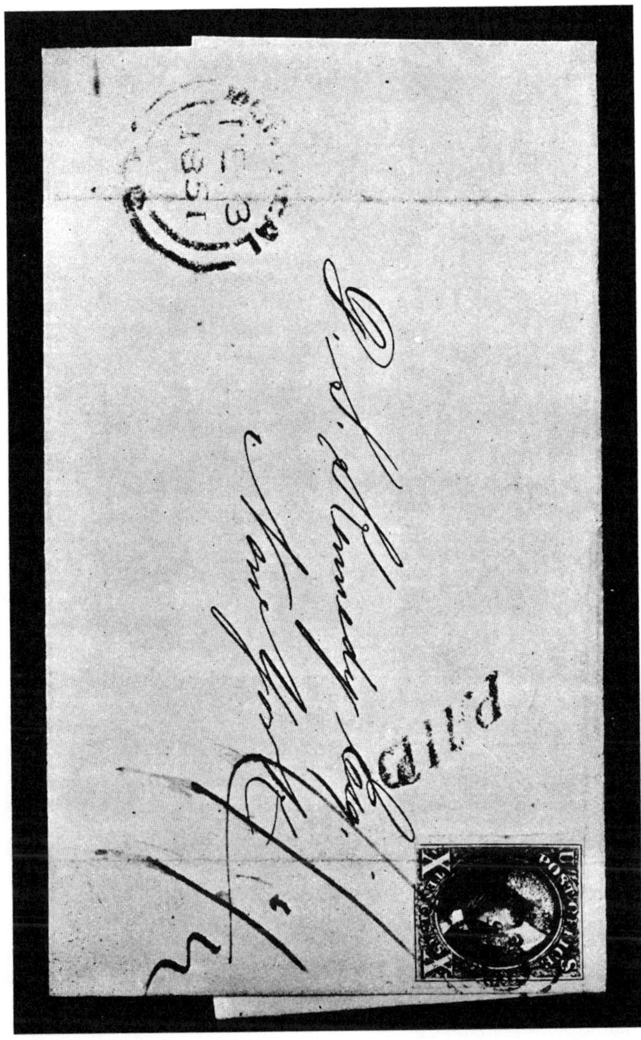

Referring to the No. 1 cover, we find inscribed in the lower left corner, "Paid to the Lines No. 20," and initialed with letters which might be "J.R." This indicates the existence of an understanding between the P.O. Departments of the two countries, relative to the assessment of rates on either side of the border, of which the postmasters concerned had been advised.

This "No. 20" refers to the individual to whom any deficiency in the rate was to be charged back. I have noted the following covers marked in this way:

From Oswego, N.Y., to Whitby, U.C., dated Feb. 11, 1850, with notation "Paid 243."

From Montreal to New York, dated Apr. 10, 1853, prepaid with a 6d Canada, with the notation in ink in upper left corner "Deficiency if any to be charged to B.H.L. 225." (The letter discloses the identity of B.H.L. as B. H. LeMoine.)

From Ingersoll to New York, dated May 23, 1856, with "Paid 6d" in red and the notation "Paid 51 W. D. & Co." (Wm. Dunn & Co.) in three lines.

It was the custom of the postmaster to keep an account for all those making frequent use of the post, in which he charged all deficiencies. From an examination of many covers I believe these charges were kept against the box number of the person or firm. This "charge account" system seems to have continued until after 1860.

DEPARTMENT ORDER NO. 1

Letters, Etc., Between Canada and the United States, Including California and Oregon.

Post Office Department,
Toronto, 2nd April, 1851.

Commencing on and from the 6th instant, Letters, Newspapers, etc., will pass through the mails between Canada and the United States, including California and Oregon, at the Rates of Postage and under the Regulations herein mentioned.

1. Letters posted at any office in Canada, addressed to any place in the United States, except California and Oregon, are to be rated with a uniform rate of six-pence, currency, per half-ounce.

2. Letters posted in any part of the United States, except California and Oregon, addressed to Canada, will be rated there with a uniform charge of ten cents, equal to sixpence, currency, per half ounce.

3. The Postage Rate on Letters passing between Canada and California and Oregon, will be a uniform charge of ninepence, currency, equal to fifteen cents per half ounce.

4. It is to be understood that the above rates include the whole charge for the transmission of a letter between any place in Canada and any place within the United States, including California and Oregon.

5. The scale for computing the charge upon letters weighing more than half ounce, will be the same as that for letters passing within the Province.

6. Pre-payment of letters passing between Canada and any place within the United States, including California and Oregon, will, in all cases, be optional.

7. Newspapers, Pamphlets, etc., posted in Canada, addressed to the United States, including California and Oregon, are . . . . to be forwarded through the post at the same rates of charge as if addressed to a place within the Province; the said rates must, however, be prepaid—as, if the ordinary Canada Rate is not paid at the time of posting

a Newspaper or Pamphlet, etc., it cannot be forwarded to the United States.

8. United States Newspapers, Pamphlets, etc., addressed to places in Canada, will be received in the Province with the American Postage thereon pre-paid—leaving the ordinary Canada Rate of charge from the Frontier Line to the place of destination, to be . . . . ; collected by the Postmaster who may deliver the same in Canada.

9-10-11. (Copies of newspapers or printed documents sent by or to publishers or editors are free of Canadian postage.)

12. The Canada Postage Stamps, when used, will be taken in the United States as evidence of pre-payment of Postage on Letters going from Canada to the United States, and in like manner the United States Postage Stamps on Letters coming into Canada, are to be taken by Postmasters in this Province as evidence of pre-payment having been made in the United States.

13. (Names of Offices in Canada through which Post communication with the United States was to be maintained and to which Postmasters were to forward mail for the United States, according to relative position of the offices.)

NOTE: The rates of postage on periodicals and other printed matter were not given in the above order, but were fully set out in Order No. 3 of 17th April, 1851.

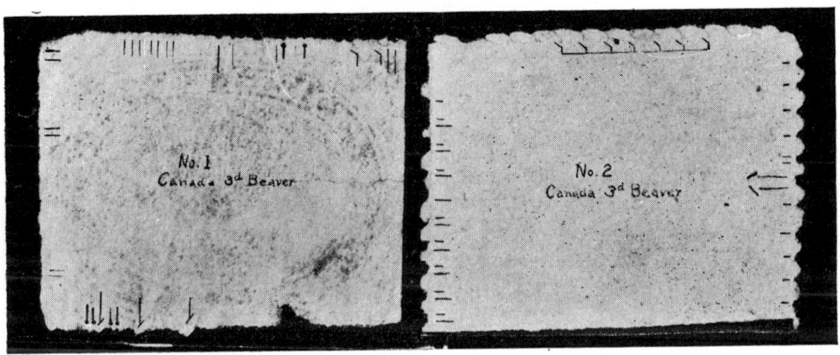

TRIAL PERFORATIONS.

The Postmaster-General, in his report for the year 1855, stated: "The Department has been led by the increasing us of postage stamps to take measures for obtaining the Canadian Postage Stamps in sheets perforated in the dividing line in the manner adopted in England, to facilitate the separation of a single stamp from the others on a sheet when required for use."

According to the records of the British American Bank Note Co., which took over the firm of Messrs. Rawdon, Wright, Hatch & Edson, makers of the first Canadian stamps, that firm never made use of any but a standard gauge 11¾ perforating machine, first used on the ½d, 3d and 6d in January, 1859.

The "measures for obtaining stamps in sheets perforated in the dividing line" must therefore have been taken locally by the P.M.G., who doubtless supplied some firm, or firms, with one or more imperforate sheets on which to experiment. As these were equivalent to cash, the number handed out would be few, and these would all be handed back to the authorities regardless of the success or failure which may have attended any effort to discover a means of perforating them. The dates of the experiments must have been as late as 1857, since the "Perce en Scie" specimen in the Tapling collection is of the brown shade issued in that year.

A considerable revenue would be derived from the Post Office Department for doing this work should a successful method of perforating the stamps be discovered. Serious efforts were doubtless made to satisfy the demands of the P.M.G. It is certain that the firm responsible for the trial perforations of the Pence issue made use of every device and expedient at their command. "These trial perforations," states Chas. J. Phillips, "are of very great interest, and I think are just as worthy of being worked out as the rouletted and serrated of Australian stamps."

It has always been understood that only the 3d stamp was experimented on, but it is now possible to examine an undoubted specimen of a 6d. It will be remembered, also, that the famous Ferrary collection contained a perforated 10d, supposed to be fraudulent, but which may also have been the result of official experiment.

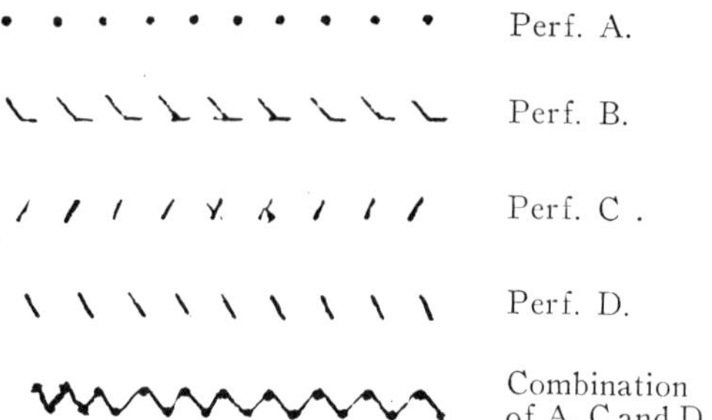

In examining stamp No. 1 it will be noted that the left side, top, and bottom show small pieces punched out of the paper, leaving holes, designated herein as "A" type. These holes do not appear in a straight horizontal line but they are regular as to spacing between.

In stamp No. 2, left and right, we find similar holes, appearing at the base of larger perforations. It would appear that these were not punched in pairs but are the result of two punchings, the second spaced slightly to one side of the first.

On all sides of stamp No. 3 (the 6d) we find holes similar to those found in stamps 1 and 2, as to size, spacing, and pairing. We are therefore on sure ground when we indicate one type of trial as Type A (Double size, as shown).

Stamp No. 1 was punched with this type three times in an effort to get the holes sufficiently close to cause the stamps to separate easily. The series of punched holes could not have been done at one stroke by setting the punching teeth close together, as in several instances one punching overlaps into another.

In stamp No. 2 we see the result of other trials. In addition to the small holes we note a consistent cut sloping to the right, with a turn at its base, apparently at an angle and not curved, as Type B (Double size, as shown.)

If we refer back to stamp No. 1 we find at the top right two cuts which correspond in spacing and angle with those in No. 2. These two stamps correspond in respect to both Types A and B.

Two sides of stamp No. 2 were severed in such a way as to leave "teeth." An examination of the cuts forming the sides of these teeth shows that they are not uniform as to spacing or as to the angle at which they are cut. The cuts to the right and the cuts to the left may or may not have been made at one operation. They appear as Type C (Double size, as shown.)

Where the Type C cuts converge, i.e., at the depth of the perforation, they run into Type A holes in pairs. Such an arrangement of oblique cuts running into one line of holes would make it possible to separate stamps so as to leave teeth, but if only one line of these holes was punched it will be seen that while the stamp illustrated shows holes at the depth of the perforations the stamp separated from this one would show evidence of these holes at the points of the perforations and not at the depths. To better understand this, look upon the black background as forming the teeth which fit into the perforations in the stamp illustrated.

It would appear that the perforation used on the right side of stamp No. 2 was a combination of Type A and Type C.

Also, the angle and spacing of the cuts on the left side of stamp No. 2 seem to correspond with the Type B cuttings on the top of the same stamp, and these cuts also run into holes of the A Type.

In stamp No. 3 one of the first details to be noted is that the point of one tooth does show a hole, indicating that this stamp was severed from another which had been perforated as described in the preceding paragraph. This hole is larger than Type A, and a similar hole may be noted at the upper right corner. The holes correspond in spacing with those in stamps 1 and 2. The above evidence would indicate stamp 3 as having been perforated and cut as in Type D (Double size, as shown).

The sheet from which stamp No. 3 was separated must, according to the foregoing, have been operated on not less than seven times. It will be seen that this method of perforating the stamps would not proceed past the experimental stage. As this sheet represented a value of fifty shillings, it would be returned whether successfully perforated or not, and there would be no reason for not placing the stamps on sale along with the regular imperforates. In fact this would be done in order to ascertain the opinion of the stamp using public as to the usefulness of sheets so treated.

Stamp No. 3, the 6d, presents a perforation puzzle that the fore-

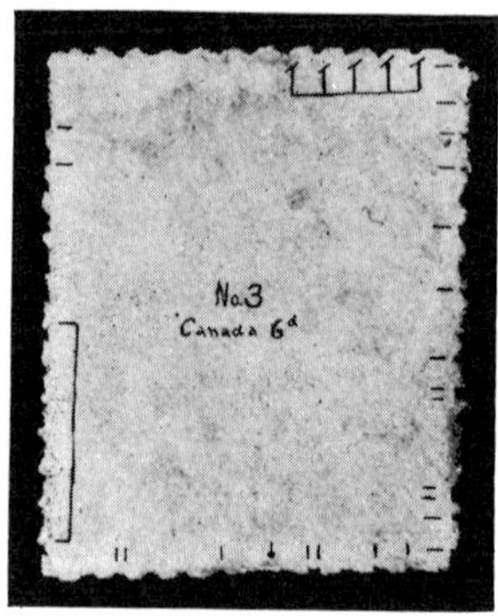

going deductions only partially solve. It not only shows unmistakable examples of A, B, C and D trials, but interesting combinations of all of these. It is undoubtedly the result of many operations in an effort to deliver stamps to the P.M.G. which would be perforated in the dividing line in such a manner as to facilitate separation.

NOTES ON THE PENCE ISSUE.

"Block of 6 cancelled "14" Goderich, U.C. In Reford collection."

½d Imperf.:

The shades vary from pale rose to a deep rose. The wove paper varies in thickness. There is an extremely thin ribbed paper.

The stamp prepaid postage on newspapers in Canada, which accounts for the comparative rarity considering the quantity issued, many having been destroyed with the papers. It was also used to make up odd rates, such as 4½d, and in strips to make up rates of 3d or 6d.

Imprint:

The stamps were printed in sheets of 120, 10 rows of 12. The imprint is in small Diamond type (See 3d Notes) occurring eight times on each sheet, reading up on the left, down on the right and upside down on bottom margin. The imprints are centered over the 3rd and 10th stamps on the top and under the 3rd and 10th stamps at the bottom. The side imprints are centered opposite stamps No. 25 and No. 85 on the left, and 36 and 96 on the right.

Re-entries and Other Varieties.

(As located by Proof Sheet in Mrs. A. R. Clarke's Collection, Toronto.)

Plate Position

4 Position dot in wide upper margin at center. "York" of imprint shows at top.

7 Position dot outside left frame line center.

11 Two heavy position dots above "A" and "P" of CANADA POSTAGE in upper margin.

12 Short entry. Bottom left outer frame lines missing or faint at corner.

18 Bottom frame line double thickness. Spot of color at top and between AL of HALF extends into oval.

22 Fine line runs parallel to inside bottom frame line; dot in N of ONE at bottom right; letters ADA POST show traces of doubling.

23 Short entry, top; heavy position dot in panel between "ONE" and "CANADA" very pronounced.

26 Doubling of "PE" and doubling of left frame line at bottom; other letters show doubling and there is a stroke of color above the last "A" of CANADA.

42 Frame line doubled at bottom left; two dots in "D" of CANADA; dot in "P" and other letters.

46 Inner frame line doubled at top left.

52 One fine parallel and one short oblique line under frame line at bottom under "HAL".

58 Letters CANA and P show signs of doubling; there are two dots at left side of "P" and dot in "EN" and stroke of color at top right of "Y" of "PENNY".

60 A fine line runs through bottom portion of letters HALF. Guide dot in panel between ONE and CANADA is very pronounced.

61 The bottom frame line is missing.

70 Single re-entry at bottom left and correspondingly inside frame line at top left and right.

72 Double re-entry at lower right and re-entry shows in all letters, particularly in lower left corner where frame lines are doubled. Correspondingly the frame lines show doubling at top and top left.

84 Left frame line at bottom doubled. Letters CANDA OSTG and PENNY show traces of doubling. Inner frame line at left extends as a fine line down to next stamp. Portion of imprint at bottom right.

93 A line through "P" of POSTAGE sloping up to the right.

96 Faint doubling of frame line at bottom left. Inner frame line extends as fine line into next stamp at top left. Imprint at right.

102 Frame line doubled at top, and bottom left. Traces of doubling in "P" of POSTAGE and "ALF." Inside frame line at top extends to left and crosses outer frame line. Below bottom frame line there is a flourish of horizontal lines to right, to left, to right, Z fashion.

111 There is a smudge of color extending through the left seriph of second "A" of CANADA, ending in a heavy dot inside the frame line of the background for the head. A smudge also shows slightly in the top right side of "D" of CANADA.

117 Stamp shows beginning of imprint at bottom. The top frame line is doubled for almost its entire length.

118 Stamp shows center portion of imprint at bottom. The top frame line is doubled for almost its entire length.

No. 120 Re-entry.

120 Double re-entry, showing at top and bottom, left, and doubling in nearly all letters.

---

a. A short diagonal line extends outward from middle of right frame line.

b. A line caused by a scratch on the plate runs horizontally but slightly sloping to upper right, cutting between letters "CA" of CANADA.

c. A flaw occurs near the inside circle at top, on left, becoming a faint smudge in the "D" of CANADA, and continuing through the seriph of lower part of A.

d. Plate flaw. A distinct flaw or line under the bottom frame line below letters "H" and "E" of HALF PENNY.

e. A line sloping to the right, almost horizontal, passes through "P" of PENNY.

Forgeries:
A lithographed forgery exists which is not dangerous, and there is an engraved forgery which need not deceive any but the most careless.

Rarities:
The Ayer collection contained a mint strip of three on ribbed paper. The Reford collection contains many choice blocks, including the one illustrated. In the author's collection there is a cover prepaid with a horizontal strip of six, including a major re-entry.

½d Perforated:
The notes on the Imperforate stamp also apply to the Perforated stamp. A lilac-rose shade might also be listed.

(Reford Collection.)

3d Beaver:
The 3d was designed by Sir Sanford Fleming, then a civil engineer and draughtsman. His original design, as described in the chapter on Essays, was not altered materially in the finished stamp.

A beaver skin was a standard of trade in the earlier days of the Hudson's Bay Co., and the coins later issued by this Company bore a beaver as an emblem of value. The beaver was later officially used along with the maple leaf in the coat-of-arms of Canada.

The 3d prepaid postage on inland letters and to Nova Scotia, New Brunswick, Cape Breton and Prince Edward Island.

The first printings are generally listed as "red" and are found on laid, wove and thin oily wove papers. Orange-vermilion may be noted in the case of the laid paper printings. On the harder wove paper the shade is brown-red and runs almost to a brown. There is a distinct rose-red shade on the thin wove.

The re-entries which come from the two plates are found on all papers, since both plates were in use throughout the entire period of issue.

Counterfeits, etc.:

There is an engraved counterfeit. The color is not correct, the paper is unlike any of the papers used for the different printings of the genuine, being a thick yellowish wove, and the design is lacking in definition. Doubtless other attempts have been made to counterfeit this popular stamp, but we have yet to see one that has been in the least successful.

The ribbed paper has been imitated by using a proof on India paper, on which finely ribbed lines are lightly embossed before mounting on similarly treated paper to give the proof the thickness of the genuine ribbed paper stamp of issue. The soft flexibility of the genuine is lacking.

Plates:

These consisted of ten horizontal rows of ten impressions. The different plate varieties identified with the two plates are found on all papers used from the beginning to the end of the issue. Both plates were therefore in use concurrently. The author believes a third plate was in use, made from "A" and "B" reliefs on the transfer roll, the first and second plate being made from the "A" relief.

Rawdon.Wright.Hatch & Edson, New-York.

Imprint (enlarged).

Imprint:

The imprint is in Diamond type upper and lower case letters, reading "Rawdon, Wright, Hatch & Edson, New-York." Length 28 mm.

The imprint occurs eight times on each sheet, reading up on the left, down on the right and upside down on the bottom. It is centered on the 3rd and 8th stamps in the vertical and horizontal rows, the beginning and ending of the imprint appearing on the 2nd and 4th, and 7th and 9th stamps in the vertical and horizontal rows. Imprint specimens are Nos. 2-3-4, 7-8-9, 11-21-31, 20-30-40, 61-71-81, 70-80-90, 92-93-94, and 97-98-99.

There is no imprint on the laid paper of 1851 and the thin paper of 1852. The red brown shade on medium wove paper, which we have identified as early as December, 1852, is found with and without imprint. It is probable, therefore, that the imprint was added to the plate, or plates, in December, 1852.

Papers:

Eight distinct varieties of paper may be listed. Paper men do not recognize "ribbed" paper, but it is nevertheless a distinct variety and easily identified. The paper described by some as "hard ribbed" is not distinctive enough to warrant listing.

There is a second variety of laid paper, thicker and whiter. One variety of paper used in the early printings corresponds in texture and appearance to the proper laid, but laid lines are not seen. Laid paper has been noted which shows the laid lines as wavy instead of straight, a fine example being a pair in the collection of Mr. J. O. Labrecque, Montreal.

This might be accepted as due to uneven shrinkage of the paper, but it is more easily explained by a bending of the wires which put the laid lines in the paper during manufacture. An accidental blow or the falling on them of a heavy tool would easily bend them out of shape and when bent back into position again they would still be far from straight, resulting in a crooked or "wavy" series of laid lines.

The thin soft ribbed is brittle and difficult to obtain in good condition. Even the thicker ribbed paper must be handled carefully to avoid damaging it.

Papers:
- A. Laid.
- B. Thin, almost pelure, laid lines not apparent.
- C. Medium white wove.
- D. Thin yellowish oily surface.
- E. Medium thick hard wove.
- F. Thin soft ribbed, very fragile.
- G. Ribbed, varying in thickness.
- H. Thick, hairy, rough.

Bisected:

The 3d is known bisected diagonally and used with two entire 3d stamps to make up the 7½d Packet Rate to Great Britain. (Lichtenstein Collection, cover from Montreal to England, July, 1856.)

Combinations:

A cover in the Lichtenstein Collection shows the 3d used with a 5c Beaver to make up the 10c rate from Montreal to New York, dated July 31, 1859.

Rarities:

Used block of 8. Reford Collection.
Mint strip of 5. "A" and "B" Reliefs. (Jarrett.)
Used strip of 6. James H. Hoffman, Mammondsport, N.Y.
Mint strip of 7. Nos. 94 to 100 Pl. ?. British Museum.

The above block of eight 3d Beavers (Reford Collection) illustrates the lack of uniformity in rocking the separate impressions on the plate. The upper right stamp is in a higher position than the upper left, although the lower right stamp is even lower than its neighbor to the left.

The skilled artisans who were employed to do work of this character usually took considerable pride in the execution of it. Some day

we may know the name of the man who made the 3d plates, when there will attach to his memory the stigma of carelessness, when in truth he may have been as scrupulously careful as any of his fellows in the trade, for the plate may have shifted its position under the pressure of the transfer roll, requiring a new adjustment each time.

3d Perf. 11¾x11¾:

The paper used for the Perforated 3d is listed as "medium hard wove," but its texture seems to differ somewhat from other wove papers, resulting in an impression that is distinctive from other printings. Copies in fine clean condition have a distinctive lustre not found in printings on the other wove papers. The earliest date known to the author is October, 1858, from Galt, U.C. The plate varieties common to the other 3d stamps may be found on the Perforated 3d.

Trial Perforations of the 3d:

The 3d Perf. 14 was probably the result of one of the last trials made locally by the P.M.G. In any event the British American Bank Note Co., which took over the firm of Rawdon, Wright, Hatch & Edson, claim they never used any but a standard gauge 11¾ machine, and it is quite possible that no gauge 14 machine was ever in the possession of the original firm. Had such a machine been in use, the Bank Note Co. would have had a record of it and would doubtless have made use of it.

The trial perforations described below are on a different paper to that used for the Perf. 11¾, and might be identified as belonging to the period referred to in the P.M.G.'s report for 1855.

1. Percé en scie—a series of parallel slanting cuts.
2. Percé en arc—cuts assume the form of an arc.
3. Close irregular pin hole perforations.

THE "CRACKED TRANSFER."

A variety often referred to as the "Cracked Plate" is really the result of a crack in the transfer roll, and since the transfer roll, Relief "A," had two such faults or cracks in the metal, it is necessary to differentiate between them. I have therefore designated one as the main variety, and the other as the minor.

When a transfer with a crack in any portion of its surface is impressed on a plate, the soft metal of the plate is forced into the crack. A crack or minute crevasse on the transfer becomes a raised line of metal on the plate. A crack may go deeper into the metal of the transfer roll than the other depressions, resulting in a line on the plate that is slightly higher than the normal surface of the plate. This fact has a definite bearing on the main cracked transfer variety, and explains the smudgy appearance of the line. Unless one studies this line carefully one is liable to fall into the error of thinking it is a "line of color" caused by a depressed line in the plate, instead of a "smudge" caused from a raised line, or ridge.

In the process of inking a plate for printing, the ink is rubbed into the depressions and off of the normal surface of the plate. Lines of color in the printed stamp represent depressions in the plate; colorless spaces or lines represent the normal surface of the plate, or any portion raised above the normal surface.

Proof impressions of the main cracked transfer variety, examined with a strong glass, disclose minute smears of ink extending irregularly away from one side of the line. Had the plate been cracked of course the ink would have been rubbed evenly into the crack and the result would have been a clearly defined constant black line, but what actually happened was this,—the irregular line or ridge caught and held some of the ink against its side and was rubbed off unevenly over the top, forming the smears.

In other words, on account of this obstruction it was impossible to wipe the plate properly, because it was not a normal surface until the imperfection had been burnished off with charcoal and oil, as was done later.

The minor "cracked transfer variety" consists of a line running from the outer white oval through the two right frame lines, to the right of "T" of POSTAGE. This is constant, but while discernible to philatelists who seek it with glasses, specifically, it might easily be overlooked on the transfer roll or plate.

PLATE I. VARIETIES.

Plate Position

2 There are two dots above the top frame line and over the "O" of POSTAGE. There is a line of color terminating in a dot or dash at bottom of "S" of POSTAGE. (The line of color under the "3" in the illustration is accidental and does not belong to the design.

No. 2, Pl. I.

12 There is a smudge in the "N" of CANADA.

33 There is a smudge in the "N" of CANADA and a line through the letters "PE" of PENCE and below in the oval.

34 The bottom figures "3" are shaded. There is doubling in the white space under "EE PENCE" and slight traces of doubling in "CAN" of CANADA.

41 There is a faint doubling of the upper frame lines above the crown at left and the left inner frame line extends to the outer at the top.

No. 47, Pl. I.

47 This is the main or major re-entry. A line through "EE PEN" is the best distinguishing feature, accompanied by lines of color under "EE PENCE." The bottom of figure "3" on lower left, lower right and top right is shaded. There are signs of re-entry above and below "POS," in and below "ANAD" and in and below "THR" of THREE, etc.

No. 56, Pl. I.

Plate
Position

56 There is a "pearl" in the center of the lower frame line, under "P" of PENCE.

62 There is a period between "THREE.PENCE," and a smudge in the "N" of CANADA.

63 There is a period between "THREE.PENCE."

64 Same as No. 63.

65 Same as No. 62.

71 Same as No. 63.

72 Same as No. 63.

No. 80, Pl. I.

80 The letters "EE PE" are blurred at top and the lower left numeral of value shows doubling. There are lines under "P" and "E" of PENCE. This is an imprint stamp.

88 The frame line is missing above the crown. The inner and outer frame lines at right are entirely missing. Variety due to imperfect "rocking in" from transfer roll.

91 The top left "3" shows doubling. There is a fine line of color on the right side of the stamp. The pearls on right and left of the crown are doubled. There are traces of color in all numerals of value. The last "A" of CANADA, "POST" of POSTAGE, and "REE PEN" of THREE PENCE show traces of re-entry.

PLATE II. VARIETIES.

Plate
Position

12 The frame line at bottom center is missing.

Plate
Position

13 A smudge of color shows above the "N" of CANADA extending across the oval line. There are doublings of the lower frame line, center and right.

15 There is a vertical curved line to right of crown running to frame.

19 The constant "cracked transfer line" at right shows as a fine line slanting down through the "OS" of POSTAGE and across the white space of the oval. This also shows clearly in Nos. 37 and 77 and faintly in most other impressions.

20 There is a short horizontal line of color across the lower portion of the upper right "3".

21 There is a line to upper left side of crown, extending through the oval line to the inner frame line at top.

22 The same as No. 21, but the line does not extend beyond the inner frame line and there is a dot under the first "E" of PENCE.

26 A line of color shows above the "N" of CANADA, extending across the oval line.

30 There is a period in the corner after the lower right "3".

31 There is a vertical scratch or line extending from the left top side of the crown through the frame lines.

32 The line to upper left side of crown as in No. 21, 22, and 31, is less pronounced and there is doubling in the frame line at left.

41 The line to upper left side of crown is as described for Nos. 21, 22 and 31, and the line through "R" of V.R. is very broad.

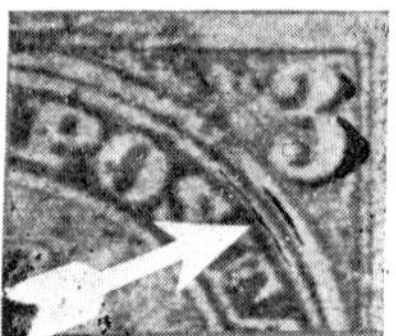

No. 42, Pl. II.

42 There is a doubling at lower left frame line and the shading of the upper right numeral "3" extends to frame line. The crack through "R" of V.R. is blurred above "R." There are doublings in the letters "STAG" of "POSTAGE" and in the oval under the upper right "3".

50 The same as in No. 26, 65 and 73. There is a period between "THREE.PENCE" and a diagonal stroke of color below the "P" of POSTAGE.

52 Variety as described for No. 21 (line at upper left side of crown) and doubling of horizontal line above the crown at left and right.

No. 53, Plate II.

Plate
Position

53 The frame line is doubled at upper left and top; there is a doubling of frame line above the crown; there is doubling in and under "STA" of POSTAGE; there are dots or lines in the "REE PENC" of THREE PENCE, "V.R." and inside of the lower ball of the left "3" there is a line of color.

No. 61, Pl. II. The left stamp of the strip (Reford Collection) is this variety.

61 The shading of the lower left "3" extends through frame line. There are lines and dots in the "E" of PENCE, lines under the "EE P" of THREE PENCE; lines in various other letters; hori-

Plate
Position

zontal lines doubled to left and right above crown, and faint re-entry showing under lower right "3".

65 Variety as described for No. 26, but the line has become a smudge. Doublings are found in nearly all the letters; lower left "3" is shaded to right; there are doublings in and under "THREE"; pearls are doubled at right top side of crown and there are two added lines at left of crown. There are lines above "P" and "O" of POSTAGE and strokes of color top and bottom in lower right "3".

66 An uneven application of the transfer shows in the lightness of the printed impression on the left side of the stamp. The proofs show a smudge between "NA" of CANADA which is barely distinguishable in the stamps, this defect in the plate having afterwards been rubbed out.

73 The line of color described in No. 26 becomes a smudge above the "N" of CANADA extending across the oval line.

75 A smudge shows above the "N" of CANADA extending across the oval line.

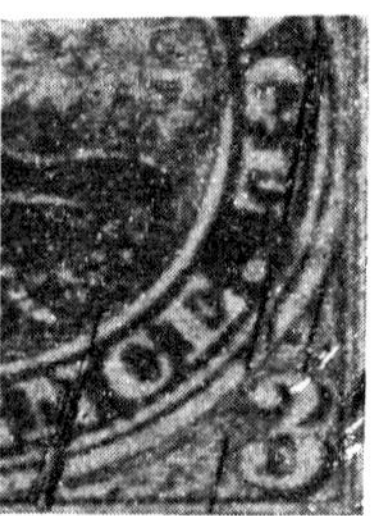

No. 31, Pl. ?.

Unidentified Varieties.

31 Two vertical parallel lines of color run through the "N" of PENCE and "GE" of POSTAGE, continuing to bottom frame line. A third line rests on the top of the "3." All stamps from this position on the plate will not show this variety, which is the result of damage to the plate after there had been printings from it. The proof sheets do not show the variety, first noted by Dr. Lewis Reford. A postmarked copy has been noted for June 22, 1857, and Col. Studd notes it on the late or thick papers. The author's copies are on the red-brown thick paper of January, 1857, the rose red of April, 1855, and the Indian red on oily surface of January, 1854, respectively.

a. There is a short line of color extending upwards from between the letters "HR" of THREE. This is imprint stamp No. 3 or No. 8, Plate ?.

b. Imprint stamp No. 14 or No. 19 shows a thick dot or line joining oval to spandrels at right of period after PENCE.

c. There is a white line under the first "E" of THREE.

Plate
Position

d. There is a horizontal line of color running from the last "E" of PENCE through outer right frame line.
e. The outer left frame line is entirely missing.
f. The imprint is doubled at top of stamp.
g. There is a stroke of color in the white space above "OS" of POSTAGE above the colored line of the oval.
h. The main "cracked die" variety shows clearly; there is a semi-circular crack beginning a downward curve in the trees just visible beyond the back of the beaver, running through the tail at the base, continuing through the rock ledge below the back of the beaver's left hind leg, just touching the foliage above the "N" of PENCE, intercepting the white inner oval above the vertical standard of the final "E" of PENCE; the minor cracked die variety is distinguishable, the line running from the outer white oval through the two right frame lines, to the right of "T" of POSTAGE. A considerable portion of the right half of the outer frame line is missing. There is a white spot between "E" and "P." There are traces of doubling in "AGE" of POSTAGE. The crown is smudgy and heavy and the lower right pearl is square in formation. The first upper right pearl is missing. (Hibbard.)
i. Scratch or flaw shows in "3" top right.
j. Scratch or flaw shows through "R" in THREE.

6d Imperforate:

The stamp shows the portrait of Albert, Prince Consort.

The printing was in sheets of 100, 10 rows of 10. The imprint is as described for the ½d, but does not exist on the thin and laid paper printings. If the author is correct in his deductions that the imprint was added to the 3d plates about December, 1852, then we may expect to find the 6d imprint about the same date.

The stamps were printed from one plate only, but a second plate was in existence which showed re-entries along the top row.

The stamp prepaid postage on letters to the United States, except California and Oregon, which required 3d additional.

The early printings on laid and thin wove are grey-violet or slate, and greenish grey. The variety "thick soft wove" is almost of the softness of blotting paper.

A sheet of proofs from the unused plate shows a doubling of the upper numerals and the letters "CANADA POSTAGE" on two stamps at the upper right corner of the plate. The guide dot noted outside and at the center of the left frame line is doubled.

6d Bisected Diagonally:

The 6d Imperforate bisected diagonally may be seen in the Lichtenstein Collection, which contains one cover from Quebec dated Jan. 10, 1859, and another April 26, 1858.

6d Perforated 11¾x11¾:

Dr. Reford fixes the date of the perforated 6d at September, 1858. The author has seen a cover which he considers genuine, prepaid with a 6d Perforated dated Montreal, July 31, 1858. (Kay Collection, Toronto.)

The high value of the stamp compared with the imperforate variety tempts counterfeiters to put perforations on the cheaper stamp. Sometimes these are brazenly referred to in auction catalogues as "privately perforated." If philatelists desire such stamps we would suggest that they do the "private perforating" themselves and save money. If in doubt about a perforated 6d, compare it with the 3d, with which it should correspond. The base of all the perforated holes in a line should rest upon any straight edge aligned with them. In the genuine there is no variation in the distance between the holes. Suspicion at once attaches to a perforated stamp which shows the ends of the teeth "squared" instead of with the rough ends which naturally result when perforated stamps are separated.

The 6d Perforated is a very rare stamp. The figures show it to be seven times as rare as the Imperf. 6d, but we know from experience that it is at least double as scarce as that.

Rarities:

6d Perforated bisected diagonally for 5c, dated May, 1859, from Toronto. First recorded by Mr. Dunbar Heath, or Messrs. Perkins, Bacon & Co., now in Lichtenstein Collection.

The Ayer Collection contained a mint pair on laid.

A specimen, fully described elsewhere in this volume, with trial perforations, was taken from a "stuck down" collection purchased in Toronto in 1888, remaining in the purchaser's possession until sold to the author in 1925.

7½d Green:

The stamp prepaid postage to Newfoundland, British West Indies (including packet rate of 4½d for sea conveyance between Halifax and Bermuda—the rate being 9d if carried by ordinary U.S. mails, British West Indies and Havana via New York.) It also prepaid book post up to ½ lb. to England. The sterling rate is also shown.

The guide dot may be noted in the frame opposite the lower left "6" of "6d Stg." There is a very slight variation in the width of the oval.

The paper, a medium hard wove, varies in thickness. Paper shrinkage accounts for a variation in the width of the oval. Of 32 copies examined, 19 measured 17½ mm. in diameter and 13 were 17 mm.

The 7½d was printed in sheets of 120. The supply received (100,080) is divisible by 120 (834 sheets) but not by 100. The imprint is in small diamond type as described for the ½d.

An engraved forgery exists which differs from the original in many details. A crude lithographic forgery also exists.

The re-entries are (1) a slight doubling in the lower right figure of value; (2) Doubling in the "X PENCE" of SIX PENCE, etc.; (3) the "K" of PACKET shows doubling, and lettering on left side shows traces of doubling; (4) there is a vertical stroke of color in "E" of POSTAGE. There is a variety showing a fine horizontal guide line across the center of the stamp.

Rarities:

The Ayer Collection contained two strips of three.

The Studd Collection contained a cover with a strip of three and a single 10d.

A superb used block of four, possibly unique, went into the Lichtenstein Collection in 1927.

10d BLUE

The 10d prepaid postage on overseas mail. Sterling equivalent of Canadian currency is shown.

The papers vary in thickness for both the white wove and the tough oily papers, and for both papers there is a light and a dark blue. There is no imprint. The stamps were printed in sheets of 120. An engraved forgery exists on wove paper and another on coarse yellowish wove. These are not dangerous.

The variation in the width of the oval was first discovered by the late Mr. W. H. Brouse, Toronto, who prepared a paper for the Royal Philatelic Society dealing with this interesting variety. The variation is due to shrinkage in the paper, which was moistened before the printing, and which contracted unevenly when drying. The narrow oval measures 17 mm. in diameter and the wide 18 mm. Mr. Chas. J. Phillips' stock of the 10d as of June, 1928, checked up as follows:

10d thin paper,	5 wide,	9 medium,	12 narrow.
10d medium paper,	8 wide,	2 medium,	0 narrow.
10d thick paper,	12 wide,	0 medium,	0 narrow.

This stamp shows a portrait of Jacques Cartier, from the original painting in the Hotel de Ville, St. Malo, Brittany, his birthplace.

"Cartier," writes Harry E. Huber, "was a French navigator, the discoverer of the Canadian River St. Lawrence. He was born in 1491. Of his early life nothing is known. On the suppression of the trade to Brazil, by Admiral Chabot, an expedition of two ships and sixty-one men was dispatched from St. Malo, under Cartier, in 1534, to look for a N.W. passage to the East. He sailed on the 20th April and reached Newfoundland on the 10th May, and at once entered the straits of Belle Isle, then known to the fishermen as the Bay of Castles. While the ships renewed their supply of wood and water at Belles Amours, on the north side of the straits, the long boats discovered that the coast farther west was barren, rocky and uninviting. In view of this Cartier set sail on the 15th June for the south side of the strait, by following which he was led down almost the whole west coast of Newfoundland. But he was disappointed in not finding a strait. During a ten-day stay in Gaspe Harbour, Cartier made friends with Huron Iroquois Indians from Quebec, two of whom he carried off with him. After more disappointments in not finding a strait, he set sail for France.

"Cartier set sail again from St. Malo in 1536 with three vessels, and anchored in August of that year in Pillage Bay, opposite Anticosti. The next day he named this bay the bay of St. Lawrence. September found him at the mouth of the Saguenay, which the two Indians, who had passed the winter in France, informed him was the name of a kingdom 'rich and wealthy in precious stone.' Again, on reaching the Island of Orleans, so named after the third son of Francis I., they told Cartier he was now in the kingdom of Canada, in reality the Huron Iroquois word for village. Leaving his two larger vessels in the St. Charles, which there enters the St. Lawrence, Cartier set off westwards with the bark and the long boats. The former grounded in Lake St. Peter, but in the latter he reached, on the 2nd of October, the Huron Iroquois village of Hochelaga on the site of the city of Montreal. Further progress was checked by the Lachine Rapids. From the top of Mount Royal, a name still in use, Cartier beheld the St. Lawrence and the Ottawa stretching away to the west. On his return to the St. Charles, where during the winter twenty-five men died of scurvy, Cartier sought further information about the rich country called Saguenay, which he was informed could be reached more easily by way of the Ottawa. In order to give Francis I. authentic information of this northern Mexico, Cartier seized the chief and eleven of the head men of the village and carried them off to France.

"Francis I. was unable to do anything further until the spring of 1541, when Cartier set sail with five vessels and took up his quarters at Cap Rouge, 9 miles above Quebec. A soldier, the seigneur de Roberval, had been chosen to lead the men to the conquest of Saguenay; but when he did not arrive, Cartier set sail for France. On reaching Newfoundland, Roberval met Cartier on his way back. In the summer of 1543 Cartier was sent out to bring home Roberval, whose attempt to make his way up the Ottawa to this mythical Saguenay had proved futile. From 1544 until his death at St. Malo in 1557, Cartier appears to have done little else than give technical advice in nautical matters and act as Portuguese interpreter."

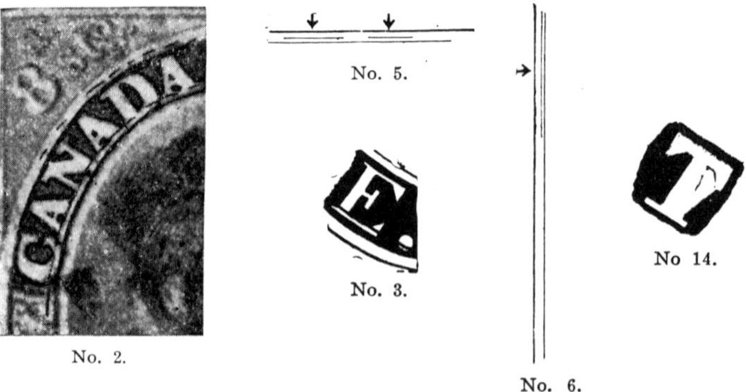

No. 2.

No. 5.

No. 3.

No. 14.

No. 6.

RE-ENTRIES AND OTHER PLATE VARIETIES.

1. Major re-entry. Most letters show doubling and there are lines in white space below letters at various points around the oval. No. 53 on plate.
2. Major re-entry. Lines through bottoms of letters CANADA, etc., and in oval, above letters.
3. Major re-entry. Letters "ANADA" and "NCE" are doubled at bottom as illustrated with letter "E" above. No. 6 on plate.
4. There is an extra line between the oval lines at left, lines appear in the letters "C" and "D" of CANADA and "GE" of POSTAGE. A line cuts the period after PENCE. The top frame line extends beyond the left frame line. There is a vertical line above the "d" of 8d at right and a spot of color under the "cy" at right.
5. There are short lines of color between the frame lines at top. No. 68 on plate.
6. There are lines of color between the frame lines at top and bottom, left side. No. 90 on plate.
7. The frame line at bottom right is doubled, and "1" of "10" and "N" of PENCE shows doubling. No. 17 on plate.
8. Between the frame lines, at left, under the "y" of "cy" there is a dot.
9. There is a dot in the shank of "P" of PENCE. No. 58 on plate.
10. There is a doubling of the frame line, top right.
11. There is a position dot back of the head and in line with the ear.
12. Retouch: The inner frame line at right has been unevenly retouched.
13. Retouch: A portion of the inner frame line at top, above "DA" of CANADA, and at left near bottom corner, has been heavily retouched.
14. The space to the left of an imaginary line from the tip of the right seriph of the "T" of TEN to the inside of the right seriph at base of the "T" of TEN is colorless, probably due to a foreign substance adhering to the plate at this point. (Clarke Collection.)
15. In stamps from the outer right vertical row, the right side may show an extremely fine vertical guide line running between the frame lines and continued from one stamp to the next. The plate was ruled with extremely fine horizontal and vertical lines in conjunction with a system of dots, to assist in the accurate laying down of the separate impressions of the die that went to make up the entire plate of 120 impressions.
16. Four fine horizontal lines extend across the white space in the oval to the left of the leaf ornamentation.

Light or Short Transfer Varieties:

Col. Studd mentions the background of the stamp outside the oval as often showing "light patches" in varying positions. Most of these are constant, and due to bad "rocking in." They assist plating. Most of the Pence and 1859 values show similar patches from the same cause.

12d BLACK.

The head is from the full length painting by Alfred Edward Chalon, R.A., ordered by the Queen for her mother, the Duchess of Kent, as a souvenir of Her Majesty's first visit to the House of Lords.

The printing was from a plate of 100 impressions, ten rows of ten, with no imprint. In the Lichtenstein Collection there are proof impressions complete from two different plates, both of which this authority claims were used.

The stamp was used as a multiple of the 3d and 6d, and for mail to Great Britain. Only five copies are known on original cover. Two of these are in the Lichtenstein Collection and one in the Reford Collection.

In New England, New York, Upper and Lower Canada, the shilling had a different value. That there might be no misunderstanding, the stamp was given a full value of twelve pence instead of one shilling. This was 12d Sterling. The 12d stamp was equivalent to 15d currency, the value of the Lower Canada shilling, and could be used to prepay 1 oz. letters, the rate for which was 7½d currency (6d Stg.) per ½ oz. The original essay (see chapter on Essays and Proofs) submitted by Sir Sanford Fleming expressed the denomination as "one shilling."

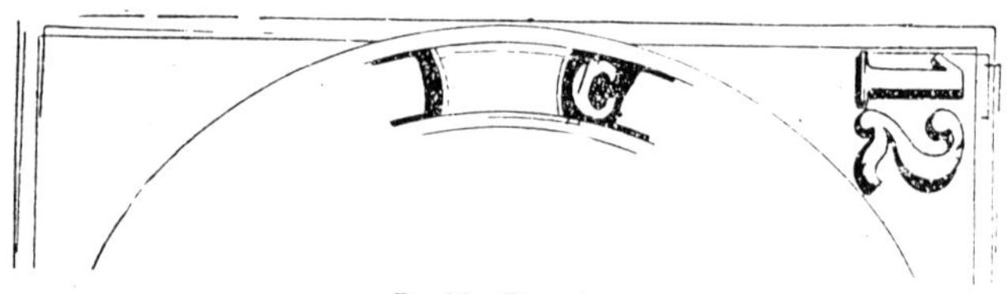

Double Re-entry.

Mr. R. Roberts, London, makes it possible for us to illustrate a re-entry which occurs on the 12d. Two faulty impressions were laid on the plate, and these occur in such a way as to clearly show the successive operations. The re-entry may be traced in several parts of the design.

All impressions from the original die differ from impressions from the plate. Proofs from the die show the two outside vertical frame lines extended beyond the horizontal frame line at the top on both sides, and there is a marked defect at the top of the letters "NCE" described in "Proofs." Three tiny projections or spikes stick out into the outer white oval below the letter E, two to the left and one heavier one to the right. These characteristics are not in evidence in plate proofs, hence the original die or the transfer roll must have been corrected. Such corrections were often made by burnishing that portion of the plate with engraver's charcoal and oil until the fault dis-

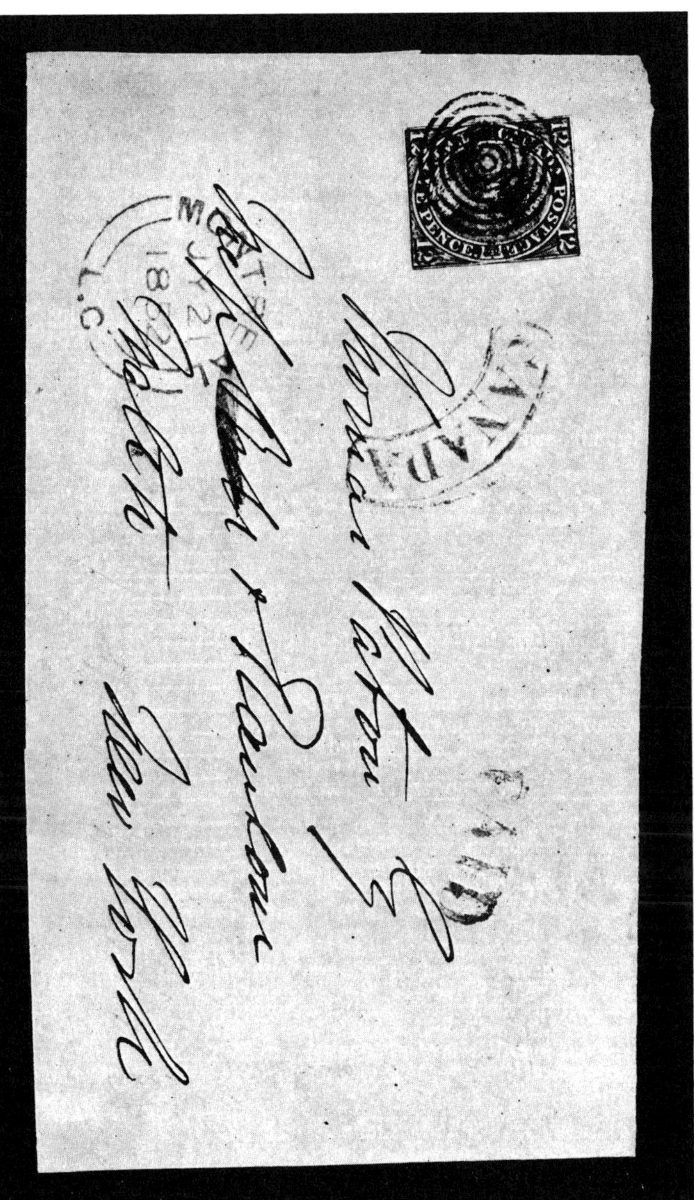

appeared. The design was then retouched on the plate. When the correction could not be made in this way, a hole was drilled in the steel from the back, leaving about $\frac{1}{32}$" of steel under the portion to be altered. This portion was then hammered to a flat surface and the new surface retouched to obtain the design required, when the plate was again hardened.

Plate proofs show a distinct additional line added to the shading of the background, running horizontally from the foot of "T" of POSTAGE into the third ornament of the crown, which does not appear in impressions from the die.

As every die proof so far examined shows the characteristics mentioned, we can only assume that a single die existed, or, if another did exist, no proofs were ever taken from it, which is improbable. The *added line* above described must therefore have been made on the transfer roll.

In the die proofs the lines made by the "graver" in roughing out the background of the letters may be noted, and the letters themselves are unfinished, the "P" of POSTAGE being a good letter for comparison. Either this die was never used or no proofs were taken from it in its finished state.

On the laid paper the laid lines show clearly and the design of the stamp shows through. On all printings the stamp is black, not grey-black. In the wove paper printings the design does not show through.

Beware of faked proofs.

Counterfeits:

No engraved forgery is known to the author.

There are many counterfeits having their origin as proofs. Die proofs did not bear the word SPECIMEN and therefore presented no difficulty to the counterfeiter in this respect, but die proofs may be recognized by the defect described in the check list of proofs. Die proofs are on thin, tough, oily paper, medium thick wove, and thin, soft India proof paper. Any attempt to make these papers look like the original is usually an apparent failure.

The greatest obstacle to the counterfeiter is the paper. Proof paper is usually mounted on other paper to give the stamp the required thickness. Often it is not necessary to use a powerful glass to discover that the texture of the paper varies on the two sides. A drop of water on India paper spreads rapidly and is absorbed. This does not happen on the harder paper used for the genuine stamp.

An accumulation of proofs, including many of the 12d, was purchased by a New York firm some years ago. Among these were several of the 12d in conjunction with another stamp. In every case where such a combination occurred in black, the 12d proof had been cut away at an earlier date.

Plate proofs were printed on soft India paper. So far as known to the author, plate proofs bore the word SPECIMEN in every case. The most dangerous counterfeit is the one made from a plate proof, carefully mounted, the word SPECIMEN removed, and a cancellation put on so as to fall over any trace of the removed letters. Such stamps are usually more of a grey-black than the original. The cancellation is on the right side where SPECIMEN is commonly found. Such stamps are usually mounted on a piece and sold "as is," with instructions not to soak.

Wove Paper:

Some experts doubt the authenticity of the wove paper variety, but we have no hesitancy in stating that the 12d was printed on wove paper and may be considered as many times more valuable than the laid paper variety. The wove papers examined show the same re-entry varieties as found on the laid papers. They were, therefore, from the plate. One theory advanced against the genuineness of the wove papers is that they were probably proofs. No plate proofs are known on anything but India paper. The stamps cannot be die proofs, for the simple reason they are printed from the plate.

Rarities.

The greatest showing of 12d blacks ever brought together will be seen in the Lichtenstein Collection, including three pairs, and more than twenty singles.

Quantities Issued:

(From an anonymous article stated to have been prepared from absolute accurate official records which appeared in 1902 in the Metropolitan Philatelist):

Date of Issue	Office	Postmaster	No. Issued
June 14, 1851	Hamilton	W. Hepburn	100
Oct. 17, 1851	Chippewa	J. Keefer	20
Nov. 13, 1851	Thorold	E. Ritchie	300
Nov. 25, 1851	Toronto	C. Berchy	200
Mar. 8, 1852	Montreal	J. Porteous	200
Sept. 14, 1852	Ingersoll	D. Phelan	100
Apr. 5, 1853	Bytown (Ottawa)	G. W. Baker	100
Oct. 20, 1853	Sherbrooke	Wm. Brooks	15
Jan. 13, 1854	Smith's Falls	Jas. Shaw	50
Jan. 20, 1854	Bytown (Ottawa)	G. W. Baker	100
Feb. 8, 1854	L'Islet	Ballantyne	15
Feb. 27, 1854	Ingersoll	Chadwick	20
Mar. 22, 1854	Sault Ste. Marie	Jos. Wilson	25
May 15, 1854	Port du Fort	McLaren	15
Oct. 21, 1854	Rowan Mills	de Blaquiere	50
Oct. 26, 1854	Melbourne	Thos. Tait	50
Oct. 27, 1854	Montreal	A. LaRocque	100
Dec. 4, 1854	Smith's Falls	Jas. Shaw	50
			1,510

It is interesting to note that during the four years the stamp remained in issue one office only, Ottawa, came back for a second supply. It would appear safe to surmise that when the stamp was withdrawn some of the offices had still a stock of them on hand. These would, presumably, be returned to Ottawa and duly destroyed. Accordingly, although 1510 is the official number issued to the post-offices, the actual number placed in circulation was probably considerably less, and may have fallen short of 1,000.

Quantities Issued (Howes' Figures):

½d	Imperf.	3,389,960	
	Perf.	789,440	
3d	Imperf.	3,100,000	
	Perf.	428,200	
6d	Imperf.	350,478	
	Perf.	52,422	
7½d		100,080	supplied.
		82,410	issued.
10d		141,000	
12d		51,000	supplied.

The quantities of ½d Imperf. and 3d Imperf. are approximately the same, but the ½d stamp having been used on newspapers was destroyed in larger numbers, accounting for its greater rarity. The remainders of the 7½d and 12d stamps were destroyed by the Government. An estimate of their rarity must be based on the numbers actually issued to postmasters.

POSTAL RATES.

From 1771 the following charges were in effect:

Letters carried not exceeding 60 miles	4½d cy.
Letters carried over 60 and not exceeding 100 miles	7d cy.
And for each additional 100 miles	2d cy.

The above rates were for a single sheet of paper weighing less than 1 oz. Even the smallest enclosure doubled the charge.

In 1843 the system of reckoning by single, double or triple sheets and enclosures was abandoned and the weight system was introduced, ½ oz. being the unit of weight. One of the many benefits of this change was that it permitted the use of envelopes. Until then the use of an envelope would have doubled the charge.

In 1851 closed mail to Great Britain via British Packet was carried for 10d per ½ oz. Closed mail per Halifax and Quebec was carried for 7½d per ½ oz. Per U.S. Packet the rate per ½ oz. was 1s 5½d.

The Postmaster-General of Great Britain in his report for 1857 gave rates in Canada as follows:

Reduced rate established in 1851. Payment in advance optional. On ordinary letters, 3d per ½ oz., on letters posted and delivered in same town, each, ½d. Newspapers free. Books ½d per oz., the weight of a single packet being limited to 4 lbs. The local rate of ½d did not come into use until 1857.

Rates to England, May 1, 1857, or earlier, were 10d per ½oz. closed mail via U.S. by British Packet; 7½d per ½ oz. closed mail via Halifax; 1s 5½d per ½ oz. closed mail via U.S. Packet; and 7½d per ½ oz. closed mail via Canadian Packet as from Oct. 1, 1856.

ISSUE OF 1859.

In 1859 a change in the country's monetary system made it necessary to issue a new series of stamps with the values in decimal currency. The change to decimal currency came into effect July 1st, 1859.

The contract for the new stamps was given to the American Bank Note Co., New York. This Company took over the dies, plates and other equipment from Messrs. Rawdon, Wright, Hatch & Edson.

The stamps followed the general design of the Pence issue. Parts of the design appearing on the transfer rolls used in making the Pence issue plates, which could not be used for the new stamps, were removed before obtaining an individual transfer roll impression for each stamp in soft steel. On this piece of steel the balance of the new design would be engraved, the steel hardened, and from these new dies would be made new transfer rolls, followed by the plate itself.

In the case of the 17c stamp, it will be noted that a small line exists between the "O" and the "S" of POSTAGE, as in the 10d, which is acceptable proof that the 10d die was used in making up the die for the 17c.

Imprint:
The sheets contain 100 stamps, ten rows of ten. The 1c, 2c, 5c, 10c, 12½c had eight imprints on each sheet, two on each side, top and bottom, reading "American Bank Note Co., New York," up on the left, down on the right, and upside down on the bottom, placed against the 3rd and 8th stamps of each marginal row of ten, except in the case of the 10c, which had the imprint centered over the space between the 3rd and 4th and the 7th and 8th stamps of each marginal row. The 17c had no imprint. It may yet be established that two plates were used for the 12½c. This would be shown by the existence of a second imprint located slightly to the left or right of the first.

Perforation:
In the Fall of 1925 Dr. Lewis Reford announced an important discovery relative to the perforations of this issue, which, he stated, came in three gauges, representing three periods. A careful checking up of dated copies by the author results in the following data, which is offered subject to revision as specialists study more material and report their findings:

From July, 1859, to April, 1863, 11¾x11¾.
From May, 1862, to Dec., 1864, 11¾x12 or 12x11¾.
From Jan., 1865, to end of issue, 12x12.

(Note: Although the compound perforation is first seen in May, 1862, it does not become general until May, 1863.)

Imperforate:
The imperforates listed are all legitimate and have been seen in unused pairs and blocks. In the case of the 1c and 5c, used covers are on record, postmarked 1860 and 1861, from Toronto and from Prescott. Mr. Pack stated that he believed the imperforates were also on sale at Kingston about the same time and that he had seen the 2c and 10c in undoubtedly early used condition. The 12½c is the blue-green shade and the 10c is in the shade of the last printings.

Papers:

The papers may be divided into many varieties, but the following five should suffice:

1. Coarse white wove.
2. Similar, but yellowish.
3. Hard, greyish wove.
4. White wove of fine texture.
5. White wove with hard finish.

The 1c and 10c have been noted on a yellowish soft wove. The author has yet to see a true ribbed paper. The wove papers sometimes show fine lines of ribbing when held to the light at an angle, but this ribbing is common to nearly all stamps and has little or nothing in common with the ribbed paper of the Pence issue.

All papers vary in thickness and the extremes give the collector "thick" or "thin" if he so desires.

Quantities Issued:

The following figures are from accounts examined by Clifton A. Howes in the Department at Ottawa. The stamp accounts for 1868 did not separate the supplies received of the 1859 issue and of the 1868 issue which commenced April, 1868, so that other published figures may differ slightly. The figures given for the 1c, 2c and 12½c are the estimated quantities according to Mr. Howes' logical deductions as given on page 88 of his book.

Received from Manufacturer to June 30, 1868.

1c	27,475,450	10c	5,799,698
2c	910,500	12½c	3,176,632
5c	39,792,172	17c	599,999

According to the statement furnished by Donald A. King, there were on hand June 30th, 1867, the following quantities:

1c	2,408,900	10c	347,000
2c	171,000	12½c	385,750
5c	1,853,200	17c	81,973

The total quantity of the 17c ordered from the manufacturers was 600,000. The total number issued and the above total on hand at the end of the issue account for but 594,999, leaving 5,001 unaccounted for.

Of the quantities issued, some would be returned by postmasters when the new issue (1868) was ready.

Faulty Perforation:

Stamps are sometimes seen which have received several strokes of the perforating machine without sufficient force to perforate holes in the paper. For the most part the perforating was done carefully, and there are few freaks.

Parcel Post:

Clause 5 of "An Act to Amend the Post Office Laws," assented to 4th May, 1859, stated: "The Postmaster-General may establish a parcel post and parcels other than letters and not containing letters may be sent by such parcel post and when so sent shall be liable to such charges for conveyance and to such regulations as the Governor-in-Council shall from time to time see fit to make." Clause 8 stated that to enclose a letter in a parcel or a newspaper posted as such was a misdemeanor. Although the Act was assented to on 4th May, 1859, the parcel post had been in operation since Jan. 1st of that year. The rate was 25c per pound and the size was not to exceed the carrying capacity of the ordinary mail bag, nor were the contents to be of a nature to injure the rest of the mail.

In 1865 the parcel post was extended to parcels passing between Canada and N.B. and N.S., and the report of that year stated that "parcels not containing letters may now be forwarded by post from one end of British North America to the other on prepayment of a uniform rate of 25c per pound."

Offsets:

An offset printing may occasionally be seen in the different values, caused through one sheet being placed on top of another on which the ink had not sufficiently dried.

1c 1859:

The stamp is subject to about the same classifications as the 5c Beaver, as to paper, perforations, and dates for changes in shade. The earlier printings are on a thick wove paper. By contrast, there is a thin, hard, bluish tinted paper about December, 1867. The only laid paper copy known to the author is the collection of A. Jephcott, Toronto. A guide dot may be noted on the left of colored oval background for the Queen's head. The stamp was used mostly on newspapers and printed circulars. An odd use of the stamp may be noted in the case of "Tax Return Forms" which were addressed and stamped on both sides for return use. The stamp enjoyed a prolonged use, one cover in the author's collection being dated as late as Feb. 6, 1891.

Variety No. 1.

Varieties:

1. A line of color crosses the lower portion of the letter 'E" of CENTS.
2. A re-entry shows in the doubling of the lower half of the outer right frame line and there is a dot under the "E" of ONE.
3. Due to poor inking possibly, there is a variety with a faint background for "One Cent."

2c 1859.

Only in recent catalogues has the real value of this stamp been hinted at to collectors. According to the statistics of issue, the stamp is nearly six times as rare as the 10c, if we take that stamp as a means of comparison. In a few years it will be as difficult a stamp to obtain as the 17c Blue. There is a considerable variation in shade, including a claret shade which is extremely hard to obtain.

In some stamps the frame line is continued, extending across the frame line which meets it at right angles.

5c Beaver:

Several plates were used for the different printings, and each offers its quota of minor varieties.

From the limited material which we have been able to study, it seems apparent that the different plates were either given hard usage or were of poor steel, which developed flaws and soft spots, necessitating constant retouching.

These stamps will long afford plenty of material for argument among the learned, and many a pleasant and instructive hour will be spent by serious philatelists deciding on the fine distinctions between re-entries, shifts and re-touches.

Worn Plates:

In 1865 we note the fine cross-hatch lines forming the background for the numerals in the corners have disappeared, and this characteristic applies to most of the stamps dated 1865 seen by the author.

Specimens are not difficult to find which show evidence of wear in the plate, but the student is warned to distinguish between wear and short entry. A short entry is caused by too light an impression of the transfer roll at any point of the design in making up the plate, giving the stamps printed from that position a faded-out appearance usually in one corner.

Bisected 5c Beaver:

A cover has been examinned, dated Montreal, Feb. 1, 1860, and addressed to Three Rivers, P.Q. The rate on such a letter would be 5c. This was prepaid by the use of three 1c stamps and a diagonal half of a 5c Beaver. The stamps and the bisected are properly tied on with a Montreal 4-ring numeral 21 cancellation.

Re-entry. Normal.

Varieties—Re-entries, Shifts, Flaws, etc.:

(Students are reminded that some varieties are not the result of re-entry or shift in the making of the plate, but are caused by a shifting or double printing at the time the impression was made. These are of course not constant.)

1. The main re-entry is illustrated above. The doubling is not as pronounced at the right side. The variety occurs but once on the plate, in use in November, 1867, or earlier. A counterfeit described as "lines painted in" need deceive no one, since it will be seen that the double lines occur on either side of a blank space wherein a single line occurs normally.

2. Re-entry. No. 93 or 98 on plate. Lines doubled above crown. (September, 1867.)

2a. Re-entry. Top frame line, lines above crown, above "DA" of CANADA and "POS" of POSTAGE, above "FIVE" and in oval below, frame line at right center, and letters of CANADA and "P" of POSTAGE doubled, with doubling of upper left "5."

3. Oval line doubled above "POS" of POSTAGE; line through bottom of "T" of POSTAGE; stroke of color in right side of "D" and "A" of CANADA, and stroke of color over the shoulder of upper left "5." The oval line over "DA" of CANADA is thick.

3a. Re-entry. Added line above "ADA" of CANADA and "POS" of POSTAGE, with line through bottom of letters "POSTA" of POSTAGE and frame line doubled right center.

4. **Log in waterfall.** This variety was discovered by Dr. Reford in 1925. It consists of a line, resembling a stick or small log, caused by a scratch on the plate, extending across the lower step of the waterfall from a position under and to the right of the fore paw of the beaver to the oval frame line above the "I" of FIVE.

5. **Oval frame lines broken at top.** This variety is illustrated below. This variety is almost in the same class as the "burr over shoulder" variety of the 17c as regards rarity.

Variety No. 5.

Variety No. 6.

6. **Oval frame line broken at bottom.** This variety is illustrated above. The author has noted the variety on cover dated Sp. 23, 1862.

Variety No. 7.

Variety No. 8.

7. **Stroke of color above lower right "5."** This variety was caused through something falling on and damaging the plate. Stamps

may be found which show evidence of an attempt to correct the damage. The variety is illustrated below.

8. **"Sun Spot" varieties.** These also are the result of plate damage. (Plate of Dec., 61.)

9. Stroke of color through the lower left portion of the "N" of CENTS. About October, 1867. (Isaac Pitblado, K.C.)

10. Stroke of color appearing diagonally in the upper left corner of the "N" of CENTS. (S. Tanner Green.)

11. Large blur covering the left side of the "C" of CENTS.

12. Defective tail to the "R" of "V.R." consisting of an oblique dash forming a cross.

13. A line of color joins the colored background of "POSTAGE" to the curved horizontal line at the left of letter "P."

14. A heavy dot or pearl joins the oval line to the colored background at the top of the "G" of POSTAGE.

15. Numerals of value, right, left, top or bottom, extend to the frame line or show traces of doubling. These are usually classed as "shifts."

16. "FIVE CEN" shows distinct doubling at bottom, and color covers lower part of these letters.

17. Upper right frame line is doubled inside.

18. Upper right frame line is doubled inside and there is a doubling of the bottom right frame line.

18a. Re-entry. Frame lines doubled above crown at left; line doubled at right of crown; inner right frame line doubled top and bottom; re-entries in all figures of value, and in letters "ANAD" of CANADA, "VE" of FIVE, "CE" of CENTS. There is a dot under the "N" of CENTS.

19. Distinct space between the letters "TA" of POSTAGE at bottom. These letters are usually run together.

20. "S" of CENTS has vertical stroke passing through it and crossing oval frame line. The letters "AN" of CANADA are doubled at bottom.

21. There is a color dot below the upper right "5" and the lower right "5" is tied to the inner frame line by shading.

22. There are two vertical strokes of color, one on the shoulder of the upper right "5" and one slightly below and to the left.

5c Beaver, Dot in "C." There is a colored dot in the "C" of CENTS which occurs in many different positions. In one variety three distinct dots occur in the "C," and in other varieties dots may be noted in the letter "V," the "E" of FIVE, and at the bottom left of "E." Dots may be noted at the top, sides and bottom of the stamp.

23. Re-entry. Frame lines doubled at lower left, and line through bottom of letters "STAGE" of POSTAGE.

24. Re-entry. Traces of re-entry in letters "I" and "E" of FIVE, "EN" of CENTS, "CA" of CANADA, and there is a vertical line inside the inner left frame line extending from "5" to a point opposite the "A" of CANADA.

25. Position dots: At the lower left corner are three strong dots, one to left of frame line, two to the right and under bottom frame line. A faint fourth dot may be noted above and to the left of the middle dot above described.

26. There is a horizontal stroke of color extending to the right from "S" of POSTAGE and under the "5."

27. There are two horizontal strokes of color extending to the right from the "flower" after CENTS, one through the frame line and the other to the oval frame line.

5c Bisected:

Although not authorized, the practice was nevertheless resorted to, with the result that we have the stamp bisected to make up the 12½c packet rate.

10c Prince Consort:

Previous writers have dealt with the shade problem by stating that "of a hundred copies probably no two would be alike." It remained for Senator J. A. Calder to contribute the most instructive chapter to the history of this stamp. At the New York Exhibition in 1926 Senator Calder's framed exhibits showed covers representing the shades supplied by the manufacturers for the twenty-seven separate orders for stamps placed by the P.O. Department. His searchings of the Departmental archives had yielded the information as to the number of orders placed and the dates and quantities. With this information as a solid foundation it was possible to separate the different printings, each of which naturally came in a different shade, sometimes so little different as to cause difficulty in identifying it at first, but more often so distinctly different as to be recognizable at once. These printings are listed below:

	Date Ordered.	Shade.	Quantity.
1.	March 16, 1859	Brownish Black and Black Brown	100,000
2.	July 12, 1859	Bright Red Purple	100,000
3.	Nov. 9, 1859	Dull Greyish Red Purple	10,000
4.	Feb. 10, 1860	Dark Purple	200,000
5.	Sept. 29, 1860	Purple	200,000
6.	March 6, 1861	Greyish Violet	200,000
7.	Aug. 13, 1861	Deep Dark Purple	200,000
8.	Jan. 23, 1862	Grey or Greyish Slate	100,000

9.	May,	1862	Dull Light Reddish Purple	200,000
10.	Sept. 2,	1862	Brownish Purple	100,000
11.	Dec. 17,	1862	Purple on Yellowish Wove	200,000
12.	Feb. 27,	1863	Grey Brown Purple	200,000
13.	Sept. 14,	1863	Greyish Brown Purple	100,000
14.	Nov. 21,	1863	Cream Purple	200,000
15.	March 1,	1864	Dull Reddish Purple	200,000
16.	May 6,	1864	Bright Greyish Purple	300,000
17.	July 9,	1864	Dark Brown Purple	200,000
18.	Nov. 28,	1864	Deep Violet	200,000
19.	Jan. 28,	1865	Dull Reddish Violet	200,000
20.	April 22,	1865	Violet	300,000
21.	Sept. 25,	1865	Bright Red Violet	300,000
22.	Feb. 24,	1866	Very Light Violet	400,000

23rd, 24th, 25th, 26th and 27th in Red Violet.

Note: The dates of issue are later than the dates given above.

Varieties:

There are several minor varieties, consisting of shifts or re-entries.

1. The shading of the bottom of the numeral at the lower right corner bottom extends over the frame line, as in the variety described for the 12½c, and the lower left "X" shows re-entry to right.
2. There are seven minute dots in the oval above "PO" of POSTAGE and two dots in the center of the right numeral "X."
3. There is a colorless spot or patch against the hair at left side of head.
4. The top frame line is doubled from a point above "D" of CANADA to right corner.
5. There is a dot in the oval above "P" of POSTAGE.

How Used:

The stamp was for domestic use on double or overweight letters and for prepayment of postage on letters to the United States. It could also be used to make up rates on letters to Great Britain or foreign countries.

Bisected:

The Ayer Collection, dispersed in 1897, contained two covers, each bearing a bisected 10c prepaying the 5c rate. The one was dated July 11, 1859—black brown, and the other Feb. 12, 1860. Both were sold by Chas. J. Phillips in 1927. Covers are also known from Bowmanville, Feb. 15, 1860, and Barrie, Nov. 5, 1860.

12½c Green:

The stamp was for prepayment of Canadian packet post rate, which was 4½c cheaper than the rate for letters sent by British packet post, a service that was more speedy and certain than the Canadian packet.

Varieties.

A guide dot may be located on the left side of the colored oval background, and in the case of the top row; an arrangement of dots along the top frame line of the stamp, at the corners, enables us to plate stamps 1 to 10.

1. Re-entry. In No. 61 on the plate the figure "1" of "12½" extends across the frame line on the bottom left. No. 71 on the plate is similar but not as pronounced.

No. 61 on Plate.

Variety No .2.

2. Re-entry. There is a fine line in the first "E" of PENCE and traces of doubling may be noted in other parts of the same stamp.
3. There is a dot of color in the right side of the base of the "2" of "12½" in lower right corner.
4. There is a stroke of color in the left side of the base of the "2" of "12½."
5. There is a plate flaw at the top of the "X" of SIX and to right, on shoulder.

17c Blue, Jacques Cartier:

This stamp was for the prepayment of the British packet post rate. By this packet, mail reached the British Isles with greater speed, justifying the increase of 4½c over the Canadian packet rate.

Papers:

The paper used was a stout wove for the most part. There is a paper that might be described as softer and more coarse than the usual, and one printing, or part of one printing, was on thick coarse yellowish wove.

Printings and Quantities:

There were twelve orders placed by the Government with the American Bank Note Company, each for 50,000 stamps. It is to be expected that the twelve printings will show twelve varieties of shade, but while this may be true, it is difficult to make any classifications after separating light blue, dark blue, bright blue, and slate blue, the latter being a quite distinctive shade.

Guide Dots:

A guide dot may be noted outside the center of the left frame line. On an imaginary horizontal line passing through this dot, other dots will be found to the left of the ear, in the ear, on the cheek, on the nose, midway between the nose and the right oval frame line, etc. In his research work. Senator Calder located all these various guide and position dots and extracted from them the solution to the plating puzzle. To use his own words: "I collected material for five years and then in five hours I was able to plate the 17c stamp."

In the white space of the oval, above and between the "O" and "S" of POSTAGE there is a stroke or line of color as described for the 10d. This portion of the original 10d die was doubtless used in making up the die for the 17c, along with the central portion.

Variety No. 1.

Varieties:

Stamps from the top row show dots along the upper frame line.

A faint perpendicular line may be noted extending from top to bottom of the stamp, on the right side, passing through the "s" of "Stg." The usual varieties caused through poor impression or inking may be noted, particularly those showing white lines above or below the letters. One, for example, shows a faint white line under the "E" and a distinct white line under the "N" of CENTS.

1. The variety "Burr over shoulder" was no doubt caused by a sharp tool or other heavy steel instrument falling on the plate.

As one plate only was used for printing the 17c stamp, this variety would be constant in the ratio of one in the hundred stamps, providing of course the accident happened at the beginning and the flaw was not remedied. You will understand that the variety is, by way of illustration, twice as rare if the plate received this flaw after six of the twelve printings had been taken from it. Senator Calder identifies the shade of the last printing, and all copies of this variety which he has examined belong to the last printing. He locates the stamp as No. 7 on the plate, but has three copies of No. 7, last printing, which do not show this flaw. It therefore follows that the flaw came during the last printing and after a portion of the order had been printed. If there are three copies of No. 7, last printing, without the flaw, then not more than 497 sheets will show No. 7 with the flaw, but it is thought the accident to the plate took place towards the last of the printing, since but five copies are known.

2. A distinct re-entry shows in the doubling of the upper portion of the left frame line, and letters "TAG."

3. A second re-entry shows a line in and above the letters "GE" of POSTAGE.

Pairs, Strips, Blocks, Covers:

Pairs, strips and blocks are quite rare. Blocks are found only in the finest collections. The Reford and Lichtenstein Collections contain some fine blocks, and a superb block went into the Fergus Collection in March, 1928. Covers are more than usually difficult to obtain.

Imperf. Pair.

1859 Issue Rarities:

1c Used block of 8—Telfer Collection, Phillips, Jan., 1928.
2c Strip of 4 with pair 12½c on cover—Jarrett Collection.
5c Used block of 8—Telfer to Phillips, Jan., 1928. Phillips to Van to Gooderham, Aug., 1928, value $175.00.
Used block of 6, one with major re-entry. Lichtenstein.
10c Strip of 3 Black Brown on cover—Telfer Collection to Phillips, 1927.
10c Bisected. The Ayer Collection, dispersed in 1897, contained two covers with bisected 10c, one dated July 11, 1859, and the other Feb. 12, 1860.
12½c Block of 4, imperf.—Lichtenstein.
Block of 4 on cover.
17c Block of 4, imperf.—Lichtenstein.
Unused block of 4 imperf.—Jarrett Collection.
Block of 6, Telfer to Phillips, Jan., 1928.

1868 ISSUE—DOMINION OF CANADA

On July 1st, 1867, the "British North America Act" combined the territory of Canada, Nova Scotia and New Brunswick into the "Dominion of Canada." Prince Edward Island, British Columbia, Rupert's Land and North West Territories were admitted later.

The stamps which appeared in April of the following year are therefore the first of the "Dominion of Canada." They were engraved and printed by The British American Bank Note Co. at Montreal and Ottawa.

Imprints.

The imprint consists of colored capitals on a narrow strip of color with bossed ends, and reads "British American Bank Note Co., Montreal and Ottawa." The strip is framed in very thin parallel lines. Entire width is 1 mm. and the length is 51 mm. This imprint is on four sides, opposite the 5th and 6th stamps, upright on the bottom margin instead of upside down as in the case of the imprint for the 1859 issue.

The ½c, 3c, 5c and 12½c values have an additional imprint at the top of the sheet, consisting of the value in large capitals 4 mm. high. In the 12½c value the letters are unshaded.

E. & C. BOTHWELL

CLUTHA MILLS

1868 Watermark. (Reduced to ½ size.)

Watermark:

The watermarked stamps show one or more letters from the complete watermark illustrated, reduced.

To Mr. J. N. Luff, the New York specialist, belongs the credit of solving the mystery of the 1868 issue watermark. The following extract illustrates Mr. Luff's methods of discovery:

"As the broadest letter measures only 12 mm., and the stamps are about 23 mm., from center to center of perforation, there are usually parts of two or three letters on each stamp. I have found a large number of single letters, pairs, portions of three letters, and in one instance a pair and parts of two letters. Of many combinations I have found several examples. I have also found quite a number of stamps showing parts of two rows of letters one above the other. Of the combinations given in the following list, I have not always found the whole of all the letters, but there has been sufficient to preclude any doubt, or the specimen has been rejected. The reader will please bear in mind that when the stamps are viewed from the back, the letters read from to right to left (at least when the sheets were placed normally in the press as is usual with the Crown and CC, CA, and other watermarks.

"The letters are plain double-lined capitals, except the third in the first line, 'C,' which is more fancy, having a decided hook at the end of the lower curve and the upper curve ending in a point, instead of being cut off squarely, as in the case of the other letters. The 'E' and 'C' are followed by periods 2½ mm. square. The initial capitals 'E,' 'C' and 'B' are 13 mm. high, the other letters 12½ mm. The upper row is about 140 mm. long, the lower about 122 mm., and the distance between the rows 11½ mm. The watermark will thus fall on 12 stamps in each sheet of one hundred. But it cannot be argued from this that the stamps with watermark are only eight times as rare as those without, as we must take into consideration the proportionately large number of sheets on ordinary unwatermarked paper. The sheets were apparently placed on the press without much care, as the letters are found reversed and inverted."

Papers:

The Montreal printings were on a thin hard semi-transparent paper. The laid paper used for the 3c is thinner and harder than the laid paper used for 1c, which is somewhat thicker than the ordinary wove papers. There is, in addition to the usual medium thick opaque wove, an extremely thick white wove of fine quality which was used for a printing of the 15c, and a fine white wove for the 3c. The 12½c blue may be noted on a rather coarse yellowish wove. One printing of the 15c was on an opaque wove paper with a hard pebbly finish.

Quantities Issued:

½c		6,500,000	
1c	Red-brown	7,500,000	?
1c	Orange and Orange-yellow	4,000,000	?
2c	(Approximate)	10,000,000	
3c			?
5c			?
6c	(Approximate)	10,000,000	
12½c		1,900,000	
15c			

Perforations:

From the beginning to the end of the issue the stamps were permorated 12x12 (slightly under) with the exception of the ½c and 15c, which appear in perforation 11½x12. We believe the last printing of the 1c, 2c, 3c, 6c and 12½c stamps was sufficiently large to supply the demand until the appearance of the corresponding values of the "Small Cents" issue.

The perforations of the ½c and 15c stamps, printed and perforated concurrently with the "Small Cents" issue, will be found to correspond in a general way with the perforations of that issue.

½c:

This stamp comes on a variety of papers and in several shades from greyish to intense black. The stamp was used until about July, 1882. A guide dot appears in the lower left corner. The watermark was first discovered about 1923 by Dr. Reford in the stock of the Scott Stamp & Coin Co. Three specimens are known to the author. The variety "Chignon not shaded" is found in several stamps in the central portion of some sheets. (Chignon: Coil of hair at back of head.)

At least two stamps in the sheet, or in some cheets (seen in a vertical pair surrounded by normal stamps), show a variety consisting of a stroke of color sloping downward until it touches the outer curved line at top of stamp above "P" of POSTAGE.

1c Orange:

In the first printing the color seems to have been a deep orange, more rare than catalogues indicate. The orange was followed by orange-yellow and pale orange-yellow. A guide dot appears close to the bottom of the design but not so far to the left as in the other stamps of the issue. The smaller stamp replaced the 1868 stamp in March, 1870.

1c Red-brown:

The total issue of 1c stamps was 11,500,000, of which probably two-thirds were red-brown. The watermark comes on both thick and thin papers. In the collection of Mrs. A. R. Clarke there is a mint block of twelve, the largest in any collection, we believe. In the author's collection there is a used block of twelve on cover, with marginal imprint.

1c Laid Paper:

There are two varieties of laid paper, one thick and the other medium. Both differ from the laid paper of the 3c, which is thinner. A specimen has been noted bearing the 4-ring cancellation 47, identified as Napanee. It is possibly worth recording this fact, as the meagre supply of the 1c on laid paper would mean that they could have been used from very few offices.

Bisected 2c.

Variety.

Variety "Double Print."

2c Green:

The variety "Lines cross at lower left" consists of a fine vertical and horizontal line crossing through a faint guide dot. In some stamps the vertical line is more to the right and runs through the design. These lines would be ruled very faintly on the plate before the separate impressions were put on it from the transfer roll, acting as a guide, and to be polished off the plate when completed. This was omitted. The 2c on laid paper was purchased in 1925 by Dr. Reford and is the only copy known.

The bisected 2c shown above seems to have been accepted as 1c, but its use in any event would be unofficial. It is unfortunately not on the entire.

In 1928 Chas. J. Phillips purchased a "lot" from Nova Scotia which included an authentic cover prepaid with a 2c and a half of a 2c, postmarked "Bridgetown, N.S., Au. 16, 1872."

3c Red.

In the variety "dry plate" the lines stand out very distinctly. The shade is pale red-brown. It is from a sheet printed from the plate when partially cleaned, or lightly inked.

In the laid papers, the earliest printing shows less of the rose shade.

In February, 1927, Mr. Eugene Telfer of Detroit showed us a specimen, late printing, with unmistakable signs of having been printed from a plate which had received a deep horizontal scratch. This scratch extended across the stamp, passing through the two figures of value and top of "PO" of POSTAGE.

The variety "dot in upper left 3" seems to be less rare than the Telfer variety above described. There is a similar variety, "dot in upper right 3." The variety "upper left 3 defective" is another example of a damaged plate variety, and may be quite rare. Still another damaged plate variety shows a vertical line of color bisecting the lower ball of the bottom left 3.

There is a forgery of the laid paper. The laid lines are too close together. The specimen in the Firth Collection is of the shade which does not belong to the date for the laid paper printing.

6c Brown:

The variety above illustrated is an example of "double printing," the sheet or portion of sheet having received two impressions. As the stamp is properly perforated it must have been separated from other similar stamps, but no others are known to the author.

In the author's collection is a "part perforated" variety with but three holes punched on the right side and with a portion of the adjoining stamp included in the separation.

The 6c Bisected Diagonally (3c rate) is known from Nova Scotia, where the practice of bisecting stamps was commonly followed. Mr. F. F. Lamb in the philatelic Journal of America records one as used from Wilmot, Feb., 1872. In the Tapling Collection in the British Museum there is a specimen on cover addressed to James W. Bancroft, Acadia College, Wolfville, N.S. The stamp was bisected by tearing in equal halves. The bisected is tied to cover by 2-ring four (Halifax).

A constant and easily detected variety consists of a doubling in the outer lines of the scroll at the top right corner. In the normal stamp there are two lines; in the variety there are three.

6c Bisected:

The 6c is listed as used bisected for the 3c rate. Such covers are mostly from Nova Scotia. The Ayer Collection, dispersed in 1897, contained two covers, each prepaid with a bisected 6c one dated July 5th, 1869, and the other Dec. 8th, 1870.

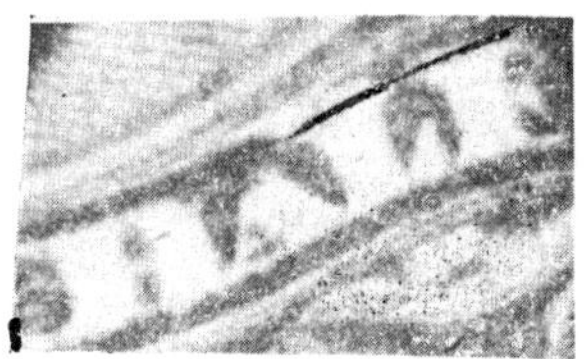

Variety.

12½c Blue:

The 12½c stamp prepaid the ordinary letter rate "By Canadian Line" to Great Britain. Until recent years the stamp was scarce in Canada but easily obtained in England, where most of them were addressed.

G. M. O'Connell reports the 12½c with a line of color through "LF" of HALF as illustrated above.

A distinct variety consists of the end of the scroll, as well as outer frame line, cut away from a point opposite the "T" of TWELVE to the bottom of the design. In some stamps the frame line remains, but the ornament has been cut away or worn. These appear only on the late shade. The author found but five examples in five hundred stamps in his collection.

The 12½c stamp has been noted with Hechler's most unofficial "Official" overprint.

A guide dot appears at the lower left corner.

From September 1st, 1878, a reduction in the postage rate on closed parcels sent by post within the Dominion came into effect. The reduction was from 12½ cents per 8 oz. to 6 cents per 4 oz. Under this change small parcels not exceeding 4 ounces in weight were passed for 6 cents instead of 12½ cents as before. The use of the 12½c stamp, therefore, decreased rapidly. In 1879 there were issued to postmasters 84,150 of these stamps, but in 1880 the number fell to 13,400, and in 1881 only 4,950 were issued. It was issued in decreasing numbers until 1888, when it disappears from the accounts.

15c:

This is a stamp that offers the true philatelist everything the heart desires, from imperforates to compound perforations, from watermarked paper to canvas ribbed, from red lilac shade to green. The stamp holds the world's record for length of service, having been on sale at post offices and available for postal duty for not less than 33 years. With the fullest appreciation of the writings of many prominent philatelists, we may express the opinion that many years will elapse and many thousands of these stamps will be examined before all their philatelic secrets are laid bare. The following represents a framework upon which to build as material offers.

The dates of issue of the different shades have been given in the priced section with reasonable accuracy, based on examination of many dated copies.

The earliest printing is on the thin or "A" paper, but this paper varies in thickness to a point where it might not be identified. The texture, however, remains unchanged.

Gum:

The gum gives a good clue to the date of the printing.
1868—Thin smooth white.
1873-1879—Dull streaky, slightly yellow.
Dec., 1879-1880—Smooth yellowish.
1880-1890—Same, but more yellowish.

Perforations:

March, 1868, to June, 1875—11¾x11¾.
July, 1875, to June, 1878—11½x11¾.
July, 1878, to —11¾x12.
1879—12x12.
Jan., 1879, to —11½x12.

Papers:

All papers vary in thickness or "weight" and the mere description "thick" or "thin" is not sufficient to distinguish any given paper.

March ,1868—Thin white wove.
May, 1868—Stout white wove.
Sept., 1869—Stout yellowish wove.
Aug., 1877—Hard stout wove.
June, 1880—Thick smooth white surface. Thick soft wove.
May, 1883—Medium wove of poorer quality than wove of Aug., 1877.

Jan., 1891—Wove of poor quality, slightly grey-toned.

The variety "heavily ribbed" is the result of the paper passing over canvas in the final stages of manufacture, instead of the metal rollers, and receiving the coarse impression of the canvas.

Small 15c:

This stamp was engraved but never issued. (See Proofs.) Proofs were printed from the plate, and the stamp is also known in finished state, with full gum.

EXTRACTS FROM "THE POST OFFICE ACT, 1867."

Section 19. On all letters transmitted by Post for any distance within Canada, except in cases herein otherwise specially provided for, there shall be charged and paid one uniform rate of three cents per half ounce in weight, any fraction of an ounce being chargeable as a half ounce, provided that such three cents postage rate be prepaid by postage stamp or in current coin at the time of posting such letters: *and when such letters are posted without prepayment being made thereon, then and in such case it shall be lawful to charge upon letters so unpaid a rate of five cents per half ounce.*

General Instructions.

Part VIII.

Section 53. If the postage be prepaid in money, the word "paid" should be stamped or written in red against the rate, thus, "PAID 3."

Section 54. If the postage be not prepaid, the rate should be marked in black. Care must be taken to use proper red and black stamping material to prevent any doubt as to the letter or packet being paid or unpaid.

Part IX.

Section 79. Letters cannot be prepaid partly in stamps and partly in money: *the postage must be prepaid either wholly in stamps or wholly in money.*

Part XXIV.

Section 283. A mutilated stamp or a stamp cut in half is not recognizable in prepayment of postage.

Part XXXIII.

Section 363. Every Courier should carry a post horn and sound the same distinctly two or three times on approaching and leaving a post office.

THE "SMALL CENTS" ISSUE.

This issue was engraved and printed by the British American Bank Note Co. in Montreal and in Ottawa. The stamps offer an inviting field to the specialist, being rich in minor varieties and affording many interesting studies. The dating of the various shades, varieties of paper, printings, cancellations, etc., are but a few of the interesting features.

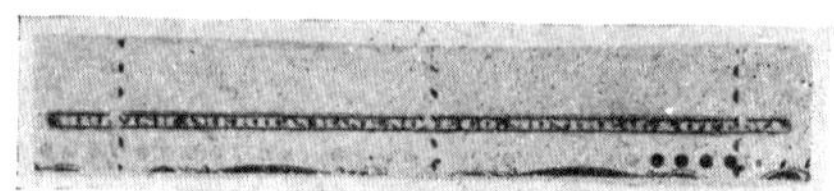

No. 1 Imprint.

Shaded letters, 4 mm. high.

Faintly shaded letters, 4 mm. high.

Imprints.

The First Imprint:

This was used until 1875, and reads "British American Bank Note Co., Montreal & Ottawa," in colorless Roman capitals on a strip of color 1 mm. high and 51 mm. long, reading up on the left, down on right. It is centered over the 4th, 5th, 6th and 7th stamps of the top row, for the 1c, 2c, 3c, 5c, 6c and 10c values.

In the 1c, 2c, 3c, 5c, 6c values, figures of value appear in shaded Roman capitals 4 mm. high over the 2nd and 3rd stamps of the top row. In the 10c these figures are unshaded. The shading is often faint in the other values.

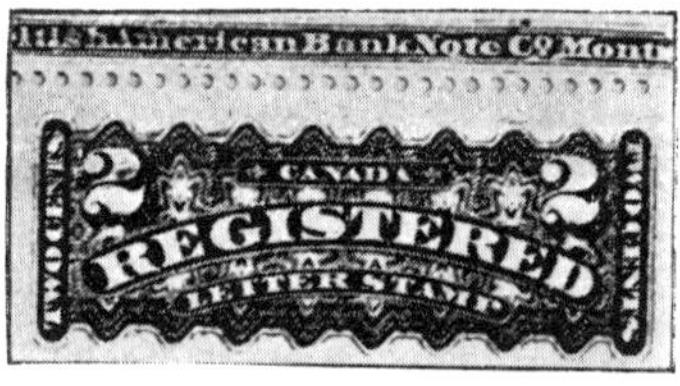

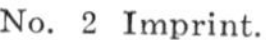

No. 2 Imprint.

Shaded letters, 6 mm. high.

The Second Imprint.

This was introduced in 1875, when the Government ordered all stamps to be printed in Montreal. It reads, on all values, "British American Bank Note Co., Montreal," in capitals and lower case letters on a colored strip 56 mm. long and 2½ mm. high, with pearled border, appearing on all sides. The top imprint commences over the 4th stamp and ends over the 7th. The bottom imprint is in corresponding position.

A full sheet of the 1c is noted by Howe with the imprint at top and bottom, and no other marginal inscriptions. The author has not seen a sheet, or large block, of the 2c bearing the Montreal (second) imprint, but it doubtless exists.

The 3c value shows "THREE" in shaded Roman capitals 6 mm. high over the first two stamps of the top row. The author has also seen "THREE CENTS" in similar lettering over the last three stamps. Howe mentions having examined a sheet on which the imprint is centered on the top and bottom row, and not appearing on the sides.

In the 6c stamp the "SIX" appears over the 9th stamp of the top row. In the 10c stamp "TEN" appears over the 9th stamp and over stamp No. 2 we find "10" in unshaded figures 6 mm. high.

The Third Imprint:

This appeared in 1888, when the Government required the Bank Note Co. to do its printing in Ottawa, the imprint reading "British American Bank Note Co., Ottawa," in design similar to the first imprint, 1 mm. high and 40 mm. long. The first printing in Ottawa from the plates with the 3rd imprint was in September, 1892, although the British American Bank Note Co. had been removed from Montreal to Ottawa early in 1888 according to the Postmaster-General's report for 1889. It will therefore be noted that there must have been printings in Ottawa from the Montreal plates with the 2nd imprint, and from plates with the 1st imprint which had been used formerly in Montreal.

The imprint occurs three times—in the middle of the top margin over the 10th and 11th stamps, twice on the bottom margin, under the 5th and 6th stamps, and again under the 15th and 16th stamps. There were no side imprints. The denomination appears in the top margin over stamps 2 and 3 at left and stamps 18 and 19 at right, in thin letters slightly under 4 mm. high reading "ONE CENT," "TWO CENT," etc. In the 3c the denomination appears over the first four and last four stamps of the top row. The ½c and 8c stamps do not have this. The words commence over the left of the 1st stamp and end over the right side of the third stamp, and again over the 18th, 19th and 20th stamps at the right, the Ottawa printings being in sheets of 200, 10 horizontal rows of 20, except the 2c stamps.

The Fourth Imprint:

This reads the same as the third, but is 49 mm. long and 2 mm. high, applied to the 2c (Ottawa) plates, which were 100 to the sheet, 10 rows of 10. The imprint was at top and bottom only. This imprint may have been used prior to the smaller one described as the third.

Plate Numbers:

Although many plates must have been used, philatelists have not as yet discovered any consistent system of identification.

GENERAL NOTES

Small Cents Issue.

Worn Plates:

Such large quantities of the 1c., 3c., 5c., and 8c. stamps were printed that many plates, especially in the case of the 3c. must have been used, and some of the plates undoubtedly remained in use for considerable periods.

Position Dots:

A position dot will be found under the design at the lower left corner on stamps from January, 1870, until September, 1888.

From 1875 a small position dot may be noted in another position—at a point where the outer rim of the circle or medallion is nearest the margin of the stamp, usually on the left side but occasionally on the right. These dots are not commonly found.

Ribbed Paper (?):

We believe the paper often classed as ribbed comes under the "A" classification, i.e., wove which after 1875 appears as a pebbly surface and in the heavier grades might be called ribbed, although actually of the same texture and showing the same pin points of light characteristic of the "A" paper. What seems to have led many astray is the appearance of parallel vertical lines on the face of the stamp, but closer examination reveals the truth that these are in the printing and not in the paper. Such varieties have been noted for the 2c., 5c. and 10c. stamps, and are listed as "ribbed printing" varieties.

Hechler's Overprint.

"Service" and "Official":

The stamps and postal stationery of this issue are occasionally seen with "SERVICE" or "OFFICIAL" over-printed in black, blue or red, vertically or diagonally, and accompanied by the Coat of Arms (in the case of stationery). These were discredited by the P.O. Department in 1885. They were done by Henry Hechler (deceased January, 1928), in Halifax, at the time of the Indian outbreak in the Canadian North-West in 1884-85. His explanation was that mail matter addressed to members of the militia of various provinces required some means of distinguishing it from ordinary mail matter in view of the prompt measures being taken to call men to the service. Although unofficial, the over-printing did not impair the postal value of the stamps and envelopes and they were permitted to pass through the mails. The large 12½c. and 15c. stamps have also been noted with the "OFFICIAL" overprint.

Bill Stamps Used Postally:

Bill stamps sometimes prepaid postage, although unauthorized. The 50c. blue, third issue, bill stamp, was occasionally confused with the

50c. blue postage stamp, and covers are met with which were prepaid by the bill stamp instead of the proper postage stamp. The author's collection contains several examples of a similar nature.

Rates of Postage:

From official notice "Post Office Department, Ottawa, 8th May, 1889."

"Changes in postage rates under authority of Post Office Act, 1889. The rate of postage upon letters posted in Canada addressed to places within the Dominion or in the U.S. will be Three Cents per ounce instead of Three Cents per half ounce as heretofore.

½c:

Printed in two panes of 100 stamps, separated by a space of 11 mm. The imprint (2nd, or Montreal) appears at top and bottom of each pane and on the left side of the left pane and the right side of the right pane. The reversed figures "1" and "2" are centered above the top imprints, 4 mm. high, for the left and right panes respectively.

The variety often referred to as "printed both sides" is the result of the printed sheets having been stacked before the impression was thoroughly dry. Some of the sheets show an impression on the back almost as clear as on the front, but in reverse of course.

Re-entries may be located, not the least of which is a distinct doubling of the corner lines at top left, under the "m" of "American" in imprint. It shows also on right side, top. (Stamp No. 5.)

The "thick white wove paper" variety has received little attention, although easily distinguished from the other papers. It is very white compared to the others, and quite opaque.

There are many shades, most of which cannot be listed without confusing the collector.

1c:

Printed in sheets of 100, 10 rows of 10 (2nd or Montreal printing) and sheets of 200, 10 horizontal rows of 20 (Ottawa printing). Sheets of the Ottawa printing show the letters A, B, C, D above the marginal imprint, one letter to each pair with imprint.

Although the orange shade lasted until 1873, a quite distinctive shade of yellow appeared about Sept., 1872. The orange shade was finally replaced by an orange-yellow, and this was followed by innumerable shades of yellow which cannot be classified or listed. In some of the yellow stamps the color permeated the paper, giving it a toned appearance.

There is a re-entry in the Montreal and Ottawa printings, consisting of the outer line at lower left slightly doubled.

Another interesting variety is one showing an extra lock of hair over the ear.

The variety "printed on both sides" is not an offset printing caused by one sheet being placed on another and taking a faint impression therefrom. It is a rare item, and I have recorded but three blocks of four and one single.

In the author's collection is a specimen (1890) with watermark "C," probably due to an accident in the manufacture of the paper.

On
H S.
M.

On 1c 1880.

The author has noted the 1c with "On H.M.S." overprinted in black. Any information would be appreciated.

Bisected Diagonally:

This bisected was used on the "Railway News," issued from New Glasgow, N.S., Thursday, Nov. 4, 1897, Friday, Nov. 5, Saturday, Nov. 6th and Monday, November 8th. Some of these papers were mailed from points other than New Glasgow bearing the stamp bisected in this manner, including Pictou, Welsford, etc.

way News.

oats, Hotels and Commercial Men.

NDENT AND NON-POLITICAL.

SDAY, NOVEMBER 4, 1897. ONE DOLLAR A YEAR

The following extract from the "Railway News" of November 11, 1897, throws light on the stamp: "The Railway News last week on account of not receiving permission from the Postmaster-General to allow papers to go through the mails free, was compelled to pay postage. No half-cent stamps being available, the P.O. Department allowed 1c stamps to be cut in half for postage. This is the first time on record, we believe, where such was allowed, and the stamps have been eagerly sought after, one dollar being paid for single stamps with the post office mark on it."

The same paper (Nov. 11, 1897) contained the following: "The Railway News, New Glasgow, will pay 25c each for the 1c Jubilee stamps cut in half bearing the post office stamp of November 5th, 6th or 8th which was allowed to pass through the mail on that date, owing to there being no regular ½c stamps available."

These "bisecteds" are without value except on the Railway News of the proper date, bearing a genuine postmark.

2c:

There is in addition to the imprint a figure "1" possibly intended as a letter "I."

The use of the 1c stamp was so general, and the rates so easily made up with the 3c and the 1c stamps, that the 2c stamp was not often called for. It is difficult to obtain dated copies. The earlier printings may be identified by the paper and the perforation, the paper being white, opaque, of a softer texture than the later papers, and often with the perforations adhering.

Although the imperforates are listed as yellow green and blue green at the same catalogue value, the yellow green imperforates, when found O.G. (brownish gum) are quite rare in comparison.

2c Bisected.

The diagonally bisected 2c is noted on a cover with an entire 2c making the 3c rate from Brantford to Elginburg in 1886. Another has been noted on cover prepaying the 1c drop letter rate, postmarked Montreal, Jan. 30, 1888, addressed to Chas. Chant, Box 1981, Montreal.

The vertical bisecteds are postmarked Halifax, and we believe the late Mr. Hechler was responsible for them. No evidence has been forthcoming to show that these were created to meet a sudden emergency.

The earlier printings of the 2c show a variety which may be designated as "white heads," the hair at top of the head showing as white space.

2c Re-entries:

The strongest re-entry is similar to the main re-entry of the 6c, and shows in the words "CENTS" and the two figures "2." In addition the scroll work at each side is doubled.

A second pronounced re-entry shows in the "2" on the left, and there is a line in the "C" of CENTS. This is the Montreal & Ottawa printing.

A third re-entry is found on the left side of the stamp, the "2" and the lower corner being doubled. This is the Ottawa printing, date about 1891.

A fourth re-entry shows the lower right corner doubled as well as the figure "2." This is the Montreal & Ottawa printing.

3c:

Printed in sheets of 100, 10 rows of 10 (Montreal printing) and sheets of 200, 10 horizontal rows of 20 (Ottawa printing). The Ottawa printings show in addition to the imprint, the letters E, G or H. The author's collection contains a top row (Montreal printing), showing a small numeral "4" to the right, 2 mm. high, in the sheet margin. Another Montreal printing, block of 12, shows "S3" in reverse, having been cut in the plate as "S3" instead of in reverse to give correct form on the printed sheet.

The shades are recorded with reasonable accuracy in the priced section of this catalogue. The stamp was in continuous use for nearly thirty years, during which period innumerable printings from many plates gave us a range of shades that will ever remain a puzzle to the specialist. The oxidized stamps are found in all shades of brown, and are even found black.

There are many varieties, which may be listed as re-entries, retouches, double-strikes or printings, plate flaws, etc.

Re-entries:

1. Line through CENTS, partial doubling. On Ottawa printings.
2. Lower left corner. Montreal and Ottawa printing.
3. Entire base line doubled. Montreal and Ottawa printing.
4. "3" doubled at right and "TS" of CENTS shows signs of doubling. Montreal print.
5. Lower left corner shows signs of doubling and also "CENT". Montreal and Ottawa printing.

Retouches:

1. Curve at top of "3" on right is cut close.
2. A retouch gives a hooked appearance to nose.

"Double Strikes, 'Kisses' or Double Printings":

(Caused by the sheet receiving a second printing, or falling lightly back on inked plate.)

1. Entire lower portion of stamp deeply shaded, upward.
2. Shading in "Canada Postage."
3. Numerals deeply shaded to right.

Damaged and Worn Plate Varieties:

1. There is a white line above and below most of the letters "Canada Postage". This is noted on stamps dated August, 1871, and later printings up to 1890.

2. About 1880 a variety appears which consists of a diagonal stroke or line of color passing through the left 3 and crossing the frame line near the bottom left. There is a dot of color under the "3".

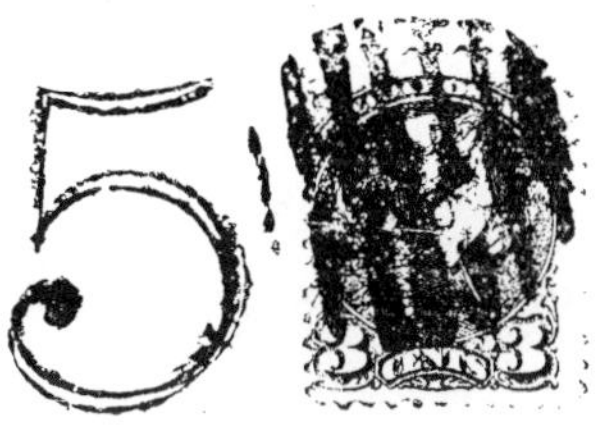

The above illustration is from a cover to which was affixed a 3c. stamp for the postage, the registration fee of 5c. being paid in cash and so indicated by the "5" stamped alongside the stamp.

5c. (Large):

When the dies were prepared for the "large cents" issue, one was made for the 5c. value, but was not used since there was no rate requiring such a denomination.

In 1875 the need for a 5c. stamp arose, and the die was brought out and a plate made, that stamps might be printed at once to take care of the demand until a 5c. stamp could be available of the same size and design as the other stamps of the issue. This smaller 5c. stamp appeared in February, 1876. It will be seen that the large 5c. stamp was in use for a few months only, although doubtless remainders were used up in the months immediately following the introduction of the smaller stamp.

During the period when no 5c. stamp existed to fill the need, postmasters made use of the "Paid 5" and the large "5" markings, and many covers so marked are in the nature of provisionals. All covers so marked would not be provisionals, for the reason that where the postage was not prepaid the recipient of the letter was charged the 3c. postage and 2c. fine, the letter being handed to him with "Paid 5" or "5" stamped in the corner. A cover with "5" and "REGISTERED" would represent 3c. postage paid plus 2c. registration. A ½ oz. cover marked "Paid 5" in red, however, might be accepted as having been so stamped in the absence of any 5c. stamp. (See "Post Office Act, 1867"). The stamp has been reported with an accidental watermark, but the author has not examined the stamp.

Small. 5c.:

Printed in sheets of 100, 10 rows of 10 (Montreal printing) and sheets of 200, 10 horizontal rows of 20 (Ottawa printing). The Ottawa printings show the letter "A" above the imprint.

The large 5c. stamp was replaced in February, 1876, by the smaller one, which conformed in size and design to the other stamps of the series. The shades, perforations and papers are covered elsewhere.

The olive shades belong to the Montreal printings. In October, 1888, the Government required all stamps to be printed in Ottawa, and shortly after this date a printing of the 5c. appeared in grey. The imperforate stamps are in the grey Ottawa printing, but bear the Montreal imprint, which had not yet been replaced with the new "Ottawa" imprint.

The stamp has been noted surcharged "2 CENTS" in two varieties. The figure "2" is 5 mm. high and "CENTS" 4 mm. high, the whole surcharge being 30 mm. in width. These are doubtless the result of amateur faking.

Re-entries:

1. There are 3 lines instead of 2 in the border of frame on right opposite "5". From Montreal and Ottawa plate.
2. All corners, and "5" on right doubled. (Ottawa printing.)
3. Doubling very noticeable in corners and top line doubled. (Ottawa printing.)
4. Slight doubling lower left corner.

6c.:

Printed in sheets of 100, 10 rows of 10 (Montreal) and sheets of 200, 10 horizontal rows of 20 (Ottawa printing). The letter "R" appears above the top imprint in the Ottawa printing.

Here is a stamp that invites attention from the student. It shows a few papers, a few printings, a few plate varieties, a few distinctive shades, a few perforations—not a rare stamp and still not too easily obtained.

The position dots identify the printings, and if one has sufficient material with which to work, even the positions on the plate. They come singly, in pairs or in groups, in varied arrangement.

The chestnut shades are often found with the "Montreal" imprint. Though this particular plate was made at Montreal the printing and ink mixing must have been done at Ottawa.

Re-entries:

1. The numerals "6" and "CENTS" show doubling to the right, and the design is doubled most of the way up the left side of the stamp. Chestnut shade, Ottawa printing.
2. The stamp to the left of the re-entry described above shows a doubling at the bottom on the left side.
3. A line runs through "CANADA POST" at the top and faint traces of doubling may be noted at bottom. Noted on cover dated February, 1873.
4. The design is doubled at lower left and lower right, the re-entry or shift occurring faintly downward (Yellow brown.)
5. Re-entry shows down left of stamp, under and around numeral "6" and in CANADA.
6. Left corner and left half base line shows doubling.
7. Right corner base line shows doubling.

Varieties:

1. Dot in P of POSTAGE. No. 2 on plate. This variety is found on both the Yellow and the Red Brown shades.
2. Diagonal stroke of color through lower right portion of right numeral 6.

The Imperfs. in chestnut shade are listed for 1891-93, but Imperfs. are known with the Montreal and Ottawa imprint 1870-75. This may have been a printing during the period 1891-93 from an old plate bearing the Montreal and Ottawa imprint.

8c.:

Printed in sheets of 100, 10 rows of 10. The shades are listed with reasonable accuracy in the priced section. Of the peculiar greenish-blue shade the author's collection contains but three copies, and the largest number known in a single collection is nine, while many of the best collections are minus this stamp altogether. Beware of the blue-grey shades chemically treated.

The total issue is given as 7,500,000. The slate-purple and blackish-purple shades are printed from a new plate. All fine lines are sharp and distinct, in contrast to earlier printings which are often smudgy and worn.

Two distinct double strikes (accidental second impressions) have been noted, one showing "Canada Postage" doubled, the other showing figures of value and "Cents" doubled.

Re-entry: Faint doubling under and above cents in white border, in white oval under bust, and thin line in letters "AD OSTA E" purple black and pale blue-grey shades.

10c.:

Printed in sheets of 100, 10 rows of 10 (Montreal) and sheets of 200, 10 horizontal rows of 20 (Ottawa).

The stamp, occurring in many distinctive shades and printings, awaits attention from the specialist.

The first printing produced a shade that collectors frequently discard as a sun-faded copy of a later printing. Mint, this shade is an exceedingly rare item.

In the 2c., 5c. and 10c. but particularly the 10c., there is a printing on the late "A" paper with the appearance of vertical ribbing, more noticeable in the background at left of head. This has been classed as a "Ribbed Printing" variety.

Small 12½c. and 15c.:

These were engraved but never issued. Particulars are given in the chapter on proofs.

20c. Vermilion:

The engraving shows Queen Victoria in widow's weeds, the design being copied from the Bill Stamps engraved twenty-five years previously. The sheets were in ten rows of ten, with imprint in a colored strip 38 mm. long and 2½ mm. high, with square ends, reading "British American Bank Note Co., Ottawa" within a pearled border, appearing at top and bottom of sheet. The Imperfs. are gummed with a brownish streaky gum. Approximately 520,000 were issued and used.

50c. Blue:

The engraving shows Queen Victoria in widow's weeds, the design being taken from the Bill Stamps engraved twenty-five years previously. The sheets were in ten rows of ten with imprint in a colored strip 38 mm. long and 2½ mm. high, with square ends, reading "British American Bank Note Co., Ottawa", within a pearled border, appearing at top and bottom of sheet. The Imperfs. are gummed with a brownish streaky gum. Approximately 520,000 were issued and used.

Re-entry: The single line between the corner ornaments over "AP" over Queen's head is found doubled, and the corner scroll work blurred. (R. W. T. Jones.)

REGISTRATION STAMPS.

The system of registering letters commenced, according to the P.M.G.'s report for the year 1856, in May, 1855, but covers dated as early as December, 1854, bear the "Registered" marking. (*See cancellations.*) From October, 1856, the rate was 1d. for letters in Canada and 3d. for letters to the U.S. The Post Office Directory for 1866 (dated October 1, 1865), gives the charge for registration in addition to the rate of postage, as follows:

To any office in Canada or British North America	2c.
" the United States	5c.
" the United Kingdom	12½c.
" British Colonies or possessions, sent via England	25c.
" France and other foreign countries via England, an amount equal to the postage.	

In all cases both postal charge and registration fee had to be prepaid.

In November, 1877, the rates were:

To offices within the Dominion of Canada	2c.
" offices in the United States	5c.
" offices in the United Kingdom	8c.

The P.M.G.'s report for 1877 states "The registration charge on registered letters between the United Kingdom and Canada has been reduced from 8c. to 5c." No reduction was made in the rate on letters to foreign countries, and the use of the 8c. Registration stamp continued for such registered letters.

A report dated early in 1878 mentioned "to foreign countries the rate is as before—eight cents", but the author has not found any report in which a reduction from "an amount equal to the postage" was put into effect, and the date of this change therefore cannot be given. The registration rate to foreign countries must have been reduced early in 1878, because the records show but 25 of the 8c. stamps issued to postmasters between July, 1878, and July, 1879.

Quantities Used.

It has not been possible to get the figures for all years. Those shown are from Howes' book, with the exception of the figures for the 5c. for the years 1878 to 1889, which are estimated on the basis of steady increase in use from 135,000 to 1877 to 500,000 in 1889. The enormous falling off in the use of the 2c. in the years from 1890 is accounted for by the change in the rate. For the same reason, the 5c. shows a large increase from the year 1890 on.

2c.

Year	Quantity
1876......	937,000
1889......	2,800,000
1890......	600,000
1891......	14,850
1892......	100
1896......	400

5c

Year	Quantity
1876......	232,000
1877......	135,000
1878......	140,000
1879......	150,000
1880......	165,000
1881......	185,000
1882......	210,000
1883......	240,000
1884......	265,000
1885......	295,000
1886......	345,000
1887......	395,000
1888......	450,000
1889......	500,000
1890......	1,450,000
1891......	1,765,000
1892......	1,900,000
1893......	2,260,000
1894......	307,000

8c.

Year	Quantity
1876......	71,950
1877......	17,200
1878......	9,400
1879......	25
	98,575
Returned as unfit for use	8,872
	89,705

In 1878 it was reported that "a lot of 75,000 of the 8c. stamps had been destroyed by order of the P.M.G." This probably means that the stamps were called in after their usefulness had ceased, and, allowing for the amount destroyed, we have approximately 40,000 actually used.

Registration Rate Increased to 5c., 1889:

A "Notice to the Public" from the Post Office Department, Ottawa, 8th May, 1889, relative to "Changes in Postage Rates Under Authority of Post Office Act, 1889," reads:

"The rate of postage upon letters posted in Canada, addressed to places within the Dominion or in the United States, will be 3 cents per ounce instead of 3 cents per half ounce as heretofore.

"Upon Drop Letters posted at an office from which letters are delivered by Letter Carrier, the postage rate will be 2 cents per ounce, instead of 1 cent per half ounce. The rate of postage upon Drop Letters, except in the cities where free delivery by Letter Carrier has been established, will be 1 cent per ounce.

"The fee for the Registration of a letter or other article of mail matter will be 5 cents upon all classes of correspondence passing within the Dominion. For the present and '*until further instructed, the registration fee may be prepared by using 2 cent Registration stamps and postage stamps to make up the amount.*'

"Letters insufficiently prepaid will be charged double the deficiency as heretofore, provided at least a partial prepayment has been made. Letters posted wholly unpaid will be sent to the Dead Letter Office for return to the writer." JOHN G. HAGGART, P.M.G.

From the above it would appear that at this date there were no 5c. Registration stamps available, but such was not the case.

Pencancelled Registration Stamps:

Many of the registration stamps are pencancelled with the registration number of the letter. "Registered" in different types is the usual cancellation, the letter "R" sometimes appears, and a town cancellation is rather rare.

Manufacturers, imprints, etc.:

The stamps were engraved and printed by the British American Bank Note Co., Montreal and Ottawa, in sheets of 50, ten horizontal rows of five each. The imprint reads "British American Bank Note Co., Montreal and Ottawa" in a pearled frame appearing four times on each sheet. In 1888 when the work was done in Ottawa instead of Montreal, new plates were made for the 5c., one hundred stamps to the sheet, ten rows of ten instead of ten rows of five, and the word "Montreal" was omitted from the imprint.

2c. Registration:

The 2c. stamp was issued for registration of letters to any post office in Canada or British North America. The imprint (No. 2) appears on all sides, with "2" in the top margin 6 mm. high, and the words TWO CENTS appear in shaded capitals over the first stamp of the top row. The stamps were in sheets of 50, ten horizontal rows of five each.

The carmine shade is quite scarce, and in mint condition is quite rare. It will be noted that the carmine stamp is sister to the 3c. carmine of October, 1888, printed at that period, in the same run of ink, and doubtless in somewhat similar quantities, since it is equally as scarce compared to the more common shades.

The brown shade is due to oxidization. Possibly the most conclusive proof is the existence of covers with the 3c. in brown (although positively never issued in that shade and therefore an oxidized stamp) and the 2c. Registration in the same shade, both stamps having oxidized to identically the same degree.

"Re-entry": The fine marginal line at left is doubled. In a second example, the lines at right are doubled showing four instead of two.

5c. Registration:
The first printing was in sheets of 50, 10 rows of 5. No. 2 imprint appears on all sides. The word FIVE appears over the first stamp in the top row.

The second printing was in September, 1892, in sheets of 100, 10 rows of 10, with No. 3 imprint.

8c. Registration:
Printed in sheets of 50. 10 rows of 5. Imprint No. 2 appears on all sides, with "8" and EIGHT in shaded Roman capitals 6 mm. high in the top margin. The first printing (100,000) was in a pale blue, the second (25,000) in a deeper shade of blue. Of a total issue of 125,000 all but 40,000 were destroyed by the Government.

In 1926 Mr. Chas. J. Phillips noted in a collection he had purchased an 8c. registered stamp that had been perforated with a combination of oblique cuts resembling Types B, C, and D of the Pence Issue trials. As there was no necessity for further experimenting after more than fifteen years of successful perforating of stamps, the only theory that can be advanced is that because of some emergency arising, an old set of cutting edges may have been locked into the machine and used. It is even possible that the instrument used for this perforating was part of the equipment used with the earlier pence stamps.

The 8c. Registered was intended for registered letters to the United Kingdom and to foreign countries. Most of the covers examined by the author are addressed to foreign countries. The stamp has also been noted many times on domestic covers, so that its use was not entirely restricted to the United Kingdom and Foreign Countries.

A full sheet of the 8c. Registered realized but $585.00 at Drew's sale in Boston on November 18th, 1927. We believe this sheet was broken up and sold in blocks which usually sell for about ten dollars per stamp.

"Upon drop letters posted at an office from which letters are delivered by letter carrier, the postage rate will be Two Cents per ounce instead of One Cent per half ounce. The rate of postage upon drop letters except in the cities where free delivery by letter carriers has been establishd, will be One Cent per ounce.

"The fee for the registration of a letter or other article of mail matter will be Five Cents upon all classes of correspondence passing within the Dominion. For the present and until further instructed the registration fee may be prepaid by using the Two Cent Registration stamps and postage to make up the amount.

"Letters insufficiently prepaid will be charged double the deficiency as heretofore, provided at least a partial prepayment has been made. Letters posted wholly unpaid will be sent to the Dead Letter Office for return to the writer."

From April 1st, 1877, the letter rate to Newfoundland was reduced from 6c. to 5c. per ½ ounce. The same reduction was effective on letters to Germany.

On July 1, 1878, Canada was admitted as a member of the General Postal Union and in consequence the rate of letter postage between Canada and all "Postal Union" countries became 5c. per ½ ounce.

Imperforate:

All values exist imperforate, including an early shade of the 3c. Some are gummed and some are not. Dr. Lewis Reford states that the first imperforates were given to Mr. Lauchlan Gibb, of Montreal, by the post office authorities in Ottawa, in recognition of his services to the Department in advising them regarding new issues, designs, etc.

In the Reford collection there are several covers addressed to Mr. Gibb or his friends. The Gibb specimens are gummed.

In the period 1896-1900 stamp collecting was given a new enthusiasm by the issue of the Jubilee set and the change from the 1870 design. At that time some 100 sheets of each denomination got out, mostly without gum. The New England Stamp Co., of Boston, got the most of these, and had difficulty in getting collectors to accept them, as both the Scott and Gibbons catalogues did not list them. Then Howes' book on Canada came out, in which it was stated that they were really on sale at Montreal and other G.P.O.'s (which statement was contradicted by Mr. Gibb in conversation with Dr. Reford). No contradiction was forthcoming from Mr. Gibb at the time, as he did not want to take part in any discussion, having sold some of his copies and not wanting to influence their value.

Mr. Gibb's standing in the philatelic world was a very high one. He was a Past-President of the Royal Philatelic Society and several times was called in to advise King George about purchases and arrangement of his B.N.A. stamps.

After Howes' book was published copies began to filter out through auctions, and finally Scott and Gibbons bought out the New England Stamp Company's stock and sold Chas. J. Phillips most of the stock at a good price. From that time they have been listed and have steadily grown in favor.

Perforations.

Perforation gauges vary. An article on perforations is meaningless if the author does not specify the gauge used in studying the stamps. What is Gauge 11 to one is Gauge 12 to another. When perforations are distinguished to the half or quarter it is imperative that all work on the same basis. The author has made use of a gauge which corresponds with the one illustrated in the notes on the 1859 issue.

A stamp perforated 11½x12 signifies (1) that two machines were used, one equipped to perforate Gauge 11½ and the other to perforate Gauge 12, or (2) that the stamps were perforated by a machine Gauge 11½ and this machine for some reason reset with combs that perforated the stamps with lines of perforations Gauge 12 at right angles to the first lines.

More than likely there were at least two machines in use. It should be borne in mind, too, that one or more of the bars containing the teeth which punched the holes might be taken out on account of defective work, and the new bars which replaced them might be of a slightly different gauge.

While we may set approximate dates between which certain perforations appeared, we must expect to find inconsistencies.

Faulty Perforating:

The stamps of this issue are sometimes found with faulty or careless perforating, which may consist of lines of perforation running diagonally through the stamp or much out of position and cutting through the design vertically or horizontally. In the 3c. and 10c. values one or more sheets were so perforated that the stamps, when separated, show the denomination at top instead of bottom of the stamp. The 3c. has been noted on cover dated December '92, uniformly perforated top and bottom but with a single vertical line of perforating passing through the center of the stamp. With the lines of perforation in this position the stamps if separated, would present a strange appearance, and the alternative would be to separate them by cutting in the vertical spaces between the stamps, which would of course be imperforate.

Six different perforations may be found in this issue. From 1880 on the gauge is consistently 12x12. It is difficult to assign any of the six earlier perforations to a particular period. We submit the following data from which deductions may be made.

January, 1870, to November, 1873, of 226 examined:

	Gauge	Machines with Gauge 11¾ and 12 used
173 were	11¾ x 11¾	First appearing Jan. '70
25 were	12 x 11¾	First appearing May '70
20 were	11¾ x 12	First appearing Jan. '71
4 were	12 x 12	First appearing Nov. '72
4 were	11½ x 12	First appearing Sept. '73

December, 1873, to July, 1876, of 186 examined:

137 were	11½ x 11¾	First appearing Dec. '73
32 were	11½ x 12	
13 were	11¾ x 11¾	
2 were	11¾ x 12	
2 were	12 x 11¾	

August, 1876, to December, 1879, of 271 examined:

68 were	11¾ x 11¾	
66 were	11½ x 11¾	
57 were	11¾ x 12	
54 were	12 x 12	Appearing 2nd time Nov. '76
16 were	12 x 11¾	
10 were	11½ x 12	

The different values may be found with double perforations, perforated diagonally, etc. The 3c. and 10c. are found so perforated that the figures of value show above the Queen's head. Major Studd reports two 3c. entires dated February and April, 1871, which are perf. 12½. Dr. Day also has a 3c. that gauges 12½.

Freaks:

Stamps printed on creased paper are found, which may be ironed out to show blank spaces across the face of the stamp. Nearly all values may be found with the design printed in reverse (offset) on the back, due to sheets having been "stacked" while the ink was still moist.

Jubilee Issue.

The Imprint at top of sheet, reads "Ottawa No. 1", etc. The ½c., 1c., 2c., 3c., 5c. and 8c. stamps were printed in sheets of 100, 10 rows of 10. The 6c., 10c., 15c., 20c., 50c., $1, $2, $3, $4 and $5 stamps were in sheets of 50, 10 horizontal rows of 5. All values in sheets of 50 as listed above were engraved to a smaller scale than those in sheets of 100, the width from outer margin to outer margin of the design across the sheet being from 2½ to 3 mm. less.

Shades:

There are distinctive shades to be found in nearly all denominations. A few are listed below:

1c. Orange-yellow, orange, oxidized to a brown-orange.
2c. Yellow-green, blue-green.
3c. Pale carmine, deep carmine.
5c. Blue, steel blue.
20c. Vermilion, pale vermilion, deep vermilion.
50c. Ultramarine, pale ultramarine.

Bisected 1c.:

This was used on the Railway News issued from New Glasgow, N.S., Nov. 4th, 6th and 8th. Copies may be found on the same paper mailed from other points, but the 13th November is the latest date noted, from Pictou, N.S. (See notes on Small 1c. Yellow.)

Plating the 8c.:

Guide or position dots which in the other values came on the plate in a position covered by a portion of the inked design when printed, occur in the 8c. stamps in positions which enable the specialist to locate them readily. In the band giving the denomination "Eight Cents" dots will be seen between the words. Stamps 1 to 10 are illustrated, each of which may be easily identified with a certain position in the top row.

8c. Jubilee

Plating the Top Row.

No. 1
No. 2
No. 3
No. 4
No. 5
No. 7
No. 6
No. 8
No. 9
No. 10

Counterfeits:

Dangerous counterfeits of the $1, $4, and $5 stamps have been seen and other values may also exist. The paper is coarse and yellowish compared with the originals.

	Quantities Issued	Plate Numbers.
½c	150,000	9
1c	8,000,000	5, 6, 15, 16
2c	2,500,000	7, 8
3c	20,000,000	1, 2, 3, 4, 11, 12, 13, 14, 28, 29, 30, 31
5c	750,000	10
6c	75,000	17
8c	200,000?	20
10c	150,000	19
15c	100,000	18
20c	100,000	
50c	100,000	23
$1	25,000	27
$2	25,000	26
$3	9,515	24
$4	9,937	22
$5	12,600	25

(The figures given for the 8c are likely in error, as more were issued than were authorized. The P.M.G. in reply to a question by Mr. Gibson in the House of Commons regarding the quantity of each denomination to be issued, stated that it was the intention to issue 25,000 of each of the $3. $4 and $5 values. For some reason unknown, there were less of each of these values.)

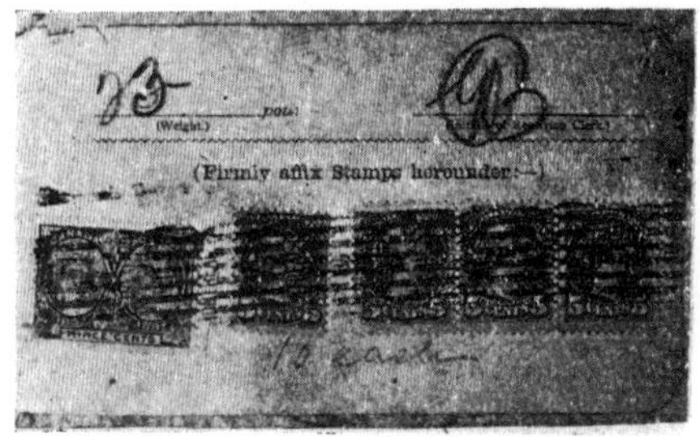

The above illustrates the use of Jubilee and other stamps to prepay postage on newspapers. Sometimes entire sheets were cancelled as a receipt for postage paid.

Queen Victoria 4-Leaf Issue.

Each sheet bore the imprint "Ottawa No. 1" or other number designating the plate.

Variations in the dimensions of these stamps may be noted, caused by uneven shrinkage of the dampened paper when drying after printing.

Imperforate:

The author has examined blocks of all values printed on the wove paper of the issued stamps.

½c.:

Mrs. A. R. Clarke's study of the ½c. stamp brought to the attention of specialists a heretofore unlisted variety, consisting of a re-entry in stamp No. 41. At top right corner, inside of frame line, there is a short vertical line in the white space between the background and the frame line.

5c.:

This value comes on a whitish paper.

2c. on 3c.:

Issued on July 28th, 1899.

4,120,000 of both the 4-Leaf and the "Numeral" 3c. stamps were surcharged "2 CENTS". The "4-Leaf" surcharges are noticeably more scarce than the "Numeral" surcharges, and in order to make comparisons we have allotted approximately one-third of the total number to the 4-Leaf surcharge, i.e., 1,375,000. The surcharged stamps are from Plates 5 and 6. Plate 5 of course being the rarer of the two. The surcharges vary considerably in thickness of type.

2c. on 3c. Inverted:

The inverted surcharge comes at the top of the stamp. Many counterfeiters have overlooked the fact that the genuine invert was caused through the sheet being printed "wrong end to," thus placing the surcharge at the opposite end of the stamp. The counterfeits of this surcharge are skilfully done for the most part and often deceive experts, but one of the cleverest is easily detected by comparison of the letter "C" with the "C" of ordinary surcharges. In the ordinary it will be found that an extension of the tip of the "C" downward would join the lower part of the letter, whereas in the counterfeit such an extension would bring the line across the lower corner of the E to the right.

Variety:

There is a distinct variety, caused by a worn or defective spot in the plate, showing a dash at the bottom and to the left of "T" of "THREE". Another shows such a dash both before and after "THREE CENTS".

6c.:

An outstanding "re-touch" variety occurs as No. 91 on the plate, consisting of a prong or extended line breaking away from the bottom frame line under the "C" of CENTS and extending to a point under the "N" when it breaks entirely away from the frame line.

Denom.	Plate No.	Quantity
½c	1	2,000,000
1c	1-2-3-4	34,000,000
2c	1-2-3-4	12,000,000
3c	1-2-3-4-5-6	44,000,000
2c on 3c	5-6	1,375,000?
5c	1	3,500,000
6c	1	500,000
8c	1	1,400,000
10c	1	500,000

Queen Victoria Numeral Issue.

The change from leaves to numerals in the lower corners was made when it was claimed that the French-speaking population of Canada had difficulty in distinguishing the values when not expressed in figures.

In this design it will be noted the Queen wears two necklaces instead of one as in the 4-Leaf stamps.

Bisecteds:

These were unauthorized but were sometimes accepted in full payment of the rates they represented when put in the mails by collectors and dealers.

½c.:

This stamp varies in size, the minimum measurement top to bottom being slightly under 21 mm. and the maximum 21½ mm.

½c.—This value comes on a yellowish or toned paper.

1c.:

This stamp comes in various shades, and on a toned paper. There is a variation in the size, as in the ½c.

1c.—This value comes on a yellowish or toned paper.

2c.:

The stamp offers a field for study in that many re-touches and re-entries may be located. There is a very distinct re-entry covering a large portion of the design, in the case of the 2c. purple. In the 2c. carmine stamps frame lines were re-touched in many places, and there are at least three distinct examples of re-entry. In the most prominent, the starting point in identifying the re-entry is at the base of the numerals of value, the re-entry showing as an added horizontal line. Shading will be noted in some of the letters. Another pronounced re-entry is similar but shows as a shadowing under the numerals of value. A third shows this same shadowing upward on the numerals of value.

The 2c. purple comes on a thick paper, from Plate 1 printings.

2c. Carmine.—This value comes on a yellowish or toned paper.
2c. Purple.—This value comes on a yellowish or toned paper.

A circular to all Postmasters dated 1st July, 1899, advised, in part—"The colour of the domestic rate postage stamp as prescribed by the Universal Postal Union is red, and it is intended to discontinue the issue of the ordinary 2c. purple-coloured stamps as soon as the present supply on hand is exhausted. This will be about July 20th, 1899. Thereafter, the Department will issue 2c. stamps in red, first, however, surcharging down to 2c. the unissued remnant of the 3c. stamps in red now in possession of the Department."

2c. Rose-purple:

This peculiar shade is possibly due to an impression taken from one of the plates used for the 2c. purple before the plate had been thoroughly cleaned for printing the 2c. carmine.

2c. Orange:

Kelton & Sloane, New York, sold a 2c. in their April, 1922, sale which was of an orange color, cancelled Nov. 17, 1902. It is either an error of color or a changling.

2c. on 3c.:

Of both the Maple Leaf and Numeral 3c. stamps 4,120,000 were surcharged, of which two-thirds were probably numerals. For convenience in making comparisons we have set a number as 2,745,000.

In the inverted surcharge variety, the same remarks apply as for the 4-Leaf stamp.

There is a printing from a worn plate in which the background of the letters "Canada Postage" is partially or wholly missing, giving the letters the appearance of block or shaded letters.

2c. Rose-Carmine, tete-beche:

These have been described in the check list as "Block of 12 in two strips of 6, right block of 6 stamps inverted making center pairs tete-beche." They are from a special plate made up for printing booklet panes, which were supplied to the public two panes or blocks of six to the booklet.

3c.:

There is a pronounced re-entry and several minor re-entries and retouches. No. 5 on plate (?) shows re-entry in tablets of value, which are doubled, and horizontal lines of shading at bottom are doubled. This is also found in the third stamp in from the left, about the centre of the sheet.

3c. Carmine.—This value comes on a yellowish or toned paper.

Imperforates:

The Imperf. 2c. carmine probably appeared some time during the period of issue. Postally used singles with exceptional margins are in the collections of Kenneth A. Millican, Edgar B. Jessup and L. Goetz. The set of numerals, imperforate in blocks, broken up by Mr. George Lowe, Toronto, in July, 1926, did not contain any 2c. stamps.

In March, 1924, two sheets of the 2c. stamp in carmine were broken up by Mr. Robertson, Montreal, at the time he sold the King Edward imperforates. These were of a bright shade of carmine but possibly no brighter than could be expected of stamps in absolutely perfect mint condition. They were not gummed and the stamps of the bottom row of one sheet had not received a proper impression, the lower portions being colorless.

Denom.	Plate No.	Quantity	Denom.	Plate No.	Quantity
½c	1		6c	1	
1c	1-2-3-4-5-6-7-8		7c	1	
2c	1 to 12		8c	1	
3c	1 to 4				
2c on 3c	5 & 6	2,745,000	10c	1	
5c	1-2-3		20c	1	500,000

About 1922 a sheet, or major portion of a sheet, of the 20c. value, was in the possession of a New York dealer, who had obtained it from Ottawa. These stamps were in mint O.G. condition. In 1927 a superb collection of proofs and imperforates was offered in Montreal and Toronto, and finally purchased by a Toronto dealer. These were contained in a specially made album of full morocco, gold lettering, with bristol leaves containing the stamps in cut-out spaces with bevelled sides, the leaves being all bevel-edged and gilded. The album and contents we believe had originally been made for the Post Office Department, or an official of the Bank Note Company.

The following year—1928—saw a new lot of imperforates put on the market by another Toronto dealer, who had obtained them when the estate of a former Post Office Department official was closed. These were at once taken up by the leading collectors, the quantity not being large. With the exception of the 7c. Olive-yellow, these were full O.G.

5c.:

This value is usually found on a bluish paper, but has been seen on a white paper.

8c. Brown-Orange:

This shade is from a printing used entirely by the T. Eaton Co. for catalogues mailing.

Map Stamps:

The "Imperial Penny Postage Commemorative Stamp" was designed by the Hon. Wm. Mulock, Postmaster-General. The quotation "We hold a vaster empire than has been" is from the Jubilee Ode by Sir Lewis Morris.

The imprint, in small capitals at top and bottom of sheet, reads "American Bank Note Co., Ottawa."

It is understood that 16,000,000 were issued. (London Philatelist VIII. '79). The plates were numbered 1, 2, 3 and 5.

Varieties:

1. Re-drawn inner line of cable at right extends into and above top cable.
2. Re-drawn inner and outer lines of cable at right extend slightly at top.
3. Right cable strongly re-touched, particularly toward bottom of stamp:

These retouches were first noted shortly after the stamps were issued, by Mr. l'Estrange Ewen. They appear on the right hand vertical row, and Mr. Ewen noted that nine of the ten stamps showed retouching. The plate was probably No. 3. Retouched stamps so far examined by the author are in the lavender shade.

4. Re-entry. Outer frame line doubled on right side, No. 27, Plate 2.
5. Stamp No. 46 on the plate shows the two most northerly islands as on the same parallel of latitude. In the normal stamps one of these islands is above and one on or slightly below the equator.
6. Stamp No. 48 on the plate shows an additional island.

There are many minor differences in the size and location of the dots of red color denoting British islands.

Forgeries:

There is a lithographic reproduction bearing a forged cancellation, circular type, reading in four lines "Montreal 24-12-98." The figures indicate that it was done in Europe as they are of the continental type not common in America.

First Use of Map Stamp:

The first letter to be despatched under Imperial Penny Postage was handed in at the G.P.O., Adelaide Street, Toronto, and bore the following endorsement.

"This is to certify that this letter was marked at the Toronto Post Office at one quarter minute past 12 o'clock on the morning of December 25th, 1898, and is the first letter to be posted and cancelled at the Toronto Post Office bearing the new Imperial Penny Postage Stamp, addressed to Great Britain.

"(Signed) JOHN CARRUTHERS,
"Assistant Postmaster."

King Edward Issue.

A Crown replaces the Maple Leaves in the upper corners. One plate sufficed for all values except the 2c., which are from Plates 1 to 14.

The Imperfs. first existed as printer's waste. An official of the P.O. Department states that in burning this waste a sheet of stamps was drawn up the chimney and fell in the street where it was picked up by someone who realized its philatelic value. This story is probably as good as any. The Department forestalled criticism for issuing unwarranted varieties by sending to the Ottawa G.P.O. stocks of the 2c. stamp in imperforate condition, printed from Plates 13 and 14 which were in use at that time. These were sold at face value as late as April, 1920, when the stock became exhausted.

In May, 1928, the Marks Stamp Company placed on the market a second lot of King Edward Imperfs., including the 2c. from Plate 2. It is understood these were among the personal effects of a former Postmaster General whose estate was being cleared up.

A sheet of the 2c. Imperf. from Plate 1 was among the Imperforate 1c., 5c., 7c. and 10c. sheets, but when these were cut into sets of pairs and blocks the owner did not include the 2c. value, considering it of low value according to standard catalogues. It was not until he had sold the two top rows of the other values, showing the date stamp of the American Bank Note Co., Ottawa, and the initials of Sir William Mulock, P.M.G., that he realized the imperforate 2c. stamps, being from Plate 1, were rare.

The tete-beche stamps are from a plate made up for printing booklet panes. These panes consisted of six stamps—two rows of three. The plate was made up to print two panes, with one pane inverted. The middle pair would, of course, be a tete-beche pair. Imperf. blocks of twelve from this plate are in the Lichtenstein, Clarke and Jarrett Collections only. These came on the market when the Marks Stamp Co. purchased certain philatelic material from the estate of a former Postmaster-General in May, 1928.

A hairline Variety is noted for the 2c., consisting of coarse parallel lines of color extending diagonally across the stamp.

2c. Guide dots may be noted in the 2c. stamps, consisting of single dots, pairs or groups of three, located so as to be hidden in the color of the numeral of value, but in rare instances falling to the left of the numeral.

A 2c. "Perce en arc" perforation was shown to the author and others in June, 1926. The cutting edges were inked to match the stamps, but we fail to see why this might make them cut any better. We consider this item an out-and-out fake.

1c.:

As in all green stamps, the shades vary. A very distinct grey-green is rare. There is a faulty perforation variety, the perforations running vertically on a line through "D" of CANADA and "E" of ONE.

5c.:

The fine cross hatching which forms the background of "Canada Postage" and "Five Cents" shows faintly in some stamps, due to the background consisting of horizontal lines only instead of horizontal and vertical. The need for retouching would exist, and a careful study of the 5c. stamps will reward the student with plenty of evidence of retouching, particularly in the background above described.

The 5c. Imperf., Plate 2, was included in the May, 1928, sale of imperforates mentioned earlier.

10c.:

There is a distinct variety consisting of a double line at left side of left tablet of value.

50c.:

The author has examined a specimen of this stamp in which "FIFTY" appears as "FHFTY". In another variety the top of the right hand "5" crosses through the oval.

Guide Dots:

These may be noted in the 2c. stamps, in pairs or groups of three, located so as to be hidden in the color of the numeral of value but in rare instances falling to the left of the numeral. Dr. Almas H. Walker, 147 Delaware Ave., Toronto, made a study of this issue and has discovered some interesting plate varieties.

Imperforates:

These came on the market in March, 1924, including the 1c., 5c., 7c. and 10c. values. The few pairs and blocks offered at auction were promptly taken up at comparatively high prices. There were two sheets of each value. These were stamped in the upper right corner with the date stamp of the American Bank Note Co., Ottawa, and in the upper left corner were initialed "W.M." (Sir. Wm. Mulock, P.M.G.). The dates were earlier than the date of issue of the ordinary stamps, the 1c., 2c. and 5c. being dated May 6th, 1903, and the 7c. and 10c. being dated June 1st, 1903.

In May, 1928, the Marks Stamp Co. placed on the market a second lot of King Edward Imperforates which, we understand, were purchased from the estate of a former Postmaster General. These were of a different shade and were from Plate 2.

The ownership of these imperforates is limited to a few collectors, as listed: (2 indicates a pair, 4 a block of four, etc.)

	Pl. 1	Pl. 2	2c. Tete-beche
Lichtenstein Collection	4		12
Clarke "	4	8	12
Jarrett "	4-12	16	12
Jeffcott "	4	4	
Reford "	20		
Kerr "	4		
Norris "	4	20	
Candler "	4	4	
Wilson "	4	4	
Telfer "	4	4	

Hair Lines:

After the plate has been made, the soft steel is bent to conform to the curvature of the rollers on which it is fitted for printing. This bending sometimes causes fine cracks to appear in the steel. If these are not completely taken out in the final burnishing or polishing (after the plate has been hardened), they show as fine lines of color, or hair-lines. These will be found to some extent in all values.

The Quebec Tercentenary Issue.

This issue commemorated the 300th anniversary of the founding of the City of Quebec by Champlain.

One stamp shows Cartier's arrival before Quebec. On the calm waters of the St. Lawrence stand in bold relief the three ships of the discoverer of Canada. "La Grande Hermione" of 120 tons, "La Petite Hermione" of 80 tons and "La Hermionette" of 40 tons.

In Champlain's narrative of his third voyage to Canada we read "with our canoes laden with provisions, our arms, and some merchandise to be given as presents to the Indians, I started on Monday, May 27th, from the Isle of Sainte Helaine, accompanied by four Frenchmen and one Indian. A salute was given in my honour from some small pieces of artillery." One stamp depicts Champlain's departure for the West. In one of the canoes Champlain's companions have already taken their places, paddle in hand, while the explorer is still on shore bidding good-bye to friends. Huber informs us that the word "Partement" in the legend "Partement pour l'Ouest" is now obsolete, this being the actual word used by Champlain.

	Quantities	Pt. Numbers
½c	2,000,000	1, 2
1c	22,530,000	3
2c	35,100,000	1, 2, 3, 4
5c	1,200,000	2
7c	700,000	1
10c	500,000	1
15c	300,000	1
20c	304,000	1

Variety in ½c.

Stamp No. 44 on the plate shows a line through bottom of the letters "ANAD" of CANADA, two dots in the "C" of CANADA, a dot on either side of "0" in 1608, a line above the "2" of "½" on the left, and a splitting of the bottom frame line at right center. This appears to have been the result of careless retouching, when the engraver's tool slipped and cut a line or prong away from the regular frame line. The other characteristics of this variety have all the appearance of a re-entry.

King George Issues.

The stamps were engraved and recess printed by the Canadian Bank Note Co., Ltd., of 234 Wellington Street, Ottawa (the Canadian subsidiary of the American Bank Note Co. of New York) on white wove paper, in sheets of 400 (20 horizontal by 20 vertical) with a margin at the top, bottom, and two sides. Plate numbers have been given where possible, from information supplied by Mr. Frederick T. Norris.

Originally the marginal inscription (in the upper margin of the two upper panes) took the form of the word OTTAWA followed by the plate number and the die number; about 1915 a new series of numbers (starting with 1) was inaugurated with the plate number preceded by the letter "A".

The inscription latterly appears normally only in the upper margin, over the 4th, 5th, 6th and 7th vertical rows of the upper left pane, and the 14th, 15th, 16th and 17th, vertical rows of the upper left pane, as T-7-OTTAWA-No.-A117, 944 A. T.

"A 117" is of course, the plate number, 944 the die number (of the 3c. denomination), while the initial "T-7" and the final "A T" are private check marks of the manufacturers.

In the lower margin of the lower left and lower right panes there is a band of beautiful engine turning, in the color of the stamp, appearing only partially, as the lower portion is usually cut off in trimming the sheets to size. (The 3c. carmine, imperforate, has the plate inscription in the lower margin of the two lower panes, and the upper margins blank). The exact significance of the private check marks cannot be learned, as "the lettering is put there for our own guidance, and cannot be of any possible interest to the general public; in fact it would be entirely contrary to our policy to disclose the information covered by these markings."

Between the 10th and 11th vertical rows, and the 10th and 11th horizontal rows, guide lines in color divide the 400 subjects into four panes of 100 stamps each (10x10) and knives passing along these guide lines (as the stamps were being perforated 12, single line) separated the sheets of 400 into Post Office Sheets of 100 stamps each. The Post Office Sheets of 100 have margins only at the top and one side (upper left and upper right panes) or at the bottom and one side (lower left and lower right panes). Of the 19 stamps in each pane or Post Office Sheet of 100, bordering on the guide lines, one is imperforate on two sides and 18 on one side.

The cross which surmounts the crown in the design has been the subject of some comment, not being a true representation of the cross on the actual crown. There are many points of difference in the crowns of the various issues.

Hairlines:

The hairline varieties listed for the 1c. and 2c. stamps are explained in the notes on the 2c. King Edward. These occur as very fine irregular lines crossing the stamp diagonally more numerous and pronounced on the 2c. than on the 1c. Of the 1c. but half the sheet of 100 shows the lines to any appreciable degree, but the entire sheet of the 2c. stamps show the hairlines throughout, sometimes as many as twenty lines crossing the stamp. In the 2c. stamp the hairline variety is from Plates 4 and 52. Plate 4 appeared in Feb., 1912

Embossed:

About April, 1925, the Georgian stamps appeared with the design so deeply impressed in the paper as to give an appearance of embossing. The Department could give no explanation and stated that no change had been made in the process of producing the stamps.

Thin Paper:

In order to obtain more stamps to the pound of paper used, an experimental run was made about October, 1924, using a thin wove paper. This did not prove satisfactory and succeeding runs were on the regular stock. This paper cannot be confused with the extremes of thin paper in the ordinary paper of issue.

Worn Plate

Worn Plates:

The stamp formerly listed as "block letter" variety is in reality the result of a worn plate. Similar, though less pronounced varieties, have since been noted.

Engine Turned Design on Sheet Margins:

The Georgian stamps are noted with an engine turned design on the bottom of the sheet. The plates are bent to form and the printing done from revolving drums. Signs of wear in the plate therefore first become apparent on that part of the plate from which the impression commences. Ordinarily a worn plate would not be noticed until the stamps of the lower row began to show poor impressions, but the use of this border design enables the pressmen to scrap a plate as soon as wear shows in the border and before it has reached the stamps.

Special Delivery, 10c. Green:

The stamps were printed in sheets of 50, 10 rows of 5. There are two types. In Type ... the numerals of value in the circle at right and left is shaded, in contrast to Type ... which shows clean-cut parallel lines.

There being few cities in Canada where a special delivery service is in operation, the use of such stamps is not common.

The Special Delivery stamps will not prepay postage. Postage stamps, however, will prepay special delivery charges. Since special delivery stamps will not prepay postage, it will be seen that nothing would be gained in affixing more than the one stamp. Collectors will please note, however, that in the interval between the introduction of the new 20c. Special Delivery stamp and the using up of the final supplies of the 10c. stamp, special delivery letters were prepaid with two 10c. special delivery stamp, to equal the new 20c. rate. The new rate was effective September, 1922, and used pairs of the 10c. Special Delivery about this date, properly date postmarked, have a peculiar value.

2

3c. Red Surcharged "2 Cents" or "Cents":

When the letter rate was restored to 2c. on July 1st, 1926, there was on hand 130,000,000 of the 3c. stamps—enough to last for twenty-five years if used for prepaying the 3c. rate to Great Britain, and representing in cost of paper, printing, gumming, perforating, etc., $15,000. It was therefore economical to surcharge these to help meet the demand for the stamp of the new denomination.

The work was entrusted to the King's Printer, and upwards of 15,000,000 of the 3c. stamps were surcharged with the one-line type in which the numeral "2" is 3 mm. high, the letters of "CENTS" 2½ mm. high, and the overall length of the surcharge, 16 mm.

The work was not satisfactory, owing to the difficulty of printing on gummed sheets, which had been perforated and cut into the regular post office sheets, and therefore impossible to feed to the presses accurately because of the varying widths or lengths of these cut sheets. Two of these sheets fed to the press accurately would result in wide variations in the position of the surcharge. The Deputy Postmaster-General ordered the stamps destroyed, but before this was actually proceeded with, 500 sheets were selected, to be distributed through the Postage Stamp Division to collectors. A letter from an official states "The entire quantity was ordered destroyed, and this was being done when an order came to save 500 sheets if possible and these were actually saved at the furnace door." The stamps were burned under supervision of an officer from the Auditor-General's Department.

The surcharged stamps were placed on sale at the Philatelic Bureau, Ottawa, on August 16th, 1926.

The plate numbers of the one-line type surcharge are 115, 116, 117, 162, 163. There exists but one sheet of Plates 162 and 163. Plates 117, 162 and 163 are in a carmine shade as compared to the others in a washed-out rose shade.

The supply was limited, and it was impossible to distribute the stamps to the various Post Offices throughout Canada. The Deputy Postmaster-General answered an enquiry as follows: "They were kept on sale at the Philatelic Bureau, at Ottawa, in order to oblige philatelists who might desire stamps of this kind. The different Post Offices know that the stamps are good for postage purposes and can be used for that purpose to pay postage to any part of the world."

Two or more stereos of 100 subjects were used for overprinting these stamps. Normally, the overprint is 16 mm. in length, but occasionally, it varies slightly. In its normal position the surcharge is over "3 CENTS" at the bottom of the stamp.

On almost every sheet there are slight imperfections in surcharging, but so insignificant that they cannot be classed as errors.

Of Plates 162 and 163, but one pane of each seems to have escaped destruction, and of these 48 of the stamps were sold to American tourists in Ottawa at the time they were placed on sale, and were used on postcards. The others were located in mint condition.

Huber states that he has seen two blocks of 25 (5x5) from the upper left corner of the upper left pane (Plate No. unknown, the margin having been removed) in which there is a badly broken "S" (lower curve) on stamps 4, 9, and 24. These would be positions 4, 14 and 44 on the 100 stamp sheets. A distinct variety has been listed, a "surcharged raised", the surcharge resting on the panels with numerals of value.

Surcharged by the Canadian Bank Note Co.:

The 2-line type surcharges were the work of the Canadian Bank Note Co., Ltd.. 1,000 sheets (100,000 stamps), were available for collectors. The distance from the top of the "2" to the bottom of "N" is 7 mm. the letters of "CENTS" are wider, and 2 mm. high, and the word measures 15 mm. in length. The figure "2" is slightly larger than in the one-line overprint.

There is a slight variation in the vertical spacing between the 8th, 9th and 10th horizontal rows, as in the one-line overprinted stamps. On the stamps of the 10th vertical row, the tail of "2" is at least ¾ mm. longer. due possibly to slipping of the sheet in printing.

Collectors are warned that, due to the poor printing and impression, differences which will be found are not constant.

The printing on each of the four sheets making up the pane is identical for both types.

Stamps of the right vertical row (2-line) show the left extremity of "2" in line with or to the right of the left extremity of the "N".

Variety in "2 CENTS":

The distance between "2 C" of the stamps on the right vertical row is slightly over 5 mm. The other stamps measure slightly over 4 mm.

1c., 2c., 3c. Imperforate:

These stamps in imperforate sheets made their appearance through the Collectors' Bureau. The imprint for the 3c., in one line reads "T-Z-OTTAWA No. A 127 944BG," and "T-Z-OTTAWA No. A 126 944 BG." The plates were numbered 126, 127, 128, 129, 130, 131 and the issue 100,000. Of the 1c. 50,000 were issued, plates 179, 180 of the 2c., 50,000 were issued, plates 188. 189.

1c. Yellow:

The stamp may be noted on a very thick wove paper, appearing in March, 1924.

2c. Rose-red:

The shades vary from pale to deep rose-red, brick red, and an aniline color which is scarce.

The 97th stamp on the sheet shows a white dot or accent over the "C" of "Cents."

The hairline variety is as described for the 1c. George and the 2c. King Edward, occurring on Plate 4, February, 1912.

2c. Green:

The shades vary from pale green to a deep blue green.

A double paper variety has been noted.

3c.:

The 3c. carmine exists in a variety known as double paper, a printing which fell on the overlapped portion of the paper, which had been joined in its manufacture.

In the 3c brown there is a variety with a dot of color resting on the bar of the H of THREE.

5c. Violet:

This stamp had been printed in blue, but International Postal Conventions made it necessary to issue the 10c. stamp in blue, and the 5c. was accordingly issued in violet.

8c. Blue:

On October 1, 1925, the foreign letter rate was reduced from 10c. to 8c., requiring a stamp of this denomination, which was printed in blue and issued September 1, 1925.

10c. Blue:

Following the raising of the International Postage Rates in 1922, the 10c. stamp was issued in blue for the new foreign letter rate.

There is a variety "Bald Spot at Back of Head".

$1 Orange Red:

The extensive use of the 50c. stamp by banks for registered mail parcels requiring postage to the value of many dollars, warranted the issue of a dollar stamp. This stamp is printed from a plate in which the design has been so deeply cut that the stamp has the appearance of an embossed stamp.

Confederation 3c. Brown:

This stamp commemorated the 50th anniversary of Confederation. The design shows the "Fathers of Confederation." The original painting by Robert Harris, President of the Royal Canadian Academy, was lost in the fire which destroyed the Parliament Buildings, in 1916. Plates 1 to 12 were used.

Confederation 3c. Brown Imperforate:

Mr. J. O. Labrecque of Montreal, was fortunate enough to obtain a large portion of the only imperforate sheet known. This has long since been broken into pairs and blocks. The author would like to record the names of collectors who possess these. 24 of the 100 stamps are accounted for as follows:

J. O. Labrecque	Blocks of 4 and 6
J. Edgar Tanguay	Blocks of 6
L. A. Davenport	Blocks of 4
Mrs. A. Russell Clarke	Blocks of 4

4c. Yellow Ochre:

This stamp was issued for convenience in prepaying postage on letters to Great Britain and Newfoundland. On July 1st, 1926, the rate was reduced to 3c.

3c. Brown Coil, Perf. 12 Horiz.:

These coils were supplied to a Montreal firm which claimed that their stamp affixing machine would not handle the regular coil stamps. Three rolls or coils had been made specially when it was found that the stamps were really for philatelic purposes. The Department later issued these coils through the Collectors' Bureau.

3c. Brown Coil, Perf. 12 Vert.:

Other standard catalogues either omit this variety entirely or do not price it. We believe it to be faked from a booklet pane of six stamps. Only a strip of more than three stamps would prove this item to be genuine.

1c. Green Coil, Perf. 8 Horiz.:

A variety similar to that described as a worn plate for the 1c. George, exists for this stamp, consisting of (a) a white triangular spot between "A P" of "CANADA POSTAGE" (b) background of some letters missing so as to give them the appearance of having been blocked out, and a large white space after "E" in POSTAGE.

2c. Rose-red Coils, Perf. 12 All Around:

There being no supply of the specially perforated sheets which are cut up for coils, an urgent demand necessitated calling into use the current 2c. Rose-red stamp in ordinary Post Office sheets, these being torn into vertical strips and pasted up for coils. About 18,000 rolls were made up, according to figures supplied by Mr. Frederick T. Norris. Mr. Norris happened to be in the Department when these were being made up, and realizing that there was nothing to distinguish them as coils he had them stamped over the "paste-up" on a number of strips. This stamp is in violet and reads "Postage Stamp Branch, May 11, 1915, P.O.D." in three lines, framed.

3c. Brown Coil, Perf. 8 Vert.:

There is a printing in an extremely pale shade, apparently from a plate which had been lightly inked.

1c. Green Horiz. Perf. 12 and 2 Holes 4½ mm. diam.:

This stamp was used for two days in July, 1918, in the Toronto General P.O., in a stamp vending machine. In addition to the horizontal Perf. 12, there are two holes 4½ mm. in diam. and 7 mm. apart, centered on the regular perforations. Teeth in the feed wheels engaged in these larger holes and made the feeding more positive, with less liability of the paper jamming. Stamps from this machine prior to the introduction of the stamps with the large holes, show two punctures where the two teeth came into operation.

The experiment was not considered a success and the sale of this coil was shortly after discontinued.

Pairs Perf. 8 Vert. and Imperf. Between:

It is believed that two only of these uncut coil sheets got out to the public. As soon as the Department became aware of their possession by collectors an attempt to destroy their value and importance was made, by issuing them at face value, in quantities. The 3c. plate, however, was no longer available and the reprints of the 1c. and 2c. are easily distinguished from the first printing.

"War Tax" Stamps:

The "Special War Revenue Act" of February, 1915 (See Revenue notes) necessitated both the Inland Revenue Department and the Post Office Department issuing stamps. In accordance with the Act, the 1c. green and 2c. carmine "WAR TAX" stamps made their appearance on April 15, 1915, to be used for paying the war tax on letters, post cards and postal money orders. They were, however, used as well on anything that required the tax, such as drugs, bank cheques, express waybills, telegrams. It also frequently happened that letters passed through the mails with the entire postage and tax combined prepaid in war tax stamps only.

The 1c. War Tax stamps differ from the ordinary 1c. green stamps in other respects than in having the wording "WAR TAX" across the lower portion of the design. Henry J. Perry, M.D., was the first student to call attention to the difference in the shape of the figures in the lower corners, the difference in spacing between the right maple leaf and the square containing the numeral of value, the space being narrower in the ordinary stamp so that a horizontal line of the background cannot pass the leaf and numeral as it does in the WAR TAX stamp. The portion of the epaulette in white is different also. The die, transfer roll and plate were carefully prepared and the finished stamp does not indicate the "hurry-up" job attributed to these stamps.

The fact that these 1c. and 2c. stamps had WAR TAX engraved on them, contributed to the confusion of the general public and even to postmasters, the Inland Revenue Department having (as explained in the Revenue Chapter) overprinted postage stamps with WAR TAX to serve their purposes. As early as March 5, 1915, the Deputy Postmaster-General, in a circular to the Postmasters, advised that "postage stamps of 5c., 20c., and 50c. denominations, impressed with the words 'WAR TAX' are being used by the Inland Revenue Department for the collection of war tax on wines, and the Postmaster is especially instructed that postage stamps of these denominations having the words WAR TAX impressed on them, are not to be accepted for postage, as they are being used exclusively for Inland Revenue purposes."

The circular of April 16th, 1915, from Ottawa, did not help matters. It read "The Postmaster has been informed that it has been decided that postage stamps upon which the words 'WAR TAX' have been printed may be accepted for prepayment of postage, and he is to amend his instructions and procedure accordingly. In no circumstances are Inland Revenue stamps to be accepted on letters, post cards, postal notes, or Post Office Money Orders."

On 22nd April, 1915, a philatelist was informed officially from Ottawa that "in so far as the Post Office Department is concerned, the

War Tax stamps have only been issued in two denominations, namely, 1c and 2c. The 2c War Tax stamp may be used on money orders, cheques, notes, and whatever the tax of that rate applies. I would also add that ordinary postage stamps may be used to pay War Tax fees, and that the Post Office War Tax stamps can be used to prepay postage charged."

It will be seen that the general misunderstanding could have but one result—the use of the 5c, 20c, and 50c overprinted stamps for the prepayment of postage, and these are known postally used, even on registered covers.

iTc (1c Tax) Stamps.

The "WAR TAX" stamps were superseded by a stamp which included the 1c tax and was sold for 3c. According to a circular to the Postmasters, from the Deputy Postmaster General, dated December 30, 1915, "This is an ordinary 2c postage stamp surcharged as follows: iTc (one cent tax). This has been issued in response to the demand of the public for a stamp having the value of 3c, so that postage and war tax might be paid by affixing one stamp. This stamp is of permanent validity."

The stamps were printed from plates which give two distinct varieties, Die I and Die 11. The die that is common in the carmine stamp is rare in the brown stamp.

Quoting from a statement by an official of the Postage Stamp Division, "Postage stamps are manufactured from a master die which is transferred to a rotary or steel wheel, then transferred to the steel plate, 400 impressions to the plate, and from the plate printed on the paper. In the case of this stamp the master die was found to be wearing out, due to the steel being soft, and a new master die was engraved, when these slight differences crept in the engraving."

Plates 15 and 16 were made from the new master die, which differed in a number of details from the original master die. The total number of stamps in carmine from these plates 15 and 16 (Die II) was 5,500,000. At this time the color of the stamp was changed from carmine to brown.

With the 2c postage, and the iTc stamp printed in the same color, it is natural that confusion resulted, and a change was found necessary. Under date of August 26, 1916, the Deputy Postamaster General notified Postmasters that, "In future these stamps will be issued in the color mentioned (brown) so as to overcome the difficulty experienced owing to the similarity in color to the ordinary 2c stamp."

New plates were needed, but were not ready, and Plates 15 and 16 were supplemented by the use of Plates 1 and 2, which had not been destroyed. Plates 1 and 2, of course, were of the old die, Die I. The use of these two old plates accounted for 450,000 stamps in brown showing Die I, the original die. Plates 15 and 16, and all subsequent plates up to the end, numbered 56, were from the new Die II.

Printings from Plate I are in a light brown shade (as seen from the imperf. sheet of Plate I and Plate II examined by the author, but the rare die iTc stamp is almost invariably seen in the dark shade. There must have been a small printing from Plate I.)

iTc Carmine, Perf. 12 horiz. x 8 vert.

This stamp was placed on sale in August, 1916, as a temporary makeshift "The manufacturers were obliged to use part of the stock which had been prepared for roll postage, and perforated sideways with the wide perforation. These sheets were then perforated endwise with the regular perforation, and issued."

Imperforate 1½c Brown.

In May, 1924, a single sheet of the 1½c brown stamp (common die) was sold to Mr. Harry Brook, of Simcoe, Ont. He sold half of the sheet to Mr. L. A. Davenport, of Toronto, and this was broken up and sold by Mr. Davenport and Mr. Geo. A. Lowe, to different specialists. Mr. Chas. J. Phillips purchased the Brook Collection, containing the other half-sheet, which was also broken up. The author would like to list the names of collectors who own these blocks. Twenty-eight of the stamps have been accounted for, as follows:

Fred Jarrett	Block of 4
Alfred Jephcott	Block of 4
Frederick T. Norris	Block of 4
J. Edgar Tanguay, M.D.	Pair 2
Mrs. A. Russell Clarke	4-4-4
Chas. J. Phillips	Strip 6
Chas. J. Phillips	Strip 4 (imprint)

In the Davenport lot of imperfs, put on the market in 1928 (see notes on Numeral Issue and King Edward Imperfs.) there was a sheet from Plate I (Rare Die) and Plate II (Rare Die), Plate I being in a lighter shade. Since the rare die 1½c brown is almost invariably seen in the dark shade, we believe the light brown stamp to be quite rare. The imperf. rare dies, imprint blocks, Plate I and Plate II, went into Mrs. A. Russell Clarke's collection.

Prior to September, 1923, when the Collectors' Bureau, P.O. Dept., Ottawa, sold the few remaining copies of the Officially Sealed stamps at a nominal price, these stamps proved exceedingly elusive. Values were upset for a time, but the stamps have again found a level.

Until the above date, the authorities took every precaution to see that no Officially Sealed stamps left the Department. From the wording we might assume that the labels were used to seal dead letters retained in the D.L.O. This is correct, but *all* dead letters were not sealed with these labels. An envelope containing correspondence of importance, and which could not be delivered to the addressee or returned to the sender who might prove his identity, was "officially sealed" by the proper official, this seal then becoming a guarantee that the contents of the envelope were intact should the rightful owner come forward. This explanation was obtained from an Ottawa philatelist of repute, whose official position made it possible for him to pursue enquiries regarding the proper use of the stamps.

Used copies show the D.L.O. postmark and are usually creased from having been used as a sticker sealing the envelope.

THE 1927 HISTORICAL AND "JUBILEE OF CONFEDERATION" ISSUE.

The Historical Issue was prepared for July 1st, 1926, but was withheld, and came out with the appearance of the "Jubilee of Confederation" stamps announced for July 1st, 1927.

Supplies had been sent to postmasters, with instructions to hold the stamps until the morning of July 1st, but these instructions were not obeyed in some offices, with the result that first-day covers are postmarked June 28th and June 29th.

On Dominion Day, 1st July, 1927, the Postmaster-General of Canada, Honourable Charles Murphy, sent to every Postmaster, and practically every publication printed in Canada, the following letter:

Ottawa, Dominion Day, July 1st, Nineteen twenty-six. To commemorate the beginning of the sixtieth year of Confederation and the restoration of Two Cent Postage, I desire to extend Greetings to the Canadian Public and to express the hope that increasing prosperity may help to bring about a further reduction in the burden of war taxation. Signed, Charles Murphy, Postmaster-General of Canada."

Another message was sent to friends and associates, which read, "To Commemorate the Beginning of the Sixtieth Year of Confederation and the Restoration of Two Cent Postage, I am sending you this Greeting Prepaid at Penny Postage Rate which is Effective from this date. Sgd. Chas. Murphy, Postmaster-General of Canada."

Quantities Issued.

5c McGee	20,000,000
12c Laurier-Macdonald	5,000,000
20c Baldwin-Lafontaine	7,000,000

2c:

This stamp has been noted with double paper.

5c Laurier.

The career of that great statesman, Sir Wilfrid Laurier, is difficult to compress into the space at our command. Laurier was the offspring of strict French Roman Catholic parents, but his education, some time in a Protestant School, and his lodging with a Presbyterian family during some of this time, undoubtedly had a permanent influence upon his mind, and showed effects throughout the rest of his life. Laurier was opposed to Confederation. He made some remarkable speeches in the Federal House in defence of Riel and the French halfbreeds in the Red River rebellion. He was a strenuous opponent to the construction of the Canadian Pacific Railway. The ultramontaine element of the Roman Catholic church in Quebec were always against him. In 1887 he became the first French Canadian to lead a Federal party; his personal supremacy was shown by his long continuance in power. The chief features of his administration were the fiscal preference of 33 1/3% in favour of goods imported into Canada from Great Britain, the dispatch of Canadian contingents to South Africa during the Boer War, the contract with the Grand Trunk Railway to construct a second transcontinental line from coast to coast (a volt face from his opposition to the C.P.R.), the assumption of Canadian Defence, the reduction of the postal rate, a tariff arrangement with the U.S.A. His attempt to bring in a Reciprocity bill caused his downfall, as the Canadian people considered that reciprocity with the U.S.A. was merely the thin edge of the wedge of annexation. A skilful party leader, an orator of no mean order, he held the affections of his party until his death in Ottawa, 1919. (Huber.)

Varieties:

There is a pronounced dot in the ball of the lower right figure 5, occurring in No. 66, Plate 2, left top pane.

A printing fell on the overlapped portion of paper joined in manufacturing, resulting in a "double paper" variety.

5c McGee.

Thomas D'Arcy McGee was an eloquent Irishman, who after a somewhat stormy career, in which he took part in the insurrection of Smith O'Brien in 1848, was compelled to flee from Ireland. He escaped to the United States and at length arrived in Montreal, where he started a newspaper and became very popular. He first entered the Canadian Parliament in 1857. Being an Irishman he was "agin" the Government, and consequently was allied with George Brown. In 1862 he became President of the Council under John Sandfield Macdonald. Later he changed his views, so that he came into close political and personal comradeship with John A. Macdonald. He was a member of the Tache-Macdonald administration in 1864, and until Confederation was accomplished, when he resigned. In 1865 he visited Ireland, and while there vehemently denounced Fenianism and the Fenians. This courageous attitude brought upon him the rage and hatred of a large bulk of that brotherhood, and probably led to his assassination. He was murdered on the night of April 7th when entering his office in Ottawa after having attended a session of Parliament. The deed was ascribed to the Fenians.

A printing fell on the overlapped portion of a roll of paper joined in manufacturing, resulting in a "double paper" variety.

Sir John A. Macdonald.

Sir John Alexander Macdonald, the first premier of the Dominion of Canada, was born in Glasgow, of Sutherlandshire parents. The family first settled in Kingston, Ontario, where he first made acquaintance with public business as an alderman of that city. In 1884 he was elected as conservative member for Kingston, and a sentence in his first address to the electors strikes the dominant note of his public career:—"I therefore need scarcely state my firm belief that the prosperity of Canada depends upon its permanent connection with the mother country, and that I shall resist to the utmost any attempt which may tend to weaken that union." He was a member of the Reform Government which passed the Rebellion Losses Bill. This caused a riot in Montreal, which ended in the burning of the houses of parliament in that city, with the ultimate result of the formation of league with the confederation of all the provinces of Canada as its objective. The Fenian raids across the American border, and other incidents of international gravity gave impulse to the movement, which was consumated in the framing of the North American Act.

Among the many benefits he showered upon Canada, must be mentioned the construction of the Canadian Pacific Railway. "The faith of Sir John," said one of his biographers, "did more to build the road than the money of Mount-Stephen." From 1878 till his death in 1891 his history is practically that of Canada.

Few political leaders had such a number of antagonistic elements to reconcile as presented themselves in the first Canadian parliament after Confederation. The man who could manage to rule a congeries of jealous factions, including Irish Catholics and Orangemen, French and English anti-federationists and agitators for independence, Conservatives and Reformers, careful economists and prodigal expansionists, was manifestly a man of unusual power and without any bias toward any creed. Such a man Macdonald proved himself to be. He made Canada a nation.

Robert Baldwin (20c) was a Canadian statesman, born at York (now Toronto), 1804, of Irish parentage, was a devoted member of the Church of England. He was many times in office and as often resigned. He steadfastly opposed any advanced views of the Liberal or Radical party, and was constantly in hot water. But even those who most bitterly attacked his measures, admitted the purity and unselfishness of his motives. After the concession of responsible government he devoted himself to bringing about a good understanding between the English and the French speaking inhabitants of Canada, and his memory is held as dear among the French Canadians as in his native province of Ontario. He died December, 1858.

Sir Louis Hippolyte Lafontaine (20c), Canadian statesman and judge, was born at S. Boucherville, Quebec, in 1807. He entered parliament 1830, and became an ardent admirer of Papineau, one of the leaders of the rebellion of 1837. Lafontaine, however, did not approve of the violent methods of his leader, and though he disapproved these tactics, he became involved in the trouble of that time and was for a short time in prison. Later he collaborated with Robert Baldwin in forming a ministry, and it was during the ministry of Lafontaine-Baldwin that the Amnesty Bill was passed, which occasioned grave riots in Montreal, personal violence to Lord Elgin, and the destruction of the Parliament buildings. He became Chief Justice of Lower Canada. Died February, 1864. (Huber.)

12c Map.

There is a variety in the 12c Map stamp, No...... in the 5th row, showing two small dots in the tail of the "2" of the lower left "12."

20c Special Delivery.

We believe the tiniest lettering on any postage stamp appears on this 20c Special Delivery. The design typifies the conveyance of mail by horse, rail, water and air. At the bottom left hand corner will be found the extremely small lettering referred to. A horseman is carrying a tiny mail bag, and careful examination will reveal that this bag bears in microscopic form the legend "Canada P. O."

Georgian Issue of October, 1928.

A letter from the Department at Ottawa reads in part: "Commemorative issues such as the Confederation issue, are always temporary issues, and as soon as practicable the service reverts to a permanent issue, which is now being done in respect to the 1c and 2c denomination in the new design.

"Other denominations are being provided for as soon as possible, and for purposes of economy, changes have not been made until it becomes necessary."

This would mean that as stocks of the Confederation and Historical issues became exhausted, replacements would be made with stamps of the new design, and such new stamps would continue in use indefinitely.

The 2c stamp was the first to go into use, and the above letter has the following interesting admission to make in this respect: "Action was required on the 2c denomination for the reason that a great many complaints have been received in regard to the 2c Confederation stamp, which was considered too large for the purpose.

5c Airmail.

Many compliments have been paid this stamp, and, as always, a few criticisms. One of these seems to be justified. It will be noted that the angels have but one pair of wings between them. Engravers have in the past put the wrong end of the telescope to the explorer's eye, engraved lions' claws on seals, and made other odd slips, but an angel from Heaven with one wing does not seem to give sufficient guarantee of speedy delivery of any messages intended for the air route.

The author has a mild criticism to make: Why issue the stamp in a shade that is "earthy" when sky blue is so appropriate.

The stamp is one of the finest examples of the engraver's art that Canada has had since the days of the 3d Beaver. Whoever he may be, we do not hesitate to say that there are few such craftsmen in the world to-day.

This beautiful stamp deserves better than to be stuck on those circus envelopes which our erring cousins to the south are so prone to use. Postal clerks who handle millions of registered and thousands of special delivery letters do not need to have their intelligence insulted by any red-white-and-blue decorations to tell them the letter prepaid with this 5c distinctive airmail stamp shouldn't be thrown in the ordinary mail bags.

BAHAMAS SPECIAL DELIVERY.

(Scott's 41) Used from Canada.

The following information is from a letter dated 2nd May, 1928, received from Mr. H. E. Atwater, Financial Superintendent, Post Office Department, Canada:

"A special delivery service between Canada and the Bahamas was inaugurated on the 1st January, 1916. This was done at the request of the Government of that country. The idea was that letters written in Canada for the Bahamas could have one of the stamps placed on them for special delivery in those islands. That country did not have a regular special delivery stamp and had a regular five penny stamp overprinted with the words "special delivery." It was understood that the number of stamps sent to Canada, i.e., 600, was to be the whole issue. These were placed on sale at four offices in Canada—Ottawa, Toronto, Westmount and Winnipeg—and about 430 were distributed in this manner.

"The Department soon discovered that these stamps were being sent to the Bahamas to two individuals by a number of stamp collectors, and that they were really not being used legitimately. The Bahamas Government had strong representations made to them from stamp collectors throughout the world that they were unable to get the stamps owing to the limited quantity, and they immediately, without the knowledge of the Department, had a further supply of 6,000 printed in England for distribution to collectors. These were slightly different, as collectors soon discovered.

"When the Department discovered this they immediately cancelled the arrangement with the Bahamas Government and ordered the balance of the stamps in the hands of the offices mentioned to be sold in any way at once.

"The action which was taken on this case by the Bahamas Post Office involved this Department in a number of inquiries which were somewhat difficult to answer, for the reason that a complete answer could not be given without an apparent criticism of another Postal Administration.

"While the Department is ready and willing at all times to furnish any information it has in its possession to persons applying for such information in respect of postage stamps that have been used in the Canadian Postal Service, it accepts no responsibility whatsoever for the correctness of such information, or its application to philatelic requirements."

January, 1916.

5d orange and black Bahamas (Scott's No. 41) overprinted at

Nassau. Bahamas, in black, "Special Delivery." Cover from Canada only $125.00

The sheets supplied Ottawa by the Bahamas Postal Authorities contained the varieties listed below:

a. Double overprint.
b. Double overprint, one inverted.
c. Inverted overprint (30).
d. Pair, one without overprint (5 pairs).

5d bright orange and grey-black (6,000). Cover from Canada only 25.00

Introduced Feb., 1903, for prepayment in cash of quantities of third class matter. Printed on wrapper or cover in black or dark blue.

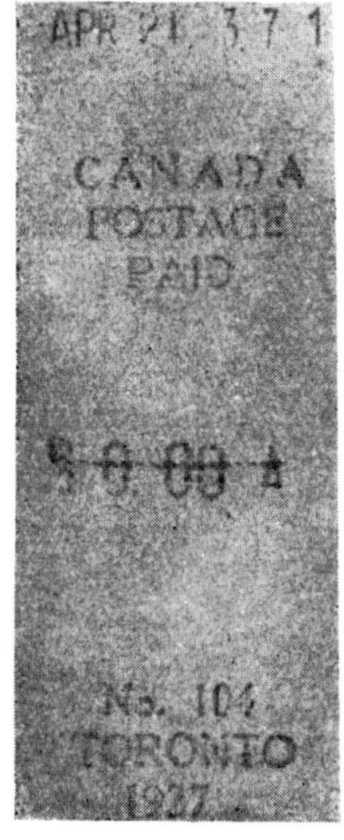

Cash Register, "Postage Paid in Cash" Labels.

On September 3rd, 1925, the P. O. Department issued Permit 100 to the Robert Simpson Co., governing the use of "Postage Paid in Cash" labels issued from cash registers used to receive and record the amount of postage paid. The official notice governing these labels reads:

"Postmasters are informed that in order to facilitate the handling and despatch of parcels posted at the large centres where extensive mailings are made, for delivery at places in the Dominion of Canada or in the United States, the Postage Paid in Cash system has been extended to parcel post. Each parcel mailed under the Postage Paid in Cash system will have affixed to it at the upper right hand corner of the address, where stamps are usually placed, an impression in red showing the amount of postage paid."

The first labels were on white gummed paper, printed by the Cash Register type in red, soon followed by violet, and in April, 1927, the Toronto General Post Office was supplied with cash register rolls printed in violet over a safety design in grey showing crown, maple leaf, and words "Canada Postage."

The wording on the labels and the arrangement is subject to too great variation to permit an accurate listing.

A wide range of "Permit Number" printed designs exist, in various colors, such as "Canada Post" enclosed in circles with "½ cent, 1926," in centre printed on the envelope in black. The variation and number is without limit.

Perforated "O.H.M.S."

In the fall of 1926 collectors noted different values of the Georgians appearing perforated O.H.M.S. The P.O. Dept. explained these as follows: "The Dept. of Militia and Defence, the Finance Dept., the Bell Telephone Co., and other companies had permission to perforate stamps as they saw fit, and purchased their own machines for so doing."

PROOFS, ESSAYS AND COLOR TRIALS.

"Die" proofs are taken from the original steel engraving, one at a time. "Plate" proofs are from the finished plate. Essays are proofs from the original steel engraving, of designs not accepted. Color trials are plate proofs in various shades of color.

Die proofs usually have ample margins. In any proof taken from a steel plate the ink is delivered from the lines in the plate to the paper pressed upon it, giving a fine sharp impression, and there is a perceptible body of ink transferred to the paper from the cut lines.

The actual beginning of a stamp is the artist's sketch showing a suggested design. If this is accepted the design is perfected and an engraving made on steel. This design may finally be discarded in favor of something more desirable, when it becomes an "essay."

Proofs are made in various colors, and a choice having been made, everything is ready for the issuing of the stamp of issue. Postal regulations may govern the color in which a stamp is issued.

Proofs are occasionally seen with heavy penwritten strokes, and a portion of the proof missing. This is a tested proof, the possibility of removing a cancellation without changing the natural coloring of the stamp having been the subject of experimentation. After pen strokes have been made on the stamp a corner is cut off and kept for comparison with the remainder after it has been subjected to chemical experiments with a view to removing the cancellation. If the shade of the treated portion differs from the shade of the part held for comparison, it is sufficient evidence that any dishonest effort to remove a cancellation would change the color of the stamp.

Particularly skilled in his art is the engraver who can in the space of a thumbnail reproduce perfect portraits of important personages, whose privilege it is to criticize the slightest defect. Many difficulties must be overcome before a satisfactory "head" has been engraved and accepted.

Sometimes one engraving of a head or central design is used for a series of stamps. The engraving for each of the other values of the set is without the centre, and the engraving of this centre is used to complete the design. The blank oval in the stamp will be slightly larger than the size of the central design to allow for any variation in the centering which would otherwise mean an overlapping at some point.

The engravings for two of the heads used for the early Canadian stamps were used in later issues. Proofs from the original engraving of the head alone, as illustrated for the 7½d are very rare. This illustration shows how a stamp design is "built up."

Proofs of stamps in color of issue bearing the word "SPECIMEN" were sent out to the chief postal administrators of all countries in the Postal Union, for purposes of reference, when a new design or change of color or any other obvious difference was made in the stamp, and if the P.O. Department deemed the difference important.

The usual number of sets surcharged "SPECIMEN" is said to be about 1,200. No single colony, however large or important, receives more than five sets of each. The higher values are not nearly so numerous. Most of these proofs are retained in official archives for reference, and only those which are superfluous or not likely to be required actually come on the market.

With very few exceptions these specimens are much more rare than the stamps which are issued to the public. Collectors as a whole have not yet realized their true philatelic interest and value, although there is evidence of no little activity on the part of advanced collectors in respect to proof collecting. The time is fast approaching when the majority of collectors will possess a showing of these specimen stamps, which add interest and value to a collection, and enable the specialist to pursue his studies to a point not possible with the actual stamps of issue.

CANADIAN POSTAL STATIONERY

By T. L. Derwent Kinton, M.A.

The field of Canadian Postal Stationery is one which has not received that measure of attention which it deserves. Even specialists, who devote their entire attention to Canadian stamps, have but a fair representation of the issues, varieties, and errors which exist in this interesting field. The stamped envelopes, postcards, letter cards and wrappers of the Dominion of Canada are well worthy of careful study, and, it is to be hoped, they will receive that measure of attention which is their due as postal issues of this country.

Stamped envelopes were first issued by New South Wales, in the year 1858. They were first issued in Canada in 1860. The month in which they appeared is a moot question, but it was early in that year. February is given by Howes, and may be correct. The earliest date the writer has seen is March 16th, 1860.

There were two values, the five cent red and the ten cent black-brown. The stock used was a good quality of laid paper, watermarked "Ca" over "POD" and was very similar to the paper used for the U.S. envelopes of the same period. They were manufactured by George F. Nesbitt of New York, for the British American Bank Note Co., who then held the contract for supplying Canadian stamps.

Only one issue of the ten cent envelope was required, but a second supply of the five cent value was called for in 1864. This resulted in a variety with a less rounded flap than that of the previous issue.

The varieties are listed in the Stationery Chapter, and in the Chapter on Essays and Proofs will be found a list of color trials on different papers. The author's collection contains three attempts at a forgery of the five cent envelope and two of the ten cent. The first of the five cent forgeries, on white wove, is extremely crude; the second, on yellow wove, is crude only as to the lettering, the centre being a good likeness of the Queen, and the embossing well done; while the third, on yellow wove, is deeply embossed and is characterized by a head of the Queen with thick lips and an oversize nose. Of the ten cent envelopes, both are on yellow wove, one corresponding to the second type of the five cent forgery, in deep chocolate, and the other corresponding to the third type of the five cent forgery, in pale brown.

After Confederation the Government did not issue stamped envelopes until October 6, 1877. This is the design illustrated and designated as Type A2. The values were 1c and 3c, and the colors were blue and red respectively. The chief point of interest in this and subsequent issues down to 1896, was the varying width of the cross vergures, or parallel laid lines running at right angles to the close laid lines of the paper. They were 18 mm. apart in the issues of 1877, and in the issues of 1888 they were 24 mm. apart. In the case of the 1c deep blue of 1896 the cross vergures were 27 mm. apart. A few envelopes of the first issue had tongued flaps, but it was evidently an experiment, as the pointed flap is the type for all remaining issues down to 1896. One further variety remains to be noted in this series, and that is a 3c envelope on wove paper.

One December 13, 1894, a special issue of 1c and 3c stamped envelopes was made by the Government for Mr. Frederick Burnett, of Brantford, who states "five thousand of the 1c and three thousand of the 3c stamped envelopes official size, on buff paper, were issued by the Post Office Department." They were evidently made to meet a special need and are the only instances of any sort in which the Post Office Department has catered to the wishes of a private firm, with the single exception of the C.P.R. Letter Sheets.

The 3c stamped envelopes that were in stock when the postal rate was lowered to two cents were surcharged with a hand stamp. The work was crudely done and many varieties in position of the surcharge resulted. Double impressions are also noted. The chief variety was a capital "C". It was evidently an error, for as soon as noted it was changed and consequently is very scarce. All previous regular issues of the 3c envelope were surcharged with the single exception of the 3c tongued flap. This adds size B of the 1877 issue to the check list of Howes.

The Edwardian and Georgian stamped envelopes require very little comment, as the design of the frame is the same in each case, and the embossed head is the only difference. Mention has already been made of the envelope designated Size F in the check list. The 1c and 2c envelopes now conform to the color changes of the stamps of the same value.

On June 14, 1895, a 2c envelope was issued. It was intended for "drop letters" or letters mailed and delivered within municipal limits. The stamp was rather fantastic in design (Type A3). The cardboard proof shown in Chapter on Proofs, in carmine, is quite possibly an essay submitted at about this time.

When the contract with the British American Bank Note Co. expired in 1897 the work was done by the King's Printer at Ottawa, a wove paper being used for the most part. Type 4 was the first issue from the King's Printer, and appeared in April, 1898. The 2c violet was issued January 2, but was changed to red in six days, to conform to postal regulations. 10,000 were issued. In addition, the size of the envelope for all values remained constant, until December of 1922, when Size F made its appearance.

The following changes have been made in the stamped envelopes:

The size of the regular stamped envelopes has been increased and is noted in the check list as Size "G". The head has been re-engraved.

The features are now sharper and the hair has a decided "combed" effect. The figure "3" has been changed. In the case of the envelopes, Size "F" the head is now embossed and the "cheap" appearance of the earlier issue is corrected. The 2c envelope has not yet appeared with this change, but will doubtless soon follow. The knife used in cutting the paper for these envelopes has been changed also and now conforms in shape with that of the regular issue. A cheap manila 1c envelope, Size "F" made its appearance in January of 1926. There will probably be further changes to conform to the color regulations and the reduction in the postal rate.

In September, 1926, the Post Office Department supplied business firms with stamped envelopes of practically any size, made to order, with advertising matter printed on the face of the envelope. Some of these have been very elaborate, and even beautiful.

RETURNED LETTER ENVELOPES.

In 1855 the Department returned undelivered letters to the sender, enclosed in a buff envelope, size 8¾ x 4⅛ inches, with inscription on face "RETURNED LETTER, Post Office Department, Official Business," in three lines, and on the inside of the flap "The enclosed letter has been opened by the proper Officer appointed for that purpose, and is returned to you as the writer thereof, for the reason thereon assigned. W. G. Griffin, Secretary."

POST CARDS

Post cards were first issued in Canada in 1871—considerably earlier than the issue of stamped envelopes for the Dominion. They were beautifully engraved and had an ornamental engine-turned border. The first issue bore the marginal imprint "British American Bank Note Co., Montreal and Ottawa," just inside the south border. A subsequent issue in 1876 omitted the "Ottawa."

In 1882 a cheaper method of production was adopted, the border was omitted and the stamp was the same as Type 2 of the wrapper stamps. The words "Canada Post Card" were enclosed in a banderole, and below it was the injunction "The address to be written on this side." Type 1 of the wrapper stamp was never used for post cards.

Blue was the normal color, but there were numerous shades.

A curious and very rare error appeared in 1884 in the case of the reply card. The stamp was printed at the left of the banderole and not at the right hand side. This is due to the design being in two pieces. It is simply a printer's error—and they are not uncommon. The claim, that this error was due to cutting the cards incorrectly is easily proven to be false by the use of a millimeter scale. The very strict order that followed the appearance of these cards, calling for their immediate return to Ottawa, is the chief cause of their scarcity. In some cases the cards and the notice for their return were received at the same time.

Subsequent issues down to 1896 followed the designs of the wrapper stamp, and the illustrations are sufficient. The large business card of 1893 proved too cumbersome and was soon discontinued.

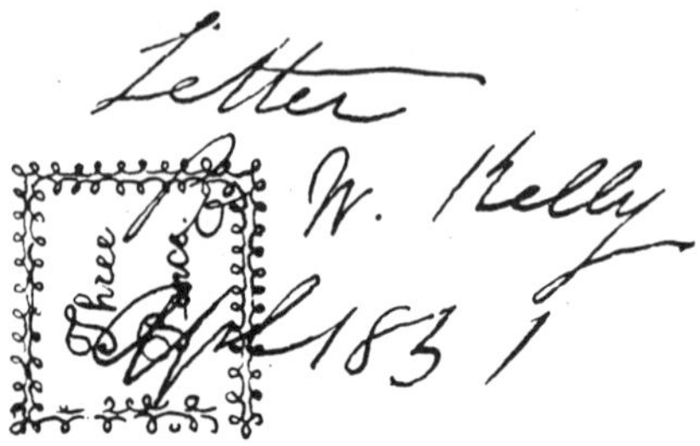

PROVISIONAL STAMPED ENVELOPE

The provisional stamped envelope illustrated, used from New Carlisle, Gaspe, Québec, April 7, 1851, addressed to Hugh Miller, Esq., Medical Hall, Toronto, C.W., must have been printed upon the initiative of Mr. R. W. Kelly, the local Postmaster, whose signature appears across the design. But one specimen ever came to the attention of philatelists, and the present whereabouts of this is not known to the author.

The 3d Beaver stamps were not issued until April 23, 1851, although an advance circular may have been sent out announcing the proposed issue. Postmasters generally made use of a brass stamp with which to mark the amount prepaid on a letter—usually 3d—and these stamps differed in design, as illustrated elsewhere. In many cases the amount was written in black ink by the Postmaster. The New Carlisle Postmaster was therefore not violating any regulations in having a "Three Pence" marking set in type and enclosed in a fancy border. Donald A. King examined this envelope in 1904 and stated: "I have shown the cover to a friend who is an expert in typography and he assures me that the printing is as old as dated."

If this marking was applied by the Postmaster to all envelopes or covers upon which a 3d rate had been prepaid, the stamped envelope illustrated would be in the same class as any envelope bearing the rate markings illustrated in the cancellation chapter. If, however, the Postmaster kept a supply of envelopes so stamped, ready for sale at 3d plus a possible fee covering the cost of the envelope, the item is an exceedingly rare and valuable provisional. The neatness with which the marking appears on the only known specimen lends strength to the theory that they were prepared in advance and sold as required. Again, Postmaster Kelly would be unlikely to perform the two operations of handstamping with this design and signing in pen and ink, when with pen and ink he could inscribe a large figure "3" to denote that the amount had been paid.

The ½c Business Reply Post Card is also an attempt to cater to the needs of the business world. Printed matter, requesting further information, is given on the back of the card. The card may be mailed if the sender merely adds his name and address. These cards are enclosed in letters and in the case of the 1c+½c Business Reply Card the ½c card is severed and returned.

According to announcements, the rate for post cards has not been altered. It may also follow in due course, as there is no reason why the letter rate should apply to post cards.

No new Postal Union card has as yet made its appearance, although the rate has been lowered from six to four cents.

In the case of the cards the designs conformed to the design of the stamps then current. Thus the Jubilee post card bore a stamp similar in design to the Jubilee stamp. The Jubilee card exists without the usual inscription in its ornamental border. The stamp alone was printed on the card. In the case of the four maple leat reply card there is a very rare error due to the reply portion being printed on the back of the message card, the reply portion being blank.

The Edwardian and Georgian cards call for little comment, with the exception of noting that Georgian cards conform to the color changes introduced in 1922.

The business post cards were introduced in 1898 and were intended to allow firms to print advertising matter on the face of the card. The inscription "The space below is reserved for the address" indicated the portion of the card that might not be used for any other purpose. It was printed in the centre of the right half of the card. In the first Georgian business card this inscription was in French as well as in English. In the next issue—about 1915—a colored line was substituted and in addition a vertical line joined it at the left. This was soon omitted and now the colored horizontal line is used to indicate the portion reserved for the address.

The Postal Union Cards are the most beautiful cards that Canada has issued. They have all been line engraved and are in a class by themselves. The 2c post card to the United Kingdom was issued just before Canada was admitted to the Postal Union. It had a border very similar to the first post cards. The first card in this series bore the inscription "Union Postale Universelle". It likewise had the ornamental border and the stamp was slightly different in design.

A new card was issued in 1896. The frame or border was omitted and the design and inscription is as shown in the illustration. It is unquestionably the handsomest card Canada has ever issued. The normal color is a brilliant orange-red, but there is a very scarce carmine shade.

Here too, subsequent issues follow the design of the stamp, but the inscription has remained the same as that of the 1896 card. The color of the stamp has been a blue of varying shade. Early in 1922 the Georgian card in this series was surcharged "6 CENTS" in reddish brown with a solid block of color over the former value. The new value was enclosed in a hollow rectangle.

LETTER CARDS

The letter cards introduced in 1893 did not prove very popular, and remained in use for about ten years. The fact that the gummed edges stuck together and that the perforated strips were easily severed, probably hastened their demise. Perf. "B"—the type in which the horizontal perforated line stops at the vertical lines, is quite scarce in both values. 1c and 3c. So far as the writer knows, the 2c value has not been found in this type of perforation. The Capital "C" surcharge is also quite scarce.

WRAPPERS

Newspaper wrappers or post bands first appeared in 1875. They were intended primarily to be used as such, but served similar useful purposes. Since 1898 the design has been the same as that of the adhesives. In 1907 the Department issued two new values, 2c and 3c, but they were not required, as the rate was soon reduced. The remainders were surcharged the next year. About this time the wrappers bore the inscription, "This wrapper to be used only by publishers for the sole purpose of mailing second-class matter to the United States." They are a special type and are not sold to the general public. The Inland Revenue Wrapper issued about 1877, is also quite scarce, and some doubt has been expressed as to whether it was ever used.

The C.P.R. letter sheet was a special issue to that corporation and was intended to be used to give a monthly statement of earnings and expenses. It was evidently an experiment, with the result that the sheets are correspondingly scarce.

Port Hood Provisionals:

These were used from Port Hood, Nova Scotia, on Jan. 5, 1899, by the Postmaster's Assistant. Donald A. King, then employed in an official capacity in the Halifax Post Office, made enquiries and the matter was investigated by the Department and an Inspector sent to Port Hood. All copies on hand—not a large number—were taken possession of by him, including used and unused. These were eventually all destroyed. Collectors are warned to leave unused copies alone, and to be extremely careful even in regard to covers. A few covers had been sold to Stanley Gibbons before the Department's Inspector arrived, and these were soon bought up by advanced collectors. On the complete cover with correct postmarks these provisionals command good prices. Those originally handled by Stanley Gibbons were stamped with the firm name on the back of the cover. Gibbons Monthly Journal for Jan., Mar., Apr., 1899, gives more details.

PROVINCE OF CANADA

A1

A3

A4

A5

A6

No.	Type		Imperforate	Unused	Used
1	*A1*	½*d*	Rose on stout wove. *Aug., 1857*	$ 30.00	$ 15.00
			a. Ribbed horiz. Feb., 1858	*85.00*	*65.00*
			b. Ribbed vert. Feb., 1858	*100.00*	*85.00*
			c. Major re-entry		*60.00*
			d. Minor re-entry		*30.00*
			f. Stitch watermark		*50.00*
			On cover $20.00; pair	*75.00*	*40.00*
			Strip 3		*90.00*
			Strip 6		*300.00*
			Block 4		*175.00*
			Block 6		*500.00*

A2

No.	Type			Unused	Used
2	*A2*	3d	Red or Orange Vermilion, *laid Ap. 23, '51*	100.00	15.00
			On cover $25.00; pair		*45.00*
			Block 4	*750.00*	*400.00*
			a. Laid lines wavy instead of straight.		

No.	Type.			Unused.	Used.
3		3d	Red or Orange Vermilion *very thin 1852*....	50.00	8.50
			On cover $17.50; pair.....................		*22.50*
4		3d	Red-brown *wove Dec., 1852*...............	25.00	5.00
			On cover $8.50; pair......................		*20.00*
			Block 4..................................		*175.00*
5		3d	Indian-red *oily surface wove Jan., 1854*.....	25.00	4.50
			On cover $8.00; pair......................		*15.00*
			Block 4..................................		*150.00*
6		3d	Rose-red *thin wove Apr., 1855*.............	35.00	7.00
			On cover $12.00; pair.....................		*20.00*
			Block 4..................................		*175.00*
7	*A2*	3d	Indian-red *whiter wove June, 1856*..........	25.00	4.50
			On cover $8.00; pair......................		*15.00*
			Block 4..................................		*150.00*
8		3d	Red-brown *thick wove Jan., 1857*...........	25.00	6.50
			On cover $12.00; pair.....................		*22.50*
			Block 4..................................		*175.00*
9		3d	Indian Red *very thin soft wove*............		
10		3d	Indian Red *thin soft ribbed Feb., '58*........	*75.00*	*22.50*
			On cover $30.00; pair.....................		*60.00*
			Block 4..................................		*350.00*
11		3d	Indian-red *thicker soft ribbed Mr., '59*.......	*75.00*	*18.00*
			On cover $30.00; pair.....................		*55.00*
			Block 4..................................		*350.00*
12		3d	Red-brown *thick hairy rough*..............	75.00	20.00
			Varieties. Different papers and shades.		
			a. Major re-entry		50.00
			aa. Major re-entry in pair with normal....		
			b. Minor re-entry		25.00
			bb. Minor re-entry in pair with normal....		
			c. Stitch watermark (wove papers)........		35.00
			d. Bisected diag. on cover with other 3d stamps or 6d to make 7½d Packet rate (hard wove paper)...........................		
			e. Cracked die (notes) laid paper.........		30.00
			f. Cracked die wove paper..............		15.00
			g. Pair one showing "Relief A" (cracked) and other "Relief B" (normal)		100.00
			h. Reford's No. 31, Pl. ?, two vertical lines of color at bottom right (notes)........		75.00
			i. Pearl in center of lower frame line......		17.50
			j. Frame line missing, No. 12, Pl. 2.......		7.50
			k. Frame line missing, No. 88, Pl. 1.......		35.00
			l. On cover with 3c U.S. (notes)		
			m. On cover with 5c Beaver (10c. rate)		
13	*A3*	6d	Grey-violet *laid My. 15, '51*...............	275.00	50.00
			a. Bisected on cover used as 3d............		
			On cover $65.00; pair $150.00............		
13x		6d	Purple black *laid Jy., '55*.................		60.00
			On cover $75.00.........................		
14		6d	Grey-violet *thin wove 1851-57*............		45.00
			a. Stitch watermark......................		
			On cover $60.00; pair $135.00.............		
15		6d	Slate grey *medium wove*..................		45.00
			On cover $60.00; pair $135.00.............		
16		6d	Greenish grey *hard wove*.................		50.00
			On cover $65.00; pair $145.00.............		

No.	Type.			Unused.	Used.
17		6d	Brown violet *medium wove 1851-57*		45.00
			a. Bisected used on cover for 3d		
			On cover $60.00; pair $135.00		
18		6d	Grey-violet *thick hard wove Jy., '57*		85.00
			On cover $110.00; pair $200.00		
19		6d	Grey-violet *thick soft wove*		85.00
			a. Bisected used on cover for 3d		
			On cover $110.00; pair $200.00		
20	*A4*	7½d	Green *wove June, 1857*	250.00	85.00
			a. Re-entry		
			b. Stitch watermark		
			On cover $125.00; pair $200.00		
			Block 4 $2500.00		
			(*See notes re width of oval*)		
21	*A5*	10d	Blue *thin tough oily wove Ja., '55*	225.00	55.00
			a. Re-entry, major		150.00
			b. Re-entry, minor		75.00
			c. Stitch watermark		100.00
			On cover $90.00; Pair $175.00		
22		10d	Blue *opaque white wove, 1857*	200.00	75.00
			a. Re-entry, major		*160.00*
			b. Re-entry, minor		*85.00*
			On cover $125.00; pair $225.00		
			(*See notes re width of oval*)		
23	*A6*	12d	Black *laid May, '51*	1750.00	1200.00
			a. Major re-entry		
			Pair $5000.00		
24		12d	Black *wove* (*S.G. lists thin and medium*)		
			Perforated 11¾ (commonly listed as 12).		
25	*A1*	½d	Rose *wove Ja., '59*	70.00	35.00
			a. Re-entry, major		*75.00*
			b. Re-entry, minor		*50.00*
			On cover $45.00; pair		*85.00*
			Block 4		*250.00*
26	*A2*	3d	Red *medium wove Oc., '58*	50.00	20.00
			a. Re-entry, Major		
			b. Re-entry, minor		
			On cover $35.00; pair		50.00
27	*A3*	6d	Grey-violet, *wove, Sept., 1858*	250.00	130.00
28			Brown-purple, *wove, June, 1859*	250.00	150.00
			On cover bisected diagonally (*No. 28*)		
			Perforated 14.		
29	*A2*	3d	Red, *medium wove, prior to Oct., 1858*		
			Trial Perforations (See notes)		
30	*A2*	3d	Red, *medium wove and early thin paper*		$ 75.00
			a. Perce en scie; b. Perce en arc; c Pinhole.		
31		6d	Grey, *medium wove* (*notes*)		250.00
32		10d	Blue (*A 10d Perforated in the Ferrary Collection was pronounced counterfeit but may have been a 'trial perforation' made at the same time as the 3d and 6d stamps*		

A7

A8

A9

A10

A11

A12

No.	Type.			Unused.	Used.
			Perforated 12 (or slightly undernotes)		
			Wove paper.		
33	*A7*	1c	Deep Rose Red, *July, 1859*	7.50	2.50
33x		1c	Rose red, pale rose red	3.00	.90
			a. Minor variety (see notes)		*5.00*
			b. Imperf. pair	*100.00*	
			c. Laid paper (notes)		*150.00*
			d. Very thick paper		*3.00*
			e. Thin soft wove paper		*5.00*
			On Cover $1.25. Used Pair $3.00		
			Used strip 5 $12.00. Block 4		*50.00*
34	*A8*	2c	Rose, *wove, Aug. 1, 1864*	10.00	8.50
			a. Minor variety (notes)		*12.00*
			b. Imperf. pair	*80.00*	
			On Cover $15.00. Used Pair $22.50		
			Used Block 4 $75.00		
			Used Strip 4 $60.00		
35		2c	Claret	12.00	10.00
36	*A9*	5c	Brick Red, *medium soft wove, July 1859*	5.00	1.50
37			Light Brick Red, *October, 1859*	4.00	1.25
38			Red, *June, 1860*	2.50	.50
			a. Major re-entry		60.00
			b. Minor re-entry		*10.00*
			c. Broken oval		*40.00*
			d. Stitch watermark		*15.00*
			e. Imperf. pair	*100.00*	
			f. Imprint copy		*1.75*
			Commoner Shades—*on cover $1.25*		
			Pair	*7.50*	*1.60*
			Strip 3 $3.50; Strip 4 $20.00; Block 4	*75.00*	*55.00*
39	*A10*	10c	Black brown, *Jy. 1, 1859*	150.00	35.00
			a. Bisected, on cover		
			On cover $45.00; Used pair $90.00		

No.	Type.			Unused.	Used.
40		10c	Bright red purple *Jy. 12, 1859*	75.00	20.00
			On cover $35.00		
41		10c	Dull greyish red purple	75.00	20.00
			On cover $35.00		
42		10c	Purple shades *4th & later printings* greyish violet *6th*	20.00	4.00
			a. Bisected on cover dated Feb. 12, 1860		
			On cover $8.00; pair	*60.00*	*12.00*
			Block 4		*85.00*
43		10c	Violet shades, *20th to 27th printings*	17.00	3.00
			a. Imperf. pair	*170.00*	
			Single on cover $6.00; pair		*9.00*
			Used strip 3 $25.00; strip 4 $35.00		
			Block 4		*75.00*
			a. Re-entry, Lower R "10" etc.		*15.00*
			b. Re-entry top frame line		*15.00*
			c. Minor Variety		*12.00*
44	*A11*	*12½c*	Pale olive green *Jy., 1859*	20.00	7.00
			On cover $12.00		
45		*12½c*	*Green*	12.00	3.25
			On cover $8.00		
46		*12½c*	Pale yellow green *Sp. '63*	12.00	3.25
			On cover $8.00		
47		12½c	Deep yellow green	12.00	3.25
			On cover $8.00; pair		*10.00*
			Used strip 4 $50.00; Block 4		*100.00*
47x		12½c	Blue green *Mr. '66*	15.00	5.00
			a. Imperf. pair	150.00	
			b. Pair Imperf. horiz.		
48	*A12*	17c	Blue, *July 1859*	17.50	8.50
			a. Re-entry		*25.00*
			b. Burr over shoulder		*75.00*
			c. On coarse yellowish wove $10.00.		
			d. Imperf. pair	*200.00*	
			On Cover, $25 00; Pair		*25.00*
			Block 4		*150.00*
49		17c	Slate Blue		12.00

A13

A14

A15

A16

A17

A18

A19

A20

DOMINION OF CANADA

No.	Type.			Paper	Unused.	Used.
			Papers: (A) *Thin hard semi-transparent, design showing through.....*			
			(B) *Ordinary wove, softer, thin to medium..............*			
			(C) *Yellowish coarse medium wove...................*			
			(D) *Fine soft white very thin to medium...............*			
			Perf. 12	Paper		
50	*A13*	½c	Black, *Mar., 1868*................	A	5.00	2.00
51		½c	Grey-black.....................	B	1.75	1.50
			a. Watermarked (notes)..........			75.00
			b. Imperf. between, pair..........			
			c. Chignon not shaded...........		*4.00*	
			d. Other minor variety...........		3.00	
52		½c	Grey-black.....................	C	1.75	1.50
			Perf. 11½x12, (1874-1878)........			
53		½c	Pale grey-black.................		4.00	2.50
			Commoner Shades.			
			On cover, pair $6.00.................			
			On cover, strip 4 $12.00..............			
			On cover, strip 6 $14.00..............			
			On cover, block 4 $25.00.............			
			Pair..............................		4.00	4.00
			Strip 3		6.00	7.00
			Block 4...........................		10.00	20.00
			Perf. 12.			
54	*A14*	1c	Brick red *March, 1868*...........	A	8.25	3.25
			a. Watermarked................		45.00	15.00
55		1c	Red brown (April, 1868)..........	B	6.00	2.50
			a. Watermarked................		*40.00*	*12.00*
56		1c	Deep red brown, LAID *Nov. 27 '68*		*375.00*	*75.00*
			Commoner Shades.			
			On cover, $4.50; pair.................		15.00	6.00
			On cover, pair $10.00................			
			On cover, strip 3 $20.00..............			
			Block of 4.........................		35.00	35.00
57		1c	Deep orange *Jan., '69*...........	B	*20.00*	*6.00*
58		1c	Orange *Jan., '69*................	B	*15.00*	*5.00*
			On cover $8.00; pair.................		32.50	12.00
			On cover, pair $12.00................			
			On cover, strip 3 $35.00..............			
			Block of 4.........................			50.00

No.	Type.			Paper.	Unused.	Used.
59		1c	Pale orange-yellow *April, 1869*	B	*12.50*	*3.75*
60		1c	Orange-yellow *July, 1869*	B	*10.00*	*3.50*
			On cover, $5.00; pair		22.50	9.00
			On cover, pair $10.00			
			On cover, strip 3 $22.50			
			Block of 4		50.00	50.00
61	*A15*	2c	Deep green *March, 1868*	A	*7.50*	*3.00*
62		2c	Green *July, 1868*	B	*6.00*	*2.50*
63		2c	Blue-green *July, 1868*	B	*6.00*	*2.25*
			a. Watermarked	B	*50.00*	*10.00*
			On cover $5.00; pair		15.00	5.50
			Strip 3			15.00
			Block 4			60.00
			Bissected vert. used on cover			
64		2c	Pale green *Nov., 1869*	B	*6.00*	*2.25*
65		2c	Pale emerald-green *1871*	BC	*6.00*	*2.25*
66		2c	LAID *see notes*			
67			*Variety (all shades), Faint lines cross at lower left*		*8.00*	*3.50*
68	*A16*	3c	Red *March, 1868*	A	12.50	2.50
			On cover $3.50 pair		*27.50*	*6.00*
			Strip 3			*15.00*
			Block 4			*40.00*
69		3c	Rose-red *May, 1868*	BC	*10.00*	*.85*
			a. Rose-red	D		*1.50*
70		3c	LAID paper *June, 1868*			*12.50*
			On cover $20.00 pair			*30.00*
			Block of 4			*200.00*
71		3c	Dull red *Jan., 1869*	B	*7.00*	*.60*
			On cover $1.50 pair		*16.00*	*2.00*
			Strip 3			*5.00*
			Block 4		*100.00*	*40.00*
			a. Variety; dot in upper left 3			*2.50*
			b. Variety, dry plate printing			*5.00*
			c. Variety, double perforated			*5.00*
			d. Watermarked letter *July, 1868*	B	*60.00*	*12.00*
			e. Watermarked stitch			*8.00*
72	*A17*	6c	Deep brown *Mar., 1868*	A	12.50	3.00
73		6c	Chocolate brown *May, 1868*	B	12.50	2.50
			a. Watermarked letter	B	*75.00*	*40.00*
			b. Watermarked stitch	B		*20.00*
74		6c	Sepia brown *Jan., 1869*	B	12.50	2.00
75		6c	Light brown, *May, 1869*	B	12.50	2.00
			a. Re-entry	*B*		*12.50*
76		6c	Yellow brown *June, 1870*	B	12.50	2.00
			On cover $7.50; pair		*20.00*	*7.50*
			Strip 3		*60.00*	*25.00*
			Block 4		*200.00*	*100.00*
77		6c	Bisected diag. *used on cover from N.S.*			
78		6c	Double printing (*notes*)			
79	*A18*	12½c	Deep blue *Mar., 1868*	A	10.00	3.50
80		12½c	Blue	B	9.00	3.00
			a. Watermarked letter	B	*45.00*	*18.00*
			b. Watermarked stitch	B		*20.00*
81		12½c	Pale blue	C	9.00	3.50

No.	Type.			Paper.	Unused.	Used.
82		12½c	Pale dull blue *Feb., 1870*	B	9.00	3.00
			Minor variety			*7.50*
			On cover $10.00 pair		*20.00*	*10.00*
			Strip 3		*40.00*	*22.50*
			Block 4		*50.00*	*60.00*
83	*A19*	15c	Deep dull purple, *Mar. 16, 1868*	A	35.00	5.00
84		15c	Pale dull purple, *May, 1868*	AB	17.50	4.00
			On cover			*15.00*
			a. Watermarked script letter	B		*75.00*
85		15c	Grey lilac *June, 1868*	B	12.50	4.00
			On cover $15.00; pair		*30.00*	*12.00*
			a. Watermarked letter			*32.50*
86		15c	Grey purple *June, 1868*	B	12.50	4.00
			On cover $15.00; pair		*30.00*	*12.00*
87		15c	Lilac *Jan., 1869*	B	10.00	3.50
			On cover, domestic rate			*7.50*
			On cover, foreign rate			*12.00*
			Pair	B	*22.50*	*10.00*
			Strip 3		*35.00*	*17.50*
			Block 4		*55.00*	*55.00*
88		15c	Grey lilac *Aug., 1874*	B	10.00	3.50
			Covers, etc., as for No. 87			
89		15c	Grey violet *Dec., 1874*	B	10.00	3.50
			Covers etc., as for No. 87			
			a. Watermarked letter	B		32.50
90		15c	Pale olive grey *Jan., 1876*	B	*15.00*	*7.50*
			On cover $15.00 (domestic)			
			On cover $20.00 (foreign)			
91		15c	Brownish grey *Aug., 1877*	B	16.50	10.00
			On cover $17.50 (domestic)			
			On cover $22.50 (foreign)			
92	*A19*	15c	Grey purple *Aug., 1877*	B	12.00	7.50
			Covers as for No. 90			
93		15c	Greenish grey *July, 1878*	B	15.00	6.50
			On cover, domestic rate $10.00			
			On cover, foreign rate $15.00			
94		15c	Grey *July, 1878*	B	15.00	5.00
			On cover, domestic rate $7.50			
			On cover, foreign rate $10.00			
95		15c	Dull grey violet *June, 1880*	B	7.50	2.50
			On cover, domestic rate $6.50			
			On cover, foreign rate $10.00			
			Block 4		32.50	25.00
96		15c	Slate violet *very thick smooth white wove paper June, 1880*			15.00
			Pair			*40.00*
97		15c	Slate violet *thick soft wove paper 1880*			10.00
			Pair			*25.00*
98		15c	Deep slate *1881-1888*	B	7.50	2.25
			On cover, domestic rate $3.50			
			On cover, foreign rate $7.50			
			Block 4			15.00
99		15c	Slate blue *1881-1888*	B	7.50	2.25
			Covers etc., as for No. 98			
			a. On hard heavily ribbed (notes)			*15.00*
100		15c	Pale green *Apr., 1891*	C		5.00
			On cover, domestic rate $10.00			

No.	Type.			Paper.	Unused.	Used.
101		15c	Pale green *soft wove paper*........			10.00
			The printings from Jan., 1891 include shades which correspond more or less to all the earlier shades, but the impression gives a slightly embossed appearance to the paper, which is of poorer quality and slightly grey.)			
102		15c	Slate violet, grey violet, etc., *from Jan., 1891*......................		3.75	1.75
			On cover, domestic rate $3.25.......			
			On cover, foreign rate $6.00........			
			Block 4.......................		16.50	12.00
103		15c	LAID PAPER (*Howes*)..........			
104		15c	IMPERFORATE, brownish purple		15.00	15.00
			Block 4.......................		*70.00*	
105		15c	Stitch watermark................			12.00
			Perf. 11½x12.			
106		15c	Grey-violet *Dec., 1874*............		25.00	10.00
107		15c	Pale olive grey *Jan., 1876*........		25.00	10.00
108		15c	Brownish grey *Aug., 1877*........		30.00	12.50
109		15c	Grey purple *Aug., 1877*..........		25.00	10.00
110		15c	Greenish grey *July, 1878*.........		25.00	10.00
111		15c	Grey (thicker paper) *July, 1878*...		25.00	10.00
			On Cover, any shade $20.00 (Domestic)......................			
			On Cover, any shade $25.00 (Foreign)			
			Perf. 11½x12.			
112	*A20*	5c	Olive green, *Oct. 1, 1875*..........	B	15.00	6.00
			a. Grey green...................	B	15.00	6.00
			On Cover $12.00; pair on cover $20.00; pair.....................		47.50	20.00
			Strip 3........................		*80.00*	*35.00*
			Block 4.......................		*175.00*	*125.00*
			Provisional Cover—see "5" in Cancellation Chapter.			

A21

A22

A23

A24

A25 A26 A27 A28

"SMALL CENTS" ISSUE

Papers, Montreal Printings.

a. *Fine quality wove, smooth surface, opaque. January, 1870. (Noted also as slightly yellowish smooth surface and as clear white but texture the same). Later, about 1875, there is a paper of the same texture but with pebbly surface which is sometimes classed as hard ribbed, especially on the thicker grades of the paper.......*

b. *Thick soft opaque wove, perforations adhering. January, 1871. (RARE)....................*

c. *Hard wove, points of light not showing through, varying from thin to medium stout but usually thin, with design showing through. Feb., 1871..................*

d. *Thin smooth surface white wove. February 10, 1871............*

Ottawa Printings.

e. *Wove, poor quality, often yellowish. February, 1888..........*

No.	Type.			Paper.	Unused.	Used.
			Perf. 12.			
113	*A21*	½c	Grey-brown *July, 1882*...........	AE	.25	.20
114		½c	Grey...........................	E	.15	.15
			a. Imperf. pair 1891-93 (10, 100)..	E	*30.00*	*30.00*
			b. Imperf. between horiz. pair.....	E	*50.00*	
			c. Offset printing on back.........	E	*.25*	*.25*
			d. Re-entry (notes)...............	E	*2.50*	*2.50*
			On cover, pair $1.00.............			
			On cover, strip 4 $2.00...........			
			On cover, strip 6 $2.25...........			
			Block 4.........................		*.75*	*1.00*
115	*A21*	½c	Grey white wove resembling......	A	.75	.75
			Pair $2.00; block 4..............		*5.00*	
			Re-entry.......................		*5.00*	
			Perf. 11¾x11¾, 11¾x12, 12x12.			
116	*A22*	1c	Orange *March, 1870*.............	A	12.50	1.75
			On cover $2.75; Pair on cover $6....			
			Strip 3 on cover $8.50; pair........		*27.50*	*4.00*
			Strip 3.........................		*40.00*	*6.50*
			Block 4.........................		*50.00*	*35.00*
117		1c	Orange-yellow *March, 1872*.......	C	4.00	.60
118		1c	Pale yellow *Sept., 1872*...........	AC	4.00	.60
119		1c	Pale Lemon-yellow *Dec., 1873*.....	A	4.00	.60
			a. Perf. 11½x12 (also orange-yellow)......................	A	*17.50*	*2.50*
			On cover $3.50; pair.............			*6.00*
120		1c	Yellow (*shades*) *Sept., 1875*.......	A	.75	.05
			a. Imperf. pair (10,100) 1878-97 ..	A	*22.50*	*22.50*
			b. Perf. 11½x12 to Aug. '77.......	A	*10.00*	*1.50*
			On cover (b) $1.75; pair...........			*3.25*
121		1c	Yellow (shades) *Feb., 1888*........	E	.50	.02

No.	Type.			Paper.	Unused.	Used.
			On cover 10c; pair on cover 25c.....			
			Strip 3 on cover 35c; strip 6 on cover $1.00; strip 3 used 25c			
			Block 4.........................		*3.00*	*4.00*
			a. Bisected on Ry. News (notes)...			*75.00*
			b. Bisected on letter cover.........			*10.00*
			c. Printed both sides............			
122	*A23*	2c	Pale and deep green *Feb., 1872....*	A	3.75	.20
			On cover $1.00; pair on cover $2.00.			
			Strip 3 on cover $4.00; pair.......		*8.00*	*.50*
			Strip 3.........................		*15.00*	*1.00*
			Block 4.........................		*25.00*	*15.00*
123		2c	Green.........................	A	1.25	.15
			a. Perf. 11½x12 (1873-78).......	A	*10.00*	*1.75*
			On cover $2.50; pair..............			*4.00*
124		2c	Green *Jan., 1888................*	E	2.50	.10
			Cover 35c; block 4................		*15.00*	*4.50*
125		2c	Blue-green *June, 1888............*	E	*2.50*	*.10*
			Cover 25c; block 4................		*15.00*	*4.50*
			Strip 3 on cover $1.00............			
			Common shades.			
			a. Imperf. pair (*1891-93 10,100*)...	E	*20.00*	*20.00*
			b. Ribbed printing..............		5.00	5.00
			c. Major re-entry...............		10.00	10.00
			d. Minor re-entry...............		5.00	5.00
			e. Bisected vert. on cover........			12.00
			f. Bisected diag. on cover........			12.00
			(*The imperforates are found in yellow-green and blue-green. The blue-green shade is not rare, but the distinctive shade of blue-green on the clear white "A" paper is the most difficult of the 2c stamps to obtain The perforations usually adhere.*)			
126	*A24*	3c	Indian red *Jan. 20, 1870..........*	A	12.50	1.25
			a. Stitch watermark..............			*8.00*
			On Cover $2.00; pair used $3.50 block 4.........................		*125.00*	*35.00*
127		3c	Pale Indian red *Sept. 9, 1870.......*	A	12.50	1.25
			On cover $2.00; pair used $3.50 block 4.........................		*125.00*	*35.00*
128		3c	Pale faded rose *Nov. 1, 1870......*	A	12.00	1.00
			On covers $2.00; pair used $3.50 block 4.........................		*125.00*	*35.00*
129		3c	Rose *Dec., 1870................*	A	12.00	1.25
			On cover $2.00; pair used $3.50 block 4.........................		*125.00*	*35.00*
130		3c	Rose *Jan. 14, 1871...............*	B	25.00	6.50
131		3c	Rose *Feb. 6, 1871................*	C	15.00	1.25
			On covers $2.00; pair used $3.50; block 4.........................		*125.00*	*35.00*
132		3c	Pale Rose *Feb. 10, 1871..........*		12.00	1.25
			On cover $2.00; pair used $3.50; block 4.........................		*125.00*	*35.00*
133		3c	Red *June 7, 1872................*	AC	10.00	.60
134		3c	Orange vermilion *Mar. 10, '73.....*	A	10.00	.50
			a. Perf. 11½x12 (*Sept., '73*)......		*10.00*	.75

No.	Type.			Paper.	Unused.	Used.
135		3c	Dull vermilion *Jan., 1875*	A	2.00	.10
			On cover .25; block 4		*12.00*	*5.50*
			a. Imperf. pair		*25.00*	*25.00*
			b. Perf. 11½x12 (to Au., '78)		*3.00*	*.75*
136		3c	Vermilion (shades) *Oct., 1877*	A	1.25	.10
			a. Imperf. pair		*17.50*	*17.50*
			b. On cover .25; block 4		*6.00*	*4.50*
137		3c	Vermilion (shades) *Feb., 1888*	E	1.00	.02
			On cover .15; block 4		*5.00*	*4.00*
138		3c	Rose-carmine *Oct. 9, 1888*	E	25.00	1.00
139		3c	Dull rose-carmine *Oct., 1888*	E	20.00	1.00
			Nos. 138-139 on cover $2.50			
			Pair		*60.00*	*3.00*
			Strip 3		*85.00*	*5.00*
			Block 4		*125.00*	*25.00*
140		3c	Bright vermilion *Apr., 1889*	E	.75	.02
			a. Imperf. pair (5000)		*17.50*	*17.50*
			On cover .15; block 4		*4.50*	*4.00*
141		3c	Bright vermilion, *analine die goes through paper July, 1894*	E	1.50	.25
			On cover .50; block 4		*10.00*	*5.00*
142		3c	Pale vermilion *Nov., 1893*	E	.75	.02
			On cover .15; block 4		*4.50*	*4.00*
			Minor Varieties.			
			Re-entry, baseline doubled	A		7.50
			Lesser re-entry			4.50
			Lower portion of design deeply shaded upward (slip printing)			5.00
			White line above and below most letters of CANADA POSTAGE (worn)	A		5.00
143	*A25*	5c	Pale olive green *Feb., 1876*	A	12.00	1.00
			a. Perf. 11½x12 1876-9		*15.00*	*2.00*
			On cover $2.50; pair		*27.50*	*3.00*
			Block 4			*30.00*
144		5c	Olive-grey *Mar., 1888*	A	8.00	.60
			On cover $2.00; block 4		*40.00*	*25.00*
145	*A25*	5c	Brownish grey *May, 1888*	E	2.50	.50
146		5c	Grey *July, 1889*	E	2.25	.35
			a. Imperf. pair 10,100 1891-93?		*30.00*	*30.00*
			b. Re-entry			*5.00*
			c. Ribbed printing		*5.00*	*5.00*
			Nos. 145-6 on cover $1.75;			
			Block 4		*15.00*	*10.00*
147	*A26*	6c	Yellow-brown *Jan., 1872*	AD	4.00	.75
			a. Perf. 11½x12 1876-9		*5.00*	*1.50*
			b. Re-entry "CANADA POST"		*20.00*	*15.00*
			On cover $2.00; pair		*9.00*	*2.00*
			Block 4		*25.00*	*30.00*
			Bisected vert. (3c) on cover Au., '86.			
			Bisected diag. (3c) on cover Ja. 13 '74			
148		6c	Chestnut *Oct., 1890*	E	3.00	.65
			a. Re-entry CENTS	E	*15.00*	*10.00*
			b. Lesser re-entry	E	*5.00*	*3.00*
			c. Imperf. pair 1891-3? 10,000	E	*25.00*	*25.00*

No.	Type.			Paper.	Unused.	Used.
			On cover $2.00; pair		*6.00*	*1.50*
			Block 4		*12.00*	*12.00*
149		6c	Pale chestnut *1891-1893*	E	2.50	.65
			a. Re-entry CENTS	E	*15.00*	*10.00*
			b. Lesser re-entry	E	*5.00*	*3.00*
			c. Imperf. pair 1891-3? 100	E	*30.00*	*30.00*
			On cover $2.00; pair		*5.50*	*1.50*
			Block 4		*12.00*	*12.00*
150		6c	Deep chocolate-brown *July, 1893*	E	3.50	.85
			Pair		*7.50*	*2.00*
			Block 4		*17.50*	*12.00*
			On cover $2.50			
151	*A27*	8c	Blue-grey *Aug., 1893*	E	4.50	.25
			a. Imperf. pair	E	*22.50*	*22.50*
			b. Worn Plate	E	*6.00*	*.50*
			On cover $1.00; pair		*9.50*	*.50*
			Block 4		*18.00*	*15.00*
152		8c	Bluish slate *Aug., 1895*	E	3.50	.20
			a. Re-entry	E	*7.00*	*3.50*
			b. Double strike	E	*4.50*	*2.50*
			c. New plate, Oc., 1896		*6.00*	*.75*
			On cover $1.00; block 4	E	*17.00*	*15.00*
153		8c	Greenish slate *Feb., 1896*	E		2.00
154		8c	Slate-purple *Nov., 1896*	E	3.50	.30
			a. Re-entry	E	*7.00*	*3.50*
			b. Double-strike	E	*4.50*	*2.50*
			On cover $1.00; Block 4	E	*17.00*	*15.00*
155		8c	Blackish purple *June, 1897*	E	4.50	.40
			a. Re-entry	E	*7.00*	*3.50*
			b. Double strike	E	*4.50*	*2.50*
			On cover $1.00; Block 4	E	*18.00*	*17.50*
156	*A28*	10c	Pale faded magenta, *Nov., 1874*	A	20.00	3.75
			On cover $8.00; pair			*9.00*
			a. Perf. 11½x12			*9.00*
157		10c	Pale to deep magenta, *Nov., '74*	A	10.00	2.25
			On cover $5.00; pair		*22.50*	*6.00*
			Block 4			*40.00*
			a. Perf. 11½x12		*20.00*	*5.00*
158		10c	Rosy-red		8.00	2.00
			On cover $5.00; pair			*5.50*
			Block 4			*35.00*
			a. Imperf. pair 100 1891-93?		*25.00*	
159		10c	Rose *Mar., 1888*		5.00	1.75
			On cover $3.50; pair		*11.00*	*4.00*
			Block 4		*23.00*	*20.00*
			a. Ribbed printing (notes)		*12.00*	*5.00*
160		10c	Pale faded salmon, *Nov., 1896*		5.00	1.75
			On cover $3.50; pair		*11.00*	*4.00*
			Block 4		*23.00*	*20.00*
161		10c	Salmon-red, *Oct., 1896*		5.00	1.75
			On cover $3.50; pair		*11.00*	*4.00*
			Block 4		*23.00*	*20.00*
162		10c	Brick red, *Oct., 1896*		5.00	1.75
			On cover $3.50; pair		*11.00*	*4.00*
			Block 4		*23.00*	*20.00*
			a. Imperf. pair (5000)		*22.50*	*22.50*

No.	Type.			Paper.	Unused.	Used.
163		10c	Pale brown *1897*		5.00	1.75
			On cover $3.50; pair		*11.00*	*4.00*
			Block 4		*23.00*	*20.00*
			a. Imperf. pair (5000)		*18.00*	

A29

A30

Perf. 12

No.	Type.			Paper.	Unused.	Used.
166	*A29*	20c	Vermilion *Feb., 17, 1893*	A	2.25	.75
			On cover $1.75; pair		*5.00*	*1.75*
			Block 4		*12.00*	*12.00*
			a. Imperf. pair		*40.00*	
167	*A30*	50c	Blue *Feb., 17, 1893*	A	1.75	.60
			On cover $1.50; pair		*5.00*	*1.50*
			Block 4		*11.00*	*8.00*
			a. Imperf. pair, deep blue		*40.00*	

A31

No.	Type.			Paper.	Unused.	Used.
168	*A31*	2c	Orange *Nov. 15th, 1875*		.75	.15
			On cover add 50c to value			
			Block 4 O.G. $5.00; on cover			*30.00*
			a. Perf. 11½x12(?)			
169		2c	Orange-red		.75	.15
			On cover add 50c to value			
			Block 4 O.G. $5.00; Block 4 on cover			*30.00*
170		2c	Vermilion		.75	.12
			On cover add 50c to value			
			Block 4 O.G. $5.00; Block 4 on cover			*30.00*
			(From May, 1889 the Registration fee was raised from 2c to 5c. Covers with 2c Registration stamps and other postage stamps to make up the rate are quite rare. Covers which show the entire postage and registration prepaid with 2c Registration stamps are extremely rare.)			
			a. Imperf. pair		*20.00*	*20.00*

No.	Type.			Unused.	Used.
171		2c	Carmine-rose *Oct., 1888*	20.00	1.00
			On cover add $2.50 to value		
			Block 4		*30.00*
172		5c	Deep green *Nov. 15, '75*	.85	.15
			On cover add 50c to value		
			Block 4 O.G. $5.00; Block 4 on cover		*30.00*
173		5c	Yellow-green	.85	.15
			On cover add 50c to value		
			Block 4 O.G. $5.00; Block 4 on cover		*30.00*
			a. Imperf. pair	*20.00*	*20.00*
174		5c	Bluish-green *1888*	1.00	.15
			On cover add 50c to value		
			Block 4 O.G. $5.50; on cover		*30.00*
175		8c	Bright blue *Nov. 15, 1875* (*40,000*)	8.00	
			Used cancelled with Town, Registered or R		*12.00*
			On cover, tied with R		*25.00*
			On cover, tied with "Town" or "Registered"		*35.00*
			Pair	*18.00*	*25.00*
			Block 4	*50.00*	
			a. Emergency Perf. (*?*) *Notes*		
176		8c	Dull blue	8.00	10.00

A32

A37

Jubilee, June 19th, 1897. Perf. 12.

No.	Type.			Unused.	Used.
180	*A32*	½c	Black, grey-black	.85	.85
			Block 4	*3.65*	*7.00*
181		1c	Orange, orange-yellow	.15	.10
			On cover .25; block 4	*.70*	*2.50*
			a. Bisected diag. on Ry. News (notes)		*75.00*
182		2c	Green, deep green	.20	.20
			On cover, .50; block 4	*.90*	*2.50*
183		3c	Carmine	.12	.03
			On cover .20; block 4	*.55*	*2.00*
184		5c	Slate blue, deep blue	.50	.30
			On cover $1.00; block 4	*2.25*	*3.00*
185		6c	Brown	3.00	3.00
			On cover $5.00; block 4	*15.00*	*15.00*
186		8c	Slate-violet	1.00	1.00
			On cover $3.50; block 4	*4.50*	*10.00*
187		10c	Purple	1.30	1.25
			On cover $3.50; block 4	*7.00*	*10.00*

No.	Type.			Unused.	Used.
188		15c	Slate	2.00	1.75
			On cover $3.50; block 4	*10.00*	*12.50*
189		20c	Deep or pale vermilion	1.50	1.50
			On cover $3.75; block 4	*7.00*	*12.50*
190		50c	Pale or bright ultramarine	1.50	1.00
			On cover $3.50; block 4	*7.00*	*6.00*
191		$1	Lake	3.75	3.75
			Block 4	*20.00*	*20.00*
192		$2	Deep violet	5.50	3.00
			Block 4	*25.00*	*25.00*
193		$3	Bistre	12.00	8.00
			Block 4	*55.00*	*40.00*
194		$4	Violet	12.00	7.50
			Block 4	*50.00*	*40.00*
195		$5	Olive-green	13.50	8.00
			Block 4	*60.00*	*50.00*

A33 A34 A35 A36

1897. 4-Leaf. Perf. 12.

No.	Type.			Unused.	Used.
196	*A33*	½c	Black *Nov., 1897*	.30	.15
197		½c	Grey-black	.08	.07
			a. Imperf. pair	*50.00*	
			b. Re-entry	*2.50*	
			On cover, pair .50; strip 6 $1.00;		
			Block 4 $1.00; off cover block 4	*.35*	*.75*
198		1c	Green *Dec., 1897*	.08	.03
			Block 4	*.40*	*.60*
			a. Imperf. pair	*50.00*	
199		2c	Violet *Dec., 1897*	.30	.09
			On cover .35; block 4	*1.35*	*1.00*
			a. Imperf. pair	*50.00*	
200		3c	Carmine *Jan., 1898*	.20	.02
			On cover .25; block 4	*.75*	*.75*
			a. Imperf. pair	*50.00*	
201	*A34*	3c	Surcharged 2c	.45	.20
			On cover .50; block 4	*2.00*	*2.50*
			a. Surcharge inverted	*25.00*	
202	*A33*	5c	Deep blue on bluish *Dec., 1897*	.30	.12
			On cover .35; block 4	*1.35*	*1.25*
			a. Imperf. pair	*50.00*	
203		6c	Brown *Dec., 1897*	1.00	.75
			On cover $1.50; block 4	*4.50*	*6.50*
			a. Imperf. pair	*50.00*	
204		8c	Orange	.75	.30
			On cover .95; block 4	*3.50*	*3.50*
			a. Imperf. pair	*50.00*	

No.	Type.			Unused.	Used.
205		10c	Brownish purple *Jan., 1898*	1.40	1.40
			On cover $2.00; pair	*3.25*	*3.25*
			Block 4	*7.00*	*9.00*
			a. Imperf. pair	*50.00*	
			1898. Numerals in all corners. Perf. 12.		
206	*A35*	½c	Black *Sept., 1898*	.08	.03
208		½c	Grey-black	.04	.02
			Pair on cover .50		
			Strip 4 on cover .60		
			Strip 6 on cover .90; block 4	*.25*	*.25*
			a. Imperf. pair	*50.00*	
209		1c	Blue-green *June, 1898*	.04	.01
			Block 4	*.25*	*.50*
			a. Imperf. pair	*50.00*	
			b. Deep green toned paper	*.25*	*.03*
210	*A35*	2c	Purple *Sept., 1898*	.20	.02
211		2c	Violet	.20	.02
			On cover .25; block 4	*.90*	*.50*
			a. Thick paper Sept., 1898	*2.50*	*.25*
			b. Imperf. pair	*50.00*	
212		2c	Rose-carmine *Aug. 20, 1899*	.15	.02
			Block 4	*.75*	*.50*
			a. Rose-purple		*.50*
			b. Imperf. pair (carmine)	*50.00*	
213		2c	Rose-carmine, block of 12 in two rows of 6, right block of 6 stamps inverted making center pairs tete-beche (notes)	100.00	
214		3c	Rose-carmine *June, 1898*	.15	.02
			Block 4	*.75*	*.75*
215	*A36*	3c	Surcharged 2c Rose-carmine	.25	.15
			On cover .35; block 4	*1.15*	*2.25*
			a. Surcharge inverted	*25.00*	
216	*A35*	5c	Slate blue on bluish *July, 1899*	.60	.10
			On cover .50; block 4	*2.75*	*.75*
			a. Imperf. pair	*50.00*	
217		5c	Prussian blue *bluish*	.75	.10
			a. On olive green	*.75*	*.10*
218		6c	Brown *Sept., 1898*	2.00	1.00
			On cover $1.75; block 4	*10.00*	*6.00*
			a. Imperf. pair	*50.00*	
219		7c	Greenish yellow *Dec. 23, 1902*	.75	.40
			On cover .75; block 4	*3.25*	*5.00*
			a. Imperf. pair	*60.00*	
220		8c	Orange yellow or deep orange, *Oct., 1898*	1.75	.65
			On cover $1.25; block 4	*6.25*	*5.00*
			a. Imperf. pair	*50.00*	
221		8c	Brown-orange *Feb., 1899*	1.00	.65
222		10c	Brownish-purple *Nov., 1898*	.85	.25
			On cover $1.00; block 4	*4.50*	*5.00*
			a. Imperf. pair	*50.00*	
223		20c	Olive green *Dec. 24, 1900*	2.50	.85
			On cover $2.50; block 4	*6.50*	*7.50*
			a. Imperf. pair	*60.00*	

D

C

A38

No.	Type.			Unused.	Used.
			PROVISIONALS—Unauthorized.		
224		2c	Purple bisected horiz. on cover....		12.50
225		2c	Purple bisected diag. on cover.....		12.50
226		3c	Rose-carmine bisected vert. on cover..............................		12.50
227	C	3c	Rose-carmine bisected vert. ⅓ used for 1c on cover.............		175.00
228	D	3c	Rose-carmine bisected vert. ⅔ used for 2c on cover.............		90.00
			(These "Port Hood Provisionals"—227 and 228, see notes—had the figures "1" or "2" in violet surcharged over the numerals of value on the stamp. The bisecting was done in such a manner as to cause two varieties of each provisional—right and left.		
229		10c	Brownish-purple bisected diag. used on cover with 2c and 7c making 10c rate (*Scott's 199th sale*)............		
			Booklet Blocks		
			June 11, 1900. Blocks of 6, 2 blocks to booklet, corner stamps imperf. two sides.		
1	*A35*	2c	Rose-carmine, *block 6*............	1.50	
			Maps *7th Dec., 1898. Perf. 12.*		
230	*A37*	2c	Lavender........................	.20	.08
231		2c	Pale lavender..................	.20	.08
232		2c	Greenish blue..................	.20	.08
233		2c	Pale greenish blue...............	.20	.08
			On cover .25; block 4..............	*.45*	*3.50*
			a. Imperf. pair, all shades........	*50.00*	
			b. Carmine color omitted..........		
			c. Carmine and ocean color omitted		
			d. Re-entry....................	*2.50*	*2.50*
			King Edward. July 1, 1903. Perf. 12.		
235	*A38*	1c	Pale green.....................	.03	.01
			Block 4........................	*.25*	*.40*
			a. Imperf. pair................	*40.00*	
236		1c	Grey-green (*Pl. 70*).............	.05	.01
237		2c	Rose-carmine (*Pl. 1 to 62*)........	.05	.01
			Block 4........................	*.25*	*.50*
			a. Imperf. pair (Pl. 13-14).......	.25	.40
			b. Imperf. pair in pale rose-carmine (Pl. 1—notes)..............	*20.00*	

No.	Type.		Unused.	Used.
		c. As above, Pl. 2	*25.00*	
		d. Block of 12 in two strips of 6, right block of 6 stamps inverted making center pairs tete-beche	*100.00*	
		e. With heavy horiz. hairlines		*2.50*
238	5c	Blue *bluish*	.25	.04
239	5c	Indigo	*.25*	*.04*
		Block 4	*1.50*	*.50*
		a. Imperf. pair (Pl. 1)	*40.00*	
		b. Imperf. pair (Pl. 2)	*50.00*	
		c. Background horiz. lines (notes)	.75	.12
		d. Re-touch variety	*1.50*	*.50*
240	7c	Olive-yellow	.40	.06
		On cover .75; Block 4	*2.00*	*1.00*
		a. Imperf. pair	*40.00*	
241	7c	Bistre *June, 1912*	1.00	.25
242	10c	Brown-lilac	.35	.09
		On cover $1.00; Block 4	*2.50*	*1.00*
		a. Imperf. pair	*40.00*	
243	10c	Dull purple	.40	.12
		On cover .75; block 4	*1.75*	*2.50*
244	20c	Olive green *Sept. 27, 1904*	1.50	.30
		On cover .75; block 4	*8.00*	*3.50*
245	50c	Deep mauve, purple, *Nov. 19, 1908*	8.00	1.30
		On cover $2.50; block 4	*50.00*	*20.00*

Booklet Blocks

		Corner stamps imperf. two sides.		
2	1c	Green (*Block 4*)	1.00	
3	2c	Rose-carmine (*Block 6*)	1.25	

A39

A40

A41

A42

A43

A44

A45

A46

No.	Type.			Unused.	Used.
			Quebec Tercentenary, July 16, 1908. Perf. 12.		
246	*A39*	½c	Sepia *Prince & Princess of Wales* . . .	.10	.10
			Block 4	*.40*	*.75*
			a. Imperf. pair	*30.00*	
			b. Re-entry (notes)	*1.75*	*1.75*
247	*A40*	1c	Blue-green	.12	.10
			Block 4	*.50*	*.75*
			a. Imperf. pair	*30.00*	
			b. Hairline	*.50*	*.50*
248	*A41*	2c	Carmine *King Edward and Queen Alexandra*	.12	.02
			Block 4	*.35*	*.50*
			a. Imperf. pair	*30.00*	
249	*A42*	5c	Indigo *Headquarters of Champlain*.	.40	.35
			On cover, .50; block 4	*1.75*	*2.75*
			a. Imperf. pair	*30.00*	
250	*A43*	7c	Olive-green	.45	.35
			On cover .75; block 4	*2.00*	*2.50*
			a. Imperf. pair	*30.00*	
251	*A44*	10c	Violet	1.00	.75
			On cover $1.50; block 4	*4.50*	*5.00*
			a. Imperf. pair	*30.00*	
252	*A45*	15c	Brown-orange *Champlain's Departure*	*1.25*	*1.00*
			On cover $2.25; block 4	*6.50*	*7.50*
			a. Imperf. pair	*30.00*	
253	*A46*	20c	Dull brown *Cartier's Arrival, Quebec*	1.25	1.25
			On cover $2.25; block 4	*5.50*	*8.00*
			a. Imperf. pair	*30.00*	
			(Some of the values are found on both toned and white paper).		

A47

A47a

A48

A49

A50

Die I

Die II.

A51

A52

No.	Type.			Unused.	Used.
			Georgian. Perf. 12.		
255	*A47*	1c	Yellow-green *Jan., 1 1912*........	.02	.01
256		1c	Blue-green.....................	.03	.01
			a. Hairlines...................	*4.00*	*1.00*
			Worn plate (*notes*)...............		
257		1c	Yellow, orange yellow *June 7, 1922*	.02	.01
			a. Imperf. pair Oct. 7, 1924.......	*1.00*	*1.00*
258		2c	Rose red *Jan. 1, 1912*............	.05	.01
			a. Hairline Feb., 1912...........	*4.00*	*.85*
			b. Accented E in CENTS........	*2.00*	*.40*
259		2c	Green *June 6, 1922 Pl. 161 up*....	.03	.01
			a. Imperf. pair Oct. 7, 1924.......	*1.00*	*1.00*
			b. Thin paper *Oct., 1924 Pl. 185-6*	*1.00*	*.50*
260		3c	Brown *Oct., 1918 Pl. 1 to 120*.....	.05	.01
261		3c	Carmine *Dec. 14, 1923 Pl. 115 to 164*...........................	.05	.01
			a. Imperf. pair Oct., 1924........	*.50*	*.50*
			Surcharged in One Line *August, 1926*		
262	*A51*	3c	Carmine surcharged 2 Cents......	.75	.90
			a. Broken "S"................	*5.00*	*5.00*
			b. Surcharge raised 4 mm. from bottom frameline.................	*1.25*	*1.50*
			c. Wide spacing "2C"..........	*1.25*	*1.50*
			Surcharged in Two Lines, *August, 1926*		
263	*A52*	3c	Carmine surcharged 2 cents.......	.35	.45
			a. Spacing variety...............	*.75*	*.90*
264	*A47*	4c	Yellow ochre *July 7, 1922*........	.07	.02
265		4c	Golden yellow..................	.60	.30
266		5c	Pale blue *Jan. 17, 1912*..........	.07	.01
267		5c	Indigo.........................	.07	.01
268		5c	Violet *Feb. 22, 1922 Pl. 16 up*.....	.07	.01
			a. Thin paper Oct., 1924 Pl. 21-22	*1.00*	*.50*
269		7c	Olive bistre *Jan. 17, 1912*........	.20	.03
270		7c	Pale sage green *1912 Pl. 6*........	.75	.25
271		7c	Golden yellow..................	.20	.04
272		7c	Red-brown *Dec. 12, 1924 Pl. 7-8*...	.12	.03
273		8c	Blue *Sept. 1, 1925*..............	.12	.02
274		10c	Reddish purple *Jan. 17, 1912*.....	.40	.03
275		10c	Brownish purple................	.24	.03
276		10c	Blue *Feb. 20, 1922 Pl. 13 to 22*....	.20	.03
277		10c	Light brown *Aug. 1, 1925 Pl. 21 up*	.14	.02
278		20c	Olive green *Jan. 20, 1912 Pl. 1 up*	.40	.06

No.	Type.			Unused.	Used.
279		50c	Grey-black *Jan. 29, 1912 Pl. 1-2-3-4*	.75	.15
280		50c	Black *Oct., 1924*	3.00	.50
281	*A47a*	$1	Red-orange *July 1, 1923*	1.15	.20
			Georgian War Tax. Perf. 12.		
290	*A48*	1c	Yellow-green *Apr. 15, 1915 Pl. 1 to 18*	.09	.02
291		2c	Carmine red *Apr. 15, 1915 Pl. 1 to 10*	.12	.03
292	*A49*	2c+1c	Carmine red *Feb., 1916 Die I*	.20	.01
			a. Die II Sept., 1916	*15.00*	*1.00*
			b. Perf. 12x8 vert. Aug. 2, 1916	*.30*	*.10*
293		2c+1c	Rose red	.50	.02
294		2c+1c	Brown *Aug. 28, 1916 Die II*	.09	.01
			a. Imperf. pair (100)	*100.00*	
295			Die I *Sept. 19, 1916 Pl. 1 & Pl. 2*	30.00	1.50
			a. Imperf. pair (200)	100.00	
			Feb. 12, 1915. Type A47 overprinted.		
296	*A50*	5c	Blue, black overprint	5.00	10.00
297		20c	Olive-green, *black overprint Pl. 3*	1.25	5.00
			a. Sage green, black overprint Pl. 2	*2.50*	
298		50c	Sepia, *red overprint*	2.50	5.00

A53

300	*A53*	3c	Brown *Sept. 15, 1917*	.12	
			a. Imperf. pair (200)	*60.00*	.03

COILS

Coil No. 2 Block No. 4

No.	Type.			Unused.	Used.
			Coils Perf. 12 horiz. were used in automatic stamp vending machines. All other coils were used in authomatic stamp affixing machines. Stamps for vending machines were in rolls of 1000. Stamps for stamp affixing machines were in rolls of 500.		
1	*A47*	1c	Green. Perf. 12 horiz............	.30	.12
			1912.		
2		1c	Green, blue-green, Perf. 8 horiz..	.75	.25
3		1c	Green. Perf. 8 vert.............	.12	.04
			July, 1918.		
4	*A47*	1c	Green (*2 large holes*) Perf. 12 horiz...........................	1.00	.25
5	*A47*	1c	Chrome-yellow Perf. 8 vert........	.08	.01
			(*The 1c green Perf. 12 vert. is faked from a booklet pane*).		
6		2c	Deep rose red Perf. 12 horiz.......	.15	.03
			May 11th, 1915 (*notes*)		
7		2c	Rose carmine Perf. 12 all around, paste-up pair with Department date..........................	5.00	
			1912		
8		2c	Carmine. Perf. 8 horiz...........	.15	.10
9		2c	Carmine. Perf. 8 vert...........	.15	.08
			Dec., 1922.		
10		2c	Yellow-green Perf. 8 vert.........	.06	.01
11		2c	Green Perf. 12 horiz. (*1924*)......	.05	.02
			Aug., 1918.		
12		3c	Brown. Perf. 8 vert.............	.18	.12
			Jan., 1921.		
13		3c	Brown. Perf. 12 horiz...........	.30	.18
14		3c	Brown. Perf. 8 horiz............	.15	.08
			(*The 3c brown perf. 12 vert. is faked from a booklet pane*).		
			April 9, 1924.		
15		3c	Carmine. Perf. 8 vert...........	.05	.02
16	*A49*	2c+1c	Carmine. Perf. 8 vert...........	.20	.06
17		2c+1c	Brown. Perf. 8 vert. Die II......	.25	.05
18		2c+1c	Brown. Perf. 8 vert. Die I.......	1.00	.20
			1926 PAIRS PERF. 8 VERT. AND IMPERF. BETWEEN HORIZ. FROM SHEETS PERFORATED INTENDED TO BE CUT HORIZONTALLY BETWEEN ROWS TO MAKE STRIPS FOR COILS. (notes).		
			1st Issue (*White Gum, Embossing not evident*).		
1	*A47*	1c	Yellow, vert. pair imperf. between..	7.50	
2		2c	Green vert. pair imperf. between...	7.50	
3		3c	Carmine vert. pair imperf. between.	7.50	
			2nd Issue, *embossed appearance, lighter shade*.		
4		1c	Yellow vert. pair imperf. between...	1.00	
5		2c	Green vert. pair imperf. between...	1.00	

No.	Type.			Unused.	Used.

Booklet Blocks.

Blocks of 4 or 6. Corner stamps imperf. two sides.

No.	Type.			Unused.	Used.
			Jan. 1912.		
1	A47	1c	Green, blue-green, yellow-green (6)	.25	
			a. Green on deeply toned (6).....	2.00	
2		1c	Dec., 1922 chrome yellow (6).....	.20	
			Dec., 1922 chrome yellow (4).....	.15	
3		2c	Carmine (6).....................		.75
4		2c	Green (4) .25; (6) .35............		
5		3c	Brown (4) .40; (6) .60............		
			Dec., 1923.		
6		3c	Rose red (4)....................	1.00	
7		3c	Carmine (4) .40; (6) .60..........		

(The December, 1922 booklets contained a block of four of the 1c yellow, 2c green and 3c brown. The December, 1923 booklets contained a block of four of the 1c yellow, 2c green and 3c carmine.)

A54

A55

A56

"Historical" Issue June 29, 1927.

No.	Type.		Perf. 12.	Unused.	Used.
305	*A54*	5c	Violet..........................	.08	.02
306	*A55*	12c	Green...........................	.20	.18
307	*A56*	20c	Carmine.........................	.30	.15

A57

A58

A59

A60

A61

No.	Type.			Unused.	Used.
			Commemorating 60th Anniversary of Confederation, June 29, 1927. Perf. 12.		
308	*A57*	1c	Orange	.02	.01
309	*A58*	2c	Green	.03	.01
310	*A59*	3c	Carmine	.04	.01
311	*A60*	5c	Violet	.06	.01
312	*A61*	12c	Blue	.18	.10

A62

			Oct., 1928. Perf. 12.		
313	*A62*	1c	Orange *Oct. 25th*	.02	.01
314		2c	Green *Oct. 16th*	.03	.01
315		3c	Carmine *Dec. 20th*	.04	.01
316		5c	Pale violet *Jan. 6th*	.07	.01
317		8c	Light blue	.10	.02

A63

A64

A64a

A65

A66

No.	Type.			Unused.	Used.
380	*A63*	10c	Green "British Columbia Mountain Scenery", *Dec. 6th*...............	.15	.02
381	*A64*	12c	Grey *Jan. 6th*..................	.15	.05
381a	*A64a*	20c	Carmine *Jan. 6th*................	.25	.10
382	*A65*	50c	Blue *Jan. 6th*	.60	.20
383	*A66*	$1	Olive *Jan. 6th*..................	1.15	.25

A100

Air Mail, Sept. 23, 1928.

390	*A100*	5c	Grey-brown....................	.10	.10

A110

A111

A112

Special Delivery, July 1, 1898. Perf. 12.

400	*A110*	10c	Green (*Pl. 1*)..................	.60	.15
401		10c	Blue-green (*Pl. 1, 1905*).......... *On cover .50*..................... *a. Used pair $1.50; dated Sept.,*	.75	.15

No.	Type.			Unused.	Used.
			1922, or later (notes) 2.50; same on cover $5.00		
			b. No shaded background for numerals "10" (Pl. 2)...............	*1.50*	*.50*
			September, 1922 Perf. 12.		
402	*A111*	20c	Scarlet........................	.30	.12
			June 29, 1927.		
403	*A112*	20c	Bright orange....................	.25	.12

A120

Postage Due.

No.	Type.			Unused.	Used.
			June 1, 1906. Perf. 12.		
410	*A120*	1c	Dull violet (*Pl. 1 & 2*)...........	.03	.03
			a. Thin experimental paper of October, 1924....................	*.50*	*.50*
411		1c	Red-violet......................	.03	.03
412		2c	Dull violet (*Pl. 1 to 4*)...........	.05	.04
			a. Thin experimental paper of October, 1924....................	*.50*	*.50*
413		2c	Red-violet......................	.05	.04
414		4c	Dull violet (*July 3, 1928*).........	.06	.04
415		5c	Dull violet (*Pl. 1 & 2*)...........	.12	.05
			a. Thin experimental paper of October, 1924....................	*.50*	*.50*
416		5c	Red-violet......................	.12	.05
417		10c	Dull violet *July 3, 1928*..........	.15	.08

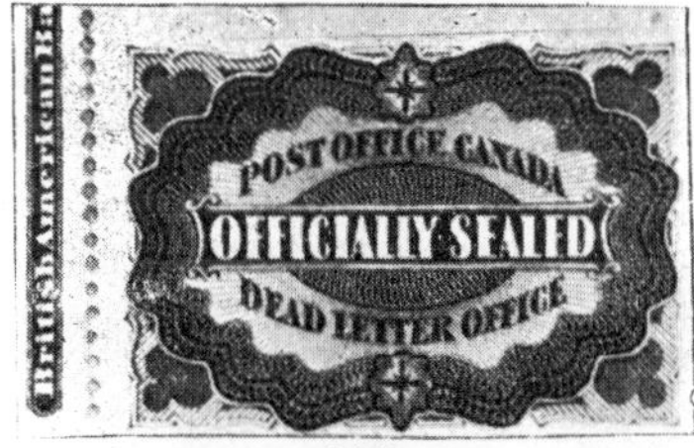

A140

A142

A141

No.	Type.		Unused.	Used.
		Officially Sealed.		
		1879. Perf. 12.		
450	*A140*	Brown on medium stout wove.....	2.50	2.50
		a. Imperf. (?)..................		
		On cover $5.00; Pair $7.50........		
		1905 Perf. 12.		
451	*A141*	Black on very thick blue wove....	5.00	10.00
		Block 4.........................	*22.50*	
		1907		
452		Black on white wove.............	1.50	2.50
		Block 4.........................	*7.50*	
		1913		
453	*A142*	Black-brown on medium stout white.........................	1.00	1.00
		Block 4.........................	*4.50*	
		(All issues were printed in sheets of fifty stamps. Plate 1 only exists for each type).		

ESSAYS.

On India Proof Paper unless otherwise specified.

E1
Enlarged.

E2
Enlarged.

1 *E1* 3d Black. *Original design by Sir Sanford Fleming, now in the Reford and Jarrett Collections.*
Nos. 1 and 2 are from a steel or copper die, on an opaque wove.

E3

E4

E5

2 *E2* 1s Black. *Original design by Sir Sanford Fleming, now in the Reford Collection.*

No.	Type.			Unused.	Used.
			On Wove. (Accepted by most specialists as Canadian Essays, but the author has never seen any evidence to prove this.)		
3	*E3*		Design by Bradbury Wilkinson. Blue Green, Brown, Violet, or Red on wove..		10.00
4	*E4*		Design by Bradbury Wilkinson. Brown, Red-Brown or Green..................		50.00

E6

E7

No.	Type.			Unused.	Used.
5	*E5*		Design by Bradbury Wilkinson. Brown, Red-Brown or Green..................		50.00
6	*E6*		From plate engraved by Ellis Co., Toronto. Only known specimen in collection of Mrs. A. R. Clarke, Toronto. Black *on red surfaced wove.*		
7	*E7*		Proof from die for centre of 7½d stamp cardboard. Green, pale green, grey, violet, red, brick red, black............		50.00
			Canada Bank Note and Printing Co. On extremely thin Japanese vegetable fibre paper, sometimes having appearance of laid paper.		

E8

E9

E10

No.	Type.			Unused.	Used.
8	*E8*	2c	Red.................................		6.00
9		2c	Green...............................		6.00
			a. *Block 4*...........................		25.00
			b. *Block 4 with sketch of running horse in black on left and "SAMPLE PROOF IMPRESSION" in margin*.........		*35.00*

No.	Type.			Unused.	Used.
			On smooth surface coated paper.		
10		1c	Orange-yellow........................		3.50
			Pale yellow.........................		*3.50*
11		2c	Olive................................		3.50
12		2c	Blue (paper blued)..................		3.50
13		2c	Brown or brownish-red...............		3.50
14		2c	Yellow-green........................		3.50
15		3c	Black...............................		3.50
16		3c	Red.................................		3.50
17		3c	Carmine.............................		3.50
			On India paper.		
18		2c	Blue................................		3.50
			(The printings on the smooth surface coated paper also come mounted on card-board. The Plate bore an imprint at the bottom.)		
19			An essay for a stamp of the intended new "Republic" was prepared by a member of Louis Reil's Cabinet, and is now, we understand, in the possession of the Catholic Hierarchy, St. Boniface, Man.		
			Engraved but never issued.		
			Plate Proofs on India Proof Paper.		
20	*E9*	12½c	Lilac...............................		25.00
21			Bright blue.........................		25.00
22	*E10*	15c	Green...............................		25.00
			Gummed and Perforated.		
23	*E9*	12½c	....		50.00
24	*E10*	15c	....		50.00

E12

No.	Type.			Unused.	Used.
25	*E12*	1c	Grey-black..........................		5.00
26		1c	Rose................................		5.00
27		1c	Pale brown..........................		5.00
28		1c	Pale blue...........................		5.00
			These cards have a rubber stamp impression on the face "SAMPLE PROOF-IMPRESSION".		

E13

E14

E15

No.	Type.			Unused.	Used.
29	*E13*	1c	Rose on cardboard *cut square*..........		5.00
			On Thin Cardboard *cut square.*		
30	*E14*	3c	Light rose pink......................		5.00
31		3c	Dark rose pink.......................		5.00
32		3c	Yellow green.........................		5.00
33		3c	Blue green...........................		5.00
			Plate Proof on India Paper. Design of issued stamp except for lines in band between CANADA and THREE (left) and POSTAGE and CENTS (right).		
34	*E15*	3c	Azure blue, blued paper...............		15.00
			a. Lines omitted.		
			(*This proof is also found mounted*).		

E16

E17

No.	Type.			Unused.	Used.
			KING EDWARD.		
			Plate never used—numerals of value colorless. Thin wove paper, gummed.		
35	*E16*	1c	Pale rose............................		12.00
		1c	Grey.................................		15.00
			(*These are also found mounted*).		
			Queen Victoria Numerals.		
36		50c	Olive green, identical with issued stamps, plate proof impression, mounted........		15.00

No.	Type.			Unused.	Used.
			Original 2c Carmine Georgian with "iTc" in white outlined in color for reproduction purposes. (See notes on War Tax issues.)		
37		2c plus 1c.	Carmine (*but one known copy*)......		
38	*E17*	10c	An "historical" set was announced as ready for sale July 1st, 1926, but the issue was withheld. In November, 1926 the Toronto Telegram illustrated three stamps including the 5c McGee, the 20c Baldwin-LaFontaine, and a 10c Laurier-Macdonald, as in the issued 12c stamp of June 29, 1927......................		

L1

L2

L3

Labrador Essays.

				Unused.	Used.
1	L1	5c	Green and Black.....................		10.00
2	L2	25c	Blue and Black......................		10.00
3	L3	$1	Green, Pink and Red.................		10.00

We invite those who delight in stamps with stories back of them to pay attention to the three stamps of Labrador inscribed "U.S.A. Post Office" illustrated above.

W. R. Patton, editor of Canada and Newfoundland Section, Philatelic Gossip, 1927, supplies a few particulars of these stamps, but first let the author state that he purchased two sets from a Montreal dealer in September, 1926. These were in perfect mint condition, with no defacing marks whatever. The dealer knew little about them except that "many years ago an American had intended to use them on the Labrador Coast and the police had seized them, the lot being destroyed with the exception of a few sets, which had been eagerly sought after by collectors at the time."

No.	Type.		Unused.	Used.

This is what Mr. Patton has to say: "There is a great stamp story behind these. I have been after it for nearly a year, but there is much to get yet. The Supt. P.O., Honolulu, got a great deal of information about these from a Private in the U.S. Army, stationed there, formerly of the Royal North West Mounted Police, who had seized them when bringing in an Eskimo prisoner from the far North, and later destroyed them in Toronto. An item in a philatelic paper published in Regina during 1910 referred to these stamps as having been seized in Montreal, however. It appears that the American gentleman who was responsible for the stamps had issued nearly One Million Dollars' worth, as I have evidence that $675,000 were destroyed by the Government, probably more."

The gentleman made a mistake in trying to annex this territory to the United States.

PROOFS

P1

P2

P3

Specimen Types.

No.	Type.		Unused.	Used.
1	½d	with 10d on one piece, on thin paper, sometimes mounted on die sunk card, Orange, yellow, brown, pink.		20.00
2	½d	Color of issue, on medium wove.		12.00
3	½d	Brown, rose, deep rose, pale rose, pale pink, pale faded rose, olive yellow, pale violet, pale violet blue, yellowish brown, salmon red, deep pink, on medium wove. .		10.00
4	½d	Included with 10d and 17 other stamps in lithographed proof sheet illustrating fine examples of Bank Note Company's engraving. Colors and shades as for No. 2 and 3. . . .		45.00
5	½d	With 10d cut out of No. 4 sheet, color of issue, distinguished by a spot of color in the lower frame line under AL of HALF		10.00
		Plate Proofs with SPECIMEN.		

No.	Type.			Unused.	Used.
6	P1	½d	Color of issue, SPECIMEN vert. green..		5.00
7			Pink, SPECIMEN vert. green.........		5.00
8			Pale brown, SPECIMEN vert. carmine.		5.00
9			Black, SPECIMEN vert. carmine.......		5.00
			a. Nos. 6-7-8-9 with major re-entry......		*12.00*
			b. Nos. 6-7-8-9 with minor re-entry......		*8.00*
			Plate Proofs without SPECIMEN.		
10		½d	Rose, pale rose, green, pale green, brown, orange, yellow, blue, pale pink........		3.00
			a. No. 10 with major re-entry..........		*10.00*
			b. No. 10 with minor re-entry..........		*6.00*
10aa		½d	Brown rose, etc.		45.00
			Brown rose, cut from sheet No. 4		6.00
			Finished Proofs, without SPECIMEN, Perf. 12, brown gum, stout wove paper.		
11		½d	Black-brown, blue, or green............		25.00
			a. No. 11 with major re-entry..........		*35.00*
			b. No. 11 with minor re-entry..........		*28.00*
			(Also seen imperf., brown rose, gummed.)		
			Plate Proofs with SPECIMEN.		
12	P1	3d	Color of issue SPECIMEN horiz. carmine		10.00
13			Black, SPECIMEN horiz. yellow		10.00
14	P3		Black, SPECIMEN diag. carmine......		10.00
15			Color of issue, SPECIMEN horiz. green..		12.00
16			Color of issue, SPECIMEN vert. green...		12.00
			a. Nos. 12 to 16 with major re-entry.....		*25.00*
			b. Nos. 12 to 16 with minor re-entry.....		*20.00*
			Plate Proofs without SPECIMEN.		
17		3d	Color of issue.........................		15.00
18		3d	Yellow, orange or black...............		10.00
			a. Nos. 17-18 with major re-entry.......		*30.00*
			b. Nos. 17-18 with minor re-entry.......		*22.50*
			Plate Proofs with SPECIMEN.		
19	*P1*	6d	Black, SPECIMEN vert. carmine......		5.00
20			Grey, Blue-grey, SPECIMEN vert. carmine............................		3.75
			a. Re-entry, Upper Left "6" double......		*12.00*
			(The stamps on the right side of the top row show a doubling of the upper left 6 and the position dot at centre left. We have never seen the stamps of issue similarly doubled. These proofs may have been taken from a plate not otherwise used, or these "entries" may have been burnished off the plate and re-entries made which showed the stamps of issue as normal stamps.)		
21			Blue, SPECIMEN vert. carmine.......		4.25
22			Black, SPECIMEN vert. yellow.......		5.00
23			Grey, SPECIMEN vert. yellow or green.		3.75
			Grey, SPECIMEN diag. carmine.......		5.00
			Plate Proofs without SPECIMEN.		
24		6d	Orange-yellow, red-lilac, purple, purple-black or dull purple..................		3.75

No.	Type.			Unused.	Used.
			Die Proofs.		
25a		7½d	Green, coarse yellowish wove, SPECIMEN in heavy type diag. in carmine...		10.00
			(This may have been from an experimental die.)		
25		7½d	Black, on manila....................		10.00
26		7½d	Black on white wove.................		10.00
			Plate Proofs with SPECIMEN.		
27	*P1*	7½d	Black, SPECIMEN vert. carmine......		4.00
28	*P3*		Black, SPECIMEN diag. blue.........		4.00
29			Orange, SPECIMEN vert. carmine.....		4.00
			Plate Proofs without SPECIMEN.		
30		7½d	Green............................		7.00
31			Yellow, orange, black...............		5.00
			Die Proofs.		
32		10d	With ½d on one piece, on thin paper, sometimes mounted on die sunk card....		20.00
33		10d	Pale pink, light brown, claret, deep lake, yellow brown, light blue, etc..........		10.00
33a		10d	With ½d and 17 others on lithographic proof sheet (No. 4). Colors as for Nos. 2 and 3...........................		45.00
33b		10d	Cut from sheet No. 4................		6.00
			Plate Proofs with SPECIMEN.		
34		10d	Black on manila SPECIMEN diag. carmine...........................		12.00
35			Blue, SPECIMEN vert. carmine.......		4.50
36			Black, SPECIMEN vert. or diag. carmine.............................		4.50
			Plate Proofs without SPECIMEN.		
37		10d	Color of issue......................		6.00
			a. With major re-entry...............		*12.00*
			b. With minor re-entry...............		*9.00*
38		10d	Black, pale olive or grey-green, pale violet, pale rose, orange, yellow ochre....		4.50
			a. With major re-entry..............		*10.00*
			b. With minor re-entry..............		*7.00*
39		10d	Black on laid paper..................		25.00
			Finished Proofs, without SPECIMEN, Perf. 12.		
40		10d	Brown or slate blue..................		30.00
			Plate Proofs with SPECIMEN.		
41		12d	Black, SPECIMEN vert. carmine right..		25.00
42		12d	Black, SPECIMEN vert. carmine left...		35.00
43		12d	Black, SPECIMEN vert. green right....		30.00
44	*P3*	12d	Black, SPECIMEN diag. carmine......		35.00
			Die Proofs, on Bond Paper, from unfinished die. (Also noted on India Paper)		
45		12d	Orange, green, blue, lilac, grey-violet, pale violet, brown, chocolate, grey-black, vermilion, bright vermilion, or deep purple............................		50.00
46		12d	Pale red-violet, Bond Paper, slip printing (*Mrs. A. R. Clarke Collection*)..........		
47		12d	With 10c 1859, green................		50.00
48		12d	With 10c 1859, blue..................		50.00
49		12d	With 10c 1859, Vermilion.............		50.00

No.	Type.			Unused.	Used.
50		12d	With 10c 1859, Black.................		50.00
50a		12d	With 10c 1859, Chocolate.............		50.00

Die Proofs (from the unfinished die) of the 12d show a defect at the top of the letters CE of PENCE. The background of the letters shows in lines resulting from the first cutting of the graver, instead of the solid mass of color as in the issued stamp and all plate proofs. The letters are unfinished, as for example the P of POSTAGE, the lines of which are thinner and sharper in the issued stamps and in plate proofs. We doubt if there exists a proof from this die in its final stage before the transfer roll was made from it.

Proofs of stamps of different issues on the same piece were made after the stamps had become obsolete. In one instance a transfer proof was taken from each of the original dies and the double proof then taken from a stone by lithographic process. Ordinarily the two dies were locked together to produce a single die proof of the two stamps.

P4

P5

P6

Proofs of the 1859 Issue, *on India Proof Paper unless otherwise stated.*

No.	Type.			Unused.	Used.
			Die Proofs, on India Paper, mounted.		
		1c	Rose................................		
			Plate Proofs with SPECIMEN.		
51	*P3*	1c	Rose, Deep Rose, SPECIMEN vert. black................................		2.75
52		1c	Rose, Deep Rose, SPECIMEN diag. black................................		3.50
			Plate Proofs without SPECIMEN.		
53		1c	Black or orange......................		2.75
54		1c	Color of issue.......................		3.50
			Die Proofs, on India Paper.		
55		2c	Deep Rose or Green..................		10.00

No.	Type.			Unused.	Used.
			Plate Proofs with SPECIMEN.		
56	*P3*	2c	Deep Rose, SPECIMEN vert. black....		4.50
57	*P4*	2c	Color of Issue SPECIMEN horiz. red...		12.00
			Plate Proofs without SPECIMEN.		
58		2c	Green, Deep Rose or Claret...........		5.00
			Die Proofs, mounted.		
		5c	Color of Issued Stamp, Black..........		
			Plate Proofs with SPECIMEN.		
59	*P3*	5c	Color of Issue SPECIMEN horiz. black.		6.50
			a. The major re-entry.................		*50.00*
			b. Major re-entry.....................		*20.00*
			c. Minor re-entry....................		*10.00*
			Plate Proofs without SPECIMEN.		
60	*P3*	5c	Color of Issue.......................		6.00
			a. The Major re-entry.................		*50.00*
			b. Major re-entry.....................		*20.00*
			c. Minor re-entry....................		*10.00*
61	*P3*	5c	Pale Yellow or Black..................		5.00
			a. The Major re-entry.................		*50.00*
			b. Major re-entry.....................		*20.00*
			c. Minor re-entry....................		*10.00*
			Die Proofs, mounted.		
		10c	Black...............................		
62		10c	With 12d, Blue on thin paper..........		50.00
63		10c	With 12d, Green on thin paper.........		50.00
64		10c	With 12d, Vermilion on thin paper.....		50.00
65		10c	With 12d, Black on thin paper.........		50.00
66		10c	With 12d, Chocolate on thin paper.....		50.00
66x		10c	Bright Vermilion.....................		25.00
			Plate Proofs with SPECIMEN.		
67	*P3*	10c	Grey-black SPECIMEN diag. carmine..		6.50
			a. Re-entry..........................		*15.00*
68	*P3*	10c	Black SPECIMEN vert. carmine.......		4.50
			a. Re-entry..........................		*15.00*
69		10c	Grey-black SPECIMEN vert. carmine..		4.50
			a. Re-entry..........................		*15.00*
70		10c	Yellow SPECIMEN horiz. carmine.....		3.00
			Plate Proofs with SPECIMEN at bottom, rubber stamp impression.		
71	*P4*	10c	Black-brown SPECIMEN horiz. carmine		12.00
72	*P4*	10c	Red-purple SPECIMEN horiz. carmine.		12.00
72x	P4	10c	Orange.............................		12.00
			Plate Proofs Without SPECIMEN.		
73		10c	Black, Grey-black, Black-brown, Pale Red-brown, Violet, Purple, Vermilion, Orange, Yellow, Green, Reddish lake....		3.50
			Die Proofs.		
74		12½c	Blue or pale blue....................		10.00
			Plate Proofs with SPECIMEN.		
75	*P5*	12½c	Green SPECIMEN vert. carmine......		3.50
76		12½c	Olive-green SPECIMEN diag. black....		3.50

No.	Type.			Unused.	Used.
			Thick letters.		
77		12½c	Grey-black SPECIMEN vert. carmine..		
			Thin letters.		
78		12½c	Grey-black SPECIMEN vert. carmine..		
			Plate Proofs without SPECIMEN.		
79		12½c	Green, blue-green, blue, pale blue, black, yellow............................		3.00
			Plate Proofs with SPECIMEN.		
80		17c	Blue SPECIMEN diag. carmine........		3.50
			a. Burr over shoulder.................		*60.00*
			b. Re-entry.........................		*12.00*
81			Blue SPECIMEN vert. carmine........		3.50
			a. Burr over shoulder.................		*60.00*
			b. Re-entry.........................		*12.00*
			Plate Proofs Without SPECIMEN.		
82		17c	Blue, ultramarine, black, orange, green, yellow-green, vermilion, chocolate......		3.50
			a. Burr over shoulder.................		*60.00*
			b. Re-entry.........................		*12.00*

Forgery (Notes)

No.	Type.			Unused.	Used.
			Proofs of 1859 Stamped Envelopes.		
82x	*S1*	5c	On laid, SAMPLE printed below stamp, *entire*..............................		12.00
82xx	*S1*	5c	Bright red on thick yellow vertically laid, *cut square*..........................		2.50
82xxx	*S1*	5c	Bright blue on white wove, under side ruled with horiz. green lines 8 mm. apart, *cut square*..........................		2.50
82xy	*S1*	5c	Deep black, brown on cream toned stout white wove, *entire*..................		
82xyx	*S2*	10c	Chocolate brown on white, *cut square*....		2.50
82xyz	*S2*	10c	Brown on vertically laid yellow, *cut square*		2.50
82z	*S2*	10c	Green, on white wove, *cut square*........		2.50
82zz	*S2*	10c	Bright red, on cream toned stout white wove, *entire*........................		
			(One, and possibly more, of the above is known on "diagonally laid" paper.)		
			1868 Issue.		
			Die Proofs, on India Paper.		
83		3c	Black.............................		12.00
84		6c	Black.............................		12.00

No.	Type.		Unused.	Used.
85	12½c	Black		12.00
86	12½c	Deep Rose		12.00
87	15c	Black		12.00
		Plate Proofs on Cardboard.		
88	½c	Color of issue or in green		6.50
89	1c	Color of issue		6.50
90	2c	Color of issue		6.50
91	3c	Color of issue or in deep lilac		6.50
92	5c	Color of issue or in grey-green		6.50
93	5c	Pale red-brown		6.50
94	12½c	Color of issue		6.50
95	15c	Deep lilac		6.50
		Plate Proofs on India.		
96	5c	Brown-rose		6.50
		Plate Proofs on Manila Glazed Surface.		
97	5c	Green		10.00
		Finished Proofs, Perf. 12, Gummed.		
98	1c	Blue		25.00
		1870 "Small Cents" Issue.		
		Die Proofs.		
99	3c	Green, pale red-brown, pale brown		12.00
100	6c	Black		12.00
101	8c	Blue (1892-93)		12.00
102	8c	Pale chestnut		12.00
103	5c	Ultramarine		12.00
		Plate Proofs. Cardboard or India.		
104	½c	Color of issue, on cardboard		5.00
105	1c	Orange, on cardboard		5.00
106	1c	Blue, on India		5.00
107	2c	Color of Issue *Cardboard*		5.00
108	3c	Color of Issue *Cardboard*		5.00
109	5c	Olive or grey *Cardboard*		5.00
110	6c	Yellow-brown *Carbdoard*		5.00
111	8c	Grey *Cardboard*		5.00
112	10c	Pale lilac, deep magenta *Cardboard*		5.00
		Finished Proofs, Perf. 12, Gummed, on Wove Paper.		
113	1c	Pale red-violet, pale violet		25.00
114	2c	Dull red, shade of 3c 1870		25.00
115	3c	Green		25.00
		Large 20c and 50c of 1893.		
		Die Proofs.		
116	20c	Deep vermilion		12.00
117	50c	Blue		12.00
		Plate Proofs.		
118	20c	Vermilion *Cardboard*		3.75
119	50c	Blue *Cardboard*		3.75

Jubilee Issue of 1897.

Plate Proofs On Soft Wove and On Cardboard.

120		½c	Grey-black	7.50
121		1c	Orange-yellow	7.50
122		2c	Green	7.50
123		3c	Carmine	7.50
124		5c	Blue	7.50
125		6c	Brown	7.50
126		8c	Slate violet	7.50
127		10c	Purple violet	7.50
128		15c	Slate	7.50
129		20c	Pale vermilion	7.50
130		50c	Pale ultramarine	7.50
131		$1	Lake	7.50
132		$2	Deep violet	7.50
133		$3	Bistre	7.50
134		$4	Violet	7.50
136		$5	Olive-green	7.50

Actual stamps as issued, but with SPECIMEN overprinted with rubber stamps, letters 2½ mm. high, with seriphs.

137	*P6*	½c	Grey-black	12.00
138		1c	Orange-yellow	12.00
139		2c	Grey	12.00
140		3c	Carmine	12.00
141		5c	Blue	12.00
142		6c	Brown	12.00
143		8c	Slate violet	12.00
144		10c	Purple violet	12.00
145		15c	Slate	12.00
146		20c	Pale vermilion	12.00
147		50c	Pale ultramarine	12.00
148		$1	Lake	12.00
149		$2	Deep violet	12.00
150		$3	Bistre	12.00
151		$4	Violet	12.00
152		$5	Olive-green	12.00

The 20c, 50c and $5 stamps have been noted with an overprint letters 2 mm. high, no seriphs.

P7

No.	Type.			Unused.	Used.
			4-Leaf Issue of 1897.		
			Die Proofs. On India paper, or mounted on white cards size 5 x 7, with Plate Number for each value and Imprint "American Bank Note Co., Ottawa" extending to either side of stamp.		
153	*P7*	½c	Grey-black, *Plate F. 102*		15.00
154		1c	Green, *Plate F. 103*		15.00
155		2c	Purple, *Plate F. 104*		15.00
156		3c	Carmine, *Plate F. 105*		7.50
157		5c	Blue, *Plate F. 106*		15.00
			a. Purple, Light Purple, on green		*17.50*
158		6c	Brown, *Plate F. 107*		15.00
159		8c	Pale orange, *Plate F. 108*		15.00
160		10c	Brown-violet, *Plate F. 109*		15.00
			The author's set, (Nos. 153 to 160) was obtained from a Toronto barrister who had collected Canadian essays and proofs, with an accompanying note that, "This set of eight proofs were printed from dies in the possession of the American Bank Note Co. at Ottawa, at the request of the P.M.G. for the purpose of presenting them to His Royal Highness the Duke of Cornwall and York (Now His Majesty King George V) who was then (1901) about to visit Canada and who was known to be an enthusiastic collector. This set was duly printed for the above purpose but mislaid and could not be found when required for presentation. When subsequently found it was presented to me by order of the then P.M.G. who had been particularly interested in the unique collection of Canadian stamps which I then had."		
			Without Plate Number or Imprint.		
161		5c	Blue on *white*		17.50
162		5c	Blue on *bluish*		17.50
163		5c	Blue on *light blue*		17.50
164		5c	Blue on *dark blue*		17.50
155		5c	Brown-violet, *greenish hard wove*		17.50
			Plate Proofs, on India Paper.		
165		½c	Grey-black		3.00
166		1c	Green		3.00
167		2c	Purple		3.00
168		3c	Carmine, deep carmine		3.00
			On Medium Thick Wove.		
169		8c	Carmine		6.00
			On Thin Greenish-blue.		
170		5c	Dull blue-grey		6.00
			On Cardboard.		
171		½c	Grey-black		2.00
172		1c	Green		2.00
173		2c	Purple		2.00
174		3c	Carmine or Orange		2.00

No.	Type.			Unused.	Used.
175		5c	Blue		2.00
176		6c	Brown		2.00
177		8c	Pale orange		2.00
178		10c	Brown violet		5.00
			On Stout Wove, Perforated 12, Gummed.		
178x		2c	Grey-black		5.00
178xx		3c	Green		5.00
			Queen Victoria Numerals.		
			Die Proofs. On India paper, or mounted on white cards size 5 x 7, with plate number for each value and imprint "American Bank Note Co., Ottawa" extending to either side of stamp.		
179	*P7*	½c	Grey-black, *Plate F. 110*		12.00
180		1c	Green, *Plate F. 111*		12.00
181		2c	Purple, *Plate F. 112*		12.00
182		3c	Carmine, *Plate F. 113*		7.50
183		5c	Blue, *Plate F. 114*		12.00
184		6c	Brown, *Plate F. 115*		12.00
185		8c	Pale orange, *Plate F. 116*		12.00
186		10c	Brown violet, *Plate F 117*		12.00
			Toned Paper.		
187		3c	Carmine, light Carmine, *Plate F. 118*		12.00
			No Plate Number or Imprint, on fine wove paper.		
188		3c	Color of issue and in various shades of carmine		5.00
			Finished Proof, Perf. 12, on Wove, Brownish Gummed.		
189		10c	Carmine		40.00
			Plate Proofs.		
		20c	Light green, mounted		10.00
		50c	Olive green, mounted		15.00
			King Edward Issue.		
			Die Proofs. With wide margins and impression of whole face of die.		
190			Mauve, dull green, dull blue, pale brown		
			Stamp as issued, but with SPECIMEN overprinted in black.		
191		20c	Olive-green, SPECIMEN horiz		12.00
			Registration Stamps.		
192		2c	Vermilion *thin paper*		4.50
193		2c	Vermilion *cardboard*		3.50
194		5c	Green *Cardboard*		3.50
195		8c	Blue *Cardboard*		5.50
			Quebec Tercentary.		
			Die Proofs.		
196		7c	Black		15.00
197		10c	Violet		15.00
			"War Tax," 1915. Die Proofs.		
198		1c	Green *mounted*		15.00

No.	Type.			Unused.	Used.
199		2c	Deep carmine *mounted*		15.00
200		2c	1Tc Red		15.00
			Georgian Issues.		
			Die Proofs. With wide margins and impression of whole face of die. Imprint "F. 211 American Bank Note Co., Ottawa."		
201		2c	Carmine rose		12.00
			Officially Sealed.		
			Plate Proof.		
202	*A140*		Brown *Stamp of 1879*		5.00

P10

P11

P12

P13

P14

P15

P16

P17

Macdonald-Cartier Centenary

Die Proofs. Dies were prepared for a Macdonald-Cartier Centenary set, but plates were never made. The beauty of these die proofs, and the historical

No.	Type.			Unused.	Used.
			interest of the set, leave little to be desired. But four sets of proofs are known, and three of these do not include P15, an alternative 10c value.		
203	*P10*	1c	Green		
204	*P11*	2c	Carmine		
205	*P12*	5c	Blue		
206	*P13*	7c	Bistre		
207	*P14*	10c	Brown violet		
208	*P15*	10c	Brown violet		
			a. Mounted, with marginal notations pertaining to alterations		
209	*P16*	20c	Olive		
210	*P17*	50c	Grey-black		

STATIONERY

Province of Canada

S1

S2

Envelopes.

March, 1860.

Laid paper, watermarked "Ca, POD". Size 5½ x 3¼.

No.	Type.			Unused.	Used.
1	*S1*	5c	Bright red, *cream toned paper, flap rounded, (Feb. 1, '60)*	4.00	6.00
			a. Deep black brown on stout white wove (error?)		
2		5c	Bright red, very white paper, flap more pointed *1864?*	6.00	10.00
3	*S2*	10c	Black-brown; cream toned paper, flap rounded *Feb. 1, '60*	10.00	25.00
			a. Bright red (error?)		

On diagonally laid white or buff envelopes watermarked "POD US". Size 5½ x 3.

No.	Type.			Unused.	Used.
4	*S1*	5c	Bright red	25.00	
5	*S2*	10c	Dark red-brown	30.00	

S3

S4

S5

DOMINION OF CANADA

Sizes

A. 5½ x 3⅛ — D. 5⅞ x 3½ — F. 9⅝ x 4⅛
B. 6 x 3⅜ — E. 6 x 3½ — G. 6½ x 3⅝
C. 10½ x 4½

No.	Type.			Unused.	Used.
			Oct. 6, '77. Laid paper, cross vergures 18 mm. apart. Pointed flap. Size A. 5½x3⅛.		
7	*S3*	1c	Pale blue, deep blue, white p..........	.25	.20
8	*S3*	3c	Red, rose, white paper................	.50	.50
			Size B. 6 x 3⅜.		
		3c	Red, rose, white paper................	.50	.50
			Size A. 5½ x 3⅛.		
9	*S3*	1c	Blue, tongued flap, *white paper*.........	25.00	35.00
10	*S3*	3c	Red, tongued flap, *white paper*.........	2.50	5.00
			Laid paper, cross vergures 24 mm. apart. Pointed flap. Oct., 1888.		
11	*S3*	1c	Blue, deep blue, *cream toned paper*......	.10	.10
12		3c	Red, carmine, *cream toned paper*........	.10	.10
			Cross Vergures 27 mm. apart. Size A. 5½ x 3⅛.		
14	*S3*	1c	Deep blue..........................	.15	.15
15	*S3*	1c	Ultramarine *1896?*....................	.05	.05
			Size B. 6 x 3⅜.		
16	*S3*	3c	Red, carmine.......................	.05	.05
17	*S3*	3c	Carmine, white wove *1895?*............	.75	.75
			Size C. 10½x4½. Burnett Envelopes. Manila amber wove paper............		
18	*S3*	1c	Ultramarine.........................	3.00	
			a. On thin manila amber wove..........	*4.50*	
19	*S3*	3c	Red................................	1.00	
			June 14, 1895. Laid paper, cream toned. Size B. 6x3⅜.		
20	*S4*	2c	Blue green..........................	.10	.10
			a. Stamp inside envelope.............	*5.00*	

No.	Type.			Unused.	Used.
			April, 1898? Wove paper, cream toned. Size D. 5⅞x3½.		
21	*S5*	3c	Bright red	.15	.10
			July 22, 1899. Wove paper cream toned. Size D. 5⅞x3½.		

S6

2c

S7

S8

No.	Type.			Unused.	Used.
22	*S6*	1c	Dark green	.10	.10
			Jan. 2, 1899.		
23	*S6*	2c	Deep violet	2.50	2.50
			Jan. 8, 1899?		
24	*S6*	2c	Vermilion	.10	.05
			a. On white paper		
			Size E. (1904) 6x3½.		
25	*S6*	1c	Dark green, *white wove*	2.50	2.50
26		2c	Bright red, *white wove*	2.50	2.50
			Feb. 6, 1899. No. 8 surcharged 2c in blue-black, lower case C.		
27	*S7*	2c	On 3c Red	.35	.50
			No. 17 surcharged.		
28	*S7*	2c	on 3c Red	4.00	5.00
			No. 12 surcharged.		
29	*S7*	2c	On 3c Red	.50	.50
			No. 16 surcharged.		
30	*S7*	2c	On 3c Red	.50	.50
			Feb. 6, 1899. Size D. 5⅞x3½. (No. 21 surcharged 2c in blue-black.		
31	*S7*	2c	On 3c. Bright red, *lower case C*	.35	.20
			a. With corner imprint "If not called for in ten days return to	.40	.25
			b. Above but without dotted line	.40	.25
32	*S7*	2c	On 3c. Bright red, *capital C*	5.00	
			EDWARDIAN.		
			On very white wove paper. Jan. 12, 1905. Size E. 6x3½.		
33		2c	Bright red	.07	.05
			a. Die re-engraved	.10	.08

No.	Type.			Unused.	Used.
			Mar. 1, 1905. Size E. 6x3½.		
34		1c	Deep blue-green, pale green...........	.07	.05
			a. Die re-engraved....................	*.10*	*.08*
			GEORGIAN.		
			On white wove paper. Same frame design as Edwardian. Size E. 6x3½.		
35		1c	Green *1912?*.........................		
36		2c	Bright red, *1912?*....................		
37		3c	Dark brown, *Aug., 1921*...............		
38		1c	Orange, *Sept. ?, 1922*................		
39		2c	Green, *Sept. ?, 1922*.................		
			Size F. Dec., 1922. Unembossed.		
41		1c	Orange.............................	.05	.05
42		2c	Green..............................	.06	.06
43		3c	Brown..............................	.07	.06
			Embossed, 1925.		
44		1c	Orange.............................	.05	.05
45		2c	Green..............................	.06	.05
46		3c	Brown *July 1926*....................	.07	.05
47		3c	Carmine............................	.07	.05
			Jan., 1926. Unembossed.		
48		1c	Orange on manila....................	.05	.04
			Oct., 1927. Unembossed.		
49		1c	Green *white wove*....................	.05	.04
			1925? Unembossed.		
50		1c	Orange various papers and sizes made to order for business firms, with printed cancellation "Canada Post Office" and seven wavy lines....................	.05	.04
			Size G. Dec., 1924. Embossed.		
51		1c	Orange *white wove*...................	.05	.04
52		2c	Green *white wove*....................	.06	.05
			a. With "From" and two dotted lines, upper left..........................	*.06*	*.05*
53		3c	Brown *white wove*....................	.08	.06
54		3c	Rose carmine *white wove*..............	.07	.05
			a. With "From" and two dotted lines, upper left..........................	*.07*	*.05*
			b. Albino..........................	*1.50*	
			Size G. July, 1926. Embossed.		
55		3c	Brown *white wove*....................	*.08*	*.05*
			Surcharged in Black, "2 CENTS".		
			Feb., 1927. Size F. Embossed.		
56	*S8*	3c	Brown *white wove*....................	.25	.25
57	*S8*	3c	Carmine *white wove*..................	.25	.25
			Size G.		
58	*S8*	3c	Brown *white wove*....................	2.50	3.50
59	*S8*	3c	Carmine *white wove*..................	2.50	3.50
			a. With "From" and two dotted lines, upper left..........................	*2.50*	*3.50*

No.	Type.			Unused.	Used.
			Size E.		
60	*S8*	3c	Brown (shades) *white wove (150 issued)*..	5.00	6.50
			Unembossed.		
			Size F.		
			Oct., 1927. Size 6⅜x6⅝.		
62		10c	Brown Registration, linen lined, embossed, sold for 11c..................	.20	.20

S12

S13

S14

WRAPPERS OR POST BANDS.

No.	Type.			Unused.	Used.
			May, 1875. Size 9½ x 5.		
70	*S12*	1c	Dark blue, *light buff paper*.............	.10	.10
			a. Stamp at left (11½ x 6½)...........	*5.00*	*5.00*
			Nov. ?, 1881. Size 11⅛ x 4⅞.		
71	*S12*	1c	Dark blue, blue, *cream paper*...........	.10	.10
			April ?, 1882. Size 11⅛ x 4⅞.		
72	*S13*	1c	Pale blue, *light buff paper*..............	.15	.15
73	*S13*	1c	Blue, *straw paper (Aug. ?, 1882)*........	.10	.10
74	*S13*	1c	Ultramarine, *cream paper (1885)*........	.10	.10
			May ?, 1887. Size 11⅛ x 4⅞.		
75	*S14*	1c	Ultramarine, *thin white paper*..........	.10	.10
76	*S14*	1c	Ultramarine, *cream paper (1888)*........	.10	.10
77	*S14*	1c	Ultramarine, *light manila paper*........	.10	.10

S15

S16

S17

No.	Type.			Unused.	Used.
			Feb. ?, 1892. Size 10⅜ x 4⅞.		
78	*S15*	1c	Dark blue, *thin straw paper*............	.10	.10
			a. Stamp half way cross wrapper.......	*5.00*	
79	*S15*	1c	Blue, *cream paper*...................	.10	.10

No.	Type.			Unused.	Used.
			Size 10¾ x 4⅞.		
80	*S15*	1c	Dark blue, *straw paper*	.10	.10
81	*S15*	1c	Black, *light buff paper* (*Feb. ?, 1894*)	.10	.10
82	*S15*	1c	Black, *light brown paper*	.10	.10
			4-Leaf Design.		
			June, 1898.		
83		1c	Dark green, *manila paper*	.10	.10
			Edwardian. Oct. ?, 1903.		
84		1c	Dark green, *manila paper*	.10	.10
			July 11, 1907. Size 15 x 6½.		

THIS WRAPPER TO BE USED ONLY BY PUBLISHERS AND FOR THE SOLE PURPOSE OF MAILING SECOND CLASS MATTER TO THE UNITED STATES.

S18

No.	Type.			Unused.	Used.
85	*S18*	1c	Dark green *manila*	.20	.25
86	*S18*	2c	Carmine *manila*	.20	.25
			Size 12 x 8.		
87	*S18*	3c	Slate violet *manila*	1.50	1.50
			June 18, 1908.		
88	*S16*	1c on 2c.	Carmine (*With S18*)	1.25	1.25
89	*S17*	1c on 3c.	Slate violet (*With S18*)	5.00	5.00
			GEORGIAN, 1912. Size 6 x 13½.		
90		1c	Green, *with S18*	.05	.05
			a. Without S18	*.10*	*.10*
91		1c	Orange, *with S18*	.05	.05
			a. Without S18	*.10*	*.10*
			POSTAGE DUE WRAPPER.		
			Oct. 2, 1908. Size 6½ x 14⅞. (*Used by Postmasters only, to return wrapper mail to publishers. Printed instructions are given in French and in English*).		
92		?	On Manila paper		

S19

S20

S21

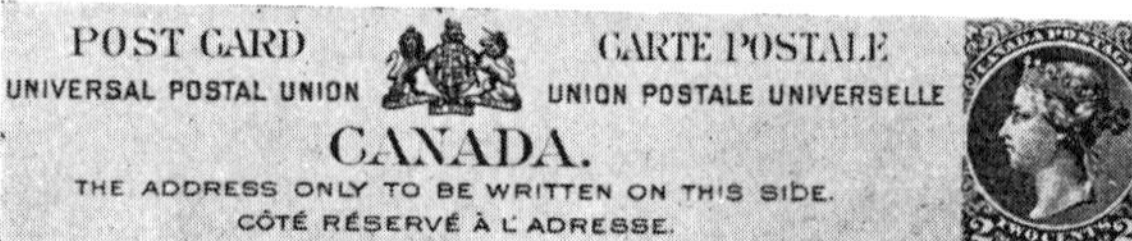

S22

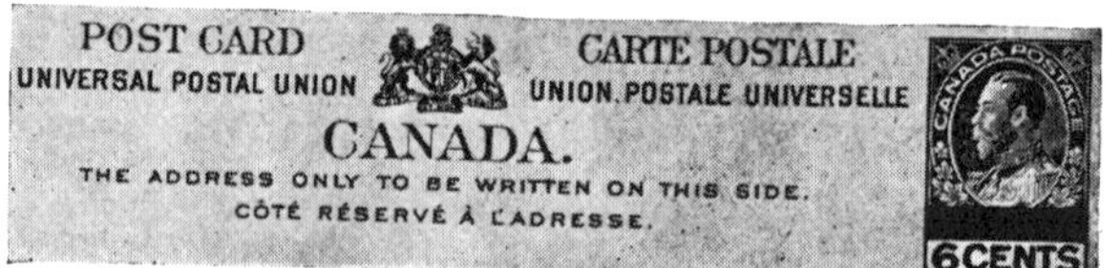

S23

S24

S25

POST CARDS

No.	Type.			Unused.	Used.
			June, 1871. Size 4⅝ x 3¼. Imprint "Montreal and Ottawa."		
100	*S19*	1c	Dull blue, deep blue, pale greenish blue, *light buff or pale buff*..................	.05	.03
			Dec., 1876?. Size 4¾ x 3. Imprint "Montreal" only.		
101	*S19*	1c	Dull blue, deep blue, pale greenish blue, *pale buff*............................	.06	.03
			Jan. 1, 1877. Size 4⅝ x 3. Inscribed "To United Kingdom."		
102	*S20*	2c	Deep yellow green, *Pale buff*...........	.06	.10
			April ?, 1882. Size 5 x 3. No frame.		
103	*S13*	1c	Light blue, pale ultramarine, *buff*.......	.05	.02
			"Reply Cards." Unused prices given are for entire unseparated card. Dec. ?, 1882. Size 5 x 3. No frame.		
104	*S13*	1c	Plus 1c Slate, *pale buff*................	.15	.15
			a. Portrait at left....................	*5.00*	
			b. Additional impression, double at bottom, inverted.....................	*15.00*	
			c. Double impression, with additional single impression at bottom inverted..	*15.00*	
			Sept. ?, 1884.		
105	*S13*	1c	Plus 1c Slate, *pale buff*................	.20	.40
			May ?, 1883.		
106	*S13*	1c	Plus 1c Slate black....................	.25	.50
			Feb. ?, 1887. Size 5 x 3.		
107	*S14*	1c	Dull blue, *pale buff*...................	.05	.01
			"Reply Cards." Unused prices are for entire unseparated card.		
108	*S14*	1c	Plus 1c Slate, *pale buff*................	.25	.75
			1888.		
109	*S14*	1c	Plus 1c. Slate green, *pale buff*.........	.15	.50
			a. Reply card on back of message card....	*10.00*	
			Dec. ?, 1891. Size 5 x 3.		
110	*S15*	1c	Dull ultramarine or pale ultramarine, *pale buff*............................	.03	.01
			"Reply Cards." Unused prices are for entire unseparated card. Dec. ?, 1892. Size 5 x 3.		
111	*S15*	1c	Plus 1c. Slate green with Type S14 on reply card, *pale buff*...................	.20	.50
			Oct. ?, 1894.		
112	*A15*	1c	Plus 1c. Grey-black, *pale buff*.........	.25	.15
			May, 1893. Size 5 x 3.		
113	*A15*	1c	Black, *pale buff*......................	.03	.01
			Large Business Card.		

No.	Type.			Unused.	Used.
			Feb. ?, 1893. Size 6 x 3⅝.		
114	*A15*	1c	Black, *pale buff*	.03	.02
			Size 5½ x 3⅜. Feb. ?, 1894.		
115	*A15*	1c	Black, *pale yellowish*	.50	.20
			April ?, 1896.		
116	*A15*	1c	Black, *rough straw*	.15	.05
			JUBILEE CARDS. (7,000,000 issued). June 19, 1897. Size 5½ x 3⅜.		
117		1c	Black, *pale buff*	.03	.01
			a. Inscriptions lacking		
			4-Leaf Design.		
			Jan. ?, 1898. Size 5½ x 3⅜.		
118		1c	Green, dark green, *pale buff*	.03	.01
			"Reply Card." June?, 1898. Size 5 x 3.		
119		1c	Plus 1c. Black, *pale buff*	.25	
			a. Reply printed on back of message card	*10.00*	
			EDWARDIAN.		
			Aug. ?, 1903. Size 5½ x 3⅜.		
120		1c	Green, *pale buff*	.03	.01
			"Reply Card." Feb. ?, 1904. Size 5 x 3.		
121		1c	Plus 1c. Black, *pale buff*	.15	.05
			GEORGIAN.		
			1912. Size 5½ x 3⅜.		
122		1c	Green, blue green on pale buff (*English*)	.03	.01
123		1c.	Green, blue green on pale buff (*English and French*)	.03	.01
			"Reply Card."		
124		1c	Plus 1c. Black on buff (*English*)	.10	.05
125		1c	Plus 1c. Black on buff (*English and French*)	.10	.05
			1915		
126		2c	Carmine (Shades) on buff (*English*)	.05	.01
127		2c	Carmine (Shades) on buff (*English and French*)	.05	.01
			July, 1917. Jubilee of Confederation, with comparative statistical data 1867-1917 relating to Canada's growth printed on left half.		
128		2c	Carmine on buff (*English*)	.15	.05
			Sept., 1922.		
130		1c	Orange on pale buff (*English*)	.05	.01
131		1c	Orange on pale buff (*Eng. and French*)	.05	.01
132		2c	Green on pale buff (*English*)	.06	.01
133		2c	Green on pale buff (*Eng. and French*)	.06	.01

No.	Type.			Unused.	Used.
			Reply Cards.		
134		1c	Plus 1c. Orange (*English*)............	.10	.10
135		1c	Plus 1c. Orange (*Eng. and French*)....	.10	.10
			BUSINESS CARDS.		
			4-Leaf Design.		
			Jan. ?, 1898. Size 5½ x 3⅜.		
136		1c	Carmine, *pale buff*....................	.05	.01
			Edwardian.		
			Dec. ?, 1903.		
137		1c	Rose, *pale buff*.......................	.05	.01
			Georgian. 1912.		
138		1c	Carmine on cream (*Fr. and English*)....	.05	.01
			1915.		
139		2c	Carmine on cream, *no inscript*..........	.06	.01
140		2c	Carmine on cream *with printed line*.....	.06	.01
			1920.		
141		1c	Green on pale buff *with printed line*......	.05	.01
142		2c	Carmine on pale buff *with printed line*...	.06	.01
			Sept., 1922.		
143		1c	Orange, pale buff, *with printed line*......	.05	.01
144		1c	Orange, *pale buff*, stamp only printed on card, printed line omitted.............	.06	.01
145		2c	Green, *as above*.......................		
			1922.		
146		2c	Green, pale buff, *with printed line*.......	.06	.01
			Jan., 1925.		
147		½c	Pale violet, *pale buff card*, "Business Reply Card" in Englsih...............	.08	.02
148		½c	As above, *inscriptions Eng. and French*..	.08	.02
149		1c	Orange regular issue plus ½c pale violet as above (*English*)...................	.15	.02
150		1c	Orange regular issue plus ½c pale violet *with inscriptions on each in Englsih and French*............................	.15	.02
			POSTAL UNION CARDS.		
			1879. Size 4⅝ x 3.		
151	*S21*	2c	Yellow-green, *pale yellowish*............	.35	.15
			Oct. ?, 1896. Size 5⅛ x 3.		
152	*S22*	2c	Orange-red, carmine, *pale buff*..........	.35	.15
			4-Leaf Design.		
			Dec. 1 ?, 1897. Size 4⅝ x 3.		
153		2c	Deep orange red, *pale buff*.............	.35	.15
154		2c	Deep blue, *cream card* (*June ?, '98*).....		
			Edwardian.		
			Feb. ?, 1904. Size 5⅛ x 3.		
155		2c	Indigo, *pale buff*.....................	.40	.25

No.	Type.			Unused.	Used.
			Georgian.		
			1912. Size $5\frac{1}{8}$ x 3.		
156		2c	Indigo, *pale buff*	.25	.15
			Sept., 1922.		
157	*S23*	6c	Indigo, *pale buff*, surcharged in reddish brown over 2c	.50	.35
			CUSTOMS POSTAL CARDS.		
			1888. Size $5\frac{1}{8}$ x $3\frac{5}{8}$.		
158		?	Plain front, *manila card*		.15
159		?	Inscriptions on front, *manila card*		.15
			LETTER CARDS		
			(Prices are for specimens with full margins.)		
			Perf. A. *The horiz and vert. lines of perforation cross at corners.*		
			Perf. B. *The horiz. line of perforation stops at the vertical.*		
			Feb. 17, 1893.		
165	*S24*	3c	Carmine *on blue-green* Perf. A	.50	.50
166	*S24*	3c	Carmine *on blue-green* Perf. B	15.00	
			Oct. ?, 1895.		
167	*S25*	1c	Black *on blue-green* Perf. A	.50	.50
168	*S25*	1c	Black *on blue-green* Perf. B	15.00	
169	*S25*	2c	Green *on blue-green* Perf. A	.50	.50
			4-Leaf Design.		
			Perf. A.		
			Dec. ?, 1897.		
170		2c	Green *on blue green*	.15	.25
171		1c	Black *on blue-green (Jan. ?, 1898)*	.30	.40
172		3c	Carmine *on blue green (Jan. ?, 1898)*	.30	.40
			Surcharged with Type S7 in blue-black. Feb. ?, 1899.		
173	*S24*	2c on 3c.	(No. 165) *Cap surcharge* Perf. A	10.00	10.00
174	*S24*	2c on 3c.	(No. 165) *Lower Case surcharge* Perf. A	.50	1.00
175	*S24*	2c on 3c.	(No. 166) *Lower Case surcharge* Perf. B	15.00	
176		2c on 3c.	(No. 172)	.25	.50
			a. Surcharged in violet	*5.00*	*5.00*
			b. Surcharge double	*5.00*	
			C.P.R. Letter Sheet.		
			1893.		
179	*S15*	1c	Black *on grey-blue laid paper*	20.00	
180		1c	Black *on white laid paper*	15.00	

OFFICIAL STATIONERY

No.	Type.			Unused.	Used.
			Inland Revenue Wrapper, Size 11 x $5\frac{1}{8}$.		
181	*A6*	1c	Dark blue, cream paper, (*?, 1879*)	10.00	10.00
182	*A6*	1c	Dark blue, cream paper, *slightly different inscription*, (*?, 1879*)	10.00	10.00
183			Marine and Fisheries O.H.M.S. Envelopes supplied lighthouse keepers for Official Reports		

No.	Type.		Unused.	Used.

Returned Letter

In April 1849 the General Post Office, Montreal, used a sheet inscribed "Returned Letter" which was addressed to the sender of an undelivered letter, the letter being enclosed. There was a printed notation on the inside reading "General Post Office, Montreal, Dead Letter Department. The enclosed letter not having been delivered for the reason assigned thereon, was opened here by the Officer appointed by Her Majesty's Postmaster General for that purpose, and it is now returned to you as the writer, on payment of the Postage. T. A. STAYNER, Dy. Postmr. Genl."

In June, 1849 a cover was used, with the inscription illustrated above.

No.		Unused.	Used.
184	Blue		10.00
185	Blue (RETURNED LETTER smaller)		10.00
186	Manila		10.00

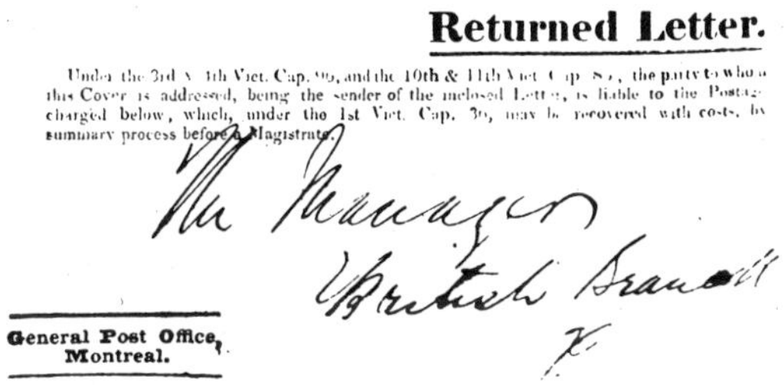

RETURNED LETTER

No. 184-5
(Reduced ½)

No. 186
(Reduced ½)

Wholesale Canada

The following list is published as a guide to the value of the more common stamps in quantities. These are the approximate prices at which dealers are prepared to supply the stamps listed. Wholesale prices fluctuate, and collectors are warned that this list will probably be useful only as a general guide for one year from date of publication.

			Per 10	Per 100	Per 1000
1872	1c	Yellow	$ .06	$ .40	
1882	2c	Green	.07	.60	

			Per 10	Per 100	Per 1000
1882	3c	Vermilion		.25	2.00
1892	8c	Grey	.60	5.50	$50.00
1897	1c	Jubilee	.30	2.75	
	2c	Jubilee	.40	3.75	
	3c	Jubilee	.10	.85	
	½c	4-Leaf	.30	2.75	
	1c	4-Leaf	.08	.50	4.00
	2c		.10	.90	8.00
	3c		.08	.70	
	2c on 3c 4-Leaf		.40	3.50	
	5c	4-Leaf	.35		
1898	½c	Numerals	.10	.65	
	1c		.05	.20	1.50
	2c	Purple	.05	.35	3.00
	2c	Carmine		.15	1.10
	2c on 3c		.30	2.75	
	5c	Blue	.35	3.00	
	7c		1.00	8.50	
	10c	Violet	.70	6.00	
	2c	Maps	.40	3.50	
	5c	REGISTRATION	.30	2.80	
1903	1c	King Edward		.10	.75
	2c	King Edward		.08	.50
	5c	King Edward	.08	.60	
	7c	King Edward	.20	1.75	
	10c	King Edward	.25	2.25	
	20c	King Edward	.90	8.50	
1908	½c	Quebec	.35	2.75	
	1c	Quebec	.30	2.50	
	2c	Quebec	.08	.65	
1912	1c	Green (George)		.06	.40
	1c	Yellow (George)		.08	.40
	2c	Carmine (George)		.05	.30
	2c	Green (George)		.05	.30
	3c	Carmine (George)		.08	.65
	3c	Brown (George)		.08	.60
	5c	Blue (George)	.05	.30	1.75
	5c	Violet (George)		.20	1.40
	4c	Olive Bistre (George)	.10	.60	5.00
	7c	Olive Bistre (George)	.10	.75	6.00
	7c	Red Brown (George)	.15	1.50	14.00
	8c	Blue (George)	.25	2.00	17.00
	10c	Plum (George)	.08	.70	
	10c	Blue (George)	.15	.85	7.50
	10c	Bistre Brown (George)	.05	.35	3.00
	20c	Olive Green (George)	.15	1.00	7.00
	50c	Grey (George)	.40	3.25	30.00
	$1	Orange (George)	.75	6.00	43.00
	1c	Green War Tax	.05	.35	2.50
	2c	Carmine War Tax	.10	.60	4.50
	2c plus 1c iTc Brown			.18	1.50
	2c plus 1c iTc Carm.			.30	2.50
	1c	Postage Due	.10	.75	5.50
	2c	Postage Due	.10	.85	6.00

		Per 10	Per 100	Per 1000
5c	Postage Due	.15	.95	7.50
3c	Brown Confederation	.08	.40	3.50
10c	Special Delivery	.50		
20c	Carmine Delivery	.60	4.00	36.00
20c	1927 Confederation	.50		
5c	1927 Historical	.15	1.25	10.00
12c	1927 Historical	1.25	12.00	
20c	1927 Historical	.30	2.50	
1c	Orange 1927 Confed.			.50
2c	Green 1927 Confed.			1.25
3c	Carmine	.04	.35	
5c	Violet		.40	.90
12c	Blue		2.00	
Coil Stamps.				
1c	Green 12 horiz.		.20	
1c	Green 8 horiz.		.40	
1c	Green 8 vert.		.08	
1c	Yellow 8 vert.			
2c	Carm ne 8 vert.		.25	2.20
	8 horiz.			
	12 horiz.			
2c	Green 8 vert.			
	12 horiz.			
3c	Brown 8 vert.	.20		
	12 horiz.			
3c	Carmine 8 vert.			
2c	plus 1c Carmine 8 vert.			
2c	plus 1c Brown 8 vert.	.15	1.10	

CANADIAN AIR MAIL

The dream, the experiment, of letters carried from city to city through the air, is now a reality. Mail was first flown in Canada on June 24th, 1918, when a few letters were carried from Montreal to Toronto. On October 1st, 1928, truckloads of Canadian mail were delivered to and received from planes traveling between our cities. These ten years will live in history as a period of aerial pioneering as full of romance, adventure, sacrifice and glory as any found in the annals of peace or war.

The next ten years will be a period of such progress as none dare predict.

Let us not forget those who have given their lives that the dream of regular airmail service might be a reality, or those brave men who take their places.

We here tender a full measure of credit to the one who has given to Canada an airmail service that ranks as one of the finest in the world—the Hon. P. J. Veniot, Postmaster-General of Canada.

Cover No.	Cachet, Stamp, etc.	
		Montreal-Toronto.
1	AC1	The first Royal Air Mail to be carried in Canada was flown by Capt. Bryan Peck from Montreal to Toronto on June 24th, 1918. This mail was composed largely of official correspondence and greetings from the Mayor and Postmaster of Montreal to the Mayor and Postmaster of Toronto, and from Military Headquarters and the General Manager of the Bank of Montreal, at Montreal, to like officials in Toronto, together with a few other letters of more or less official import.

AC1

Cover No. | Cachet, Stamp, etc.

Arrangements for this flight were made by Mr. E. Greenwood, Treasurer of the Aerial League of the British Empire, who acted as aerial postmaster, under authority issued by Mr. R. F. Coulter, Deputy Postmaster General, and through the courtesy and assistance of Mr. J. E. Leonard, Postmaster at Montreal, Mr. Greenwood was supplied with a new mail bag, suitable for air work, and a special cancellation stamp was prepared in triangular form, showing the historic importance of the event. This bore the date "23-6-18," as may be seen from the illustration, Type AC1.

Mr. Greenwood, as Acting Aerial Postmaster, cancelled all the letters that were to go on the flight, and registered some of them. He then sealed the bag, and handed it over to Capt. Peck who, on Sunday afternoon, June 23rd, made an ascent at 4.35 p.m. Unfortunately the weather was extremely bad, the clouds were very low, and Capt. Peck was forced to descend after a short flight. He left, however, early the next morning, and arrived at Toronto at 4.55

In any further correspondence on this subject please quote

No.

Chief Post Office Superintendent,

CANADA.

EASTERN DIVISION.

MONTREAL, 22nd. June 1918.

Dear Mr. Greenwood:-

Following our conversation yesterday, our messenger will hand you herewith a small bag for delivery to the Postmaster at Toronto.

With thanks, believe me,

Yours very truly,

[signature]

Chief P.O. Supt. Eastern Canada.

E. Greenwood, Esq.,
Treasurer of the
Montreal Branch of the
Aerial League.
MONTREAL.

Correspondence and Original First Flight Cover, Toronto-Montreal.

Cover No.	Cachet, Stamp, etc.	

p.m. on Monday, June 24th. The mail was rushed by motor to the General Post Office in Toronto, where it was received by Postmaster W. E. Lemon. This flight occupied almost exactly six hours, about forty minutes being lost through landing at Kingston for gasoline. One passenger was carried on the trip. Full records of the flight appeared in the daily press of that date.

The mail bag contained 124 covers. The pilot received a few letters after the bag was closed, and these also bore proper postmarks and cancellation. **Flown Cover** $250.00

2 **Calgary-Edmonton.**

On July 9th, 1918, Katherine Stinson is recorded as having made a mail-carrying flight between these cities. No special cachets were used, and we fear that these covers, if any survived for philately, have long since lost their identity. The author has never seen one, nor have we been able to learn of the existence of one in any of the important collections.

Toronto-Ottawa (with return).

3 AC2 The Aero Club of Canada had authority from the Dominion

Cover No.	Cachet, Stamp, etc.	
	AC3	Government to issue a label which would designate mail to
	AS1	be delivered at Leaside Flying Field, and from there flown

to the Capital—Ottawa—and return. These letters had to carry the correct amount of postage, and the label was affixed on the back of the envelope in accordance with regulations. The label did not prepay postage and was not a postage stamp in any sense, but without it the letter would not go by aeroplane from one point to the other. The labels were printed in the printing department of the United Typewriter Co., Toronto, on commercial gummed stock, Perf. 12. They were printed two on a piece, the paper being previously perforated and divided into pairs. An impression was made on the left half of the piece, which was then turned so that the second impression covered the right half. This was necessary, as there was but one block from which to print. All pairs are tête bêche. Specimens from the first "run" (about 194) were shown to the Secretary, at which time it was pointed out that numerals might be put in the lower corners to denote the value. This was done when the balance of the order was printed. The Secretary retained this first lot, and these, without the numerals of value, were the stamps which were affixed to covers and flown.

The red color depicting the airship bursting into flames was a happy thought on the part of the printer, who used battered type, plugged into the electro, to give the suggestion of flame in a second run through the presses. There is no record of the actual number of stamps which did not go through the second time to receive the red color, but these would probably number about six, we are informed by the printer who did the work.

3,000 were printed and the block returned to the Club, now disbanded. It is doubtful if any of the stamps without numerals of value and without the red color were ever used on flown covers.

Under date July 2, 1920, the Secretary, P.O. Dept., Canada, writes: " . . . . no postage stamps were issued by the Department in connnection with aerial mail flights. Stickers were, however, gotten up by the Aero Club of Canada, 30 Yonge St., Toronto, and these were sold to be affixed to the back of letters carried by aeroplane. There is no objection on the part of the Department to the use of stickers, provided they comply with the postal regulations. One regulation on the point reads: 'The affixing on the face or address side of letters or other mail matter of stamps issued in the interest of charitable or other institutions, etc., is not permitted, but there is no objection to such stamps being placed on the back of letters or other mail matter as stickers, provided they do not resemble postage stamps in form and design and do not bear numerals or indications of value. Letters or other mail matter bearing stamps of charitable institutions, etc., on the face, will be returned to the senders as violating the postal regulations.' "

Cover No.	Cachet, Stamp, etc.		

AS1

AERIAL MAIL
AUG 27 1918
TORONTO CANADA

AC2

AC3

Cover No.	Cachet, Stamp, etc.		
		Flown Covers.	
		Aug. 26th, 27th, Sept. 4th, 1918.	
		a. No figures of value	90.00
		b. With figures of value	125.00
		Return—Ottawa-Toronto.	
4	AC2	Aug. 27th and Sept. 4th, 1918.	
	AC3	a. No figures of value	90.00
	AS1	b. With figures of value	125.00
		STAMPS. (Aug. 27, 1918. Perf. 12.)	
	AS1	25c Black and red on *wove* (*2800*)	3.00
		Pair tête-bêche	9.00
		a. Figures of value omitted (*194*)	15.00
		Pair tête-bêche	30.00
		b. Figures of value and red color omitted (*6*)	
		The above prices are for stamps as commonly found without gum.	
		O.G. stamps list at double cat.	

Cover No. | Cachet, Stamp, etc.

Vancouver-Seattle, U.S.A.

5 A special cachet was used, reading, in three lines, "Via Airplane Mail—First Flight—Vancouver, B.C., to Seattle." Flown Cover (*Feb. 17, 1919*) $100.00

Vancouver-Vernon-Lethbridge-Calgary.

6 **"First Flight Over the Rockies," Aug. 5, 1919.**
Only a few covers were carried by Aviator Capt. Hoy. These received a special cachet in red, "1st B.C.—Alberta Aerial Post." **Flown Cover** $300.00

Toronto-New York, Aug. 25, 1919.

7 AC6 AS2 This flight, with special stamp, was intended to commemorate the first International Aerial Mail Service, from the Canadian National Exhibition Grounds to the Hudson River at New York. The stamp was used in the same way as the Toronto-Ottawa stamp. 3,000 per printed, in sheets of 10. Envelopes were stamped, "Aerial Mail Aug. 25, 1919, Toronto Canada," within a border, in blue, accompanied by the usual postal markings of that date—"Toronto-date-Ont." and "Canadian National Exhibition-Toronto-Date" in four lines. Although the quantity is given as 3,000, we are of the opinion that there was a large "over-run" in the printing.

AS2

AERIAL MAIL
AUG 25 1919
TORONTO, CANADA.

AC6

Owing to a re-adjustment of the forms in the press, or because the stamps were printed in two lots, one printing shows a lack of proper registration between the colors, which leaves a white space across the design from the last O of TORONTO to the N of NEW YORK.
Flown Cover $40.00

STAMPS. (Perf. 12.)

AS2 $1 Red and blue 2.00
a. "Out of Register." (*See notes.*)
b. Printed both sides 10.00
(*O.G. stamps list at 3 times cat.*)

8 **Victoria-Nanaimo. Aug. 16, 1919.**
The mail bag with 96 letters was handed to the pilot at noon and delivered three hours later to the Postmaster at Nanaimo. Covers had to be inscribed "Via Aeroplane" in

Cover No.	Cachet, Stamp, etc.	

order to receive departure and arrival postmarks. A private cachet was used, and the covers are to be distinguished also by departure and arrival postmarks. **Flown Cover** 75.00

9 **Truro-Charlottetown (with return). Sept. 29, 1919.**
In connection with the annual Charlottetown Exhibition. Covers bear hand-written inscription, "Via Aeroplane" or "Via Aerial Post." The postage was prepaid in the regular way by current Canadian stamps and no airmail stamp or label was used. Covers are authenticated by the P.O. date stamp, "Truro (Nova Scotia) 1 P.M." and "Charlottetown (Prince Edward Island) 2 P.M." of the same date. Nine covers were carried and 30 on the return trip.
Flown Cover 250.00
Return, Charlottetown-Truro 175.00

10 **Toronto-Hamilton (and return). May, 1920.**
A special label was issued in connection with a flight on the occasion of the Grand Army of Canada Carnival. These sold for $1.00. The mail from Toronto consisted of 5 letters, and from Hamilton to Toronto, 24 letters.
Flown Cover 250.00
Return, Hamilton-Toronto 175.00

STAMPS.
$1.00 Black on white wove .... ?

11 **Victoria-Seattle, U.S.A. Oct. 15, 1920.**
Cachet in black, "Airplane Service." About 50 covers were carried. **Flown Cover** 50.00

12 **Vancouver-Seattle. Mar., 1921.**
Covers are distinguished by the cachet of Flight No. 5 of Feb. 17, 1919, which was again used. Few covers were carried or have survived for collectors. **Flown Cover** 25.00

13 **First Trans-Canada Flight.**
Although not a mail-carrying flight, we think the achievement of Lt.-Col. Leckie and Major Hobbs in flying across Canada from Halifax to Vancouver is worthy of record in this brief history of aerial mail flights which broke the trails over which the mailbags now pass daily.
On October 7th, 1920, Lt.-Col. Leckie and Major Hobbs commenced the flight at 8 a.m., from Halifax. A mishap to their Fairey Seaplane caused a forced landing three hours later. Transferring to an H.S. 2L machine, they proceeded to Riviere du Loup, P.Q., where they transferred to another machine and completed their journey to Ottawa. The 820 miles from Halifax was completed at 12.40 p.m. on Oct. 8th. Engine trouble delayed them and they did not leave Ottawa until 8.30 a.m. on the 9th. Winnipeg was reached at 7.40 p.m. on the 10th. From Winnipeg to Vancouver was finished in three sections.

14 AC10 **Halifax-St. Johns, Newfoundland. Jan. 20, 1922.**
Mail for this flight bore the current postage stamps, which were cancelled with type AC10 in violet. The Georgian 1c

Cover No.	Cachet, Stamp, etc.		

yellow, 2c green, 5c violet, 10c blue and 20c green have been seen so cancelled. The plane was wrecked and the mail was later carried by steamer, the covers bearing a backstamp with a date some time later than the receiving stamp. **Covers** 5.00

AC10

15 **Lethbridge, Alberta, to Ottawa, Ontario, via Minot, North Dakota, U.S.A. June 22, 1922.**

Lieut. H. H. Fitzsimmons set out from Lethbridge, carrying 993 covers. He was forced to land at Minot, North Dakota, U.S.A., and from this point the mail was forwarded by the usual means. Three different types of envelopes with special wording were used, as follows:

a. "Greeting via the First Canadian Air Mail Plane from Lethbridge, Alta. The Little City with the Big Future."

b. Similar, with "Southern Alberta, the Land of Irrigation and Sunshine, Greets You."

c. Yellow envelope with "Greetings," etc., "—from the Crow's Nest Pass."

The ordinary postal cancellation "Register All Letters of Value" was used. The envelopes were sold at $1.00. The towns of Macleod, Pincher Creek and Blairmore were advertised on the back. **Flown Cover** 35.00

AS4
(Reduced ½.)

16 AS4 **Haileybury-Rouyn, Laurentide Air Service, from Sept. 11, 1924.**

On Sept. 11, 1924, the Laurentide Air Service, Limited, contracted to carry mail from Haileybury, Ontario, and Angliers, Quebec, into the Rouyn country. Of the first issue, with zigzag roulette, the printing was 200 in the form of booklets of 8 stamps (four pairs) bound at the left. The Company sold the stamps at a face value of 25c.

Flown Cover. Prepaid with 25c Green, rouletted left side and bottom, or left side and top 200.00

Cover No.	Cachet, Stamp, etc.		
17	AS5	In October, 1924, there was a second printing of stamps in similar form to the first, but rouletted horizontally and bound at the top, giving one stamp (the bottom of the pair) imperf. both sides and bottom, and the other stamp rouletted top and bottom, with sides imperf. The issue was 2,000. **Flown Cover.** (From October, 1924.) Prepaid with 25c Green, rouletted horizontally	15.00

AC12

Laurentide Winter Flights.
A special cachet, AC12, was used, dated 1924, but these flights did not take place until January of 1925.

Cancellations and Cachets on Winter Flight covers.
Covers were cancelled at the Post Office Jan. 3rd but an accident to the plane delayed the flight until the 12th January, when the same covers were again cancelled with the new date. About 100 letters (bearing 2nd, 3rd and 4th issue stamps) were carried. A special cachet was used, Type AC12, reading "Larder Lake" or "Three Rivers."

18	AS5	**Larder Lake-Rouyn. (Winter Flight, Jan., 1925.)**	
	AC12	**Flown Cover.** Prepaid with 25c Green, horizontal roulette	20.00
		a. Signed by pilot	35.00
19	AS5	**Three Rivers-Rouyn. (Winter Flight, Jan., 1925.)**	
	AC12	**Flown Cover.** Prepaid with 25c Green, horizontal roulette	25.00
		STAMPS.	
	AS4	**1st issue.** (*Sept. 11, 1924.*)	
		25c Green, rouletted left side and bottom, or left side and top	25.00
	AS5	**2nd issue.** (*Oct., 1924.*)	
		25c Green, horizontal roulette	3.00
	AS6	**3rd issue.** The words "Canada 1924" appear in the sun, and the color is changed to red. (*Oct. 17, 1924.*)	
		25c Red, horizontal roulette	1.50
	AS7	**4th issue.** (*Oct. 17, 1924.*) Perforated 13 and printed 20 to sheet.	
		25c Red	1.50

Cover No.	Cachet, Stamp, etc.		
20	AS6	**Flown Covers,** prepaid with 3rd issue stamps. 25c Red (3rd issue), horizontal roulette, Haileybury-Rouyn or Rouyn-Haileybury, from Oct. 17, 1924	8.00
	AS7	a. Prepaid with 4th issue	8.00
21	AS6 AC12	**Winter Flights.** *(Jan., 1925.)* Larder Lake or Three Rivers to Rouyn, prepaid with 25c Red (3rd issue), horizontal roulette	15.00
		a. Signed by pilot	25.00
22	AS7	**Covers,** from Oct. 17 and Oct. 24, 1924, prepaid with 25c Red, Perf. 13	8.00
23	AS7 AC12	**Winter Flights.** *(Jan. 21, 1925.)* Prepaid with 25c Red, Perf. 13, bearing Larder Lake cachet	14.00
		a. Signed by pilot H. L. L. Pot	25.00
24		Bearing Three Rivers cachet	15.00
		a. Signed by pilot H. L. L. Pot	35.00
25	AS7 AC12	**Flown Covers,** Winter Flight, prepaid with 4th issue 25c Red, Perf. 13, from Three Rivers or Larder Lake to Rouyn, without special Winter Flight cachet	8.00

AS8

AC13

26 AC13 AS8 **Estevan-Winnipeg. Oct. 1st, 1924.**

An official date stamp and special cancellation was used, with authority of the P.O. Department. Flight-Lieutenant E. A. Alton carried the mail in a Curtis biplane, the purpose of the flight being to advertise the rich coal-bearing area in Saskatchewan, particularly in the Estevan district. Only one bag of mail was carried. An original air label or vignette was used, sold at $1.00, depicting an aeroplane in the clouds, above the town of Estevan, and showing a mine and its tipple, with shaft sinking beneath the ground and a miner with mine car working at the face of a coal seam. The words "First Saskatchewan Aerial Mail" are shown above the coal seam and the words "Estevan-Winnipeg, October 1st, 1924," are shown on the label beneath the coal seam. 1,028 of the labels were printed, on red gummed paper with the printing in black. The original design was created by Donald Dunbar, editor of the Mercury, of Este-

Cover No. | Cachet, Stamp, etc.

van. The postage stamps were cancelled with Type AC13 in pale violet. The covers also bear a rubber stamped impression in pale violet or pale blue showing a biplane about one inch in width. Covers are backstamped "Winnipeg, Man., October 1st, 1924, 10.30 P.M."

Flown Cover. $1 Red and black on Special env. (400) 4.00

a. Signed by pilot (100) 15.00

b. Special envelope without label (850) 2.50

c. Special envelope without label and with special cancellation and Estevan postmark over stamps 10.00

d. Same as "c" but with pilot's signature 15.00

e. Same as "c," but with U.S. 2c Postage postmarked Wahpeton, N.D., September 26th, 1924-5 P.M. 22.50

f. Same as "e" but with pilot's signature (3 known).

STAMPS.

AS8 $1 Red and blue, imperf. 5.00

FIRST EXPERIMENTAL FLIGHT
HAILEYBURY TO ROUYN LAKE

AC14

27 AC14 **Northern Air Service, Limited, Haileybury-Rouyn (and return).**

Experimental Flight (and return), May 18, 1925.

These covers bear a cachet in purple reading in two lines, "First Experimental Flight—Haileybury to Rouyn Lake" (or Rouyn Lake to Haileybury) and are back stamped on the same date—May 18th, 1925. Eight covers were carried each way. **Flown Cover** 150.00

AS9

NORTHERN AIR SERVICE LTD.
FIRST FLIGHT
ROUYN, QUE. TO HAILEYBURY, ONT.
B.W. Broatch
Pilot

AC16

FIRST FLIGHT

AC15

Cover No.	Cachet, Stamp, etc.		
		Extract from Canadian Official Postal Guide of July, 1925: "Air Mail Service to Rouyn, P.Q., resumed. Permission has been granted the Northern Air Service, Limited, Haileybury, Ont., operating an aerial service five times per week between Haileybury, Ont., and Rouyn, P.Q., to convey such mail matter as is offered for conveyance by this service, provided the senders assume all risk. The requirements for this mail are:	
		1. "By Aerial Mail" to be prominently written on the address side.	
		2. The usual Canadian postage to be affixed on the address side.	
		3. A special aerial sticker sold by the Company or its agents, representing a charge of 25 cents, to be placed on the reverse side, in payment of the special charge for transmission by aerial service, which has been fixed by those making the flight."	
28	AS9	**Flown Cover.** (*June 27, 1925.*)	
	AC16	Prepaid with 25c Blue, Northern Air Service stamp, with cachet AC15, "Northern Air Service Ltd. First Flight, Haileybury, Ont., to Rouyn, Que." (or Rouyn, Que., to Haileybury, Ont.) and signed by Pilot B. W. Broatch. (*About 400 carried*)	4.00
		a. Unsigned (*50 each way*)	5.00
	AC15	b. Unsigned, with "FIRST FLIGHT" in single line in violet	8.00
29	AS9	Later dates either direction	2.50
		STAMPS.	
	AS9	Printed in sheets of 20, four rows of 5 with third and fourth rows inverted, making all vertical pairs from the middle of the sheet (second and third rows) tête-bêche. (*4,000.*) Also printed in booklets of two leaves of four stamps each to the booklet.	
		25c Blue, O.G.	1.50
		a. Pair tête-bêche, O.G.	6.00
		(Stamps without gum should be discounted one-third.)	

RED LAKE GOLD FIELDS.

At the height of the Red Lake gold rush an airmail service was inaugurated which reduced the time necessary for mail delivery from seven days to a few hours, flying over a wilderness of rock, snow and ice.

AC17

Cover No.	Cachet, Stamp, etc.	
30	AS10 AC17	**Rolling Portage (Hudson)-Red Lake (and return), (Mar. 6, 1926).**

The first flight (official) was on March 6th, 1926. Covers bear a distinguishing cachet, type AC17. The postal authorities sanctioned the use of a special stamp to cover the additional 25c fee. These were printed in red on a yellow background of shaded zig-zag lines. There is a wide variation in the shades, from pale yellow to orange. Sheets of eight stamps were prepared, each sheet consisting of two horizontal rows of four, and the background wholly covering each vertical pair of stamps, leaving white margins for the vertical perforations. The second and third of the upper row, and each stamp of the lower row show minor varities, one, a variety in the border design of leaves, being quite rare. Types of varieties may be distinguished by the "dot and dash" design above and below

AS10

"AIR SERVICE." The four types are:

a. Upper line ends in a small rosette—5th and 7th.
b. Both lines end in dashes—1st and 3rd.
c. Lines at right end in a dot above and a dash below—2nd and 4th.
d. Start with a dash and end with a dot—6th and 8th.

These varieties are identical in the 2nd, or Swastika background, printing.

The first flight (March 6th) covers in addition to the special first flight cachet received an oval cachet reading "Kenora-Received-Mar. 6, 1926 (Red Lake)" in pale blue. All covers have this Kenora cachet, but all covers do not have the first flight cachet AC17. This Kenora cachet is known on other than first flight covers.

		Flown Cover. Stamp with wavy background	7.00
		Return flight	7.00
		a. With minor variety	8.00
31	AS10	Regular Service Flight, stamp with wavy background, ordinary P.O. cancellations	2.50

Cover No.	Cachet, Stamp, etc.		
32	AS10	Regular Service Flight, stamp with wavy background, cachet AC18	
		a. Ditto, with rare cachet AC19	
33	AS11	Regular Service Flight, second issue stamp with Swastika background, ordinary P.O. cancellations	2.50

AC18

AC19

STAMPS. (*Perf. 11½.*)

AS10	25c Red on yellow, background wavy lines (*2,504*)	2.00
	a. Imperf. pair	15.00
AS11	25c Red on yellow, background Swastika (*2,000*)	1.75
	(Varieties same as first issue.)	
	a. Imperf. pair	12.50
	b. Imperf. pair, one stamp with "Air Service" inverted	20.00

AS12

Elliot-Fairchild Service to Red Lake.

The new company issued stamps somewhat similar to the Jack V. Elliot issue, printed in red on a yellow background of Swastika emblems covering the whole area of the printing surface, leaving white margins around each sheet of eight. The two upper leaves of the Elliot design were removed to allow space for the more lengthy first line of type and the word "FIRST" was omitted, but the variation in the remaining leaves, etc., occur exactly as in the first and second Elliot issues.

A further variety is a tall "r" in "Fairchild" which is repeated on the second and fourth stamps of each sheet.

The Elliot-Fairchild people lost or relinquished their contract to the Patricia Airways & Exploration Co., which did

Cover No.	Cachet, Stamp, etc.		
		not officially commence operations until July 7th. The Patricia plane—the Lark—was on the ground, however, from April 12th. The first flight of the Lark after arrival was on April 15th, 1926, but mail had been received at Sioux Lookout and held for this flight. Such mail bears the date stamp of April 7th.	
		Flown Covers, *(Apr. 15, 1926.)*	
34	AS12	**Rolling Portage (Hudson) to Red Lake,** prepaid with 25c Red on yellow, Swastika background	20.00
35	AS12	Red Lake-Rolling Portage-Hudson, do.	20.00
36	AS12	Regular Service Flights, later dates	2.50
		Sioux Lookout-Red Lake. *(Apr. 15, 1926.)*	
37	AS12	25c Red on yellow, Swastika background	20.00
38	AS12	Regular Service Flights, later dates	2.50
		On June 27th the Patricia people commenced to fly in with the accumulated mail which bore the Elliot-Fairchild stamps and the Jack V. Elliot stamps. These were cancelled in blue or black with a 4-line cachet in a rectangle and also with a single line cachet, generally placed across the stamp, reading "Patricia Airways & Exploration, Ltd."	
39		**Flown Cover. June 27, 1926.**	
	AS10 AS11	25c Red on yellow Jack Elliot with wavy lines and with Swastika background	7.00
	AS12	25c Red on yellow Elliot-Fairchild	20.00
		STAMPS. *(2,504)*	
	AS12	25c Red on yellow, background Swastika	1.50
		a. Words "Air Service" inverted.	

AS13

The Elliot-Fairchilds Air Service issued a new stamp in April, 1926, type AS13, which appears on covers from April 15th. The total issue was 5,600, blue on white wove.

Cover No.	Cachet, Stamp, etc.		
40	AS13	**Flown Cover.... April 15, 1926.**	
		Hudson (Rolling Portage)-Red Lake.	
		25c Blue *(60)*	7.50
		a. Prepaid with tête-bêche pair *(10)*	45.00
		b. Flown in by courtesy Patricia Airways Co. *(June 27, 1926)*	3.00

Cover No.	Cachet, Stamp, etc.		
41		**Elliot-Fairchild Haileybury-Rouyn Service.**	
	AS13	Rouyn-Haileybury (*May 27, 1926*) prepaid with 25c blue (*45*)	7.50
42	AS13	Haileybury-Rouyn (*June 1, 1926*) prepaid with 25c blue (*45*)	7.50
43	AS12	The Elliot-Fairchilds Air Service, Ltd., using their new "Plane Over Boat" stamp, AS13, issued instructions that letters franked with the 25c Red and Yellow Swastika background, Red Lake Service stamps, were not to be accepted. The author has seen such covers, from which the Red Lake stamps had been torn (but with pieces adhering) and the blue Elliot-Fairchild stamps affixed. After June 30th the Red Lake stamps and the Elliot-Fairchild stamps were superseded by those of the Patricia Company. The Post Office Department later ruled that the 25c Red and Yellow Swastika background stamps could be used. A letter from the P.O. Department reads in part: "Arrangements have been made by the Post Office Department with the Patricia Co. to carry temporarily any letters bearing Elliot-Fairchild air stickers."	
		STAMPS. (*Apr. 15, 1926.*)	
	AS13	25c Blue	.60
		a. Tête-bêche pair (*50*)	10.00

AS14

		A new stamp was prepared, with an issue of 5,000, printed five to the sheet, and sold at 25c face value. 400 covers were carried on the first flight and 410 on the return trip, all signed by the pilot.	
	AS14	25c Red	1.50
		Flown Cover. (*Aug. 13, 1926.*)	
		Rouyn-Haileybury (with return).	
45	AS14	Prepaid with 25c Red	3.50
		a. Prepaid with Elliot-Fairchild AS12 (*Aug. 12*).	

AS15

Cover No.	Cachet, Stamp, etc.		
		FAIRCHILD AIR TRANSPORT.	
46		**Haileybury-Rouyn Service.**	

The intrepid Jack V. Elliot now disappears from the picture (although not from the air) and the stamps of the next issue read "Fairchild Air Transport Limited," similar in general design to the Elliot-Fairchild stamps of the preceding issue. 5,000 was the total issue, 10 stamps to the sheet. 500 covers were carried in, and 517 out on the return trip, all signed.

Flown Covers. (*Oct. 20, 1926.*)

Haileybury-Rouyn (and return).

	AS15	Prepaid with 25c blue signed by pilot	3.50
		a. With tête-bêche pair (7)	15.00

STAMPS.

	AS15.	25c Blue	1.25
		a. Tête-bêche pair	3.50
	AS15	25c Ultramarine (issued but not seen on flown cover)	1.25
		a. Tête-bêche pair	3.50

(Printed in tête-bêche horiz. pairs and tête-bêche vert.—*15 sheets—pairs.*)

AS16

PATRICIA AIRWAYS & EXPLORATION CO.

Sioux Lookout-Red Lake Service.

This Company was given the mail carrying contract, to commence July 7th, 1926. Their new plane, the "Lark," had been on the ground since April 12th, when she arrived from New York. The details of this flight from New York are supplied by O. W. R. Smith, Toronto, and certified correct by Pilot Capt. W. R. Maxwell, as follows:

March 21, 1926. Left New York with 2 passengers. After rough travelling reached Buffalo, 330 miles. 75 letters were carried, but as there was no time to obtain official sanction, they were not franked with stamps at New York, this being done at Toronto. A cachet, however, distinguishes these letters.

March 22. Left Buffalo and reached Toronto, 110 miles.

March 27. Plane left Toronto and reached Sudbury, 225 miles. A mail of 134 letters had been collected for this trip, and together with the 75 letters brought from New York, 209 in all, were handed by the Postmaster at Toronto to the

Cachet,
Cover Stamp,
No. etc.

pilot. All these letters bear the Toronto date stamp of various dates. A mail of 45 letters was taken on at Sudbury. The Postmaster-General at Ottawa officially sanctioned this plane to carry mail on the trip to Red Lake, and this service was accordingly advertised in the press.
March 30. Skis were fitted in place of wheels, but again weather delayed progress.
April 2. Left Sudbury, and after being forced down by weather at Lake Vermillion, eventually reached Pogamasing, 100 miles. A mail of 20 letters was taken on board at this place. Attempts to proceed on the 3rd and 4th were failures.
April 6. Left Pogamasing and after encountering terrific weather was forced down on Lake Como, an uninhabited place 12 miles west of Chapleau, the crew being forced to eat their emergency rations.
April 7. Left Lake Como and was forced down at Lake Oba, 12 miles from the nearest settlement, but eventually reached Amyot on Lake Hegwazu, some 80 miles in direct line.
April 8. Left Amyot and, favored by the best weather of the trip, reached Lake Nipigon, 210 miles, where the fuel cache was placed.
April 10. Left Lake Nipigon and, after being forced down by disengaged oil feed, reached Sioux Lookout, 145 miles.
April 12. Left Sioux Lookout and reached objective at Red Lake, 120 miles. A mail of 25 letters was carried on this leg. In the Red Lake Post Office a cachet was placed on the 134 letters brought from Toronto. All letters are backstamped at Red Lake, Ont., April 12th.

First Official Flights.
On July 7th, 1926, the first official flights took place. All covers handled through the Company's Toronto office received the First Flight cachet, type AC14, but a small number of covers not sent north through the Company's office were carried to and from Sioux Lookout without this cachet on the first day, July 7th.

Sale of Stamps.
The stamps were on sale previous to July 7th in order to facilitate the delivery of mail to Sioux Lookout, the new base, in time for the July 7th first official flight. The stamps were obtainable at Post Offices in Toronto (June 28th), Ottawa, Montreal, Winnipeg, Hamilton, Sudbury, North Bay, Cobalt, Temiskaming, Haileybury, Sioux Lookout, and Red Lake.
The stamp was designed by Arthur J. Algate of the Map Specialty Co., Toronto, assisted by Fred Jarrett. In the preparation of the stamps 10 pt. heavy gothic was selected, but proved too heavy for the balance of the design and was changed to 6 pt. engravers gothic. There are two or three sheets in the heavier type, and a few are known to be postally used. The change to the 6 pt. was not satisfactory until the type had been leaded to give slightly wider spacing, and the stamps printed in 6pt. set close (two or three sheets)

Cover No.	Cachet, Stamp, etc.		
		we believe were the ones filed in the P.O. Department. Of the stamp in the final 6 pt. leaded printing, 61 sheets, 488 copies, were overprinted with bottom tablet in blue appearing as blue black for official use, but the color is not easy to distinguish from the regular moss green color, of which there were 1,600 sheets, 12,800 stamps. Of the Woman Lake stamps (50c instead of 25c) there were 517 sheets, 4,136 stamps, and about 125 of these bore the initials F.E.D. (Davidson), President of the Company, in script, applied with a rubber stamp in green. The 50c Woman Lake stamp exists without the small printing at the bottom of the stamp. All stamps were printed in sheets of 8 with marginal inscription showing service intended and total value.	
47		**New York-Toronto-Red Lake** with special cachet, signed by pilot. With the exception of three covers, these are not postmarked at New York, but are postmarked at Toronto...	15.00
48		**Toronto to Red Lake.** Official Post Office flight, service advertised in press, no special stamp required, postage two cents, senders to assume all risk. These covers bear a 5-line cachet in green reading, 'This letter was carried by aeroplane on official mail-carrying flight from Toronto to Red Lake." Left Toronto March 27th, 1926, stopping at several places due to weather conditions. Back-stamped Red Lake, April 12th, 1926. 114 covers, unsigned, and 20 signed, were carried	15.00
		a. Signed *(20)*	22.50
49		**Sudbury-Red Lake.** This flight, on March 29th, carried 45 covers, all signed	18.00
50		**Pogamasing-Sioux Lookout.** Apr. 6, 1926. 20 covers, all signed	22.50
51		**Sioux Lookout-Red Lake.** Apr. 12, 1926. 25 covers were carried, all backstamped Red Lake, Apr. 12th, 1926........	22.50

AC22
a. "Woman Lake."
b. "Birch Lake."

Cover No.	Cachet, Stamp, etc.		
		Cancellations.	
		A special cachet, AC22, in blue green, was used for the first flight covers. A few are known in red. The Woman Lake covers had the Government postage stamp cancelled with the Canadian National Exhibition obliteration and are also seen cancelled with a rubber stamp supplied hurriedly to fill the need in the new post office.	

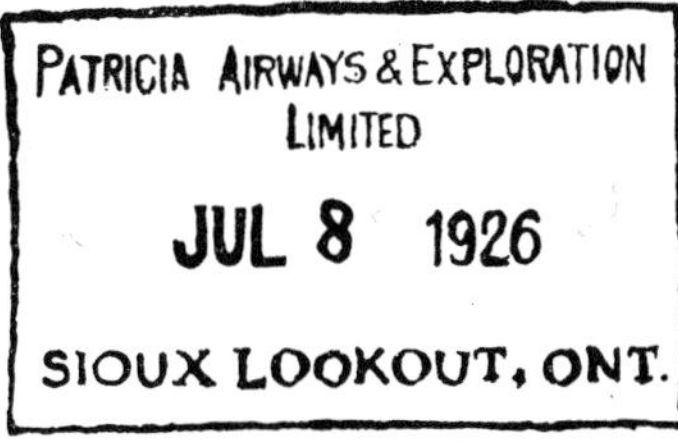

AC23 (In green)

AC24 (In green)

Cover No.	Cachet, Stamp, etc.		
		Flown Covers.	
		Sioux Lookout-Red Lake. *July 7, 1926.*	
52	AC22	25c Yellow *(415)*	4.00
	AS16	a. Stamp with variety, Small t in TO *(2 known to exist).*	
53		Return flight *(770)*	3.50
54	AC23 AS16	Regular Service Flight	1.50
		Sioux Lookout-Pine Ridge. July 7, 1926.	
55	AS16	25c Yellow *(125)*	6.50
56	AC22	Return flight *(140)*	6.50
57		Regular service flight	2.00
		Sioux Lookout-Woman Lake. Aug. 2, 1926.	
58	AS16	50c Blue *(216)*	5.00
59	AC22	Return flight *(450)*	4.50
60	AC24	Regular service flight	2.00
		Sioux Lookout-Birch Lake. Aug. 2, 1926.	
61	AS16	50c Blue *(123)*	6.50
62	AC22	Return flight *(105)*	6.50
63	AC24	Regular service flight	2.50
		STAMPS.	
		July 1, 1926. Perf. 11½. *(12,830).*	
	AS16	25c Green and Red on Yellow, 3 bottom lines printed in moss green (Red Lake)	2.00
		(The paper ordinarily used was yellow-orange, but a pale yellow shade is known.)	
		a. Three lower lines of wording omitted.	
		b. Imperf. pair	15.00
		(Proofs exist.)	
	AS16	25c Green and Red on Yellow, three bottom lines printed in blue black *(350)*	6.50
		a. Small "t" in TO *(50)*	10.00

Cover No.	Cachet, Stamp, etc.		
	AS16	50c Greenish-blue (Woman Lake, etc.)	3.00
		a. Variety three lower lines omitted.	
		b. Overprinted "Special Delivery to Pine Ridge" in blue.	
		c. Initialed by Davidson, President.	
		d. Imperf. pair	15.00
		(Proofs in indigo blue on blue are known).	

AS17

		April 1, 1927. Perf. 11½.	
64	AS17	Yellow stamp overprinted as above in bright red ascending to right (*1,200*) (First flight April 9). Stamp	1.50
		Flown cover	4.00
		May 2nd, 1927.	
65	AS17	Greenish-blue with overprint as above (*770*). Stamp	2.50
		Flown cover	5.50
		a. "N" of ROUYN partly missing (*110*) Stamp	3.25
		May 20, 1927.	
66	AS17	Yellow stamp as above but overprint in deep red (*500*)	2.25
		Flown cover	4.00
67	AS17	Greenish blue stamp, as above (*544*). Stamp	3.00
		Flown cover	5.50
		a. As above, overprint in black (1 sheet).	
	AS17	Yellow stamp, overprint as above in deep red on stamp with three bottom lines printed in blue black (*14*)	
	AS17	Yellow stamp as above, overprint in bright red on stamp with variety small "t" in TO (2 known to exist)	
	AS17	Yellow stamp as above but overprint in deep red, double, one inverted	
		Sept. 1st, 1927.	
	AS16	Yellow stamp as above, with additional overprint "Special Air Service Sioux Lookout and Red Lake District, 5 cents" descending to right, in *black*	
		Sept. 1, 1927.	
68	AS16	Original 25c yellow overprinted in *black*, "Special Air Service Sioux Lookout and Red Lake District 5 cents" ascending to right (*200*). Stamp	4.50
		Flown Cover	6.50

Cover No.	Cachet, Stamp, etc.		
69	AS16	Original 25c yellow, overprint in black, descending to right *(8 known to exist)*	
		Flown Cover	25.00
70	AS16	Original 25c yellow, overprinted in *red* "Special Air Service Sioux Lookout and Red Lake District 5 cents" descending to right (*200*). Stamp	4.50
		Flown Cover	6.50

AS19

71	AS19	Original 25c yellow with "Haileybury and Rouyn 10 cents" in red ascending to right, and with additional overprint in *black* "Red Lake" descending to right. Stamp	7.50
		a. "Red Lake" inverted	9.00
		Flown Cover	10.00
		May 20, 1927.	
72	AS19	Original 50c greenish-blue overprinted in *dark red,* "Haileybury and Rouyn 10 cents" ascending to right, with additional overprint in *black,* "RED LAKE" descending to right (*20*)	7.50
		a. "Red Lake" inverted	9.00
		Flown Cover	10.00
		Sept. 1st, 1927.	
73	AS16	Original 50c greenish-blue overprinted in *black* "Special Air Service—Sioux Lookout-and-Red Lake District—5 cents," in five lines, ascending to right (*200*). Stamp	4.50
		Flown Cover	6.50
		a. in *deep red* (*200*)	4.50
		Flown Cover	6.50
	AS16	Overprint as above, in *bright red,* descending to right. (*Very rare.*)	
		June 1st, 1927.	
74	AS16	Original 50c greenish-blue overprinted in *violet* with rubber stamp "Red Lake" ascending to right (*50*). Stamp	10.00
		Flown Cover	15.00
		June 11, 1927. Rouletted. (Total, 17,496.)	
76	AS20	Stamp with same format as original 25c yellow, but with face value 5c, rouletted, without inscription at bottom of stamp and with "Red Lake" omitted from borders, surcharged in *green* ascending to right, "Special Air Service	

Cover No.	Cachet, Stamp, etc.		
		Sioux Lookout and Red Lake District 5 cents." (*4,448*)	1.00
		Cover, 1st day, July 1, 1927	3.50
		a. Overprinted in black (*1,368*)	2.00

AS20

77	AS20	Stamp as described, overprint in smaller type, in *green*	.75
		Flown Cover	2.50
78		Overprint as above, *black*	.75
		Flown Cover	3.00
79	AS17	Stamp as described but overprint "Haileybury and Rouyn 10 cents" in *red* ascending to right (*4,608*)	.75
		Flown Cover	4.00
80	AS19	Stamp as described overprinted in *red*, "Haileybury and Rouyn 10 cents" ascending to right and "RED LAKE" descending to right	4.00
		Flown Covers (*100*)	6.00
		a. As above but "RED LAKE" overprint inverted	5.00
		Flown Covers	7.00

AS21

81	AS21	Stamp as described overprinted in green as above, "Special Air Service Sioux Lookout and Red Lake District 5 cents" descending to right (*1,368*)	.75
		a. As above, overprint in *red* (*1,368*)	.75
		b. As above, overprint in *black* (*1,368*)	.75
		Flown Covers	3.00

Cover No.	Cachet, Stamp, etc.		
82	AS20	Stamp as described overprinted "Special Air Service Sioux Lookout and Red Lake District 5 cents" ascending, small type, in *red*	.75
		a. In *black*	.75
		b. In *green*	.75
		Flown Covers	3.00
		c. Overprint in *red* inverted (*16*)	7.50
		Flown Covers	20.00
		Sept. 1, 1927.	
83	AS21	Stamp as described overprinted "Special Air Service Sioux	
	AS17	Lookout and Red Lake District 5 cents" descending to right, "Haileybury," etc., Type AS17, up to right; in *black* (*500*)	2.00
		Flown Cover	4.00
84		As above but "Special Air Service Sioux Lookout and Red Lake District 5 cents" in small type	1.50
		Flown Cover	4.00
		As above but "Special Air Service" etc. inverted	7.50
85	AS	**Sept. 17, 1927.**	
		Stamp as described, with carmine overprint "RED LAKE" (*1,450*) descending	.75
		Flown Cover	3.00
		a. Overprint inverted, two directions (*200*)	1.50
		Flown Cover	5.00
		b. Plane inverted (*48*)	9.00
		c. Overprint in *pale green* (*1,450*)	.75
		Flown Cover	3.00
		d. Overprint in *pale green* inverted descending to left (*100*)	1.50
		Flown Cover	5.00
		e. Overprint in *green* inverted ascending to left (*100*)	1.50
		Flown Cover	5.00
		f. Overprint in *black* normal (*1,380*)	.75
		Flown Cover	3.00
		g. Overprint in *black* inverted descending to left (*200*)	1.50
		Flown Cover	5.00
		(One sheet of this variety is known with the two lower stamps without overprint.)	
		h. Imperf., RED LAKE in *carmine* descending to right	7.50
		i. Imperf., RED LAKE in *carmine* ascending to right	7.50
		j. Imperf., RED LAKE in *carmine* inverted	7.50
		k. Pair, showing varieties "i," "j"	15.00
		l. Imperf. pair, RED LAKE in green, one normal descending to right, other inverted	15.00
		Original stamp as described (June 11, 1927) without overprint	3.00

"Between April 12th, 1926, and Sept. 12th, 1927, the Company's records show 1,539 flights, 897 hours in the air, 77,257 miles flown, 750 passengers carried, 76,276 lbs. of freight and express and 8,416 lbs. of mail carried."

Cover No.	Cachet, Stamp, etc.		

Western Canada Airways Service to Red Lake and other Gold Fields.

The Western Canada Airways contract began on May 10th, 1927, when the first flight took place. The Company's planes had been on the ground earlier, however, and during the spring of 1927 mail was carried by courtesy for the Patricia Airways. These covers, from March 4th, 1927, bore the Patricia stamps.

AS28

AS29

Flown Covers (Patricias), Courtesy of Western Canada Airways; from Mar. 4, 1927.

86 Rolling Portage-Red Lake (*return*) 7.50

Apr. 9, 1927.

87 Haileybury-Rouyn, with Patricia stamp ....

The beginning of the contract was celebrated on May 10th, 1927, with a flight from Rolling Portage to Red Lake and Gold Pines, carrying 353 letters. 389 letters were brought out, about 15 signed by the pilot. A special first-flight cachet was used.

The stamps were on sale at the Winnipeg G.P.O. and other principal cities of the Dominion, May 1st, 1927. These were printed in sheets of fifty.

Flown Covers. May 10, 1927.

Rolling Portage-Red Lake or Gold Pines.

88	AS28	10c Pink and black	4.00
	AC25	Return	4.00
		a. Signed by Pilot Stevenson	12.00
		2nd Flight—covers without cachet, with 4-line cachet, and with 2-line cachet, catalogue from	1.00

June 1st, 1927.

Long Lake-Gold Pines-Lac Du Bonnet-Slate Lake-Rice Lake. 387 covers were carried in by Pilot Stevenson and the same number out. These bore a special cachet in red or violet, "First Flight-Aerial Mail-Central Manitoba Mining District-Western Canada Airways, Ltd." in an oval with outline of plane in center. This was accompanied by a 4-line cachet in red or blue, "Western Canada Airways Limited June 3 (in error) 1927 Lac Du Bonnet, Man."

89	AS28	Lac Du Bonnet, Man.-Long Lake	12.00
90	AS28	Lac Du Bonnet, Man.-Slate Lake	12.00
91	AS28	Lac Du Bonnet, Man.-Rice Lake	12.00
92	AS28	Rice Lake-Lac Du Bonnet, Man.	12.00
		a. Any of above signed by pilot	15.00

Cover No.	Cachet, Stamp, etc.		
		July 1st, 1927.	
		Rolling Portage-Red Lake.	
93	AS29 AC26	A special flight was made, called the Jubilee Flight, covers bearing the new Jubilee stamp, and a special cachet in the form of a large Maple Leaf, similar to Type AC26 applied in red, blue, or violet, inscribed "Red Lake." (*90 covers*)	10.00
		a. Return	10.00
94		**Rolling Portage-Gold Pines** (*92*)	10.00
		a. Either flight, 93 or 94, signed by pilot (*35*)	15.00
		July 1st, 1927.	
		With similar cachet (AC26) with exception that words "Red Lake" replaced by "Central Manitoba."	
95	AS29	Lac Du Bonnet-Rice Lake (*72*)	11.00
96	AC26	Lac Du Bonnet-Long Lake (*73*)	11.00
97		Lac Du Bonnet-Slate Lake (*73*)	11.00
		a. Any of above signed by pilot (*17*)	15.00
98		Rice Lake-Lac Du Bonnet (*218*) signed	5.00
		Aug. 14, 1927.	
99	AC27	**Cormorant Lake and Cold Lake**. 202 covers were carried to Gold Lake (*101 signed*) and 201 to Cormorant Lake, of which 101 were signed. Cold Lake covers also have Cormorant Lake cachet, but Cormorant Lake covers have that cachet only, on front. The special cachet in violet was used, Type AC27	4.50
		a. Signed by pilot	7.50

AC26

AC27

Cover No.	Cachet, Stamp, etc.		
		Dec. 23, 1927.	
100	AS28 AC26 AC27	**The Pas-Flin Flon Mine,** with special Maple Leaf cachet in violet, Type AC17 and green cancellation AC18	2.00
		a. Return via Schist Lake	2.00
101		The Pas-Gold Lake	2.00

Cover No.	Cachet, Stamp, etc.		
		STAMPS.	
		May 1, 1927.	
	AS28	10c Black, pink background (*732 sheets of 50*)	.50
		a. Pair imperf. between	
		Later Printing.	
		Black, dull red background	.25
		a. Pair imperf. between	
		Jubilee Issue, July 1, 1927.	
	AS28	10c Black, orange-buff background	1.00
		(In March, 1928, the Western Canada Airways, Ltd., was the largest aviation company in Canada, with twenty-two machines in operation. By October, 1928, the number had been increased to over thirty machines.)	

AS30

102 AS30 **Whitehorse-Mayo-Dawson. ...Nov. 7, 1927.**

The monoplane "Queen of the Yukon," a sister of Col. Charles Lindbergh's plane, intended for use in the Yukon, arrived in Vancouver on Sept. 27th, 1927, after a flight from Los Angeles which included numerous stops en route. The machine, piloted by A. D. Cruickshanks, former Royal Air Force Lieutenant, carried four passengers, including one woman and an infant. It was later shipped north to link up Whitehorse, Mayo, Dawson and other Yukon points during the winter, fitted with skis. Ordinarily it takes twelve to fourteen days to carry mail between Whitehorse and Dawson during the winter, but the use of a plane cuts this to five hours.

The story of the first mail-carrying flight is one of adventure and hardship. Navigating his plane through temperature at times as low as 40 degrees below zero, Pilot Andrew Cruickshanks on Nov. 7th, 1927, carried the mail from Whitehorse to Mayo and Dawson, Alaska, a distance of more than 500 miles, in four hours and a half. The plane was a Ryan monoplane made by the B. F. Mahoney Corp. of San Diego, Calif. Dog sled stations are maintained along the route in case of forced landing. The trip takes over two weeks by dog sled, incurring even greater dangers than making it by air.

The stamps, quantity 12,000, were of the denomination of 25c, lithographed in blue, and rouletted, books of 100, 10 stamps to the sheet.

Cover No.	Cachet, Stamp, etc.		
		Flown Cover (The author has been unable to locate any of these.)	
103	AS30	**Second Flight, Nov. 24th, 1927.** The plane leaving Whitehorse on Nov. 24th was forced owing to very cold weather to land 50 miles from Mayo. Mail was carried into Mayo by dog team, reaching there Dec. 4th, Werneckie 5th, Keno Hill 6th, and Dawson on the 8th. The covers, with red an blue strips, had the Canadian 2c stamp and the Yukon Airways & Exploration Company's 25c blue stamp. Flown cover	3.00
104	AS30	**April 13th, 1928,** with small box cachet in brown. Whitehorse-Atlin (or return)	1.25
105	AS30	Whitehorse-Carcross (or return)	1.25
106	AS30	Carcross-Atlin (or return)	1.25
		STAMPS.	
	AS30	25c Blue, lithographed, rouletted top and bottom, imperf. at sides	1.00

AS31

PATRICIA AIRWAYS, LTD.

On Oct. 17, 1927, Patricia Airways and Exploration, Limited, ceased operations. The new company in the meantime had continued the mail service, but bore no relation to the former company. Patricia Airways Ltd. used a yellow stamp similar to the first Patricia Exploration stamp but with "Patricia Airways, Limited," in script type. "Northern Ontario" in small capitals and "CANADA" in larger capitals. The face value was 10c. First flight covers bear a Maple Leaf cachet similar to AC22 in red.

		May 9th, 1927.	
107	AS31	*Red Lake-Sioux Lookout* (*81*)	7.00
		a. Signed by pilot	10.00
108	AS31	Sioux Lookout to Clearwater Lake (*93*)	7.00
109	AS31	Sioux Lookout to Red Lake (*97*)	7.00
110	AS31	Sioux Lookout to Rainbow Lake (*25*)	10.00
111	AS31	Rainbow Lake-Sioux Lookout (*25*)	10.00
112	AS31	Gold Pines-Sioux Lookout (*124*)	5.00
113	AS31	Sioux Lookout-Gold Pines (*187*)	5.00
114	AS31	Jackson Manion-Sioux Lookout (*101*)	6.00

a. With rare violet cachet, AC26 .... 12.00

115 AS31 Sioux Lookout-Narrow Lake *(57)* 8.00

116 AS31 Narrow Lake-Sioux Lookout *(45)* 8.00

117 AS31 Gold Pines-Jackson Manion *(62)* 8.00

118 AS31 Red Lake-Gold Pines *(72)* 8.00

119 AS31 Jackson Manion-Gold Pines *(80)* 8.00

STAMPS.

AS31 10c Green and red on yellow .... .50

120 **Montreal-Vancouver** (no mail carried). **September, 1926.** In September, 1926, Squadron-Leader A. Earl Godfrey of the Royal Canadian Air Force piloted a seaplane from east to west, starting from Montreal and completing the journey at Jericho Beach, Vancouver, where the Pacific coast station of the Royal Canadian Air Force is located. His final "hop" was from a lake west of Edmonton, through the Rocky Mountains, to Vancouver, a distance of 720 miles, covered in seven hours and twenty minutes. Squadron-Leader Godfrey was not seeking to establish a speed record, the flight taking ten days from Montreal to Vancouver, although he was delayed by weather unfavorable for flying at several points along his route.

121 **London, Canada, to London, England. June, 1927.** The history of this unfortunate flight, a private venture for a $25,000 prize offered by Charles Burns, President of the Carling Breweries, Ltd., may be read in the daily press of London and Toronto, Canada, for June and July, 1927.

The following from the Toronto Globe gives details that are bound to be of greater interest as time passes: "The London to London flight for the $25,000 prize offered by Charles Burns, President of the Carling Breweries, Ltd., assumed a new phase this afternoon with the selection of an aviator now in its final stages. Eighty Canadian fliers are competing for the opportunity to participate in the flight. Londoners are beginning to wage war over who shall have the honor of going as passengers, if passengers are carried. To-day Rev. Roy D. Mess, Rector of St. David's Anglican Church and Chairman of the Board of Education, formally entered his application, basing his claim on the fact that he was born in London, England, and is now a citizen of London, Canada. To-night Ald. Dickson F. Glass formally lodged with Mr. Burns an offer of $3,000 for his fare if he is carried on the London-to-London plane. Ald. Glass does not want to be the first passenger over but he wants a place in world history as the first man who paid his fare in the air route to Europe." One wonders what the emotions of these gentlemen were on reading the last chapter of this ill-fated adventure: "Plane believed lost at sea." The fliers were compelled by fog to land at Caribou, Maine, reaching Harbour Grace, Newfoundland, on Sept. 5th. Nothing further was heard from them after leaving that point. 100 copies of a special stamp were printed, approved by the Post Office Department. These were on white wove, perf. 12, printed in olive green with a background in yellow. The Post Office Department made up a direct despatch on London containing special letters to the weight of about two pounds. Dealers paid $25.00 on the understanding that the special stamp would be placed on any letter they forwarded for delivery overseas. A few of the stamps are said to have been given out by special favor. All mail was of course lost at sea.

AIR FLICHT ABANDONED
LETTER RETURNED

AC28

AC29

122 AC28 AC29 **Montreal-Vancouver.** It is said that this flight was cancelled because satisfactory insurance arrangements could not be made. Those who sent envelopes to be mailed from Montreal received them back again from the Inspection Division, Dead Letter Office, Ottawa, on July 19, 1927. As it is only a question of time till such a trans-Canada flight will take place (Postmaster-General Veniot speaking at Rawdon, Que., on Jan. 14, 1927, prophesied that in a short time mail from Montreal would be in Vancouver within twenty-four hours), the plans for this flight may here be recorded for comparison with any successful later flight.

The pilot was to have been Captain Edward Dobbin, flying from Montreal to Sault Ste. Marie, from there to Winnipeg, on to Medicine Hat (some claim MacLeod, Alta.), and from there to his destination on the Pacific Coast. Capt. Dobbin (Canadian Air Force) visited Winnipeg in June and made landing arrangements in that city. The plane to be used was a De Haviland Moth, shipped to Canada on the Empress of Australia from England. This plane is of 80 horsepower and therefore not particularly high-powered, but very fast. Capt. Dobbin had hoped to make the journey in from forty-two to forty-eight hours flying time. The flight was included in the programme of notable events scheduled in connection with Canada's Jubilee of Confederation, 1867-1927.

The electric cancelling machine in Montreal was supplied with a special cancellation for the flight. This read, "Air Flight, Montreal-Vancouver, July, 1927." Covers bear "Air flight abandoned, letter returned" in violet.

Covers (returned) dated July 8, 1927 .... 1.00

123 AS32 **Victoria-Vancouver,** July 23rd, 1928.

On July 23rd, 1928, the British Columbia Airways, Ltd., of Victoria, B.C., carried their first bag of mail to Vancouver. The cancellation on the covers shows that they were despatched 2.30 p.m. July 23rd, arriving at Vancouver

P.O. at 4 p.m. the same day, with the Vancouver backstamp. Each envelope was stamped on the face by the Victoria Post Office in black, "First Flight-Air Mail-Victoria-Vancouver, B.C.," in three lines, by a type-set rubber stamp. About 400 were sent over, of which approximately 200 were mailed by the Victoria Chamber of Commerce to other like organizations. Most of these covers were not saved for collections. The public was first notified that 5c in addition to the regular postage would be necessary, but on the morning of the flight Mr. Gardiner, P.M., kindly

AS32

allowed letters to go at the ordinary postal rates, an act of courtesy much appreciated by the senders. Covers therefore are to be had showing either 7c or a 2c rate, as some were handed in for mailing the day before.

This flight was followed by the regular twice-a-day service on Aug. 3rd. By this time the B.C. Airways, Ltd., had received from the printers the supply of their own 5c Air Mail stamps, which were sold to be affixed on the back. The first regular flight left Victoria at 11 a.m. on August 3rd, arriving at Vancouver 12.30 p.m. the same day. The Victoria P.O. again applied a cachet in the same type as before, but reading "First Regular Flight-Air Mail-Victoria-Vancouver, B.C.," in three lines. Collectors will note the difference in these two "first" flights, the latter of which is the "first regular" flight.

In the First Regular Flight there were 600 letters, and these bore, on the back, the B.C. Airways Air Mail stamps.

Flown Covers. July 23rd, 1928.

AS32 Victoria to Vancouver 7.50

Flown Covers. First Regular Flight, Aug. 3rd, 1928.

124 AS32 Victoria to Vancouver 3.00

STAMPS.

AS32 5c Ultramarine. Lithographed by Colonist Printing & Publishing Co., Victoria, sheets of eleven rows of five stamps, rouletted .... .50

(The same plane also made two trips a day to Seattle with passengers, but no arrangement had been made to carry mail pending international arrangements.)

GOVERNMENT SERVICE, 2c RATE

125 **Leamington-Pelee Island. Dec. 14, 1927.**

This was an official Government attempt to get mail from

Cover No.	Cachet, Stamp, etc.		

Leamington (mainland) to Pelee Island, a distance of about nineteen miles. The Toronto Mail and Empire for Nov. 27th, 1927, stated: "The air mail service . . . . will be inaugurated within a few weeks. Bids have been asked for on a ship capable of carrying a maximum of 300 pounds of mail. Four trips per week will be made." The first mail was scheduled for Dec. 14th. Covers are postmarked Leamington, Dec. 14th, and Pelee Island, Dec. 14th. Covers addressed from Toronto Dec. 14th are postmarked Leamington, Dec. 15th, and Pelee Island, Dec. 19th, the second flight apparently being four days later. This service is instituted for the winter season after Lake Erie becomes frozen over and boat mail is impossible to this island.

Covers, Dec. 14, 1927 .... 3.00

Return ....

Later or 2nd Flight.

126 Toronto-Leamington-Pelee Island 1.75

127 **Rimouski-Father Point-Montreal.**

In April, 1927, Hon. P. J. Veniot, Postmaster-General, called for tenders for an aerial mail service between Father Point and Montreal, with the end in view of speeding up the mail arriving from overseas by liner.

The first attempt to pick up the mail from a liner at Father Point resulted in failure, the plane crashing into the dock through being too heavily loaded and unable to rise. This was on Sept. 16th, 1927.

On Oct. 27th, 1927, the Toronto Globe carried the following news: "The first air mail delivery off a transatlantic liner was made to Ottawa to-day. At 12.56 p.m. the Fairchild monoplane G-CAIH swooped down on the waters of the Ottawa River and landed a bag of mail from the Canadian Pacific Steamship Montroyal. The mail came to Quebec from Father Point. The Fairchild Aviation Company took the Ottawa bag at Quebec and added another Quebec-Ottawa bag to it. The plane, operated by Pilot H. M. Pasmore, and Air Engineer A. Kahre, left Quebec at 10.31 and arrived here at 12.56, the trip taking 2 hours 25 minutes. This mail, which was delivered with the usual afternoon mail to-day, would ordinarily have reached its destination to-morrow afternoon or Saturday morning. "It was an exceptionally good flight. The visibility was good all the way," said Mr. Pasmore, the pilot. "If the future flights are as successful as this one the service will be a regular one," stated a post office official. "This flight was only experimental but it proved highly successful." It is expected that the plane will go back Saturday morning to catch the steamship Regina and deliver Ottawa mail to her. One of the fliers expressed the hope that he might be allowed to fly over the boat and drop the mail sacks on the deck. Flown Covers 2.50

128 **Montreal-Rimouski.** Sept. 16, 1927.

All first-class mail received in the Montreal P.O. on Sept. 21, 1927, up to 10.30 a.m., for overseas, was despatched by airplane to Rimouski, Quebec, to be put on liner which had

Cover No.	Cachet, Stamp, etc.

already left Quebec City. Newspapers carried notices of this flight, which was successful. Chris. Goulden's covers (Century Stamp Co.) were stamped in blue "First Flight, Montreal to Rimouski," in two lines in the upper left, and "Via Air Mail" in lower left.

The hydroplane of the Canadian Airways Limited left Montreal at 1.15 p.m. and arrived at Rimouski at 5.15, several hours before the arrival of the Empress of Australia. Captain Mulcahy, pilot, carried 500 pounds of mail. There was no extra charge for mail so carried. Flown covers...... 5.00

Dec. 26th, 1927.

129 **LaMailbaie (Murray Bay) to Seven Islands.**

The plane for this service was flown from New York to Murray Bay, carrying, we understand, a private mail, which was dropped at Quebec. The only cover from this mail that we have seen was from "Hotel Astor" in New York, stamped in black "New York-Quebec" at top and in lower left "Air Mail."

In the official Seven Islands flight mail was taken on the plane on Christmas Eve, 1927, the plane leaving Pointe-au-Pu Wharf at 10.15 a.m. Christmas day, arriving at Seven Islands at 2.30 p.m. that day, where the mail was delivered to the Post Office and marked "26th." Mail left there at noon of the 27th, arriving Murray Bay 3.50 p.m. the same day, at Quebec 1.40 p.m. Dec. 28th.

On its return trip from Seven Islands the plane landed at Shelter Bay with and for mail. Mr. Goulden (Century Stamp Co.) states, "The mail coming out would be much scarcer than the mail going in, as the mail going out would be by dog team or wait for a later trip of the plane. I had only two letters out on the 27th. The Ontario Paper Co. does considerable business in Shelter Bay." Flown cover 4.00

a. Return, Seven Islands-Shelter Bay ....

b. Return, Shelter Bay-Murray Bay ....

130 **Moncton-Magdalene Islands. Jan. 11, 1928.**

This plane left Moncton, N.B., at noon on the 11th January, 1928, reaching Grindstone, Magdalene Islands, at 1.30 p.m., leaving there on return trip at 2.07, landing at Cape Tormentine (which is 10 miles from Moncton) at about 4 p.m. As a snowstorm was prevailing the plane remained there for the night. A newspaper despatch of the above date stated: "Inhabitants of these isolated islands of the Gulf of St. Lawrence thronged the shore at Grindstone to-day when a wireless message stated that the first mail plane inaugurating a regular winter service to the islands had left Moncton at noon. An hour and a half later the hum of the motor was heard and just one hour and 35 minutes after the hop off from Moncton the plane flown by E. J. Cooper made a graceful landing on the water and transferred 700 pounds of mail to a waiting boat." A despatch from Port Elgin, N.S., stated, "The first trip of the aerial mail service between Moncton, N.B., and the Magdalene Islands was carried out successfully to-day, but

Cover No.	Cachet, Stamp, etc.

Pilot E. J. Cooper and his companion, making the return trip, ran into a blinding snowstorm on approaching the New Brunswick shore, and landed in a cove at North Shore near here about 4 o'clock. Cooper said they would hop off for Moncton with the next high tide if the weather cleared sufficiently." Figures for the number of letters carried are not available. We understand a Winnipeg dealer had 300, the Century Stamp Co. had some, and there were, doubtless, other parcels.

Flown Cover 2.50

131 **Jan. 23, 1928.**

Canadian Government Service to Mining Districts. Mail flown in as formerly, but all charges covered by 2c postage. Rolling Portage-Red Lake-Gold Pines, flown covers ....

132 Red Lake-Gold Pines-Woman Lake-Narrow Lake, flown covers ....

133 **Moncton-Charlottetown. Feb. 19, 1928.**

Under instructions from the Postmaster-General, Inspector Whear proceeded to Moncton on Friday, February 17th, to meet Inspector Griffith of Saint John to make arrangements in connection with the new airmail service.

On arriving at Moncton word had been received ordering the plane to Murray Bay, Quebec, and advising that a new plane would be sent from New York, and the service would not start until Saturday, 25th February. The pilot stated that weather conditions were not favorable to permit flying to Murray Bay, that he would receive a telegram on Saturday morning, Feb. 18th, and if weather conditions still continued unfavorable for flying to Murray Bay he would make the flight to Charlottetown.

In view of this possibility, Prince Edward Island (Charlottetown) mails were put off at Moncton and taken to the Moncton Post Office and made up for the air route, but as the weather was not very favorable Saturday morning and no definite assurance could be obtained from the pilot, the mails were again ordered to the trains. The Charlottetown postmaster received a wire on Saturday night that the mails were being forwarded by special train leaving for Tormentine (where transfer is made to car ferry), crossing over Sunday morning. But on Sunday morning, Feb. 19th, the Charlottetown postmaster received a telephone call from the Moncton postmaster that the plane would leave at 11.15 and arrive about noon. The plane did not leave, however, until after 12.30 and arrived at Charlottetown at 1.13 p.m., bringing one bag of local mail from the Moncton post office. The pilot left Charlottetown at 1.40 and reached Moncton at 3 p.m. on the return trip.

The plane left Moncton (Pilot Cooper) with practically no mail, owing to the more or less uncertainty of the arrangements and the suddenness of the flight. The largest lot of letters consisted of a bundle of 100 of the current King George 2c stamped envelopes (embossed), evidently put in the mail bag at the last moment, the party having no time

Cover No.	Cachet, Stamp, etc.		

to address them. These received the Moncton date stamp but were refused the Charlottetown backstamp, and after some correspondence were returned to the Moncton postmaster. Less than 100 actual letters were carried, many addressed to inland points on the Island, where they would be destroyed. Those addressed to Charlottetown individuals or business firms, about forty in all, were rounded up by an enterprising collector. These are postmarked "Moncton 11 A.M.-Feb. 19-1928-N.B." and backstamped "Charlottetown 1.30 p.m. Feb. 19-1928-PEI."

The official nature of this flight may be still better understood when it is pointed out that the unsatisfactory mail service to Prince Edward Island had been the subject of complaint on the part of the Hon. J. A. McDonald. On February 24th, replying to statements made by Mr. McDonald, the Postmaster-General is reported to have said, "That is right—they asked for it last week and they received it within 48 hours of the request." It will be seen that the question of a more regular and expeditious service to Prince Edward Island had been given serious and prompt attention, and that the P.M.G. himself was responsible for the improved service and indirectly this first flight.

Flown cover 12.50

2nd Flight. Covers are postmarked "Moncton-12-MR-3 28-N.B." and backstamped "Charlottetown-3 p.m.-Mar. 3-1928-P.E.I." 3.00

3rd Flight. Covers postmarked "Moncton-12-MR-10-28-N.B." and backstamped "Charlottetown-3 P.M.-Mar. 10-1928-P.E.I." Flown covers 3.00

134 **Feb. 19th, 1928, Charlottetown-Moncton.**

The return flight from Charlottetown to Moncton on Sunday afternoon of February 19th carried 300 lbs. of mail (a small portion of which would be letters) and a few bore the Charlottetown date stamp and the Moncton backstamp. About 30 covers are known to have been preserved.

The letters originated for the most part at country points and bear such postmarks on the face, with no Charlottetown postmark. With the exception of the few destined to Moncton itself, they were not backstamped at Moncton.

Flown covers with the Charlottetown postmark, 12.30 p.m., on face, backstamped "Moncton-16-Feb. 19-28-N.B." 15.00

With other P.E.I. town postmark and Moncton backstamp... 15.00

135 **2nd Flight.** The second flight was on Saturday, March 3rd, when a limited mail was carried either way. Covers are postmarked "Charlottetown-1.30 P.M.-Mar 3, 1928-P.E.I." and backstamped "Moncton-18-Mar. 3-28-N.B." Flown covers 5.00

135a **3rd Flight.** Covers are postmarked "Charlottetown-2 P.M.-Mar. 10-1928-P.E.I." and backstamped "Moncton-17-MR 10-28-N.B." Flown covers 3.50

135b **4th Flight**. Covers are postmarked "Charlottetown-12.30 P.M.-Mar. 17-1828-P.E.I." and backstamped "Moncton-13-MR-18-28-N.B." Flown covers 2.75

136 **March 3rd, 1928, Middle Sackville-Charlottetown.**

Mail from Halifax, Sydney, St. John, Montreal, Toronto,

Cover No.	Cachet, Stamp, etc.		

Boston, New York and other points was assembled at Middle Sackville and picked up by plane from Crystal Lake, leaving 2.10 p.m. and landing on the ice off west end of Richmond street at 2.31, making the trip in 21 minutes. The inland mail was despatched by the afternoon trains, so that it reached its destination in Prince and Kings Counties Saturday evening instead of Monday noon or Monday evening. This means that for some sections of the Island mail was delivered 48 hours earlier. In Charlottetown is was delivered five and a half hours earlier. An immense crowd of people were on hand to greet the plane and witness the hop-off. The plane left at 2.50 p.m., carrying 250 pounds of mail.

With the exception of letters from Middle Sackville, bearing that postmark, the mail carried on this flight has no value, as it has no distinguishing marks to show that it was transferred to the plane at Crystal Lake, Middle Sackville.

Flown Covers, with Middle Sackville postmark and Charlottetown backstamp (about 10 known) 35.00

Middle-Sackville-Charlottetown, Mar. 10, 1928.

137 A second flight was made on Saturday, March 10th, 1928, which included a few covers from Middle Sackville, so postmarked. Both first and second flight covers were all addressed to one party, who holds a letter to this effect from the Middle Sackville postmaster. The covers are postmarked "Middle Sackville P.M. MR 10-28-N.B." and backstamped "Charlottetown-3 p.m.-Mar. 10-1928-P.E.I." About 30 flown. **Flown Covers** 15.00

138 **Charlottetown-Magdalen Islands, First Direct Flight.** Postmarked "Charlottetown 11.30 a.m. Mar. 11-1928-P.E.I.." Backstamped "Grindstone a.m. Mar. 11-28 P.Q." Flown cover 17.50

138a **Charlottetown-Magdalen Islands,** via Moncton. On Friday, March 9th, the plane in service from Moncton to Magdalen Islands could not make a landing on arrival at Magdalen Islands and returned to .Charlottetown rather than carry the mails back to Moncton. On Saturday, March 10th, the plane came from Moncton and picked up this mail, together with a small bag made up by the Charlottetown postmaster for the Magdalen Islands, returning to Moncton and flying from there to the Magdalen Islands the following day, March 11th.

Flown Covers, Charlottetown March 10th, Magdalen Islands, March 11th 15.00

Magdalen Islands-Charlottetown, via Moncton.

139 The first through flight covers were held pending first flight from Grindstone Island, reaching Moncton and being postmarked "Moncton 9 P.M. Mar. 2-1928-N.B.," leaving Moncton by airmail next day, postmarked "Moncton 12-MR 3-28-N.B." and backstamped "Charlottetown-3 p.m.-Mar. 3-1928-P.E.I." 12.50

Cover No. | Cachet, Stamp, etc.

139a **Magdalen Islands-Charlottetown, via Moncton. 2nd Flight.** These covers are postmarked 'Grindstone Is. A.M. March Ɛ (3 reversed) 28-P.Q." Backstamped "Moncton-12-MR 7-28-N.B." also "Charlottetown P.E.I.-20-MR-8-28-Canada." Flown cover 5.00

140 **Toronto-Montreal-Father Point.**
Ottawa-Montreal-Father Point.

On May 5th, 1928, mail was flown from Toronto and Ottawa to Montreal and thence to Father Point to connect with a transatlantic liner. Mail to Montreal bore in the lower left corner the marking illustrated, and mail from Montreal to Toronto on May 6th bore a similar marking reading "To Toronto."

This mail, postmarked in Toronto April 4th and 5th, arrived in Europe nearly ten days in advance of registered mail sent by ordinary service.

Postmaster Victor Gaudet, Montreal, used a special envelope with red and blue line, and printed in lower left corner in blue, "VIA AIR MAIL." Enclosed was a letter over his signature giving details of this flight, and much useful information regarding the future airmail services of Canada. The mail picked up at Father Point would not receive any distinguishing mark there, but on arrival in Toronto would receive the special marking above illustrated. A letter dated May 14th, 1928, regarding mail from Rimouski (Father Point) reads in part: "—that part of the service between Quai de Rimouski and Montreal is exclusively for the purpose of carrying British and foreign mails, that is to say, no mail is carried by air from Quai de Rimouski to Montreal that is not taken off the transatlantic liner at Father Point, and no mail is carried by air to Quai de Rimouski that is not intended to be transported by steamer to British and foreign points."

THIS MAIL WAS CARRIED BY
POSTAL AIRPLANE
TO MONTREAL

AC30

On May 6th, 1928, an enthusiastic reception was tendered the pilot of the first mail plane to land in Toronto, when thousands of spectators crowded Leaside Field to see J. H. St. Martin glide down out of a clear sky with his cargo of letters. They were the first letters "by air" to Toronto, and this significant milestone in the postal service apparently captured the imagination of the thousands of persons who crowded the field, for they greeted the appearance of the plane with wild acclaim.

Most of the mail was off the steamer Empress of Scotland. Pilot St. Martin made splendid time in his trip here. Leav-

Cover No.	Cachet, Stamp, etc.	

ing Montreal at 1 p.m., he arrived at Leaside Field at 4.30, covering the distance in three and a half hours. He was met on his arrival by one of the trucks of the P.O. Department. The mail was postmarked in Montreal 10 a.m. May 6th. Mail postmarked Montreal, May 5th, and bearing cancellation AC30, was forwarded to Toronto by train.

Flown Covers, May 5th, 1928.

Toronto to Montreal 1.50

141 AC30 Montreal to Toronto, May 6th, 10 a.m. 3.00

142 **Rimouski-Montreal.**

On May 29th, 1928, the "Domestic Mail" service was inaugurated from Rimouski to Montreal. Previous flights from Father Point (Rimouski) carried ship mail only and the pilots did not deliver or pick up mail at Rimouski. Official covers were used, banded in red, white and blue diagonally at either end, and typewritten in upper left, "Premiere envolee officielle des depeches aeriennes de Rimouski Despatch" and in the lower left corner appears the post office cancellation AC30.

The "Second Domestic Mail" from Rimouski was carried on June 15th, 1928.

Flown Covers, *First,* May 29, 1928, to Montreal or Toronto 5.00

142 Second, June 15, 1928, to Montreal or Toronto .... .75

	Rimouski-Montreal	Montreal-Toronto	Total
Air mileage	350	310	660
Rail mileage	372	333	705
Flying time, hours	4½	3½	8
Rail time, hours..........	12	9	21

143 **Canadian National Exhibition Flights** to Hamilton, London and Windsor, and from Montreal, Ottawa and Kingston to Toronto.

The Post Office Department made an announcement under date August 1st, from Ottawa, as follows:

"By authority of the Postmaster-General a special air mail flight will be undertaken on the 29th August, 1928, from the Canadian National Exhibition Grounds at Toronto to Toronto to Windsor, Ontario. This is a special flight to commemorate not only the Golden Jubilee of the Canadian National Exhibition but also the first Annual Aircraft Show. The flight will be via Hamilton, Ontario, and London, Ontario. All mail offered and prepaid at the rate of five cents for the first ounce and ten cents for each succeeding ounce will be conveyed on this flight. All covers should bear in the top left-hand corner the words:

"Via Special Air Mail Flight—"
"Toronto-Windsor"
or "Toronto-London"
or "Toronto-Hamilton"

depending on the wish of the sender, but any covers marked for this flight without definite instruction to the contrary will be carried by air through to Windsor.

The postmaster at Toronto will be furnished with special

Cover No.	Cachet. Stamp, etc.

separate cachets covering the three above alternatives and a special impression of such cachet will be made (according to the wish of the sender) on all properly prepaid covers reaching the postmaster, Toronto, for inclusion on this flight. However, these special cachets will be used only on such covers as are sent to the postmaster at Toronto bearing Canadian postage stamps.

All covers so prepaid and marked will be date-stamped at the Canadian National Exhibition Grounds at Toronto and back-stamped at the point at which they leave the plane and will bear in addition, the special cachet commemorative of the occasion.

All other covers bearing the correct amount of postage in U.S.A. stamps reaching Toronto in the ordinary mails from points in the U.S.A. in time to connect with this flight will also be included but will not bear the special cachet.

All covers conveyed on this flight addressed to points beyond the territory covered by the plane will go forward to the addressees at the conclusion of the flight in the ordinary way."

Surmounting considerable obstacles in the way of fog, rain and adverse winds the special air mail flights arranged to salute the fiftieth anniversary of the Canadian National Exhibition were completed only slightly off schedule. They were due to terminate on the lake off the Exhibition Grounds at about 12 o'clock. The plane from Windsor, London and Hamilton arrived at 12.55 p.m., and the one from Quebec, Montreal, Ottawa and Kingston came down off the foot of York street at 1.45 p.m. (August 24th, 1928).

These brought 850 pounds of mail, including many letters of greetings to the Exhibition from Government officials and other prominent persons, and a number of Canadian Pacific air express packages.

The big amphibian plane from Windsor was piloted by Capt. Jack Caldwell, and the one from Quebec by Capt. Romeo Vachon, who piloted one of the planes which went to the aid of the Bremen fliers when they landed on Greenley Island. Both reported difficult weather conditions over the greater part of their courses, and stated they had to navigate by compass for long stretches.

Included in the mail which arrived from Windsor was a letter from Mayor Jackson to Thomas Bradshaw, president of the Exhibition. It read in part: "This letter will travel by the first air mail service from the Border Cities and will carry to you hearty greetings and sincere wishes that the 1928 Canadian National Exhibition will be the greatest and most successful ever promoted." A few moments later letters from the Ottawa plane, which landed in the Bay, were delivered to the president. They all bore greetings and best wishes for the success of the Exhibition, from Rt. Hon. Macknzie King, Premier of Canada; Hon. Peter Heenan, Minister of Labor; Hon. Charles A. Dunning, Hon. Charles Stewart, Hon. P. J. Veniot, Hon. Robert Forke, Hon. James Malcolm, Hon. J. A. Robb.

Cover No.	Cachet, Stamp, etc.

On August 29th the planes left for Windsor (including Hamilton and London) and Quebec (including Kingston, Ottawa and Montreal).
Sixteen Special Cachets were used, the Quebec-Toronto and Toronto-Quebec cachets being duplicated in French.

FLOWN COVERS

To Toronto Aug. 24, 1928.		Return Flights Aug. 29th, 1928.	
a. Windsor-Toronto	1.00	Toronto-Windsor	1.00
b. London-Toronto	1.00	Toronto-London	1.00
c. Hamilton-Toronto	1.00	Toronto-Hamilton	1.00
d. Kingston-Toronto	1.00	Toronto-Kingston	1.00
e. Ottawa-Toronto	1.00	Toronto-Ottawa	1.00
f. Montreal-Toronto (via Ottawa)	1.00	Toronto-Montreal (via Ottawa	1.00
g. Quebec-Toronto	1.00	Toronto-Quebec	1.00

144 **Ottawa-Vancouver, Sept. 5th-Sept. 8th, 1928.**

A special 2-line cachet in blue-black on the face of the cover at right beneath the current 5c postage stamp reads, "Plane left Ottawa 7 a.m. Feb. 5—arrived Vancouver 6 p.m. Sept. 8." The 5c postage stamp was cancelled "Ottawa, Sept. 2nd, 6 a.m., 1928, Ont." "INSURE YOUR PARCELS AT THE POST OFFICE." On the left there is a cachet in a double-lined rectangular shield reading, in six lines, "Special—Trans-Canada Flight—Ottawa—to—Vancouver—February, 1928," in purple. Covers are backstamped "Vancouver, Sept. 8, 6.30 p.m., 1928, B.C." A few were signed by pilot. To the best of the author's information there were between 500 and 600 covers. The following is from the Canadian Philatelist, Vol. 1, No. 2: "As far as collectors were concerned, except, perhaps, those of Ottawa who were in the good graces of officials, they didn't have a chance. Why, I don't know, but the whole affair was very mysterious and apparently was hurriedly conceived, for as late as August 28th, eight days before the flight commenced, the Post Office Department refused to give any information. It may be, however, that it was not able to do so. However, Major A. E. Godfrey, of the R.C.A.F., left Ottawa flying a Fairchild seaplane, on September 5th, at 7 a.m., for Vancouver, carrying a small "very special" pouch of letters. He arrived there at 6 p.m., September 8th, after covering the distance of 3,300 miles in thirty-two hours flying time. This flight was said to have been for the purpose of testing the feasibility of a trans-continental air mail service. It was feasible alright, but not for collectors. We shall now play the game of "Who has the covers?" Press announcements caused the Ottawa post office to be flooded with covers from all over North America, but, unfortunately, they ALL arrived too late."

Flown Covers 10.00

(Any covers seen by the author were addressed in pencil to a Mr. Herring.)

Cover No.	Cachet, Stamp, etc.		
145		**Moose Jaw-Winnipeg, Aug. 17th, 1928.**	

The postmark is "Moose Jaw, 10.30 a.m., Aug. 17, 1928, Sask." The covers are backstamped "Winnipeg, 8.30 p.m., Aug. 17, 1928, Man." A label, perforated top and bottom, printed in red between two horizontal borders, in four lines, reads "Air Mail—Moose Jaw to Winnipeg—August. 17th, 1928—Moose Jaw Flying Club Limited." Collectors were given absolutely no notice of this flight, which was "pulled off," to use the language of the prairies, upon receipt of telegraphic authority from Ottawa. It is understood about 100 covers were carried. Covers seen by the author, like the Ottawa-Vancouver covers, were addressed in pencil to a Mr. Herring.

Flown Covers 5.00

146 AC30 **Toronto-Montreal-Albany. First Official Daily Service Flight, Oct. 1, 1928.**

Flown Cover .... .30

Flown Cover, Albany-Montreal-Toronto .... .35

Flown Cover, earlier bi-weekly service, with AC30 and new airmail stamp, Toronto-Montreal Sp. 22, 1928 .... 1.25

A Departmental Notice under date Aug. 21, 1928, reads: "The first International Air Mail Service between Canada and the United States will be inaugurated on or about Sept. 15th, 1928, with the first air mail flight from Montreal, Quebec, to Albany, N.Y. All mail offered and prepaid at the rate of 5c for the first ounce and 10c for each succeeding ounce or fraction thereof, will be conveyed. All covers should bear in the top left hand corner the words: 'Via First Air Mail Flight, Montreal-Albany.'

"The postmaster at Montreal will be furnished with a special cachet and an impression of such cachet will be made on all properly prepaid covers reaching him for inclusion on this flight.

"Senders of mail from Montreal to Albany who desire such mail re-forwarded from Albany under cover should forward to the postmaster at Albany a stamped addressed envelope for use in returning such mail to the sender together with any special instructions considered necessary. This stamped addressed envelope should bear U.S.A. postage stamps."

(Editor's Note: The double rate for the 2nd ounce was to discourage the use of airmails for small or lightweight parcels of bulk.)

STAMP. (See Title Page.)

A100 5c Grey-brown .... .10

Toronto Notes.

The "Mail and Empire" carried the following news on the morning of Oct. 2nd:

"Two heavily laden planes soared above the Leaside Landing Field outside Toronto yesterday and opened a new era in the annals of transportation in the Dominion. By the general public the event which marked the inauguration of

Cachet,
Cover Stamp,
No. etc.

daily mail and express service by air between Toronto and New York with Montreal as an intermediate point, was hardly noticed. In Montreal formal ceremonies marked the occasion, but Toronto took the inaugural of the air mail service as a matter of course. A small group of officials of the Post Office and the Canadian Pacific Express Co. were on hand to give a send-off to Pilot Wallace and his plane, which sprang into the sky at 9.45 a.m., Montreal-bound. A still smaller group welcomed the Montreal plane as it landed at Leaside at 3.10 p.m., having accomplished a trip through fog and cloud in three hours and twenty-five minutes.

"Mail and express trucks were waiting with motors already going as the heavy plane dropped from the sky and came to a standstill on the field. Ten bags of mail and about 20 express packages were unloaded and reloaded in the space of a moment, and the vehicles clattered off down Yonge street. At 4.15 p.m. an express consignment for the Robert Simpson Company, despatched from Montreal in the morning, was on display in the window of Toronto's department store. Goods shipped from Montreal had come from destination to destination in less than five hours.

Montreal Notes

"Late editions of New York morning newspapers were in the hands of Montreal readers at noon to-day with the ink scarcely dry on the paper when Montreal, Toronto and New York (via Albany) were linked up with an air mail service that will henceforth be conducted on a regular schedule. The formal opening of the new service was staged at the St. Hubert airport, Montreal, accompanied by one of the most elaborate aerial exhibitions ever witnessed in Canada.

"Over fifteen thousand people were on the spacious grounds of the flying field to see the arrival and departure of the mail planes, while high dignitaries of the United States and Canadian Governments participated in the ceremonies. A perfect Autumn day favored the occasion, and throughout the morning and forenoon the sky was dotted with the darting planes in exhibitions of stunt flying, racing and 'joy riding,' the whole proceedings being carried out with a smoothness and lack of accident of any kind.

"Some fifty airplanes, including four Siskin fighters of the Royal Canadian Air Force, who flew in formation, looped, zoomed, rolled and bombed a corner of the airdrome with smoke bombs, and units from the local flying clubs, and the first all-metal plane to be manufactured in Canada, a product of the local company, participated in the exhibition.

"The international air mail service became an accomplished fact when there swept into the flying field in all the glory of the brilliant sunshine that greeted the new Moth, an airplane from Albany, N.Y., laden with mails for Montreal and Toronto. The machine whirled to its resting place at 11.20, only five minutes after it was due to arrive, and five minutes later another plane swung gracefully into the air

Cachet,
Cover Stamp,
No. etc.

and sped away for Toronto, and Canada's two great cities were linked together by air. Shortly after this the mail plane from Rimouski arrived, carrying trans-atlantic mails.

"Later the City of Montreal tendered a luncheon to the invited guests and among those present were: Hon. William Phillips, U.S. Minister to Canada; W. I. Glover, Second Assistant Postmaster-General of the U.S.; Hon. Narcisse Perodeau, Lieut.-Governor of the Province; Hon. P. J. Veniot, Postmaster-General of Canada; Hon. Lucien Cannon, Solicitor-General; Premier L. A. Taschereau of Quebec; C. J. Desbarats, Deputy Minister of Defence; Mayor Camilien Houde, of Montreal, and Victor Gaudet, K.C., postmaster at Montreal."

"I predict for Canada a new era of airmindedness," said Mr. Glover. "People are going to take to the air. The Post Office is the pulse of the nation, and your Post Office is leading the way in commercial aviation. The people will follow."

Hon. Mr. Veniot talked of the warm sentiments which existed between Canadians and Americans and said the new international service would work further in that direction.

Winnipeg-Regina-Calgary-Edmonton-Saskatoon Government Service. Dec. 10, 1928, and continuing daily except Sundays until Dec. 29, 1928.

An announcement was sent out by authority of the Postmaster-General, dated Ottawa, Canada, November, 1928, to the effect that special air mail flights would be undertaken as above stated. The following flights were enumerated:

(1) Winnipeg, Manitoba, to Regina, leaving Winnipeg 9.15 a.m. and arriving Regina 12.15 p.m.

(2) Regina, Sask., to Calgary, Alta., leaving Regina promptly on arrival of plane from Winnipeg. Arriving Calgary 4.15 p.m., in time to connect with westbound trains from that point.

(3) Regina, Sask., to Edmonton, Alta., via Saskatoon leaving Regina promptly on arrival of plane from Winnipeg, arriving Edmonton 5.15 p.m.

(4) Edmonton, Alta., to Regina, via Saskatoon, leaving Edmonton 7.00 a.m., arriving Regina 11.45 a.m.

(5) Calgary, Alta., to Regina, leaving Calgary 7.00 a.m., arriving Regina 11.30 a.m.

(6) Regina to Winnipeg, leaving Regina 12.00 noon, arriving Winnipeg 4.15 p.m. or in time to connect with eastbound and southbound mail trains.

Only first-class mail matter prepaid at the air mail rate of 5 cents for first ounce and 10 cents for each succeeding ounce or fraction thereof will be conveyed on these flights. Registered mail properly prepaid will be accepted for conveyance. Special delivery letters will also be carried if properly prepaid both as regards air mail postage and special delivery charge.

In order to commemorate the inauguration of the first

Cover No.	Cachet, Stamp, etc.	

official air mail services in the Prairie Provinces, the following special cachets will be used:

Winnipeg-Regina,	Saskatoon-Winnipeg,
Winnipeg-Calgary,	Regina-Calgary,
Winnipeg-Edmonton,	Regina-Edmonton,
Winnipeg-Saskatoon,	Regina-Winnipeg,
Calgary-Regina,	Regina-Saskatoon,
Calgary-Winnipeg,	Edmonton-Regina,
Saskatoon-Edmonton.	Edmonton-Winnipeg,
Saskatoon-Regina,	Edmonton-Saskatoon.

These special cachets will be used only on such covers as are sent to the different postmasters bearing Canadian postage at the air mail rate. All covers conveyed on these flights addressed to points beyond the terminus, will be placed in the ordinary mails at that point and will go forward in the ordinary way.

NEWFOUNDLAND AIR MAILS

1 N200 **Hawker Flight, May 18, 1919.**

This flight was an attempt to cross the Atlantic, in competition for the London Daily Mail prize. The 3c Caribou stamps were overprinted for use on correspondence carried by Hawker, Type AS1. 200 were overprinted. Of these 95 were used on letters, 18 were damaged and destroyed, 11 were used as presentation copies, and the remaining 76 were sold. The price of those sold was fixed at $25.00 each. The flight was attempted on May 18th, ending in failure. Hawker was rescued from the ocean after flying 1,100 miles. Most of the covers were damaged by water. The postmaster placed his initials "J.A.R." on the back of all stamps.

Flown Cover, ... 500.00

Stamps, unused, $500.00; used 450.00

(There is a forgery of the stamp in which "April" appears "APRIL."

2 **Capt. Raynham's Martinsyde Flight, May 18, 1919.**

Anxious to win the contest over Hawker, Raynham took off later in the same day, carrying 60 covers, most of which were franked with ordinary Newfoundland postage stamps. Three are known with the inscription in manuscript, "Aerial Atlantic Mail, J.A.R." This plane was partially wrecked in starting. It is believed that another lot of 25 letters was added to the mail bag in July. A second attempt again met with accident and the mail was finally carried to England by Capt. Raynham and delivered to the Post Office January 7, 1920. The covers are backstamped London, Jan. 7, 1920. A few covers bearing privately overprinted stamps were included in this mail, the overprint reading: "1st Atlantic—Air Post—Martinsyde—Raynham—Morgan." This was unauthorized, but several covers franked with these stamps came through in the regular way. The 1c, 2c, 3c and 24c values of the 1919 issue were so overprinted.

Covers (not flown) 60.00

a. With manuscript inscription on stamp 200.00

b. With unofficial 5-line overprint ....

Cover No.	Cachet, Stamp, etc.	

3 N201 **Alcock-Brown FIRST FLIGHT ACROSS THE ATLANTIC—June 14th, 1919.**

On June 14th Alcock and Brown took off from St. Johns, Newfoundland, landing in Ireland the next day. The mail was forwarded to London two days later. Covers bear the St. John's postmark of June 10th to 13th and the London receiving cancellation of June 18th. The stamps used were the 15c Scarlet Cabot, which had been overprinted "Trans-Atlantic Air Post 1919 ONE DOLLAR." As a token of appreciation of this flight, the British Government knighted Alcock (Sir John) and Brown was given important promotions.

Flown Cover 200.00
Stamps, unused (10,000) 8.00
a. No comma after "AIR POST" 12.00
b. No stop after "1919" 24.00

Handley-Page, June 15, 1919.

4 N201 A Handley-Page machine was ready for the trans-Atlantic hop, and on June 15th, 1919, an attempt was made. This was unsuccessful on account of engine trouble developing, and the machine returned. Covers may be distinguished by the St. John's postmark of June 9, 1919, 5 p.m., or Harbour Grace, A.M. June 14, 1919, either one or both of these postmarks appearing on the cover. Covers were stamped with the overprinted 15c Cabot.

Cover (not flown) 45.00

After deciding to abandon the trans-Atlantic flight, permission was given by the Postmaster-General to carry mail to the United States, the flight to terminate at Greenport, Long Island. Leaving Harbour Grace at 5 p.m. local time, for Long Island, the "Atlantic" was compelled to land at Parrsboro, Nova Scotia, at 5.30 a.m. the following morning, on account of a bursting oil tube. Dr. Robinson used every effort to have the Handley-Page trans-Atlantic mail transferred to the R-34 and flown to England on its return flight. The Handley-Page mail, however, missed connections and was forwarded to England by steamer.

5 **Handley-Page, Parrsboro, Nova Scotia, to Greenport, New York, Oct. 9, 1929.**

On October 9th, just before noon, the Handley-Page resumed the trip from Parrsboro, N.S., and at 11 o'clock that night landed at Greenport, Long Island, a distance of 800 miles in 11 hours and 5 minutes. A small mail was carried, franked with ordinary Canadian postage stamps and cancelled "PARRSBORO, N.S., A.M. OCT. 9, 1919."

Flown Cover 100.00

6 **St. John's-St. Anthony, Feb. 26, 1921.**

Major Cotton made several mail-carrying flights in 1921 and 1922. Covers were usually stamped "Per Aerial Mail." "AIR POST ST. ANTHONY" appears on covers carried on this flight.

Flown Cover (scarce) ....

Cover No. | Cachet, Stamp, etc.

7 **St. John's-St. Anthony (via Botwood), March 1, 1921.**
(200 carried.) This flight was unsuccessful and the mail was returned to St. John's. A special cachet, "Air Post St. Anthony" in black, was used.
Cover 3.00

8 **St. John's-Fogo via Botwood, March 28, 1921.**
A special cachet, "Airpost Fogo," was used. The flight was completed in 30 minutes. Covers are dated St. John's, Mar. 10, Fogo March 28th. 200 covers were carried.
Flown Cover 4.00

9 **Botwood-Halifax, November, 1921.**
A total of 14,000 of the 35c Red Cabot stamps were overprinted "AIR MAIL-Halifax, N.S.-1921" for a mail-carrying flight from Botwood, Newfoundland, to Halifax, Nova Scotia. Attempts were made in December, 1921, and January, 1922, to make the flight, the mail consisting of 5,000 letters. The covers were afterwards mailed by the ordinary route.
Covers 4.00
Cover franked with stamp, no stop after "1921" (10 in sheet) 6.00
Cover franked with stamp with stop after "1921" (4 in sheet) 7.00
No stop after "1921" (2 in sheet) 8.50

STAMPS.
35c Cabot, overprinted, unused $3.00, used 3.00
Inverted surcharge, unused 75.00
(For minor varieties see Catalogue Section, B.N.A. Book.)

10 **St. Anthony, Apr. 20, 1922.**
Major Cotton carried a few covers from St. Anthony on the above date, stamped "Per Aerial Mail" in magenta with "Post Office-Apr. 20, 1922-St. Anthony, Nf'l'd." in a rectangle. (*Scarce.*)

11 **St. John's-Cartwright, Labrador, Feb. 8, 1923.**
The flight was held up at Botwood and continued May 16th, arriving at Cartwright same day. Covers are postmarked "Cartwright, May 16, 23, Newf'd." The return trip was made on May 17th, receiving cancellation at St. John's 2.30 p.m. and "AERIAL MAIL" in heavy type on face of cover.
Flown Covers 30.00

12 **St. John's (Trepassey) to Rome, Pinedo, Flight, May 23, 1927.**

Notes by Harry E. Huber in Mekeel's Weekly

Col. Francesco de Pinedo started on his four-continent flight at Cagliari, Italy, February 13th, 1927, and flew to Africa and South America; thence to the United States via Haiti and Cuba. At Roosevelt Lake, Arizona, his plane was burned, and another craft was sent out to replace it. In this, the "Santa Maria II," he flew over eastern and

Cachet,
Cover Stamp,
No. etc.

southern United States, and across Canada to Quebec, leaving there on Wednesday morning, May 18, 1927, for Shippegan, New Brunswick.

In the St. John's, Newfoundland, daily papers of May 18th, there appeared the following Post Office Notice relative to a limited air mail which it was planned to despatch to Italy and the neighboring countries, by Col. de Pinedo's plane:

"Post Office Notice. Air Mail Per De Pinedo via Trepassey, Newfoundland. A limited number of letters, not exceeding 1 ounce in weight, prepaid with a sixty-cent Newfoundland postage stamp, endorsed 'Via Air Mail,' will be accepted at the General Post Office, and forwarded to Trespassey, for transmission by Air Mail to Italy, up to 5 p.m. Thursday, 19th inst. Letters for this despatch should be handed into the Minister of Posts' Office (Upper Flat, G.P.O.) between the hours of 10 a.m. and 5 p.m. It would be advisable for senders to have their address noted on back of letter. The despatch of this mail is subject to consent and courtesy of Commander Francesco de Pinedo. Signed, W. J. Woodford, Minister, Post and Telegraphs, G.P.O., May 18, 1927."

For the prepayment of postage on this air mail, the Minister of Posts and Telegraphs authorized the overprinting, in red, of 300 of the 60c black Cabot series of 1897, in three lines:

These stamps were sold only to those presenting letters for inclusion in the air mail and as the mail was limited in weight (approximately 3 lbs., 255 letters) many were disappointed. Most of the stamps were purchased on the 18th May, and the few remaining were sold the next morning.

The 60c Cabot was considered the most appropriate for overprinting, as the stamp portrays King Henry VII, by whom letters patent were granted on March 5, 1497, to John Cabot (a native of Genoa), and his three sons, to take possession on behalf of England of any new lands which they might discover.

In the mail was an official communication from the Prime Minister, Hon. W. S. Monroe, addressed to H. E. Benito Mussolini, Premier and Minister of Foreign Affairs, Italy.

"Prime Minister's Office, St. John's, Newfoundland, May 19, 1927. Your Excellency: Your great country, already associated with Newfoundland, through the discovery of our Island by John Cabot, of Genoa, in 1497, is again linked with Newfoundland by the glorious air flight of Commander Pinedo.

"I take advantage of this first and historic Air Mail between Newfoundland and Italy to extend to your Excellency, and through you to Their Majesties and the people of Italy, cordial greetings and sentiments of friendship and goodwill, from the people of Newfoundland.

"Commander Pinedo carries with him our sincere concern for his safety, and the hope that he may successfully finish his historic journey. (Signed) W. S. Monroe, Prime Minister."

Cover No.	Cachet, Stamp, etc.

The mail was sent down to Trepassey, by rail, on the morning of Friday, May 20th, and at 6 o'clock that afternoon, just a few hours before Capt. Chas. A. Lindbergh passed over Newfoundland on his historic non-stop flight of 33½ hours from New York to Paris, the "Santa Maria II" arrived at Trepassey Bay, on the southern coast of the Avalon peninsula, about 80 miles south of St. John's, having flown from Shippegan, N.B., in five hours.

At 2.58 a.m. Eastern daylight saving time, on Monday, May 23, 1927, they took off for Rome, via the Azores, passing over St. John's, at 3.12 a.m. But later in the day, unable to make headway against the strong winds, and gas running low, it was necessary to alight on the ocean about 200 miles north of their objective. Near the landing spot was the three-master Portuguese fishing schooner "Infanta Sagres," bound for the Grand Banks, which rescued the aviators and took the plane in tow. On the 26th, the schooner was relieved by the Italian S.S. Superga, and the machine and crew were brought into port at Horta, in the Azores, Monday morning, May 30th.

Repairs were made and on June 10th the flight was continued; first flying from Horta to the place where the plane was forced down, and then to Ponta Delagada, so as to retain the continuity of the flight. Leaving Ponta Delagada on the 11th, they arrived at Lison that afternoon; at Barcelona on the 13th; and the final leg to Italy was accomplished on the 16th, landing at Ostia, at the mouth of the Tiber, 15 miles from Rome.

The overprint is in red in three lines, "Air Mail" (initial caps only) measuring 13mm, "De Pinedo" (all caps) 17½mm, and "1927," 7mm. The overall height from the bottom of "1927" to the top of "M" of "Mail" is 10mm.

On covers the overprinted stamp is cancelled by one of the electric postmarking machines at the G.P.O., St. John's, a single lined circle (21mm) lettered "St. John's N'fld.—1927" around the inside, with the date and hour in two lines in the center, 'May 20-10-A.M." At the right is a flag of seven wavy lines, with the fourth one cut short at the left and the numeral "1" inserted. On the face also is the cancellation of "Trepassey, Newf'd" (in circular form but without the usual outer circle), with the date in the center in two lines, "My 21-27."

I have seen two covers, addressed to the Postmaster at Rome, which have face markings as above described for St. John's and Trepassey. These have the handstamping on the back, "Roma Centro Corrispondenze Ordinairie" in a single lined circle, 31mm, with the date across the center in a single line "15.6.-27.10." This is evidently an error, as Commander de Pinedo did not arrive at Ostia until the afternoon of June 16th.

Two other covers, addressed in care of a business house in Liverpool, England, have face markings of St. John's and Trepassey as above, but on the back above the electric machine (not handstamp) cancellation of "Roma Centro" between two concentric circles, 25 and 15mm, with the dating

Cover No.	Cachet, Stamp, etc.

in three lines in the center, "19-20-22. VI-1927," and to the right the five line advertising slogan, within a single lined frame (50x22mm) "Le Piu Belle Terme—Del Monde—Salsomaggiore—Periodo di cura—Marzo-Novembre." Owing to the fact that the British P.O. Department abolished some years ago (just as in the U.S.) the practice of backstamping, there is no evidence to show that delivery of these letters was effected in Liverpool, on June 24th or 25th.

In addition to the air mail bearing the overprinted 60c Cabot stamp, a small supplementary mail, of approximately 75 letters, with 60c Cabot stamps not overprinted, was also conveyed by Commander de Pinedo from Trepassey, Nfld., to Ostia, Italy.

These do not have the face marking of St. John's and the Trepassey cancellation (My 21-27) appears alongside but not on the stamp. On receipt at Rome, the 60c Cabot stamp was handstamp cancelled "Roma Centro Corrispondenze Ordinarie" with the date across the centre in one line, "22.6.27.17."

On the back is the electric machine cancellation (and the advertising slogan), described above, but with the dating given as "16-17-22.VI—1927."

Twenty of these letters were sent in care of the American Consul at Rome, and are backstamped additionally in purple, 'American Consulate-General—June 23, 1927—Rome, Italy" within a single lined horizontal rectangle, measuring 2 in. x 1 in.

The sending of this supplementary mail, with the ordinary 60c overprinted stamp, was done principally to satisfy some business people of St. John's, who had presented letters for the mail, after the overprinted stamps had been disposed of. There was complaint that sufficient time had not been given in which to prepare letters for this mail, the advertisement having appeared in the daily papers of May 18th and the stamps having been completely sold out by the following morning.

As a matter of fact, it was not certain that the mail, even after it had been prepared, would be taken by Commander de Pinedo, and for this reason Mr. W. J. O'Neill, the Private Secretary of the Minister of Posts and Telegraphs, went down to Trepassey, with the air mail, to interview Commander de Pinedo on his arrival Friday evening, May 21st. In previous cases, Commander de Pinedo had refused to take a mail,—a case in point being that which the Postal Administration of Haiti, at Port au Prince, had prepared after receiving the assurance of the Italian Charge d'Affaires that a small mail would be accepted. Yet when Commander de Pinedo arrived he refused absolutely to take the mail prepared, claiming that he had always met with mishap when mail had been carried."

Flown Covers 175.00

a. With stamp not overprinted (approximately 75) ....

STAMPS.

60c Cabot, overprinted, unused 350.00

Vancouver Island

From June 20, 1864, to Nov. 1, 1865, (when replaced by a proper 3d stamp on the mainland—British Columbia—) the British Columbia and Vancouver's Island 2½d stamp was sold at Victoria Post Office for 3d and did duty as a 3d stamp on letters to New Westminster (3d rate) and inland British Columbia post offices (6d rate). The author has no knowledge of the quantity of 2½d stamps used from Vancouver Island between the above dates, but there is a record of 28 sheets having been purchased, July 20, 1865, from the British Columbia authorities.

The Colony of Vancouver Island changed from Pence Currency to Decimal Currency in 1862—about three years prior to the issue of the 5c and 10c stamps.

Records so far available show that the supply of 5c and 10c stamps received from the makers, Thos. De La Rue & Co., London, England, included both the Imperforate and the Perf. 14, and that these were issued in July 1865. Used copies of the Imperf. stamps have not been noted earlier than 1866. These were used from Victoria.

The Perforated 5c is found in a deep rose and a pale rose shade. The Imperf. 5c is known only in the deep rose shade.

(Readers are referred to notes on British Columbia Express Companies.)

The 5c and 10c stamps were engraved and printed in sheets of 240 (Perf. 14 by a single line machine) each sheet made up of four panes of 60 stamps each—six horizontal rows of ten stamps. The gum is white. In addition to the "Crown CC" watermark for each stamp there are marginal watermarks reading "Crown Colonies" up on the two right panes and down on the two left panes, and across the sheet, in the centre alley or gutter, as the space is known to the manufacturers.

On Nov. 19, 1866, the Colonies of Vancouver Island and British Columbia were consolidated as one territory, called British Columbia, after which date the current stamps of each colony were distributed and used throughout the combined territory.

British Columbia and Vancouver's Island

The British Columbia and Vancouver's Island stamp (2½d) was engraved and printed on thin hard wove paper of a yellowish tint, in sheets of 240 (Perf. 14 by a single line machine) by Thos. De La Rue & Co., London, each sheet made up of four panes of 60 stamps each—six horizontal rows of ten stamps. "Price: 2½d per Label, 1s 3d per Row of Six, 12.0.6d per Sheet of Sixty" appears in the left margin, reading up, and in the right margin reading down on the two left and right panes respectively, centered opposite the centre six stamps in the vertical rows. "Postage Two Pence Half-penny" in single line capitals extends across the panes at the bottom of the two top panes and at the top of the two lower panes. A control number appears opposite stamp No. 2 in the upper left pane, stamp No. 5 in the upper right, No. 56 in the lower left, and No. 59 in the lower right.

The shades vary from light brown and pale dull red to reddish rose and pink.

The stamp was issued for use jointly of the Colony of British Columbia and the Colony of Vancouver's Island, but was mostly used for inland postage in British Columbia.

The supply left London in December 1859 but the earliest known cover is dated July 30, 1860.

The imperf. copy in the Historical Archives at Victoria was purchased in London. The Ayer Collection contained six copies, including one copy which was thought to have been genuinely used, but no properly authenticated used copy is known. Hitt states that these are reprints which never went to the Colony officially. It is quite possible that they did reach the Colony unofficially and that copies could have been used inadvertently.

From June 20, 1864, to Nov. 1, 1865 (when a British Columbia 3d stamp made its appearance) the 2½d stamp was sold for 3d in the Post Offices of both Colonies and did duty as a 3d stamp on letters between British Columbia and Vancouver Island posted at Victoria or New Westminster. The author has no knowledge of the quantity of 2½d stamps used from Vancouver Island between these dates, but there is a record o 28 sheets having been purchased, July 20, 1865, from the British Columbia authorities.

British Columbia

A proclamation covering both Colonies (Vancouver Island and British Columbia), was issued May 4th, 1859, authorizing Express Companies to carry the mails. A charge of 5c or 2½d per letter was fixed. This went to the Colony. The payment of this charge was shown by the use of several types of rubber stamp franks. The Express Companies made their own charges in addition to the 2½d charge. The use of adhesives did not begin to supercede the use of stamped franks until 11th November, 1866, when the Colonies were combined and the stamps distributed for use in the combined territory called "British Columbia."

All stamps were engraved and printed in sheets of 240 by Thos. De La Rue & Co., London, England, each sheet made up of four panes of 60 stamps each—six horizontal rows of ten stamps.

In addition to the "Crown CC" watermark for each stamp there are marginal watermarks reading "Crown Colonies" up on the two right panes and down on the two left panes, and across the sheet in the centre alley or gutter, as the space is known to the manufacturers.

A control number appears opposite stamp No. 2 in the upper left pane, stamp No. 5 in the upper right, No. 56 in the lower left, and No. 59 in the lower right. Plate numbers are also shown.

The design for the 3d stamp is thought to have originated in the Colony. It was but slightly altered for the official issue. The 3d blue, and the same design in various colors with values surcharged, is on white wove paper. The second shipment of the 3d stamp (light blue, 1867) is on a thinner white wove paper. The gum is white in both cases.

The 3d stamp was accepted at a value of 6¼c in making up the 25c rate to distant inland points after March 13, 1867. The Postal Act of March 1867 gave new rates of postage computed in cents and accordingly a supply of 2c, 5c, 10c, 25c, 50c and $1 values had been ordered from London. To save expense the makers used the existing plate of the 3d, printing the supplies for each denomination in a distinctive color and then overprinting the value on the bottom of the stamp.

The 2c stamp was for the newspaper rate. Despite the large quantity sent to the Colony (2,115,600) the stamp is not common. Most of the copies used on newspapers were lost to collectors. The stamp, with other values, was on sale to dealers before being retired, the majority of the stamps being sold as unused remainders.

The 10c and $1 Perf. 14 were never issued to the Postal authorities in the Colony and are therefore not found in used condition. Although all the "remainders" in the Colony were destroyed, some small lots of stamps were kept as samples by the Crown Agents for the Colonies in London, and it is believed that there was a leakage from this source between 1897 and 1900. (Monthly Journal, Jan. 31, 1900, by C. J. Phillips). The stamps that then appeared were: 50 copies of 2½d imperforate; and between 50 and 75 each of the Perf. 14 10c red lilac and $1 green, and perf. 12½ $1 green. A few years later most other values perf. 14 turned up in small blocks, which Mr. Phillips believes were from the "Haslett" stock secured by Mr. H. Griebert. The Perf. 12½ stamps sent to the Colony were all issued and there were no remainders. A certain number of the 5c and 25c Perf. 14 were issued and used, but the great bulk of all these values were destroyed as remainders in 1871.

Mr. C. J. Phillips states that the Perf. 14 $1 was almost unobtainable in the old days and was missing in the finest collections. It came on the market about 1898 with the lot described above.

One-sixth of all the stamps Perf. 14 had a blank tab to the right or left side. There are no straight edges, though stamps are seen on original cover with these tabs cut off.

Hitt refers to an Imperf. 50c from the Ferrary collection, now owned by Mr. Lichtenstein, on which the margins are entirely satisfactory, although nothing is known of its origin. A second specimen came to light in 1924 and was examined by the same expert, who declared it genuine.

Forgeries:

The surcharged stamps have been cleverly forged. Album Weeds lists a forgery lithographed on stout yellowish paper, unsurfaced, perf. 12½, in which the v-shaped middle of the M of Columbia comes down level with the upright legs of the letter, and the G of Postage is a distinct C, the surcharge being well done.

The author has a set which first became known to him in 1926, although possibly of earlier date, in which the lithographing is remarkably well done, the colors almost identical, the perforations exactly 14, and the cancellation "35" an exact reproduction. The surcharging is poorly done and need not deceive anyone, with the exception of the TWO CENT stamp.

There is a "1 Dollar" forgery in which the word is spelled "Doller."

Prior to Jan. 17, 1869, the stamps of British Columbia were for use inland and between the Mainland and the Island. After that date rates to the United Kingdom, prepaid by these stamps, were established. At the same time rates were established to the United States, Canada, Prince Edward Island and Newfoundland, which could be prepaid by these stamps. These rates necessitated higher values up to One Dollar.

After the consolidation of the two Colonies, the current stamps of each colony were distributed and used throughout the combined territory. In 1871, after British Columbia became a Province in the Dominion of Canada (Confederation) all remainders were burned. A document certifying to the fact that these stamps had been burned and setting forth the number of each value so destroyed, was signed by the official sent to the Colony to perform this duty. These figures are not available to the author, but when published they will show collectors the quantities of these stamps actually used, by the simple expedient of subtracting the quantities burned from the quantities sent to the Colony. The publication of these figures will have a strong effect on the market value of British Columbia stamps, particularly the $1 which is more rare than collectors realize.

British Columbia ceased to be a Crown Colony on July 20, 1871, when she was admitted to the Dominion of Canada as one of the most important Provinces.

LIST OF EARLY POST OFFICES IN BRITISH COLUMBIA

(From "The Gazette" April 14, 1866)

Office	Postmaster
Antler	
New Westminster	W. R. Spalding, P.M.G.
Hope	A. S. Hall
Douglas	Richard White
Lillooet	T. H. Sharwood
Yale	L. Agassiz
Lytton	W. M. Cochran
Ashcroft (mail for Big Bend District forwarded)	C. F. Cornwall
Clinton	J. Champness
Lake La Hache	W. Anderson
Soda Creek	J. T. Sanay
Quesnelmouth	F. Mevor
Quesnelle	
Van Winkle	L. Cahn
William's Creek	
William's Lake	
Fort Shepherd	John Lane
Columbia River, Big Bend	
District	
Kootenay	

The following offices may be added as having been omitted from the above list or having been opened at a later date:

Barkerville	Hope	150 Mile House

Burrard Inlet	Kamloops	Sooke
Cache Creek	Langley	Spence's Bridge
Chemainas	Maple Bay	Sinnas
Comox	Nanaimo	Victoria
Cowichan	Nicola Lake	Skeena
Dunkeed	Okanagon	Chilliwack
Duck & Pringle's	Okanagon Mission	Pavillion
Esquimalt	Omineca	

POSTAL RATES FROM VANCOUVER ISLAND AND BRITISH COLUMBIA

The first Directory in the Colony, published in 1860, contained a table of rates of postage from the Colony to different countries, viz.:

Rates of Postage from Vancouver Island and British Columbia

Countries	Not over ¼ oz.	Not over ½ oz.	Payment
Aspinwall	...	20c	Compulsory
Australia, via England	...	48c	Compulsory
Austria	...	40c	Optional
Belgium, via France	26c	47c	Optional
British N. A. Provinces	...	20c	Optional
Cape of Good Hope	...	43c	Compulsory
Chili	...	39c	Compulsory
Cuba	...	25c	Compulsory
China, by private ship from San Francisco	...	15c	Compulsory
Denmark	...	45c	Optional
France	25c	50c	Optional
German States	...	40c	Optional
Great Britain and Ireland	...	34c	Optional
Greece	...	47c	Optional
Holland, via France	31c	57c	Optional
Mexico	...	25c	Compulsory
Norway	...	56c	Optional
Panama	...	25c	Compulsory
Peru	...	32c	Compulsory
Poland	...	47c	Optional
Portugal	...	68c	Compulsory
Prussia	...	40c	Optional
Russia	...	48c	Optional
Sandwich Islands	...	15c	Compulsory
Spain, via France	48c	...	Compulsory
Sweden	...	52c	Optional
Switzerland	...	48c	Optional
West Indies	...	30c	Compulsory

These rates include Colonial Postage of 5c on every half ounce. Prepayment was optional on the U.S. postage. The rates are in cents on account of the money circulating being U.S. currency.

In the Directory of 1863 there is a list of rates on letters and papers between nine offices. The charge on letters ranged from 5d to 4s, based on destination. Papers were carried for 2½d within a certain zone and 5d outside of that zone. Prepayment was compulsory. As at that date but one stamp (2½d) was available, it is obvious that as a general rule postage was prepaid in cash.

Rates Reduced in 1864

A considerable reduction was made in the rates as shown by a notice in the Gazette dated 8th June, 1864, as follows:

Between Br. Columbia and Vancouver Island, delivered at Victoria or New Westminster, for each letter under ½ ounce................ 3d
And for every additional ½ ounce or fractional excess.............. 3d
For each newspaper.. 1d
On all letters and papers to and from abroad, and delivered or mailed at New Westminster, in addition to foreign postage, for each letter under ½ ounce.. 3d
And for every additional ½ ounce or fractional excess.............. 3d
For each newspaper.. 1d
Between a Post Office at any one place in the Colony and a Post Office at any other place in the Colony, in all cases to be prepaid, for each letter under ½ ounce.. 6d
And for every additional ½ ounce or fractional excess.............. 6d
For each Newspaper.. 6d

N.B. Parcels or Packages other than newspapers, and not exceeding 8 ounces in weight, will be charged at the letter rate of 6d per ½ ounce. No parcels can be taken exceeding eight ounces in weight.

(Sgd.) Warner R. Spalding, P.M.G.

It will be noted that the rates were 3d and 6d and multiples of these amounts, but the only stamp available was the 2½d stamp. Three days after the promulgation of the above Notice another one was published which gave the 2½d stamp the value of 3d. This notice read:

"On and after the 20th day of June, 1864, all letters and mail matter liable to postage must be prepaid. Until other stamps shall have been substituted, there will be issued for the prepayment of postage the postage stamps at present in use, bearing the mark 2½d, for which the sum of 3d will in future be charged.

(Sgd.) Warner R. Spalding, P.M.G., General Post Office, 11th June, 1864."

As there was no 1d stamp for the prepayment of the newspaper rate' the charge on newspapers had to be paid in cash.

The proper 3d stamp was issued in November 1865. An Official Notice concerning this stamp appeared in the Gazette, as follows:

"General Post Office, 28th Sept., 1865. It having been found necessary to issue a new postage stamp to meet the requirements of the Postal Ordinance 1864, notice is hereby given that, from and after the 1st of Nov. next, the stamp at present in use will not be received by the Post Office Department. Persons in possession of the stamp at present in use may exchange the same, on application at any of the Post Offices of British Columbia, on or after the 1st of November. (Sgd.) Warner R. Spalding, Postmaster-General."

Changes in Rates for Decimal Currency

When the currency was changed in 1867 a series of six stamps was issued and changes were made in the postal rates.

On March 20, 1867, and Act was passed changing the currency to the decimal system of dollars and cents. The following clauses are taken from a new Postal Ordinance Act which became law March 13th, 1867:

"........that on every letter deposited in or passing through any Post Office in the Colony, and not exceeding ½ oz. in weight, there shall be paid a postage according to the following scale:

At or between Victoria, or any Post Office in Vancouver Island, and New Westminster, or any Port in the Colony........ 5 Cents

Between Vancouver Island or New Westminster and Clinton, or Savana's Ferry.......................................12½ Cents

Beyond those distances.................................. 25 Cents
Between any two Post Offices above Yale, Hope and Douglas. 12½ Cents"

A substantial reduction in rates was brought about in 1868, but in 1869 a new list of foreign postal rates was issued in which the charges were increased in many cases. The rates given in the Directory of 1869 are the last rates published prior to the entry of the Colony into the Dominion of Canada in 1871.

Additional postage was charged for every additional half ounce or fraction thereof.

On every single newspaper deposited in or passing through any post office in the Colony the rate was 2c.

From the above it would appear that there was a demand for a 12½c stamp, but no such value was issued.

Poole, in his excellent handbook (Mekeel's Weekly) points out that there were no copper coins in the Colony and one could not spend less than 5c. It would therefore seem that the 12½c rate was prepaid by three 5c stamps or a 5c and a 10c stamp.

Specimens:

Specimens are very rare, but are known to exist in two types on nearly all stamps.

QUANTITIES ISSUED

2½d	Dull rose.......	235,440	10c	Perf. 12½.......	4,800
3d	Deep blue......	111,360		Perf. 14.........	241,920
	Light blue......	1,063,440	25c	Perf. 12½.......	4,800
2c	Brown.........	2,115,600		Perf. 14.........	475,280
5c	Perf. 12½......	4,800	50c	Perf. 12½.......	4,800
	Perf. 14........	244,320		Perf. 14.........	571,760
			$1	Perf. 12½.......	4,800
				Perf. 14.........	117,600

Quantities Destroyed

On August 26th, 1871, Gilbert E. Griffin, an Inspector from the P.O. Department, Ottawa, destroyed by fire, all stamps remaining, as follows:

5c....................	146,400	10c..................	120,000
25c....................	451,680	50c..................	508,080
$1....................	117,600		

Including both 14 and 12½ Perf.

The official document, with samples of each of the above stamps attached thereto, with the above amounts certified as having been destroyed by Mr. Griffin, is now in the collection of Mr. A. F. Lichtenstein.

Quantities Used

The following figures are obtained by subtraction. These figures will not be an accurate guide to relative rarity, however, as the class of mail on which the stamp was used is an important factor. While the $1 is the scarcest stamp, the 10c comes next, although the figures show four times as many used as the 25c. A possibly explanation is that the 10c stamp was used largely on mail to mining camps and fewer survived.

2½d	235,440	5c Vancouver	114,000
10c Vancouver	111,360	3d	1,174,800
2c	2,115,600	5c	102,720
10c	126,720	25c	28,400
50c	68,480	$1	4,800

Rarities

Under this heading will be listed any outstanding philatelic item which may come to the author's attention through sale by auction, private purchase or personal knowledge.

Description

2½d Perf. 14, Full sheet of four panes. Part of the "Mayfair Find" of 1925 auctioned by the Bond Street Auction Rooms, London, and purchased by A. F. Lichtenstein.

3d Imperf. Pair, mint, ?.
3d Perf., Mint and Used Blocks of Four, owned by A. F. Lichtenstein.
3d Used Block of Four from two severed pairs, purchased from Lincoln in London, by Fred Jarrett, 1927.
2½d Imperf. Block of Four.
2c Pane of 60, collection of A. F. Lichtenstein.
50c Imperf. Block of Four. A. F. Lichtenstein.

Early Mail Carriers

In British Columbia and Vancouver Island

(Much of the information which follows is from Poole's Handbook)

Hudson's Bay Company.

Victoria existed as a Hudson's Bay Post in 1844 (then called Fort Camousan). In 1849 a lease was granted to the Hudson's Bay Company for colonizing purposes. The mainland had been leased previously to the same Company for trading purposes. In compliance with the charter, the "Norman Morrison" arrived at Esquimalt (adjacent to Victoria) in March 1850 with 80 immigrants. These were under engagement to serve the Hudson's Bay Company for five years, receiving £25 per annum with food and lodging. The "Norman Morrison", five and a half months at sea—the usual time—brought a mail from England for the Muirs, the coal miners at Fort Rupert, and Capt. Grant and his retinue at Sooke, these having come out a few months previously. The ship sailed for England after a few months.

This annual visit of the Hudson's Bay ship does not mean that the Colony received but one mail per year. In 1849 the California gold rush took place, bringing thousands to the Coast and necessitating a mail service on the part of the United States Government, which was soon extended to Oregon and Puget Sound. Victoria therefore had facilities for communicating other than the annual Hudson's Bay ship. It will be remembered, too, that from the foundation of the Colony coastwise shipping called at Victoria and would carry mail.

In March 1850, H.M.S. Dover brought to the Colony Governor Blanchard, and with him, doubtless, a mail for the colonists.

British Columbia depended almost entirely on the postal service of the United States for communication with outside points. It is true that a Hudson's Bay Brigade crossed the continent annually from Hudson's Bay to Fort Vancouver on the Columbia, carrying dispatches and letters, but these had to do with Company's business or were private communications between friends in the service.

About 1850 communications between Victoria and the mainland of British Columbia became more frequent. J. W. McKay had charge of the service. A canoe would leave Victoria carrying dispatches for Nesqually, where Dr. Tolmie had charge. Tolmie sent the dispatch box or bag on horseback to the Hudson's Bay Post at Cowlitz River; from there it was forwarded to Fort Vancouver and thence the letters went by any suitable conveyance occurring to their destination.

In the reply of the Legislative Assembly to the request of Governor Douglas, in April 1857, for a Post Office, the Govenrment acknowledged its debt to the Hudson's Bay Company as follows: "The Assembly acknowledge the Colony to be under great obligations to the Hudson's Bay Company for the kind and liberal manner in which they have carried gratuitously the letters from the American shores to this island."

Government Post Office at Victoria.

On April 21, 1857, Governor Douglas recommended to the Legislative Assembly that means should be provided for initiating a postal service. At that time the business of the General Post Office was being transacted within a public building and letters were exposed under conditions that were not seemed safe. To be exact, the letters were kept in the office of the Hudson's Bay Company accountant, Mr. Finlayson.

Notwithstanding the fact that the Legislative Assembly replied that "the letters were so few that they would not pay one-tenth part of the contemplated outlay" and that there were no funds to establish a Post Office, Governor Douglas appointed Captain Sangster as Postmaster, who occupied as an office a small house built by Mr. Yates in the Fort yard. At this date the canoe service to the mainland had been supplemented by a schooner or more, including Jimmy Jones' "Wild Pigeon" and later the American steamer "Major Tomkins" which was shortly wrecked at the entrance of the harbor.

Barnard's Carbiboo Express.

From November 1861 to about 1868 Barnard operated a local express carrying packages and letters. Twenty-five varieties of franked envelopes were issued, some on U.S. stamped envelopes and some combined with Wells, Fargo Co. printed franks. Typeset adhesives were also used, in nearly forty varieties or types. There are dangerous counterfeits. There is a circular handstamp which is quite rare.

The "Paid" or "Collect" labels printed in black on colored paper were pasted on letters and packages by the company's employees in conjunction with the 2½d British Columbia and Vancouver Island stamps.

The hand press on which the labels were printed was the first to be brought into the district, and is now in the museum of Saint Ann's Academy, Victoria.

Dietz & Nelson's British Columbia and Victoria Express:

About 1868 Barnard was succeeded by the firm of Dietz & Nelson, which firm used several labels, printed in black on glazed vermilion paper, used in conjunction with British Columbia stamps. Between 1862 and 1868 Dietz & Nelson operated from Victoria to British Columbia, using envelopes with their printed frank. They also used a circular handstamp which is found obliterating British Columbia stamps. Hitt mentions four adhesives. One of these was inscribed "Dietz & Nelson's B. C. & V.— Express From Victoria" with small vignettes depicting a steamer and railroad train between the second and third lines. The others, slightly differing in type, are inscribed in four lines.

Forwarded by
Dietz's and Nelson's
British Columbia and Victoria
Express

Upper Columbia Co. Used a perforated label in pink reading "U.C. Co. 5c" with typeset border.

Freeman and Gerow & Johnson are listed as mail carriers but details are not available.

Wells, Fargo & Co.

The sudden influx of a mining population following the discovery of gold on the Pacific Coast, brought with it the Express Companies that handled transportation and mails, for which they issued their own franks, printed envelopes and adhesives. In 1858 the Fraser River gold excitement occurred and steamers brought passengers up the Coast in thousands. Many of the private Express Companies in California and Oregon extended their activities to include British Columbia and Vancouver Island, where the Government had been slow in establishing post routes and postal services were uncertain at best with no provision for carrying valuables in the mails.

In July, 1858, Wells Fargo & Co. established an Express in Victoria, operating on Vancouver Island, and on the mainland through other companies.

Envelopes were sold with the Company's title on them. There were no stamps, but when the supply was received later these Wells, Fargo envelopes had to bear a local stamp. American stamps could be obtained at their office.

After 1860 the United States mail steamer came to Victoria once and subsequently twice a week. The San Francisco boat every month or oftener. This boat received a subsidy from the Colonial Government. The continuance of this boat service became one of the terms of Confederation, so important was it considered.

The wells, Fargo Co. took the envelopes in quantity to the Post Office and paid the postage in cash, and the Post Office then stamped these Wells, Fargo Co. envelopes with its official seal. There were two types of this seal, one a circle enclosing a crown, and inscription.

The following is from an article by E. L. Pemberton in Stamp Collector's Magazine for Sept. 1, 1869:

"Wells, Fargo & Co. have offices throughout the North American British Territory of British Columbia and Vancouver Island. As the English law will not allow Wells, Fargo & Co. to carry letters they affix the government stamps upon their own franked envelopes, have the stamps cancelled at the Post Office, and then forward them in their own conveyances. For this reason they charge for every letter to or from the English possession 5 cents, in coin, additional to their rates, to pay the colonial government postage. Hence we find letters coming to England from British Columbia, per Wells, Fargo & Co., show the United States embossed stamp, Wells, Fargo & Co's. printed frank, and the British Columbia 5c."

Before the introduction of postage stamps the envelopes of Wells, Fargo & Co. were passed by the Post Office by being stamped "Post Office Victoria, V.I., in blue, oval form with Royal Arms in centre. This was also used for a cancellation at first.

British Columbia and Victoria Express Company:

This Company used envelopes with the Company name printed along the top, and along the bottom, in captials "PAID FROM VICTORIA TO LYTTON OR LILOOET", etc. The envelopes were franked by the Government Post Office with a handstruck frank in black.

Ballou's Pioneer Fraser River Express.

Ballou & Co's Cariboo Express, Paid.

Ballou's Pioneer Fraser River Express operated between New Westminster (and probably Hope) from June 1858 to the fall of 1859 when Jaffray took over the business. It was subsequently subsidized by Barnard and continued until October 1862. Franked envelopes were used.

In February 1928 an unusual item came to the attention of philatelists, an unused Ballou's Pioneer Fraser River Express envelope franked with the New Westminster postmark frank in red.

Ballou & Co's Cariboo Express used their own envelopes, franked with a fancy oblong frame woodcut with rounded corners, and bearing the handstamp frank in red "New Westminster, British Columbia, Post Office."

Pioneer Line Fraser River Steamers.

John Irving operated the Pioneer Line of Fraser River Steamers, carrying mail from New Westminster to Sumas and other points. A cover in the author's collection dated Ja 18 '81 is back-stamped in pale violet "Pioneer Line, Fraser River Steamers" in double-lined circle, the date appearing "Jan. 18, 1881" across the centre with an ornament above.

A1

BRITISH COLUMBIA & VANCOUVER ISLAND, 1860. Imperforate.

No Watermark.

				Unused.	Used.
1	*A1*	2½d	Pale dull red	150.00	
			July 30, 1860. Perf. 14, no watermark.		
2		2½d	Deep reddish rose	15.00	20.00
		2½d	Pale reddish rose		
			On Cover $40.00.		
			(235,440 of both Imperforate and Perforate were printed.)		
			From June 20th 1864 to November 1st 1865 the 2½d was sold for 3d and did duty as a 3d stamp.		

A2

Vancouver Island.

				Unused.	Used.
			July 1865. Watermark Crown CC, **Imperf.**		
1	*A2*	5c	Rose	750.00	475.00
			On cover $600.00.		
			Perf. 14.		
2		5c	Rose or Pale Rose	15.00	15.00
			On cover $25.00.		
			a. Inverted watermark		
			(Of both Imperf. and Perf. 14 114,000 were printed.)		

July, 1865. Watermark Crown CC, **Imperf.**

No.	Type.			Unused.	Used.
3		10c	Blue	125.00	90.00
			On cover 125.00.		
			Perf. 14.		
4		10c	Blue	16.00	16.00
			a. Inverted watermark	*20.00*	*20.00*
			On cover $25.00.		
			(Of both Imperf. and Perf. 14 111,360 were printed).		
			Other Vancouver Island Covers:		
			June 20th, 1864 to Nov. 1st, 1865 Perf. 14.		
	A1	2½d	Dull Rose used from Vancouver Island, with identifying postmarks		
		5c	Rose, Imperf		600.00
		5c	Rose, Perf. on cover to inland points dated prior to August, 1866		50.00
		5c	Rose, Perf. 14, on cover to New Westminster, Capital of British Columbia, dated prior to Aug., 1866		
		10c	Blue, Perf. 14, to inland points dated prior to August, 1866		
		10c	Blue, Perf. 14, to New Westminster, capital of British Columbia, prior to August, 1866		

A3

A4

A5

No.	Type.			Unused.	Used.
			British Columbia.		
			Nov. 1, 1865. Watermark Crown CC, Perf. 14, on White wove paper.		
1	*A3*	3d	Deep blue (*111,360*)	9.00	9.00
			1867. Thinner White wove paper.		
2		3d	Light blue (1,063,440)	3.00	4.00
			a. Inverted watermark		
			b. Imperf		*100.00*
			On cover, $25.00; Pair, $10.00; Block 4	*25.00*	*150.00*
			The 3d stamps printed in various colors and surcharged for different decimal values.		
			Perf. 14, November, 1867.		
3	*A4*	2c	Brown, black surcharge (2,115,600)	2.50	7.50
			On cover, $25.00; Block 4	*17.50*	
			Perf. 14, April, 1869.		
4	*A5*	5c	Pale red *Black surch.* (244,320)	10.00	10.00
5		10c	Lake *Blue surch.* (241,920)	50.00	

No.	Type.			Unused.	Used.
6		25c	Yellow *Violet surcharge* (475,280).......	8.00	8.00
			a. Orange yellow, violet surcharge.......		
			On cover, $20.00; block 4..............	50.00	
7		50c	Mauve, red surcharge (*571,760*)........	17.50	
			a. Mauve, imperf....................		
8		$1	Pale green, *green surcharge* (*117,600*)....	60.00	
			Perf. 12½. April, 1869. (*4,800 of each value.*)		
9		5c	Pale red, *black surch*..................	50.00	50.00
10		10c	Lake, *blue surch*.....................	50.00	50.00
11		25c	Yellow, *violet surch*..................	50.00	50.00
12		50c	Mauve, *red surch*....................	50.00	50.00
13		$1	Pale green, *green surch*................	60.00	75.00

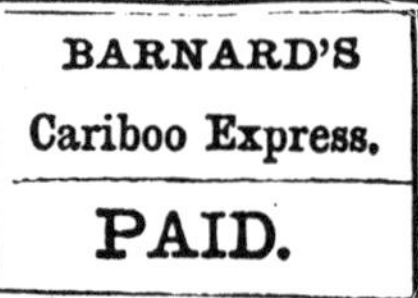

A6

A7

BARNARD'S
Cariboo Express.
COLLECT.

A8

No.	Type.			Unused.	Used.
2	*A6*		Red, imperf.........................		25.00
3	*A7*		Red, imperf.........................		25.00
4	*A8*		Green, imperf.......................		40.00
			(There are nearly forty varieties. Beware of dangerous forgeries.)		
			British Columbia Covers.		
		2½d	Dated earlier than June 20, 1864.......		35.00
		2½d	Between British Columbia and Vancouver Island delivered at Victoria or New Westminster prepaid with 2½d between June 20th, 1864 and Nov. 1st, 1865..............................		100.00
			(*During this period the 2½d was sold as a 3d stamp—see notes.*)		

(A) Specimen.

(B) Essay.

Nearly all the stamps of this Colony are known with "Specimen" as above, in two

No.	Type.		Unused.	Used.
		types. The author would be glad to know of any collections containing these.		
A	2½d	Imperf. Specimen in black, diagonally reading down........................ (dark shade)		50.00
?	2c	Color of issue on heavy paper..........		
?	5c	Perf. 12½ overprinted "Cancelled".....		
B	3d	Essay................................ *Die proofs are known, in trial colors.*		

NEW BRUNSWICK

The pence stamps were engraved and printed by Messrs. Perkins, Bacon & Co., London. The design shows the Royal Crown and Heraldic Flowers of the United Kingdom. The paper is a medium soft wove with a bluish tint. Each sheet consisted of 160 stamps

Remainders.

The Postmaster General's report for 1859 says, in reference to the Pence Issue remainders, "The principal part of those remaining on hand are unfit for sale, having been damaged by being stored in the vault which was so damp as to cause them to mould and the color to run."

3d Watermarked.

The watermark is a large double-lined 3 in one instance and double-lined letter H in another, these specimens possibly being unique. It is thought that paper used for printing the stamps of another colony accidentally became mixed with that used for printing the New Brunswick stamps.

1s.

The early impressions (there was probably but one printing) are pinkish-mauve in shade and are listed as "bright violet." The later impressions are in darker shade of mauve or dull violet and are less rare. 50,000 New Brunswick shilling stamps were ordered as compared with 250,000 for Nova Scotia.

"Cents Issue."

Engraved and printed by the American Bank Note Co., New York, in sheets of 100, 10 rows of 10. The imprint, in small type, appears on the four sides. Three distinct papers may be noted, as follows:

A. Medium white wove, for all values.

B. Medium yellowish wove for 10c (less common).

C. Finely ribbed soft white for 1c, 10c, 12½c and 17c. This paper is quite rare.

Remainders of the "Cents" Issue.

The great majority of the unused stamps of this issue are noted without gum. They are remainders which became soaked when the St. John Customs House in which they were stored was damaged by fire.

1c

The 1c stamp is noted with double perforations between horizontal pair.

Variety.

5c

An outstanding variety occurs once to each sheet (No. 60) of the 5c consisting of what may be named a "long pendant" from left ear, caused doubtless by an engraving tool having dropped on the plate.

The double impression variety of the 5c is the result of faulty press work and is not a plate variety.

10c

A double impression variety similar to the 5c is noted, but this is not a plate variety.

It is possible to locate re-entries in which there is a distinct doubling of the left frame line.

The fine lines with which the plate was ruled off before starting to make the impressions are traceable in many stamps.

Connell 5c Brown.

Charles Connell, Postmaster-General of New Brunswick, authorized the issue of the 5c stamp bearing his portrait, and the stamps were printed, but owing to severe criticism they were never placed on sale. The stamp was replaced by one bearing the portrait of Queen Victoria. A few copies were retained as souvenirs when the stock was destroyed, and some are known postally used. It is my personal opinion that a check up of the number of postally used copies in existence, would cause the experts to completely revise the many pretty tales that are told about this stamp,

6d used in combination with 1c and 3c U.S., 1851. (*Lichtenstein Collection*).

all tending to enhance its rarity. For a stamp of which the Postmaster General retained a copy for himself, and presented an odd one to his close personal friends, the stamp comes up too frequently in auctions. The Ayer collection contained three unused and one used, and I have the temerity to suggest that all the leading collections of today contain one or more copies, used or unused. As will be noted, the stamp comes on the market repeatedly.

Beware of forgeries, and proofs that have been mounted and perforated.

The re-entry is similar to that illustrated for the 12d Canada, appearing as triple corners, due to false impressions of the transfer roll.

"Bisecteds" by Donald A. King.

"I have been unable to find any official notice in the Royal Gazette authorizing the use of any of these mutilated stamps; but an interesting article, published in the Philatelic Record for October, 1886, clearly shows the reason for the bisection of the 3d. As the article points out, no half specimen of this value is known used by itself, but the variety is always found in connection with other 3d stamps or a 6d stamp. The paper then goes on to say that the half stamp was used to make up the letter rate to England, which was 6d Sterling the ½ oz., equal to 7½ Cy., or for letters forwarded via the United States and British Packet, 8d Sterling, equal to 10d Cy. I have found that the former rate was in existence on May 1, 1856, and it had probably been in use some time previous to that date. The latter rate came into operation on Jan. 1, 1857. Besides the letter rates to England we learn from the following notice published in the Royal Gazette for Sept. 16, 1857, that two of the new rates on Pamphlets, mentioned therein, could only be made up by using half of the 3d stamp with other values.

> "On and after the 1st day of October next the following will be the rates on Pamphlets sent from N.B. to Great Britain via Halifax, viz., for a packet, not exceeding 4 oz. in weight, 3d Stg. 4d Cy.
>
> For a packet exceeding 4 oz. and not exceeding half a pound, 6d Stg. 7½d Cy.
>
> For a packet exceeding half a pound and not exceeding one pound, 1s Stg. 1s 3d Cy.

And so on, increasing 7½d Cy. for every additional ½ lb. or fraction.

There was no stipulation that the above rates must necessarily be prepaid, and I have no doubt from the following notice, which was published in the British Postal Guide for October 1, 1859, that correspondence between the United Kingdom and all the North American Colonies was frequently forwarded either wholly or only partly prepaid from both sides.

"Letters for Nova Scotia, New Brunswick, and Newfoundland, if posted unpaid or insufficiently prepaid, are now charged on delivery with a fine of 6d. each in addition to the postage."

"This addition of a fine of 6d upon unpaid or insufficiently prepaid letters would naturally cause senders to be anxious to see that their correspondence was properly stamped, and consequently a good many more cut stamps would be required after the appearance of this notice, which no doubt was published in New Brunswick the same as in Nova Scotia. We should therefore expect to find a greater number of half 3d stamps postmarked after Oct. 1, 1859, than previously. As regards the bisection of the 6d and 1s value, there was not the same reason; but the varieties are probably due to one or perhaps both of these causes (a) the public seeing the 3d allowed to be used in this way may have concluded the two other stamps might be similarly employed and not having the value required at the moment manufactured it out of either the 6d or 1s (b) or it may be that certain offices fell short of 3d and 6d stamps and issued the halves of the two other values provisionally until a fresh supply of the required value as obtained."

Bisecteds of the "Cents" issue.

Owing to the Connell stamp being discredited, no 5c stamp was available when the issue was put in circulation in May, 1860. Pending the preparation of a new plate the public had to make up the 5c rate by using 1c stamps, an inconvenience which was surmounted by halving the 10c stamp and using the half as a 5c stamp. Both vertical and diagonal halves are known, the vertical being the rarer. Bogus splits of this nature were made up by two young collectors named Coombs in St. John, N.B., in 1892 and the early part of 1893.

The 5c rate was also made by using two 2c and a diagonal half of another. But long before the 2c stamp made its appearance there was a plentiful supply of 5c stamps and no necessity existed for such a provisional. It is possible that this variety was made for collectors, but we must remember that the custom of using bisected stamps had been countenanced by the authorities for some time and such a provisional might therefore have done postal duty in a regular manner.

Parcels Post.

New Brunswick was one of the first, if not *the* first colony to inaugurate a Parcels Post. The following is from the Royal Gazette Jan. 19, 1859—"From the 1st February next a parcel, not weighing over 2 lbs., will be conveyed by mail between any of the Post Offices in New Brunswick. They must be prepaid at the following rates by postage stamps only: Not exceeding 1 lb., 1s 3d; over 1 lb. and not exceeding 2 lbs., 2s 3d."

Counterfeits.

Crude counterfeits of all the stamps are known. There is, however, an engraved forgery of the 3d, 6d and 1s stamps which might be considered dangerous. When comparisons are made, it differs in many respects, such as figures, lettering, shade, paper, etc., but under some conditions, and if one is too prone to accept things for what they are represented, the forgery might be taken as an original. Its outstanding defect is the brightness of the coloring. These have a catalogue value of $10.00 each.

There is a fairly good forgery of the Connell stamp, described in the Monthly Journal for Sept., 1900. This closely follows the original in paper and perforation, but the color is not as deep as in the original. The design is faithfully reproduced with the exception of the "5" on the upper left side."

1½d on Half of 3d in Red (Bogus).

This was supposed to have been used on local or drop letters some time in 1860. The surcharge was applied twice on each 3d stamp, the purchaser dividing the stamps as required. The drop letter rate in Fredericton and St. John, the only towns where letter carriers were employed, was 1d and not 1½d, and this 1d was paid in cash.

Reprints:

Reprints on hard wove paper were made in 1890, during the regime of P.M.G. Haggard, who authorized 5 sheets of each value to be printed. Some were given to collectors, and the balance eventually were handed over to Mr. A. G. Blair, Minister of Railways and Canals, Ottawa, in 1897. Mr. Blair's son later sold them to Mr. J. M. Bartels of New York. There originally existed 800 of each of the three values, but the quantity purchased by Mr. Bartels was as follows: 3d Pale Orange, 768; 6d Bluish Black, 770; 1s Violet Black, 716. One sheet of the 1s stamps was badly blurred in the printing, from careless pulling from the plate it would appear. This sheet bore the notation in the corner "43 N.G.".

Postal Rates.

The Report of the Postmaster General of Great Britain for 1857 furnishes us with a list of the rates in force at the time of the introduction of stamps, as follows:

Letters not exceeding ½ oz. . . . . 3d Cy.
Above ½ oz. not exceeding 1 oz. . . . . 6d Cy.
Every additional ½ oz. . . . . 3d Cy.
Prepayment optional.

(Above rates did not apply to packet letters to or from United Kingdom and letters to or from Newfoundland and U.S.)

Letters delivered at St. John and Fredericton, the only offices where where letter carriers were employed, were taxed 1d (1½d Cy.) in addition.

Letters to or from the United Kingdom via Halifax, 1s Stg. or 1s 3d Cy.

Same, via New York, 1s 2d Stg. or 1s 5½d Cy. Prepayment optional. Rates increased according to scale. Newspapers conveyed free. Books, etc., to or from the United Kingdom were subject to the following charges, prepayment compulsory: Single volume not exceeding ½ lb. weight, 7½d Cy. Above ½ lb. not over 1 lb., 1/3d Cy., and above 1 lb. not over 2 lb., 2/6d Cy. Rates increasing according to scale.

1859 Rates

Letters to or from the United Kingdom and New Brunswick not exceeding ½ oz., 6d Stg., 7½d Cy. Letters for Bermuda and Newfoundland, not exceeding ½ oz., 6½d Stg., 8d Cy. Letters for West Indies not exceeding ½ oz., 10½d Stg., 1s 1d Cy.

Prepayment was compulsory on the initial ½ oz., optional on the balance should the letter exceed the ½ oz. except in the case of West Indies mail which had to be paid in advance.

The following is found in the Royal Gazette for Aug. 3, 1859:

"Part 9, Sect. 2, Post Office Regulations is repealed and following adopted: Printed books, periodical publications or pamphlets, under sixteen ounces in weight, can be forwarded by post in New Brunswick at the rate of ½d per oz. Printed music will be allowed to pass through post in New Brunswick under same regulations as pamphlets. Printed circulars, catalogues, hand bills and prices current posted in New Brunswick will be liable to a rate of ½d each, subject to the following regulations—postage must be prepaid, each must be in a cover unsealed, or if sealed, open at the end or side; the word 'Circular' 'Catalogue' 'Hand Bill' or 'Price Current' as the case may be, must be written or printed on the face of the cover; and each package must weigh under ½ oz. Any of the above mentioned, however, coming into New Brunswick by post from U.S., Canada, Nova Scotia, or P.E.I., will be subject to ½d postage to be collected on delivery and must be taxed accordingly. Signed Charles Connell, P.M.G."

The Postage on the above must, I think, have been prepaid in money until the issue of the One Cent stamp in May, 1860; for it is difficult to see how a half penny value could have been improvised out of the three stamps then current."

Quantities:

There is a record of but one requisition or supply of the pence stamps. The quantities shown were ordered along with the first supply for Nova Scotia, by the Hon. Jos. Howe, Provincial Secretary for Nova Scotia, who apparently had authority, while in London, to settle upon the design to be used for the New Brunswick stamps and place orders for such quantities as might be required. In placing the order for Nova Scotia stamps in the quantities shown elsewhere, he recommended that a similar quantity be supplied for New Brunswick, at the same time suggesting that the quantity be doubled if thought insufficient. It is evident that the quantity was not doubled, as had this been done the pence stamps would have been placed on an almost equal footing as to scarcity with those of Nova Scotia whereas we know by their relative scarcity that they are not. It is well to bear in mind, also, that the business section of St. John, where old correspondence bearing these stamps would exist, was visited by more than one fire which swept everything before it.

Some explanation seems to be required with respect to the quantity of 12½c stamps. The figures shown are taken from Poole's handbook on New Brunswick published by Severn-Wylie-Jewett Co., Beverly, Mass. No indication is given as to the source of the information, which doubtless is reliable, but if 400,000 of the 12½c stamps was delivered a very large portion must have been destroyed, as the stamp is of much greater scarcity than the 1c of which 200,000 was the supply.

Variety "long ear pendant" No. 60 on sheet.

Denomination	*Sheets*	*Stamps*
3d (Ordered Jy. 8, '51)	2,500	400,000
6d (Ordered Jy. 8, '51)	625	100,000
1s (Ordered Jy. 8, '51)	312½	50,000
1c		200,000
2c		
5c Connell		(Destroyed)
5c A4 all shades		500,000
10c		200,000
12½c		400,000
17c		100,000

NEW BRUNSWICK

Sept., 1851. Imperf.

No.	Type.			Unused.	Used.
1	*A1*	3d	Red, pale red........................	65.00	25.00
			On cover $35.00; pair..................		*60.00*
			Strip 3............................		*125.00*
			a. Watermarked double lined 3.........		*100.00*
			b. Watermarked double lined H.........		*100.00*
2		6d	Olive yellow.........................	200.00	100.00
			On cover $125.00......................		
3		6d	Orange-yellow........................	200.00	100.00
			On cover $125.00......................		
4		1s	Bright or dull violet..................	800.00	400.00
			On cover $600.00......................		
			On cover with 3d $700.00...............		

A2

A3

A4

A5

A6

A7

A8

May, 1860-1863. Perf. 12.

No.	Type.			Unused.	Used.
5	*A2*	1c	Brown purple May, 1860 (AC)	2.00	2.00
			On cover $4.50; block 4	*12.00*	
6		1c	Grey purple (AC)	.75	1.00
			On cover $2.50; block 4	*4.00*	
7		1c	Dull claret	1.00	1.25
			On cover $3.00; block 4	*6.00*	
			a. Pair imperf. vert.	*20.00*	
8	*A3*	2c	Orange 1863 (A)	.50	1.75
			a. On cover $3.00; block 4	*2.50*	
9		2c	Orange-yellow (A)	.30	1.00
			On cover $2.00; block 4	*1.50*	
10	*A4*	5c	Brown (Connell) (A)	350.00	
			On cover $500.00		
			a. Re-entry (see Proofs)		
11	*A5*	5c	Yellowgreen May, 1860 (A)	.15	.40
			On cover $1.00; block 4	*.75*	
			a. Long ear pendant (notes)	*5.00*	
12		5c	Green	.15	.40
			On cover $1.00; block 4	*.75*	
			a. Long ear pendant (notes)	*5.00*	
			b. Double strike	*2.50*	
13		5c	Deep olive green Dec., 1863	15.00	2.50
			On cover $4.00; block 4		*25.00*
			a. Long ear pendant (notes)	*25.00*	
14		5c	Pale olive-green	25.00	5.00
			a. Long ear pendant (notes)		15.00
15	*A6*	10c	Red 1860 (ABC)	.75	1.25
			a. Major re-entry	*10.00*	
			b. Double strike	*3.00*	
			On cover $2.50; block 4	*3.50*	*25.00*
16	*A7*	12½c	Blue *1860* (AC)	1.00	1.75
			On cover $5.00; Block 4	*4.75*	
17	*A8*	17c	Black *1860* (AC)	1.75	3.50
			On cover $10.00; block 4	*9.00*	

Bisecteds making double 7½d. rate. Note "tying on" cancellation.

Bisected, properly tied to cover and London postmark proving necessity for 7½d. combination.

Bisecteds or Splits

Values are given for covers in good condition. The bisected stamp must be properly "tied" to the cover. The amount represented by the stamps must agree with the rate required between the points designated by the Postmarks. A 7½d cover (two 3d and a split 3d for example) addressed to an inland or local post office would be contrary to any rate for such letters, and would therefore be examined with suspicion. Values as given do not apply to splits "on pieces of original cover." We have noted auction prices of $35.00 for such a "piece" as compared to $135.00 for a similar bisected on the entire cover. Unless the piece of cover happens to contain all the necessary postmarks, we do not believe it would be of interest to the more advanced collectors. Bisecteds on pieces of cover trimmed to approximate size of stamp, have little value, and bisecteds off cover are best obtained by the simple expedient of buying damaged stamps and cutting away the half which is torn, thinned, heavily cancelled or partially missing.

Two 6d and diag. ½ of 6d (1s 3d rate)	$200.00
6d, 3d and diag. ½ of 3d (10½d rate)	250.00
6d and diag. ½ of 6d (9d rate)	250.00
Diag. ½ of 1s and diag. ½ of 3d (7½d rate)	750.00
Diag. ½ of 1s and vert. ½ of 3d (7½d rate)	850.00
6d and ¼ of 6d (7½d rate)	
6d and diag. ½ of 3d (7½d rate)	225.00
Two 3d and diag. ½ of 3d (7½d rate)	185.00
Two 3d and vert. ½ of 3d (7½d rate)	200.00

Diag. ½ of 1s (6d rate)	
3d and diag. ½ of 3d (4½d rate)	
1s quartered, square (3d rate)	250.00

1s quartered, triangle (3d rate)	250.00
6d diag. ½ (3d rate)	150.00
Diag. ½ of 3d (1½d rate)	
Two halves of 6d (6d rate) (Aug., 1858)	175.00

2c vert. ½ (noted on authentic cover from Woodstock).	
10c vert. ½	50.00
10c diag. ½	35.00
2c diag. ½ with two 2c (5c rate)	
10c and diag. ½ of 10c (15c rate)	75.00

ESSAYS, REPRINTS AND PROOFS

1890. Reprints on stout white paper.

3d Pale orange	$5.00
6d Bluish black	5.00
1s Violet black	10.00

Essays.

1c Black, cardboard	25.00
2c Black, cardboard	25.00

Die Proofs on India.

1c Black, No. 130 above design	25.00
2c Black, green, magenta	
5c Blue (Connell) mounted or unmounted	25.00
12½c Black	25.00
17c Black, Orange	25.00

Plate Proofs, on India.

1c Colors of issue	
1c Orange, pale carmine	
2c Black, pale magenta, green, orange, mounted or unmounted	
5c Queens Head, colors of issue	
5c Orange	
5c Connell, Color of Issue	25.00
5c Connell, Color of Issue (thick paper)	35.00
5c Connell, Orange	5.00
5c Connell, Color of Issue, with SPECIMEN	15.00
a. (All shades) Re-entry	
10c Light and dark vermilion	
12½c Blue, yellow orange	
17c Black, orange	

Proofs.

Proofs and color trials exist for the "Cents Issue" in a number of shades. Proofs of the Connell stamp are much sought after, coming in a brown shade somewhat lighter than the shade of the issued stamp, without or with SPECIMEN vertically in carmine.

NEWFOUNDLAND

Notes on Pence Issues.

The author acknowledges the source of most of the information regarding the Pence Issues as from the worthy pen of Chas. J. Phillips, in his excellent "Philatelic Classics." We doubt if any individual philatelist has in his experience handled more of these early stamps than Mr. Phillips.

Paper.

The study of the papers on which the early stamps are printed is of prime importance, as some varieties are of a high degree of rarity.

The first paper may be described as thick, white, heavy opaque. The second paper is of medium thickness and fairly opaque. The third paper is thin, hard, and semi-transparent. The "rose" shades are ordinarily on this paper.

Watermarks.

The "rose" shades (1862-63) come on watermarked paper, the watermark consisting of the maker's name "STACEY WISE 1858". This is found on a small percentage of the sheets. Watermarks are not found on any other Newfoundland stamps.

Shades.

There are some distinctive shades in the early printings. In the 1862-63 printings a shade is noted which may be described as Rose Claret. Any abnormal shade is always worth a place in the album and will command good prices in the future.

Fakes and Forgeries.

There are ordinary forgeries which should not deceive anyone. There are others which constitute a real menace to the unwary. In Belgium some clever artists have been taking the "rose" stamps of 1862-63 and painting them over to imitate the scarlet-vermilion and orange issues. The painting is wonderfully done and deceives even the careful philatelist, but of course the papers are not quite right.

Forged Cancellations.

The "rose" shades of 1862-63, of which it is possible to get unused copies at reasonable prices, are cancelled to give them the higher value for used specimens. The faked cancellations are usually on the later printings in fresh and brighter colors. The "bar" cancellation is the one usually faked, but the bars in the fakes are too pale and the lines not sharp and well defined as in the originals.

Mr. Phillips records having (1927) seen the stamps of 1866 to 1879 cancelled with ten bars arranged in oval forms, in dull blue ink which goes clearly right through the stamps and shows on the back. He states that in his opinion no such ink was used in Newfoundland at this period.

Bisections.

Fakes on portions of covers and even whole covers have been seen of several of the Pence Issues. The biggest find of genuine bisections was that made by the Burger Bros. many years ago. These were all addressed to Tucker Bros., Baltimore. Under no circumstances add a bisected "rose" stamp to your collection until it has been passed on by someone who has handled enough of Newfoundland early issues to gain the necessary experience. The 6c Dull rose 1868-73 and the 10c black (ship) have been noted on cover bisected, accepted by the P.O. and late as 1896. Such bisecteds were not justified by any shortage of stamps.

Repaired Stamps.

Someone in Belgium or France, or both, is rebacking stamps to duplicate the paper, and adding margins where necessary. The work is done by a master hand and even the experienced collector has been deceived. Sometimes the outer framelines are drawn or painted in. Even if soaked, it is important that you leave them in the water for a half hour or more. Don't buy bargains.

Rarities.

Fine used pair of 6d Scarlet Vermilion (Ayer Colletcion). Used pair of 6d Orange (Ayer Collection). Cover dated July 7, 1863 with ½ of 1/ rose and ½ of 8d rose used to make up 10d rate—Ayer Collection to Ferrary to Lichtenstein 1926. "Tucker Find" cover dated Feb. 29, (Leap Year) 1860 prepaid by ½ of 8d used as 4d. Warren H. Colson, sold about 1927, a cover with a 2d Scarlet, described as with enormous margins; half of 1d No. 1, and a whole 1d, in conjunction with a 10c black, 1866 to make 13c rate.

In Dec. 1928, there was sold by auction in London, England, a cover bearing a strip of 3 of the 2d orange-vermilion, which is believed to be unique.

Notes on Different Values.

1d Brown Violet.

The re-entry consists of a doubling of the upper right numeral of value and the letters "LAND".

3d Green.

The 1860 printing of the 3d was 76,000 and in 1889 the remainders consisted of 1,029 stamps, which Mr. Phillips thinks went largely to Whitfield, King & Co. These are now scattered and even pairs are difficult to obtain.

6d Rose.

There was a rather large "remainder" of 29,937, and supplies could be bought at face in Newfoundland until about 1917, when they weer exhausted. The stamp will now rise consistently in value.

6½d.

This stamp was very little in demand. Very few copies were used and the bulk of the unused were saved and passed into the hands of collectors.

The rarest Newfoundland stamp is the 6½d Orange on "B" paper. There is no record of the printing in the published figures of the invoices of Perkins Bacon & Co. but this stamp does exist. Quite possibly only one sheet of twenty stamps was printed and this not issued.

8d.

This stamp was for a rate little used and most of the stamps went into collections. Many of the 8d Scarlet were bisected for the 4d rate. The 8d Rose was never issued although a few may have been passed through the post at later dates than the early 60's.

1/.

Of this stamp in the orange shade 1,000 were printed. Of the 12d black Canada 1510 copies were issued. The Newfoundland stamp catalogues $500.00 and the Canada $1250.00. Either the Newfoundland stamp is undervalued or we must attribute $500.00 of value of the 12d to popularity.

The 1/ orange on laid is known both with horizontal and vertical laid lines. At least one sheet of 20 of each must have been printed. It has never been seen used.

Quantities Issued.

1p	Brown violet	1857	70,000
	Reddish brown	1862–63	(1 sheet?)
	Purple brown		10,080
2p	Scarlet vermilion	1857	3,000
	Orange	1860	5,000
	Rose	1862–63	10,000
3p	Green	1857	16,000
		1860	76,000
4p	Scarlet vermilion	1857	5,000
	Orange	1860	5,000
	Rose	1862–63	35,000
5p	Violet brown	1857	11,000
	Brown violet	1860	20,000
	Reddish brown	1862–63	10,000
6p	Scarlet vermilion	1857	5,000
	Orange	1860	10,000
	Rose	1862–63	70,000
6½p	Scarlet vermilion	1857	2,000
	Orange	1860	20 ?
	Rose	1862–63	15,000
8p	Scarlet vermilion	1857	8,000
	Rose	1862–63	10,000
1s	Scarlet vermilion	1857	2,000
	Orange	1860	1,000
	Orange, laid p.	1860	40 ?
	Rose	1862–63	25,000

1c on 3c of November, 1897.

Type I.

Black surcharge	31,920
Red surcharge	40 ?
Red over black	40 ?

Type II.

Black surcharge	6,384
Red surcharge	....
Red over black	....

Type III.

Black surcharge	1,596
Red surcharge	2
Red over black	2

(Figures based on 798 sheets surcharged in black, 1 in red and 1 in red over black.)

5c Brown Seal, 1866.

The re-entry consists of a doubling of the frame line at the lower right. The stamp also shows that the plate developed a flaw in the steel or became damaged in some way, the lower corner being incomplete. The bottom row of stamps may be distinguished from the other rows by the absence of the position dot outside the frame line at lower right.

12c Puce Brown, 1890-94.
This is a printing from the old American Bank Note Co. plate, by the British American Bank Note Co.

24c Blue, 1866.
The author has not had an opportunity of studying any large blocks of this stamp, but from the few seen it is suggested that a systematic study will reveal several minor varieties, such as a dot of color in the upper part of the left "2."

1c Violet, 1868.

1c Brown Purple, 1868-73.
The 1c Violet of 1868 was engraved and printed by the National Bank Note Co., New York. The 1c Brown Purple was re-engraved and printed by the American Bank Note Co., New York. In the "National" the triangular white space between the ends of the band carrying the words "ONE CENT" and the oval is about half the size of the white space in the American Bank Note Co.'s stamp.

5c Black Seal, 1868.
The re-entry is that described and illustrated for the 5c Brown Seal, and the remarks as to plate flaw and position dots apply.

6c Carmine Lake, 1894.
This shade is from a printing by the British American Bank Note Co., Montreal, from the old American Bank Note Company plate.

5c Blue Seal (Rouletted) 1876-79.
The re-entry is that described and illustrated for the 5c Brown Seal. The remarks as to plate flaw and position dots apply.

Re-issues of 1896-7.
These were re-issued for postal purposes and are not reprints. The colors are generally brighter than those of the original stamps. The gum is yellowish instead of white.

5c Blue Seal (1887 and 1894).
Three distinct shades of blue exist, which have been listed as pale blue, dark blue and bright blue, but unfortunately catalogue makers do not seem to agree on which is bright blue and which is pale blue. The minor variety listed consists of a plate flaw appearing as an added scroll or ornament at top right side.

10c Black 1887.
The variety "CE" of CENTS is illustrated above.

½c, 1c, 2c, 3c Re-issue of 1896.
These may be distinguished by the gum, which is yellowish instead of white. The colors are generally brighter than the colors of the earlier issues.

3c Slate 1890.

This stamp was engraved and printed by the British American Bank Note Co., Ottawa. The shades listed represent the main variations.

A variety may be found in which the paper is colored through, in a salmon pink shade. This is from a shipment of stamps wrecked in transit and later rescued from the salt water.

Cabot Series of June 24, 1897.

(For the greater portion of the data for this and succeeding issues we are indebted to Harry E. Huber, whose articles in Mekeel's Weekly, the Stamp Herald, Philatelic Gossip, etc., represent the most comprehensive studies available.)

The Cabot Series commemorated the 60th anniversary of Queen Victoria's ascension to the Throne, and the 400th anniversary of the discovery of the Island by John Cabot. The stamps are line engraved and printed by the American Bank Note Co. of New York, in sheets of 100, perforated 12 single line.

Quantities.

1c	400,000	10c	200,000
2c	400,000	12c	200,000
3c	1,000,000	15c	200,000
4c	400,000	24c	100,000
5c	400,000	30c	100,000
6c	400,000	35c	100,000
8c	200,000	60c	100,000

The dies, rolls and plates were destroyed on June 23rd, 1897. On January 4th, 1900, there remained 2,658 copies of the 3c and 11,342 copies of the 5c, which were then burned.

60c Surcharged (Essay).

In December, 1918, a shortage of 2c stamps occurred. Pending the issue of the Caribou series (January 2nd, 1919), plans were made for surcharging the 60c Cabot stamps, of which there was a surplus still in stock. A sheet of 100 of the 60c black Cabot was overprinted in red in three lines "TWO-2-CENTS" but the work was not proceeded with and the stamps were not issued in this form.

Remainders.

Several times inventory was taken of the Cabot remainders, preparatory to destruction, but the orders were stayed, and the stamps returned to the vaults, to be brought forth as emergencies arose. In November, 1920, orders were given to deface the remainders of the 24c, 30c, 35c and 60c Cabot stamps and then burn them. For defacement the "St. John's, N.F." cancelling stamp was used, with the date "NOV.-26-1920" in three lines in the center, applied in red, once to each block of four. After face value of $175.00 had been defaced the orders were countermanded, and the defaced stamps were later sold to a collector in St. John's at 10% below face.

1c on 3c of 1890.

In September, 1897, the stocks of the 1c Cabot becoming exhausted, 800 sheets of the 3c 1890 stamps were surcharged. The stamps being in sheets of 50, this represented a total issue of 40,000, containing Types "A," "B" and "C" in the proportion of 32,000, 6,400 and 1,600 respectively. It is probable that the above figures include the printings in red and the printing in red over black, in the original experiments.

Stamps 1 to 40 (1st 4 rows) are Type A; Nos. 41 to 48 inclusive are Type B, and Nos. 49 and 50 are Type C. A complete sheet was sold in 1928 for $200.00 by the Marks Stamp Co.

Stanley Gibbons mentions that one sheet was surcharged in red, and as this was indistinct it was further surcharged in black.

Herman Focke, writing in Mekeel's for Dec. 27, 1926, states: "I have it on the authority of my late friend, Mr. Peter G. Tessier of St. John's, one of Newfoundland's greatest collectors and specialists, and also from a Mr. Reichardt, who resided at St. John's at the time when these provisionals appeared, that both the stamp with the red surcharge only and the one with surcharge in red and black were issued in the regular way and were obtainable at the P.O. in the first days of October, 1897.

That the stamp with surcharge in red, and the stamp with surcharge in black over red, had franking value and was legitimately used, is the opinion of Mr. Focke, who reports having seen at least two covers with postage prepaid by these stamps.

The 3c stamp was issued in a variety of shades and the stock of stamps on hand when the surcharging was done seems to have included most, if not all, of these shades, as slate, grey lilac, lilac, slate violet, and possibly the brown-lilac.

The 1st stamp in the 5th row (No. 41) varies in the width of the spacing between "ONE" and "CENT" the entire surcharge being about 1¼ mm. wider.

Mr. Frank B. Gooch, of Washington, D.C., was a correspondent of P. G. Tessier at the time the 1c on 3c stamps were issued, and states that Mr. Tessier wrote him that the Post Office refused to sell any of these provisional stamps at the stamp window, and required that mail matter be brought to the office, when the stamps would be affixed by postal authorities.

"Paid All."

In the collection of Frank B. Gooch, mentioned above, there is a cover bearing the marking "Paid All" within a circle. In the interval between the exhausting of the supply of the 1c Cabot and the arrival of the 1c on 3c surcharges, the Post Office was forced to adopt this means of handling the mail, which was brought to the post office and stamped and after the postage had been paid in cash.

ROYAL SERIES, 1897-1901.

In his report for the year ended June 30, 1926, the Minister of Posts and Telegraphs, Hon. William Woodford, stated that a new series of postage stamps would be issued as needed, and that "the 4c purple, used within the Empire, will have a portrait of H.R.H. the Prince of Wales, the greatest and most popular of Empire visitors." It was suggested that this one denomination be issued on the birthday of His Royal Highness, June 23rd, but shortness of time made this impossible.

In a letter dated June 14th, 1897, the Postmaster-General of Newfoundland, J. O. Fraser, informed all Postmasters "that on and after the 24th June instant, the stamps at present in use are to be called in, to be replaced by those of the Cabot issue," and further, that "you will please at once make a requisition for all stamps required for the use of the public in your settlement, and return all stamps on hand of the present series, retaining only sufficient for the public requirements while your order goes to the General Post Office."

The Cabot series was issued June 24, 1897, to commemorate the 400th anniversary of the discovery of the Island by John Cabot, on June 24, 1497, and the 60th year of Queen Victoria's reign (born May 24th, 1819. Her Majesty succeeded to the throne on June 20, 1837.)

The stock of the 1c running out, sale was restricted until the 3c 1890 stamps could be surcharged. Mail matter was taken in with cash and handstamped "Paid All" in a circle. This procedure continued until December, 1897, when the first two denominations of the Royal Family series (representing four generations), 1c carmine, Queen Victoria, and 2c orange, Prince of Wales (later King Edward VII) were issued.

In June of the following year the 1c and 2c were re-issued in green and vermilion, respectively (more nearly meeting the colour requirements of the Universal Postal Union) along with a 3c denomination, orange, portraying the features of Princess Alexandra of Wales. Two months later (August) the ½c olive green appeared, picturing Prince Edward (born June 23rd, 1894), the present Prince of Wales. On the 5c blue, issued in June, 1899, the Duke of York (the present King George V) made his first philatelic appearance. Queen Victoria died on January 22, 1901, and King Edward VII ascended the throne. In October of that year while the Prince and Princess of Wales (the present King George V and Queen Mary) were on Empire tour, and visiting Newfoundland, the Royal series of postage stamps was completed by the issue of a 4c denomination, violet, presenting a likeness of Princess Mary of Wales.

These stamps were line engraved and recess printed by the American Bank Note Co. of New York, and perforated single line 12, in sheets of 100 (10x10), with margins on all four sides. These are plain, except that in the lower margin, under the 5th and 6th stamps, the printer's name appears in small coloured caps, "AMERICAN BANK NOTE CO., NEW YORK." Under each stamp of the sheet is the printer's imprint, "American Bank Note Co., N.Y." in small coloured caps.

A consignment of the 1c, 2c and 3c received in 1907 was on thinner paper than used for the earlier printings; the 4c exists only on the thinner paper.

Under date of November 7, 1899, the Postmaster-General of Newfoundland gave notice that "on the 2nd January, 1900, all obsolete postage stamps will be destroyed, and that after that date the only stamps that will be on sale by the Postal Department will be the ½c, 1c, 2c, 3c, 5c of the Royal issue, and the 4c, 6c, 8c, 10c, 12c, 15c, 24c, 30c, 35c and 60c of the Cabot issue."

On January 4, 1900, 49,717 of the 2c orange (Codfish); 40,638 of the 3c slate (Queen Victoria); 104,569 of the 5c blue (Seal), along with quantities of the higher denominations of obsolete series, 6c, 10c, 12c, 24c were burned.

On Christmas Day, 1898, penny letter postage was introduced "between any place in Newfoundland and the United Kingdom, and such of the possessions of the British Empire as may adopt the same rate of postage." In 1908 the inland letter rate was reduced to 2c, and on May 1, 1909, this rate was made effective to the U.S., and vice versa.

In April, 1908, the Red Cross S.S. Silvia was wrecked en route from New York to St. John's and a consignment of 2c and 5c postage stamps, valued at $100,000, was washed ashore on the Island of Cuttyhunk, Mass. One fisherwoman was said to have secured all the 5c stamps—some of these were given away, and some sold. A representative of the American Bank Note Co. immediately proceeded to the scene, and according to the postal officials of Newfoundland, all the stamps were recovered, destroyed, and the order duplicated. However, as many sheets of the 2c Royal series, without gum, later came on the market, it is doubtful if *all* the stamps were recovered. However, the stamps of the Royal series were never demonetised, and continued on sale at the G.P.O. until exhausted.

In September, 1908, the 2c Map design stamp was issued, the last to be supplied by the American Bank Note Co. to the Newfoundland Government, as the postage stamp printing contract was given to Messrs. Whitehead, Morris & Co., Ltd., England, who produced the Guy Tercentenary or Colonising series.

On May 17, 1918, a war tax of 1c was imposed on every "prepaid letter and letter packet posted in Newfoundland." A consignment of 1c and 2c Coronation series was en route from England. There had been no previous intimation of a change in the rate and no preparations had been made by the Post Office Dept. to provide additional quantities of this denomination. (Only the 1c, 2c and 5c of the Coronation series were being reprinted, and the remainder stocks of the Cabot series was being used for denominations above 5c.)

The need for 3c stamps was imperative, and as the American Bank Note Co. of New York still retained the original 3c Royal series plate, wire was sent them to make a reprinting as quickly as possible. The stamps reached St. John's late in June, 1918, and were issued when the old stock became exhausted. The colour is reddish orange, and the paper has a bluish tinge, which distinguishes this printing from the earlier ones.

"GUY" ISSUE.

"To John Guy, and the company of merchants and adventurers of the City of London and Bristol, belongs the credit for the first serious attempt at peopling the island of Newfoundland," says Harry E. Huber in his notes on the Newfoundland Guy Tercentenary issue published in the Stamp Herald for February, 1928. "The scheme," he continues, "had been mooted for a long time, but finally, in 1610, King James I of England granted John Guy, of Bristol, a charter to colonize the island, between Cape St. Mary's and Cape Bonavista, and with 39 men, he arrived in the "Endeavour" in June, 1610. He set up his staff house at Cupids in Conception Bay, and there built three houses, stores, wharves, and a fort. (Later, the town of Mosquito was founded.) On a second voyage, in 1612, he was accompanied by a clergyman, Rev. Erasmus Stourton, and in the following year, the first white child of European parents was born at Cupids. The colony, however, suffered in various ways from the adventurers or fishing admirals, who burned his mill, and harrassed the settlers, and the colonization was never a permanent success, though it struggled along for a time.

"In 1910 plans were formulated to celebrate the 300th anniversary of the founding of the first settlements in Conception Bay, and on February 1, 1910, Mr. H. J. B. Woods, who succeeded Mr. J. O. Fraser, in 1902, as Postmaster-General of Newfoundland, wrote: "The issue of a commemorative stamp in connection with the Guy Memorial Celebration, has been suggested. There can be no objection to such an issue if confined to stamps of the smaller denominations, as they are always in demand for postage, even if there should be but a limited demand from stamp collectors, which of late seems to be falling off."

"A series of postage stamps, commemorative of the Guy Tercentenary ,was decided upon, and in the St. John's 'Daily News,' of August 12, 1910, there appeared the following notice:

"GENERAL POST OFFICE

"On and after the 15th instant, Guy Tercentenary Postage Stamps will be for sale at St. John's and Conception Bay Post Offices, and at the end of the month, generally, at all Post Offices in Newfoundland. The issue contains 11 varieties, 1, 2, 3, 4, 5, 6, 8, 10, 12 and 15 cents, one of each costing 75 cents.

"Signed, Geo. W. LeMessurier,
"Acting Postmaster-General."

"The stamps were designed and poorly lithographed on white wove unwatermarked paper, by Messrs. Whitehead, Morris & Co., Ltd., London, England, who had supplied the Island Government with bonds, but they had no previous experience with postage stamp printing. The appearance of the stamps was no credit to them, and complaints having been made, a Mr. E. R. Morris of the printing firm made a special trip to Newfoundland to confer with the authorities and explain the difficulties which had beset them.

"The 1c, 2c and 5c were printed in sheets of 200 stamps (2 panes of 100 each, 10x10), separated by a margin 38 mm. wide, which was afterwards cut down the middle to form two Post Office sheets of 100 stamps each. The other denominations were printed from stones of 100 subjects only. Of the 1c perforated 12x11, at least one sheet, not separated, was sent out and issued as a 200 stamp sheet.

The 2c is incorrectly inscribed, as the arms are those granted to the Colony, not the Company, by Borough Charter of January 1, 1637, and registered by the College of Heralds, in London. These arms are described in the original grant as follows:—

" . . . . And whereas for the greater honor and splendour of the country and the people therein inhabiting, it is and will be necessary that there be proper and peculiar arms thereunto belonging, to be used in all such cases as arms are wont to be, by other nations and countries. Upon the request unto me made . . . . . I have accordingly, for the purpose before recited, devised, set forth and contrived, the arms and ensigns hereafter described:—

"That is to say, gules a cross argent; in the first quarter of the escutcheon a lion passant guardant crowned or; in the second a unicorn passant of the second armed, maned and unguled of the third gorged with a crown whereunto is affixed a chain passing between his forelegs and reflexed over his back of the last; in the third as in the second;

in the fourth as in the first. And for the Crest, upon an 'healme' mantled gules doubled argent and a wreath or and gules an elk proper, the escutcheon supported by two savages of the clime proper armed and appareled according to their guise when they go to war; and under all in a scroll, this motto 'Quaerite Primo Regnum Dei.'"

(A cross super-imposed upon the shield, divides into quarters, in the first and fourth of which is a crowned lion, and in the second and third a silver unicorn. Around the neck of the unicorn is a crown, to which is attached a chain. The crest is a Caribou; two white Indians are the supporters.)

The arms consist first of all of a cross based on St. George, though of different colour; the lion is based on the lion in the arms of England, and the unicorn was used as the supporters of the Kings of Scotland, and taken as one of the supporters of the King of England at the union of England and Scotland. The term "gules" of course means "red," and "a unicorn passant of the second" means "a unicorn of the second colour stated in the blazon, i.e., argent (silver)." Similarly, the words "of the third" mean "or (gold)." The translation of the motto is "Seek ye first the Kingdom of God."

The supporters and motto do not appear in the stamp design.

On the 6c the inscription is also incorrect as Sir Francis Bacon never assumed the title of Lord Bacon. When he was raised to the peerage in 1618, he took the title of Lord Verulam.

The subjects on the 9c and 10c denominations are not connected with Guy's colonizing venture, but rather with Newfoundland's great pulp paper industry. The paper mills of the Anglo-Newfoundland Development Co. at Grand Falls (16 hours run from St. John's, by the trans-insular railway) is one of the largest paper producing plants in the world. It was built to supply pulp for the publishing interests of Lord Northcliffe and his associates.

The death of King Edward VII (12c) on May 10, 1910, brought to the throne King George V. The 15c stamp of this series was the first issued (a trifle over 90 days) after King George's accession to the throne.

Complete sets of these stamps were sold in small envelopes inscribed "Newfoundland—1610—1910—Issue of Newfoundland Stamps to Commemorate the 300th Anniversary of the earliest settlement in the British Empire made in Conception Bay, Newfoundland, in June, 1610."

In the first consignment were 50,000 each of the five lower denominations, and 10,000 each of the higher, and it was for the reason of limited quantity that the stamps were first placed on sale at only St. John's and the Conception Bay Post Office.

In the first printing of the 6c the word "Colonization" appeared with a reversed "Z," or a malformed "S," in addition to numerous flaws. In the second printing the "Z" was partially corrected, but the flaws continued, and it was not until a later printing, that the flaws were entirely eliminated and this "Z" correctly formed.

At least one sheet each of the 5c, 6c (first printing) and 12c were sent out imperforate and issued.

At first all denominations were perforated 12 horizontally as well as vertically, but later consignments of the 1c, 2c and 5c came in a variety of perforations, i.e., 12x14 (1c, 2c and 5c), 12x11 (1c), 11½x11 (1c), and 12x11½ (2c).

All four varieties of the 1c exist with the lower bar of the "E" of "NEWFOUNDLAND" missing, making it a letter "F," on the 41st stamp of the right pane. In the perf. 12 variety, only, the 42nd stamp on the right pane has a somewhat similar error, "JAMRS," the lower portion of the "E" being malformed.

A block of the 1c is known variously perforated, 11, 11½, 12, 12½ and 14, probably printer's waste, but sent to Newfoundland and issued. The imperf. vertically 1c occurs between the 1st and 2nd vertical rows.

The 6c and 10c exhausted in December, 1910, and by February only the 1c, 2c, 3c, 4c, 5c and 8c were to be had.

The stamps were originally intended to be printed from line engraved plates (and die proofs in black exist of all denominations), but time was limited and the first supplies were printed from lithographic stones.

On January 31, 1911, a supply of the 6c was received at St. John's, printed from an engraved plate; the 8c, 9c, 10c, 12c and 15c followed a week later. The stamps were perforated 14, single line, and printed on very hard white paper, in shades quite different from the lithographic prints. On the 6c the "Z" is correctly formed; the letters of SIX CENTS greatly strengthened, and the background of the tablet of value is colourless instead of being vertically lined.

The 8c and 10c from engravel plates are known imperforate.

The quantities printed from engraved plates were very small, as the Coronation series, 1c to 15c, was in preparation, and issued June 19, 1911.

By June the 10c had exhausted; the 8c followed in September, and the other values were not to be had byNovember. The five lower denominations (printed only lithographically) continued on sale for some months. As a matter of fact, the 5c was still to be had in 1914 (October 1st), when a large quantity, approximately 50,000, were overprinted in red, in three lines, "Money Order Stamp Tax Only."

"Money Order Stamp Tax Only" on 5c Guy Series.

Money Orders were classed as Bills of Exchange, and although Sect. 5 of the Act which came into operation on the 1st day of October, 1914, made postage stamps receivable for these taxes, a specially marked stamp was considered desirable by the P.O. Department as a check on the issuing offices. A large quantity of the 5c Guy Tercentenary series of August 15, 1910, "View of Cupids," perf. 14x12 on very soft white paper, was in the vaults at St. John's. Full sheets of these, 100, 10x10, were overprinted in carmine (1st printing) and vermilion (2nd printing) at the offices of the "Royal Gazette" at St. John's. The horizontal measurements of the three lines are 22, 18 and 7½ mm. respectively. The overall vertical measurements is 7½ mm.

Several varieties occurred in the overprinting. On some the period after "only" is missing. On others the right upward branch of the "y" is broken. Normally, the "l" of "only" is slightly to the right of the "p" of "Stamp," but occasionally the vertical strokes of the two letters are in exact alignment.

The stamp, although paid for by the purchaser of the Money Order, was attached by the issuing clerk. When first sent to the outport offices some postmasters, not understanding the special purpose for which the stamps were intended, sold them as ordinary postage stamps and as such they were used, and passed through the post untaxed. Very few are so known and these should be classed as interesting curiosities, as they were never authorized for postal use. The stamps were dealt with only by the Money Order Division of the Post Office Department. The fact that the stamp was attached, by the clerk, to the Money Order, seems to have been considered sufficient evidence of use, as in only a few cases were the stamps ever cancelled. Copies without gum have probably been detached from Money Orders.

After eight months the tax was cancelled by the passing on June 5, 1915, of Act 6 George V, "Stamp Duties Act." Following the passage of the rescinding Act the unused stamps in the outport offices were recalled for destruction.

No official statement was ever made as to the quantity of stamps overprinted for use on Money Orders, but in the year ending June 30, 1915, 260 Money Order Offices were in operation and 70,906 Money Orders were issued, totalling $871,344.28. As the tax on Money Orders was collected for eight months of this period, approximately 50,000 stamps must have been overprinted. Close check was kept, so that very few, with gum, reached the public, even through favor. In March, 1919, an accumulation of paid Money Orders, whose term of usefulness had expired, was destroyed, and shortly afterwards, the stamp without gum appeared on the market in quantity, due, it is said, to the fact that about 1,000 stamps escaped the flames and reached the public through a Government employee.

In the fall of 1920, a small lot of 400 stamps, with gum, came on the market, the majority being in blocks (no complete sheets), the largest of which was of 35, from the lower right corner. On all of these the period after "only" was missing. A block of 25 stamps from the lower left corner had the period on all stamps save numbers 19, 20 and 25. A reconstructed sheet showed that 60 stamps were without the period, and 40 with the period.

CORONATION SERIES, 1911.

The stamps were engraved and printed by Messrs. Whitehead, Morris & Co., Ltd., London, in sheets of 100 (10x10), unwatermarked, with cross marks in all four margins to aid in centering the perforation. The 1c, 2c, 3c, 4c, 5c and 10c are comb perforated 13½x14, and the other values single line 14. On the 15c is shown the Seal of the Colony (not the Arms as incorrectly given in the Post Office notice sent out announcing this issue).

The 2c "blurred impression" was the result of a carelessly executed printing from the engraved plates. It is distinguishable from the regular printing by the smudgy appearance and rose-red shade instead of the deep rich red of the ordinary stamp.

The first consignment of these stamps consisted of the following quantities:

1c	50,000		8c (both shades)	2,000
2c	50,000		9c	2,000
3c	10,000		10c	10,000
4c	25,000		12c	2,000
5c	100,000		15c	2,000
6c	2,000			

The first printing of the 8c was in aniline blue, with the color showing through to the back, but early in September another lot was received, in blue-green.

Of the 1c, 2 c and 5c printings were made as needed until 1918, and they exist with both comb and single line perforation; the former is the commoner. The other values, however, exhausted by the end of the year—December, 1911.

When the Coronation series appeared on June 19, 1911, the whole of the Cabot series save the 1c, 2c, 3c and 5c was to be had at the G.P.O.; all values of the Royal series, except the 2c; the 2c Map, lithographed low values of the Guy series, and some values in the Guy engraved type. But by January, 1915, much of this stock had been used, and the only low values available were the 1c, 2c and 5c Coronation series (which had been reprinted), 3c and 4c Royal series, 4c Cabot and 5c Guy. From 6c upwards the stamps were of the Cabot series.

A printing of the 2c Coronation series sent out in 1916 was so blurred in appearance that it was thought to have been surface printed or produced by lithography, rather than from the original line engraved plate. The fine lines of engraving in the background merged into one another; the color was rose-red instead of carmine, and the majority was perforated single line 14 (it exists also with the comb 13½x14 perforation).

However, the changed appearance of the stamp was explained to be due to conditions occasioned by the war, i.e., scarcity of skilled labor and materials, dyes, etc. Messrs. Whitehead, Morris & Co., the printers, under date of May 3, 1921, wrote:—

"The whole of the Coronation issue postage stamps have been supplied by us to the Newfoundland Government . . . printed direct from engraved plates. The sheet . . . which you suggest has been lithographed . . . . is from a reprint supplied during the war, when it was impossible to obtain the same quality of color as used for the first supply: you will appreciate there will be isolated sheets showing some defects, produced under the abnormal conditions prevailing. We assure you . . . . that the whole of the Coronation issue is plate printed."

The only low value stamps available in May, 1918, were the 1c, 2c and 5c Coronation, and the 3c and 4c of the Royal series. The higher values were of the Cabot series, 6c through to 60c with the exception of the 10c, which had exhausted in April, 1918.

From May 17, 1918, a war tax of 1c was imposed on all inland, Empire, and foreign letters. At that time the stock of the 3c stamps, Royal series, was only 200,000, and it was necessary to secure additional quantity immediately from the American Bank Note Co. of New York, who held the plate of the 3c of the Royal series, to tide over until the

Caribou series (issued January 2nd, 1919, was in readiness.

When the war taxes of 5c and 10c on telegrams came into force on May 17, 1918, no 10c stamp was available, and this so increased the pressure on the stock of the 5c Coronation that it exhausted in September. A reprinting from the 5c Coronation plate was cancelled, when it was learned that the stamps could not reach St. John's before the Caribou series would be in hand.

Shortage of 1c, 2c, 3c—Provisional Stamping of Envelopes.
With the great demand for the lower denomination stamps caused by the increased postal rates, the telegram tax, and fiscal duties, the stock was so reduced by the middle of December, 1918, that the outport offices were instructed to conserve stock as much as possible. At St. John's, commencing December 24th, stamps of 1c, 2c and 3c denominations were not sold except for fiscal purposes. Letters and postal matter requiring these rates, were taken over the counter for cash. If the destination was abroad, postage stamps were attached by the P.O. clerks, but if for local or inland delivery, they were rubber stamped in violet, "POSTAGE PAID—G.P.O.—St. John's, Newf'l'd." The postmark was then applied as usual. Letters from the outports were forwarded to St. John's, with cash, and there rubber stamped. This procedure was in force from December 24th to December 31st, 1918, when Str. Graciana arrived. When it was learned that the Caribou series was on board, sale was resumed of the 1c and 2c Coronation and 3c Royal stamps.

In all, the following quantities of Coronation stamps were printed:

1c	19,938,400	8c	20,000
2c	26,065,500	9c	20,000
3c	50,000	10c	22,000
4c	50,000	12c	20,000
5c	1,035,800	15c	20,000
6c	30,000		

CARIBOU ISSUE.

On January 2, 1919, the Caribou stamps appeared, commemorating the services of the Newfoundland contingent in the War 1914-18 Each denomination is inscribed with the name of an action in which Newfoundland troops participated.

From Harry E. Huber's notes we learn that in 1917 a badge was designed by orders of Lt.-Col. Whittaker, for the Depot Battalion of the Royal Newfoundland Regiment, quartered at Ayr, bearing the figure of a Caribou over a ribbon lettered "Terra Nova." The phrase "Trail of the Caribou" perpetuated by Dr. J. Alex. Robinson, Postmaster-General of Newfoundland, 1916-1918, in the Caribou series of postage stamps issued January 2, 1919, was originated by Lt.-Col. T. Nangle, R.C. Chaplain with the Royal Newfoundland Regiment, and was used by him to advertise a lecture which he gave in St. John's while the war was on, on the activities of the Royal Newfoundland Regiment.

In addition to being pictured on the 4c of the Guy series, and all denominations of the Caribou series, the Caribou appears on the 6c of the Cabot series of June 24, 1897, and on the 9c of the pictorial series of July 9, 1923. Incidentally, it is not a Caribou's head that is shown on the Caribou series, nor that of a moose, but rather a composite.

Quantities.

6c .... 48,400 8c .... 50,000 24c 50,000 36c 50,000

Forgeries.

The 4c and 8c values have been forged, by the letterpress process, and are printed in an ink slightly of a lighter shade than the genuine copies. They are on a white wove paper, of a thicker quality than the original. The 8c has been found to be printed upon a paper that is watermarked with a small four-leaf design. The forged copies vary very slightly from the originals, the outstanding features being as follows:

1. The framework immediately to the left of the head of the Caribou consists of only one line whereas in the original there are two.
2. In the top right hand corner of the framework the lines forming the background are indistinct, and in the center, at the top, under the letter T, the framework is broken, whereas in the original the framework is continuous.
3. The figure 4 (bottom left) is shaded in the forgery, instead of standing out clearly. The perforations are practically the same.

PROVISIONALS OF 1920.

New supplies of the 2c and 3c Caribou stamps, being late in arriving, caused a sudden shortage in these two values. The 15c, 30c and 35c stamps of 1897, of which there was a plentiful supply still on hand, were surcharged to relieve the situation, and were in use from the 13th to the 25th of September, 1920.

50,000 of the 15c stamps were overprinted "THREE CENTS" and delivered on Sept. 11th and 13th.

The first 3,000 of the 15c Cabot stamps were surcharged "THREE CENTS" from a setting of 25 (5x5), in which the two horizontal bars were spaced 10½ mm. As the materials at the bottom of the 15c stamp were not obliterated by the lower bar, the spacing was changed to 13½ mm. and the balance (47,000) of the 15c overprinted.

From the first setting with the 10½ mm. spacing of bars, one pane of 25 of the 6c red brown Cabot was overprinted in red, and one pane in black, to ascertain in which color the surcharge would be most distinctive. However, as the 6c Caribou had exhausted in November, 1919, and the 6c Cabot was much in demand for use on foreign letters, it was decided to use instead the 15c Cabot.

These two panes of 25 each of the "THREE CENTS" on 6c Cabot were sold at face to a resident of St. John's in October, 1921, and later offered for sale in the United States. One copy of each passed through the post at the surcharged value. That with the red overprint was used in conjunction with a 5c Caribou (letter and registration rate to the States was then 8c), on a letter addressed to a dealer in New York State. In addition to the large "R" in oval, the envelope was rubber stamped in red, "Registered—No. 512—Nov. 11, 1921—St. John's, N.F." The stamps themselves bore the obliteration of graduated bars forming an oval. The date of the receiving postmark was Nov. 18, 1921. The stamps are essays.

The regularly surcharged stamps were on sale at the G.P.O., St. John's, at 9 a.m. on Sept. 13th, and the supply was exhausted at 6 p.m. on the 14th. The authorities state that to avoid speculation each applicant on the first day received but one stamp, and on the second day this was stopped and only those with letters addressed abroad could obtain the stamps. Other letters were handed to the postal clerks with the necessary postage in cash, and the stamps affixed by the clerks.

We believe the authorities stopped speculation in these stamps by the public, but we have still to be shown that no speculation took place. If the above little story holds together we would find the bulk of these stamps in unused singles scattered throughout the world—admitting that Newfoundland carries on a heavy correspondence with the rest of the world—and not in blocks and sheets, unused, in quantities, to be had up to 1926 at least.

At 9 a.m. of the 15th the 35c surcharged "THREE CENTS" was placed on sale. The stamps were available until 6 p.m. of the 25th. 50,000 of these were surcharged. The variety "lower bar missing" occurs in the 15th stamp of the sheet counting from left to right, but is not found in all sheets. The 14th and 21st stamps of the same sheet had part of the lower bar missing.

The 30c surcharged "Two Cents" (50,000) were on sale from noon of the 23rd until 6 p.m. of the 25th.

On account of the 2c tax on receipts and cheques paid by affixing a two-cent stamp, each person was allowed to purchase from five to ten stamps, and business houses up to 500 by producing an order proving they were required for use as above. This had to be signed by the Asst. Postmaster before the order was filled.

"THREE CENTS" on 35c Inverted (?)

Writing in regard to the inverted overprint on the 35c Cabot, Harry E. Huber states: "This seems to have been based on the report of a St. John's (Nfld.) correspondent in March, 1923, that a sheet of this variety had been found. On subsequent investigation it was learned that about November, 1922, a resident of St. John's told a clerk in the General Post Office that he had 100 of these 35c stamps with inverted surcharge. But an offer of $25.00 each was refused, as was also a request to see the stamps. Had the stamps actually existed (with genuine overprint) in this condition, it was believed that "the owner would have fallen all over himself in his hurry to get the $2,500.00."

1923 PICTORIAL ISSUE.

This series of fourteen stamps illustrate for the most part the scenery for which Newfoundland is famous.

Quantities.

6c .... 100,000 9c .... 50,000 11c 100,000 24c 25,000

ISSUE OF JANUARY 3, 1928.

10c Purple.

"In the new series of Newfoundland postage stamps issued in January, 1928," writes Harry E. Huber, "the design of the 10c purple has been fixed upon by the Minister of Posts and Telegraphs, Hon. W. J. Woodford, as the National War Memorial, in honor of those who gave their lives by sea and land for the defence of the British Empire in the Great War, 1914-1918. The Memorial was unveiled on 1st July, 1925, the eighth anniversary of the Beaumont Hamel battle, by Field Marshal Earl Haig, who with Lady Haig, arrived from England on the Cunard Liner "Caronia" on June 29th. Naval detachments from British (H.M.S. Constance), French (Ville d'Ys) and American (Lawrence, Brooks and Hatfield), men-of-war in port, participated in the ceremonies.

The War Memorial, which is of Italian granite and bronze, was designed and modelled by Messrs. F. V. Blunstone, R.S.B.S., and Gilbert Bayes, R.S.B.S., and stands on King's Beach, St. John's East (opposite the landing pier of the Red Cross Line), near the spot where Sir Humphrey Gilbert on August 5, 1583, read his commission from Queen Elizabeth empowering him in her name to take possession of the island. The Royal Arms cut in lead were affixed to a post, a salute fired, and the flag of England raised. This was the first official hoisting of the English flag in "English Dominions across the sea," and incidentally the founding of the British Empire.

Surmounting the Memorial is the allegorical figure of Freedom, with an uplifted torch in one hand, a sword in the other, on a granite pedestal, at the sides of which at the base are figures representing the Royal Newfoundland Regiment (soldier) at the left; Royal Naval Reserve of Newfoundland (sailor) at the right; and in a central position, facing front, a woodsman and a seaman in oilskins, representative of the Newfoundland Forestry Corps and the Newfoundland Merchant Marine.

The Memorial was made possible by public subscription of $50,000, raised between 1922 and 1923—(A slogan die inserted in the electric cancelling machine at the G.P.O. and first used March 14, 1922, read, "Have you contributed to the War Memorial?")—through the efforts of Lt.-Col. T. Nangle, who during the war was R. C. Chaplain, with the Newfoundland Regiment. After the Armistice he was appointed Graves Commissioner, and looked after the many burying places of Newfoundlanders in France, Flanders and the Gallipoli. On returning to Newfoundland in 1923, he was elected President of the Great War Veterans Association.

On July 5, 1925, a dedicatory tablet of bronze placed on the Memorial, was unveiled by Governor Sir William Allardyce, K.C.M.G., reading: "To the Glory of God—and—in Perpetual Remembrance—of —One Hundred and Ninety-two Men of the Newfoundland Royal Naval Reserve, Thirteen Hundred Men of the Royal Newfoundland Regiment, and One Hundred and Nineteen Men of the Newfoundland Mercantile Marine, who gave their lives by sea and land for the defence of the British Empire in the Great War 1914-1918; For enduring witness, also, the services of the men of this Island who, during that war, fought, not without honour, in the Navies and Armies of their Empire: this Monument is erected by their fellow countrymen. —'Let us give glory unto the Lord and declare His praise in the Islands.' Isaiah 42: 12."

9c Green.

In June, 1928, the stocks of the 9c stamp became exhausted. Official notification was to the effect that there would be no reprint. The early shortage of this stamp, of a denomination not commonly used, would indicate the activities of speculators not more than a mile from the G.P.O.

15c Blue.

The stamp shows the famous Vickers-Vimy plane in which the late Sir John Alcock, with Sir Arthur Whitten Brown, accomplished the *first non-stop transatlantic flight* in 1919. The plane is shown rising from Lester's Field, St. John's, where it took off on the great adventure.

N1

N2

N3

N4

N5

N6

N7

N8

Papers (A) Thick opaque 1857.
(B) Medium fairly opaque 1860.
(C) Thin hard semi-transparent.

No.	Type.			Unused.	Used.
1	*N1*	1p	Brown violet (A) *1857*	9.00	12.50
			On cover $20.00; block 4	*30.00*	
			a. Re-entry		*50.00*
2		1p	Violet brown (A)	9.00	20.00
			On cover $30.00; block 4	*40.00*	
			a. Watermarked		
3		1p	Reddish brown (B) *1862-3*	500.00	
4		1p	Purple brown (C)	12.00	20.00
			On cover $35.00; block 4	*55.00*	
			a. Watermark, entire sheet $300.00; single	*25.00*	
5	*N2*	2p	Scarlet vermilion (A) *1857*	700.00	350.00
			On cover $450.00.		
6		2p	Orange (B) *1860*	50.00	100.00
			On cover $150.00.		
7		2p	Rose (C) *1862-3*	20.00	40.00
			a. Watermarked	*30.00*	
			On cover	*55.00*	
8		2p	Rose (A) *1862*	40.00	75.00
9	*N3*	3p	Green (A) *1857*	20.00	50.00
10		3p	Green (B) *1860*	6.00	10.00
			A cover $17.50; block 4	*30.00*	
			a. Watermarked (C)		
11	*N4*	4p	Scarlet vermilion (A) *1857*	500.00	200.00
			On cover $		
			Half used as 2p on cover		

No.	Type.			Unused.	Used.
12		4p	Orange (B) *1860*	200.00	100.00
			On cover $175.00		
			a. Half used as 2d on cover		
13		4p	Rose (C) *1862-3*	1.75	7.50
			On cover $12.00; block 4	*9.00*	
			Entire sheet, $50.00; Watermarked, $75.00; single	*2.25*	
			Half used as 2p on cover		
14		4p	Rose (A)	5.00	25.00
			Block 4	*22.50*	
15	*N4*	5p	Violet brown (A) *1857*	7.00	15.00
			On cover $25.00; block 4	*30.00*	
16		5p	Brown violet (B) *1860*	9.00	15.00
			On cover $25.00; block 4	*40.00*	
			a. Watermarked		
17		5p	Reddish brown (C) *1862-63*	3.50	10.00
			On cover $17.50; block 4	*16.00*	
			Entire sheet, $100.00		
18		5p	Orange brown (C)	*4.00*	*12.00*
			On cover $17.50; block 4	*20.00*	
19	*N5*	6p	Scarlet vermilion (A) *1857*	600.00	200.00
20		6p	Orange (B) *1860*	300.00	75.00
21		6p	Rose (C) *1862-3*	1.25	5.00
			On cover $7.60; block 4	*6.00*	*50.00*
			Half used as 3p on cover		*200.00*
			a. With portion of watermark	*1.50*	
			b. Entire sheet	*40.00*	
			c. Watermarked sheet	*50.00*	
22		6p	Rose (A)		
23	*N6*	6½p	Scarlet vermilion (A) *1857*	125.00	150.00
24		6½p	Orange (B) *1860*	1250.00	
25		6½p	Rose (C) *1862-3*	6.00	25.00
			On cover $100.00; block 4	*25.00*	
26		6½p	Rose (A)		
27	*N7*	8p	Scarlet vermilion (A) *1857*	20.00	40.00
			On cover $60.00; block 4	*95.00*	
			Half used as 4p on cover		*150.00*
28		8p	Rose (C) *1862-3*	6.00	50.00
			Block 4	*30.00*	
29		8p	Rose (A)		
30	*N8*	1s	Scarlet vermilion (A) *1857*	750.00	400.00
			a. Half used as 6p on cover		
31		1s	Orange (B) *1860*	1200.00	500.00
			a. Half used as 6p on cover		
32		1s	Orange LAID PAPER *1860*	1250.00	
33		1s	Rose (C) *1962-3*	2.50	12.50
			On cover, $18.00; block 4	*12.50*	
			Entire sheet, $100.00		
			Half used as 6p on cover		
34		1s	Rose (A)		

N9

N10

N11

N12

N13

N14

No.	Type.			Unused.	Used.
			1866. Perf. 12.		
35	*N9*	2c	Green	3.00	2.50
			On cover $5.00; block 4	*20.00*	
			a. Thin yellowish paper	*4.00*	*4.00*
			b. Half used as 1c on cover		
36	*N10*	5c	Brown, *thin yellowish paper*	30.00	20.00
			On cover $27.50; block 4	*200.00*	
			a. Half used as 2½c on cover		
			b. Re-entry	*100.00*	*75.00*
			c. No guide dot		
37	*N11*	10c	Black	7.50	3.50
			On cover $5.00; block 4	*40.00*	
			a. Thin yellowish paper	*8.50*	*5.00*
			b. Half used as 5c on cover		
38	*N12*	12c	Pale red brown	1.25	1.25
			On cover $2.50; block 4	*6.00*	
			a. Thin yellowish paper	*15.00*	*10.00*
			b. Half used as 6c on cover		
39		12c	Puce brown *1890-94*	2.00	2.00
			On cover $2.50; block 4	*7.50*	
40	*N13*	13c	Orange, *thin yellowish paper*	3.50	3.50
			On cover $6.00; block 4	*25.00*	
41	*N14*	24c	Blue (*thin paper*)	1.00	1.25
			Block 4	*5.00*	
42		24c	Blue, *medium white wove paper*	15.00	10.00

N15

N16

N17

No.	Type.			Unused.	Used.
			1868		
			Engraved and printed by National Bank Note Co. New York.		
43	*N15*	1c	Violet	3.00	3.00
			On cover $5.00; block 4	*16.00*	
			1868-73.		
			Re-engraved and printed by American Bank Note Co., New York. (*Triangular white space under T of CENT is larger than National design*).		
44	*N16*	1c	Brown purple	3.50	3.50
			On cover $5.50; block 4	*17.00*	
45	*N17*	3c	Vermilion	10.00	7.50
			On cover $12.00; block 4	*75.00*	
46		3c	Blue	6.00	2.75
			On cover $4.50; block 4	*40.00*	
47	*N10*	5c	Black, *white wove*	17.50	15.00
			On cover $25.00; block 4	*100.00*	
			a. Re-entry	*100.00*	*75.00*
			b. No guide dot	*25.00*	*22.50*
48	*N17*	6c	Dull rose	.50	.50
			On cover $1.00; block 4	*2.25*	*6.00*
49		6c	Carmine lake *1894*	1.00	1.00
			On cover $1.75; block 4	*5.00*	
			1876-79 Rouletted.		
50		1c	Brown lilac	6.00	4.00
			On cover $7.50; block 4	*35.00*	
51	*N9*	2c	Green	4.00	3.00
			On cover $6.50; block 4	*25.00*	
52	*N17*	3c	Blue	5.00	1.00
			On cover $2.25; Block 4	*25.00*	
53	*N10*	5c	Blue	6.00	.80
			On cover $2.50; block 4	*50.00*	
			a. Re-entry	*100.00*	*15.00*
			b. No guide dot	*15.00*	*5.00*
			c. Imperf. pair		

N18

N19

N20

N21

N22

N23

No.	Type.			Unused.	Used.
			Engraved and printed by British American Bank Note Co., Montreal.		
			Perf. 12.		
54	*N18*	½c	Rose red, 1887	.35	.35
			On cover $1.00; block 4	*1.75*	*2.00*
55		½c	Black, 1894	.20	.20
			On cover $1.00; block 4	*1.25*	*1.50*
56		½c	Orange red *re-issue*, 1896	1.00	1.00
			On cover $1.50; block 4	*5.50*	*6.00*
57	*N19*	1c	Violet brown, 1880	.75	.75
			On cover $1.25; block 4	*4.50*	
58		1c	Grey brown, 1880	2.00	2.00
			On cover $3.00; block 4	*9.00*	
59		1c	Deep green, 1887	.20	.50
			On cover $1.00; block 4	*1.00*	
60		1c	Grey green, 1887	.50	.50
			On cover $1.00; block 4	*2.50*	
61		1c	Brown *re-issue*, 1896	.70	.50
			On cover .75; block 4	*3.50*	
62		1c	Green *re-issue*, 1896	1.00	.50
			On cover $1.00; block 4	*5.00*	
63	*N20*	2c	Yellow green, 1880	2.50	1.25
			On cover $2.00; block 4	*11.50*	
64		2c	Red orange, 1887	.25	.25
			On cover .75; block 4	*1.00*	
			a. Imperf. pair	*20.00*	
65		2c	Green *re-issue*, 1896	.75	.75
			On cover $1.25; block 4	*4.00*	
66	*N21*	3c	Blue, 1880	1.75	.35
			On cover $1.00; block 4	*8.50*	
67		3c	Deep brown, 1887	2.50	.75
			On cover $2.00; block 4	*15.00*	*5.00*
68		3c	Deep blue *re-issue*, 1896-7	2.00	1.00
			On cover $2.00; block 4	*9.00*	
69		3c	Chocolate brown *re-issue*, 1896-7	1.50	1.75
			On cover $2.50; block 4	*8.00*	*5.00*
70	*N22*	5c	Pale blue, 1880	3.00	.50
			On cover $1.00; block 4	*15.00*	
71		5c	Dark blue, 1887	3.00	.50
			On cover $1.00; block 4	*15.00*	
72		5c	Bright blue, 1894	1.00	.50
			On cover $1.00; block 4	*5.00*	
			a. Minor variety—all shades		*2.00*

N24

Type I. Type II. Type III.

No.	Type.			Unused.	Used.
73	*N23*	10c	Black, 1887	3.00	2.50
			On cover $3.75; block 4	*15.00*	
			a. Hairline CE of CENT	*7.50*	
			1890. Perf. 12.		
74	*N24*	3c	Slate	1.25	.10
			On cover .25; block 4	*10.00*	
75		3c	Grey lilac	1.00	.10
			On cover .25; block 4	*7.50*	
76		3c	Brown lilac	1.00	.15
			On cover .35; block 4	*10.00*	
77		3c	Lilac	1.00	.15
			On cover .35; block 4	*10.00*	
78		3c	Slate violet	1.25	.25
			On cover .75; block 4	*12.00*	
			a. Pair, imperf. horiz.	*40.00*	
			Nov., 1897. Surcharged "One Cent".		
79	*N24*		Type I, black, thick letters	2.50	2.50
			a. Red surcharge		
			b. Red over black		
80			Type II, black, thinner letters	6.00	6.00
			a. Red surcharge		
			b. Red over black		
81			Type III, black, no seriphs	30.00	35.00
			a. Red surcharge		
			b. Red over black		
			Block of 4 showing all types	60.00	
			Pair showing Types II and III	40.00	

N25

N26

N27

N28

N29

N30

N31

N32

N33

N34

N35

N36

N37

N38

No.	Type.		**1897. Cabot Issue.**	Unused.	Used.
82	*N25*	1c	Deep green	.25	.25
			Block 4	*1.25*	*1.50*
83	*N26*	2c	Carmine lake	.25	.25
			Block 4	*1.25*	*1.50*
84	*N27*	3c	Ultramarine	.25	.10
			Block 4	*1.25*	*1.50*
85	*N28*	4c	Olive green	.25	.25
			On cover .50; block 4	*1.25*	*1.50*
86	*N29*	5c	Violet	.25	.25
			On cover .50; block 4	*1.25*	*1.50*
87	*N30*	6c	Red brown	.25	.25
			On cover .50; block 4	*1.25*	*1.50*
88	*N31*	8c	Red orange	.50	.50
			On cover .75; block 4	*2.25*	*2.50*
89	*N32*	10c	Black Brown	.75	.75
			On cover $1.00; block 4	*3.50*	*3.50*
90	*N33*	12c	Dark blue	.60	.60
			On cover $1.00; block 4	*3.00*	*3.00*
91	*N34*	15c	Scarlet	.60	.60
			On cover $1.00; block 4	*3.00*	*3.50*
92	*N35*	24c	Grey violet	1.00	1.00
			On cover $1.50; block 4	*5.00*	*5.00*
93	*N36*	30c	Slate	1.25	1.25
			On cover $1.75; block 4	*6.00*	*6.00*
94	*N37*	35c	Red	1.50	1.50
			On cover $1.75; block 4	*10.00*	*10.00*
95	*N38*	60c	Black	1.75	1.75
			On cover $2.25; block 4	*10.00*	*10.00*

N39

N40

N41

N42

N43

No.	Type.			Unused.	Used.
			1897-1901. Perf. 12.		
96	*N39*	½c	Olive green Prince Edward *Aug., 1898*...	.04	.02
			Block 4............................	.25	.40
			a. Imperf. pair....................	40.00	
97	*N40*	1c	Carmine rose Queen Victoria *Dec., 1897*.	.12	.10
			Block 4............................	.60	.50
			a. Vert. pair imperf. between..........		
100	*N40*	1c	Blue green *June, 1898*................	.08	.02
			Block 4............................	.50	.35
101	*N40*	1c	Myrtle green(thin).................	.15	.02
			Block 4............................	.75	.35
			a. Vert. pair imperf. between..........	30.00	
98	*N41*	2c	Orange King Edward VII *Dec., 1897*....	.25	.18
			Block 4............................	1.25	1.50
99		2c	Vermilion King Edward VII *June, 1898*.	.08	.03
			Block 4............................	.50	.35
			a. Imperf. pair....................	40.00	
			b. Imperf. pair on cover..............	55.00	
102	*N42*	3c	Orange Queen Alexandra *June, 1898*....	.18	.05
			Block 4............................	.90	.50
			a. Imperf. pair....................	50.00	
103		3c	Reddish orange *bluish paper June, 1918*.		
104	*N43*	5c	Blue Duke of York (George V) *June, 1899*	.25	.10
			On cover .35; block 4.................	1.50	
			a. Vert. pair imperf. between..........	30.00	

N44

N45

No.	Type.			Unused.	Used.
			Oct., 1901. Perf. 12.		
105	*N44*	4c	Violet *Princess (Mary) of Wales*........	.40	.25
			On cover .50; block 4..................	*1.75*	*1.75*
			a. Imperf. pair......................		*24.00*
			Sept., 1908. Perf. 12.		
106	*N45*	2c	Rose carmine........................	.15	.04

N46  N47

N48  N49  N50

N51  N52  N52

N54  N55  N56

			Aug. 15, 1910. Lithographed. Guy Issue.		
107	*N46*	1c	Deep green Perf. 12..................	.25	.25
			a. Perf. 12x11......................	*.15*	*.06*
			b. Perf. 11½x11.....................	*.15*	*.06*
			c. Perf. 12x14½.....................	*.20*	*.12*
			d. Horiz. pair imperf. between 12x11 and		

No.	Type.			Unused.	Used.
			12x14	*40.00*	
			e. Vert. pair imperf. between 11½x11	*40.00*	
			f. "NFW" for new (all perfs. except 12x11½)	*2.75*	
			g. "JANES" for JAMES Perf. 12		
			h. Dot before POSTAGE (all perfs. except 12x11½)		
			i. Dash between "One-Cent" (all perfs. except 12x11½)		
108	*N47*	2c	Carmine Perf. 12	*.20*	*.12*
			a. Perf. 12x14½	*.50*	*.06*
			b. Horiz. pair imperf. between (12x14½)		
			c. Perf. 12x11½		
			d. Variety, leaf on left front leg of Unicorn on top of cross		
			e. Colorless spot at back of lion, lower right Coat of Arms		
109	*N48*	3c	Brown olive Perf. 12	1.25	1.25
			On cover $1.50; block 4	*6.00*	*7.00*
110	*N49*	4c	Dull violet Perf. 12	1.25	1.25
			On cover $1.50; block 4	*6.00*	*7.00*
111	*N50*	5c	Ultramarine Perf. 12	1.00	1.00
			a. Imperf. pair		
			b. Perf. 14½x12	*.50*	*.25*
112	*N51*	6c	Claret Perf. 12	3.00	3.00
			On cover $3.75; block 4	*15.00*	
			a. Imperf. pair		
			b. "Z" of "COLONIZATION" reversed	*1.75*	*1.75*
113	*N52*	8c	Pale brown Perf. 12	1.75	1.75
			Block 4	*8.00*	
114	*N53*	9c	Olive green Perf. 12	*1.75*	*1.75*
			Block 4	*8.00*	
115	*N54*	10c	Violet black Perf. 12	2.00	2.00
			Block 4	*9.50*	
116	*N55*	12c	Lilac brown Perf. 12	2.00	2.00
			Block 4	*9.50*	
			a. Imperf. pair		
117	*N56*	15c	Grey black Perf. 12	3.00	3.00
			Block 4	*15.00*	

January, February, 1911. Perf. 14½.

			ENGRAVED,		
118	*N51*	6c	Brown violet	2.00	2.50
			Imperf. block 4	*600.00*	
119	*N52*	8c	Bistre Brown	4.50	5.00
			a. Imperf. pair	*300.00*	
120	*N53*	9c	Olive green	4.25	5.00
			a. Imperf. block 4	*600.00*	
121	*N54*	10c	Violet black	4.50	5.00
			a. Imperf. pair	*300.00*	
122	*N55*	12c	Red brown	4.50	5.00
			a. Imperf. block 4	*600.00*	
123	*N56*	15c	Slate green	5.50	5.50
			a. Imperf. block 4	*600.00*	

N57

N58

N59

N60

N61

N62

N63

N64

N65

N66

N67

No.	Type.			Unused.	Used.
			June 19, 1911. Perf. 13½x14 or 14x14.		
			Royal Family Issue commemorating coronation of King George V.		
124	*N57*	1c	Yellow green *13½x14 and 14x14*	.05	.02
125	*N58*	2c	Carmine *13½x14 and 14x14*	.08	.02
126		2c	Carmine *13½x14 and 14x14, Blurred Impression, 1917*	.25	.05
127	*N59*	3c	Red brown	.50	.50
			Block 4	*2.25*	
128	*N60*	4c	Violet	.50	.50
			Block 4	*2.25*	
129	*N61*	5c	Ultramarine *Perf. 13½x14 and 14x14*	.25	.08
			Block 4	*1.15*	
130	*N62*	6c	Black *Perf. 13½x14 and 14x14*	1.00	1.00
			Block 4	*5.00*	
131	*N63*	8c	Peacock blue *Perf. 13½x14 and 14x14*	5.00	5.00
			Block 4	*25.00*	
132		8c	Paper colored through *13½x14 and 14x14*	3.00	3.00
133	*N64*	9c	Blue violet *Perf. 13½x14 and 14x14*	1.00	1.00
134	*N65*	10c	Dark green	1.25	1.25
135	*N66*	12c	Plum *Perf. 13½x14 and 14x14*	1.25	1.25
			a. Imperf. pair	*16.00*	
136	*N67*	15c	Magenta *Perf. 13½x14 and 14x14*	1.25	1.25
			a. Imperf. pair	*12.00*	

No.	Type.			Unused.	Used.
			Dec. 24th, 1918 to Dec. 31st, 1918.		
137			Envelopes stamped "Postage Paid G.P.O. St. Johns Newf'l'd." in violet (notes)....		

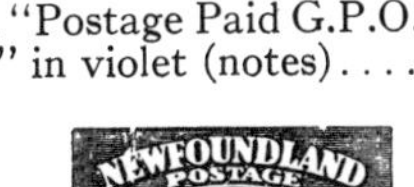

N69

N70

Jan. 2nd, 1919. Perf. 14. Trail of the Caribou Issue.

No.	Type.			Unused.	Used.
138	*N69*	1c	Green..........................	.04	.02
139	*N70*	2c	Scarlet or Carmine Red...............	.06	.02
140		3c	Red brown (*Gueudecourt*).............	.08	.04
			Block 4..........................	.40	.30
141		4c	Violet (*Beaumont Hamel*).............	.20	.20
			Block 4..........................	*1.00*	*1.20*
142		5c	Ultramarine........................	.25	.15
			Block 4..........................	*1.15*	*1.00*
143		6c	Grey (*Monchy*)......................	1.00	1.00
			Block 4..........................	*5.00*	*5.00*
144		8c	Magenta...........................	1.00	1.00
			Block 4..........................	*5.00*	*5.00*
145		10c	Dark green (*Steenbeck*).............	.40	.40
			Block 4..........................	*2.00*	*2.40*
146	*N70*	12c	Orange............................	.75	.75
			Block 4..........................	*4.00*	*4.75*
147		15c	Dark blue (Langemarck).............	1.00	1.00
			Block 4..........................	*5.00*	*6.00*
148		24c	Bistre (Cambrai)....................	1.00	1.00
			Block 4..........................	*5.00*	*6.50*
149		36c	Olive green (Combles)...............	1.50	1.50
			Block 4..........................	*7.00*	*8.00*

N71

N72

N73

Sept. 11th to 25th, 1920.
Stamps of 1897 Surcharged.

Sept. 11th, 1920. *(2975)*

No.	Type.			Unused.	Used.
150	*N71*	3c on 15c.	Scarlet *bars 10½ mm. apart*........	6.00	6.00
			a. Inverted surcharged (25)............	*150.00*	

No.	Type.			Unused.	Used.
			Sept. 13th, 1920. (47,000).		
151	*N71*	3c on 15c.	Scarlet *bars 13½mm. apart*.........	1.75	1.75
			Sept. 14th, 1920 (49,000).		
152	*N72*	3c on 35c.	Red..............................	1.50	1.50
			a. Lower bar omitted (1000)............	*25.00*	
			b. THREE omitted (stamps 13 and 14 of a few panes).......................		
			c. Lower portion only THREE showing..	*100.00*	
			d. Top of NTS of CENTS missing......		
			Sept. 23rd, 1920.		
153	*N73*	2c on 30c.	Slate...........................	1.25	1.25
			a. Inverted surcharged (50)...........	*75.00*	

N74  N75  N76

N77  N78  N79  N80

N81  N82  N83  N84

N85  N86  N87

			July 9, 1923.		
154	*N74*	1c	Grey green *Perf. 14x14*................	.03	.02
155	*N75*	2c	Carmine *Perf. 14x14*...................	.06	.03
156	*N76*	3c	Brown *Perf. 14x14 and 13½x14*.........	.08	.02

No.	Type.			Unused.	Used.
157	*N77*	4c	Brown-violet *Perf. 14x14 and 13½x14*	.12	.06
158	*N78*	5c	Ultramarine *Perf. 14x14 and 13½x14*	.15	.06
159	*N79*	6c	Grey-black *Perf. 14x13½*	.18	.10
160	*N80*	8c	Dull violet *Perf. 14x13½*	.24	.12
161	*N81*	9c	Slate green *Perf. 14x13½*	.85	.75
			Block 4	*4.25*	*4.75*
162	*N82*	10c	Dark violet *Perf. 13½x14*	.30	.15
			Block 4	*1.50*	*1.25*
163	*N83*	11c	Olive green *Perf. 14x13½*	.40	.25
			Block 4	*2.00*	*2.00*
164	*N84*	12c	Lake *Perf. 14x13½ and 14x14*	.45	.20
			Block 4	*2.00*	*2.00*
165	*N85*	15c	Deep blue *Perf. 13½x14 and 14x14*	.50	.25
			Block 4	*2.50*	*2.00*
			April 28, 1924.		
166	*N86*	20c	Red brown *Perf. 14x13½*	.60	.30
			Block 4	*3.00*	*2.00*
			April 22, 1924.		
167	*N87*	24c	Black brown *Perf. 14x14 and 13½x14*	1.50	1.25
			Block 4	*8.00*	*8.00*

N88

N89

N90

N91

N92

N93

N94

N95

N96

N97

N98

N99

N100

No.	Type.			Unused.	Used.
			Jan. 3rd, 1928. Perf. 12.		
168	*N88*	1c	Green	.03	.01
169	*N89*	2c	Red	.05	.02
170	*N90*	3c	Brown	.06	.02
171	*N91*	4c	Purple	.08	.02
172	*N92*	5c	Grey	.10	.02
173	*N93*	6c	Blue	.12	.04
174	*N94*	8c	Lavender	.16	.05
175	*N95*	9c	Green	2.50	2.50
176	*N96*	10c	Purple	1.50	.75
177	*N97*	12c	Maroon	.24	.07
178	*N98*	15c	Blue	.30	.10
179	*N99*	20c	Grey	.40	.15
180	*N97*	28c	Grey-green (Dec. 1928)	.50	.20
181	*N100*	30c	Sepia	.75	.35

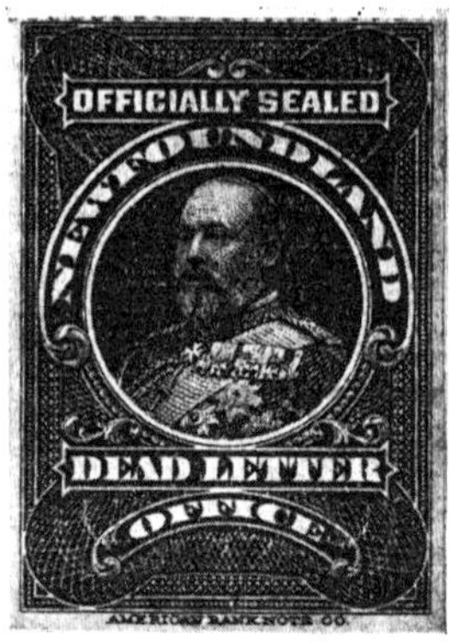

N110

N110	No denomination, black or blue wove	10.00
	Block 4	*45.00*

FIRST
TRANS-
ATLANTIC
AIR POST
April, 1919.

N200

N201

N202

Air Mail
DE PINEDO
1927

N203

No.	Type.			Unused.	Used.
			May 18, 1919, overprinted in black.		
200	*N200*	3c	Caribou overprinted..................	500.00	450.00
			(There is a forgery in which "April" appears "APRIL")		
			14th June, 1919, overprinted in black.		
201	*N201*	15c	Cabot overprinted....................	8.00	
			a. No comma after "AIR POST".......	*12.00*	
			b. No period after "1919".............	*24.00*	
			c. No comma (Air Post) no period (1919)		
			(Total issue 10,000)		
			Nov., 1921. Overprinted in black. *(14,000)*		
202	*N202*	35c	Cabot overprinted....................	3.00	3.00
			a. Inverted surcharge (50 from Plates 2 and 18) (narrow and wide space between air mail)..........................	*75.00*	
			Stamps with wide space between "Air Mail."		
			b. No stop after "1921" (10 in sheet)....	*3.50*	
			c. "1921" moved to right (1 in sheet)....		
			d. Stop after "1921" (7 in sheet)........	*4.50*	
			Stamps with narrow space between "Air Mail."		
			e. Stop after "1921" (4 in sheet)........	*4.50*	
			f. No stop after "1921" (2 in sheet).....	*6.00*	
			g. "1921" moved to right, no stop, (1 in sheet)		
			May 18, 1927. Overprinted in red (300).		
203	*N203*	60c	Cabot overprinted....................	350.00	150.00

ESSAYS

Normal Minor Doub'ing Major Doubling

N38	60c	Black surcharged in red in three lines "TWO-2-CENTS" *(100)*.............		25.00
		a. Double impression in Mrs. A. R. Clarke collection..........................		
		Sept. 1920 *(Notes on Cabot issue)*		
N71	6c	Red-brown surcharged in red "THREE CENTS" (25)........................		
		a. Surcharged in black (25)............		
N73	30c	Slate, surcharged "TWO CENTS" in red (25)............................		

Essays for Air Mail Stamps.

During the summer of 1919, Messrs. Whitehead, Morris & Co., Ltd., at the request of the Postmaster General, Dr. J. Alex. Robinson, submitted three designs for proposed air mail stamps. This gave rise to the rumor that special stamps were being prepared for issue when the Prince of Wales visited the island on August 12th and 13th, 1919, just as the 4c of the Royal series (Queen Mary was brought out in October, 1901, when Their Majesties (then Prince and Princess of Wales) visited St. John's, while on Empire tour. (Harry E. Huber).

Proofs

The following list is far from complete. The author would appreciate the co-operation of Newfoundland specialists in building up this check list.

1857:

1d. . . . .
2d. . . . .
3d Black (cardboard) $12.00
4d. . . . .
5d Black (cardboard) 12.00
6d. . . . .
6½d Black (cardboard) 12.00
8d. . . . .
1s. . . . .
1d to 1s on B paper, with SPECIMEN diag., seriphed letters, each stamp. 10.00

1866:

2c Issued stamp overprinted "RECOM:" in black reading, normal and inverted.
5c Brown (die) 12.00
6c Brown, black, brown orange, deep rose red 6.00
10c. . . . .
12c. . . . .
13c. . . . .
24c Color of issue, (Plate, on India) 2.00

1868:

1c. . . . .
3c. . . . .
5c. . . . .
6c. . . . .

1880:

1c. . . . .
2c. . . . .
3c. . . . .
5c Blue (die) 10.00

1887:

½c. . . . .
10c. . . . .

1890-94:

3c. . . . .

1897 Cabot:

1c. . . . .
2c. . . . .
3c. . . . .
4c. . . . .
5c. . . . .
6c. . . . .
8c. . . . .
10c. . . . .
12c. . . . .
15c. . . . .
24c. . . . .
30c. . . . .
35c. . . . .
60c. . . . .

1898-99:

1c. . . . .
2c. . . . .
½c. . . . .
3c. . . . .
5c. . . . .

1901:

4c. . . . .

1908:

2c. . . . .

1910 Guy:

1c. . . . .
2c. . . . .
3c. . . . .
4c. . . . .
5c. . . . .
6c. . . . .
8c. . . . .
9c. . . . .
10c. . . . .
12c. . . . .
15c. . . . .

1911 Royal Family:

1c. . . . .
2c. . . . .

3c. . . . .
4c. . . . .
5c. . . . .
6c. . . . .
8c. . . . .
9c. . . . .
10c. . . . .
12c. . . . .
15c. . . . .

1918 Caribou:

1c. . . . .
2c. . . . .
3c. . . . .
4c. . . . .
5c. . . . .
6c. . . . .
8c. . . . .
10c. . . . .
12c. . . . .
15c. . . . .
24c. . . . .
36c. . . . .

1923-24:

1c. . . . .
2c. . . . .
3c. . . . .
4c. . . . .
5c. . . . .
6c. . . . .
8c. . . . .
9c. . . . .
10c. . . . .
11c. . . . .
12c. . . . .
15c. . . . .
20c. . . . .
24c. . . . .

NS1

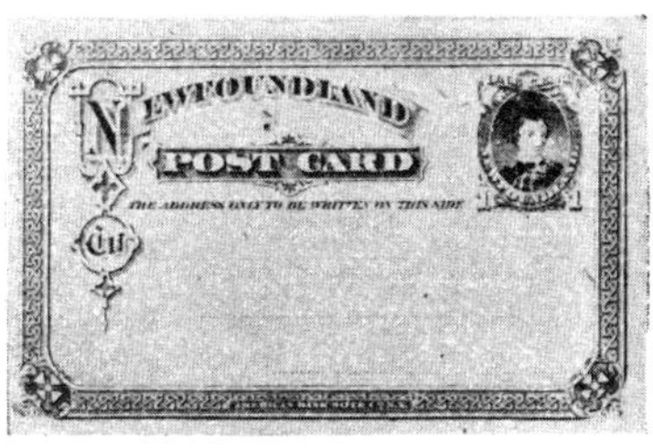

NS2

NS3

NS4

NS5

NS6

NS7

NS8

No.	Type.			Unused.	Used.
1	NS1	1c	Green engraved by British American Bank Note Co., Montreal.............	.15	.10
2	NS2	1c	Green, engraved by American Bank Note Co., N.Y.......................	.15	.10
3	NS3	1c	Green, engraved by American Bank Note Co., N.Y...........................	.15	.10
4	NS4	1c	Green...............................	.02	.02
			Universal Postal Union.		
5	NS5	2c	Vermilion, engraved by American Bank Note Company, New York............	.25	.15
6	NS6	2c	Red orange, engraved by British American Bank Note Co., Montreal.........	.25	.15
7	NS7	2c+2c.	Bright red (Reply card)..............	.25	.15
8	NS8	2c	Vermilion (*Queen Alexandra*)...........		

NS9

Envelopes.

1	NS9	5c	Ultramarine or Pale Blue (Embossed)...
2		4c	Ultramarine (*Queen Victoria*)...........
3		3c	Violet (*Queen Victoria*)................

Wholesale Values

The following are the prices at which the more common Newfoundland stamps may be purchased from dealers at time of going to press, January 1929.

			Per 10	Per 100	Per 1000
1887	1c	Green	$ .80		
	2c	Red orange	.85		
	3c	Brown	2.50	$20.00	
1890	3c	Slate	.35	2.75	
1897	1c	Green Cabot	.80		
	2c	Carmine Cabot	.80		
	3c	Ultramarine Cabot	.35	2.85	
	4c	Olive green Cabot	.90		
	6c	Red brown Cabot	.75		
1898–99	1c	Olive green	.60		
	2c	Vermilion	.07		
	1c	Green	.06	.45	
	3c	Orange	.10	.75	
	5c	Blue	.40		
1901	4c	Violet	1.15		
1908	2c	Carmine	.12		
1910	2c	Carmine	.12	1.00	
1911	1c	Green	.04	.30	
	2c	Carmine	.04	.30	
	5c	Ultramarine	.35		
1918	1c	Green Caribou	.04	.35	
	2c	Scarlet Caribou	.05	.45	
	3c	Red Brown	.05	.40	
	4c	Violet	.20	1.90	
	5c	Ultramarine Caribou	.20	1.90	
1923–24	1c	Green	.04	.30	
	2c	Carmine	.04	.30	
	3c	Brown	.04	.30	
	4c	Brown Violet	.15	1.15	
	5c	Ultramarine	.12	1.00	
	6c	Grey Black	.35		
	8c	Dull Violet	.50		
	9c	Slate Green	.40		

A rare cover in the Lichtenstein Collection

The stamps were engraved and printed by Messrs. Perkins, Bacon & Petch, and supplied through Mr. Trelawney Saunders, with the exception of the last requisition which was supplied through a Mr. Stamford. All values were printed in sheets of 160 stamps, with the exception of the 1d which was printed in sheets of 120 for greater convenience in computing values. For example, two sheets of 160 each would amount each to £1.6.4 while two sheets of 120 each would amount to £1.0.0.

The 1d stamp is on a distinctly bluish paper. Specimens on whiter paper are probably those from which the color has been discharged.

There are forgeries which may be detected at once by any collector at all familiar with Nova Scotia stamps. The best of these is on a paper that is thin and quite different from the original. The workmanship is crude.

3d Blue.
For the most part the stamps come in slightly blued paper. Donald A. King states that the last requisition in 1857 included a few sheets on intensely blue paper. None of the stamps occur on a true white paper, but by comparison with the blued paper they may be classed as white. The stamps are often tinted blue on the face by the ink or because the plates were not thoroughly cleaned.

Of several forgeries of the 3d none are dangerous except two engraved ones attributed to the original engraver. On one of these he shows "facsimile" printed in small black type above the word "Postage."

6d Green.
Donald A. King states that the last shipment of stamps in 1857 included stamps on an intensely blued paper and that he has seen but four specimens of the 6d.

In the most successful counterfeit of the 6d the distinguishing feature is in the figure "6" which appears four times on the stamp, these figures being of a different shape and less heavy than in the genuine. No other forgery is at all dangerous. The lithographed forgeries in blue-green and yellow-green are quite crude.

1s Purple.
There are several counterfeits of the shilling stamps. The lithographed ones are of course easily detected, but an engraved forgery exists which might deceive. This Forgery is in demand by specialists and has a catalogue value of $10.00.

"Cents" Issue

The Province adopted a monetary system of dollars and cents in 1859. The new stamps were engraved and printed by the American Bank Note Co., New York, in sheets of 100, 10 rows of 10, with imprint top bottom and sides.

In the case of the 1c and 5c stamps, and possibly the other values as well, the plate was ruled with a vertical line at the left, in which guide dots were placed at regular intervals. A faint horizontal line passes through this dot. The 1c and 5c stamps in fine condition from the left side of the plate often show faint traces of these lines and dots.

1c Black.
The shades are grey to jet black. With the remainders purchased by Stanley Gibbons a single sheet (50 pairs) of the 1c was found which was not perforated vertically. The black shades on thin paper are the earliest printings.

2c Grey-purple.
The shades are grey-purple, slate-purple, dull purple and purple, the earlier printings on the the thin paper.

5c Blue.
An added paper variety is listed for 5c which may exist for other values It is similar to the ordinary wove papers in texture, but is quite thick by comparison.

Variety, 10c. Variety, 12½c.

8½c Green.
The variety "E in EIGHT unshaded" occurs as Nos. 33 and 94 in the sheet.

10c Vermilion.
The variety "Scroll incomplete at left" occurs as Nos. 32, 34, 57 and 85

in the sheet.

The variety "Stroke of color over S of SCOTIA" occurs in No. 76 in the sheet.

There is a variety showing the "O" broken in SCOTIA.

12½c Black.
The variety "Defective ornament at upper left" occurs as Nos. 38, 48 and 58 in the sheet.

The variety "Three dashes of color at upper left corner of scroll" occurs as No. 91 in the sheet.

There is a variety "Line of color extending upward from the right eye-brow."

Counterfeits:
The different values have been counterfeited with fair success, the 1c and 2c in two shades. The shades and paper correspond to the originals sufficiently to deceive, but the lettering of SCOTIA will not bear close inspection.

Another printing of these forgeries appears on thicker wove paper, with a wider perforation (illustrated above) and in shades that do not correspond to the originals. These bear the word "SPECIMEN" in a curved line inside the oval at bottom.

There is a crude lithographic forgery of all values, cancelled with ten curved vertical bars, enclosed with eight horizontal bars, four above and four below.

Reprints:
The four pence stamps were reprinted on thin hard white paper in 1890, prior to the plates being destroyed. The 1d is in a dark shade of brown which does not correspond with the original. The 6d is deep green and the 1s is violet black. It is not difficult to distinguish the reprints from the originals.

Remainders:
After Nova Scotia entered confederation the stamps of the Province ceased to be used. The remainders were later purchased by Messrs. A. A. Bartlett and Donald A. King for $18,000 and gradually put in the market through Stanley Gibbons, we believe. There were no remainders of the 5c stamps.

Rates:
In 1842, '51, '53, '54, and '56 measures were successively adopted for the establishment of a low rate of postage. On letters not exceeding ½ oz., 3d.; above ½ oz. and not exceeding 1 oz., 6d; above 1 oz. and not exceed-

ing 1½ oz., 9d, and so on in proportion. Letters posted and delivered in the same town charged 1d only per ½ oz. Newspapers conveyed free. Printed circulars, prices current, handbills, etc,. 1d. per oz. The rates to England on May 1st, 1856 were: Not above ½ oz. "direct" 7½d; by U.S. and British Packet 10d; by U.S. Packet, 1s 5½d.—(From Report of the Postmaster-General of Great Britain, 1857).

Edmund A. Smith Collection, Halifax, N.S.

Rarities:

Under this heading will be listed any outstanding philatelic items which may come to the attention of the auther, through sale by auction, private purchase or personal knowledge.

The Ayer Collection contained 11 unused and 37 used 1d, mostly in pairs and blocks; a block of 8 unused 3d dark blue; and a block of 12 unused pale blue; a block of four of the 6d dark green, used, and 35 used 6d yellow green including seversl strips.

The majority of the mint blocks of the 3d in existence today may be found in the Lichtenstein Collection, A mint block of six is in the collection of the author, and a specialist in Halifax possesses what is probably the largest mint block in any collection.

The Lichtenstein Collection contains two pairs of the 1s Cold Violet.

The same collection contains a mint block of twelve of the 5c in mint condition. A strip of five of the 2c on cover, and a 10c with 2c on cover—an unusual rate—are typical of many interesting items in this collection.

Bisected Stamps or "Splits".

The P. M. G.'s report for 1853 says: "To remedy to some extent the serious inconvenience said to be experienced by merchants and others in consequence of there being no seven and one half penny currency postage stamps by which parties who feel desirous could thus prepay their letters in England, and not wishing to put the Province to any further expense in having another "die"prepared, I considered it expedient to allow half stamps to be used with those now in use to obviate the want of accommodation complained of; and a circular was accordingly forwarded to my deputies, and a note issued to the public to the effect that letters could be prepaid to England by stamps, by parties using a Six Pence or two Three Penny stamps together with half of a Three Penny stamp. The Three Penny Stamp to be cut diagonally and the half to be equivalent to 1½d. The Three Penny stamp alone to be used for that purpose."

Although authority was given for bisecting the 3d stamp only, other values were bisected, vertically as well as horizontally, and the use of such fractions was allowed without question.

The value of any bisected stamp depends upon the cover, and the stamp must be well "tied on" by the cancellation. The postmarks should prove that the rate prepaid by the stamp is the proper rate, as, for example, a rate of 7½d made up by a "split" Should properly be on a cover addressed to England and bearing British postmarks; if found on a cover to an addressee in the Province it would be more than likely a fake.

Bisected "Cents" Issue.

There was no necessity for bisected stamps in this issue, but they nevertheless were used and passed without question. They were invariably cut diagonally.

Counterfeits were made up in the early nineties by the Coombes brothers in St. John, N.B. Counterfeits may be detected by the following tests:

1. Rate made up must correspond to the rate required as shown by cover
2. Cancellation must be correct.
3. Traces of surplus gum about edges of stamps.
4. Evidence of "tieing on" cancellation having been added on top of another.
5. Cancellation out of register between stamp and cover showing that an effort was made to attach stamp or half stamp to cancellation already on cover.

Quantities Issued.

		July 8, 1851			May 12, 1853	
		Sheets	Stamps		Sheets	Stamps
	3d........	2,500	400,000	1d........	200	24,000
	6d........	625	100,000			
	1s........	312½	50,000			
Totals:	3d........		2,000,000	6d........		500,000

		July 2, 1857	
		Sheets	Stamps
	3d........	10,000	1,600,000
	6d........	2,500	400,000
	1s........	1,250	200,000
Totals:	1s........	·	250,000

1c.......	1,150,000	5c......	3,950,000	10c.......	1,000,000
2c......	100,000	8½c....	600,000	12½c.....	600,000

An order dated May 12, 1853, s on record requesting 200 sheets of 1d stamps. The Postmaster at Amherst was supplied with 60 of the 1d stamps on June 30, 1853. The requisition would account for but 24,000, but the stamp is not nearly so rare as this small supply would indicate and we may be assured that a second and perhaps a third order was placed for a much larger supply.

In estimating the relative rarity of Nova Scotia and New Brunswick stamps a factor to be considered is the populations of the two Colonies. Nova Scotias population was about 35% greater than that of New Brunswick.

For more detailed notes of quantities requisitioned for and delivered see London Philatelist Vol. 24,P. 31, E. D. Bacon.

A1

A2

No.	Type.			Unused.	Used.
			Imperforate, stout wove paper.		
1	*A1*	1d	Red-brown *May, 1853*................	85.00	35.00
			a. Re-entry........................		*50.00*
			On cover $50.00. Pair..............		*100.00*
			Strip of three......................		*150.00*
2	*A2*	3d	Very dark blue *Sept. 1, '51*............	50.00	20.00
3			Bright blue........................	25.00	7.00
			On cover $10.00. Pair..............		*18.00*
			Block of four......................	*175.00*	
4			Pale blue (*Nov., 1857*)...............	30.00	10.00
5		6d	Yellow-green *Sept. 1, '51*............	70.00	45.00
			Cover $60.00. Pair..................		*150.00*
6			Blue-green *Sept. 1, '57*..............	150.00	65.00
			a. Deeply blued paper................		
7		1s	Light violet *Sept. 1, '51*..............	750.00	300.00
			On cover ......; Pair................		
8			Deeper violet......................	650.00	275.00

A3

A4

A5

Perf. 12. On sale Oct. 1, 1860, except 2c May 11, 1863.

No.	Type.			Unused.	Used.
			PAPERS: A—Thin hard wove; B—Thick soft wove; C—Yellowish wove; D—White wove.		
9	*A3*	1c	Black, Papers CD	1.75	2.50
10			Grey-black, Papers D	.75	1.50
			On cover $3.50; pair		5.00
			Strip of 5		25.00
			Block of 4		20.00
			a. Imperf. vert. pair	*40.00*	
11	*A3*	2c	Grey-purple, Paper D	1.00	1.75
			a. Yellowish "C" paper	*7.50*	*3.50*
			On cover $4.00; Pair	*2.00*	*4.00*
			Strip 3	*3.00*	*7.00*
			Block of 4	*4.50*	*25.00*
			b. Rose lilac	*1.50*	*2.25*
12	*A3*	5c	Blue, Papers A	7.50	1.50
			a. Yellowish "C" Paper	*12.00*	*2.00*
			b. Deep blue, Paper D	*7.50*	*1.75*
			c. Deep or Pale Blue, Paper A	*10.00*	*1.75*
			d. Blue, Paper B	*10.00*	*2.00*
			On cover $1.75; Pair		*5.00*
			Strip of 3		*7.50*
			Block of 4	*100.00*	*25.00*
13	*A4*	8½c	Deep green, Papers C	1.25	5.00
			On cover $60.00; Pair	*2.50*	*15.00*
			Strip 3	*3.75*	*25.00*
			Block of 4	*5.00*	
			a. Unshaded E in EIGHT	*2.50*	
14			Yellow green, Paper C	1.50	5.00
			a. Yellow green, Paper D	*12.00*	*12.00*
15	*A4*	10c	Vermilion, Paper C	3.00	3.50
			On cover $6.00; Pair	*6.00*	*10.00*
			Strip of 3	*9.00*	*15.00*
			Block of 4	*12.00*	
			Vermilion, Paper D	10.00	7.00
			a. Stitch watermark		*15.00*
			b. Incomplete scroll	*10.00*	*7.50*
			c. Stroke over S of SCOTIA	*12.00*	*10.00*
16	*A5*	12½c	Black, Paper A	3.00	3.50
			Black, Paper C	2.50	2.75
			On cover $15.00; Pair	*5.00*	*7.00*
			Strip of 3	*7.50*	*12.00*
			Block of 4	*11.00*	
			Black, Paper D	8.50	2.00
17		12½c	Grey-black, Paper C	2.50	3.50
			Grey-black, Paper D	5.00	7.00
			a. Incomplete ornament	*5.00*	
			b. 3 strokes of color, left	*6.00*	

A6

A7

A8

A9

A8

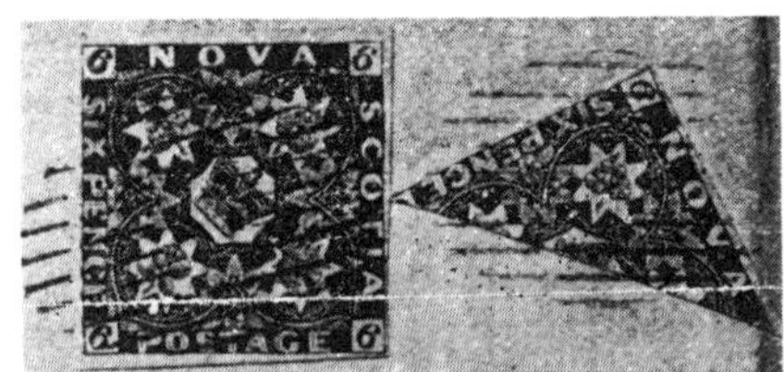

A10

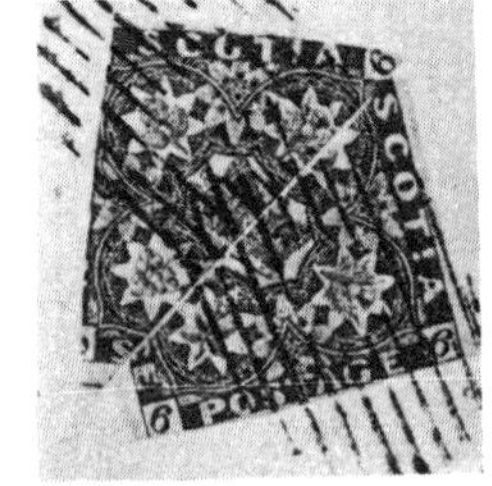

A11

A12

A13

A14

No.	Type.			Unused.	Used.
			Catalogue of "Splits" or Bisecteds. Values given are for Covers Only.		
18		1d	Bisected diag. for ½d rate.............		
19		3d	Bisected diag. with 3d for 4½d.........		
20	*A9*	3d	Dark Blue Bisected diag. with 1s bisected diag. for 7½d rate....................	600.00	
21	*A7*	3d	Dark Blue bisected diag. with 6d yellow green for 7½d rate..................	150.00	
22	*A8*	3d	Light blue bisected diag. with 6d dark green for 7½d rate..................	165.00	
23		1d	Bisected diag. with 1d and 6d yellow green for 7½d......................		
24	*A6*	3d	Dark blue bisected diag. with two 3d for 7½d rate..........................	110.00	

No.	Type.			Unused.	Used.
25	*A6*	3d	Light blue bisected diag. with two 3d for 7½d rate	125.00	
26		3d	Dark blue bisected diag. with 3d and three 6d yellow-green for 1s 10½d	200.00	
27	*A10*	6d	Yellow-green bisected diag. with 6d for 9d		
28		6d	6d Yellow-green quartered with 6d for 7½d		
29	*A13*	6d	Yellow-green bisected diag. for 3d		
30	*A13*	6d	Dark green bisected diag. for 3d		
31	*A13*	6d	Dark green on deep blue bisected diag. for 3d (*Lunenburg, Dec. 7, '59*)		
32	*A12*	6d	Dark green bisected vert.		
33		1s	Quartered for 3d		
34		1s	Violet bisected diag. for 6d		
35	*A11*	6d	Bisected diag., two bisecteds on one piece for 1s		
36		6d	Bisected diag., used with 3d bisected diag. on one piece for 6d rate		
			(As an indication of the depreciation in value of a bisected when "on piece of cover" only, a diagonal half of 3d used with a 6d for the 7½d rate, described as "on piece" and tied on, sold at Drew's Nov. 18, 1927, auction for $30.00 although catalogued over one hundred.)		
37		1c	Bisected for ½c		
38		2c	Bisected for 1c		
39		5c	Bisected for 2c (*county rate*)		
40		2c	Bisected and used with two 2c for 5c		
41		1c	Bisected and used with 8½c and 1c for 10c rate		
42		1c	Bisected and used with 10c and 2c for 12½c		
43		1c	Bisected and used with 12½c for 13c		
44		2c	Bisected, with 12½c for 13c		
45		2c	Bisected with 2c and 10c for 13c rate		
46		5c	Bisected with two 5c for 12½c		
47	*A*	10c	Bisected vert. for 5c		$50.00
48	*A14*		Bisected diag. for 5c		50.00
49	*A*	10c	Bisected, with 10c for 15c rate		50.00

I would further suggest the Head to be something similar to that represented in the margin, the field to be blue instead of Red, or any other Colour His Excellency would prefer. —

PROOFS ESSAYS AND COLOR TRIALS

Original Essay for 3d, with Postmaster Woodgate's suggestions.

The essay illustrated above, originally in the possession of Donald A. King, Halifax, is from the sketch submitted by A. Woodgate, Postmaster, Halifax, to the Honourable Joseph Howe, Provincial Secretary. Alongside we give a reproduction of that portion of Mr. Woodgate's accompanying letter dated April 21, 1851, having reference to his sketch.

An essay of the 6d exists, with the figure "6" enclosed in an octagen in the centre of a minute pattern of white and rose. "Six" is above and "Pence" below, with "Nova Scotia" on the left and right sides. The figure of value also appears in each of the four corners.

There is an essay of the 2c from which the stamp as issued was copied, as it is similar in all but a few minor details, which were improved upon in the finished design. It is on coarse soft thick wove paper, Perf. 10, color of original, surcharged "Specimen" in carmine.

Proofs of the "Cents Issue" were printed by the American Bank Note Co. in almost every conceivable shade, with and without the word "Specimen," on India paper and mounted on cardboard.

A B C
Specimen Types.

Counterfeit
with Specimen.

No.	Type.			Unused.	Used.
			A—Thin Letters. B—Seriphed Letters. C—Thick Letters.		
			Die Proofs.		
		1c	Grey-black, Black, Pale Violet, Grey....		$10.00
		2c	Grey-violet..........................		
		5c	Color of Issue, Black..................		
		8½c	Pale violet..........................		12.50
			Pale magenta..........................		10.00
		10c	Black................................		7.50
		12½c	Black................................		7.50
			Plate Proofs.		
		1c	Orange, Green, Grey-black, Black Lavender, Violet..........................		
		2c	Orange, Yellow.......................		
		5c	Black, specimen type A in gold.........		5.00
			Black, specimen type A in carmine.....		3.50
			Black, vert. pair, specimen type A one gold, one carmine....................		10.00
		5c	Black, Dark blue, Pale blue, Orange....		
		5c	Color of Issue, on thick wove..........		12.50
			Color of Issue, on India...............		7.50
		8½c	Black, Vermilion, Pale orange, Blue green, Yellow green...................		5.00
		10c	Orange, Black, Green, Deep Vermilion, Pale Red, Blue, Brown................		5.00
		12½c	Green, Orange, Black.................		

No.	Type.		Unused.	Used.
		Perforated Plate Proofs.		
	1c	Green, on thin wove..................		
		Color Trials.		
	1c	Various shades, soft tints..............		
	2c	Various shades, soft tints..............		
	5c	Various shades, soft tints..............		
	8½c	Various shades, soft tints..............		
	10c	Various shades, soft tints..............		
	12½c	Various shades, soft tints..............		
		Lithographed counterfeit "specimen"...		2.50
		Engraved all denominations...........		
		Engraved all denominations, without "specimen"........................		3.50

PRINCE EDWARD ISLAND

The Colony of Prince Edward Island offers a wonderful field for the specialist. The stamps abound in varieties, as might be expected in stamps printed from electrotype plates.

In the preparation of this chapter the author acknowledges much valuable information from the writings of Donald King, R.E.R.Dalwich, B. Goodfeellow, Henry C. Hitt, and P. L. Pemberton.

Manufacturers:
All stamps with the exception of the 4½d, were electrotyped and printed by Mr. Charles Whiting, Beaufort House, Strand, London, England.

Process of Manufacture:
From the original die of the stamp a mould was made in some hard substance, probably type metal. From this mould successive electros were taken. Sixty of these 'clichees' were then locked together (in the case of the 2d and 30 or 50 for the plates of the other values) and from this 'plate' the stamps were printed.

P. L. Pemberton claims (Philatelic Journal Nov. 1927) that the process followed was not to make sixty individual moulds from the die, and produce sixty individual electros from these moulds, but that successive electros were taken from the one mould. In the case of the 2d he points out Nos. 15 and 56 in the plate which are distinguishable from the other 58 impressions and may be traced back to the die, which he has examined. Examination of the stamps in sheet form, and comparison with the plate, shows that 58 electros were taken from one mould and 2 from another. From this it is quite evident that wax molds were not used, but that the moulds were made of some hard substance.

Stamps Superseded by those of Canada.

Prince Edward Island entered Confederation and became a Province of the Dominion of Canada on July 1, 1873, after which date the stamps of Canada were used.

DIES AND PLATES

Writing for the London Philatelist, 1893, Mr. J. A. Tilleard describes the dies and plates as follows: "They consisted of the completed dies of the 1d, 2d, 3d, and 9d, and of the 1c, 3c, 4c and 6c stamps. With them were found an engraving on wood of the head employed for the Cents Issue, and a reproduction on copper of the same, and also a metal plate of the head used for the Pence stamps. In addition to these there was an engraving on brass of a stamp, finished with the exception of the inscription, in form similar to the 3d stamp, although the details of the background are not the same. As the head also varies in several small particulars, I should imagine this was probably prepared before the stamp was issued as finally decided upon, and was not adopted. The electrotype plates were those of the 2d, 4d, 3c and 12c, and, in the case of the 3c there were parts of impressions in red and in black pasted on the back of the wooden block." These dies and plates were acquired for the Royal Philatatelic Society to avoid danger of reprints being made.

Stamp		Plate
2d Perf. 9	60 stamps	6 horiz. rows of 10.
3d Perf. 9	30 stamps	6 horiz rows of 5.
6d Perf. 9	30 stamps	6 horiz rows of 5.
1d 2nd issue	30 stamps	6 horiz rows of 5.
2d 2nd issue	60 stamps	6 horiz rows of 10.
3d 2nd issue	30 stamps	6 horiz rows of 5.
4d 2nd issue	30 stamps	6 horiz rows of 5.
6d 2nd issue	30 stamps	6 horiz rows of 5.
9d 2nd issue	30 stamps	6 horiz. rows of 5.
4½d	120 stamps	2 panes each with 10 rows of 6.
1c	100 stamps	10 rows of 10.
2c	100 stamps	10 rows of 10.
3c	100 stamps	10 rows of 10.
4c	100 stamps	10 rows of 10.
6c	100 stamps	10 rows of 10.
12c	100 stamps	10 rows of 10.

(Probably from two plates clamped one above the other.)

RATES

The uniform rate fixed by the first Post Office Act, passed May 15, 1851, on letters transmitted by post within P.E.I. to any part of the British North America, except Newfoundland, Bermuda and the West India Islands, was 3d currency the 1-2 oz.,payment optiomal. 3d was added for each additional 1-2 oz. or fraction up to ten ounces.

Unpaid letters for Nova Scotia and Cape Breton were liable to a fine of 3d in addition to the above rates.

Letters to be forwarded to Newfoundland or Bermuda were liable to a charge of 9d currency per half ounce, 3d of which had to be prepaid.

Letters to the United States via St. John, N.B., were subject to charge of 6d for every letter not exceeding 1-2 ounce.

Letters to California were subject to a charge of 9d per 1-2 ounce.

Letters via Halifax, to and from the United States, were subject to the British packet postage charge of 6d, as well as the Colonial one of 3d (9d per 1-2 ounce) independent of the United States rate of postage.

The rate on letters between any part of P.E.I. and the United Kingdom was 6d stg. or 9d cy. the 1-2 ounce, at the option of the sender, but letters posted unpaid were liable to a fine of 6d stg. each in addition to the postage.

Soldiers and Seamen could send and receive letters not to exceed 1-2 ounce at the rate of 1d each on letters for Canada, New Brunswick and Nova Scotia, and 1d stg. each on letters for Newfoundland, West Indies and England, provided the 1d was paid at the time the letter was posted and the name of the soldier or sailor, class or description, name of ship, regiment, corps or detachment to which he belonged, was specified in the direction of the letter received, or stated on letters sent.

The Royal Gazette of May 27th, 1870, stated that "On and after the first of June next the postage on paid letters for Gr. Brit. will be 3d sterling per 1-2 ounce, instead of 6d stg., as at present."

The Royal Gazette of June 10, 1870, stated that "Postage on letters for the Dominion of Canada, will be 3d cy. each rate; for the U.S. 4d cy.; for Gr. Brit. 4 1-2d cy. Newspapers for Newfoundland and West Indies, 1d stg. each rate; for Australia, New Zealand, etc., 2d stg. each rate. Newspapers for Gr. Britian, U.S. and the Dominion of Canada forwarded free."

The rate per 1-2 ounce to Gr. Britain was 4 1-2d if paid in local currency, but only 3d if paid in English coin, or sterling.

Commencing Nov. 1, 1868, the rate per 1-2 ounce, prepaid, on letters to British Columbia, California, and Oregon, was 6d.

Commencing Nov. 1, 1868, the rate on a single letter to the U.S. was 4d, and the same charge for each additional half ounce or fraction.

Parcel Post.

A parcel post rate was fixed at 1s 3d for any weight not exceeding 1 lb. and 1s 3d for each lb. up to 3 lbs. The sender wrote "By parcel post" above the address. In addition to any shortage in prepayment a fine of 6d was collected upon delivery. For an additional fee of 3d any parcel could be registered.

Registration.

The first Post Office Act, passed May 15, 1851, provided for the transmisslon of any "letter, book or other packet paying full letter rate," by registered mail upon prepayment of an additional fee of 6d. The fee was 10d stg. on letters passing through England for foreign countries and British Colonies.

Quantities Issued

(From information supplied to
London Philatelist 1914 by B. Goodfellow.)

The P.O. Accounts for the fiscal year ending March 1861 include an account of £57 paid to Mr. Whiting for 250,000 Perf. 9 stamps. It is assumed that these were in the following proportions:

2d......150,000 3d......40,000 6d......60,000

And in March, 1862, an account appears for £23.8.10. This is assumed to have been for stamps in the following proportions:

1d......40,000 9d......60,000

In the March, 1863, accounts, Mr. Whiting is credited with £100 and £25.3.2 for, say 800,000 stamps, at possibly 3s per 1,000, including 1d yellow 2d rose, 3d blue, 6d yellow green, 9d red-lilac, and possibly 4d on toned paper.

In Nov. 1865, a payment of £25.6.10 was made to Mr. Whiting for, say 200,000 stamps (the price for reprinting only would naturally be less), and these stamps were probably the 6d blue green, 9d red-lilac, and possibly the 4d toned paper, if these were not in the March 1863 lot.

For the 1867-8 issues, on coarse paper, payment was made in 1867 of £73.1.3. for, say 750,000 stamps, as the price for reprinting would be less, and these are estimated to include 250,000 of the 2d. rose, 250,000 of the 3d blue, and 250.000 of the 4d black.

On March 14th 1874 there remained in the Treasury the following stamps, of a face value of approximately $90,961.00 which were sold for the sum of $1,100.00:

2d	241,000	(Mostly coarse white paper.)
3d	226,000	(Mostly coarse white paper).
4d	277,000	(Mostly coarse white paper).
4½d	42,600	
6d	21,000	(Nearly all blue green shade).
9d	100,000	(All red lilac shade).
1c	124,500	
2c	75,000	
3c	10,000	
4c	94,000	(In addition there were 143,000 mixed stamps including
6c	162,000	a large number of the 1d).
12c	143,000	

Mr. Tilleard, in the London Philatelist (Vol. 11), gives the following figures concerning the quantities of the Cents Issue supplied to the Colony:

1c	294,500	4c	200,000
2c	100,000	6c	300,000
3c	290,000	12c	200,000

Quantities Used:

Having the quantities supplied to the Colony and the quantities sold as remainders, it is a simple matter to ascertain the quantities used, as follows:

1c	170,000	4c	106,000
2c	25,000	6c	138,000
3c	280,000	12c	35,000

Covers:

Prince Edward Island covers are rare. In many cases they are found pen-cancelled. The paper is of the cheapest and it is difficult to get covers in good condition. Only a small percentage are found with cancellations which tie the stamp on. The use of bisected stamps was not common. Stamps prepaying rates to foreign countries are of the greatest rarity.

Rarities:

2d Perf. 9Block of 15, mint. From Goodfellow Collection to Lichtenstein Collection 1926.

2d Imperf. claret shade, half sheet, mint. From Goodfellow to Lichtenstein collection 1926.

2d Rouletted—2 singles. From Goodfellow Collection to Lichtenstein Collection 1926.

2d & 6d Perf. 9 on cover, sold at Auction 1927.

Horiz. strip 3, Perf. 9, 2d, on cover—Crosby Collection.

2c & 6c on cover, sold at Auction 1927.

3d Bideford Provincial, Goodfellow to Lichtenstein 1926.

6c bisected, on cover, tied by Paid 3 in red, Auction 1927.

4d	Brown, quarter sheet, mint, *in author's collection* . . . .
1d	Yellow-orange, full mint sheet, *in author's collection* . . . .

2d Rouletted:

This rare stamp was discovered in October 1888 by Donald A. King, who states, "It was in a large quantity of used stamps P.E.I. from Charlottetown. They were mostly the 2d Perf. 9, and only one specimen was found. The papers from which this lot came eventually fell into the possession of a friend, who was fortunate enough to discover four more. Up to the present these are all the specimens known, and rank among the greatest rarities. The paper is the same as that of the other values, and the color is a deep rose, with almost a shade of the claret tint of the Perforated."

2d Perf. 9.

Because of the wide perforation and poor quality of paper used, the stamp was easily torn in separating and is rare in fine condition. The shades include pale rose, dull rose, claret, rose carmine, and brownish rose.

3d Second Issue.

The double impressions noted is the result of the sheet receiving two impressions, the second being out of register with the first.

1½d
PAID

3d Bisected:

I have seen the lower portion of a 3d Bisected (in the collection of F. G. Morant, Kamloops), tied to a piece of the original cover with "PAID", in red.

The piece of cover was of a paper commonly used on the Island. The "1½d PAID" illustrated above tied a diagonally bisected 3d to cover.

4d Black:

The stamp is listed as issued early in 1867, but the fact that it exists on the yellowish (B) paper is evidence that a supply was in the Post Office in 1865.

The supply on hand of the 4d on yellowish paper proved more than sufficient for the requirements up to 1871, but a consignment received from the manufacturer in 1867 included more 4d stamps, which were on bluish paper. Only a few copies of the 4d stamps of this last consignment were used, which accounts for the large number of 4d stamps on bluish paper in the remainders. It will be seen that the 4d on the bluish paper on used condition is rare.

4½d Brown:

This is one of the best designed stamps ever issued for any country. It was engraved and printed by the "British American Bank Note Co. of Montreal and Ottawa", whose imprint appears at top of the sheet, printed in rows of 10, sheets of 120.

6d Second Issue:

As in the case of the 4d it would appear that the supply on yellowish paper was sufficient, and the last consignment—on bluish paper—was not used. Used copies on the bluish paper are rarely seen.

9d.

This stamp (and the 4½d) shows the equivalent in Sterling. 9d of the Island Currency equalled 6d Sterling. The currency was more depreciated than that of the other Colonies, where 7½d currency equalled 6d Sterling. The Perf. 11 and the Perf. 11½ x 12 are noted with a second horizontal line of perforation about 1-8″ from top row.

2c Blue.

The 3c stamp would naturally be in more common use than the others. Fewer of these remained in 1874 than of any other value, with the exception of the 2c of which 75,000 were on hand.

"Bideford" Provisional:

Donald A. King makes note of a cover prepaid with a square of white paper stamped 3d, which had been recognized as prepaying postage and had been cancelled. This provisional was in the specialized collection of Mr. B. Goodfellow, who states "The square of white paper was part of the margin of the sheet and showed part of the Gauge 9 Perforation. It was pen-marked "3d" No Stamp."

Bogus Stamps.

A cleverly designed bogus 4c stamp was circulated soon after the issue of the genuine stamp in 1872. It was lithographed, the design imitating the 3d value of the pence issue, and existed in sheets of 100 stamps. It is often seen with a false postmark struck across the face of the stamp to disarm suspicion.

A 10c stamp of a dull mauve color became known in 1872. It is similar in design to the 3d, of which it is apparently a copy, though the general appearance is rougher. The perforation is Gauge 12. It was issued at the same time as the "Cents" issue of 1872, of which it was supposed to form a part, by an enterprising dealer, probably S. Allan Taylor, of Boston.

Counterfeits:

There is a poorly lithographed forgery of the 4½d brown.

A lithographed forgery of the 4c green became known in 1872, said to have been made by Allan Taylor of Boston. As it was discovered almost at once, very few could have been sold, and it is therefore extremely rare to-day. The points of difference between the genuine and the forgery are as follows:

1. In the genuine the crown of the head of the portrait does not touch the frame and there is a space between it and the frame along the whole length. In the forgery the crown of the head touches the frame along a certain distance and in a direct line under the letters "DW" of word "EDWARD" in the inscription in the upper margin.

2. In the genuine the square discs in the lower angles containing figure 4 are a trifle higher than the band running between them inscribed with the value. In the forgery these discs do not project above the intervening band inscribed with the value.

3. In the genuine there is a clear space between the letter "O" in "POSTAGE" on the first line of the inscription, and the letter "E" of "PRINCE" in the second line. In the forgery the letter "O" touches the letter "E" of "PRINCE" on the second line.

4. In the genuine there is a vertical line of dots fine outside the exterior row of fine horizontal lines which forms part of the ground on right side. In other words, each of these horizontal lines is succeeded by a dot. In the forgery the line of dots is absent.

Bisecteds:

The issue of the 2d, 3d and 6d stamps did not provide for 1d, 1½d and other rates, and the necessity for bisected stamps immediately arose. A notice over the signature of L. C. Owen, P.M.G., dated Dec. 26, 1860, appeared in the Royal Gazette of Jan. 1, 1861, published at Charlottetown which stated "The blue or red stamp (3d or 2d) will be received for payment of half the sum it indicates, if cut in two diagonally."

The 1d stamps (diag. half of 2d) were presumably used on soldiers' and seamens' letters, which were carried at that rate to—and received from—Canada, New Brunswick and Nova Scotia. There was a 4 oz. book post rate of 6d to most of the Colonies and doubtless this bisect was also used in conjunction with the 6d.

The 1½d stamps (diag. half of 3d) were for use on newspapers addressed to Newfoundland or Bermuda. (Clause 17 of P.O. Act, 1860).

Although the values were sufficient to cover all rates, the practice of bisecting the stamps continued. It would seem that when a person did not have a stamp of the required value he was permitted to cut any stamps to obtain the required rate. The bisects listed are the only ones used to any extent, but all values are said to have been halved. Collectors should obtain a guarantee or the opinion of an expert before purchasing bisects, and these should not be considered unless on the entire cover or sufficient of it to show postmarks received at point of mailing and destination.

The stamps that exist in imperforate condition are really proofs, but being on paper that closely resembles the papers of issue they are usually classed as imperforates by the advanced collectors.

The gum varies, but is usually yellowish, unevenly distributed upon the surface, and liable to crack. Care must be taken with unsevered blocks of the earlier printings as the brittle nature of the gum causes the stamps to separate easily. The gum of the earlier printings may be said to vary from white to thick dull brown, but the two extremes are not often seen. When the brown gum is used it has a decided effect upon the appearance of the stamp. The 1c stamp is noted in such condition that the design is seen with difficulty owing to the effect of this brown gum permeating the paper. The gum on the last assignment received from the printers was white.

Perforations:

It is almost impossible to give a complete list of the perforations owing to the innumerable and inconsistent varieties which are noted.

The first issue was uniformly perforated with Gauge 9 machine which made a single line of small holes in one direction, so that the horizontal and vertical lines had to be made in two operations. This resulted in poor perforations at the corners where the lines crossed. When one or more lines of perforations were accidently skipped the pairs were of course imperforate between.

This gauge was too wide and it was almost impossible to separate the stamps without tearing them. The poor quality of the paper contributed to the difficulty. Perf. 9 stamps are rare in good condition.

After the Perf. 9 gauge was discarded there appears to have been several single line perforating machines in use. One was uniform, Gauge 11, and a later one was anything between 11 and 12½. This later machine varied in different parts of its length, so that varieties of compound perforations resulted. Three distinct sizes of holes may be noted.

Sometimes the line of perforations did not extend the full width or length of the sheet, necessitating a second operation, and this extension of the line of perforations did not fall so as to make a continuous straight line of perforations, but varied to right or left.

The variety Perf. 11½ x 12 seems to be constant and we have listed it separately, but all perforations between 11 and 12½ are listed as compound. For convenient reference we have classified the varieties as follows:

A. Perf. 11
B. Perf. 11½ x 12
C. Perf. Compound
D. Perf. 12½ x 13 Small Holes
E. Perf. 12 Large Holes

Papers:
Early printing—
A. Soft opaque paper, and
B. a similar, but thinner paper.
Last printing—
C. Thin white hard wove.
D. Thin bluish-white hard wove.
E. Coarse bluish (mesh).

The (E) paper was used only for the 4d Black of 1867. B. Goodfellow writing in reference to this paper in Oct. 1927, states "Of the 4d Black on the coarse bluish (mesh) paper I had but two used specimens. All other cancelled copies I have seen of this value were with forged or spurious postmarks."

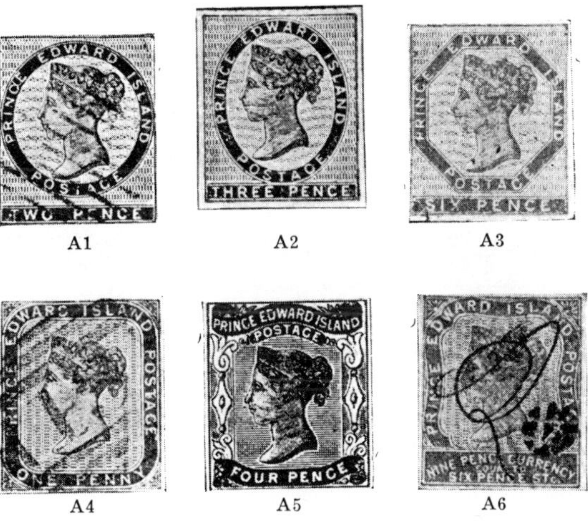

A1 A2 A3
A4 A5 A6

No.	Type.			Unused.	Used.
			First Issue, Perf. 9. Paper A.		
1	*A1*	2d	Rose *Jan. 1, '61 to Au., '64*............	$17.50	$10.00
			Rose Carmine......................	*18.50*	*10.50*
			a. Pair Imperf. Horiz.................	*150.00*	
			b. Pair Imperf. Vert..................	*150.00*	
			On cover $17.50; pair..................		*30.00*
			Single 1a on cover $50.00..............		
			Single 1b on cover $50.00..............		

No.	Type.			Unused.	Used.
			Rouletted.		
2		2d	Rose (*notes*)		
3	*A2*	3d	Blue *Jan. 1, '61 to Ap., '63*	40.00	25.00
			a. Double impression		*50.00*
			b. "Bideford" Provisional on cover		
			c. Cover with diag. half used as 1½d		
			On cover $60.00; Pair		*60.00*
4		3d	Pale blue	50.00	25.00
5	*A3*	6d	Yellow-green *Jan. 1, '61 to Ap., '63*	30.00	18.00
			On cover $45.00		
			Second Issue, Perf. 11.		
6	*A4*	1d	Brown-orange *Feb. 11, '62-65* (B)	3.75	5.00
			On cover $10.00; Imperf. pair		
7	*A2*	3d	Deep blue (B)	.60	3.00
			On cover $5.00; Pair	*1.20*	*5.00*
8	*A5*	4d	Black *1867* (AB)	3.00	2.50
			On cover $10.00; Pair	*7.00*	*7.00*
			a. Rare Paper E (see notes)		
9	*A3*	6d	Blue-green *1863-68* (AB)	2.50	3.50
			On cover $10.00; Pair	*5.00*	*10.00*
10			Yellow-green *Dec. 15, '66-Nov., '67* (BCD)	9.00	3.50
			Imperf. pair		
11			Blue-green *Aug. 4, '69-Mar., '70* (BCD)		
12	*A6*	9d	Bluish-lilac *Mar. 29, '62-Feb., '67* (B)	12.00	7.50
13			Dull mauve *Mar. 29, '62-Feb., '67* (B)	12.00	7.50
14			Lilac *1862* (B)	2.00	4.00
			On cover $25.00; pair	*4.50*	*12.00*
			Imperf. pair		
			Pair imperf. vertically		
			Diag. ½ used as 4½d on cover		
			Second Issue, Perf. 11½x12.		
15	*A4*	1d	Yellow-orange *June 23, '67-70* (B)	2.25	4.00
			On cover $9.00; pair	*4.50*	*10.00*
			Strip 3	*7.00*	*16.00*
			Imperf. Pair		
16		1d	Orange-buff *1865* (B)	5.00	5.00
17	*A1*	2d	Rose *1863 to May, '71* (AB)	1.25	1.75
			a. Diag. ½ used as 1d on cover	*10.00*	
			b. Pair imperf. between vert. (B)	*10.00*	
			c. "TWC" for "TWO" (E)	*15.00*	
			On cover $5.00; pair	*1.00*	*3.75*
18		2d	Rose-pink *1867 to 1868* (CDE)	1.25	1.75
			On cover $5.00; pair	*1.00*	*5.00*
19	*A2*	3d	Blue *1867 to Aug., '71* (BCDE)	.50	3.00
			a. Pair imperf. horiz.	*10.00*	
			b. Diag. half used as 1½d cover		
			On cover $5.00; pair	*.80*	*7.00*
20	*A5*	4d	Black *Mar. 3, '70* (DE)	3.40	7.50
			a. Pair imperf. horiz.	*10.00*	
			b. Imperf. pair	*10.00*	
			c. Diag. ½ used as 2d on cover		
			On cover $15.00; pair	*1.00*	*20.00*
21	*A3*	6d	Yellow-green *Dec. 15, '66-Nov., '67* (BCD)	9.00	3.50
			On cover $10.00; pair	*20.00*	*10.00*
22		6d	Blue-green *Aug. 4, '69-Mar., '70* (BCD)	3.00	3.50
			On cover $10.00; pair	*20.00*	*10.00*

No.	Type.			Unused.	Used.
23	*A6*	9d	Lilac *1962* (B)	2.00	3.00
			On cover $9.00; Pair	*4.50*	*8.00*
24		9d	Reddish-mauve *May 18, '68-July, '71*	3.00	3.00
			a. Pair imperf. vert.		
			On cover $;Pair		
			Diag. ½ used as 4½d on cover		
25		1d	Yellow orange	5.00	4.25
			Perf., Compound of 11 and 11½x12.		
25x	*A1*	2d	Rose *'63 to May '71* (AB)	5.00	2.75
			On cover $5.75; Pair	*12.00*	*6.50*
			a. Pair imperf. vert.	*15.00*	
			b. "TWC" for TWO	*15.00*	
26	*A2*	3d	Blue, *'67-Aug., '71* (BCDE)	7.50	4.50
			a. Pair imperf. horiz.		
			b. Imperf. pair	*10.00*	
			c. Imperf. pair with 4d stamp on other side	*15.00*	
			d. Diag. ½ used as 1½d on cover		
27	*A5*	4d	Black, *Mar. 3, '70*	.40	7.50
			On cover $15.00; pair	*.90*	
28	*A3*	6d	Yellow-green, *Dec. 15, '66-Nov., '67* (BCD)	9.00	5.50
			On cover $12.00		
29		6d	Blue-green, *Aug. 4, '69-Mar., '70* (BCD)	9.00	5.50
			On cover $12.00		
30	*A6*	9d	Reddish-mauve, *May 18, '68-July, '71*		7.50
			a. Imperf. vert.		
			b. Imperf. pair		
			c. Diag. ½ used as 4½d on cover		

A7

No.	Type.			Unused.	Used.
			Perf. 12 on White Wove.		
31	*A7*	4½d	Brown, yellow-brown, *June 1, '70*	4.00	5.00
			On cover $15.00; Pair	*9.00*	*15.00*
			Block of 4	*25.00*	

A8

A9

A10

A11 A12 A13

No.	Type.			Unused.	Used.
			Third Issue, Jan. 1872, on soft opaque (B) paper.		
32	*A8*	1c	Orange, yellow-orange and brown-orange, Perf. B and C.	.75	3.00
			a. On (C) paper		
			b. Imperf. pair	*10.00*	
			Cover $5.00; pair	*1.20*	*7.00*
			Strip 3	*1.80*	*15.00*
33	*A9*	2c	Ultramarine, Perf. D and E.	.75	10.00
			On cover $20.00; pair	*1.50*	
			a. Imperf. pair		
			b. Diag. ½ used as 1c on cover		
34	*A10*	3c	Rose, Perf. B	3.00	1.75
			a. Imperf. pair		
			Cover $6.00; pair	*7.25*	*4.50*
			b. Diag. half used as 1½c on cover		
			c. Stop between PRINCE EDWARD	*7.50*	*7.50*
			c. Stop between PRINCE EDWARD.	7.50	7.50
35	*A11*	4c	Yellow-green, Perf. D and E.	.60	4.00
			Cover $10.00; pair	*1.25*	*10.00*
			a. Imperf. pair		
			b. On (C) paper		
			c. Deep green, Perf. 12 small holes		
36	*A12*	6c	Black, Perf. 12 small holes and D.	.50	4.00
			a. Imperf. pair		
			Pair imperf. vert.	*30.00*	
			On Cover $35.00; pair	*1.00*	*10.00*
			Diag. vert. or horiz. half used as 3c on cover		
37	*A13*	12c	Reddish-mauve, Perf. D and E.	.50	12.00
			On cover $35.00		
			a. Imperf. pair		
			Bisecteds or "Splits".		
		1d	Bisected diag. (*Perf. 11½x12*) with 4d for 4½d rate.		
		2d	Bisected diag. for 1d (Ap. 19, '67)		
		2d	Biescted diag. (*Perf. 9*) and 2d Perf. 9 for 3d rate		
		2d	Bisected. diag. (*Perf. 11½x12*) with 2d for 3d rate (*Oct. 9, '68*)		
		2d	Bisected vert. (*Perf. 11½x12*) with 2d for 3d rate.		
		3d	Bisected diag. (*Perf. 9*) with 3d Perf. 9 for 4½d rate		
		3d	Bisected diag. (*Perf. 11½x12*) with 3d for 4½d rate (*1867-8*)		

No.	Type.			Unused.	Used.
		3d	Bisected diag. with five 3d (*Perf. 11½x12*) for 1s 4½d.		
		4d	Bisected diag. for 2d rate.		$35.00
		4d	Bisected vert. for 2d rate.		30.00
		6d	Bisected diag. (Perf. 9).		
		6d	Bisected diag. (*Perf. 11½x12*) 1870.		
		6d	Bisected diag. (*Blue-green, Perf. Compound 1868*).		
		9d	Bisected diag. (*Perf. 11½x12*) with MS surcharge "4½d".		
		2c	Bisected diag. with 2c.		
		2c	Bisected vert. with 2c.		
		6c	Bisected diag. Jy. 10, '72.		
		6c	Bisected diag. with 2c for 5c rate (*Charlottetown, Jy. 10, '72*).		
		6c	Bisected vert. and horiz.		
		12c	Bisected diag.		
		3c	Bisected diag. (*Jan. '72*).		
		4c	Bisected diag.		
			(The earliest issue of the 2d, 3d and 6d stamps did not provide for the 1d 1½d and other rates and the necessity for bisected stamps immediately arose.)		
			Imperforates. (B Paper).		
1	*A4*	1d	Yellow-orange, *June 23, 1867-70*.		
			Imperf. pair.		$10.00
2	*A1*	2d	Rose, *1863 to May, 1871*.		
			Imperf. pair.		10.00
3	*A2*	3d	Blue, *1867 to Aug., 1871*.		
			Imperf. pair.		10.00
4			Imperf. pair with 4d stamp on other side		15.00
5	*A5*	4d	Black, *Mar. 3, 1870*.		
			Imperf. pair.		*10.00*
6			*Imperf. pair with 3d stamp on other side*. .		*15.00*
7	*A8*	1c	Orange-yellow, *Jan., '72*.		
			Imperf. pair.		*10.00*
8	*A12*	6c	Black, *Jan., 1872*.		
			Imperf. pair.		*10.00*

PROOFS AND ESSAYS

A14

A15

An article in the London Philatelist by Mr. J. A. Tilleard, (Jan., 1893) was illustrated by proofs on thick plate paper in black ink, the impression being taken from the original plates, the property of the Royal Philatelic Society.

Some of these were from the entire plate while others were proofs of individual stamps, of both pence and cents issue, from the die.

The plate proofs bore the inscription underneath "Proofs from original plate of.........value." The die proofs bore the inscription underneath "Proofs from dies of stamps of Pence Issue" and a similar inscription for the cents issue.

The article illustrated "A proof from original engraved plate of head for pence issue." This is on a solid square background. There is a similar head for the cents issue.

There is a great variety of plate proofs on thin paper, including the 3d in dark blue and the 4d in black. A die proof of the 4d exists printed on a solid square background in the color of the impression and exists also in dark blue, brick red, brick red, brown reddish, and black. There is no inscription.

Many of the proofs are accepted as imperforates, being printed on similar paper and in the same colors as the stamps of issue.

1	*A7*	4½d	Brown, die proof......................	$10.00
2	*A14*	6d	Black, on thin India..................	25.00
3			Dull rose on thin India................ *(Nos. 2 and 3 are from a plate made by the British American Bank Note Co., similar in design to the 4½d stamp. The stamp was never introduced, and proofs are rare enough to substantiate the theory that but one proof sheet in each color ever existed.)*	25.00
4	?	1c	Preliminary proof in black, prior to final touching up of die, with pencil instructions to printer as to colors of stamps. *(In Lichtenstein Collection)*............	
5			Suggested design, (never used) for pence issue, proofs in color. *(In Lichtenstein Collection)*..........................	
6		1c	Black, plate proof....................	5.00
7	*A15*	3c	Blue, Essay on thick soft wove of poor quality, *Perf. 12*.....................	10.00
			Bogus Stamps and Counterfeits.	
1	*A7*	4½d	Brown, crude lithograph...............	.50
2	*A11*	4c	Green *(see notes)*....................	5.00
3	*A16*	10c	Mauve on thick hard wove of poor quality, Perf. 12 (Bogus)..............	2.50
			a. Maroon..........................	
4		2c	Pink, lithographed....................	2.50
5	*A16*	10c	Pink *(Bogus)*.........................	2.50
6	*A17*	15c	Blue *(Bogus)*.........................	2.50
7	*A18*	10c	Pink, perforated and cancelled, *(Bogus)*.	7.50
9	*A7*	15c	Ultramarine *(Bogus)*..................	

A16

A17

A18

MINOR VARIETIES.

The stamps are designated by number on the plate, counting from left to right from the top row down.

1d No. 7. Full stop above "L" in "ISLAND."

No. 10. White line above "N" in "ISLAND" broken, filled with solid color for about ⅛ in.

No. 30. No cross bar to "A" in "ISLAND."

3d No. 2. White circle and colored dot in centre before "P" in "PRINCE."

No. 10. Full stop between "E" and "D" in "EDWARD."

No. 12. "I" in "ISLAND" with white dash at top making it look like inverted L. Full stop at top bar of last "E" in "THREE PENCE."
Full stop after "R" of "THREE."

No. 19. Full stop after "EDWARD" in line with top of "D."

No. 23. Full stop between "P" and "O" in "POSTAGE."

1d In the earlier Perf. B printing of the 1d an outer frame line is noted 1 mm. from the design, usually cut into by the perforations. This is distinct and unbroken in the case of marginal stops, and liable to show faintly or in sections between stamps.

2d No. 30. Part of "T" in "TWO" cut off, making it look like inverted I. Full stop after "T" in "TWO."

No. 49. The "O" in "TWO" is broken, appearing as "TWC."

No. .... Left half of "A" in "EDWARD" missing.

4d Portions of an outer frame line may be noted at a distance of 1 mm. from the design, similar to the variety noted for the 1d.

9d No. 9. Two full stops, one above the other, after "STG."

9d Portions of an outer frame may be noted 1 mm. from the design. These occur infrequently as compared with the 1d and 4d, and in the later printings become more and more indistinct.

No. 10. Full stop before "S" in "STG." apparently put there instead of after "STG," which has none.

3c Nos. 7, 27, 47, 67 and 87. Full stop between "PRINCE" and "EDWARD."

REVENUE STAMPS

Appreciation is expressed for assistance from Senator J. A. Calder, Dr. F. S. McCall, F. A. Norris, J. Delano Bartlett, Col. Ernest F. Würtele, C. H. Dunham, S. Norris Oughtred, Chas. S. Thompson, and many others, without whose co-operation the present chapter, which we believe to be the most comprehensive yet published, would have been impossible.

FIRST ISSUE BILL STAMPS, 1864.

Printed from stereotypes, these stamps show many varieties and variations.

The variety SFVEN, No. 91 on the plate, is a temptation to the faker, who uses blue ink to match the color of the stamp, with which he paints out enough of the "E" to change it to an "F." He overlooks an important detail, however. Always look for the break in the oval under the "N" of CANADA.

Some collectors are under the impression that the plate was retouched to give No. 91 (7c value) a correct stamp. The plate was not altered, and the stamp which has been passed as the "retouched error" showing the "E" (that had been an "F") with peculiarities which distinguish it, is No. 54. It is further identified by a circular white spot inside the oval above the "C" of CANADA and an accent above the "E" of CENTS.

CONSTANT VARIETIES

Found in First Issue Bill Stamps

Ref. No.	No. on Plate	
		1c Stamp.
V1		Defective E of ONE, period under left of T in STAMP, oval broken between NA of CANADA.
V2		Period in center of T of CENT.
V3		Left figure 1 is defective at bottom; there is a stroke of color above the second L of BILL.
V4		There is a dot in the N of ONE; the outer oval is broken at left opposite shield; C of CENT is defective.
V5		There is a spot of color at point of chin.

Ref. No.	No. on Plate	
V6		There is a spot of color under A of STAMP and spots of color in background under chin above C.
V7		There is a colorless spot after the last A of CANADA and at bottom left of T of CENT.
V8		The bottom left of E of CENT is defective.
V9		The oval is broken under first A of CANADA.
		2c Stamp.
V1		Inner frameline, top center, wavy instead of straight; white spot in right side of shield at right, between STAMP and CANADA.
V2		Many of the squares formed by the cross hatching in the background run together in such a way as to give the appearance of small circles within the squares.
V3		There is a spot of color in the oval above S of STAMP.
V4		There is a white dot under the left of T in CENTS.
		3c Stamp.
V1		Second L of BILL has dot at top left.
V2		Defects join RE of THREE.
V3		The M has period and defective left side.
V4		There is a white dot before C of Canada, portions of frame line missing at left, dent in frame line at upper left, and white spot in cross hatching at left of left shield.
V5		There is a spot of color and line is broken at last A in CANADA; there is a period on frame line under N of CENTS.
V6		There is a colorless stroke joining oval line to side across cross hatching at left of left shield, and a colorless stroke above the first L of BILL.
V7		There is a spot of color in throat, a stroke of color touching neck opposite C of CANADA and white spot in cross hatching to right of last A in CANADA.
V8		There are spots of color in background above head and behind hair under P of STAMP.
V9		There is a heavy blob of color under the right numeral 3.
		4c Stamp.
V1		Outer frameline, right and left sides, broken.
V2		Colorless dash under N.
V3		Left end of panel with FOUR CENTS broken at corners.
V4		Colored dash above N of CANADA.
V5		White dot between EN of CENTS and colored dot in N.
V6		Spot of color in background to left of P of STAMP.
		5c Stamp.
V1		GANADA for CANADA.
V2		A dash runs from neck across oval between AN of CANADA; F runs to frameline at left bottom.
V3		A colored dot joins the panel with FIVE CENTS to frame line above C.
V4		There is a colored dot midway between the chin and C of CANADA.
V5		There is a dot of color in the cross hatching at lower right and above S of CENTS.
V6		The A of STAMP is defective; there is a spot of color at back of neck and above A of CANADA.
V7		There is a colorless flaw at back of neck and above A of CANADA; another in left spandrel on right at bottom.

Ref. No.	No. on Plate	
V8		The left side of right shield, at center, is defective.
V9		There is a colored spot in the oval above B of BILL.
V10		There is a white spot after P of STAMP and a colored spot between frame lines at right opposite bottom of shield.

6c Stamp.

Ref. No.	No. on Plate	
V1		There is a spot of color midway between top of head and S of STAMP.
V2		The frame line is defective below S of SIX.
V3		There is a white space in front of mouth.
V4		The panel with SIX CENTS is defective at left end.
V5		The cross hatching below the last A of CANADA and above the S of CENTS is damaged.
V6		The cross hatching below the last A of CANADA and above the T of CENTS has a colored dot, and there is a colorless stroke joining S of SIX to bottom of panel.
V7		A spot of color rests on oval line above and between BI of BILL.
V8		The outer frame line at lower left has a spot of color; there is a spot of color below the ear; and top frame lines are broken.
V9		There is a flaw in and above the C of CANADA; a colorless spot under right numeral 6.
V10		In the shield and above C of CANADA there is a heavy spot of color.
V11		There is a dot of color in the panel with SIX CENTS after the S of CENTS, which almost rests on frame line.
V12		The left frame lines are patched and wavy.
V13		There is a small white cross in cross hatching at center right.
V14		The outer right frame line is broken and inner frame line bent opposite A of CANADA and lines do not join at lower left corner.
V15		There is a dash of color in left frame line opposite panel with SIX CENTS and end of panel is defective.
V16		There is a stroke of color and a dot in the frame line under first A of CANADA.
V17		There is a colorless spot back of neck and above D of CANADA.
V18		There is a flaw of color back of the neck and above A of CANADA.
V19		There is a white spot above the head and S of STAMP, and another below and to right of right numeral 6.
V20		P of STAMP is defective and oval is bent in.
V21		There is a colorless flaw between NA of CANADA.
V22		The point of the neck has a stroke of color.
V23		There is a colorless flaw in cross hatching opposite second A of CANADA.
V24		Re-entry. Left frame line doubled, re-entries showing in oval above AMP, and in X of SIX, CEN, and STAMP. Lower portion of C of CENTS missing and a flaw in plate shows as a slanting line from top to bottom, cutting face across temple and cheek.

7c Stamp.

Ref. No.	No. on Plate	
V1	3	There is a spot of color below the chin and above CA of CANADA.
V2	26	There is a heavy dot of color in the oval line at left center.
V3	29	The point of the spandrel below first A of CANADA is defective; there is a colorless stroke at left of C in CENTS.

Ref. No.	No. on Plate	
V4	31	There is a heavy spot of color below the chin.
V5	32	There is a colorless dot in the D and a colorless dash before the last A of CANADA.
V6	36	The oval line is broken between DA of Canada.
V7	41	The second E in SEVEN is broad; there is a dot of color in front of the chin.
V8	43	The S of SEVEN is defective; the oval line is broken under the second A of CANADA.
V9	54	The first E of SEVEN is defective; there is a colorless spot in front of the chin and above C.
V10	58	There is a spot of color in the cross hatching at right opposite and below P of STAMP.
V11	59	EV of SEVEN is joined at top.
V12	61	S of STAMP defective; and defective under S of CENTS.
V13	62	Lower left corner is colored; there is a long colorless stroke at back of neck and a colorless dot in the mouth.
V15	64	Bottom of V of SEVEN defective.
V16	65	There is a period between CA of CANADA.
V17	72	There is a line of color in first A and a heavy colorless space after the second A of CANADA. There is a dot inside the left frame line opposite and above C of CANADA, and a dot above A of STAMP.
V18	73	There is a dot above the E of CENTS.
V19	75	The corner of the lower right spandrel is defective; there is a dot in the right numeral 7; in the neck; and to the left of the right inner frame line opposite A.
V20	81	There is a white spot in the cross hatching under C of CANADA.
V21	84	The N of SEVEN is defective; there is a large white dot under the M of STAMP.
V22	91	The first E of SEVEN is an F. The oval is broken under N of CANADA. There is a small white dash at the left of the first A of CANADA.
V23	92	The inner frame line at left is heavy opposite A of CANADA.
V24	93	There is a dot of color above the "I" of BILL.
V25	94	Between the outer and inner frame line at left below B of BILL there is a dot, and inside the inner frame line at left above C of CANADA there is a dot.
V26	95	There is a white dot before the C and a heavy colored dot in the D of CANADA.
		8c Stamp.
V1	15	The E of EIGHT is defective.
V2	19	The N of CENTS is defective at left.
V3	21	There is a white vertical stroke down the neck and a vertical white dot between TS of CENTS at bottom.
V4	29	There is a heavy plate flaw in the hair below M of stamp.
V5	32	There is a stroke of color between the outer and inner frame lines at right opposite P.
V6	34	There is a flow between LL of BILL and a horizontal white stroke in the cross hatching above TS of CENTS.
V7	35	The C of CANADA has a white dash inside.
V8	36	There is a colored dot in the cheek; the oval is broken above B of Bill.
V9	41	The spandrel is defective above L of BILL; there is a white dot in the C of CANADA.
V10	47	The D of CANADA at right bottom is broken; there is a dot in the N of CENTS.

Ref. No.	No. on Plate	
V11	48	There is a dot in the oval above the second L of BILL.
V12	51	There is a colorless dash in the D of CANADA and a colorless dash above C of CENTS.
V13	52	The H of EIGHT is defective at top.
V14	62	There is a white spot under S of STAMP; the E of EIGHT is defective.
V15	63	There is a colored spot under the first A and a white line after the last A of CANADA.
V16	68	There is a white spot at bottom between NT of CENTS; also in back ground at right of head.
V17	81	The oval is broken between NA of CANADA; there is a dot in the right side of H of EIGHT.
V18	85	There is a white spot below B of BILL and there are white spots under TS of CENTS.
V19	91	There is a dot of color in the I of BILL and inside the left frame line opposite numeral 8.
V20	96	There are dots of color in the oval above IL of BILL.
V21	97	There is a white dot above NA of CANADA and a white spot under the N of CENTS.
V22	98	There is a white spot in the cross hatching below DA of CANADA.

9c Stamp.

V1	The left of T of CENTS is defective; there is a stroke of color in A of STAMP; and a defect midway between N of CENTS and second A of CANADA
V2	There is a flaw in the oval line above C of CANADA.
V3	The frame line is broken at bottom under TS.
V4	The panel with NINE CENTS has a colorless dot at extreme right. There is a flaw in the background above and between DA of CANADA.
V5	The lower left frame line is joined to the panel by a stroke of color at bottom; there is a colored dot under E of NINE.
V6	There is a white dot before C of CENTS.
V7	There is a small colored circle in the cross hatching, at side, above S of CENTS.
V8	There is a colored dot beneath the inner frame line above and to the right of left numeral 9, and a white spot in the corner at left of left numeral 9.
V9	There is a colored dot in the oval to the left of B in BILL.
V10	There is a colored dot below the frame line at upper left and above numeral 9. There is a white dot to the left of the 9.
V11	The colored background of CANADA extends into the oval above and below C of CANADA.
V12	There is a colored dot in the white space midway between the E of NINE and A of CANADA.

10c Stamp

V1	The cross hatching runs together under DA of CANADA and the outer frame line is broken at left opposite B of BILL; there is a colorless dash midway between N and tip of neck.
V2	There is a spot of color in neck, at front.
V3	There is a flaw in the colored background of D of CANADA; there is a colorless spot in the right shield below P, and the outer frame lines at right have dots of color near bottom.

Ref. No.	No. on Plate	
V4		A white spot joins NT of CENTS at top and there is a white spot after BILL at top.
V5		The P of STAMP is all white.
V6		There is a white spot at right of last A of CANADA and a stroke of color in the N of CENTS.
V7		There is a white stroke at the top of the colored background of CANADA at left.
V8		The bridge of the nose is defective.
V13		There are two colored dots in the white space midway between N of NINE and A of CANADA.
V14		There is a white spot below the S of CENTS and in the cross hatching below and between CA of CANADA.

20c Stamp.

V1		There is a colored flaw in the shield below P of STAMP.
V2		There is a period between AM of STAMP at top.
V3		The bottom of the E of CENTS is defective and the bottom frame line between EN of CENTS is broken by flaw.
V4		There is a period between CA of CANADA and the left side of W in TWENTY is defective.

30c Stamp.

V1		There is a stroke of white in front of the nose.
V2		A large spot of white almost joins AN of CANADA.
V3		The EN of CENTS is defective.

40c Stamp.

V1		There is a spot of color in the background to left of B of BILL.
V2		There is a squared spot of color at back of the neck.

50c Stamp.

$1 Stamp.

V1		The outer frame line is broken at top right.

$2 Stamp.

V1		There is a piece out of the top of the D in DOLLARS.
V2		There is a colored flaw in the cross hatching to the left of B in BILL and a dot in C of CANADA.
V3		There is a colored flaw in the background at back of the neck, a dot in front of the neck, and a flaw in the cross hatching at left side opposite C of CANADA.
V4		There is a colored dot between the outer and inner frame lines at left opposite B of BILL, and a colored dot in S of STAMP.

$3 Stamp.

V1		STAMR for STAMP.
V2	5	There is a colorless flaw in the background back of the head and close to the oval line.
V3	6	There is a colored flaw above the first A of CANADA.
V4	7	There is a colored flaw above the C of CANADA.
V5	9	The frame line is broken at bottom left.
V6	11	There is a colored dot in the oval below CA of CANADA.
V7	15	There is a large colored spot between the frame lines at left opposite $.
V8	16	There is a dot of color in the cross hatching below D of CANADA.
V9	17	There is a colored flaw in the cross hatching under D of CANADA.

Ref. No.	No. on Plate	
V10	18	A stroke of color runs to frame line at bottom below second E of THREE.
V11	19	The second A of CANADA is defective at bottom and there is a white spot below S of DOLLARS.
V12	29	There is a flaw in the background above D of CANADA.
V13	31	The oval is broken opposite P of STAMP.
V14	32	There is a spot of color above the frame line at bottom left above T.
V15	46	There is a white spot in the shield at left and above second A of Canada.

Second Issue Bill Stamps, 1865.

The second issue of the Bill Stamp series appeared in the early months of 1865 and all values were apparently issued long before the stock of the preceding type became exhausted.

The One Dollar value is printed in red with green centre and also with the same colors reversed, but as the varieties are found used concurrently, and there is little difference in their scarcity, it does not seem likely one was an error. Possibly green was the original color decided upon for the frame, but as the two higher values had the frame in red, it may be that it was found more convenient to print all the frames in color. The $1 stamp has horizontal lines within the inner circle of the frame, which do not appear on the proofs, which were likely added by a third printing as they vary greatly in irregularity of outline.

The Two Dollar value with its red frame and lilac centre, and the three dollar value with its blue centre and red frame vary but little, except that the lines between the centre medallion and the frame has a difference of the number of lines, three appearing on the two dollar value and four in the three dollar. These appear in circle form and entirely different to the horizontal lines that appear on the one dollar value.

All of the values of this issue were line engraved and printed in sheets of 100, ten rows of ten. The same style of marginal inscriptions as on the postage stamps of the 1859 issue is found—"American Bank Note Co., New York"—in minute letters of the type known as "diamond." This is repeated twice in each margin, reading up on the left, down on the right, and down on the bottom as on the top margin. The imprint is placed against the third and eighth stamp on all four sides. In the margin usually—but not on all values—on the left in bold block type, about 4½ mm. high the value of the stamps, as NINE CENTS, appears. (From notes by E. E. Goodchild in Stamp Herald.)

Third Issue Bill Stamps.

The watermark listed in this third series is that found in the 1868 postal issues.

The value of $500.00 placed on the $2.00 inverted center is not in error. We have seen more of the 12d Black postage stamps than we have seen of this inverted center. The author would like to have the names of collectors whose collections include this stamp.

Excise Stamps Surcharged 3/16c, 3/8c, 3/4c.

To meet the requirements for stamps of the above values for Match Tax, a quantity of the Excise stamps was surcharged on November, 1927, with the above values.

A collector in 1927 was shown a sheet with the trial printing in red on the ¼c stamps. This had the surcharge inverted, and the surcharge was missing on the right vertical row. The sheet was run through again and printed in black. What the ultimate end of this sheet was we do not know, but it was more than likely destroyed by Department officers.

Customs Duty.

These stamps are affixed to printed matter mailed to Canada from foreign countries. They represent a fiscal tax collected by the Post Office Department.

War Tax Stamps

At the session of the Canadian Parliament in February, 1915, Finance Minister White introduced Bill No. 76, "The Special War Revenue Act" to "supplement the revenue required to meet the war expenditure." That part of the Act of interest to philatelists is quoted below:

"No person shall issue a cheque payable at or by a bank unless there is affixed an adhesive stamp or unless there has been impressed by means of a die a stamp of the value of two cents, and every adhesive stamp affixed to a cheque shall be cancelled by the bank at which the cheque is payable at or before the time of payment.

"No person shall transfer a bill of exchange or promissory note to a bank as to make the bank the holder thereof, unless there is affixed an adhesive stamp, or unless there is impressed by means of a die a stamp of the value of two cents, and every stamp so affixed shall be cancelled by the bank at the time of delivery or transfer.

"Every person who issues a cheque payable at or by a bank to which there is not affixed an adhesive stamp or on which there is not impressed by a die or stamp, of the value of two cents, shall be liable to a penalty not exceeding fifty dollars.

"Every express company carrying on business in Canada shall, before the issue of a money order or travelers' cheque, affix thereto an adhesive stamp of the value of two cents and the company may charge the two cents to, and collect the same from, the purchaser of the order or cheque.

"No money order shall be issued under the provisions of the Post Office Act until there has been affixed a postage stamp of the value of two cents to be paid for by the purchaser of the order. The postmaster or other officer of the Department shall cancel the stamp by imprinting thereon the date stamp of the office issuing the order.

"No postal note shall be issued under the provisions of the Post Office Act unless there is affixed a postage stamp of the value of one cent to be paid for by the purchaser of the order.

"On every letter and post card for transmission by post for any distance within Canada, and on every letter and post card not intended for transmission through the mails, but for posting and delivery at the same post office, there shall be levied and collected, a tax of one cent to be affixed thereto, at or before the time of posting the letter or post card; but such tax shall not be levied or collected on any letter or post card entitled to the privilege of free transmission under the provisions of the Post Office Act, nor on any letter or post card if the levying and collecting of such tax would be contrary to the provisions of the Universal Postal Convention concluded between Canada and certain other counntries. The stamps so affixed shall be cancelled by the postmaster whose duty is to cancel the postage stamps affixed to such letters and post cards in prepayment of postage.

"The Postmaster-General may by regulation provide, in case a postage stamp of the denomination of one cent is not affixed to the letter or post card as required by subsection of this paragraph, that the letter or post card—

(a) shall not be forwarded by post or delivered to the addressee, but shall be returned through the dead letter office to the writer or sender;

(b) If addressed to any place in Canada shall be forwarded to its destination charged with the payment of two cents by the person to whom it is addressed, and on neglect or refusal by the person to whom it is addressed to pay the two cents the letter shall be returned to the sender, through the dead letter office; or

(c) shall otherwise be dealt with as regulation provides.

"Every person importing, selling, or manufacturing any bottle or package containing, (a) proprietary or patent medicine; (b) perfumery; (c) wine of grape, nonsparkling; or (d) champagne or sparkling wine, shall at or before the time of sale affix to every bottle or package an adhesive stamp of the requisite value as mentioned in the schedule in this part.

(a) A proprietary or patent medicine .... one cent

(b) Perfumery the retail price of each bottle or package thereof being twenty-five cents or less .... one cent
more than twenty-five cents.
each additional or fractional part of twenty-five cents.......... one cent

(c) Wine of grape, non-sparkling, each bottle containing
one pint or less ....three cents
One pint to one quart .... five cents
For each quart or fractional part ....five cents

(d) Champagne or sparkling wine, each bottle containing
one half pint or less .... thirteen cents
One half pint to one pint .... twenty-five cents

"The person selling, importing, manufacturing, or producing, whose duty is to affix a stamp, under this section shall, at the time the stamp is affixed, cancel same by writing on or across the stamp, initials or other marks of identification together with the date of such writing, or otherwise cancel the stamp in accordance with the regulations made by the Minister (of Finance.)

"Every person required by this Act to cancel a stamp affixed to a bottle or package in the manner prescribed by or under the provisions of this part, who fails or neglects to do so shall incur a penalty of not less than fifty dollars, and not exceeding two hundred and fifty dollars.

'Postage stamps of a requisite value may in lieu of stamps prepared be used in the fulfilment and discharge of any requirement under this part that adhesive stamps be affixed.

"Affix to the said bottle or package an adhesive stamp of the requisite value as mentioned in the schedule and cancel same at the time of affixing.

"Postage stamps of required value may be used."

"WAR TAX" on 5c, 20c, 50c Georgian.

On February 12th, 1915, a tax on wines came into effect, and the stamps for this new tax had to be prepared in a hurry. The Inland Revenue Department obtained a supply of the 5c, 20c and 50c postage stamps and surcharged them diagonlly "WAR TAX" in black. Sheets from plates 2 and 3 were surcharged, plate 2 being the rarest. The values required by the Act were 5c, 25c and 50c, but as there were no postage stamps of the 25c denomination it was necessary to use the 5c and 20c together.

Confusion resulted among the stamp-taxed public. The Post Office had issued 1c and 2c stamps which were supposed to be "tax" stamps, but which were later given triple status, being accepted for "war tax on letters, etc.," "tax on proprietary or patent medicines, etc.," and "ordinary postage." Next appeared the Inland Revenue stamps (postage stamps surcharged) which gave no inkling as to their identity as Inland Revenue stamps. The confusion was not lessened by reference to the official circular from the Post Office Department dated April 16, 1915, quoted in the Notes on Postal Issues, which clearly read "postage stamps on which the words "WAR TAX" have been printed may be accepted for prepayment of postage." The Inland Revenue stamps were therefore used postally and are known on registered mail, which would be less apt to be passed carelessly and must have been accepted as fully prepaid by the use of the Inland Revenue stamps surcharged "WAR TAX."

It is generally known that the 5c unused is very scarce, as most of the issue was used the first day of issue, and the issue was so unexpected that philatelists and dealers were hardly aware of their existence before they were replaced by a second printing which read, "Inland Revenue War Tax" in four lines diagonally.

"WAR TAX" Regular Issue, April, 1915.

This issue was printed in sheets of 200 stamps divided into two panes of one hundred each. The 1c and 2c were also issued in coils, and later in booklet form.

"WAR TAX" Ribbon or Strip Stamps.

These were intended to go over bottles, being broken when the bottles were opened, and then rendered of no further value.

"WAR TAX" Embossed from Die on Cheques, etc.

Shortly after June, 1915, a circular went out from the Inland Revenue Department to banks, reading as follows: "Bankers wishing to use cheques stamped with a die, will supply the Inland Revenue Department at Ottawa with blank cheques in sheets, not books. The Department will have the die embossed on the cheques, charging for the work necessary thereof, plus the cost of the stamps. Embossed stamps need not be cancelled."

The die was in the form of an oval, with white embossed letters, on a red background. At the top following the curve of the oval is the word CANADA, just below is the Crown. In a curved line running beneath the crown and coming up on each side reads Inland Revenue. In the middle and at each side is WAR TAX. Next the beaver is shown and beneath him in a straight line across reads TWO CENTS. The remainder of the lower portion of the OVAL is filled with five maple leaves, the symbol of the Dominion.

1c and 2c WAR TAX Postage Stamps Used for Revenue.

Under the Act, quoted in the Notes on Postage Stamps, it will be seen that the 1c and 2c "WAR TAX" postage stamps could be used for revenue purposes, and these have therefore been listed as revenues. The ordinary 1c and 2c King George postage were also used as revenues.

ALBERTA LAW STAMPS

The following exhaustive study is by Senator J. A. Calder in "Canadian Stamp Collector," October, 1922. The author also desires to acknowledge assistance from Dr. F. S. McCall, B.A., D.D., in preparing the check list.

FIRST ISSUE

The first issue was printed at the office of the Edmonton Bulletin, Edmonton, Alberta. The date the first order was given cannot now be ascertained. The stamps were authorized for use on October 1st, 1906. The number of stamps of all denominations delivered by the printers totalled 97,092, of a face value of $37,774.40. On Sept. 26th, 1914, the remainder of these stamps was destroyed. No information is available as to the quantities of each value destroyed, but their total face value amounted to $20,856.55.

The paper used was ordinary wove of medium weight without watermark, and of a light creamy white variety. The stamps were printed in sheets containing four horizontal rows of three stamps each or twelve stamps to the sheet. Some of the sheets are imperforate on two sides—usually the top and right—and some on four sides. All perforations are 12. (In one lot of the 25c the perforation is serrated. Note by Dr. McCall.)

Of this issue there was evidently more than one printing. This is indicated by the different coloured inks used in printing stamps of the same denomination and by the appearance of errors and varieties in sheets of stamps of the same value.

When the first order for these stamps was given, it was intended that different coloured stamps of the same denomination should be used for different services—vermilion stamps for Actions, yellow for Bills of Exchange and Chattel Mortgages, green for Lien Notes and purple for Estates. While orders were given to the printers for these colours, much carelessness was shown by the Bulletin office in producing them as is indicated by the reference list appended hereto. There is evidence to show that court officers were instructed to use the different coloured stamps for the purposes mentioned, but owing to shortage of stamps, complications in accounting, and for other obvious reasons the practice soon fell into disuse and was abandoned.

According to the official record, the following is a list of these stamps first ordered:

10c stamp—Vermilion, yellow and purple.
20c stamp—Vermilion.
25c stamp—Vermilion and green.
50c stamp—Vermilion and green.
75c stamp—Vermilion.
1.00 stamp—Vermilion.

On December 20th, 1906, the following varieties were also ordered from the printers:
25c stamp—Green, yellow and purple.
1.00 stamp—Vermilion.
And on January 8th, 1907, a further order was given for 10c stamps —purple (200 sheets).

The official record approved by the Provincial Auditor shows the total stamps of the first issue ordered to be:

	Vermilion.	Yellow.	Green.	Purple.	Total.
10c	16,728	5,376		6,744	28,848
20c	2,148				2,148
25c	10,248	4,152	3,168	3,348	20,916
50c	21,764		5,208		26,972
75c	9,852				9,852
1.00	8,356				8,356
	69,096	9,528	8,376	10,092	97,092

As intimated above, this official record is not accurate as regards the colours of the stamps supplied. It does, however, indicate the total number of stamps ordered and delivered.

The stamps of this first issue were printed on an ordinary printing press and the design and lettering used were set by hand. The design on each stamp measures 37 x 35 millimeters. It consists in the first place of a fancy scroll background made up of six blocks or units of similar character so arranged in three horizontal rows of two blocks each as to give the whole the appearance of a single or solid design. Upon examination, however, it will be noted that these blocks are not always arranged in the same way, with the result that throughout the first issue series there are several distinct varieties on this account.

The background referred to was first printed on the stamps in different colours. Afterwards the sheets were run through the press the second time for the purpose of designating the use and denomination of the stamps. The words "Alberta" and "Law Stamp" are printed in fancy type in the centre of each stamp in two lines; the word "cents" is printed near the top and bottom of each stamp in uniform plain type and the value in plain type figures is inserted in each corner opposite the word "cents."

There were two distinct issues of the dollar stamp. In one printing the value is indicated by the dollar sign followed by the figure "1" printed in each corner. In the other, instead of the dollar sign, the words "one dollar" are printed in plain type across the top and bottom.

As previously intimated, because of the method followed in handsetting these stamps, there are naturally numerous errors and varieties. The chief of these are as follows:

Scroll Background Varieties

On each stamp each of the six blocks or units of the background design has three circular corners and one corner with three points. The location of the three-pointed corners is not always the same. For descriptive purposes, if it is assumed that the normal background scroll design has the three-pointed corner of each of the six blocks or units in its northeast corner, the following combinations will be found:

Locations of Three-pointed Corners.

Var.	1st Block	2nd Block	3rd Block	4th Block	5th Block	6th Block
A	N.E.	N.E.	N.E.	N.E.	N E.	N.E.
B	N.E.	S.E.	N.E.	N.E .	N.E.	N.E.
C	S.W.	S.E.	N.E.	N.E.	N.E.	N.E.
D	S.W.	S.E.	N.E.	N.E.	N.W.	N.E.
E	S.W.	S.E.	N.E.	N.E.	N.W.	N.W.
F	S.W.	S.W.	S.W.	S.W.	S.W.	S.W.

The location of these varieties of scroll background in sheets of twelve stamps indicates at least four distinct settings. In the following illustrations, each small square represents a stamp and the letters A, B, C, D, etc., the variety of scroll background on each stamp of the sheet:

—1—	—2—	—3—	—4—
D D D	D D D	A A A	A A A
D C D	D C D	A A A	A A A
D A E	D A D	A A A	A A A
D B D	D B D	A A A	A A F

Referring to the Reference List of the first issue of Alberta Law stamps, it will be found that sheets of the following numbers were printed, namely:

Type 1—Nos. 1, 2, 5, 10, 11, 12, 13, 14, 15, 16, 17, 18, 19, 20.
Type 2—Nos. 3, 4, 6.
Type 3—Nos. 7, 8, 9.
Type 4—No. 21.

To illustrate: The scroll background of a sheet of No. 1 (10c mauve and green) is arranged as indicated by type 1 above. The background of the first stamp has its blocks arranged as indicated by variety "D." In this variety the three-pointed corner of the first block is in the S.W. corner; of the second, in the S.E.; of the third, fourth and sixth in the N.E.; and of the fifth in the N.W. Similarly the 8th stamp in a sheet of No. 1, has its background arranged as indicated by variety "A" or in other words the three-pointed corners of all the blocks are in the N.E.

As a further illustration the scroll background of sheets of No. 21 (the "one dollar" stamp) is of type 4. The first eleven stamps of the sheet have all their three-pointed corners in the N.E. Whereas in the twelfth stamp they are all in the S.W. (Varieties "A" and "F" respectively.)

From the above description, it will be noted that in each sheet of twelve stamps the following varieties are to be found:

Type 1—Variety A—Once.
" B—Once.
" C—Once.
" D—8 times.
" E—Once.
" E—Once.
" F—None.
Type 2—Variety A—Once.
" B—Once.
" C—Once.
" D—9 times.
" E—None.
" F—None.
Type 3—Variety A—12 times.
Type 4—Variety A—11 times.
" F—Once.

Broken Scroll Varieties.

Among the many varieties of these are four that are readily noticeable, which for descriptive purposes are numbered: G, H, I and J.

G—Part of the scroll is missing near the three-pointed corner in the 2nd block of the background, in the fifth stamp in each sheet of Nos. 1, 2, 3, 4, 5, 6, 10, 11, 12, 13, 14, 15, 16, 17, 18, 19 and 20.

H—Is similar to G, except that it occurs in the fourth block of the 2nd stamp in each sheet of Nos. 7, 8 and 9.

I—The top part of the scroll block is missing or very badly broken in the 6th block of the 9th stamp in each sheet of Nos. 1, 2, 5, 10, 11, 12, 13, 14, 15, 16, 17, 18, 19 and 20.

J—Is similar to I, except that the block is broken or missing to the right instead at the top. This variety occurs in the 6th block of the 9th stamp in each sheet of Nos. 3 and 6.

The existence and location of these broken scroll varieties clearly indicate five distinct settings for the printing of the scroll backgrounds of stamps of the first issue, namely, the four indicated above—G, H, I and J—and that of stamp No. 4 (in reference list) in which the broken varieties I or J do not appear.

Fancy "L" Varieties.

L—Throughout the entire series of the first issue the letter "L" in the word "Law" in the 5th, 10th and 12th stamps in each sheet has an extra stroke to the right and differs otherwise from the same letter as it appears on all other stamps.

The existence of this variety appearing always on the same stamps in each of twelve would indicate that the words "Alberta Law Stamp" were hand set once only and were used for all printings.

In some sheets of the 25c stamps there is a dot between the 2 and 5, occurring once in the sheet.

Small "2" Varieties.

These occur only in the 25c stamps where occasionally a distinctly smaller and thinner "2" is used in the figures of value. These varieties appear in all sheets of Nos. 7, 8, 9, 13 and 15, as follows:

L—The 3rd stamp in each sheet has a small "2" in N.W.
M—The 5th stamp in each sheet has a small "2" in N.W.
N—The 6th stamp in each sheet has a small "2" in N.W. and N.E.
O—The 11th stamp in each sheet has a small "2" in N.W. and S.W.

The small "2" varieties do not appear in sheets of Nos. 10, 14 and 16. They may possibly be found in sheets of Nos. 11 and 12. It will thus be seen there were at least two distinct settings and printings of this denomination or value of the 25c stamps.

Raised "O" Varieties.

These are found in certain of the 10c and 20c stamps only, the figure "O" being printed higher than the "1" or "2." The following is a list of these:

P—Raised "O" in N.W. of 1st stamp in each sheet of Nos. 1 and 5.
Q—Raised "O" in S.W. of 9th stamp in each sheet of Nos. 1 and 5.
R—Raised "O" in S.E. of 12th stamp in each sheet of No. 6.

In the 10c values the raised "O" varieties occur only in sheets of Nos. 1 and 5. They are missing in Nos. 2, 3 and 4.

Lowered "O" Varieties.

These are similar to the last except that the figure "O" is lowered. They occur in the 10c and 50c values only, as follows:

S—Lowered "O" in N.E. of 7th stamp in each sheet of Nos. 1 and 5.
T—Lowered "O" in N.E. of 11th stamp in each sheet of Nos. 1 and 5.
U—Lowered "O" in N.W. of 11th stamp in each sheet of Nos. 17 and 18.

In the 10c values the lowered "O" varieties appear only in sheets of Nos. 1 and 5. They are missing in Nos. 2, 3 and 4.

Broken "O" Varieties.

These consist of a broken "O" which has the appearance of a reversed "C." They are found in the 10c and 20c values only as follows:

V—Broken "O" in S.W. of 4th stamp in each sheet of Nos. 2, 3 and 4.

W—Broken "O" in N.W. of 7th stamp in each sheet of Nos. 2, 3 and 4.

X—Broken "O" in N.W. and S.E. of 7th stamp in each sheet of No. 6.

In the 10c values the broken "O" varieties appear only in sheets of Nos. 2, 3 and 4. They are missing in Nos. 1 and 5.

From the above description of raised, lowered and broken "O's" it will be noted there were two distinct settings and printings of the 10c values. Sheets of Nos. 1 and 5 have stamps with both raised and lowered "O's" whereas Nos. 2, 3 and 4 have the broken "O" varieties.

Wide "N" Variety.

This occurs only in the "one dollar" stamp:
Y—Wide "N" in "one" at the top in the 4th stamp of sheet.

Thin "E" Variety

This also occurs only in the "one dollar" stamp:
Z—Thin "E" in "one" at the bottom in the 11th and 12th stamps of sheet.

Narrow $1 Varieties.

AA—These are found in the "$1" variety—12th stamp. The distance between the figures "1" at the top and bottom of each stamp measures 26½ millimeters as compared with 28½ millimeters in the normal variety.

Double Printed Scroll Background Variety.

BB—These are known to exist in the "one dollar" and other stamps, where the scroll background is distinctly double printed.

Other Minor Varieties.

There are many of these as it is doubtful if any two stamps in any sheet of 12 are alike.

SECOND ISSUE.

The second issue of Alberta Law Stamps was designed and lithographed by Bullman Bros., of Winnipeg, Manitoba. The design, which measures 40 x 25 millimeters, shows the figure of Justice standing and blindfolded. The words "Alberta Law Stamp" appear in two curved lines at the top and the words cents or dollars in a straight line at the bottom. The denomination of the stamps is indicated by figures in each corner.

All stamps are printed on white unwatermarked wove paper and are perforated 12. They were issued in sheets of 25—five horizontal rows of five stamps each.

Negotiations for the printing of these stamps were commenced with Bullman Bros. on October 4th, 1906. Proofs of the cent values were approved on December 28th, 1906, and of the dollar values on April 11th, 1907.

In some of the 25c sheets there is a dot between 2.5 of some stamps. There are double print varieties.

The varieties listed occur once in the sheet.

The first order for stamps of this issue was placed with Bullman Bros. on March 13th, 1907, as follows:

5c—5 books of 200 leaves each, 25 stamps to leaf—25,000 stamps.
10c—15 books of 200 leaves each, 25 stamps to leaf—75,000 stamps.
20c—5 books of 200 leaves each, 25 stamps to leaf—25,000 stamps.
25c—15 books of 200 leaves each, 25 stamps to leaf—75,000 stamps.
50c—15 books of 200 leaves each, 25 stamps to leaf—75,000 stamps.
75c—15 books of 200 leaves each, 25 stamps to leaf—75,000 stamps.
$1.00—5 books of 200 leaves each, 25 stamps to leaf—25,000 stamps.
$2.00—5 books of 200 leaves each, 25 stamps to leaf—25,000 stamps.
$3.00—15 books of 200 leaves each, 25 stamps to leaf—75,000 stamps.
$5.00—5 books of 200 leaves each, 25 stamps to leaf—25,000 stamps.
Total books, 100. Total stamps, 500,000.

Bullman Bros. agreed to print these at a cost of $350.00.

In compliance with the order given, stamps were received from Bullman Bros. as follows:

	May 17, 1907.	June 18, 1907.	Aug. 6, 1907.	Nov. 23, 1907.	Totals.
5c	5,000	5,000	10,000		20,000
10c	5,000	5,000	5,000	55,000	70,000
20c	5,000		20,000		25,000
25c	5,000	5,000	65,000		75,000
50c	5,000	15,000		50,000	70,000
75c	5,000	10,000	5,000	55,000	75,000
$1.00	5,000	10,000	10,000		25,000
$2.00	5,000	10,000	5,000		20,000
$3.00	5,000	10,000		60,000	75,000
$5.00	5,000	5,000	15,000		25,000

May, 50,000; June, 75,000; August, 135,000; November, 220,000; totals, 480,000.

On September 30th, 1908, a further order was given to Bullman Bros. for the following supply of stamps:

5c	15,000	25c	15,000	$1.00	25,000
10c	10,000	50c	10,000	$2.00	15,000

The filling of this order doubtless accounts for the shades appearing in these values. Those of the 5c, $1.00 and $2.00 are quite marked.

On June 2nd, 1910, the Attorney-General's Department instructed the Government printer to proceed to Winnipeg for the purpose of arranging for and supervising the destruction of the original engraving, the transfers, plates and remaining stock of this issue of Alberta Law Stamps. These instructions were doubtless carried out.

THIRD ISSUE

The third issue of Alberta Law Stamps was designed by the American Bank Note Company of Ottawa. They are line engraved and are perforated 12. The paper used is of a white unwatermarked wove variety. The design, which measures 40½ x 25 millimeters, represents the figure of Justice seated and not blindfolded. The name of the engraver appears on each stamp in small plain letters at the bottom. The word "cents" appears in a straight line, and the word "Alberta" in a curved line at the top; the words "Law Stamp" are in a straight line immediately below the figure of Justice; the value in words appears in two straight lines at the bottom and the denomination in figures appears in the four corners.

Negotiations for the printing of these stamps were apparently carried on prior to January 31st, 1910. On that date the company was advised certain quantities of stamps of different denominations would be required.

The first order for these stamps was given on February 5th, 1910. They were to be printed in sheets of 50—five horizontal rows of ten stamps each. The following is a list of those ordered:

5c	25,000	25c	50,000	$1.00	50,000	$5.00	2,000
10c	50,000	50c	50,000	$2.00	10,000	$10.00	1,000
20c	25,000	75c	10,000	$3.00	5,000	Total	278,000

The first stamps of the issue were received at Edmonton on May 3rd, 1910. Between that date and July 15th, 1921, many orders for these stamps were given. The total quantities received during this period were as follows:

5c	125,000	25c	1,080,000	$1.00	310,000	$5.00	5,000
10c	600,000	50c	425,000	$2.00	185,000	$10.00	14,500
20c	74,950	75c	228,000	$3.00	10,000		

These figures give a total of 3,057,450 stamps, with a face value of $1,614,740.

MANITOBA LAW STAMPS.

By Senator J. A. Calder, in Canadian Stamp Collector,

January, 1922.

The Manitoba Law Stamp Act, 1875, provided that law stamps should be used on legal documents from and after a date to be fixed by Order-in-Council. This order, passed on April 20th, 1877, fixed May 1st of the same year as the date upon which the use of stamps was to become compulsory. Law stamps continued to be used in Manitoba until June 1st, 1901, when they were abolished.

The regular issues of these stamps are oblong in shape and are engraved bearing the design of a figure of Justice standing and holding in her uplifted hand a pair of balances. The 10, 20, 25 and 50-cent values have the words "Manitoba Law Stamp" in two curved lines at the top and the value at the bottom. The $1.00 and $2.00 stamps have the value at the top and immediately beneath the value in curved lines the word "Manitoba" and across the bottom the words "Law Stamp."

There are two distinct types of the regular issues printed from different dies. The first type has nine scrolls or scallops down each side and all stamps are perforated 12. The second type has only six such scrolls. The surcharged varieties of this second type are all perforated 12½ and the unsurcharged varieties are perforated 11—at times approaching 11¼ or even 11½.

The paper used for all the regular issues is of a white wove variety, unwatermarked, and of medium thickness except in the case of the surcharged varieties of the second type. In all of these the paper used is thicker and much softer and is therefore more easily torn.

The color of the stamps of the first type varies from a light yellow green to a blue green; that of the second type, surcharged, is of a uniform deep olive green, that of the second type, unsurcharged, ranges from yellow green through olive and blue greens to a deep black blue green.

Prior to May 30th, 1892, all stamps issued were surcharged in some form or other, in many cases two surcharges being used. These surcharges indicate the purpose for which the moneys derived from the sale of stamps were to be used. When stamps were first issued two funds were designated, namely, "The Consolidated Revenue Fund," for which stamps were surcharged C.F. and the Law Society Fund surcharged "L.S." At first stamps of these two varieties had to be used on all legal documents. The use of 'L.S." stamps was abolished from April 29th, 1884, and of "C.F." stamps from July 1st, 1886. On this latter date stamps were issued for two new funds which were created, namely, "The Administration of Justice Fee Fund" surcharged "J.F." and "The Building Fund" surcharged "B.F." The use of "B.F." stamps was abolished on March 5th, 1889, and of "J.F." stamps on May 30th, 1892.

Stamps bearing two surcharges such as "C.F." and "J.F."—"C.F." and "B.F."—"L.S.' and "J.F." and "L.S." and "B.F." are accounted for by the fact that when the use of "C.F." and "L.S." stamps was abolished the remainder of the supplies on hand were again surcharged for the purpose of designating the new funds created.

In the case of all regular issues the surcharge "C.F." was printed on the centre of the stamps in large block type in black and the surcharge "L.S." in similar type but in blue black. Stamps bearing two surcharges one of which is either "J.F." or "B.F.," had the latter surcharges stamped thereon by hand in red or violet ink and as a consequence these surcharges vary considerably in appearance, depending upon the care and pressure used. These second surcharges were placed in any position on the stamps but chiefly diagonally reading either up or down.

When certain of the old stocks with the two surcharges ran out the new stamps ordered were unsurcharged and as required the letters "J.F." or "B.F." were similarly hand stamped thereon. Of these the 10c was first received on March 12th, 1887, and the 25c and 50c on September 14th, 1888. Later on, stamps of the first type were ordered with the letters "J.F." printed thereon. There were two varieties of these—the one with large blue block letters being received in stock on August 26th, 1889 (25c, 50c and $1.00) and the other with smaller blue block letters on May 29th, 1890 (20c) and on September 17th, 1891 (50c).

On May 30th, 1892, the use of unsurcharged stamps was authorized, but the surcharged varieties on hand continued in use at the same time until they were exhausted. Unsurcharged stamps of both types were used. The use of all law stamps was abolished on June 1st, 1901.

All stamps of the regular issue, first type, were supplied by the British American Bank Note Company, and those of the second type by the Bishop Engraving Company of Winnipeg. This latter Company received its first order in 1885, when it was asked to supply all values surcharged "C.F." None of the $2.00 stamps of this issue were ever used. They were subsequently all destroyed. Both of these companies received orders from time to time, which doubtless accounts for the shading in colors.

In addition to the above described regular issues, various provisional stamps were used from time to time. The first of these appeared in the latter part of June and early in July, 1877. They were printed on yellow orange paper, imperforate and unwatermarked, bearing the coat of arms of Great Britain and small letters "C.F." in black. Each stamp is numbered and signed by A. Begg (Auditor and Queen's Printer). So far as is known they were in use for about two weeks and it is estimated less than one hundred copies of each of the denominations, 10c, 20c and 25c, were supplied. The use of these provisionals was occasioned by the exhaustion of the supply of the regular issue of "C.F." stamps of the same denomination.

In the last week of October, 1877, the supply of the regular 25c "C.F." stamps again became exhausted and the second series of provisional stamps were issued and used for about three weeks. They were similar to the first provisionals, but not numbered. Some of them are signed by E. W. Romans (Deputy Provincial Treasurer); others are initialed by E.W.R. or by D.C. (Carey, Prothonatary); a few were initialed by both E.W.R. and D.C.; still others were neither signed nor initialed.

The third provisional issue made its appearance in September, 1881, when certain values of both the "C.F." and "L.S." regular issues ran out. These provisionals are also imperforate and are similar in design to the first provisionals except that the coat of arms printed in black is much smaller. The paper used was unwatermarked white wove and small letters "C.F." or "L.S." were surcharged in violet or purple ink with a rubber hand stamp. Occasionally the surcharge was written with indelible pencil and in some instances they were initialed by E.M. (Ed. Marston, Registrar and Clerk of Court), who received the document bearing these stamps.

Forgeries.

Forgeries of the 1st, 2nd and 3rd Provisionals exist which might easily deceive a collector who had not previously seen the genuine stamps. The paper, however, is not of the right color for the first and second provisionals and is too thin for the third. The surcharging of the initials or signatures is not well done. The numerals of value are in too bright a shade on the 1st and 2nd Issues and too pale on the 3rd issue.

4th Provisional Issue.

The 4th Provisional issue appeared about the third week in September, 1882, when there was a shortage of the regular 10c and 20c "C.F." values and "L.S." stamps of the same denominations were surcharged "C.F." in purple ink, the surcharge being of the same type as that of the 3rd Provisional issue. These are considered the rarest of all the Manitoba Law Stamps.

During the period the use of both "L.S." and "C.F." stamps was compulsory, mistakes frequently occurred in placing correct stamps on documents. In many instances these mistakes were rectified by Court officers pen-stroking the surcharge "C.F." and inserting in red or black ink "L.S." or vice versa. These surcharges are regarded as oddities rather than provisionals.

After April 29th, 1884, the "L.S." stamps were no longer required. Some of them were pen-stroked and surcharged "C.F." with red or black ink. The only values which appeared in this form in any number were the 10c and 50c. They should be regarded as the 5th Provisional issue.

In the latter part of 1884 and in 1885 the 6th Provisional issues made their appearance. They consisted of the 10c, 20c or 50c values of the remaining "L.S." stamps being surcharged with the letters "C.F." in red by means of a hand stamp. There were three distinct varieties of this surcharge—small round letters, large round letters and long narrow letters.

QUEBEC ASSURANCE STAMPS

The first "E" in License would appear to be a corrected error, the right arm of the top of the "E" appears above the line as if engraved after. The dollar values do not appear in this way. The stamp was placed in use as provided for by the Statutes of Quebec, Cap. VII, as follows:

1. Every assurer, carrying on in this province any business of Assurance, other than that of Marine Assurance exclusively, shall be bound to take out a license, before the first day of May in each year, from the revenue officer of the district wherein is situated his principal place of business or head agency, and to remain continually under license.

2. The price of such license shall consist in the payment to the Crown for the use of this Province, at the time of the issue or delivery of any policy of assurance, except of Marine Assurance, and at the time of the making or delivery of each premium receipt a renewal, respecting any policy issued before or after the coming into force of this Act, of a sum computed at the rate of three per cent. as to Assurance against fire, or of one per cent. to other Assurances for each hundred dollars a fraction of one hundred dollars of the amount

received as premium or renewal of Assurance, by the Assurer, his agent or employee.

And such payment shall be made by means of one or more adhesive stamps equivalent in value to the amount required, to be affixed by the Assurer, his agents, officers, or employees, on the policy of assurance, receipt or renewal, as the case may be, at the time of drawing up, issue or delivery thereof.

3. When the amount to be paid, in value of the preceding section, shall include a fraction of a cent, such shall be reckoned as one cent.

(Sections four to twelve relate as to the liabilities under this Act for non-fulfilment of any section provides for the name in which same shall be cancelled and states in section twelve: "The stamps required as the cost of the license in virtue of this Act, shall only be so required from and after the first day of the month of May next." (May 1st, 1876.)

QUEBEC PROHIBITION STAMPS

Statutes of Quebec, Cap. 18.

An Act to provide for the prohibition of the sale of intoxicating liquors and to amend the Quebec License Law in certain cases. Section 21 reads as follows:

"No person, except the authorized vendor, shall purchase intoxicating liquors for exclusively medicinal, industrial, mechanical, scientific or artistic purposes, without paying at the time of the purchase a duty equivalent to five per cent. of the purchase price.

In computing the amount of the duty, any fraction of a cent shall be considered as one cent.

The duty shall be collected by the licensee selling such intoxicating liquors by means of adhesive stamps, equivalent to the amount thereof, affixed by him in the receptacle of the intoxicating liquors and thereon obliterated by him at the time the purchase is made, in accordance with the regulations made by the Provincial Treasurer.

The stamps so used shall be only those supplied by the Provincial Treasurer, or by any officer authorized by him and shall be in such form as may be prescribed by the Provincial Treasurer."

Weights and Measures.

Collectors are warned that unused Weights and Measures stamps are guarded with the utmost strictness by officers and the possession of uncancelled current Weights and Measures stamps may cause trouble to the collector and possible dismissal of the officer from whom they were originally procured.

A1 A2 A3

A4 A5 A6 A7

BILL STAMPS

Province of Canada

1864. On white wove, perforated 12½x12½, 12½x13½, 13½x12½ and 13½x13½.

No.	Type		Perf. 12½x12½ Unused	Used	12½x13½ Unused	Used
1001	A1	1c Blue	.07	.05	.25	.20
		a. Figure 1 broken	2.50	2.00	6.00	5.00
		b. (Perf. 13½x12½)				
1002		2c Blue	.07	.05	1.50	1.25
1003		3c Blue	.07	.05	.12	.10
		a. (Perf. 13½x12½)				
1004		4c Blue	.10	.06	.12	.10
1005		5c Blue	.12	.08	.50	.40
		a. GANADA for CANADA	7.00	6.00	7.00	6.00
1006		6c Blue	.07	.05	.12	.10
		a. (Perf. 13½x12½)				
1007		7c Blue	.35	.30	2.50	2.00
		a. Error SFVEN	10.00	10.00	10.00	10.00

No.	Type		Perf. 12½x12½ Unused	Used.	12½x13½ Unused	Used
1008		8c Blue	.20	.15	.35	.30
1009		9c Blue	.12	.10	.12	.10
		a. (Perf. 13½x12½)				
1010		10c Blue	.18	.15	.18	.15
1011		20c Blue	.18	.15	.18	.15
1012		30c Blue	.30	.25	.30	.25
1013		40c Blue	.25	.20	.60	.50
1014	A1	50c Blue	......	......	.30	.25
1015	A2	$1 Blue	1.50	1.25	1.50	1.25
1016		$2 Blue	1.50	1.25	1.50	1.25
1017		$3 Blue	3.50	3.00	3.50	3.00
		a. STAMR for STAMP	7.00	6.00	7.00	6.00
		b. Vertical pair, imperf. between	......	......	10.00	......

No.	Type		Perf 13½x12½ Unused	Used.	13½x13½ Unused	Used
1001	A1	1c Blue	.25	.20	.12	.10
		a. Figure 1 broken	6.00	5.00	5.00	4.00
1002		2c Blue	......	?	1.25	1.00
1003		3c Blue	.20	.15	.12	.10
1004		4c Blue	......	?	.12	.10
1005		5c Blue	......	?	1.50	1.25
		a. GANADA for CANADA	......	......	10.00	10.00
1006		6c Blue	.20	.15	.12	.10
1007		7c Blue	.60	.50	.35	.30
		a. Error SFVEN	10.00	10.00	10.00	10.00
1008		8c Blue	.50	.40	.35	.30
1009		9c Blue	.20	.15	.12	.10
1010		10c Blue	?		?	
1011		20c Blue	?		?	
1012		30c Blue	?		?	
1013		40c Blue	?		?	
1014		50c Blue	?		?	
1015	A2	$1 Blue	1.75	1.50	1.75	1.50
1016		$2 Blue	?		?	
1017		$3 Blue	?		?	

2nd Issue. April, 1865. Perf. 13½x13½. On hard wove paper varying from thin transparent to thick almost opaque, and on opaque wove paper.

No.	Type.		Unused.	Used.
1018	A4	10c Blue	.10	.05
1019		20c Blue	.20	.10
		a. Imperf. pair	5.00	......
1020		30c Blue	.20	.10
		a. Imperf. pair	5.00	......
1021		40c Blue	.40	.20
		a. Imperf. pair	5.00	......
1022		50c Blue	.40	.20
		a. Imperf. pair	5.00	......

No.	Type.		Unused.	Used.
		3rd Issue. May, 1865. Perf. 12x12. On hard wove paper varying from thin transparent to thick almost opaque, and on opaque wove.		
1023	A3	1c Red	.10	.05
1024		2c Red	.10	.05
1025		3c Red	.10	.05
1026		4c Red	.30	.15
1027		5c Red	.10	.05
1028		6c Red	.10	.05
1029		7c Red	.50	.30
1030		8c Red	.50	.30
1031		9c Red	.10	.05
1032	A4	10c Dark blue	5.00	2.50
1033		20c Dark blue	?	
1034		30c Dark blue	?	
1035		30c Red	1.00	.50
1036		40c Dark blue	?	
		a. Vertical pair, imperf. between	5.00	.....
		b. Perf. 12 horiz. x 13½	.....	12.00
1037		50c Dark blue	4.00	2.00
1038	A5	$1 Red, green center	2.00	1.00
		a. Imperf. pair	10.00	10.00
1039		$1 Green, red center	2.00	1.00
		a. Imperf. pair	10.00	10.00
1040		$2 Red, violet center	5.00	2.50
		a. Imperf. pair	10.00	10.00
1041		$3 Red, blue center	10.00	10.00
		Dominion of Canada		
		February, 1868. Thin hard transparent wove paper. Perf. 12x12. (In December, 1873 Perf. 11½x11¾ appears, and in January, 1874, Perf. 11½x12 appears.)		
1050	A6	1c Brown	.25	.05
1051		2c Brown	1.00	.50
1052		2c Orange	.25	.05
1053		3c Deep green	1.00	.05
1054		4c Brown	.40	.07
1055		5c Orange	.25	.05
1056		6c Deep green	1.00	.05
1057		7c Orange	.50	.10
1058		8c Brown	.50	.10
1059		9c Deep green	1.00	.05
1060		10c Blue	.50	.15
1061		20c Blue	.50	.15
1062		30c Blue	.50	.15
1063		40c Blue	.75	.20
1064		50c Blue	.75	.20
1065	A7	$1 Dark blue, black center	5.00	1.00
1066		$2 Red, black center	8.00	2.00
1067		$3 Green, black center	10.00	3.50
		September, 1868. Thin to medium wove.		
1068	A6	1c Brown	.10	.05
		a. Stitch watermark	.....	2.5J
1069		2c Brown	1.00	.40
		a. On brown experimental paper	.....	.....
		b. Imperf. pair	.....	.....

No.	Type.		Unused.	Used.
1070		2c Orange	.10	.05
1071		3c Green	.05	.02
		a. Watermarked	.....	5.00
		b. Imperf. pair	.....	5.00
		c. Double printing	.....	.....
1072		4c Brown	.10	.05
1073		5c Orange	.10	.03
1074		6c Green	.05	.02
1075		7c Orange	.10	.05
1076		8c Brown	.15	.06
1077		9c Green	.05	.02
1078		10c Blue	.10	.05
1079		20c Blue	.10	.05
1080		30c Blue	.10	.05
1081		40c Blue	.20	.10
1082		50c Blue	.20	.10
1083	A7	$1 Blue, black center	1.50	.35
		a. Imperf. pair	6.00	.....
1084		$2 Red, black center	4.00	1.00
		a. Center inverted	.....	500.00
1085		$3 Light green, black center	7.50	2.50
		a. Imperf. pair	15.00	.....

(The 1c, 2c and 3c postage of the 1868 issue were sometimes used instead of Bill Stamps, affixed to notes, and bearing bank and commercial cancellations.)

A8

CUSTOMS DUTY

1912. Perf. 12.

No.	Type		Unused	Used
1100	A8	1c Green	.02	.02
1101		2c Carmine	.03	.02
1102		2c Red	.10	.03
1103		5c Brown	.06	.04
1104		10c Blue	.12	.07

1918. Used at Niagara Falls, Ont. Canada War Tax Stamps, Type A11, surcharged "Customs Duty" with rubber stamp.

1105	1c Orange, black surcharge		
1106	1c Orange, violet surcharge		

Current 1c Georgian Postage surcharged as above.

1107	1c Green, black surcharge		
1108	1c Green, violet surcharge		

A9

A10

A11

A12

A13

14

February 12th, 1915. 1st Provisional Issue.

No.	Type.			Unused.	Used.
1150	A9	5c	Blue, black surcharge	5.00	2.00
1151		20c	Olive green, black surcharge (Pl. 3)	1.25	1.50
1152		20c	Sage green, black surcharge (Pl. 2)	2.50	3.00
1153		50c	Black brown, red surcharge	2.50	2.00
			February 13th, 1915. 2nd Provisional Issue.		
1154	A10	5c	Blue, black surcharge	.25	.25
			a. Hairline variety	.....	.....
1155		20c	Olive green, black surcharge	.50	.50
1156		50c	Black brown, red surcharge	1.50	1.50
			April, 1915. Perf. 12.		
1157	A11	1c	Orange	.02	.01
			a. Coil, perf. 8 horiz.	.03	.02
1158		2c	Brown	.03	.02
			a. Coil, perf. 8 horiz.	.35	.25
			b. Perf. 12x8	.....	.....
1159		3c	Green	.04	.03
1160		4c	Blue	.05	.03
1161		5c	Olive yellow	.06	.03
1162		8c	Brown	.09	.06
1163		10c	Olive green	.11	.06
1164		13c	Vermilion	.15	.15
1165		25c	Carmine	.35	.30
1166		50c	Brown	1.00	.30
			Booklets, 6 Stamps to Pane		
1167	A11	1c	Orange (24 stamps)		
			(48 stamps)		

No.	Type.		Unused.	Used.
1168		2c Brown (12 stamps)		
		(24 stamps)		
		(48 stamps)		

Postage Used Fiscally.

No.	Type.		Unused.	Used.
1169		1c Green Georgian		
1170		2c Carmine Georgian		...

Georgian "War Tax" Postage Used Fiscally.

No.	Type.		Unused.	Used.
1171		1c Green		
1172		2c Carmine		

1915. Government Die Embossed on Bank Cheques.

No.	Type.		Unused.	Used.
1173	A12	2c Red cut square	.25	.....
1174		2c Red (rectangular) cut square	.25	.....

Excise Stamps, for Luxury Tax.

No.	Type.		Unused.	Used.
1180	A13	¼c Olive	.02	.02
1181		½c Carmine	.02	.02
1182		6c Orange	.07	.05
1183		7c Brown	.08	.05
1184		9c Violet	.10	.05
1185		15c Dark orange	.16	.15
1186		20c Olive yellow	.25	.05
1187		30c Yellow brown	.35	.10
1188		40c Purple	.50	.15
1189		60c Blue	.75	.15
1190		70c Dark olive green	1.00	.15
1191		80c Carmine	1.00	.20
1192		90c Chocolate brown	1.25	.20
1193		$1 Olive yellow (2 shades)	1.25	.04
1194		$2 Green	2.25	.10
1195		$3 Orange	3.25	.40
1196		$4 Light brown	4.50	.40
1197		$5 Vermilion	5.50	.40
1198		$10 Orange	11.00	.60
1199		$100 Green	.....	6.00

Bilingual.

No.	Type.		Unused.	Used.
1205	A14	2c Blue	.03	.02
1206		2c Blue (coil)	.04	.04
1207		4c Blue	.05	.02
1208		6c Blue	.07	.02
1209		8c Blue	.09	.03
1210		10c Blue	.12	.03
1211		20c Blue	.25	.05
1212		50c Blue	.55	.05

A15

A16

War Tax Strip Stamps for Use on Wines, Tobacco, Etc., ¾″ x 7½″.

No.	Type			Unused	Used
		June, 1915. Rouletted.			
1225	A15	5c	Black	......	.25
1226		10c	Black	......	.20
1227		13c	Black	......	.30
1228		25c	Black	......	.40
1229		50c	Black	......	.30
		1917. Rouletted.			
1230	A16	5c	Black	......	.15
1231		20c	Black	......	.30

A17

A18

A19

November, 1927. Excise Stamps, Type A13, surcharged for Match Box Stamps.

No.	Type		Unused	Used
1250	A17	$\frac{3}{16}$c on ¼c Olive	.05	.05
1251	A18	⅜c on ½c Carmine	.05	.05
1252	A19	¾c on 1c Orange	.05	.05

A30

A31

A32

SUPREME COURT

1876. Control numbers in red. Perf. 12x11½.

No.	Type.			Used.
1350	A30	10c	Blue	.60
1351		20c	Blue	1.25
1352		25c	Blue	.50
1353		50c	Blue	.75
1354		$1	Blue	.75
1355		$5	Blue	1.25

Perf. 12x12.

No.	Type.			Used.
1356	A31	10c	Blue	.60
1357		20c	Blue	1.25
1358		25c	Blue	.50
1359		50c	Blue	.75
1360		$1	Blue	.75
1361		$5	Blue	1.25
			a. With control numbers in blue.	

1897. Widowed Queen. Perf. 11½x11½.

No.	Type.			Used.
1362	A31	10c	Dark or light blue, red control	.40
1363		$1	Dark or light blue, red or blue control	.50
1364		$5	Dark or light blue, red control	2.00
1365		$5	Black, blue control	2.00

1915. King George.

No.	Type.			Used.
1366	A32	25c	Blue, red control	.35
1367		50c	Blue, blue control	.75
1368		$1	Blue, blue control	1.50

Rouletted.

No.	Type.			Used.
1369	A32	10c	Blue, blue control	.....
1370		50c	Blue, blue control	.....

(These stamps were never issued for use without control numbers.)

Note: Cigarette, Snuff and Tobacco Stamps are being written up and will appear in a future edition.

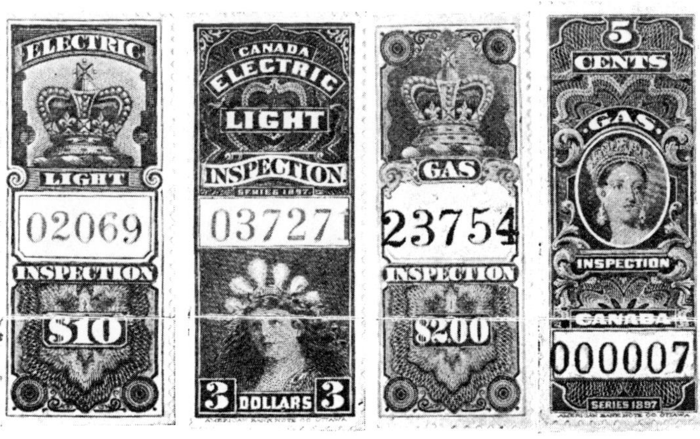

A35 A36 A37 A38

ELECTRIC LIGHT INSPECTION.

1895. Perf. 12. Blue control numbers.

No.	Type.		Used.
1375	A35	25c Vermilion	.25
1376		50c Vermilion	.15
1377		$1 Vermilion	.15
1378		$2 Vermilion	.20
1379		$3 Vermilion	.30
1380		$5 Vermilion	1.50
1381		$10 Vermilion	1.00
		a. Part perf.	.....

1900.

No.	Type.		Used.
1382	A36	25c Carmine	.10
1383		25c Vermilion	.30
1384		50c Vermilion	.10
1385		60c Vermilion	.15
1386		75c Vermilion	.15
1387		$1 Vermilion	.20
1388		$2 Vermilion	.20
1389		$3 Vermilion	.50
1390		$5 Vermilion	1.50
1391		$10 Vermilion	.75

GAS INPECTION.

1875. Perf. 12. Red control numbers, 4½ mm. high.

No.	Type.		Used.
1395	A37	5c Blue	3.00
1396		25c Blue	.10
1397		50c Blue	.15
1398		$1 Blue	.20
1399		$1.50 Blue	.30
1400		$2 Blue	.20
1401		$3 Blue	.50
1402		$4 Blue	.60
1403		$10 Blue	1.00

Control numbers 3½ mm. high.

No.	Type.		Used.
1404	A37	5c Blue	2.00
1405		25c Blue	.05
1406		50c Blue	.05
1407		$1 Blue	.10
1408		$1.50 Blue	2.00
1409		$2 Blue	.25
1410		$3 Blue	.30
1411		$4 Blue	.40
1412		$10 Blue	1.00

1897. Perf. 12. Queen Victoria. Red control numbers.

No.	Type.		Used.
1413	A38	5c Blue	2.00
1414		25c Blue	.05
1415		50c Blue	.05
1416		60c Blue (White Label)	.10
		a. Rouletted	.....
1417		75c Blue (White Label)	.75
1418		$1 Blue	.25
1419		$1.50 Blue	1.00
1420		$2 Blue ......(White Label)	.10
1421		$4 Blue	1.00
1422		$10 Blue (White Label)	.65

J. Delano Bartlett, of El Paso, Texas, reports the 60c value in rouletted form. He writes: "I have 8 copies which were all from the same sheet. All are nicely centered and a close comparison with the spacing of other stamps proves that they were not made from perforated stamps. All are dated 1913 and initialed H.G.R.." Dr. McCall of Edmonton also reports the existence of these rouletted stamps.

1915. King George. Red control numbers.

1423	A38	$3 Blue	.35

No.	Type.		Used.
	1923-1924. King George. Blue control numbers, white labels.		
1424	A38	25c Blue	.05
1425		50c Blue	.05
1426		60c Blue	.10
1427		$1	.25
1428		$2	.10
1429		$3	.25
1430		$4	.75
1431		$10	.65

A40 A41 A42 A43

WEIGHTS AND MEASURES.

1876. Large red control numbers at top.

1435	A40	5c Black	.40
1436		10c Black	.25
1437		15c Black	.30
1438		20c Black	.30
1439		30c Black	1.00

Red control numbers 4½ mm. high across center.

1440	A40	1c Blue	1.00
1441		2c Blue	1.25
1442		30c Blue	.20
1443		50c Blue	.10

No.	Type.		Used.
1444		$1 Blue	.20
1445		$1.50 Blue	.25
1446		$2 Blue	.30

Red control numbers 3½ mm. high across center.

No.	Type.		Used.
1452	A40	1c Black	.75
1453		2c Black	.75
1454		5c Black	.20
1455		10c Black	.60
1456		15c Black	.60
1457		20c Black	.15
1458		30c Black	.....
1459		50c Black	.10
1460		$1 Black	.40

1887. Small control numbers in blue across center.

No.	Type.		Used.
1461	A40	1c Black	.20
1462		2c Black	.25
1463		5c Black	.10
1464		10c Black	.10
1465		15c Black	.10
1466		20c Black	.05
1467		30c Black	.10
1468		50c Black	.10
1469		$1 Black	.15
1470		$1.50 Black	.15
1471		$2 Black	.15
1472		Red, no denomination	.50

(Two, and possibly three, numbering machines were used, showing slightly different figures.)

1897. Red control numbers.

No.	Type.		Used.
1475	A41	5c Black	.25
1476		10c Black	.40
1477		15c Black	.25
1478		20c Black	.15
1479		30c Black	.15
1480		50c Black	.05
1481		75c Black	.10
1482		$1 Black	.15
1483		$1.50 Black	.40
1484		$1.50 Black (white label)	.50
1485		$2 Black	.30

1906. (Series 1897.) King Edward. Red control numbers.

No.	Type.		Used.
1486	A42	$5 Black	1.00
1487		$10 Black	1.00

Blue control numbers. (1916-23.)

No.	Type.		Used.
1488		$5 Black	1.00
1489		$10 Black	1.00

King George.

No.	Type.		Used.
1490	A43	$2 Black, red control (1915)	.40
1491		20c Black, blue control (1916-23)	.50
1492		$2 Black, blue control (1916-23)	.40

1916 to 1923. Blue control numbers.

No.	Type.		Used.
1493	A41	5c Black	.....

No.	Type.		Used.
1494		10c Black	.10
1495		15c Black	.....
1496		30c Black	.15
1497		50c Black	.....
1498		75c Black	.15
1499		$1 Black	.10
1500		$1.50 Black (white label)	.20

It is illegal to possess Electric, Gas, or Weights and Measures stamps in unused condition.

Stamps with no control numbers or imperforate were never issued for use in that form and are classed as proofs.

CANADA MEDICINE STAMPS.

For use on bottles of old stock, indicating "Free From Taxation."

1501 No denomination

A44

A45

A46

ALBERTA LAW STAMPS.

First Issue, 1906-07. Perf. 12. Printed on creamy white wove paper by "The Edmonton Bulletin." Fancy scroll background in various colors. The first color given is that of the scroll and the second that of the lettering indicating the value.

No.	Type.		Unpunched	Punched
1505	A44	10c Mauve and green (2 shades)	2.50	1.25
		a. Broken scroll	7.50	3.75
		b. Fancy "L"	5.00	2.50
		c. Raised "O"	5.00	2.50
		d. Lowered "O"	5.00	2.50
1506		10c Olive yellow and green (2 shades)	2.50	1.25
		a. Broken scroll	7.50	3.75
		b. Fancy "L"	5.00	2.50
		c. Raised "O"	5.00	2.50

No.	Type.		Unpunched.	Punched.
		d. Lowered "O"	5.00	2.50
1507		10c Red or brown red and green	1.50	.75
		a. Broken scroll	4.50	2.25
		b. Fancy "L"	3.00	1.50
		c. Broken "O"	.300	1.50
		(In some sheets stamp No. 9 has no broken scroll.)		
1508	A44	10c Red and black (3 shades)	1.50	.75
		a. Broken scroll (?)	4.50	2.25
		b. Fancy "L"	3.00	1.50
		c. Broken "O"	.300	1.50
1509		10c Olive yellow and black	2.00	1.00
		a. Broken scroll	6.00	3.00
		b. Fancy "L"	4.00	2.00
		c. Raised "O"	4.00	2.00
		d. Lowered "O"	4.00	2.00
1510		20c Red and green (2 shades)	6.00	3.00
		a. Broken scroll	12.00	9.00
		b. Fancy "L"	12.00	6.00
		c. Raised "O"	12.00	6.00
1511		25c Brown red and black	2.50	1.25
		a. Broken scroll	7.50	3.75
		b. Fancy "L"	5.00	2.50
		c. Small "2"	5.00	2.50
		d. Period between 2.5	7.50	3.75
		e. Serrated edge	13.00	6.50
1512		25c Olive yellow and black (3 shades)	2.50	1.25
		a. Broken scroll	7.50	3.75
		b. Fancy "L"	5.00	2.50
		c. Small "2"	5.00	2.50
1513		25c Grey and Black	2.50	1.25
		a. Broken scroll	7.50	3.75
		b. Fancy "L"	5.00	2.50
		c. Small "2"	5.00	2.50
1514		25c Grey green and black	2.50	1.25
		a. Broken scroll	7.50	3.75
		b. Fancy "L"	5.00	2.50
		c. Small "2"	5.00	2.50
1515		25c Olive green and black	2.50	1.25
		a. Broken scroll	7.50	3.75
		b. Fancy "L"	5.00	2.50
1516		25c Red and black	2.50	1.25
		a. Fancy "L"	5.00	2.50
		(This sheet has pointed corners in the N.E. position of all stamps, and same arrangement of scrolls as "One Dollar" stamps.)		
1517	A44	25c Mauve and black	3.50	1.75
		a. Broken scroll	10.50	5.25
		b. Fancy "L"	7.00	3.50
1518		25c Red and green	1.50	.75
		a. Broken scroll	4.50	2.25
		b. Fancy "L"	3.00	1.50
		c. Period between 2.5	4.50	2.25
1519		50c Olive green and green (2 shades)	2.50	1.25
		a. Broken scroll	7.50	3.75
		b. Fancy "L"	5.00	2.50
		c. Raised "O"	5.00	2.50
		d. Lowered "O"	5.00	2.50

No.	Type.		Unpunched.	Punched.
1520		50c Red and green	1.50	.75
		a. Broken scroll	4.50	2.25
		b. Fancy "L"	3.00	1.50
		c. Raised "O"	3.00	1.50
		d. Lowered "O"	3.00	1.50
		(This sheet is imperforate and perforated at bottom, and there are two varieties of broken scrolls, one of which is quite rare.)		
1521		75c Red and green	2.00	1.00
		a. Broken scroll	6.00	3.00
		b. Fancy "L"	4.00	2.00
1522		$1 Red and green (3 shades)	2.00	1.00
		a. Broken scroll	6.00	3.00
		b. Fancy "L"	4.00	2.00
		c. Narrow space between $ signs	6.00	3.00
1523		"One Dollar" brown and black	2.50	1.25
		a. Fancy "L"	5.00	2.50
		b. Wide "N"	7.50	3.75
		c. Thin "E"	5.00	2.50
		d. Double scroll caused by second impression	......	......
		Second Issue. March, 1907, to May, 1910. Justice standing. Perf. 12. Lithographed by Bullman Bros., Winnipeg.		
1524	A45	5c Pearl grey (3 shades)	2.00	1.00
		a. Grey dot above W of LAW (Grey shade only)	......	......
		b. White dot on top of right pillar below P of STAMP	......	......
		c. White dot under 5 at top of stamp	......	......
1525		10c Orange, yellow-orange	1.50	.75
		a. Broken E of CENTS	6.00	3.00
		b. "0" of "10" defective, S.E. corner	......	......
1526		20c Red brown (2 shades)	3.00	1.50
		a. Broken RT in ALBERTA caused by brown blot	......	......
		b. Brown dots on left pillar above middle ornament	......	......
		c. White dot in left border	......	......
		d. White dot or break in top of left pillar and broken A in left side of A	......	......
1527		25c Red, bright red	2.00	1.00
		a. "2" defective, N.W. corner	6.00	3.00
		b. White blot on lower part of 2 in N.W. corner	......	......
		c. White spot under L in ALBERTA	......	......
		d. Red dot in lower curved part of 5 in N.E. corner	......	......
		e. White blurred line to the lower left of 2 in N.W. corner	......	......
		f. White line over 5 in N.W. corner	......	......
		g. Defective N in CENTS.		
		h. White dot over T in ALBERTA	......	......
		i. White line under B in ALBERTA	......	......
		j. Broken white line in top of 5 in N.E. corner	......	......

No.	Type.		Unpunched.	Punched.
		k. White dot under S in CENTS	......	......
		l. White dot over E in CENTS and white dot to the left of 2	......	......
		m. Dark red border to right of pillar above middle ornament	......	......
		n. White dot on robe of goddess	......	......
		o. Red bottom to right pillar above base	......	......
		p. Red dot over A in LAW	......	......
		q. Red dot in 5, S.W. corner.		
1528		50c Green, blue green	.80	.40
		a. White dot in border of left pillar	......	......
		b. White break under L of ALBERTA	......	......
1529		75c Blue, bluish violet	1.00	.50
		a. No point at the left of the 7 in top right hand corner	......	......
		b. No scroll or border of the word Alberta at top of stamp	......	......
		c. Broken 7 and 5 caused by dark purple blots	......	......
1530		$1 Blue, dark blue, violet blue	1.50	.75
		a. Right side of "A" of ALBERTA extended downward	4.00	2.00
		b. Right side of "A" of ALBERTA broken	4.00	2.00
		c. White line at top of A in first A of ALBERTA	......	......
		d. White dots at top of left pillar	......	......
		e. White line under AR of DOLLAR	......	......
1531		$2 Light or dark red brown	2.00	1.00
1532		$2 Lake (3 shades)	3.00	1.50
		a. Dot over "A" in DOLLARS	......	......
1533		$3 Grey black (2 shades)	4.00	2.00
		a. Dot after "3" in S.W.	8.00	4.00
		b. Dot in N.E. "3"	8.00	4.00
		c. Background of scroll or border under ALBERTA light in color	......	......
		d. Border of scroll at top of ALBERTA broken by heavy inking and top of ER blotted	......	......
		e. White dot under R in ALBERTA.		
1534		$5 Yellow ochre (2 shades)	6.00	3.00
		a. Dot under second "A" in ALBERTA		

Third Issue. 1913. Justice seated. Steel engraved. Perf. 12. Printed by the American Bank Note Co., Ottawa.

No.	Type.		Unpunched.	Punched.
1535	A46	5c Yellow brown (2 shades)	.50	.25
1536		10c Olive green (3 shades)	.40	.20
1537		20c Brown violet	1.50	.75
1538		25c Lake red (5 shades)	.40	.20
1539		50c Green, blue green (3 shades)	.60	.30
1540		75c Violet or light purple (3 shades)	1.00	.50
1541		$1 Blue, steel blue (2 shades)	1.00	.50
1542		$2 Steel grey (2 shades)	1.50	.75
1543		$3 Brown (2 shades)	5.00	2.50
1544		$5 Black	8.00	4.00
1545		$10 Black or brown (2 shades)	10.00	5.00

A47

Double Printing

BRITISH COLUMBIA LAW STAMPS.

No.	Type.		Used.
		1st Issue, 1879. Perf. 12. Engraved.	
1550	A47	10c Blue, "Law Stamp" in color	.35
1551		30c Blue, "Law Stamp" in color	.35
1552		50c Blue, "Law Stamp" colorless	.40
1553		$1 Blue	.75
		2nd Issue, 1887. Lithographed. Heavy dark background to figure. No inside shading to border line of triangular ornamental top corners. Small 3-leaf pattern top corners. Drape from shoulder cross-hatched shading.	
1554		10c Black, grey black	2.00
		a. Double printing	25.00
1555		30c Red, rose	2.25
1556		50c Brown, yellow brown	2.50
1557		$1 Blue	3.00
1557a		$5 Deep rose red	10.00
		3rd Issue, 1889. Lithographed. Perf. 11. On yellowish paper. Words "Law Stamp" in white block letters. Shading, below arch over figure and partly down sides. Drapery has oblique shading. Thin cross lines between double-line border round figure.	
1558		10c Black	.30
1559		30c Red	.50
1560		50c Violet brown	.50
1561		$1 Blue	.75
		(All values are found on watermarked paper.)	
		4th Issue, 1889. Lithographed. Figure almost entirely white, no shading. Vertical arm. Oblique shading on drape. Light cloud effect behind head.	
1562		10c Blue black	.....
1563		30c Orange	.....
1564		50c Brown	.....
1565		$1 Blue	.....

No.	Type.		Used.
		5th Issue, 1891. Lithographed on white paper. Perf. 11. Right arm holding scales inclined outward to elbow. Drape at back cross hatch shading. Figure well shaded. Right knee exposed.	
1566		10c Dark blue (die recut)	.....
1567		10c Black	.60
1568		25c Green	.....
1569		30c Carmine ("Law Stamp" colored letters)	.....
1570		30c Orange, red orange, as above	.60
1571		50c Red brown, dark brown, as above	.75
1572		$1 Blue	.....
1573		10c Black	.40
1574		30c Carmine rose	.75
1575		50c Brown	.75
1576		$1 Blue	1.50
		(The 10c and $1 have been reported with pin perf. 12.)	
		6th Issue, 1898. Lithographed. Distinguished from all others by drape covering knee.	
1577		10c Grey black	.....
1578		25c Green	1.00
1579		30c Carmine	.....
1580		30c Orange, brown orange	.....
1581		50c Dull brown, bright brown	.40
1582		$1 Blue, bright blue	1.00
		7th Issue, 1900. Engraved. Arm vertical, knee exposed, back drape oblique only, figure has shading distinctly. No light cloud effect behind head.	
1583		10c Dull black	.....
1584		25c Dull green (?)	.....
1585		30c Carmine (?)	.....
1586		30c Orange brown, orange yellow	.....
1587		50c Dark brown, light brown	.....
1588		$1 Deep blue, light blue	.....
1589		$5 Red	.....

A49

A50 (Reduced)

CAPE BRETON LAW STAMPS.

Provisionals. Wove paper, initialed and dated.

No.	Type.		Used.
1593	?	25c	10.00
1594	?	50c	10.00
1595	A49	25c Red, engraved	2.50
1596		50c Blue, engraved	2.50
1597	A50	25c Red, lithographed	2.50
1598	A50	50c Blue, lithographed	2.50

A51

A52

A53

DAWSON MINING COURT.

1903. Perf. 12. Engravel by American Bank Note Co., Ottawa.

No.	Type.		Used.
1600	A51	10c Vermilion	.60
1601		25c "	.60
1602		50c "	1.00
1603		$1 "	2.00
1604		$2 "	2.00
1605		$3 "	3.00

LOWER CANADA LAW.

1864. Perf. 12. Engraved by American Bank Note Co., New York.

No.	Type.		Used.
1606	A52	10c Green	.05
		a. Raised period after C	.15
		b. Raised period after L and C	.15
		c. Raised period after L	.15
1607		20c Green	.05
		a. Raised period after C	.15
		b. Lowered period after L	.15
		c. No period after C	1.00
1608		30c Green	.05
		a. Raised period after C	.15
		c. Raised period after L	.15
1609		40c Green	.07
		a. Raised period after L and C	.20
		b. Lowered period after L	.20
		c. Raised period after L	.20

No.	Type.		Used.
1610		50c Green	.05
		a. Raised period after C	.15
		b. Raised period after L and C	.15
1611		60c Green	.07
		a. Raised period after C	.20
1612		70c Green	.50
		a. Raised period after L and C	1.50
1613		80c Green	.20
		a. Raised period after C	.60
1614		90c Green	.50
1615		$1 Green and black	.10
		a. Raised period after C	.30
1617		$2 Green and black	.20
		a. Raised period after C	.60
1618		$3 Green and black	.40
1619		$4 Green and black	.60
1620		$5 Green and black	.75

(All values come on thick and thin papers.)

LOWER CANADA REGISTRATION.

December 12, 1866. Perf. 12.

No.	Type.		Used.
1621	A53	5c Brown red	.40
1622		15c Brown red	.60
1623		30c Brown red	.75
1624		5c Vermilion	.75
1625		15c Vermilion	.40
1626		30c Vermilion	.50

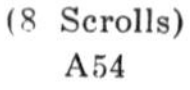
(8 Scrolls)
A54

(6 Scrolls)
A55

A57

A56

MANITOBA.

No.	Type.		Used.
		May 1st, 1877, to April 29th, 1884. Surcharged L.S. in block type, blue black.	
1630	A54	10c Green	.20
1631		20c Green	.25
1632		25c Green	2.50
1633		50c Green	.20
		a. Thin letters L.S.	.....
1634		$1 Green	1.50
1635		$2 Green	2.50
		May 1st, 1877, to July 1st, 1886. Surcharged C.F. in black with block type.	
1636	A54	10c Green	.15
1637		20c Green	.15
1638		25c Green	.10
1639		50c Green	.10
1640		$1 Green	.15
1641		$2 Green	1.50
		1st Provisional Issue. In use late June and early July, 1877. Yellow orange paper, imperforate. Value in red, coat of arms and C.F. in black. All stamps numbered and signed by A. Begg.	
1641	A56	10c	50.00
1642		20c	50.00
1643		25c	50.00
		2nd Provisional Issue. In use late October and in November, 1877. Similar to last but signed or initialed by officers other than A. Begg.	
1644	A56	10c (Signed by E. W. Romans)	50.00
1645		20c (Signed by E. W. Romans)	50.00
1646		25c (Signed by E. W. Romans)	50.00
1647		25c (Initialed E. W. R.)	50.00
1648		25c (Initialed D. C.) (Carey)	50.00
1649		25c (Initialed E. W. R. and D. C.)	50.00
1650		25c (Without either signature or initial)	50.00

No.	Type.		Used.
		3rd Provisional Issue. In use about September 15th to 23rd, 1881. White paper, imperforate, coat of arms smaller than 1st and 2nd Provisionals, printed in black, surcharged with rubber stamp either C.F. or L.S. in violet or purple, or surcharged with indelible pencil and with or without initials of E. M. (Ed. Marston.)	
		Surcharged C.F. with rubber stamp.	
1651	A57	10c	25.00
1652		20c	25.00
1653		50c	25.00
1654		$1	25.00
		Surcharged L.S. with rubber stamp.	
1655	A57	10c	25.00
1656		20c	25.00
1657		50c	25.00
1658		$1	25.00
		Surcharged C.F. with indelible pencil. With or without initials E.M.	
1659	A57	10c	25.00
		(There may have been other values.)	
		Surcharged L.S. with indelible pencil. With or without initials E.M.	
1660	A57	50c	25.00
		(There may have been other values.)	
		4th Provisional Issue. In use about third week in September, 1882. L.S. stamps of first type surcharged at top and bottom, with small letters C.F. in purple ink by hand stamp similar to that used in 3rd Provisional Issue.	
1661	A54	10c	7.00
1662		20c	7.00
		5th Provisional Issue. Used after April 29th, 1884. L.S. stamps of first type with L.S. pen stroked and C.F. written in red or black ink.	
1663	A54	10c	4.00
1664		50c	3.00
		6th Provisional Issue. In use late 1884 and early 1885. L.S. stamps of first type surcharged C.F. in red with hand stamp.	
		C.F. in large round letters stamped vertically and reading up or down.	
1665	A54	10c	25.00
1666		20c	25.00
1667		50c	25.00
		C.F. in small round letters stamped vertically and reading up or down.	
1668	A54	10c	25.00
1669		50c	25.00

No.	Type.		Used.
		C.F. in long narrow letters stamped vertically and reading up.	
1670	A54	10c	25.00
		Nos. 1665 to 1670 have been priced in previous catalogues at $10, but we believe the value given more nearly approximates the worth of these exceedingly rare varieties	
		Pen stroked varieties of L.S. surcharged C.F. in ink, and C.F. surcharged L.S. should be regarded as oddities rather than provisionals, when used during the period when both of these stamps were in issue. There are many varieties, some of which are initialed by Ed. Marston.	
		1885-1886. Surcharged C.F. in black, large block type.	
1671	A55	10c Green	4.00
1672		$1 Green	5.00
		July 1st, 1886, to March 5th, 1889. First type L.S. stamps surcharged B.F. with hand stamp in red.	
1673	A54	10c Green	25.00
1674		20c Green	25.00
1675		25c Green	.50
1676		50c Green	25.00
1677		$1 Green	4.00
1678		$2 Green	25.00
		July 1st, 1886, to March 5th, 1889. First type C.F. stamps surcharged B.F. with hand stamp in red.	
1679	A54	10c Green	4.00
1680		20c Green	1.50
1681		25c Green	.75
1682		50c Green	1.00
1683		$1 Green	8.00
1684		$2 Green	4.00
		July 1st, 1886, to March 5th, 1889. Second type of C.F. stamps surcharged B.F. with hand stamp in red.	
1685	A55	10c Green	4.00
1686		20c Green	1.50
1687		25c Green	.75
1688		50c Green	1.00
1689		$1 Green	4.00
		Surcharged only with B.F. stamped in red. In use after Nos. 43 to 59 became exhausted and until March 5th, 1889.	
1690	A54	10c Green	.50
1691		25c Green	15.00
1692		50c Green	.50
		July 1st, 1886, to May 20th, 1892. First type L.S. stamps surcharged J.F. with hand stamp in red.	
1693	A54	10c Green	2.00
1694		20c Green	1.00
1695		25c Green	.30
1696		50c Green	2.00
1697		$1 Green	1.00
1698		$2 Green	8.00

No.	Type.		Used.
		July 1st, 1886, to May 30th, 1892. First type C.F. stamps surcharged J.F. with hfand stamp in red.	
1699	A54	10c Green	.50
1700		20c Green	.30
1701		25c Green	.50
1702		50c Green	.25
1703		$1 Green	3.00
1704		$2 Green	4.00
		July 1st, 1886, to May 30th, 1892. Second type C.F. stamps surcharged J.F. in red with hand stamp.	
1705	A55	10c Green	1.25
1706		20c Green	1.75
1707		25c Green	.75
1708		50c Green	.75
1709		$1 Green	2.50
		Issued after Nos. 63 to 79 became exhausted and used until May 30th, 1892. First type surcharged only with J.F. stamped in red.	
1710	A54	10c Green	.25
1711		25c Green	.25
1712		50c Green	.40
		August 26th, 1889, to May 30th, 1892. First type surcharged only with J.F. in dark blue, large type.	
1713	A54	25c Green	.50
1714		50c Green	.35
1715		$1 Green	.50
		Used until May 30th, 1892. **First type surcharged only with J.F. in dark blue, small type.**	
1716	A54	20c Green (May 29, 1890)	.50
1717		50c Green (Sept. 17, 1891)	.50
		J.F. in red on first type with B.F. in red. (Bartlett Collection.)	
1718	A54	10c Green	.....
		(The above dates indicate the periods during which the various varieties of B.F. and J.F. stamps could be used. As supplies ran out the other varieties indicated below took their place.)	
		May 30th, 1892, until exhausted, not later than June 1st, 1901. **Unsurcharged.**	
1719	A54	10c Green	.15
1720		20c Green	.20
1721		25c Green	.10
1722		50c Green	.10
1723		$1 Green	.20
		April, 1897, to June 1st, 1901. **Unsurcharged.**	
1724	A54	10c Green	1.50
		a. Imperf. between	.....
1725		25c Green	1.00
1726		50c Green	1.50
1727		$1 Green	2.00

No.	Type.		Used.
1728		10c Deep blue green	1.00
1729		25c Deep blue green	1.00
1730		50c Deep blue green	.75
1731		$1 Deep blue green	1.25
		Proofs in orange red on India	2.50

A58

A59

NEW BRUNSWICK LAW.

1884. Perf. 12½. Engraved.

1750	A58	10c Blue	.45
1751		20c Blue	.65
1752		50c Blue	.65
1753		$2 Blue	1.00

1887 and 1890. Engraved.

1754	A58	10c Yellow	.60
1755		20c Red	.60
1756		50c Brown	.80

Lithographed.

1757	A58	$5 Green	2.00

1900. Lithographed.

1758		20c Red	.....
1759		50c Brown	.....
1760		$1 Violet	.....
1761		$5 Green	.....

NEW BRUNSWICK PROBATE.

1895. Various Perfs.

1762	A59	10c Yellow	.50
1763		20c Red	.50
1764		50c Brown	.75
1765		$2 Blue	1.50
1766		$5 Green	2.00
1767		$20 Purple	4.50

A60

A61

A63

A64

A65

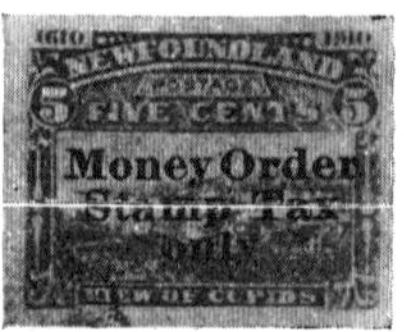

A66

NEWFOUNDLAND REVENUE

No.	Type.		Used.
		American Bank Note Co.	
1775	A60	5c Orange red	.50
1776		10c Brown	.15
1777		25c Blue	.15
1778		50c Yellow orange	.20
1779		75c Black	.60
1780		$1 Green	.50
1781		$5 Maroon	2.00
1782		$20 Pale brown	6.00
1783		$25 Slate	7.00
1784		$50	.....
1785		$100	.....
		With Head of King Edward VII.	
1786	A61	5c	.....
1787		10c	.....
1788		25c Blue	.50
1789		50c Black	.50
1790		$1 Green	1.00
1791		$5 Lilac	3.00
1792		$20	.....

No.	Type.			Used.
		With Head of George V.		
1793	A61	5c Orange vermilion		.05
1794		10c Olive green		.10
1795		25c Blue		.20
1796		50c Slate		.30
1797		$1 Green		.30
1798		$5 Purple lilac		1.50
1799		$20		.....

Cigarettes.

Numbered rectangular label with blank space for date of export and place from which exported to be written in. No denomination.

Head of Edward VII.

1801	A63	10 Violet (shades)		.30
1802		100 Green		.30

Head of George V, Series 1913.

1803	A64	5 Green		.10

Customs Duty.

July 1, 1925. Rouletted. Engraved by British American Bank Note Co., Ltd., Ottawa. Size 33½x25 mm. Used for payment of duty on advertising matter entering Newfoundland. Prince of Wales in uniform of Welsh Guards.

1815	A65	1c Green		.....
1816		3c Yellow brown		.....
1817		5c Violet		.....

Stamp Tax on Customs Entries.

1818		20c denomination		.....
		(Current postage stamps are used.)		
		Oct. 1, 1914. Perf. 14x12. Carmine overprint.		
1825	A66	5c Ultramarine	1.20	.40
		a. No period	.80	.60
		b. Broken "y"	.....	.....
		5c Deep blue	1.20	.40
		a. No period	.80	.60
		b. Broken "y"	.....	.....
		1915. Perf. 14x12. Vermilion overprint.		
1827		5c Ultramarine	1.20	.40
		a. No period	.80	.60
		b. Broken "y"	.....	.....
		c. Vertical overprint	5.00	.....
1828		5c Deep blue	1.20	.40
		a. No period	.80	.60
		b. Broken "y"	.....	.....

A69

A71

NOVA SCOTIA BILL STAMPS.

No.	Type.			Used.
		3rd Issue Canada Bill Stamps Overprinted "N.S." in Black.		
1830	A69	1c Brown	.30	.15
1831		2c Orange	.30	.15
1832		3c Green	.30	.15
1833		4c Brown	1.50	.75
1834		5c Orange	.40	.20
1835		6c Green	.30	.15
1836		7c Orange	2.00	1.00
1837		8c Brown	2.00	1.00
1838		9c Green	.30	.15
1839		10c Blue	.75	.40
1840		20c Blue	1.00	.50
1841		30c Blue	1.00	.50
1842		40c Blue	1.25	.60
1943.		50c Blue	1.50	.75
		Surcharged at Top.		
1844		$1 Blue, black center	3.50	2.50
1845		$2 Red, black center	10.00	5.00
1846		$3 Green, black center	15.00	8.00

(A second type of '"N.S." appears on late issues, all values, in the paler shades and thicker papers. These may be counterfeit.)

HALIFAX (NOVA SCOTIA) LAW LIBRARY.

Halifax (Nova Scotia) Law Library.
1879. Perf. 12½.

1850	A71	25c Green	.85	.75
		1903. Perf. 14.		
1851		25c Green	.50	.40
1852		50c Green	.85	.75

A72

A73

A74

ONTARIO LAW STAMPS.

No.	Type.			Used.
		1864. Perf. 12. Overprinted "C.F." (Consolidated Fund) in blue. Thin paper.		
1860	A72	5c Green	......	.25
		a. Dropped period after C	......	......
1861		10c Green	......	.04
		a. Raised period after F	......	......
1862		20c Green	......	.06
		a. Raised period after F	......	......
1863		30c Green	......	.08
1864		40c Green	......	.40
		a. Dropped period after C	......	......
1865		50c Green	......	.05
		a. Raised period after F	......	......
1866		60c Green	......	.20
		a. Raised period after F	......	......
1867		70c Green	......	1.25
		a. Perf. at top, rouletted bottom and sides	......	......
1868		80c Green	......	1.00
1869		90c Green	......	1.50
1870		$1 Green and black	......	.20
1871		$2 Green and black	......	.75
1872		$3 Green and black	......	3.00
1873		$4 Green and black	......	5.00
1874		$5 Green and black	......	6.00

(Some values are noted on stout wove paper. Bartlett records a set "with fine scollop cuts." All cuts touch the design on all sides, and all stamps are unused, with gum.

No.	Type.			Used.
		Overprinted "F.F." (Fee Fund) in yellow.		
1880	A73	5c Green (rouletted)	......	......

No.	Type.			Used.
1881		10c Green	......	.05
		a. Raised period after 2nd F	......	......
1882		20c Green	......	.05
		a. Raised period after 2nd F	......	......
1883		30c Green	......	.05
		a. Raised period after 2nd F	......	......
		b. Raised periods	......	......
1884		40c Green	......	.06
		a. Raised period after 2nd F	......	......
		b. Raised periods	......	......
1885		50c Green	......	.06
1886		60c Green	......	.08
		a. Vert. perfs. cut 1st F	1.50	......
1887		70c Green	15.00	......
1888		80c Green	......	1.25
		a. Raised period after 1st F	......	......
1889		90c Green	......	1.50
1890		$1 Green and black	......	.10
		a. Raised periods	......	......
1891		$2 Green and black	......	.60
		a. Raised period after 1st F	......	......
1892		$3 Green and black	......	2.00
		a. Raised periods	......	......
1893		$4 Green and black	......	3.00
		a. Raised periods	......	......
1894		$5 Green and black	......	5.00
1895		20c Blue green	......	.08
1896		60c Blue green	......	.15
1897		80c Blue green	......	1.50
		(The 70c denomination may be a perforated proof. It has not been seen used. In some stamps the letter "F" of the overprint has a base. Bartlett records a full set with scallops or roulettes as for the "C.F." stamps, as well as a rouletted 5c of which he saw a part sheet.)		
		Overprinted "L.S." (Law Society) in carmine.		
1900	A74	5c Green (rouletted)	......	......
1901		10c Green (rouletted)	......	......
1902		20c Green	......	.12
		a. Raised period after S	......	......
1903		30c Green	......	.12
1904		40c Green	......	.20
1905		50c Green	......	.06
		a. Raised period after L	......	......
		b. Raised period after S	......	......
		c. Raised period after LS	......	......
		d. Dropped period after L	......	......
1906		60c Green	......	.25
		a. Dropped period after L	......	......
1907		70c Green	......	2.00
1908		80c Green	......	1.50
1909		90c Green	......	3.00
1910		$1 Green and black	......	.10

No.	Type.			Used.
1911		$2 Green and black	......	.50
		a. Overprint in black	......	......
1912		$3 Green and black	......	3.00
1913		$4 Green and black	......	6.00
1914		$5 Green and black	......	6.00
		a. Raised period after S	......	......

(The CF, FF and LS stamps were reprinted, the reprints being for the most part in a darker shade.)

A75

A76

A77

A78

A79

ONTARIO LAW.

1871. Perf. 12. Engraved by British American Bank Note Co., Montreal and Ottawa.

1925	A75	5c Red	.30
1926		10c Red	.02
1927		20c Red	.02
		a. Imperf. pair	......

No.	Type.		Used.
1928		30c Red	.02
1929		40c Red	.04
1930		50c Red	.02
		a. Imperf. pair	......
1931		60c Red	.10
1932		70c Red	1.00
1933		80c Red	1.00
1934		90c Red	1.00
1935		$1 Red	.03
1936		$2 Red	.75
1937		$3 Red	2.00
1938		$4 Red	5.00
		Perf. 12½.	
1939	A75	10c Red	......
1940		30c Red	......
1941		60c Red	......
1942		$1 Red	......
1943		$2 Red	......
		(There are numerous shades of all values. The 10c, 20c and 50c are known part perf.)	
		1911.	
1944	A75	30c Green	......
		1912.	
1945	A76	$4 Green on greenish	......
1946	A77	$5 Blue	......
		$10 Orange	......
1947	A78	$20 Brown	......
1948	A79	$50 Purple	......

Jan., 1929. Similar designs, engraved smaller size, denominations 5c, 10c, 20c, 30c, 50c, $1, $2, $3, $4, $5, $20, $50. ......

A80

A81

A82

A83

A84

ONTARIO STOCK TRANSFER.

1st Issue. 1910. Perf. 12.

No.	Type.		Used.
1960	A80	2c Red	.10
1961		10c Green	.25
1962		20c Brown	.35
1963		50c Purple	.75
1964		$1 Blue	.....
1965		$2 Grey	.....
1966		$10 Orange	.....

2nd Issue.

No.	Type.		Used.
1967	A81	3c on 2c Red	.25

3rd Issue.

No.	Type.		Used.
1968	A80	3c Green	.15
1969		15c Brown	.30
1970		30c Blue	.45
1971		60c Olive green	.85
1972		$1.50 Claret	.....
1973		$3 Reddish brown	.....
1974		$5 Purple	.....
1975		$15 Violet	.....

4th Issue. 1926.

"Stock Transfer Tax" overprinted in black on Luxury Tax stamps. Type 84.

No.	Type.		Used.
1976	A82	3c on 2½m Red brown	.....
1977	A83	— on 6m Blue	.....

ONTARIO LUXURY TAX.

No.	Type.		Used.
1978	· 1	2½ on 2m Red brown	.....
1979		1c on 1m Green	.....
1980	A84	2½m Red brown	.08
1981		1c Green	.....
1982		6c Blue	.15

In error stamps of the denomination of 2m were supplied and the entire printing returned to be surcharged 2½m. The order for 1c stamps was filled in error with a stamp of the denomination of 1m and this printing was likewise overprinted "1 Cent."

"Luxury Tax" Overprinted on Ontario Law.

No.	Type.		Used.
1983		50c Vermilion overprinted (about 200)	10.00

A84x

GASOLINE TAX.

In use November and December, 1928. The Government found that some of the oil companies were unable to make satisfactory tax returns covering sales of gasoline. These stamps were sold to smaller companies who levied the tax directly on the purchaser. In sheets of 50 with imprint "British American Bank Note Co., Montreal and Ottawa," above stamps 5 and 6, below 45 and 46 reading upside down, and reading up opposite No. 21 on the left and down opposite No. 30 on the right. Slight defects which are constant and might be listed as minor varieties occur in No. 22, N of CENTS; No. 26 and No. 37, T of CENTS.

No.	Type	Description	Unused	Used
1990	A84x	3c on 5c Ontario Law	.75	.75
1991		3c on 40c Ontario Law	.50	.50
1992		3c on 50c Ontario Law	.50	.50
1993		3c on 60c Ontario Law	.50	.50
1994		3c on 70c Ontario Law	.50	.50
1995		15c on 60c Ontario Law	.50	.50
1996		15c on 70c Ontario Law	.50	.50
1997		15c on 80c Ontario Law	.50	.50
1998		15c on 90c Ontario Law	.75	.75

ONTARIO LAW, JANUARY, 1929.

A series of stamps of smaller size was in preparation at time of going to press, expected to be available in January, 1929. The author was informed that all remainders of the large size stamps would be destroyed.

A85

A86

A87

QUEBEC LAW STAMPS.

1871. Perf. 12.

No.	Type	Description	Used
2000	A85	10c Red	.02
2001		20c Red	.04
2002		30c Red	.04
2003		40c Red	.05
2004		50c Red	.02
2005		60c Red	.12
2006		70c Red	.20
2007		80c Red	.12
		a. Imperf. horiz.	.....

No.	Type.		Used.
2008		90c Red	.30
2009	A86	$1 Blue (2 shades)	.04
		a. Imperf.	.....
2010		$2 Blue (2 shades)	.10
		a. Imperf.	.....
2011		$3 Blue (2 shades)	.20
		a. Imperf.	.....
2012		$4 Blue (2 shades)	.35
		a. Imperf.	.....
2013		$5 Blue (2 shades)	.30
		a. Imperf.	.....

(The imperforates examined have been on thick wove, pen cancelled, and may be proofs.)
(In the denominations from 10c to 90c there are from twelve to twenty-three shades. The blue stamps may be divided into several shades.)

1890.

2014		$10 Yellow	1.50
2015		$20 Green	3.00
2016		$30 Violet	5.00

1893. Shades from grey to near-black, and from mauve to violet, also a greenish tint.

2017	A85	10c	.02
2018		20c	.05
2019		30c	.02
2020		40c	.02
2021		50c	.02
2022		60c	.60
2023		70c	.15
2024		80c	.15
2025		90c	.35
2026	A86	$1 Green	.05
2027		$2 Green	.10
2028		$3 Green	.25
2029		$4 Green	.25
2030		$5 Green	.25
2031		$10 Blue	1.25
2032		$20 Yellow	2.50
2033		$30 Vermilion	3.50

1906.

2034	A85	10c Light violet-brown	.05
2035		20c Light violet-brown	.10
2036		40c Black	.25
2037		50c Black	.30
2038		60c Black	.50
2039		70c Blue	.60
2040		80c Blue	.30
2041		90c Bluish-purple	.60
2042	A86	$1 Carmine	.75
2043		$2 Brown	.40
2044		$3 Orange	.50
2045		$4 Brown	.50
2046		$5 Carmine	.75

1912.

No.	Type.		Used.
2050	A87	10c Green	.03
2051		20c Blue	.08
2052		30c Red	.06
2053		40c Light brown	.10
2054		50c Black	.08
2055		60c Olive	.50
2056		70c Yellow brown	.50
2057		80c Dark brown	.35
2058		90c Red brown	.75
2059		$1 Scarlet	.10
2060		$2 Purple	.15
2061		$3 Green	.35
2062		$4 Black or grey	.50
2063		$5 Blue	.75
2064		$10 Violet brown	1.25
2065		$20 Red brown	......

1924. Overprinted in red, "Honoraires Fees" in two lines diagonally to right. Used to check up amounts due to Prothonotary.

No.	Type.		Used.
2067	A87	10c Green, red overprint	......
2068		20c Blue, red overprint	......
2069		30c Red, black overprint	......
2070		40c Light brown, red overprint	......
2071		50c Black, red overprint	......
2072		60c Olive, red overprint	......
2073		70c Yellow brown, red overprint	......
2074		80c Dark brown, red overprint	......
2075		90c Red brown, red overprint	......
2076		$1 Scarlet, black overprint	......
2077		$2 Purple, red overprint	......
2078		$3 Green, red overprint	......
2079		$4 Black, red overprint	......
2080		$5 Blue, red overprint	......
2081		$10 Violet brown, red overprint	......
2082		$20 Red brown, red overprint	......
2083		$30 Green, red overprint	......

1924. Overprinted (a) 'Bankruptcy Act Loi de Faillite" or (b) "Loi De Faillite Bankruptcy Act" in two lines.

No.	Type.		Used.
2085	A87	10c Green (b) in red	......
2086		20c Blue (a) in red	......
2087		40c Brown (b) in red	......
2088		50c Black (a) in red	......
2089		$1 Scarlet (a) in black	......
2090		$2 Purple (a) in red	......
2091		$3 Green (b) in red	......
2092		$4 Black (b) in red	......
2093		$5 Blue (b) in red	......

A89

A90

A91

LICENSE.

No.	Type.		Used.
		1889. Perf. 12½.	
2095	A89	$2 Brown (shades)	.25
2096		$2 Grey	.30
		1906.	
2097		$7 Olive	3.00
2098		$25 Red	.....

Provisional License. Quebec Law Stamps surcharged "License."
1893.

2099	$5 Green, red surcharge	.....
	1906.	
2100	$5 Red, blue-black surcharge	.....
	1912.	
2101	$5 Blue, red surcharge	.....

PROHIBITION.

May 1, 1919. Perf. 12.

2102	A90	1c Orange	.10
2103		2c Blue	.15
2104		5c Light brown	.30
2105		5c Red brown	.20
2106		10c Light brown	.50
2107		10c Black	.40

No.	Type.		Used.
2108		20c Vermilion	.80
2109		50c Dark brown	1.00
2110		$1 Olive green	1.50
2111		$5 Blue green	8.00
2112		$10 Violet brown	10.00

ASSURANCE.

May 1st, 1876. Perf. 12. On white wove.

No.	Type.		Used.
2115	A91	1c Green	.25
2116		2c Green	.20
2117		3c Green	.20
2118		4c Green	.30
2119		5c Green	.25
2120		10c Green	.50
2121		20c Green	.75
2122		30c Green	1.00
2123		40c Green	1.50
		a. Perf. 12x11.	
2124		50c Green	1.50
		a. Perf. 12x11.	
2125		$1 Violet	3.00
2126		$2 Violet	5.00
2127		$3 Violet	15.00
2128		$4 Violet	15.00
2129		$5 Violet	20.00

A92

A93

A94

REGISTRATION

1871. Perf. 12.

No.	Type.		Used.
2130	A92	2c Green	.25
2131		5c Green	.06
2132		15c Green	.10
2133		30c Green	.10
2134		50c Green	.30

(Stamps on papers that may be classed as "toned" are due to a thin deposit of ink having been left on the plate after cleaning.)

No.	Type.		Used.
2135		$1 Vermilion (shades)	.35
2136		$2 Vermilion (shades)	.50
2137		$5 Vermilion (shades)	3.00

1906.

2138	A92	30c Blue	.25
2139		30c Ultramarine	.30
2140		50c Black	.50
2141		$1 Carmine	.75
2142		$1 Scarlet	.75
2143		$2 Brown	.75

1918. Perf. 12.

2144	A93	5c Black	.10
2145		10c Brown orange	.15
2146		15c Green	.25
2147		20c Green	.30
2148		30c Blue	.20
2149		50c Brown (shades)	.30
2150		$1 Pale olive	.40
2151		$2 Light brown	.40
2152		$5 Purple	3.00
2153		$5 Mauve	3.00

STOCK TRANSFER.

1907. Perf. 12.

2154	A94	2c Blue	.25
2155		10c Carmine	.30
2156		20c Black	.50
2157		50c Yellow	.50
2158		$1 Red	1.00
2159		$2 Brown	1.00
2160		$10 Purple	.....
2161		$30 Green	.....

Bilingual.

2162		2c Blue	.05
2163		10c Olive	.10
2164		20c Slate	.25
2165		50c Orange buff	.40
2166		$1 Red	.40
2167		$2 Brown	.60
2168		$10 Purple	.....
2169		$30 Green	.....

A96

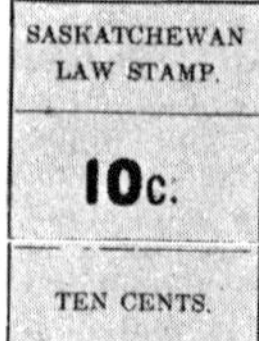

A97 (Reduced)

A98

A99

SASKATCHEWAN LAW STAMPS.

1907.

1st Issue, 1st Printing, by "The Regina Leader." The distance between the word "cents" or "dollars" and the bottom frame line is about 3 mm. Perf. 12.

No.	Type.		Used.
3000	A96	5c, Light green scroll, blue value on white	3.50
		a. No period	......
		b. Small period	......
		c. Large round period	......
		d. Large square period	......
3001		10c, Light brownish scroll, blue value on reddish pink	3.00
		a. No period	......
		b. Small period	......
		c. Large round period	......
		d. Large square period	......
3002		20c, Bluish-green scroll, black value on bright blue	2.50
		a. No period	......
		b. Small period	......
		c. Large round period	......
		d. Large square period	......
3003		25c, Dark green scroll, brown value on bright green	2.50
		a. No period	......
		b. Small period	......
		c. Large round period	......
		d. Large square period	......
3004		50c, Yellowish green scroll, dark green value on deep yellow	2.50
		a. No period	......
		b. Small period	......
		c. Large round period	......
		d. Large square period	......
3005		75c, Brown scroll, black value on bright deep red	4.50
		a. No period	......
		b. Small period	......
		c. Large round period	......
		d. Large square period	......

No.	Type		Used.
3006		$1, Light green scroll, brown value on white	......
3007		$2, Light brownish scroll, blue value on reddish pink	......
3008		$3, Bluish green scroll, brown value on bright blue	......
3009		$5, Dark green scroll, black value on bright deep green	......
3010		$10, Yellowish green scroll, black value on deep yellow	......
3011		$20, Brown scroll, black value on bright deep red	......

1908.

2nd Printing, by "The Regina Leader." The distance between the word "Cents" or "dollars" and the bottom frame line is about 2 mm. Perf. 12.

No.	Type		Used.
3012		5c, Light green scroll, blue value on white	3.00
		a. Inverted	......
3013		10c, Light brown scroll, black value on reddish pink	2.00
		a. No dot after C	......
3014		25c, Dark green scroll, black value on bright green	2.50
3015		50c, Greyish scroll, black value on orange yellow	2.50
3016		75c, Brown scroll, black value on bright deep red	3.50
3017		$1, Light green scroll, brown value on white	3.00
3018		$2, Light brown scroll, black value on reddish pink	4.00
3019		$3, Bluish green scroll, black value on bright blue	5.00

Second Issue. Printed by "The Regina Leader."
Perf. 12.

No.	Type		Used.
3020	A97	5c, Black on greenish scroll	......
3021		10c, Black on greenish scroll	2.50
		a. No dot after c in 10c	......
		b. Small round dot after c	......
		c. Large round dot after c	......
		d. Square dot after c	......
3022		20c, Black on greenish scroll	2.50
3023		25c, Black on greenish scroll	2.50
		a. No dot after c in 10c	......
		b. Small round dot after c	......
		c. Large round dot after c	......
		d. Square dot after c	......
3024		50c, Black on greenish scroll	2.50
		a. No dot after c in 10c	......
		b. Small round dot after c	......
		c. Large round dot after c	......
		d. Square dot after c	......
3025		75c, Black on greenish scroll	4.00
		a. No dot after c in 10c	......
		b. Small round dot after c	......
		c. Large round dot after c	......
		d. Square dot after c	......
3026		$1 Black on greenish scroll	2.50
3027		$2	4.00
3028		$3	5.00
3029		$5	15.00
3030		$10	......
3031		$20	......

Third Issue. Engraved by the American Bank Note Co., Ottawa. Perf. 12.

No.	Type.		Used.
3032	A98	5c Steel blue	.50
3033		10c Lake	.50
3034		20c Olive green	.75
3035		25c Lilac	.60
3036		50c Light red-brown	.40
3037		75c Olive brown	.50
3038		$1 Olive grey	.60
3039		$2 Light brown	.65
3040		$3 Grey green	.80
3041		$5 Blue green	2.00
3042		$10 Grey brown	3.00
3043		$20 Red	10.00

YUKON TERRITORIAL COURT.

1903. Perf. 12. Engraved by American Bank Note Co., Ottawa

3045	A99	10c Blue	.40
3046		25c Blue	.80
3047		50c Blue	1.00
3048		$1 Blue	2.00
3049		$2 Blue	3.00
3050		$3 Blue	4.00

A100

A101

A102

TELEGRAPH FRANKS.

Canadian Pacific Railways.

No.	Type	Date		
3055	A100	1887	Black, red control number	1.00
3056		1888	(None issued)	......
3057		1889	Black, red control number	1.00
3058		1890	Black, red control number	1.00
3059		1891	Black, red control number	1.00

No.	Type.		Used.
3060		1892 Black, red control number	1.00
3061		1893 Black, red control number	1.00
3062		1894 Black, red control number	.75
3063		1895 Black, red control number	.75
3064		1896 Black, red control number	.75
3065		1897 Black, red control number	.60
3066		1898 Black, red control number	.60
3067		1899 Black, red control number	.60
3068		1900 Black, red control number	.60
3069		1901 Black, red control number	.50
3070		1902 Blue, red control number	.50
3071		1903 Brown, blue control number	.50
3072		1904 Slate, red control number	.50
3073		1905 Black, red control number	.50
3074		1906 Black, blue control number	.50
3075		1907 Black, blue control number	.40
3076		1908 Black, blue control number	.40
3077		1909 Black, blue control number	.40
3078		1910 Black, red control number	.40
3079		1911 Black, red control number	.40
3080		1912 Black, red control number	.40
3081		1913 Black, red control number	.40
3082		1914 Black, red control number	.40
3083		1915 Black, blue control number	.40
3084		1916 Black, red control number	.40
3085		1917 Black, blue control number	.40
3086		1918 Black, blue control number	.40
3087		1919 Black, blue control number	.40
3088		1920 Black, blue control number	.40
3089		1921 Black, red control number	.40
3090		1922 Black, red control number	.40
3091		1923 Black, red control number	.40
3092		1924 Black, red control number	.40
3093		1925 Black, red control number	.40
3094		1926 Black, red control number	.40
3095		1927 Black, red control number	.40

Great North Western Telegraph Company.

No.	Type	Date	
3100	A101	1890 Blue, red control number	2.00
3101		1891 Red, blue control number	2.00
3102		1892 Green, black control number	2.00
3103		1893 Brown, black control number	2.00
3104		1894 Black, red control number	2.00
3105		1895 Violet, red control number	2.00
3106		1896 Red, blue control number	1.75
3107		1897 Blue, red control number	1.75
3108		1898 Green, red control number	1.75
3109		1899 Brown, red control number	1.00
3110		1900 Red, red control number	1.00
3111		1901 Green, red control number	1.00
3112		1902 Black, red control number	.50
3113		1903 Brown, red control number	.50
3114		1904 Blue, red control number	.50
3115		1905 Red, blue control number	.50
3116		1906 Green, red control number	.50
3117		1907 Brown, red control number	.40

No.	Type.		Used.
3118		1908 Purple, red control number	.40
3119		1909 Blue, red control number	.40
3120		1910 Red, blue control number	.40
3121		1911 Black, red control number	.40
3122		1912 Black, red control number	.35
3123		1913 Blue, red control number	.35
3124		1914 Black, red control number	.35
3125		1915 Green, red control number	.30
3126		1916 Black, red control number	.30
3127		1917 Blue, red control number	.30
3128		1918 Slate, red control number	.30
3129		1919 Black, red control number	.30
3130		1920 Black, lilac control number	.30

Grand Trunk Pacific Railway.

No.	Type	Date	
3131	A102	1916 Black, red control number	.....
		1918 Black, red control number	.....

Canadian National Railways.

(A union of the G.N.W., C.N.R. and G.T.P.)

3135	1921 Black, red control number	.....
3136	1922 Red, red control number	.....
3137	1923 Green, red control number (two varieties)	.....
3138	1924 (None issued).	
3139	1925 (None issued).	
3140	1926 Ultramarine, red control number	.....

Algoma Central Railway.

3145 This Railway with head offices at Sault Ste. Marie, issued a Telegraph Frank in the '90's, blue, of same size as the G.N.W. The author has seen but one specimen, and a thorough search of the Head Office records has failed to uncover others.

CANADA RAILWAY STAMPS.

Dominion Express Company.

Imperforate.

3150	4c Black on grey,	"1 lb. and under"	.....
3151	8c	"Over 1 lb."	.....
3152	10c Black on lilac,	"Over 2 lbs."	.....
3153	15c Black on yellow,	"Over 5 lbs."	.....
3154	20c	"Over 10 lbs."	.....
3154	25c	"Over 15 lbs."	.....

1902. Surcharged in violet, "Newspapers only" one cent a pound.

3155 1c on 4c Black and grey

Canadian Express Company.

3156 A set was printed, in black and red on white paper........................ ......

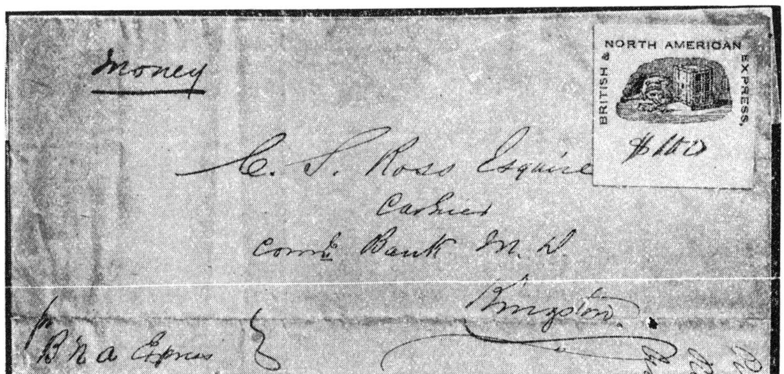

A105

EXPRESS LABELS—ON MONEY PACKAGES OR LETTERS.
1854.
British and North American Express.

3160 A105 Thick yellow wove 25.00

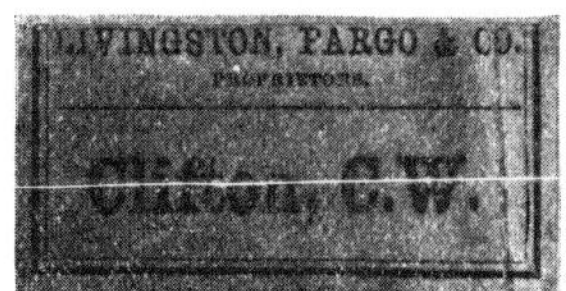

A106

A107

A108

MONEY PACKAGE.

(83) FORWARDED BY

American Merchants

UNION EXPRESS CO.

FROM

Brantford, Ont.

A109

A110x

No. Type. Used.

Livingston, Fargo & Co.

3163 A106 Black on white wove, surface colored brick red (Clifton, Ont.) 5.00

American Express Co.

Black on white wove, surface colored brick red ....

3164 A107 Suspension Bridge 5.00

3165 A108 17mm. between outer frame lines top and bottom, Oct. 7, 1861 (Toronto) 5.00

3166 22 mm. between outer frame lines top and bottom, Jan. 2, 1862 .... 5.00

20th January, 1871.

American Merchants Union Express Co.

3170 A109 Typeset adhesive on white wove, surface colored brick red, used from Suspension Bridge, Toronto, Brantford, etc. .....

A110  A111  A111

Montreal Local.

3175 A110x 5c Blue, Perf .12 ,on white wove 6.00

TELEPHONE FRANKS.

Bell Telephone Company of Canada, Limited.

3080 Messenger Service. Perf. 11. Black. No date or value.

Design, "Messenger Service Prepaid," left side, top, and left side; "B. T. Co." at bottom; running messenger in medallion ....

3081 Message Frank, dated 18..... ....

3082 Message Frank, dated 189.... Blue paper, red control number .....

Perf. 11 to 14. Red control number.

3084 A110 1900 10c Black on yellow ....

3085 15c Black on blue ....

3086 25c Black on white ....

3087 1901 10c ....

3088 15c ....

3089 25c ....

3090 1902 10c ....

3091 15c ....

3092 25c ....

3093 1903 10c ....

3094 15c ....

3095 25c ....

No.	Type.			Used.
3096		1904	10c	......
3097			15c	......
3098			25c	......
3099		1905	10c	......
3100			15c	......
3101			25c	......
3102		1906	10c	......
3103			15c	......
3104			25c	......
3105		1907	10c	......
3106			15c	......
3107			25c	......

1907. Perforated or Rouletted.

No.	Type	Date	Series A		Series B		Series C	
3110	A111	1907			5c red	.50		
3111					25c blue	.50		
3112		1908			5c red	.50		
3113					25c blue	.50		
3114		1909	5c yellow	.50	5c red	.50		
3115			25c black	.50	25c blue	.50		
3116		1910	5c yellow	.50	5c red	.50	5c green	.50
3117			25c black	.50	25c blue	.50	25c purple brown	.50
3118		1911	5c yellow	.50	5c red	.50	5c green	.50
3119			25c black	.50	25c blue	.50	25c purple brown	.50
3120		1912	5c yellow	.50			5c green	.50
3121			25c blue	.50			25c purple brown	.50
3122		1913	5c yellow	.50			5c green	.50
3123			25c blue	.50			25c purple brown	.50
3124		1914	5c yellow	.50				
3125			25c blue	.50				
3126		1915	5c yellow	.50				
3127			25c blue	.50				
3128		1916	5c yellow	.15				
3129			25c blue	.15				
3130		1917	5c yellow	.15				
3131			25c blue	.15				
3132		1918	5c yellow	.15				
3133			25c blue	.15				
3134		1919	5c yellow	.15				
3135			25c blue	.15				
3136		1920	5c yellow	.15				
3137			25c blue	.15				
3138		1921	5c yellow	.15				
3139			25c blue	.15				
3140		1922	5c yellow	.15				
3141			25c blue	.15				
3142		1923	5c yellow	.15				
3143			25c blue	.15				
3144		1924	5c yellow	.15				
3145			25c blue	.15				
3146		1925	5c yellow	.15				
3147			25c blue	.15				
3148		1926	5c yellow	.15				
3149			25c blue	.15				
3150		1927	5c yellow	.15				
3151			25c blue	.15				

A112

A113

ALBERTA GOVERNMENT TELEPHONES.

Before 1910.

3155 A112 5c Light brown, lilac control ....
3156 25c Grey ....

Dated 1909.

3157 5c Light brown ....
3158 25c Grey ....

MANITOBA GOVERNMENT TELEPHONES.

1908.

3160 A113 5c Red, red control ....
3161 25c Blue, red control ....

1909.

3162 5c Red, red control ....
3163 25c Blue, red control ....

1910.

3164 5c Red, red control ....
3165 25c Blue, red control ....

1911.

3166 5c Brown lilac, red control ....
3167 25c Green, red control ....

A114

A115

A116

BRITISH COLUMBIA TELEPHONE COMPANY SERVICE FRANKS.

No.	Type	Date		Series
3170	A114	1910	No value, Green	A—Dated
3171	A115	1911	No value, Green	SB (Undated)
3172		1912	No value, Green	SC (Undated)
3173		1913	No value, Green	SD (Undated)
3174		1914	No value, Blue	SE (Undated)
3175		1915	No value, Brown	SF (Undated)
3176		1916	No value, Green	SG (Undated)
3177		1917	No value, Blue	SH (Undated)
3178		1918	No value, Green	SI (Undated)
3179		1919	No value, Blue	SJ (Undated)
3180		1920	No value, Green	SK (Undated)
3181		1921	No value, Brown	SL (Undated)
3182		1922	No value, Green	SM (Undated)
3183		1923	No value, Dark brown	SN (Undated)
3184		1924	No value.	SP (Undated)
3184		1925	No value.	SQ (Undated)
3185		1926	No value, Green	SR (Undated)
3186		1927	No value, Reddish brown	SS (Undated)

(In the 1927 type the Series letters are much smaller than in the earlier stamps.)

BRITISH COLUMBIA TELEPHONE COMPANY MESSAGE COUPON.

No.	Type	Date	Value	Color	
3187	A116	1911	5c	Orange red	......
3188			25c	Blue	......
3189			$1	Green	......
3190		1912	5c	Olive green	......
3191			25c	Red brown	......
3192			$1	Violet	......
3193		1913	5c	Black	......
3194			25c	Red	......
3195			$1	Brown	......
3196		1914	5c	Blue green	......
3197			25c	Blue	......
3198			$1	Olive	......
3199		1915	5c	Red brown	......
3200			25c	Vermilion	......
3201			$1	Yellow brown	......
3202		1916	5c	Black	......
3203			25c	Blue	......
3204			$1	Green	......
3205		1917	5c	Brown	......
3206			25c	Orange	......
3207			$1	Olive	......
3208		1918	5c	Blue	......
3209			25c	Black	......
3210			$1	Dark purple	......
3211		1919	5c	Green	......
3212			25c	Red	......
3213			$1	Dark brown	......
3214		1920	5c	Brown	......
3215			25c	Blue	......
3216			$1	Olive	......

3217 1921 5c Brown ....
3218 25c Red ....
3219 $1 Grey ....
3220 1922 5c Green ....
3221 25c Yellow brown ....
3222 $1 Blue ....
3223 1923 5c Brown ....
3224 25c Purple ....
3225 $1 Vermilion ....
3226 1924 5c Green ....
3227 25c Blue ....
3228 $1 Green ....
3229 1925 5c Yellow brown ....
3230 25c Red ....
3231 $1 Brown ....
1926
1927

SASKATCHEWAN GOVERNMENT TELEPHONES.

(Franks are long narrow type.)

1st Issue, 1909. Printed in black on colored papers, "Coupon—Saskatchewan Telephone Company, Ltd., 190..." and numbered vertically at left; denomination "10 Cents" etc. overprinted in red large letters.

3232 10c Light yellow paper ....
3233 15c Blue paper ....
3234 25c Rose paper ....
3234a 50c Dark yellow paper ....
3234b 1.00 White paper ....

Control A.

3235 5c Black, red control ....
3236 25c Grey, red control ....
3237 25c Blue, red control ....

Control B.

3238 5c Yellow ....
3239 25c Green ....

Control C.

3240 5c Black ....
a. Small c, small number.
3241 25c Blue ....
a. Small c, small number.

KING TELEPHONE COLLECTION.

(In Bartlett Collection.)

3250 1c Brown ....

REVENUE PROOFS.

(Initial listing—incomplete.)

Canada Bill, 2nd Issue.

1c Vermilion ....
4c Blue ....
6c Sepia brown ....
8c Blue ....
30c Green ....
50c Mauve ....
$2 Yellow brown, black center ....

Canada Bill, 3rd Issue.

	2c Green	......
	4c Lake (Die Proof)	......
	5c Blue (Die Proof)	......
	6c Deep green	......
	10c Blue	......
	20c Lake	......
	30c Green	......
	40c Violet	......
	$1 Color of Issue	......
	$3 Lake, black center	......

WEIGHTS AND MEASURES.

A40	Red, no denomination	.50
A40	1c Black	1.00
	2c Black	1.00
	5c Black	1.00
	10c Black	1.00
	15c Black	1.00
	20c Black	1.00
	30c Black	1.50
	50c Black	1.00
	$1 Black	1.00
	$1.50 Black	1.00
	$2 Black	1.00

A35 **Perf. or Imperf.**

A37 **Electric and Gas Inspection, as above.**

Manitoba Law

A55	50c Red on India paper	2.50

Ontario Law

Types A72, A73, A52, A74 without "C.F.", "F.F.", "L.C." or "L.S."

10c Green	2.50
10c Blue	2.50
20c Orange	2.50
40c Orange	2.50
50c Green	2.50
60c Green	2.50
70c Green	2.50
80c Green	2.50
90c Green	2.50
$1 Green	2.50
$2 Green	2.50
$2 Light purple	2.50
f. "S.C." in panel in ochre	4.00
$3 Green	2.50

Ontario Law "C.F."

India paper, mounted or unmounted.

A72	5c Green	2.50
	10c Green	2.50
	20c Green	2.50
	a. Top of "F" missing	3.50

	30c Green	2.50
	40c Green	2.50
	a. Purple brown "C.F." in ochre	3.50
	50c Green	2.50
	60c Green	2.50
	70c Green	2.50
	80c Green	2.50
	a. Purple brown 'C.F. ...in green	3.50...
	90c Green	2.50
	$1 Green	2.50
	$2 Green	2.50
	a. "C.F." in green	2.50
	$3 Green	2.50
	$4 Green	2.50
	$5 Green	2.50

"F.F."

A73	5c Green	2.50
	10c Green	2.50
	20c Green	2.50
	30c Green	2.50
	40c Green	2.50
	50c Green	2.50
	60c Green	2.50
	8c Green	2.50
	90c Green	2.50
	$2 Green	2.50
	$4 Green	2.50
	$5 Green	2.50

"L.C."

A52	60c Green	2.50
	80c Green	2.50
	a. Purple brown, "L.C." in blue	3.50
	5c Blue	3.00
	30c Blue	3.00

"S" Only in Red

	40c Blue	4.00
	80c Blue	4.00
	$5 Blue	4.00

"L.S."

A74	10c Green	2.50
	20c Green	2.50
	30c Green	2.50
	40c Green	2.50
	50c Green	2.50
	60c Green	2.50
	70c Green	2.50
	80c Green	2.50
	90c Green	2.50
	$1 Green	2.50
	$2 Green	2.50
	$3 Green	2.50
	$5 Green	2.50
	a. "L.S." in deep purple	2.50

TYPICAL EARLY CANCELLATIONS

Late Fee

Steamboat

Pembina

Type 587 Cancelling ½d Pair
(Reford Collection)

"Numerals 16 in bars"
Entire identifying Hamilton

POSTMARKS AND CANCELLATIONS.

Collectors are now devoting considerable attention to the study of cancellations, thereby obtaining added pleasure and education from their stamps. It is fitting that we should be familiar with the distinctive markings which cancel the stamps in our collections, many of these being as official as the stamps themselves.

In the case of some stamps which are many times more rare in used condition than otherwise, it is quite necessary that the collector possess a knowledge of cancellations.

Cancellations may be forged, but the forger will not possess the knowledge of the collector whom he tries to deceive.

The value of cancellations is governed by the law of supply and demand, with condition playing an important part. With early Canadian stamps the value of the stamp has to be considered in addition to the postmark value, but postal markings on common issues are often more sought after than the stamps on which they are found.

Cancellations have been valued in this catalogue at prices which collectors are now paying. No object exists for discounting these values. Prices may vary considerably for somewhat similar items, but nevertheless sound values are rapidly being arrived at. Future editions of this catalogue will show substantial increases. All values given refer to cancellations on stamps off cover unless otherwise stated.

Values are given for cancellations on the cheaper stamps, but not always for the higher values. With these as a guide collectors should be able to estimate the value of the rarer stamps with distinctive cancellations. Because a 10c stamp has a cancellation which makes it worth $1.00, it does not follow that a $10.00 stamp with a rare cancellation increases in value ten times. The collector buys the stamp because of the added interest which the cancellation imparts to it; he may buy the cancellation irrespective of the stamp itself; or he may be influenced by the combination of rare stamp and rare cancellation. The collector will be able, by comparing prices, to arrive at the relative rarity of different cancellations.

Values are for good specimens of the stamp with the cancellation at least 75% on the stamp where this is possible. When the stamp is very fine and the cancellation clearly defined and well centered, it is worth more than catalogue.

Postmasters were instructed to "carefully postmark letters on the address side with the name of the post office, the month and day of the month, and, except when prepaid by postage stamps, to mark the rate of postage in plain figures.

Most of the early postmarks were also used as cancellations.

No attempt has been made to list cancellations appearing after 1900, with the exception of those possessing some particular significance.

Postmarks on Cover.

The catalogue value of a cover may be ascertained by computing the value of the different postal markings. The values given refer to postal markings *on the face of the cover.*

Removing Cancellations to Defraud the Government.

John G. Hendy, in his "History of the Postmarks of the British Isles," states that at the time the first adhesive stamp was issued, Rowland Hill wrote: "All sorts of tricks are being played by the public, who are exercising their ingenuity in devising contrivances for removing the obliteration by chemical agents and other means." Stamps were often washed in isinglass or something which would act as a varnish before the letter was posted, and the obliterating ink falling on this varnish was easily removed by soap and water. This practice was followed in Canada and it is possible that the changes in the paper used for the 3d printings were made in an effort to obtain a paper which would defeat any attempt to remove the obliteration.

About 1859 the duplex form of postmark was introduced, when the date and the obliteration were both struck at the same time, the dated postmark appearing to the left of the cancellation. It was against regulations to cancel the stamp with the postmark, as when this was done no date record of the letter was available should the stamp be removed. The duplex cancellations, consisting of "town in circle" type with parallel bars, was supplied to twenty-two offices, including Montreal, London, Hamilton, Toronto, Guelph, etc. Here we have one branch of cancellation collecting where the collector of moderate means may achieve completeness.

In April, 1894, however, Postmasters who applied for an "obliterator" were sent a printed notification stating that "the use of the special Postage Stamp Obliterator has been discontinued and the ordinary

Montreal (21)

Prescott (35)
Reford Collection

office Dated Stamp is in all cases to be made to serve the double purpose of dated stamp and obliterator." This accounts for the fact that stamps date postmarked in 1894 and later are much more common than earlier ones.

Colored Cancellations.

Where no color is given it is understood the cancellation or postmark appears in black. It is difficult to compile anything of an accurate nature on colored cancellations. A postmaster might alternately use green stamping ink one day and black the next. Some offices had different colors in use at the same period. There are cases, however, where one color was used consistently, as for instance Belleville in blue or Queenston in green.

In this catalogue, cancellations not specifically listed in color are to be understood as appearing in black.

Dates of Appearance.

Although dates are given in many cases, it is not improbable that such cancellations or postmarks were used earlier. The author has merely noted the earliest date at which a marking has been seen. It is equally impossible, except in a few instances, to give the period over which a cancellation was used, as many are still in use, or, if not in use are still in the post offices and may, in some emergency, be again called out.

Cork Cancellations.

Postmasters displayed considerable ingenuity in designing cancellations for their offices. These home products had a lifetime of a few days or a few months depending on the volume of mail handled through that office. It is possible to list or identify but a small percentage of the varieties. The number of offices and multiplicity of types makes it impossible to list more than a representative selection.

Pen Cancellations.

An extract from Post Office Department Circular dated Toronto, 21st April, 1851, reads: 'Stamps so affixed are to be immediately cancelled in the office in which the letter or packet may be deposited, with an instrument to be furnished for that purpose. In Post Offices not so furnished the stamps are to be cancelled by marking a cross (X) on each with a pen." About 1855 a distinctive cancellation, consisting of a number within four concentric rings, was given to 52 offices. There were, as early as 1851, 601 offices in Canada, so that these numeral cancellations represent the fifty-two most important cities and towns of that date.

In some instances covers are known to have been forwarded without the stamp being cancelled, when the postmaster at the next forwarding point, or at destination, cancelled it with his numeral cancellation. This explains an occasional inconsistency in the identity of a numeral. The following list, however, has been thoroughly identified.

Identity of 4-Ring Numeral Cancellations.

These numbers were allotted alphabetically.

Number	*Office*	*Number*	*Office*
1.	Barrie, U.C.	20.	Melbourne, U.C.
2.	Belleville, U.C.	21.	Montreal, L.C.
3.	Berlin, U.C.	22.	Napanee, U.C.
4.	Bowmanville, U.C.	23.	Niagara, U.C.
5.	Brantford, U.C.	24.	Oakville, U.C.
6.	Brighton, U.C.	25.	Oshawa, U.C.
7.	Collingwood Harbor.	26.	Owen Sound, U.C.
8.	Chatham, U.C.	27.	Ottawa, U.C.
9.	(See Notes.)	28.	Paris, U.C.
10.	Cobourg, C.W.	29.	Perth, U.C.
11.	Cornwall, U.C.	30.	Peterboro, U.C.
12.	Dundas, U.C.	31.	Picton, U.C.
13.	Galt, U.C.	32.	Port Dover, U.C.
14.	Goderich, U.C.	33.	Port Hope, U.C.
15.	Guelph, U.C.	34.	Port Sarnia, U.C.
16.	Hamilton, U.C.	35.	Prescott, U.C.
17.	Ingersoll, U.C.	36.	Preston, U.C. (?)
18.	Kingston, U.C.	37.	Quebec, L.C.
19.	London, U.C.	38.	St. Catharines, U.C.

39. St. Hyacinthe, L.C.
40. St. Thomas, U.C.
41. Sandwich, U.C.
42. Sherbrooke, L.C.
43. Simcoe, U.C.
44. Smith's Falls, U.C.
45. Stanstead, L.C.
46. Stratford, U.C.
47. Three Rivers, L.C.
48. Thorold, U.C.
49. Whitby, U.C.
50. Windsor, U.C.
51. Brockville, U.C.
52. Clifton, U.C.

Numerals (on Stampless Covers) Cancelling Rate Mark.

The rate markings, or due markings, when applied in error were cancelled, and such covers have been listed and priced. These are particularly desirable when the error of taxing a letter which should have been "FREE" of postage, has been noted at a forwarding office and the cancellation of that office applied over the "due" marking to assure the letter of delivery without payment.

Identity of 2-Ring Numeral Cancellations.

The 2-ring numeral cancellations used for the 1868 issue were allotted according to the size or importance of the office.

Numeral.	*Office.*
1.	Montreal.
2.	Toronto.
3.	Quebec.
4.	Halifax.
5.	Hamilton.
6.	London.
7.	St. John, N.B.
8.	Ottawa.
9.	Kingston.
10.	Sydney, N.S.
11.	Fredericton, N.B.
12.	St. Catharines West, Ont.
13.	Belleville, Ont.
14.	Guelph, Ont.
15.	Brantford.
16.	
17.	St. Hyacinthe, P.Q. (?)
18.	Yarmouth, N.S.
19.	Peterboro, Ont.
20.	
21.	Goderich.
22.	
23.	Woodstock, Ont.
24.	Stratford, C.W.
25.	New Glasgow, N.S.
26.	Windsor, C.W.
27.	Ingersoll.
28.	Sarnia.
29.	Cobourg.
30.	Pictou, N.S.
31.	
32.	Barrie.
33.	Sherbrooke, C.E.
34.	Branchton, U.C.
35.	Lindsay, C.W.
36.	St. Johns, C.E.
37.	
38.	Bowmanville.
39.	
40.	Cornwall.
41.	St. Mary's, C.W.
42.	
43.	Windsor, N.S.
44.	Owen Sound.
45.	Perth.
46.	Dundas.
47.	Napanee.
48.	Simcoe.
49.	Prescott.
50.	St. Andrew's, N.B.
51.	Picton.
52.	Caledon, U.C.
53.	
54.	Truro, N.S.
55.	Berlin, C.W.
56.	Brampton, Ont.
57.	
58.	Aylmer, U.C.
59.	Clinton, U.C.
60.	

Stampless Covers.

The growing interest in these covers make it advisable to give prices, based on amounts realized by private sale and by auction. Within the past few years this material has come out of obscurity to a position where it commands value. This addition to the British North America

Book will, I trust, be of assistance to philatelists seeking information in a field not heretofore covered.

Values have been given for all markings which may appear on and add value to a stampless cover. If the value of a cover lies in its postal marking, we believe it is logical to proceed on the plan that a cover with two catalogued markings is worth the combined price of those two. For example, a cover with "PAID 6" in red may be worth $1.00, but the same cover with "Too Late" would be worth the original catalogue value of $1.00 plus the value put on the "Too Late" marking, thus bringing it up to $2.00. If "Registered" appeared also, another 25c would be added.

The essential features of stampless covers may be listed as follows:

1. Town and date, value depending on color and type, which may become of secondary importance on account of:

2. Rate marking, value depending on color, type, and whether usual or unusual rate.

3. Carrier, such as SHIP, Railway, etc.

4. Contributory markings, as "Too Late," "Registered," "Advertised," "FREE," etc.

A cover may have value because of "Quebec" in red with rate pen-written, but the same cover with the additional marking, "Steamship Letter," is collected for the latter marking, and the former marking becomes contributory to its value. We ask collectors to bear with us in this first attempt to catalogue a difficult group. We believe, however, that if stampless covers are looked up under these headings, no confusion will arise.

New Brunswick Cancellations.

A considerable quantity of sheets of various denominations on hand after Confederation were retained by Mr. Malcolm A. McLeod, a Post Office Inspector, also a stamp collector, who, about two years subsequently, in response to the demand for used copies, had some circular rubber cancellations prepared with the names 'Richibucto," "Hampton," "Sussex" and other towns in the Province. With these he cancelled a large part of his holdings.

Nova Scotia.

When A. Woodgate, in April, 1851, submitted to the Provincial Secretary a design for a postage stamp, he appended a suggestion for a cancellation. This design is illustrated above. It exists on the margin of Mr. Woodgate's letter to the Provincial Secretary, a portion of which is illustrated in the Chapter on Proofs. It is interesting to note that the gridiron type of cancelling instrument supplied to the offices followed the above suggestion, using an oval containing vertical parallel bars with space for a numeral to designate the Post Office.

Donald A. King traced the "5c" and the "10" cancellations (illustrated in Due & Paid Markings) to Baddeck, N.S., where Postmaster Robert Elmsley stated he had made his own cancelling instrument of wood, in these designs. It will be noted that the figures "5" or "10" were likely to appear on any stamps prepaying letters to the United States after 1854 when a treaty was arranged in which among other things it was agreed that the rate should be 3d per ½ oz., and that all prepaid letters from Nova Scotia to the U.S. should be stamped on the face "Paid 5 Cents" or "Paid 10 Cents." This marking may have been struck occasionally on the stamp, giving it the appearance of a surcharge.

Prince Edward Island Cancellations.

A knowledge of the postal markings of this Colony is very necessary to the serious collector. Large quantities of unused stamps were on hand when the Colony entered into the Dominion Confederation, and relatively small quantities of genuinely used stamps exist. The early postmarks are usually found on the left of the envelope or on the back, and rarely found obliterating the stamp. It was not until late in the sixties that the Department issued a wooden handle with a cork in it, which the local postmasters cut in any design they fancied. Prior to that date it was customary to pencancel the stamp, or, if this was not done at point of mailing, it was cancelled when it passed through the Charlottetown Post Office.

The Station Master was often the Postmaster also. This resulted in the use of the railway ticket date stamper being used as a cancelling instrument.

Stampless covers seem to be quite scarce. The Goodfellow Collection, sold in 1926 to Mr. A. F. Lichtenstein, contained several types of franks and postmarks used prior to the issue of stamps.

RING CANCELLATIONS

Types 1 to 4 illustrate the first official cancellations or obliterators, introduced April 1851. These were cut individually and subsequent orders did not always correspond with the original rings. There are many variations, but we believe the four variations illustrated will be a sufficient guide.

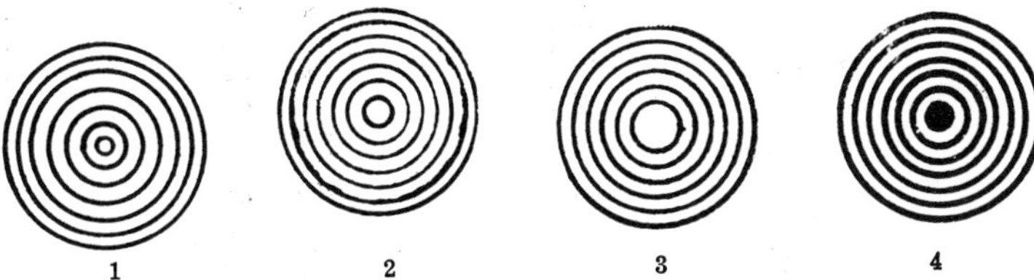

1 2 3 4

When cancellation color is not given it is found in Black. When a stamp comes in different colors the color shown in italics is the color of the stamp.

Type	Used on		Value
1 to 4	1851 3d.	....	$15.00
		Blue........	16.50
		Red.........	22.00
		Green.......	25.00
		Brown......	18.00
	1855 3d.	Green.......	8.00
	1855 3d.	....	4.50
		Blue........	5.50
		Red........	9.00
		Green.......	12.00
		Brown......	9.00
	(Drummondville used Green July 1855)		
	1857 ½d.	....	15.00
		Blue........	17.50
		Green.......	20.00
	3d.	Blue........	6.00
	6d.	....	
		Blue........	
		Red.........	
		Green.......	
	7½d.	....	
		Blue........	
		Green.......	
	10d.	....	
		Blue........	
	12d.	....	
		Green.......	
	1859 1c.	....	1.00
		Blue........	1.50
		Red........	2.00
		Green.......	2.50
	5c.	....	.50
1 to 4	1859 5c.		
	Blue.		
	Hamilton Ap. '65		.75
	Amherstburg Oct. '66		1.50
	Whitfield July '60		
	Red...............		3.00

Type	Used on		Value
	?Green..............		1.50
	?Orange.............		1.75
	1859 10c.	....	3.00
		Blue........	4.50
		Red........	7.00
		Green.......	10.00
	12½c.	....	2.50
		Blue........	5.00
		Red.........	7.00
	17c.	....	
		Red.........	12.00
	1864 2c.	....	
		Blue........	
	1868 ½c.	....	1.50
		Blue........	1.75
		Red.........	2.75
		Green.......	2.75
		Brown......	2.50
		Orange......	3.50
	1c.	*Brown*	3.00
	1c.	*Yellow*	4.50
		Green.......	6.00
	1c.	*Orange*	6.00
	2c.	....	1.75
	3c.	....	.85
		Blue........	1.00
		Red.........	1.75
		Green.......	1.75
		Brown......	1.75
		Orange......	1.75
	6c.	....	2.25
		Blue........	2.50
		Green.......	4.00
	12½c.	....	2.75
		Orange......	4.50
	1869 15c.	*Violet*	4.00
		Red Lilac	4.00
	1885 15c.	*Grey*	2.50
	1870 1c.	*Orange*	1.25

Type	Used on			Value
			Red..........	2.00
		1c.	Common Shades....	.10
			Blue.........	.10
			Carmine.....	.40
			Purple.......	.10
			Red..........	.30
			Green........	.75
			Brown.......	.40
1 to 4	1870	2c.	.............$	.40
		2c.	Common shades....	.10
			Blue.........	.25
			Carmine.....	.10
			Purple.......	.10
			Red..........	.30
			Green........	1.00
			Brown.......	.40
	1870-73	3c.	....	.30
			Blue.........	.45
			Red.........	.75
			Green........	1.00
			Brown.......	1.00
			Purple.......	.50
			Violet.......	.50
			Pink.........	.75
	1888	3c.	*Carmine Rose*	.75
			Purple.......	1.00
		3c.	Common shades....	.03
			Blue.........	.10
			Carmine.....	.10
			Purple.......	.10
			Violet.......	.10
			Red.........	.30
			Green........	1.00
			Brown.......	.40
			Pink.........	.25
	1875	5c.	Large........	5.00
			Blue.........	6.00
		5c.	Small........	.35
			Green........	.60
			Orange.......	.75
	1888	5c.	*Grey*	.20
			Blue.........	.35
	1878	6c.	*Brown*	.50
			Green........	1.00
	1890	6c.	*Red Brown*...	1.10
			Green........	1.50
	1882	½c.	....	.20
	1893	8c.	*Grey Shades*..	.40
			Purple........	.60
			Violet........	.60
	1874	10c.	*Lilac*........	1.75
	1888	10c.	*Rose*	1.75
	1896	10c.	*Red*	1.75
	1893	20c.	Vermilion....	.75
		50c.	Blue.........	.75
	1875	2c.	Orange Reg'd	.20
		2c.	Vermil. "	.20

Type	Used on			Value
		2c.	Carmine "	.60
1 to 4	1875	5c.	Registered...$	.20
		8c.	Blue Reg'd..	8.00
	1897	½c.	Jub..........	1.10
		1c.	Jub..........	.20
		2c.	Jub..........	.20
		3c.	Jub..........	.20
		5c.	Jub..........	.50
		6c.	Jub..........	2.25
		8c.	Jub..........	1.10
		10c.	Jub..........	
		15c.	Jub..........	
		20c.	Jub..........	
		50c.	Jub..........	
		$1	Jub..........	
		$2	Jub..........	
		$3	Jub..........	
		$3	Jub..........	
		$5	Jub..........	
		½c.	4-leaf........	.15
		1c.	4-leaf........	.15
		2c.	4-leaf........	.15
		3c.	4-leaf........	.15
		4c.	Surcharge...	.25
		5c.	4-leaf........	.15
		6c.	4-leaf........	1.00
		8c.	4-leaf........	.40
		10c.	4-leaf........	1.50
	1898	½c.	Map.........	.15
		½c.	Numeral....	.10
		1c.	Numeral....	.10
		2c.	Purple.......	.10
		2c.	Carmine....	.10
		3c.	Numeral....	.12
		3c.	Surcharge...	.20
		5c.	Numeral....	.25
		6c.	Numeral....	1.25
		7c.	Numeral....	.40
		8c.	Numeral....	.65
		10c.	Numeral....	.30
		20c.	Numeral....	.90
	1903	1c.	King Ed.....	.10
		2c.	King Ed.....	.10
		5c.	King Ed.....	.10
		7c.	King Ed.....	.15
		10c.	King Ed.....	.15
		20c.	King Ed.....	.40
		50c.	King Ed.....	1.75
1 to 4	1908	1c.	Quebec......$	.15
		2c.	Quebec......	.15
		5c.	Quebec......	.40

(This type of cancellation continued in use in smaller offices and may be found on any late stamp).

Type	Used on			Value
4a	1855	3d.	....	$5.00
5	1868	3c.	....	.85
	1870	3c.	....	.85
		3c.	Common shades....	.25

4 RINGS

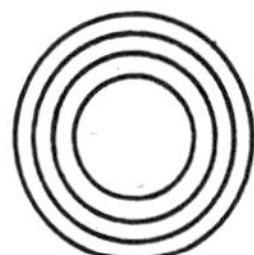

VERY LARGE CENTRE

4a

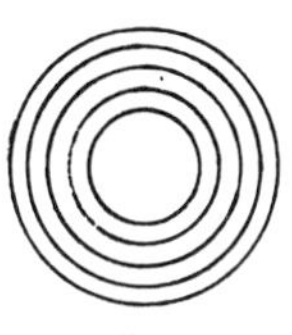

5

6

Type	Used on		Value
6	Cut into 4, 6, 8 or more segments, and with segments cut into sections.		
	1859	1c.	
		5c.	.60
	1868	3c.	1.50
	1880	1c.	.25
		3c.	.25
		15c.	2.50

6

8

L

Type	Used on		Value
7	1859	5c. Blue	1.25
8	1898	3c. Q.V. Num.	.25
	(Widder Station)		
9	1859	1c.	1.25
		5c.	.60
		10c.	3.25
		12½c.	4.00
		17c.	
	1864	2c.	
	1868	3c.	1.00
10	1859	5c. Blue	.75
11	1859	5c.	.50
	1868	3c.	1.00

10

11

12

Type	Used on		Value
12	Used by Prince Ed. Is.		
	1885-97	3c. (Canada)	.15

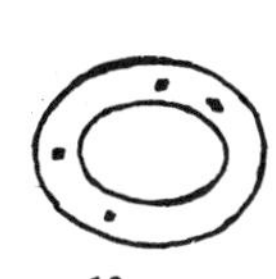

13

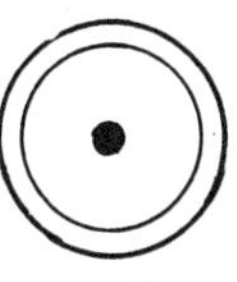

14

a. Larger dot.

Type	Used on		Value
	Red		
13	1868	2c.	$ 4.00
	1870	1c. *Orange*	3.00
14	1875	3c.	.60
14a	1880	3c.	.35

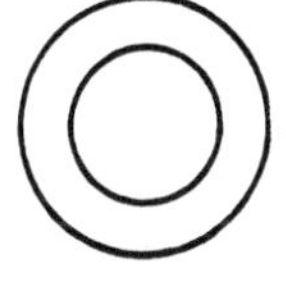

15

16

Type	Used on		Value
15	1885	3c. Violet	.40
16	North Wakefield, C.E., May 1880.		
	1880	1c.	.15
		2c.	.15
		3c.	.15

17

18

Type	Used on		Value
17	1880	3c.	.30
		Violet	.50
	Kincardine U.C. Ja. 62		
	1859	5c.	1.00
18	1868	2c.	2.00

Type	Used on			Value
		3c.		1.25
		6c.		2.50
		12½c.		3.25
	1873	6c.	*Yel. Brown*	1.00
			Purple	1.50
	1885	3c.	Red Canc.	.50

19 20

Type	Used on			Value
19	1868	2c.		2.00
		3c.		.80
		12½c.		3.00
	1870	3c.		.60
	1880	3c.		.40
			Green	.75
	1882	½c.		.30
20	1882	3c.		.30

21 22

Type	Used on			Value
21	1880	3c.		.40
22	1868	12½c.		$3.00
	1870	1c.	*Orange*	1.50
		2c.	*Green*	.50
		3c.		.75
	1872	1c.	*Yellow*	.15
		2c.		.20
		3c.	Common shades	.15
	1882	½c.		.20
	1888	3c.	*Carmine*	.75
		5c.		.25
		10c.		1.50
	1896	10c.	*Red*	1.50
	1890	6c.	*Red Brown*	1.15
	1896	8c.	Shades	.45
	1893	20c.		.60
		50c.		.60
	1875	2c.	Orange Reg'd	.25
		2c.	Vermilion "	.25
		2c.	Carmine "	.70
		5c.	Green "	.25

23 24

Type	Used on			Value
23	General Use			
	1880	1c.		.20
		2c.		.15
		3c.		.20
			Violet	.35
		15c.		1.75
24	Toronto Oct. 1880			
	1880	1c.		.15
		2c.		.20
		3c.		.15
			Violet	.25
		5c.		.30
			Brown	.50
		6c.	*Yel Brown*	.40
		6c.	*Red Brown*	1.10
	1880	15c.		2.00
	1880	15c.	*Slate Violet on Thick*	15.00

25 26

Type	Used on			Value
25	Thickness and diameter of rings vary. On all stamps to and including Q.V. Numerals.			
	1878	15c.		$2.25
		1c.		.20
		3c.		.25
			Purple	.50
			Violet	.50
			Pink	.50
			Brown	.75
			Green	.75
	1887	3c.	Carmine	.75
		5c.	Grey	.20
			Violet	.35
			Brown	.50
	1887	3c.	Carmine	
		5c.	*Grey*	
		6c.	*Yellow Brown*	
			Blue	.40
			Green	.60
	1885	15c.		

Type	Found on		Value
	1893 8c.	Blue	.50
		Purple	.75
26	Cobourg.		
	1875 1c.		.10
	2c.		.10
	3c.		.15

27 28

Type	Found on		Value
27	Nanaimo Sept. 1886		
	1886 1c.		.10
	2c.		.10
	3c.		.15
28	1880 1c.		.15
	3c.		.15

29 30

Type	Found on		Value
29	1890 1c.		.20
	3c.		.30
30	1885 1c.		.20
	3c.		.30

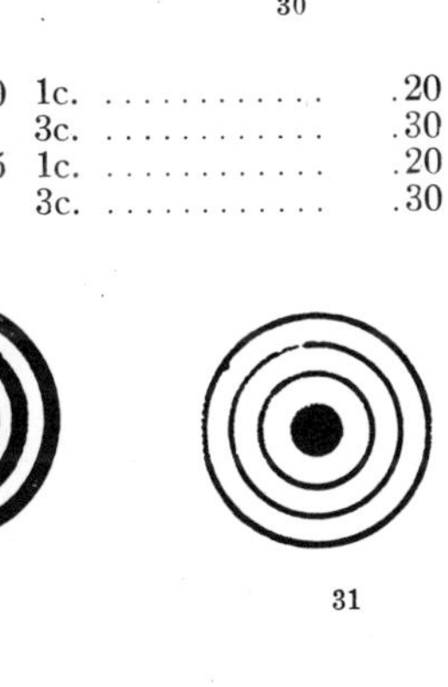

30a 31

Type	Found on		Value
30a	1880	Newfoundland	
	5c.	Seal	.85
	1876 5c.	Seal rouletted	1.25
31	1880 1c.	$	.20
	3c.		.30

32 33

Type	Found on		Value
	Pownal, P.E.I. Dec. 1888		
	1882 3c.		.40
	1888 3c.		.40
	(Wider inner ring)		
32	Oshawa, Ont. Oct. '82		
33	Montague Bridge, P.E.I. Mar. 1873.		
	1873 1c.		.20
	3c.		.30

34 35

Type	Found on		Value
34	Worn, as illustrated.		
	1880 2c.	Orange Reg'd	.25
	2c.	Vermilion "	.25
	2c.	Carmine "	.60
	5c.	Green "	.25
	1882 ½c.		.25
	1888 3c.	*Carmine*	.60
	3c.	Common Shades	.15
	10c.	*Rose*	1.50
	Clean-cut circles.		
	1868 ½c.		1.50
	1866 5c.	Nova Scotia	1.75
	1874 10c.	*Lilac*	1.75
	1873 3c.	*Orange Red*	.40
35	1868 12½c.		3.00

36 37

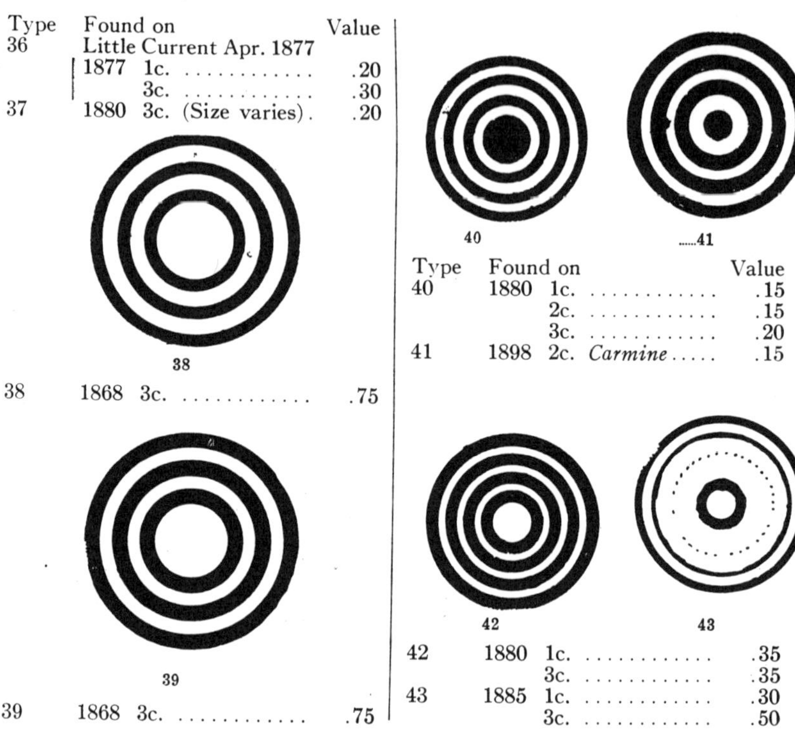

Type	Found on		Value
36	Little Current Apr. 1877		
	1877	1c.	.20
		3c.	.30
37	1880	3c. (Size varies)	.20

38

38	1868	3c.	.75

39

39	1868	3c.	.75

40 41

Type	Found on		Value
40	1880	1c.	.15
		2c.	.15
		3c.	.20
41	1898	2c. *Carmine*	.15

42 43

42	1880	1c.	.35
		3c.	.35
43	1885	1c.	.30
		3c.	.50

ATLANTIC NAVAL CANCELLATIONS

Stanley Gibbons' 1926 Catalogue referred to these interesting and valuable cancellations as follows: "From a study of official records, Mr. C. F. Dendy Marshall, M.A., has ascertained that the obliterations listed as Naval Stations were actually allotted to various mail boats for use on letters posted on board or to the Foreign Branch, London, for letters not postmarked until arrival. The fact that these obliterations are found on sailors' letters is due to the practice of warships transferring their letters to any mail boat sighted."

Mr. Marshall fixes the date as from 14th June, 1859.

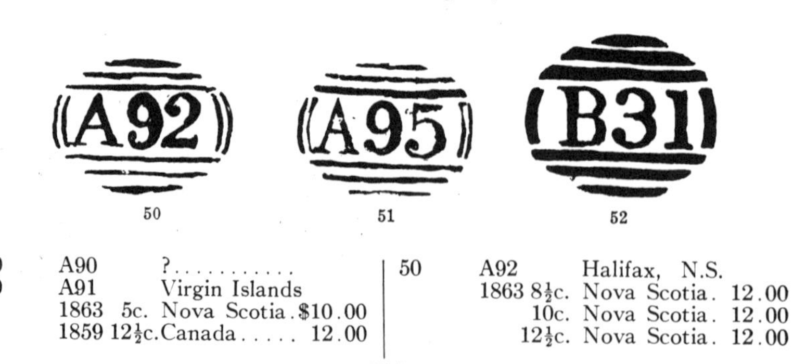

50 51 52

50	A90	?	
50	A91	Virgin Islands	
	1863 5c.	Nova Scotia	$10.00
	1859 12½c.	Canada	12.00
50	A92	Halifax, N.S.	
	1863 8½c.	Nova Scotia	12.00
	10c.	Nova Scotia	12.00
	12½c.	Nova Scotia	12.00

Type
50 A93 ?...........
50 A94 ?...........

51 A95 ?...........
3d. Nova Scotia. 15.00
1c. Nova Scotia. 15.00
10c. 12.00
12½c. 12.00

51 A96 ?...........

51 A97 ....
1865 10c. Nova Scotia. 12.00
12½c. Nova Scotia. 12.00

A98 12½c. Nova Scotia.

52 B17 "North American" Allan Line Steamer

52 B18 "North Briton" Allan Line Steamer....

52 B27 "Hungarian" Allan Line Steamer, First use December 19, 1958.......

52 B28 Allan Line Steamer....

25 B29 "Anglo-Saxon" Allan Line Steamer

52 B30 Mailboat, Allan Line..

52 B31 Mailboat, Allan Line
4½d. Prince Ed. Isl.$10.00
3c. Prince Ed. Isl. 6.50

PACIFIC NAVAL STATIONS

A79, A80, A81 China; A82, A83, A84, A85, A86 Shanghai; A87, A88 Pechili China; A89.

BRITISH COLUMBIA AND VANCOUVER ISLAND NUMERALS

This Colony used a numeral of the same type as the Atlantic Naval Station cancellations, the numerals running as high as 36. Many of these numerals were rarely used, and we doubt if some were ever used. The partially identified list follows:

Type
1. New Westminster.....
2. Douglas.............
3. Hope................
4. Yale (?).............
5. Lytton..............
6. Similkameen..........
7. Rock Creek...........
8. Cayoosh.............
9. Alexander (?).........
10. William's Creek (?)....
11. ....
12. Quesnel mouth ? ......
13. ....
14. ....
15. ....
16. ....
17. ....
18. ....
19. ....
20. ....
21. ....
22. ....
23. ....
24. ....
25. ....
26. Langley Prairie........
27. ....
28. Burrard Inlet.........
29. ....
30. ....
31. ....
32. ....
33. ....
34. ....
35. Victoria.............
36. Nanaimo.............

60 61

60 New Westminster (1)
5c. V.I. Perf......
2½d. ....
Blue........
Red.........

Type Found on Value

5c. Perf. 12½
Blue........
25c. Perf. 14.....
Blue........
1868 3c. Canada
Blue........ $7.00
1870 3c. Canada
Blue........ 5.00

60 (3) Hope.
2½d. ....

61 Yale. (4?).
2½d. ....
Red........
3d. Blue........
Red.........

61 Lytton (5)
2½d. Blue........
5c. Rose Perf.
Blue........

61 Rock Creek (7)
3d. Blue Canc.

61 Cayoosh (8).
2½d. ....

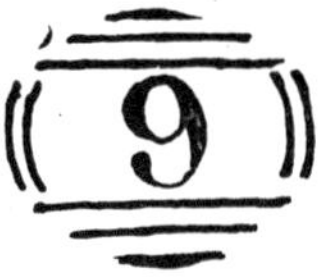

62

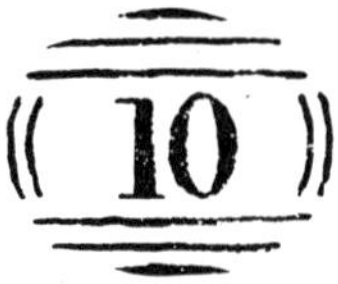

63

62 Alexander (?) (9)
5c. Vancouver
Perf...... 20.00

63 William's Creek (10?)
In Blue:....
10c. Perf.
2½d. ....
3d. ....
2c. ....
50c. Perf. 12½

63 (13?)
10c.
Blue........

63 (19?)................
3d. ....

63 (20?)................
25c. Perf........

63 (22?)
2½d. ....
Blue........

63 (24?)
5c. Rose Vancouver
Island, Imperf.
Blue........
5c. Rose Vancouver
Island, Perf.
Black.......
Blue........

63 Langley Prairie (26)
5c. Rose Vancouver
Island, Imperf.
Blue........
5c. Rose Vancouver
Island, Perf.
Black.......
Blue........
5c. Perf. 14
Black.......

63 (27?)
1872 *Canada* 1c.
Yellow...... $5.00
Canada 3c.
Red........ 5.00

63 Burrard Inlet (28)
3d. Br. Col.
Blue........

63 (31?)................
3d. ....

63 (33?)
3d. Br. Col......
1872 3c. Canada..... 5.00

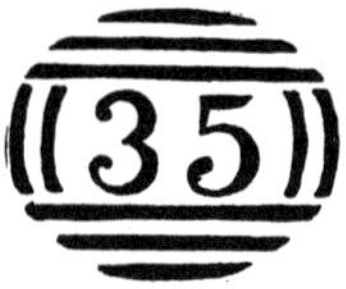

64

64 Victoria (35)
5c. Rose, Perf.
Vanc. Island
10c. Blue, Perf.
Vanc. Island
2c. Perf. 14.....
5c. Perf 14......
Blue ....
25c. Perf. 14.....
Blue ....
3d. ....
Blue........
Green.......
5c. Perf. 12½....
10c. Perf. 12½....
25c. Perf. 12½....
50c. Perf. 12½....
$1 Perf. 12½....
1868 3c. Canada..... 7.00
2c. Canada...... 9.00
6c. Canada..... 7.50
1870 3c. Canada..... 5.00
1872 3c. Canada..... 5.00

70

Type	Found on	Value
70	Charlottetown, P.E.I. Oct. 1864.	
	1864 2d. Perf. 9......	
	3d. Perf. 9......	
	6d. Perf 9.......	
70	1864 1d.	$4.50
	1864 2d. Perf. 11, etc..	3.00
	3d. Perf. 11, etc..	3.50
	4d. Perf. 11, etc..	5.00
	4½d. Perf. 12.....	6.00
	6d. Perf. 11, etc..	5.00
	9d. Perf. 11, etc..	5.50
	1872 1c.	4.50
	2c.	
	3c.	3.00
	4c.	6.00
	6c.	5.50
	12c.	

71

Type	Found on	Value
71	Bristol, England	
	1859 5c. Canada.....	1.50
	12½c. Canada.....	
	1868 3c. Canada.....	1.50
71	(Numeral 53).........	
	1859 1c. Canada.....	1.50

72

Type	Found on	Value
72	1851 6d. Nova Scotia.	

72a

Type	Found on	Value
72a	Newfoundland	
	1880 5c. Seal Black.......	$1.00
	1866 10c.	4.50
	12c.	2.50

4-RING NUMERAL CANCELLATIONS

Color is black unless otherwise stated.

80

Type	Found on	Value
80	(1) Barrie, U.C.	
	1855 3d.	$6.00
	1857 ½d.	
	6d., 7½d., 10d.	
	1859 1c.	3.00
	5c.	1.75
	10c.	5.00
	12½c.	
	17c.	
	1864 2c.	10.00
	1868 3c.	1.50
	Stampless cover, numeral 1 cancelling "3" due marking applied in error	3.00
80	(2) Belleville, U.C.	
	1857 ½d. Blue	
	1855 3d. Blue	6.00
	6d. Blue	
	1859 1c.	2.00
	5c. Blue	1.25
80	1859 10c. Blue	$6.00
	12½c. Blue	6.00
	1868 1c. Brown, Blue.	
	1c. Orange, Blue.	
	1c. Yellow, Blue.	
	2c. Blue	
	3c. Blue	1.50
	12½c. Blue	
	1870 15c. Red Lilac Blue	
	15c. Violet, Blue.	
	1875 5c. (large), Blue.	
	Stampless cover, numeral 2 cancelling "3" applied in error	3.00
80	(3) Berlin, U.C.	
	1857 ½c.	
	1855 3d.	6.00
	6d., 7½d., 10d.	
	1859 1c.	2.50
	5c.	1.50
	10c.	6.00
	12½c.	7.50
	17c.	7.00
	1864 2c.	10.00
	Stampless cover, numeral 3 cancelling "7" due marking applied in error	3.00
80	(4) Bowmanville, U.C.	
	1857 ½c.	
	1855 3d.	6.50
	6d., 7½d., 10d.	
	1859 1c.	
	5c.	1.75
	10c.	
	12½c.	

Type	Found on	Value
	17c.	
	1864 2c.	
	Stampless cover, numeral 4 cancelling "7" due marking applied in error	3.00
	Heavy Battered Impression	
	1868 1c. Brown	
	1c. Yellow	
	1c. Orange	
	2c.	
	3c.	1.50
	12½c.	
	1870 1c. Orange	
	3c. Rose	1.25
80	(5) Brantford, U.C.	
	1857 ½d.	
	Blue	
	1855 3d.	5.00
	Blue	6.50
	1859 1c.	2.00
	Blue	2.50
	5c.	1.75
	Blue	2.25
	10c.	6.00
	12½c.	7.00
	17c.	
	1864 2c.	
	1868 1c. Orange, Blue.	
	2c. Blue	
	3c. Blue	1.50
	(6) Brighton, U.C.	
	1857 ½d.	
	1855 3d.	6.50
	6d., 7½d., 10d.	
	(7) Collingwood Harbor, U.C.	
	1857 ½d.	
	3d.	8.00
	6d., 7½d., 10d.	
	1859 1c.	3.00
	5c.	2.50
	10c.	7.00
	12½c.	8.00
	Stampless cover, numeral 7 cancelling "12½" applied in error	3.00
	(8) Chatham, U.C.	
	1857 ½d.	
	1855 3d.	6.00
	6d., 7½d., 10d.	
	1859 1c.	2.50
	5c.	1.50
	10c.	6.00
	12½c.	
	17c.	

Type	Found on	Value
	1864 2c.	
	1868 1c. Yellow	
	1c. Orange	
	2c.	
	3c.	1.50
	12½c.	
	1875 5c. (large)	
	Stampless cover, numeral 8 cancelling "Paid 5" applied in error	3.00
80	(9) Not issued, to avoid conflicting with Numeral 6.	
	(10) Cobourg, C.W.	
	1857 ½d.	
	1855 3d.	$5.00
	6d., 7½d.	
	1859 1c.	1.50
	5c.	.75
	10c.	5.80
	12½c.	6.50
	17c.	
	1864 2c.	
	1868 1c. Yellow	
	1c. Orange	
	2c.	
	3c.	1.50
	6c.	
	12½c.	
	1875 5c. (large)	
	Stampless cover, numeral 10 cancelling "7c." applied in error	3.00
	(11) Cornwall, U.C.	
	1857 ½d.	
	1855 3d.	6.50
	6d., 7½d., 10d.	
	1859 1c.	2.00
	5c.	1.25
	10c.	6.00
	12½c.	
	17c.	
	1864 2c.	
	(12) Dundas, U.C.	
	1857 ½d.	
	1855 3d.	6.00
	6d., 7½d., 10d.	
	1859 1c.	2.50
	5c.	1.50
	10c.	6.00
	12½c.	
	17c.	
	1864 2c.	10.00
	1868 1c. Brown	7.00
	(13) Galt, U.C.	
	1857 ½d.	
	1855 3d.	5.50

Type	Found on	Value
	6d., 7½d., 10d.	
80	1859 1c.	$2.00
	5c.	1.50
	10c., 12½c., 17c.	
	1868 1c. Yellow	
	1c. Orange	
	2c.	
	3c.	1.50
	6c.	
	12½c.	
	1870 1c. Orange	
	1875 1c. Yellow	
	5c. (small)	
	(large)	
	3c.	1.00
	½c.	
	Stampless cover, numeral 13 cancelling "unpaid "7" applied in error	3.00
	(14) Goderich, U.C.	
	1857 ½d.	
	1855 3d.	7.00
	6d., 7½d., 10d.	
	1859 5c.	1.50
	Stampless cover, numeral 14 cancelling "unpaid 7" applied in error	3.00
	(15) Guelph, U.C.	3.00
	1857 ½d.	
	1855 3d.	5.50
	6d., 7½d., 10d.	
	1859 1c.	2.00
	5c.	1.25
	10c.	6.00
	12½c.	7.50
	17c.	
	1864 2c.	10.00
	1868 1c. Yellow	
	2c.	
	3c.	1.50
	12½c.	
	1875 5c. (small)	
	(large)	
	Stampless cover, numeral 15 cancelling due marking "3" applied in error	3.00
	(16) Hamilton, U.C.	
	1857 ½d.	
	1855 3d.	5.50
	6d., 7½d., 10d.	
	1859 1c.	2.00
	5c.	1.25
	10c.	5.00
	12½c.	5.00
	17c.	

Type	Found on	Value
	1864 2c.	
	Stampless cover, numeral 16 cancelling due marking "3" applied in error	3.00
80	(17) Ingersoll, U.C.	
	1857 ½d.	
	1855 3d.	$6.50
	Red	
	6d., 7½d.	
	10d.	
	Red	
	1859 1c.	2.25
	5c.	1.75
	10c.	6.50
	12½c.	7.50
	17c.	
	1864 2c.	
	1868 1c. Yellow	
	1c. Orange	
	2c.	
	3c.	1.50
	12½c.	
	1875 5c. (small)	
	(18) Kingston, U.C.	
	1857 ½d.	
	1855 3d.	5.00
	6d., 7½d., 10d.	
	1859 1c.	1.75
	5c.	1.00
	10c.	5.00
	12½c.	6.25
	17c.	10.00
	1864 2c.	
	Stampless cover, numeral 18 cancelling due marking "7" applied in error	3.00
	(19) London, U.C.	
	1857 ½d.	
	1855 3d.	5.00
	6d., 7½d., 10d.	
	1859 1c.	1.75
	5c.	1.00
	Blue	2.00
	10c.	5.00
	Blue	7.00
	12½c.	5.00
	Blue	7.50
	17c.	10.00
	Blue	
	Stampless cover, numeral 19 cancelling due marking "3" applied in error	3.00
	1868 1c. Yellow	
	1c. Orange	
	Blue	

Type	Found on	Value
	2c.	
	3c.	1.50
	Blue	2.00
	12½c.	
80	(20) Melbourne, U.C.	
	1857 ½d.	
	1855 3d.	$6.00
	6d., 7½d., 10d.	
	1859 1c.	2.50
	5c.	1.75
	10c.	5.50
	12½c.	6.75
	17c.	
	1868 1c. Yellow	
	1c. Orange	
	3c.	2.00
	6c.	
	1875 5c. (large)	
	(small)	
	1870 1c. Orange	
	1875 1c.	
	½c.	
	3c.	

21 21 21

i ii iii

Type	Found on	Value
	(21) Montreal, L.C. Exists in at least three types. (Type i. introduced Dec. 1857, Type ii. introduced Dec. 1859)	
	1857 ½d.	
	1855 3d.	$5.50
	6d., 7½d., 10d.	
	1859 1c.	1.75
	5c.	1.00
	10c.	4.50
	12½c.	4.75
	17c.	10.00
	1864 2c.	
	1868 ½c.	
	1c. Yellow	
	1c. Orange	
	1c. Brown	
	2c.	
	3c.	1.00
	12½c.	
	15c. Red Lilac	
	1875 5c. (large)	
	(small)	
80	(22) Napanee, U.C.	
	1857 ½d.	
	1855 3d.	$7.00

Type	Found on	Value
	6d., 7½d., 10d.	
	1859 1c.	2.50
	5c.	1.25
	10c.	5.00
	12½c.	6.00
	17c.	7.50
	1868 1c. Yellow	
	1c. Orange	
	1c. Brown	
	2c.	
	3c.	1.50
	12½c.	
	1875 5c. (small)	
	Stampless cover, numeral 22 cancelling due marking "7" applied in error	3.00
	(23) Niagara, U.C.	
	1857 ½d.	
	1855 3d.	6.00
	6d., 7½d., 10d.	
	1859 1c.	3.00
	5c.	2.00
	10c.	6.50
	12½c.	7.50
	17c.	12.00
	1868 1c. Yellow	
	1c. Orange	
	1c. Brown	
	2c.	
	3c.	1.50
	12½c.	
	1870 1c. Orange	1.50
	3c.	1.50
	1880 ½c.	
	1c.	
	(24) Oakville, U.C.	
	1857 ½d.	
	1855 3d.	6.50
	6d., 7½d., 10d.	
	1859 1c.	2.50
	5c.	1.75
	10c.	6.00
	12½c.	7.00
	17c.	
	1868 1c. Yellow	
	1c. Brown	
	2c.	
	3c.	1.50
	12½c.	
80	(25) **Oshawa, U.C.**	
	1857 ½d.	
	1855 3d.	7.00
	6d., 7½d., 10d.	
	1859 1c.	2.50
	5c.	1.50
	Red	2.75
	10c.	5.00

Type	Found on	Value
	12½c.	5.75
	17c.	
	1868 1c. Brown	
	(26) **Owen Sound, U.C.**	
	1857 ½d.	
	1855 3d.	6.00
	6d., 7½d., 10d.	
	1859 1c.	2.50
	5c.	1.50
	10c.	6.00
	12½c.	7.00
	17c.	10.00
	1868 1c. Yellow	
	1c. Orange	
	1c. Brown	
	2c.	
	3c.	1.50
	1870 1c. Orange	1.50
	3c.	1.50
	1882 ½c.	
	1c.	.50
	Stampless cover, numeral "26" cancelling "Paid 5" applied in error	3.00
	(27) **Ottawa, U.C.** There are two types. In Type i. the "7" is rounded at base. In Type ii. the "7" is squared at base.	
	1857 ½d.	
	1855 3d.	5.50
	6d., 7½d., 10d.	
	1859 1c.	2.00
	5c.	1.25
	10c.	5.00
	12½c.	6.00
	17c.	
	1864 2c.	
	1868 1c. Brown	
	2c.	
	3c.	1.50
	6c.	
	12½c.	
	1870 15c.	
	1885 2c. Registd	1.00
	Stampless cover, numeral 27 cancelling due marking "7" applied in error	3.00
80	(28) **Paris, U.C.**	
	1857 ½d.	
	1855 3d.	6.50
	6d., 7½d., 10d.	
	1859 1c.	2.00
	5c.	1.00
	10c.	5.00
	12½c.	6.00
	17c.	10.00

Type	Found on	Value
	(29) Perth, U.C.	
	1857 ½d.	
	1855 3d.	6.00
	6d., 7½d., 10d.	
	1859 1c.	2.50
	5c.	1.25
	10c.	6.00
	12½c.	7.00
	17c.	10.00
	1868 3c.	1.75
	1870 1c.	1.75
	3c.	1.75
	1882 ½c.	
	1c.	.50
	Stampless cover, numeral 29 cancelling due marking "3" applied in error	3.00
	(30) Peterboro, U.C. (Norwood, U.C. noted with this numeral)	
	1857 ½d.	
	1855 3d.	5.50
	6d., 7½d., 10d.	
	1859 1c.	2.50
	5c.	1.25
	10c.	6.00
	12½c.	7.00
	17c.	10.00
	1868 1c. Brown	
	2c.	
	3c.	1.50
	12½c.	
	Stampless cover, numeral "30" cancelling "unpaid 7" applied in error	3.00
	(31) Picton, U.C.	
	1857 ½d.	
	1855 3d.	6.00
	6d., 7½d., 10d.	
80	1859 1c.	$2.50
	5c.	1.25
	10c.	6.00
	12½c.	7.00
	17c.	10.00
	5c. Stamped Envelop, entire	7.00
	(May 19 to June '62) 5c. Green	3.50
	1868 1c. Brown	
	1c. Yellow	
	12½c.	
	Stampless cover, numeral 31 cancelling "unpaid 7" applied in error	3.00

Type	Found on	Value
	(32) Port Dover, U.C.	
	1857 ½d.	
	1855 3d.	7.00
	6d., 7½d., 10d.	
	1859 1c.	3.00
	5c.	1.50
	10c.	6.50
	12½c.	7.50
	17c.	
	1868 1c. Brown	
	2c.	
	3c.	1.50
	1870 1c. Orange	1.50
	3c.	1.50
	1882 ½c.	
	1c.	.50
	(33) Port Hope, U.C.	
	1857 ½d.	
	1855 3d.	6.00
	6d., 7½d., 10d.	
	1859 1c.	
	5c.	1.75
	10c., 12½c., 17c.	
	1868 1c. Brown	
	1c. Yellow	
	2c.	
	3c.	1.50
	12½c.	
	Stampless cover, numeral 33 in green cancelling due marking "1" applied in error	3.00
	(34) Port Sarnia, U.C.	
	1857 ½d.	
	1855 3d.	6.75
	6d., 7½d., 10d.	
	1859 1c.	2.75
	5c.	1.50
	10c.	6.50
	12½c.	7.50
	17c.	
	Stampless cover, numeral cancelling "7" applied in error	3.00
80	**(35) Prescott, U.C.**	
	1857 ½d.	
	1855 3d.	6.00
	6d., 7½d., 10d.	
	1859 1c.	2.50
	5c.	1.50
	10c.	6.00
	12½c.	7.00
	17c.	
	1868 1c. Brown	
	1c. Yellow	
	2c.	
	3c.	1.50

Type	Found on	Value
	(36) **Preston, U.C. ?**	
	1857 ½d.	
	1855 3d.	7.00
	6d., 7½d., 10d.	
	1859 1c.	
	5c.	2.00
	10c.	6.00
	12½c.	7.00
	17c.	10.00
	1868 1c. Brown	
	1c. Yellow	
	2c.	
	3c.	1.50
	12½c.	
	(37) **Quebec, L.C.**	
	1857 ½d.	
	1855 3d.	5.50
	6d., 7½d., 10d.	
	1859 1c.	1.75
	5c.	1.05
	10c.	5.00
	12½c.	5.50
	17c.	10.00
	1864 2c.	7.00
	1868 1c. Brown	
	1c. Yellow	
	1c. Orange	
	2c.	
	3c.	1.25
	6c.	
	12½c.	
	15c. Violet	
	15c. Red Lilac	
	1875 5c. (small)	
	5c. (large)	
	Stampless cover, numeral struck in upper right corner	2.00
80	(38) **St. Catharines, U.C.**	
	1857 ½d.	
	Brown	
	1855 3d.	$5.50
	6d., 7½d., 10d.	
	1859 1c.	2.50
	5c.	1.50
	10c.	6.00
	12½c.	6.50
	17c.	12.00
	1864 2c.	
	1868 1c. Brown	
	3c.	1.50
	12½c.	
	1870 1c. Orange	1.50
	3c.	1.50
	1882 ½c.	
	1c.	

Type	Found on	Value
	(39) **St. Hyacinthe, L.C.**	
	1857 ½d.	
	1855 3d.	6.00
	6d.	
	1859 1c.	2.50
	5c.	1.50
	10c.	6.00
	12½c.	7.00
	17c.	
	(40) **St. Thomas, U.C.**	
	1857 ½d.	
	1855 3d.	6.50
	6d.	
	1859 1c.	2.50
	5c.	1.50
	10c.	7.00
	12½c.	8.00
	17c.	12.00
	(41) **Sandwich, U.C.**	
	1857 ½d.	7.00
	1855 3d.	7.00
	6d., 7½d., 10d.	
	1859 1c.	3.00
	5c.	2.00
	1870 1c. Orange	1.75
	3c.	1.75
	1880 1c.	.50
	3c.	.50
	6c. Yellow Brown	
	Stampless cover, numeral cancelling "unpaid" applied in error	3.00
80	(42) **Sherbrooke, L.C.**	
	1857 ½d.	
	1855 3d.	$6.00
	6d., 7½d.	
	1859 1c.	3.50
	5c.	2.00
	10c.	6.50
	(43) **Simcoe, U.C.**	
	1857 ½d.	
	1855 3d.	6.00
	6d., 7½d.	
	1859 1c.	2.50
	5c.	2.00
	10c.	6.50
	(44) **Smith's Falls, U.C.**	
	1857 ½d.	
	1855 3d.	7.00
	6d., 7½d., 10d.	
	1859 1c.	5.00
	5c.	2.50
	10c.	8.00
	12½c.	9.00
	17c.	15.00

Type	Found on	Value
	1868 1c. Brown	
	1c. Yellow	
	1c. Orange	
	2c.	
	3c.	1.50
	6c.	
	12½c.	
	15c. Red Lilac	
	1870 1c. Orange	1.50
	3c.	1.50
	1882 ½c.	
	1c.	.50
	3c.	.50
	(45) **Stanstead, L.C.**	
	1857 ½d.	
	1855 3d.	7.00
	Blue	8.50
	6d., 7½d., 10d.	
	1859 1c.	3.00
	5c.	2.00
	Blue	2.50
	10c.	6.50
	12½c.	7.50
	1870 1c. Orange	
	3c.	1.50
	Blue	
80	1872 6c. Yellow Brown	
	Blue	
	1882 ½c.	
	1890 3c.	
	1897 3c. 4-Leaf	
	(46) **Stratford, U.C.**	
	1857 ½d.	
	1855 3d.	6.00
	6d., 7½d.	
	1859 1c.	3.00
	5c.	2.75
	10c.	7.00
	12½c.	8.00
	17c.	15.00
	Stampless cover, numeral struck in upper right corner	2.00
	(47) **Three Rivers, L.C.**	
	1857 ½d.	
	1855 3d.	6.00
	Blue	
	6d., 7½d., 10d.	
	1859 1c.	2.50
	5c.	1.50
	Blue	2.75
	10c.	6.00
	12½c.	7.50
	17c.	11.00
	1868 1c. Yellow	
	1c. Orange	
	2c.	

Type	Found on	Value
	3c.	1.50
	Blue	
	6c.	
	12½c.	
	(48) **Thorold, U.C.**	
	1857 ½d.	
	1855 3d.	7.00
	1859 1c.	3.00
	5c.	2.00
	10c.	7.00
	12½c.	8.00
	(49) **Whitby, U.C.**	
	1857 ½d.	
	1855 3d.	6.50
	6d., 7½d., 10d.	
	1859 1c.	2.00
	5c.	1.25
	10c.	6.00
	12½c.	7.00
	17c.	10.00
	1864 2c.	10.00
80	From Oct. 1864 to Aug. 1865	
	1864 1c. Blue	$3.00
	2c. Blue	12.00
	5c. Blue	2.00
	10c. Blue	7.00
	12½c. Blue	8.00
	17c. Blue	12.00
	1868 3c.	1.50
	Stampless cover, numeral struck in upper right corner	2.00
	(50) **Windsor, U.C.** (Kingsville mail was sometimes cancelled at Windsor with Numeral 50).	
	1857 ½d.	
	1855 3d.	6.00
	1859 1c.	3.00
	5c.	2.00
	1864 2c.	10.00
	1868 3c.	2.50
	Stampless cover, numeral cancelling "7" applied in error	3.00
	(51) **Brockville, U.C.**	
	1857 ½d.	
	3d.	6.00
	6d.	
	1859 1c.	2.50
	5c.	1.25
	10c.	5.50
	12½c.	6.50
	17c.	11.00

Type	Found on	Value
	1868 1c. Brown......	
	2c.	
	3c.	1.50
	6c.	
	Stampless cover, numeral cancelling "7" applied in error.....	3.00

(52) **Clifton, U.C.**

	1857 ½d.	
	1855 3d.	6.00
	6d.	
	1859 1c.	2.50
	5c.	1.50
	1868 3c.	2.50
	12½c.	
	1870 1c. Orange......	1.50
	3c.	1.50
	1880 1c.	.50
	1882 ½c.	

81

81	1868 1c. Brown......	
	3c.	$1.50

82  83

82	1880 3c.	1.25
83	(Actual diam. 22 mm.)	
	1868 3c.	1.25

84  85

Type	Found on	Value
84	1868 3c.	1.25
85	1868 1c. Brown......	
	3c.	3.00

86  87

86	1868 3c.	1.50
87	1868 3c.	2.00

88  89

88	1868 3c.	1.75
88a	(Through Cloth)......	
	1868 3c.	2.00
89	1868 3c.	2.00

90  91

90	1868 3c.	1.50
	1870 3c.	
91	1868 3c.	1.50
	12½c.	

92  93

92	(Outer circles thicker)	
	1868 3c.	1.50
93	1880 3c. Blue........	1.00

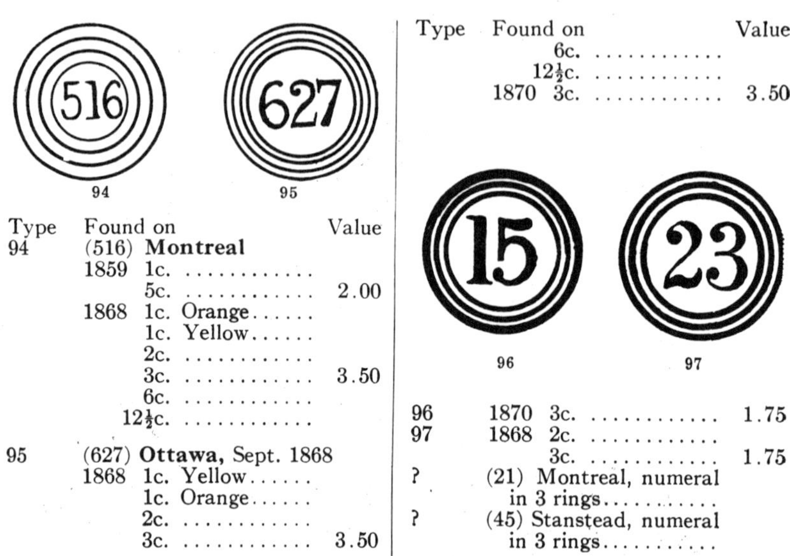

94 95

Type	Found on		Value
94	(516) **Montreal**		
	1859	1c.	
		5c.	2.00
	1868	1c. Orange	
		1c. Yellow	
		2c.	
		3c.	3.50
		6c.	
		12½c.	
95	(627) **Ottawa,** Sept. 1868		
	1868	1c. Yellow	
		1c. Orange	
		2c.	
		3c.	3.50

Type	Found on		Value
		6c.	
		12½c.	
	1870	3c.	3.50

96 97

Type	Found on		Value
96	1870	3c.	1.75
97	1868	2c.	
		3c.	1.75
?	(21) Montreal, numeral in 3 rings		
?	(45) Stanstead, numeral in 3 rings		

2-RING NUMERALS

Numbers allotted according to importance of office and not alphabetically. Color is black unless otherwise stated.

100

Type	Found on		Value
100	(1) **Montreal**		
	1868	½c.	
		1c. Brown	5.00
		1c. Yellow	5.00
		1c. Orange	7.00
		2c.	3.00
		3c.	1.75
		6c.	3.00
		12½c.	3.00
	1870	15c.	4.00
		1c. Orange	1.50
		3c.	1.25
	1875	5c. (large)	10.00
101	Through Cloth		
	1868	1c. Yellow	5.00
		1c. Orange	6.00
	1870	15c.	

Type	Found on		Value
100	(2) **Toronto**		
	1868	½c.	5.00
		1c. Brown	5.00
		1c. Yellow	5.00
		1c. Orange	7.00
		2c.	3.75
		3c.	1.75
		6c.	4.00
		12½c.	4.00
	1870	15c.	4.00
		1c. Orange	1.50
		3c.	1.25
	1875	5c. (large)	10.00
	1880	1c.	.40
101	Through Cloth		
	1868	3c.	2.00
100	(3) **Quebec**		
	1868	½c.	5.00
		1c. Brown	5.00
		1c. Yellow	5.00
		1c. Orange	7.00
100	1868	2c.	$3.75
		3c.	1.75
		6c.	4.00
		12½c.	4.00
	1870	1c. Orange	1.50
		3c.	1.25

Type	Found on			Value
	1875	5c.	(large)	10.00
	1874	15c.		
	1880	1c.		
		2c.		
		3c.		

Type	Found on			Value
100	(4) **Halifax**			
	1868	½c.		3.00
		1c.	Brown	4.50
		1c.	Yellow	4.50
		1c.	Orange	7.00
		2c.		3.75
		3c.		2.50
		6c.		4.50
		12½c.		4.50
	1870	1c.	Orange	1.50
		3c.		1.50
	1875	5c.	(large)	
		15c.		

Type	Found on			Value
100	(5) **Hamilton**			
	1868	½c.		5.00
			Violet	6.00
		1c.	Brown	4.00
		1c.	Yellow	3.00
		1c.	Orange	6.00
		2c.		3.00
			Red	6.00
		3c.		1.75
		6c.		3.00
		12½c.		4.00
	1870	1c.	Orange	1.50
		2c.		
		3c.		1.75
		15c.		
	1875	1c.	Yellow	
		5c.		
	1880	1c.	Yellow	

102

Type	Found on			Value
102	(6) **London.** (Rings Broken at base distinguishing 6 and 9).			
	1868	1c.	Yellow	$4.00
		1c.	Orange	
		1c.	Brown	4.00
		2c.		3.50
		3c.		1.50
		6c.		3.75
		12½c.		4.75
	1870	1c.	Orange	
		3c.		
		15c.		
	1875	1c.	Yellow	
		5c.	(large)	

100

Type	Found on			Value
100	(7) **St. John, N.B.**			
	1868	½c.		$1.90
		1c.	Brown	3.50
		1c.	Yellow	3.50
		1c.	Orange	5.50
		2c.		3.00
		3c.		1.50
		6c.		3.00
		12½c.		3.00
	1870	1c.	Orange	1.75
		3c.		1.00
		15c.		2.75
	1875	5c.	(small)	1.00
	1880	1c.		.35
		6c.	Yellow Brown	1.00
	(8) **Ottawa** (?)			
	1868	½c.		
		3c.		2.50
		6c.		5.50
		12½c.		6.00
	1870	15c.		4.00
	(9) **Kingston**			
	1868	½c.		
		1c.	Brown	
		1c.	Yellow	7.00
		1c.	Orange	
		2c.		
		3c.		3.00
		6c.		5.00
		12½c.		7.00
	1870	1c.	Orange	
		3c.		
		15c.		
	1875	1c.	Yellow	
		5c.	(large)	

10

103
Diam. 23 mm.

(10) Sydney, N.S.

1868 ½c. ....
1c. Brown...... 6.00
1c. Yellow...... 6.00
1c. Orange......
2c. 6.00
3c. 1.75
6c. ....
12½c. 7.00
1870 1c. Orange......
2c. .... .75
Blue........ 1.00
100 1870 3c. $1.05
Blue........ 1.00
6c. Yel. Brown.. 1.00
Blue........ 1.75
15c. ....

(11) Fredericton, N.B.

1868 ½c. ....
1c. Brown...... 4.00
1c. Yellow...... 4.00
1c. Orange...... 5.50
2c. 3.00
3c. 1.50
6c. 3.25
12½c. 3.25
1870 1c. Orange...... 1.75
3c. 1.10
15c. 3.75
1875 1c. Yellow...... .65
5c. (small)...... .35
6c. .... .75
Thicker Numerals.
1880 3c. 1.00

(12) St. Catharines West, Ont.

1868 ½c. ....
1c. Brown......
1c. Yellow...... 5.00
1c. Orange......
2c. 6.00
3c. 1.50
6c. 6.00
12½c. 6.50
1870 1c. Orange...... 1.75
2c. 1.25
3c. 1.25

Type Found on Value
15c. 3.75
1875 1c. Yellow...... .50

(13) Belleville, Ont.

1868 ½c. ....
1c. Brown...... 4.00
1c. Yellow...... 4.00
1c. Orange......
2c. 4.00
3c. 1.50
6c. 4.00
12½c. ....
15c. 5.00
100 1870 1c. Orange...... $1.75
3c. 1.25
1875 1c. Yellow...... .50

(14) Guelph

1868 1c. Brown......
1c. Yellow...... 4.00
1c. Orange......
2c. ....
3c. 1.50
6c. 6.00
12½c. ....
15c. ....
1870 3c. 1.25

(15) Brantford

1868 ½c. ....
1c. Yellow...... 5.00
1c. Brown......
1c. Orange......
2c. 5.00
3c. 1.50
6c. 5.00
12½c. 6.00
15c. ....
1870 1c. Orange......
3c. ....

(16) (?)
1868 1c. Yellow......

(17) St. Hyacinthe, P.Q. (?)

1868 ½c. ....
1c. Brown......
1c. Yellow......
1c. Orange......
2c. ....
3c. 5.00
6c. ....
1870 ½c. ....
1c. Orange......
3c. ....

(18) Yarmouth, N.S.

Shelburne, N.S., sometimes appears with this numeral.

1868 ½c. ....
1c. Brown...... 5.00

Type	Found on		Value
		1c. Yellow......	
		1c. Orange......	
		2c.	
		3c.	1.75
100	1868	6c.	4.00
		12½c.	4.50
	1870	1c. Orange......	
		3c.	
	1875	1c. Yellow......	
		5c. (large)......	

103x
Diam. 23 mm.

Type	Found on		Value
103x	(18) **Kingston,** Ap. '66.		
100	(19) **Peterboro, Ont.**		
	1868	½c.	
		1c. Brown......	4.00
		1c. Yellow......	
		2c.	
		3c.	1.75
		6c.	4.50
		15c.	7.00
	1870	1c. Orange......	
		3c.	
	1875	5c. (large)......	10.00
	1897	3c. 4-Leaf......	
	(20)	(?)..........	
	1868	1c. Yellow......	10.00
		2c.	10.00
		3c.	4.00
	(21) **Goderich**		
	1868	½c.	
		1c. Brown......	
		1c. Yellow......	
		1c. Orange......	
		2c.	4.50
		3c.	1.75
		6c.	5.00
		12½c.	
		15c.	
	1870	1c. Orange......	
		3c.	
	Thicker Numerals, Dec. 1872		
	1872	3c.	

Type	Found on		Value
	(22)	(?)..........	
	1868	3c.	1.75
		6c.	6.00
	1876	1c.	
		3c.	
100	(23) **Woodstock**		
	1868	½c.	
		1c. Brown......	
		1c. Yellow......	5.50
		1c. Orange......	
		2c.	
		3c.	1.75
		6c.	5.50
	1870	1c Orange......	
		3c.	1.50
	1875	1c. Yellow......	
		5c. (small)......	
	(24) **Stratford, C.W.**		
	1868	½c.	
		1c. Brown......	
		1c. Yellow......	5.00
		1c. Orange......	
		3c.	1.75
		6c.	
	1870	1c. Orange......	
		3c.	
	(25) **New Glasgow, N.S.**		
	1868	½c.	
		1c. Brown......	5.00
		1c. Yellow......	
		2c.	
		3c.	1.75
		6c.	
	(26) **Windsor, C.W.** Leamington sometimes appears with this numeral.		
	1868	½c.	$5.00
		1c. Brown......	
		1c. Yellow......	
		1c. Orange......	
		2c.	
		3c.	1.75
		6c.	5.50
		12½c.	
		15c.	
	1870	1c. Orange......	
		3c.	1.75
	(27) **Ingersoll**		
	1868	½c.	
		1c. Brown......	4.50
		1c. Yellow......	
		1c. Orange......	
100	1868	2c.	$4.50
		3c.	1.75
		6c.	

Type	Found on	Value
	12½c.	
	15c.	5.00
	1870 3c.	1.75
	1880 3c.	.75
	(28) **Sarnia**	
	1868 ½c.	
	1c. Brown......	
	1c. Yellow......	
	1c. Orange......	
	2c.	5.00
	3c.	1.75
	6c.	
	12½c.	
	15c.	5.00
	1870 3c.	1.75
	1875 5c. (large)......	10.00
	(29) **Cobourg**	
	1868 ½c.	
	1c. Brown......	
	1c. Yellow......	
	1c. Orange........	
	2c.	
	3c.	1.75
	6c.	6.00
	12½c.	
	15c.	
	1870 3c.	1.75
	(30) **Pictou, N.S.**	
	1868 ½c.	
	1c. Brown......	
	1c. Yellow......	5.75
	1c. Orange......	
	2c.	5.75
	3c.	1.75
	6c.	
	12½c.	6.75
	15c.	7.00
	1870 3c.	1.75
	188? 6c. Yellow Brown	
	1897 3c. Jubilee......	.60
101	Through Cloth.	
	1868 3c.	2.25
100	(31) (?).........	
	1868 3c.	$5.00
	(32) **Barrie**	
	1868 ½c.	
	1c. Yellow......	6.00
	1c. Brown......	
	2c.	6.00
	3c.	1.75
	3c. May 21, 1869 Green.......	2.00
	6c.	6.00
	12½c.	
	1870 3c.	1.75

(33) **Sherbrooke, C.E.** Covers from Eaton, 18 miles from Sherbrooke, are noted with Numeral 33. Eaton was once the County Seat of Compton County. When the railway was built in the 70's it touched Cookshire which then became the County Seat.

Type	Found on	Value
	1868 ½c.	
	1c. Yellow......	6.00
	1c. Orange......	
	1c. Brown......	
	2c.	6.00
	3c.	1.50
	6c.	
	12½c.	
	1870 1c. Orange......	
	3c.	1.50
	1872 6c. Yellow Brown	
	(34) **Branchton, U.C.**	
	1868 ½c.	
	1c. Brown......	
	3c.	4.00
	6c.	
	1870 1c. Orange......	
	3c.	4.00
	1875 1c. Yellow......	
	3c. Common Shade.......	
	(35) **Lindsay, C.W.**	
	1868 ½c.	6.00
	1c. Brown......	
	2c.	6.00
	3c.	2.00
	6c.	
	12½c.	7.00
100	1868 15c.	
	1870 1c. Orange......	
	3c.	$2.00
	(36) **St. Johns, C.E.**	
	1868 ½c.	
	1c. Yellow......	
	1c. Orange......	
	1c. Brown......	
	2c.	6.00
	3c.	1.75
	6c.	
	12½c.	
	15c.	
	1870 1c. Orange......	
	3c.	1.75

Type	Found on			Value
	1875	1c.	Yellow	
		5c.	(large)	10.00
		10c.		
	(37)		(?)	
	1868	½c.		
		1c.	Brown	6.00
		2c.		6.00
		3c.		1.75
		6c.		
	1870	3c.		1.75
	(38) **Bowmanville**			
	1868	½c.		
		1c.	Brown	
		1c.	Yellow	
		2c.		
		3c.		1.75
		6c.		
	1870	1c.	Orange	
		3c.		1.75
	1875	5c.	(large)	

101

Type	Found on			Value
	(39)		(?)	
	1868	½c.		
		1c.	Brown	
		1c.	Yellow	6.00
		2c.		6.00
		3c.		1.75
		6c.		
	1870	3c.		1.75
	1987	3c.	4-Leaf	
101	1868		Through Cloth.	
		3c.		2.00
	Thinner numerals, narrow circles.			
		3c.		1.75
100	(40) **Cornwall**			
	1868	½c.		
		1c.	Yellow	$5.50
		1c.	Orange	
		1c.	Brown	
		2c.		5.50
		3c.		1.75
		6c.		6.00
		15c.		
	1870	1c.	Orange	
		2c.		
		3c.		1.25
	1875	5c.	(small)	

Type	Found on			Value
	1885	1c.	Yellow	.40
		2c.		.40
		3c.		.50
		5c.		
		6c.	Yellow Brown	
		10c.		
		2c.	Registered	
	1897		Still in use.	
	(41) **St. Mary's, C.W.**			
	1868	1c.	Yellow	5.50
		1c.	Orange	
		1c.	Brown	
		2c.		
		3c.		1.75
		6c.		5.50
		15c.		
	1870	1c.	Orange	
		3c.		
	1875	1c.	Yellow	
		3c.		
		6c.		
		5c.	(large)	10.00
	1880	5c.		
	1897		Still in use.	
	(42)		(?)	
	1868	3c.		5.00
	(43) **Windsor, N.S.**			
	1868	1c.	Brown	
		1c.	Yellow	
		2c.		
		3c.		2.50
		6c.		
	1870	1c.	Orange	
		3c.		1.75
100	(44) **Owen Sound**			
	1868	1c.	Brown	
		1c.	Yellow	
		3c.		$2.00
		6c.		6.00
	1870	1c.	Orange	
		3c.		2.00
	(45) **Perth**			
	1868	1c.	Brown	5.00
		1c.	Yellow	5.00
		3c.		1.75
		6c.		
	1870	1c.	Orange	
		2c.		
		3c.		1.75
		5c.	(large)	
	1880	1c.	Yellow	
	1897	3c.	4-Leaf	
		3c.	Q.V. Numeral	
	(46) **Dundas**			
	1868	1c.	Brown	
		1c.	Yellow	

Type	Found on		Value
		3c.	1.75
		6c.	6.00
	1870	1c. Orange	
		3c.	1.75
	(47)	**Napanee**	
	1868	1c. Brown	
		2c.	
		3c.	1.75
		6c.	5.50
		12½c.	7.00
	1870	1c. Orange	
		3c.	1.75
	(48)	**Simcoe**	
	1868	1c. Brown	
		1c. Yellow	5.00
		1c. Orange	
		3c.	1.75
	1870	1c. Orange	
		3c.	1.75
	(49)	**Prescott**	
	1868	1c. Brown	
		1c. Yellow	
100	1868	2c.	5.00
		3c.	1.75
		6c.	7.00
	1870	1c. Orange	
		3c.	1.75
	(50)	St. Andrews, N.B.	
	1868	1c. Brown	
		1c. Yellow	
		2c.	6.00
		3c.	1.75
	1870	1c. Orange	
		2c.	
		3c.	1.75
	1897	1c. Jubilee	1.00
		2c. Jubilee	1.05
		3c. Jubilee	.75
		5c.	1.00
	(51)	**Picton**	
	1868	1c. Brown	
		1c. Yellow	
		3c.	3.50
	(52)	**Caledon, U.C.**	
	1868	1c. Brown	6.00
		1c. Yellow	6.00
		2c.	
		3c.	1.75
		6c.	
		12½c.	8.00
	1870	1c. Orange	
		3c.	1.75
	1876	2c. Verm. Regist.	
	(53)	(?)	
	1868	½c.	

Type	Found on		Value
		1c. Brown	
		1c. Yellow	4.50
		2c.	
		3c.	1.75
		6c.	
	1870	3c.	1.75
	1880	1c. Yellow	
		3c.	1.00
100	(54)	**Truro, N.S.**	
	1868	1c. Brown	
		1c. Yellow	
		½c.	
		2c.	5.50
		3c.	1.75
		6c.	
	1870	15c.	
		3c.	1.75
	(55)	**Berlin, C.W.**	
	1868	½c.	
		1c. Brown	
		1c. Yellow	5.50
		2c.	
		3c.	1.75
		6c.	
		15c.	
	1870	1c. Orange	
		3c.	1.75
	(56)	**Brampton, Ont.**	
	1868	½c.	
		2c.	
		3c.	4.00
		6c.	
	1870	1c. Orange	
		3c.	1.75
		6c. Yel. Brown	

104

Type	Found on		Value
	(57)	(?)	
	1868	½c.	
		1c. Brown	
		1c. Yellow	
		2c.	6.50
		3c.	4.50
		6c.	
104		Worn State	
		3c.	1.75
	1870	3c.	2.00

Type	Found on		Value
100	(58) **Aylmer, U.C.** This numeral also noted on St. Thomas, Ont. covers.		
	1868 ½c.	....	
	1c. Brown	......	
	1c. Yellow	......	
	1c. Orange	......	
	2c.	....	
	3c.	....	1.50
	6c.	....	6.00
	1870 1c. Orange	......	
	3c.	....	1.50
	(59) **Clinton, U.C.**		
	1868 3c.	....	3.00
	1870 3c.	....	3.00
	(60) (?)	....	
	1868 ½c.	....	
	1c. Yellow	......	
	1c. Orange	......	
	2c.	....	
	3c.	....	4.00
	6c.	....	
	12½c.	....	
	1870 1c. Orange	......	
	3c.	....	3.50

105   105 Late State

Type	Found on		Value
105	Type 100 with circles cut.		
	1872 3c.	....	1.50
	1c.	....	1.25
	1880 1c.	....	.75

106   107

Type	Found on		Value
106	(4) **Watson's Corners, U.C.** In use from Nov. 18, 1872, to June 18, 1875.		

Type	Found on		Value
	1872 1c.	....	2.50
	2c.	....	2.50
	3c.	....	2.50
107	(13) (?)	....	
	1870 3c. Rose	....	1.50
107	(23) (?)	....	
	1870 3c. Rose	....	1.50

108   109

Type	Found on		Value
	(17) (?)	....	
108	1868 3c.	....	$1.75
109	(19) (?)	....	
	1868 1c. Brown	......	
	1c. Yellow	......	
	3c.	....	1.75

110   111

Type	Found on		Value
110	(12) (?)	....	
	1868 3c.	....	2.00
111	(21) (?)	....	
	1889 3c.	....	1.00
	Figuresnot as high	....	
	3c. Q.V. Numeral Black	....	.75

112

Type	Found on		Value
112	(37) **Quebec, L.C.**		
	1859 1c.	....	
	5c.	....	1.00
	10c.	....	
	12½c.	....	4.00
	17c.	....	
	1864 2c.	....	

113 114

Type	Found on	Value
113	(37) **Quebec, L.C.**	
	1859 1c.	
	5c.	1.50
	1868 3c.	1.50
114	(37) **Quebec, L.C.**	
	1859 1c.	
	5c.	1.50
	12½c.	
	1868 1c. Brown	
	2c.	
	3c.	1.50
	12½c.	

115 116

Type	Found on	Value
115	**Hamilton,** Mar., 1858	
	1858 ½d.	
	3d.	7.00
	6d.	
	1859 1c.	
	5c.	2.00
	10c.	
	Belleville, bars at different angle.	
115	1858 ½d.	
	3d.	
116	**Hamilton,** Mar. 1858.	
	1858 ½d.	
	3d.	6.50
	6d.	
	1859 1c.	
	5c.	1.75
	10c.	

117 118

Type	Found on	Value
117	**Fredericton, N.B.** May, 1872.	
	1872 1c. Orange	
	3c. Rose	1.00
	15c.	
	1880 1c.	
	(With 8 bars)	
	1868 3c.	1.25
	12½c.	
	1870 3c.	
118	1875 1c. Yellow	$0.60
	3c.	.75
	10c.	2.00
	Numeral 242	
	1897 5c. Q.V. 4-Leaf	.50

119 120

Type	Found on	Value
119	1868 6c.	4.00
120	**Guelph**	
	1868 1c. Yellow	1.25
	3c.	1.75
	1870 3c.	1.50

121 122

Type	Found on	Value
121	**Walkerton, C.W.**	
	1868 6c.	4.00
	1870 3c.	2.00
122	(?)	
	1880 1c. Yellow	1.25

123

Type	Found on		Value
123	(?)	....	
	1868 3c.	....	2.00

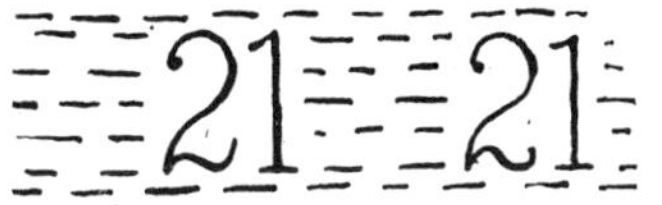

124

124	**Montreal,** Feb. 1858		
	1858 3d. Ribbed P....		20.00
	½d.	....	
	6d., 7½d., 10d.	....	
	1869 1c.	....	
	5c.	....	2.50
	12½c.	....	8.50
	1868 3c.	....	2.50
	1889 1c. Yellow......		2.50
	2c.	....	3.00
	3c.	....	3.50
	6c.	....	4.00
	10c.	....	4.00

125

126

125	(?)	....	
	1870 3c.	....	1.50
126	(?)	....	
	1859 1c.	....	2.50

127

127	**Prince Edward Island**		
	1872 3c. Rose........		2.50
128	**Toronto**		
	1868 1c. Brown......		
	1c. Yellow......		
	1c. Orange......		
	3c.	....	1.50
	1874 15c.	....	2.25

128

129

130

131

Type	Found on		Value
129	**Toronto**		
	1868 1c. Brown......		
	1c. Yellow......		
	1c. Orange......		

Type	Found on		Value
	3c.	....	1.75
130	**Toronto**		
	1868 3c.	....	1.75

132 133 134 135

136 137 138 139

Type	Found on	Value
131	**Toronto**	
	1868 1c. Yellow....	
	1c. Orange....	
	1c. Brown....	
	3c.	1.75
132	**Toronto**	
	1868 1c. Yellow......	
	3c.	1.75
133	**Toronto**, Aug. 1868	
	1869 1c. Yellow......	
	1c. Orange......	
	1c. Brown......	
	3c.	1.75
134	**Toronto**	
	1868 1c. Yellow......	
	3c.	1.75
135	**Toronto**	
	1868 1c. Yellow......	
	3c.	1.75
	12½c.	
136	**Toronto**	
	1868 1c. Yellow......	
	3c.	1.75
137	**Toronto**	
	1868 1c. Yellow......	
	3c.	1.75

Type	Found on	Value
138	**Toronto**	
	1868 1c. Yellow......	
	3c.	1.75
139	**Toronto**, Nov. 1869	
	1869 1c. Yellow......	
	1c. Orange......	
	1c. Brown......	1.75
	3c.	

140 141

Type	Found on	Value
140	**Toronto**	
	1868 1c. Yellow......	
	3c.	1.75
	1870 1c. Orange......	3.00
	3c.	2.50
141	**Toronto.** Cork, with steel "2" inserted" (in leaf, inverted).	
	1870 1c.	2.00
	3c.	1.50

142 143 144 145

146 147 148 149

150 151 152 153

154 155 156 157

Type	Found on		Value
142	**Ottawa** (?)		
	1868	3c.	1.75
		1c. Yellow......	
143	**Ottawa** (?)		
	1868	1c. Yellow......	
		2c.	
		3c.	1.75
		6c.	3.50

Type	Found on		Value
144	**Ottawa**, 1868		
	1868	1c. Yellow......	
		1c. Orange......	
		2c.	
		3c.	1.75
		6c.	3.50
		12½c.	
	1870	3c.	1.75
		15c.	

Type	Found on		Value
145	**Ottawa,** 1868		
	1868	1c. Yellow......	
		1c. Brown......	
		3c.	1.75
		6c.	3.50
		12½c.	
145	1868	15c.	
	1870	3c.	$1.75
146	**Ottawa,** 1868		
	1868	1c. Yellow......	
		1c. Brown......	
		3c.	1.75
		6c.	3.50
		12½c.	
		15c.	
	1870	3c.	1.75
147	**Kingston**		
	1870	3c.	1.75
148	**Kingston**		
	1868	1c. Yellow......	
		3c.	1.75
149	**Kingston**		
	1868	1c. Yellow......	
		3c.	1.75
		6c.	
150	**Kingston**		
	1868	1c. Yellow......	3.00
		3c.	1.75
		12½c.	
151	**Kingston**		
	1868	1c. Yellow......	
		3c.	1.75
152	**Kingston**		
	1868	3c.	1.75
		12½c.	
		15c.	
153	**Kingston**		
	1868	1c. Yellow......	
		1c. Orange......	
		1c. Brown......	
		2c.	
		3c.	$1.75
		6c	
		12½c	
		15c.	
	1870	3c.	1.75
		2c.	
154	**Kingston**		
	1868	1c. Brown......	
		1c. Yellow......	
		1c. Orange......	
		2c.	
		3c.	1.75

Type	Found on		Value
		6c.	
		12½c.	
		15c.	
	1870	1c. Orange......	
		3c.	1.75
155	**Kingston**		
	1868	1c. Brown......	
		1c. Yellow......	
		1c. Orange......	
		3c.	1.75
		6c.	
		12½c.	
	1870	15c.	
		1c. Orange......	1.75
156	**Kingston**		
	1868	1c. Yellow......	
		3c.	$1.75
		6c.	
	1870	1c. Orange......	
		3c.	1.75
157	**Kingston**		
	1868	1c. Yellow......	
		1c. Brown......	
		2c.	
		3c.	1.75
	1870	1c. Orange......	
		3c.	1.75

158 159

Type	Found on		Value
158	**Kingston**		
	1870	3c.	1.75
	1872	2c.	
	1868	6c.	
159	**Kingston**		
	1868	1c. Yellow......	
		1c. Brown......	
		3c.	1.75

160

Type	Found on	Value
160	**London.** (Duplex—"dater" and "killer" attached).	
	1868 1c. Yellow......	
	2c.	
	3c.	$1.00
	6c.	
	12½c.	
	1c. Brown......	
	15c.	
	1870 1c. Orange......	
	3c.	1.00
	1880 1c. Yellow......	
	2c.	
	3c.	
	5c.	
	6c.	
	10c.	

161

161	**London.** (Duplex)	
	1868 1c. Yellow......	
	1c. Brown......	
	2c.	
	3c.	$1.00
	6c.	
	12½c.	
	1870 1c. Orange......	
	3c.	1.00

162

162	**Hamilton.** Jan. 1871.	
	1868 2c.	
	6c.	
	1870 3c.	.75
	1c. Orange......	
	1870 3c.	.75
	Blue........	1.00

163

Type	Found on	Value
163	**Hamilton.** (In Nov. 1876, the numeral 5 Type 162 was mutilated by 2 vertical and two diagonal cuts).	
	1875 1c. Yellow......	$ .25
	2c.	.35
	3c.	.25
	5c.	.35
	6c.	1.25
	10c.	

164

164	**Ottawa.** 1885	
	1885 1c. Yellow......	.10
	2c.	.20
	3c.	.15
	5c.	.25
	6c.	
164	1893 8c.	$ .50
	1886 15c.	
	1892 15c.	
	1897 1c. Q.V. Numeral	.10
	2c.	.10
	10c.	.50
	1887 3c. Carmine Rose	.75

165

166

165	**Ottawa.** Jan. 1882.	
	1882 1c. Yellow......	.10
	2c.	.20

Type	Found on	Value
	3c.	.15
	5c.	.25
	6c.	
	1883 15c.	
	10c.	
	1887 3c. Carmine Rose	.75
166	**St. John, N.B.** Aug. 1887	
	1887 1c. Yellow......	.10
	2c.	.20
	3c.	.15
	5c.	.25
	6c.	
	10c.	
	3c. Carmine Rose	.75

167

Type	Found on	Value
167	**St. John, N.B.** Sept. 1881	
	Numeral thicker than Type 166.	
	1881 1c. Yellow......	.10
	2c.	.20
	3c.	.15
	1887 3c. Carmine Rose	.75
	1881 5c.	.25
	6c.	
	10c.	

168 169

Type	Found on	Value
168	**Toronto.** Sept. 1881.	
	1881 1c. Yellow......	.10
	2c.	.20
	3c.	.15
168	5c.	$ .25
	6c.	
	10c.	
	1887 3c. Carmine Rose	.75

Type	Found on	Value
169	**Montreal.** Sept. 1881.	
	1881 1c. Yellow......	.10
	2c.	.20
	3c.	.15
	5c.	.25
	6c.	
	10c.	1.75
	1887 3c. Carmine Rose	.75

170 171

Type	Found on	Value
170	**St. John, N.B.** Sept. 1881.	
	1881 1c. Yellow......	.10
	2c.	.20
	3c.	.15
	5c.	.25
	6c.	
	10c.	
	1887 3c. Carmine Rose	.75
170a	3rd bar from top or bottom cut away for circle.............	
170b	Numeral shorter and thicker............	
170c	Bars vertical instead of horizontal..........	
171	**Toronto.** Nov. 1880.	
	1880 1c. Yellow......	.10
	2c.	.20
	3c.	.15
	5c.	.25
	6c.	
	10c.	
	1887 3c. Carmine Rose	.75
	1897 1c. Q.V. 4-Leaf..	.10
	2c.	.10
	3c.	.15
	1c. Q.V. Numeral	.10
	2c.	.10
	3c.	.15
	St. John, N.B. July 1889.	
171	11 Bars, thick numeral.	
	1c. Yellow......	$ .10
	2c.	.20
	3c.	.15

Type	Found on	Value
171a	**Toronto.** 7 Vertical Bars, April 1885. (Sub-stations), values are for the commoner low numbers.	
	Numeral 1—Toronto.	
	2—Parkdale.	
	3—Spadina Ave.	
	4—Yorkville.	
	5—Riverside.	
	1885 1c. Yellow......	.10
	2c.	.20
	3c.	.10
	5c.	.25
	6c.	
	10c.	
	1887 3c. Carmine Rose	.75
	1897 1c. Q.V. 4-Leaf..	.10
	2c.	.10
	1c. Q.V. Numeral	.10
	2c.	.10
	3c. Jub.........	.12

173

Type	Found on	Value
173	**St. John, N.B.**	
	1881 1c. Yellow......	.25
	3c.	.25
	New Brunswick	
	1860 10c.	1.50

174

Type	Found on	Value
174	(?)	
	1880 1c. Yellow......	.20
	3c.	.20

Type	Found on	Value
a	1890 Middle bar, right, missing	
	3c.	.30

175

Type	Found on	Value
175	(?)	
	1870 3c.	.75

176  177

Type	Found on	Value
176	1880 1c. Yellow......	$ .25
	2c.	.35
	3c.	.35
177	1870 3c.	1.25

178  179

Type	Found on	Value
	New Brunswick	
178	1860 12½c.Blue........	3.00
179	**Shrewsbury, England**	
	1859 12½c............	3.50
	1868 6c.	3.50

180 181

Type	Found on		Value
180	Numerals 1 to 9 designating Montreal Sub-offices. 1917 All Georgian Stamps.		
181	1880	3c.	.50

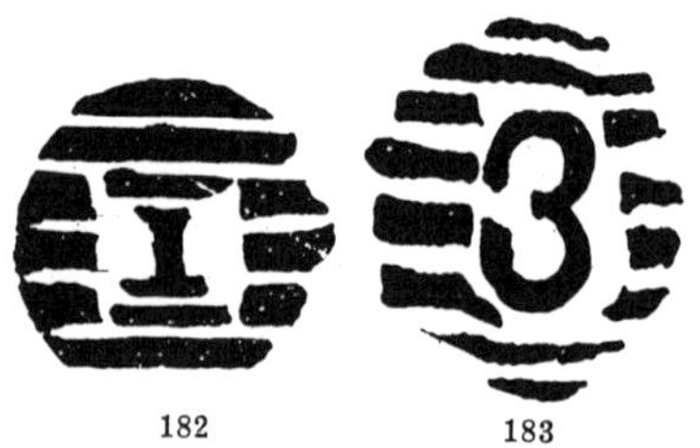

182 183

182	1880	3c.	.25
183	1870	1c. Orange.	
		3c.	.75
	1880	1c. Yellow.	.25
		3c	.30

184 185

184	1890	3c	$ .20
		1c. Yellow.	.15
185	1879	3c.	.35

185x 186

Type	Found on		Value
185x	1890	1c. Yellow.	.20
		3c.	.25
	1897	1c. Jubilee.	.35
		3c. Jubilee.	.25
186	1890	1c. Yellow.	.15
		3c.	.20

187

Simcoe. Aug. 1893.

187	1893	3c.	.25
		1c. Yellow.	.20

188 189

188	1880	1c. Yellow.	.15
		3c.	.20
189	1874	3c.	.25
		1c. Yellow.	.25

190 190

190	1890	1c. Yellow.	.25
		3c.	.40
191	1875	1c. Yellow, Blue.	.40
		3c. Blue.	.50

New Brunswick Grids.

192

Type	Found on	Value
192	(1) **St. John, N.B.**	
	1851 3d.	
	6d. 1s	
	1860 1c. Grey, Purple.	
	2c. Orange	
	5c. Green	
	10c. Red	
	12½c. Blue	
	17c. Black	
	Canada	
	1868 ½c.	
	1c. Brown	
	1c. Yellow	
	1c. Orange	
	2c.	
	3c.	2.00
	6c.	
	1870 1c. Orange	
	3c.	1.50
	(2) (?)	
	1851 3d.	
	1860 5c. Green	
	10c. Red	
	Canada	
	1868 ½c.	
	1c. Brown	
	2c.	
	3c.	2.00
	6c.	
	1870 3c.	1.00
	(3) **Woodstock, N.B.**	
	1851 3d.	
	1860 5c. Green	
	10c. Red	
	Canada	
	1890 3c.	.35
	(On all values to 8c. Grey 1894).	
	(4) (?)	
	1851 3d.	
	1860 5c. Green	
	(5) (?)	
	1851 3d.	
	1860 5c. Green	
	(6) **Edmunston, N.B.**	
	1851 3d.	
	6d. 1s	
192	1860 1c. Grey, Purple	
	2c. Orange	
	5c. Green	
	10c. Red	
	12½c. Blue	
	17c. Black	

Type	Found on	Value
	Canada	
	1868 3c.	1.75
	6c.	
	1870 3c.	1.25
	1880 3c.	.60
	(7) (?)	
	(8) **Chatham, N.B.**	
	1851 3d.	
	6d.	
	Green	
	1s	
	(The engraved forgeries of the 3d., 6d., 1s stamps are cancelled with a counterfeit Numeral 8).	
	1860 1c. Grey, Purple	
	2c. Orange	
	5c. Green	
	10c. Red	
	12½c. Blue	
	17c. Black	
	(9) **Grand Falls, N.B.**	
	1851 3d.	
	1880 3c. Canada	.40
	(10) W. O. Whites Cove	
	1880 3c. Canada	.50
	1890 3c.	.40
	(11) **Dorchester.** Noted on cover from Rosedale, Dec. 1894.	
	1851 3d.	
	(12) Edwardstown (?).. Edmunston (?)...	
	1851 3d.	
	(13) **Fredericton, N.B.**	
	1851 3d.	
	6d. 1s	
192	1860 1c. Grey, Purple.	
	2c. Orange	
	5c. Green	
	10c. Red	
	12½c. Blue	
	17c. Black	
	Canada	
	1868 1c. Brown	
	3c.	
	(14) **Gagetown, N.B.**	
	1851 3d.	
	(15) **Hampton Ferry N.B.**	
	1851 3d.	

Type | Found on | Value

(16) **Harvey, N.B.**
1851 3d. . . . .

(17) **Salisbury, N.B.**
1851 3d. . . . .

(18) (?). . . . .

(19) **Memramcook, N.B.**
1851 3d. . . . .
1892 3c. Canada . . . . .

(20) (?). . . . .

(21) **Hillsborough, N.B.**
1851 3d. . . . .

(22) (?). . . . .

(23) **Richibucto, N.B.**
1851 3d. . . . .
6d. 1s . . . .

(24) **Sackville, N.B.**
1851 3d. . . . .
6d. 1s . . . .

(25) (?). . . . .

(26) **Shediac** (Via Sheffield).
1851 3d. . . . .
6d. 1s . . . .

Letters from Shediac routed via Sheffield often received the Sheffield postmark and cancellation. Gridiron cancellations, Type 192, were used, without numbers, by Springfield, Summer. . . .d, Penobsquis, Coles Island, Hopewell Mill, etc.

192 (27) (?). . . . .

(28) **St. George, N.B.**
1851 3d. . . . .
6d. . . . .

(29) (?). . . . .

Type | Found on | Value

(30) **St. Stephen, N.B.**
1851 3d. . . . .
1885 3c. Canada 50

(31) (?). . . . .

(32) (?). . . . .
1880 3c. Canada 50

(33) **Wicklow, N.B.**
1851 3d. . . . .

(34) **Colebrook, N.B.**
1851 3d. . . . .

(35) **Upper Peel, N.B.**
1851 3d. . . . .

193

193 Rubber Stamp for Cancelling Parcels.
St. John, Fredericton, Montreal, Toronto, May 1883, Numerals 1 to 6.
1883 1c. Yellow 05
2c. 10
3c. 20
8c. 50
1897 3c. Q.V. 4-Leaf . . .10
5c. 60
2c. Q.V. Numeral .10
3c. 10

193a Toronto. (Long and short bar replaces "ONT." —(May 1883). . . . . . .

193b Toronto. "Toronto, Can." with date in centre and numerals 1 to 12, double lined oval, July 1892. . . . .

193c Same as 193 but larger
1892 All Values . . . .

225 225a 226

227 228 229

230 232 230x

233 234 235

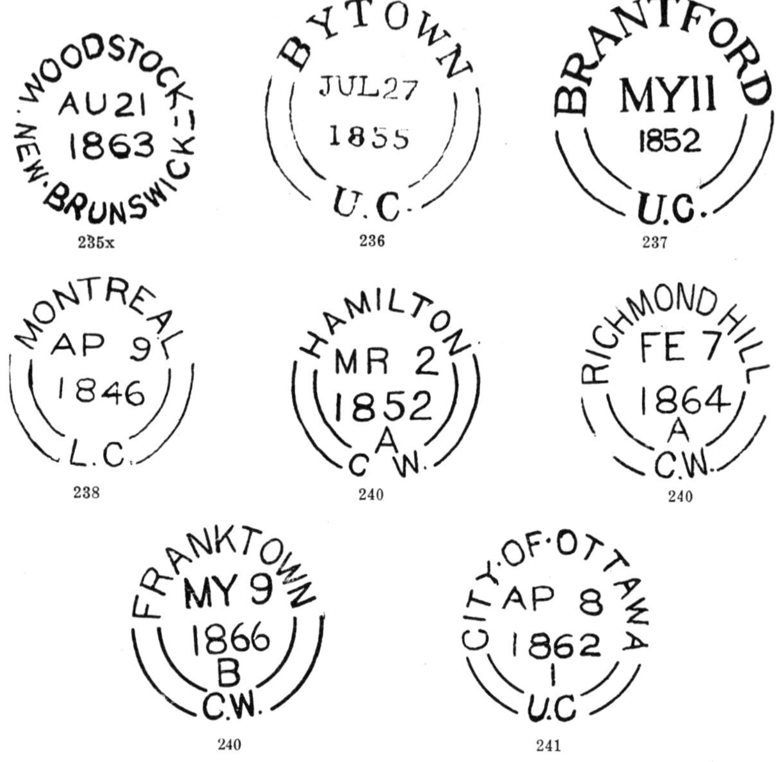

235x — 236 — 237

238 — 240 — 240

240 — 241

TYPES OF TOWN POSTMARKS

The earliest known type was used in London, England, in 1660. The earliest type noted for British North America is dated September 18th, 1790.

Type	Noted on	Value
225	STAMPLESS COVER Black....... Halifax, Sept. 1790.... (Rate stamped or written)	$6.00
226	STAMPLESS COVER Black....... Quebec, Aug. 1814..... (Rate stamped or written)	4.00
227	STAMPLESS COVER Black....... Halifax, March 1837... (Rate stamped or written)	3.50

Type	Noted on	Value
a.	The four dots are hollow, with square period at center bottom (July '39)................	

227x

Type	Found on	Value
227x	Spence, Ont., Jy. '76... Black.......	
	1876 3c............	2.00
	On Cover....	7.50
228	Halifax, Oct. 6, 1841, Black..............$	.50
	New Brunswick. General use Black.......	.50
229	St. Andrews, N.B., Ap. '53, West Flamboro, U.C., De. '45, etc... Black.......$	.50
	Blue........	.75
	Amherstburg, Ju. '55 Chatham, N.B. Ju. 1856	
a.	Date written in Black, Gananoque, Dec. 1844...............	.75
230	New Brunswick Black.......	
230x	St. John, N.B., Sept. 15, 1852...............	
	Stampless Cover, Howard, U.C., Dec. '48; Colchester, U.C., Oc. '54; Aldborough, U. C., Ap. '55; Fenelon Falls, U.C., No. '58 (larger)............	.35

231 231x

Type	Found on	Value
231	Nova Scotia. Stampless Cover. July, 1837 Rate written in.......	.50
231x	New Brunswick Stampless Cover Brown......	
	St. Stephen, N.B., May 1840, with rate written in.............	1.00
	Blue........	
	St. Stephen, N.B., May 1840, with rate written in.............	1.00
	Green.......	
	St. Andrews, N.B., with rate written in......	1.50
232	St. John, N.B., Mr. '53 Black, adds to val. of cover..............	.10
a.	Penetanguishene, U. C., Feb. 12, 1865, "12" pen written.........	.75
233	General use, incl. new Brunswick Black, from Oct. 1851	
234	General use, incl. New Brunswick, from Jan. 1848	
	Stampless Cover......	.50
	Blue, Holyrood, U.C., Sp. '64.............	.60
	Euphrasia, C.W., Fe. '52................	.60
	Brown, Waterloo-Kingston, U.C., Ap. '55..	.60
	Green, Bobcaygeon, Oc. '57................	.75
a.	Date typeset	
b.	"3 Paid" stamped over Type 234 with Paid appearing in center	
	Brown, W.O. New Mills Ap. '56.............	1.50
235	General use	.30
a.	Manitowaning "1 Ap.". above year 1852.....	.80
235x	General use..........	.40
	Cancellation 1860 5c. Green, N.B..	1.00
236-7	General use, Nov. 1839 Stampless Covers	
	Queenston, U.C. 1846..	.50
	Quebec, L.C., 1855....	.50
	Bytown, U.C., Ja. '47.	.60
	Red, Bytown, U.C....	.75
	Belleville, Mr. '48...	.75
	Niagara, No. '39....	.90
	Sandwich, U.C., Fe. '48 to Ju. '51.....	.75
	Carmine, London, May May '40...	.75
	Stanstead, L. C., No. '46	.75
	Bronze - Brown, Sandwich, U.C., No. '54..	.75
	Blue, Amherstburg, Ju. '55 to Mr. '72.......	.50
a.	Date written in Mattsville Mr. '59; Indiana, U.C. Jy. '54..	.35
	Fenelon Falls, My. '58.	.35
	Green, Nassagaweya, Fe. '71............	.75
b.	Year omitted Queenston, Fe. '46.....	.35
	Appearing on Stamps	

Type	Found on	Value
236-7	1853 3d. (Cobourg) . . .	8.00
	1854 3d. (Stanstead) . .	8.00
	1858 3d. (Quebec)	
	Toronto, U.C	
	1851 3d. laid	
	6d. laid	
	1853 3d.	7.00
	1857 ½d.	
	7½d.	
236-7	1859 1c.	
	5c.	1.50
	Blue	
	1853 3d.	$ 8.00
	Green	
	1857 ½d.	
238	General use, Ja. '46	
	Stampless Cover. (Catalogue value is computed by addition of values given for all postmarks)	
	Black	.25
	Red:	
	Delhi, U.C., Ja. '73	.50
	Omemee, U.C., Oc. '57	.50
	Montreal, L.C., Mr. '48	.25
	Berlin, U.C., Ja. '54	.30
	Oshawa, U.C., Ju. '60 . .	.30
	Blue, Markham, U.C., Jy. '61	.50
	Pembroke, U.C., My. '67	.45
	Green, Craigleith, Ja. '62 (day of month written in)	1.00
a.	Date written in, red, Lonsdale, U.C., Ju. '54	.50
	Vernonville, U.C., Ju. '57	.50

Type	Stampless Cover	Value
a.	C. E. or C. W. instead of L. C., U. C	
	Bronze-Brown, Lindsay, Jy. '55	
b.	No letters at bottom.	
	Appearing on Stamps	
238	Montreal, Sherbrooke, Stratford, Strathroy, Wingham.	
	1856 3d.	$6.00
	Eaton.	
	1852 3d. Red	
	Hamilton, U.C.	
	1857 ½d.	
	Red	
	Green	
	1859 1c.	
	Blue	

Type	Stampless Cover	Value
	5c.	
	Blue	
	12½c.	
a.	Sharon, C.W.	
	1862 10c. Red	
	1868 3c.	
	Blue	
b.	Hamilton, U.C., Ju. 8, 1858.	
	1858 ½d.	

239

Type	Stampless Cover	Value
239	Russell, C.W., with "3" July 15, 1857.	
	Stampless Cover with Paid	.50
	With Registered	.75
240	Letters "A," "B," etc., beneath the year date have no special significance. Each stamper in Liverpool and London offices retained his own date stamp, with initial letter to distinguish it, and similar date stamps were supplied to the Colony. Figures were sometimes used, and occasionally one meets with a type showing a short dash (—) under the year date. Canadian postmarks are sometimes seen in which the letter or figure has been plugged in carelessly and appears inverted or on its side.	
	Stampless Cover; Cat. val. is total of all markings listed.	
	With written rate, Black	$ .25
	With "3" or "Paid 3", Black	.50
	With "6" or "Paid 6", Black	.75
	With either of above in red	1.00
	With "Paid" and written rate, Red	.25
	Warsaw, U.C., De. '63, Brown-red	.25

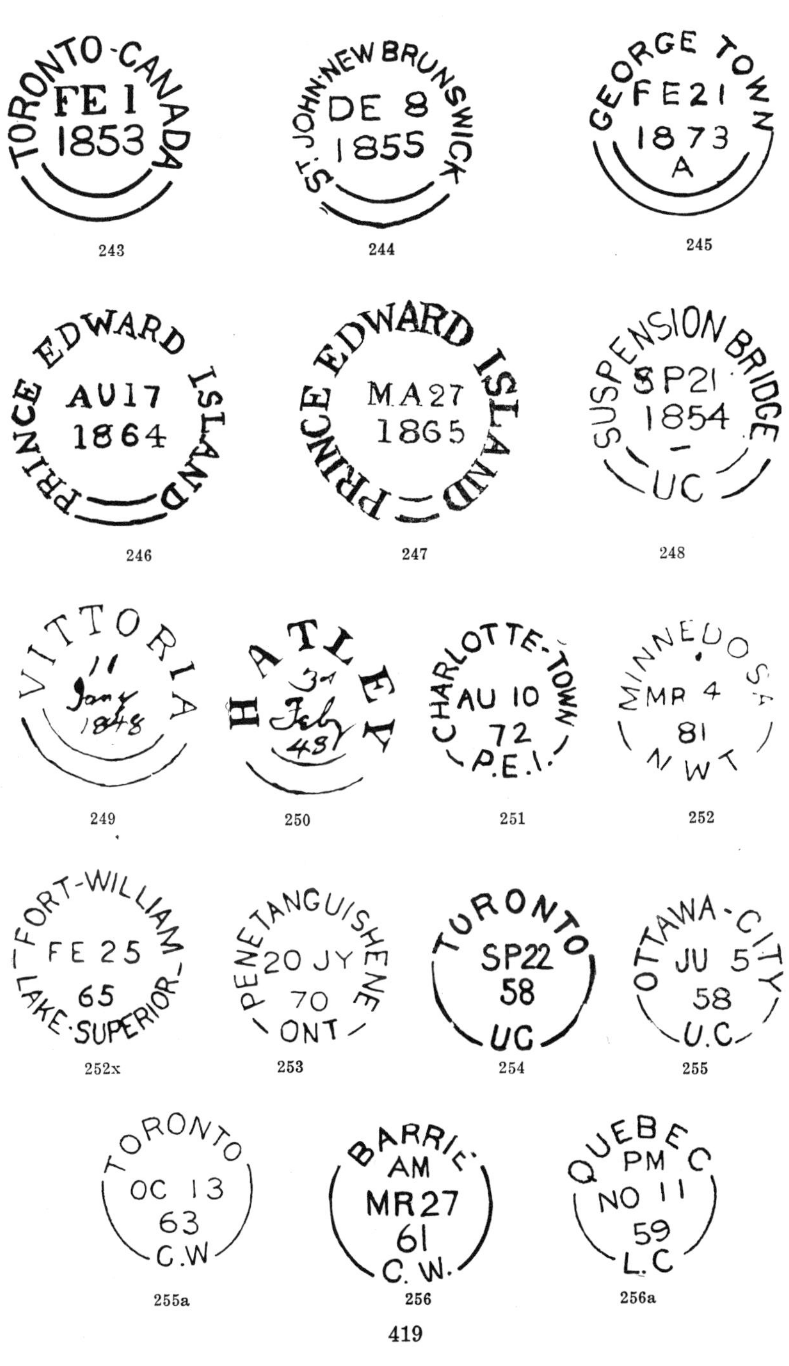

243 244 245

246 247 248

249 250 251 252

252x 253 254 255

255a 256 256a

Type	Noted on Stamps	Value
240	1857 ½d.	
	Green	
	1851 3d.	
	1853 3d.	7.00
	6d. 7½d.	

Conway, C.W.

	1859 5c. Green	$2.00

Sharon, C.W.

	1862 5c. Orange	3.00

Whitfield, U.C.

	1860 5c. Red	2.00
	1859 1c.	
	5c.	.75
	10c.	
	12½c.	
	17c.	
	1864 2c.	
	1868 2c.	
	3c.	1.00
	Blue	
	Red	
	Green	
	1870 1c. Orange	1.25
	Red	
	Green	

Number instead of letter under date.

241	1859 1c.	$1.25
	5c.	1.00
	1868 3c.	1.00
	(Used by Fitzroy Harbor, C.W. (O Ja. '56)	
	Warsaw, U.C., Mr. '59 (0)	

St. Martins, N. B., Nov. 1866.

	1866 5c. New Brunswick	1.00

PARIS·D.P.O. AU 21 62 C.W.

242

Type	Noted on Stamps	Value
	General use.	
242	Black	
	1859 1c.	
	5c.	.75
	10c.	
242	1870 1c. Orange	
	2c.	
	3c.	$ .75
	1871 3c.	.75
	Blue	.90
	Stampless Covers	
	Green, Madoc, U.C., No. '66	.15
	General use.	
243	Stampless Cover, Black, Oc. '50	
	With Paid and rate	.75
	Red	1.00
	Appearing on Stamps.	
	1853 3d.	7.00
a.	Letter under date.	
	Ottawa "O", Sept. 1862	
	1859 12½c.	
b.	Space for dates plugged with cork.	
	Smiths Falls, Black	
	1880 1c. Yellow	.25
	3c.	.25
	Halifax, N.S., Jan. 1861.	
243	1861 5c. Nova Scotia.	2.50
244	New Brunswick. General use.	
	Black, from Ap. 1852, on 3d. and all "Cents" issue	
	1d. Amherst, Oc.17, 1856	
a.	Date written in.	
245	Black	
	Georgetown, P.E.I., Mr. '65	
	2d. Rose	2.00
	3c. Rose	2.25
	Brown	
	Prince. Town, P.E.I ...	
	1865 2d.	
	Aylmer, Ottawa, My. '58, Black	
	Adds to val. of cover ...	.75
a.	No letter under date ...	
	Black	.75

Prince Edward Island, Nov. 1855 to 1868.

246	1863 2d. Rose	$3.00
	1d. Brown-Orange	5.00
	1867 3d. Blue	4.00
a.	Date in small type, and period replaces lines	

Type	Found on	Value
	at bottom, Jan. 1868	
b.	Figure 4 under date (No. significance)........	
	Prince Edward Island (From No. '46)......	
247	1865 1d. Orange-Buff.	4.50
	2d. Rose........	3.00
	3d. Blue........	4.00
248	General use.	
	1854 3d.	7.00
249	General use from 1830 in Black............	
	Stampless Cover.	
	1830	.50
a.	Date typeset, two lines.	
	Quebec, Nov. 28, 1831.	.50
	In Red.	
250	Stampless Cover.	
	Richmond, L.C., Nov. 1846...............	.75
	Hatley, Feb. 1848......	.75
	Black, Gananoque, Fe. '41................	
	Perth, My. '39........	
	Cobourg, Oc. '38; Little Nation, Fe. '39......	
	Georgeville...........	
a.	Ville-Drummond, Nov. 1846, with no curved lines...............	.75
	Prince Edward Island, Mar. 1870.	
251	In Black.	
	1865 1d. Orange B....	$4.50
	2d. Rose........	3.00
	3d. Blue........	4.00
	4d. Black.......	
	6d. Bluish G....	
	9d. Bluish Lilac.	
	1872 3c Rose.........	3.00
a.	No hyphen, to May, 1878.	
	North West Territories.	
252	In Black.	
	1881 1c. Yellow.......	.25
	2c.	.25
	3c.	.20
	Little Ridge, N.B., Apr. 1865.	
	1865 5c. New Bruns..	1.00
252x	Fort William, Lake Superior, Ja. '65, Blue...	
	Add to val. of cover....	.75
	General use. In Black.	
253	1868 3c.	.75
	1870 1c. Orange......	

Type	Found on	Value
	2c.	
	3c.	.75
	6c.	
	10c.	
	1875 5c. small.......	.25
	1880 1c. Yellow......	.15
	2c.	.20
	3c.	.10
	5c.	.20
	6c.	
	10c.	
	Blue, Cathcart, Ont., Sp. '94............	
	1894 5c.	1.00
a.	C. W. instead Ont.....	
	Ultramarine, Frankfort, Mr. '67............	.50
	In Violet.	
	1880 1c. Yellow......	.20
	2c.	.35
	3c.	.25
	5c.	.35
	6c.	
	10c.	
a.	"N.S. Canada" instead "Ont.".............	
	1868 ½c.	1.50

VICTORIA B.C. CANADA

253x

Type	Found on	Value
253x	1890 3c.	.40
	15c.	2.00
	In Black. General use. (Diam. varies.)	
254-5	1858 ½d.	
	3d.	7.00
	3d. Ribbed......	
	6d. 7½d.........	
	1859 1c.	
	5c.	.75
	10c.	
	1868 3c.	.75
	In Blue.	
	Claremont, U.C.	
	1864 5c.	1.50
	Yorkville, U.C., Ju. to Sp. 1866.	
	1866 12½c.............	4.50
	1868 3c.	1.50
	6c.	

Type	Found on	Value
	In Green.	
	Wroxeter, U.C., Ju. '62.	.85
	Hamilton Ap., 1869.	
	1869 3c.	3.50
	Yorkville, Ju. 1865.	
	1865 5c.	2.50
	Rosy Red, Toronto, C. W., Fe. '69	
	Center Blank or date written in.	
255a.	Stampless Cover	
	Black, Millbridge, C.W. No. '66	.20
	Black (Cancellation)	
	Cloyne, U.C.	
	1868 3c.	1.50
	1870 3c.	1.00
255a	CW or CE replaces UC, LC (Canada West, Canada East, Upper Canada, Lower Canada)	
	In Black. General use.	
	1858 ½d.	
	3d.	
	3d. Ribbed	
	6d. 7½d.	
	1859 1c.	
	5c.	
	10c.	
	1868 3c.	

255b

Type	Found on	Value
255b.	1870 1c. Orange	$1.75
	3c.	1.50
	"Ont." replaces "C.W."	
254-5		
	Brick-Red, Milton West Ju. '70	.50
	Black	.10
	Blue, Owen Sound, Oc. '82	
	Blue, Vankleek Hill, Mr. '71	
255	Stampless Cover.	
	In Red, with Free	1.00

Type	Found on	Value
256	"AM" or "PM" above date	
256a.	Black No. 59	
	In Black.	
	1859 1c.	
	5c.	
	10c.	
	12½c.	
	17c.	
	1864 2c.	
	1868 1c. Yellow	
	1c. Orange	
	1c. Brown	
	2c.	
	3c.	
	6c.	
	12½c.	
	1875 5c. (large)	
	5c. (small)	
	15c.	
	1870 1c. Orange	
	3c.	
	1872 1c.	
	2c.	
	3c.	
	1880 1c. Yellow	
	2c.	
	3c.	
	5c.	
	6c. Yellow Brown	
	10c.	
	1896 8c.	
	In Blue.	
	1859 1c.	
	5c.	
	1864 2c.	
	Struck through canvas. Toronto, Feb. 17, 1869 to Mar. 30th, 1869, in Black	
	1869 3c.	$1.25
	(Griffith, C.W., pen written late Nov. '61)	
256b.	"Q" replaces "CE"	

257 258

Type	Found on	Value
257	1871 3c.	$ .75
258	Black	

259

260

Type	Found on	Value
259	General use.	
	Black.	
	1859 5c.	
	1868 3c.	
	1870 3c.	
	Blue.	
	1870 3c.	
259a.	"Ont." or "Que." replaces CE, CW......	
260	1877 1c. Yellow......	$ .20
	3c.	.30

261

261	Stampless Cover.	
	Black.	
	With rate written in...	$1.25
	Blue.	
	St. John, Jy. 8, 1852...	

262

262	Stampless Cover.	
	Black.	

Type	Found on	Value
	With rate written in...	1.25
	1851 6d............	
a.	All letters in same type as Brunswick Jy. 23, 1855.........	

263

263	Backs of covers.......	
	Black.......	

264

264	General use...........	
	Black.......	
	1855 3d.	$7.00
	Red........	
	1855 3d.	9.00

265

265	Black.......	
	1859 1c.	
	5c.	1.00
	10c.	
	12½c.	
	1868 1c. Brown......	
	3c.	1.25
	6c.	

266

Type	Found on		Value
266	**New Brunswick.**		
	"Way Office".		
	Black.......		
	1872	2c.	
		3c.	$ .75

267 268

267	St. John and Yarmouth.		
	Black.......		
	1871	3c.	.75
268	Black.......		
	1876	3c.	.30

269 270

271 172

269	Black.	General use.
		Ju. 1879............
270	Black.	Ja. 1887......
271	Black.	Ap. 1882......
272	Black.	De. 1882......

280 281 285

286 286x 286xx

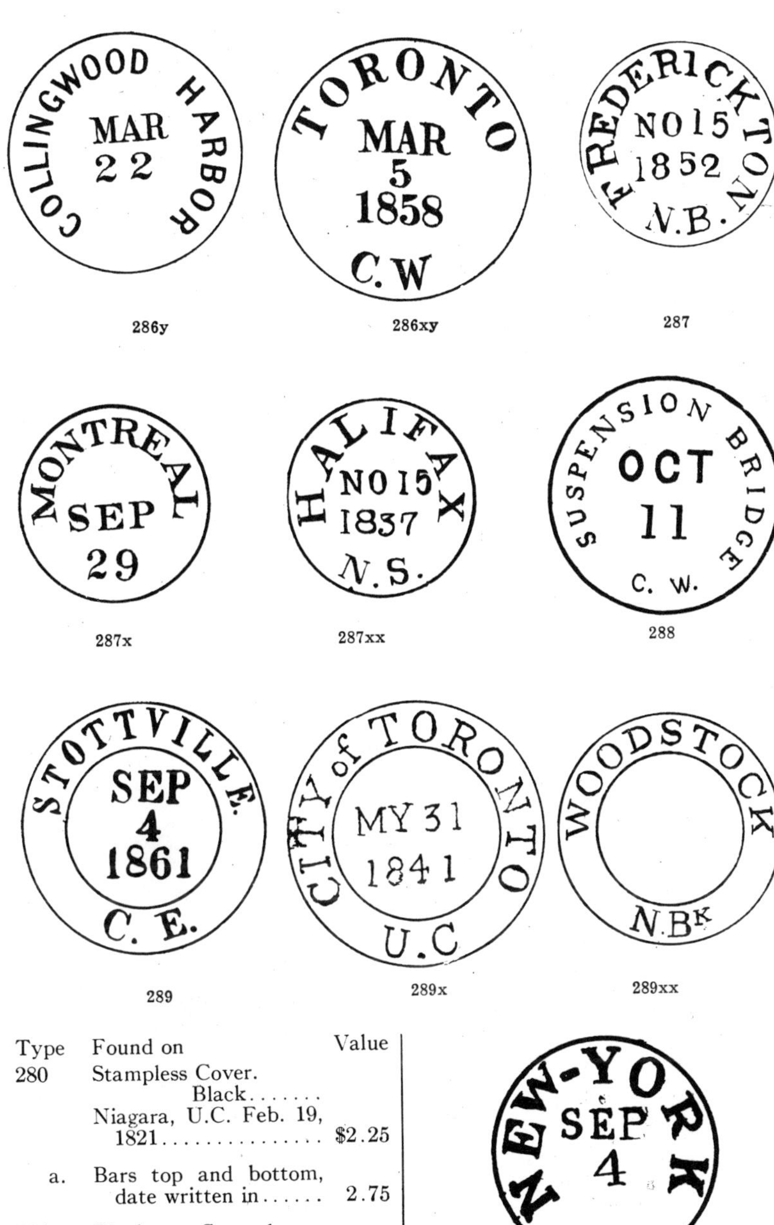

286y — 286xy — 287

287x — 287xx — 288

289 — 289x — 289xx

282

Type	Found on	Value
280	Stampless Cover. Black.......	
	Niagara, U.C. Feb. 19, 1821...............	$2.25
a.	Bars top and bottom, date written in......	2.75
281	Black. General use, 1856...............	
	Stratford, C.W., 1856..	

Type	Found on	Value
282	Nova Scotia and New Brunswick covers....	
	Black.......	
	1851 3d. Nova Scotia.	
	3d. New Brunswick......	
a.	Letters 4 mm. high and "10 Cts" at bottom..	
b.	"Boston" instead New York...............	
	Black.......	
	1851 3d. Nova Scotia.	
	3d. New Brunswick......	

283

Stampless Cover. Fort Garry via Fort Ripley. (Very rare)....

(In 1853 the establishment of a Post Office at Fort Ripley, Minnesota, by the U.S. P.O. Dept. led the settlers at Fort Garry (Winnipeg) to open an office and to exchange mails monthly. Four years later the U.S. extended the service to Pembina, N. Dakota, on the border of the Hudson's Bay Territory, and Fort Garry had the advantage of a shorter route as well as being free of the censorship of the Hudson's Bay Co. The Postmaster at Fort Garry having no Canadian postage stamps until 1857 (when a supply was sent out) made a cash charge to cover postage to Pembina and sold U.S. stamps to prepay the rate from Pembina to destination.

283	1857 3d.	
	7½d.	

284

Type	Found on	Value
284	Adds to val. of cover...	$ .50
285	Stampless Cover.	
	York, Au. '33, also with inner circle.........	
	Kingston. Nov. 1830.	
	Red, Brick-Red.	
	Adds to val. of cover...	.75
	Dated earlier than 1840	1.50

285x

285x	Adds to val. of cover....	.75
	With "3" in circle, black	2.00
	"Bytown, U.C., De. 23, 1839" brown-red....	
	Adds to value of cover.	.75

285xx

285xx	1882 1c.	.25
	3c.	.35
	2c. Regist......	.25
286	Stampless Cover.	
	Toronto, Hamilton, etc., from Ju. '41........	
	Black.......	$ .30
286a.	⅓ larger.............	.60

Type	Found on	Value
286x	St. John's, L.C., Black.	.30
286xx	Hamilton, red, adds to val. of cover........	.50
	Red.........	
	Toronto, Au. '60......	.40
286y.	Collingwood Harbour, Black, 1864.........	
286xy.	Toronto, March, 1858, Black..............	
287	Black. No. '51.......	.25
	Red. No. '51........	.50
287x	Black, Montreal.......	$1.00
287xx	Black. No. '37.......	
	Stampless Cover, rate written.............	.50

Type	Found on	Value
288	Black.	
	1854 3d.	7.00
	1859 5c.	1.50
	1864	
a.	N.Y. instead of C.W. Aug. 1854..........	
289	Stampless Cover.	
	Adds to value.........	.50
289x	Stampless Cover	
	Black, May 1841......	
	Toronto or Montreal (smaller size) in red, Oc. 1836...........	
	With Paid, rate written	$ .75

290

290x

290xx

290xxx

290xy

291

291x

291xx

294

292

293

297

Type	Found on	Value
289xx	Stampless Cover.	
	Dec. 1839; Stouffville, U.C. Au. '48; St. Andrew's, N.B., Ju. '41 Black.......	.50
	Haldimand, U.C., Au. '47; Asphodel, Fe. '57; (outer circle bent) Red........	1.75
290	Stampless Cover.	
	Rate stamped or written................	
	Black.......	
	Kingsey, L.C., Ap. 1846	.50
	Port Hope, Mr. 1853...	.50
	Vienna, U.C., Feb. 1845	
	Red........	
	Mohawk, Jy. 1840.....	.75
	Dannville, L.C., No. 1846...............	.75
	Stouffville, Nov. 1846 to Aug. 1848..........	
a.	Typeset date, Sp. 1839.	
b.	35 or 37 mm. diam....	
	Black.......	
	Toronto..............	.50
c.	31 mm. diam.........	
	Black.......	
	York, Ap. 1858 to Oc. 1861................	.50
290x	Stampless Cover.	
	Adds to value.........	.50
290xx	Stampless Cover.	
	Red, adds to value....	1.00
290xxx	Stampless Cover.	
	Black, Au. '38, adds to value.............	.85
290xy	Stampless Cover.	
	Black, Ju. '41, adds to value.............	.85
291	Stampless Cover.	
	Black.......	
	Riviere du Loup, Mar. 1848...............	.75

Type	Found on	Value
291x	Oshawa Money Order Office, Oc. '82.......	
	Adds to value of cover.	.20
291xx	Montreal Post Office, Black.............	.60
292	**Prince Edward Island.**	
	De. 1863...........	
	Black.......	
	1863 2d. Perf. 9......	
	3d. Perf. 9......	
	6d. Perf. 9......	
	1863 1d. Brown Orange	....
	2d. Rose........	
	3d. Blue........	
	4d. Black.......	
	6d. Bluish Green.	
	9d. Bluish Lilac.	
a.	Double lined circle De. 1864..............	
294	Stampless Black Cover.	.50
	Ingersol Ju. '57.......	
	Quebec Oc. '58........	
	Stamps.	
	1859 1c.	.75
	Red........	
	St. Hyacinthe, C.E. Au. 1857...............	
a.	Month followed by date and year.	
	Red. Quebec Au. '60..	
aa.	Letter above month.	
	Toronto May 4, 1856 "A"...............	
	Owen Sound, May 8, 1867 "A"..........	
	Port Hope, Oct. 14, 1857 "B"..........	
	City of Ottawa, June 10, 1858 "C".......	
	"B" 22 July, 1859.....	
	Cancellation.	
	1859 5c.	.85

295

Type	Found on	Value
	British postmark.	
295	1864 2c.	$12.00
	1865 1c. (Glasgow) ...	2.00

296

296	This type supplied to a few offices only, did not wear well and had a short life.	
	Add to val. of cover....	
296	London, Canada, Aug. 17, 1857............	$ .75
296a.	London, C.W., Apr. 28 (larger)............	.75
296b.	Barrie, C.W., "B-29-Jun." solid "1857" double figures.......	.58

296cc

296cc.	Bentinck, B., 1859, Feb. 16, C.W., solid......	1.00

296c

Type	Found on	Value
296c.	Bentinck, C.W., "1861-Jan.-7" solid........	1.50
	1861 12½c..........	4.00
296d.	Cobourg, C.W. "C-Jul-13" solid "1869" double, single circle.....	.95
296e.	Cobourg, C.W., "A" double "Jan. 17-1857" solid, single circle....	.95
296f.	Cobourg, C.W., "A" double "Jul. 12," solid, "1858" double......	.95
296g.	Hamilton, C.W. "Aug.-5" solid "1857" double	.95
296h.	Three Rivers, L.C., "D-24-Aug." solid, "1859" double.............	.85
296i.	Owen Sound "C-19-Aug.-1856" solid "C. W." solid...........	.95
296j.	Quebec, C.E., "Nov.-5" solid "1862" double................	.85
296k.	Quebec, C.E., "13 Dec." solid "1857" double, "C.E." solid........	.85
296l.	Port Hope............	
296m.	Brantford............	

298

299

Prince Edward Island.

298	Black. (Reduced drawing)...............	
	1863 3d. Perf. 9.. ...	
299	Black. 1871.........	

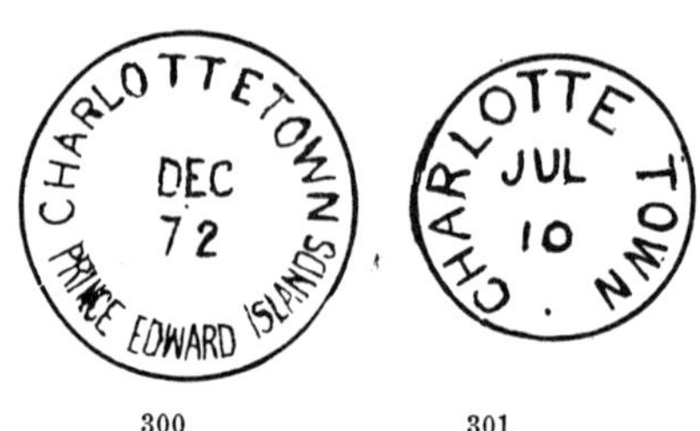

300 301

Type	Noted on	Value
300	Black. 1872..........	
301	Red Brown...........	
	Diagonal half of 6c. used with 2c. (This cancellation is thought to be a European counterfeit.)	
	1872 1c. Orange......	
	2c. Ultramarine.	
	3c. Rose........	
	4c. Yel. Green...	
	6c. Black.......	
	12c. Mauve......	

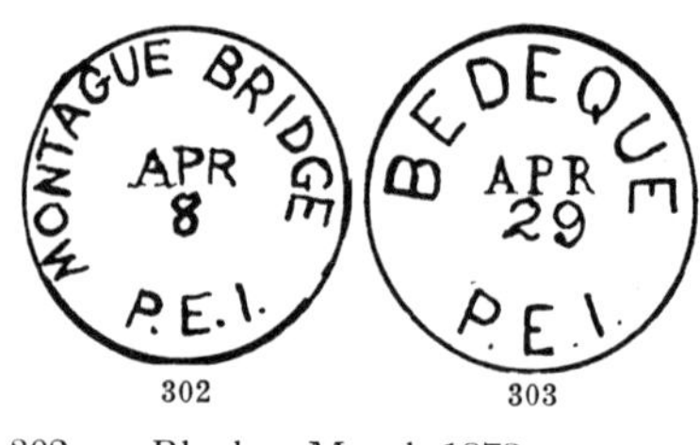

302 303

302	Black. March 1873...	
	1872 3c. Rose........	
303	Black. April 1878....	
	Canada.	
	1878 1c. Yellow......	$ .10
	3c.	.10

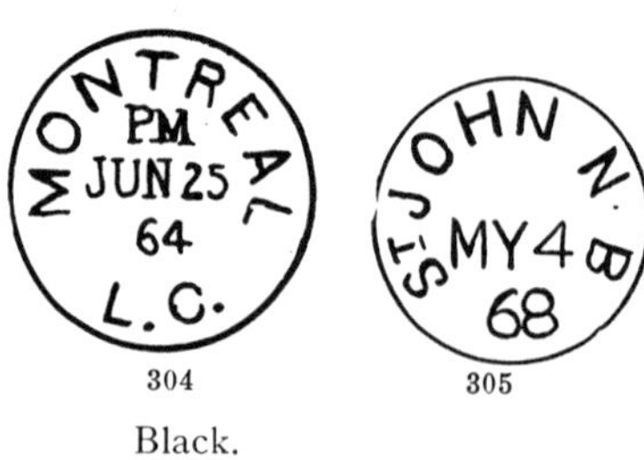

304 305

	Black.	
304	1859 5c.	$1.25

Type	Found on	Value
305	Black. General use, May 1860.	
	1860 5c.	.60
	1c.	
	10c.	
	17c.	
	12½c.	
	1864 2c.	
	1868 3c.	.80
	1870 1c. Orange......	
	2c.	
	3c.	.80
	Blue.	
	1870 3c.	1.00

306 307

306	Black. General use, May '64.	
	1867 5c. Beaver......	.60
	1c.	
	5c.	
	10c.	
	12½c.	
	17c.	
	1864 2c.	
	1868 3c.	.80
	1870 1c. Orange......	
	3c.	.80
	Blue.	
	1867 1c.	
	5c. Beaver......	1.00
	10c.	
	12½c.	
	17c.	
	1864 2c.	
	1868 3c.	1.00
	1870 3c.	1.10
a.	Letters "A", "B" or "C" above month........	
307	Black. General use.	
	1868 5c. Blue Nova Scotia..............	$1.50
	Canada.	
	1868 1c. Orange......	
	1c. Yellow......	
	1c. Brown......	
	2c.	
	3c.	.80
	6c.	
	12½c.	
	15c.	
	1870 1c. Orange......	

Type		Value
	3c.	
	Blue.	
	1870 3c.	1.10
a.	"A" above month, Oc. 1867.	
	Nova Scotia.	
	Black.	
	1867 1c. Black.......	
	2c. Grey-Purple.	
	5c. Blue........	
	8½c. Green.......	
	12½c. Black.......	
	Canada.	
	Black.	
	1868 1c. Brown......	
	1c. Yellow......	
	1c. Orange......	
	2c.	
	3c.	
	6c.	
	12½c.	
	15c.	
	1875 5c. (Large).....	
b.	"AM" above date. Sept. 1870.	
	Black.	
	1870 1c. Orange......	
	3c.	

308

309

Type		Value
308	**British Columbia.**	
	Date stamps (Type 308, 309) were introduced early in 1868 and were supplied through the British Consul at San Francisco.	
	Black.	
	1869 5c. Perf. 14.....	$12.00
309	Blue.	
	1869 5c. Perf. 14.....	12.50
	Black.	
	1869 5c. Perf. 14.....	12.50

309x

Type		Value
309x	Black. Duplex, with Cog Wheel cancellation.	
	1865. British Columbia and Vancouver Island stamps.............	

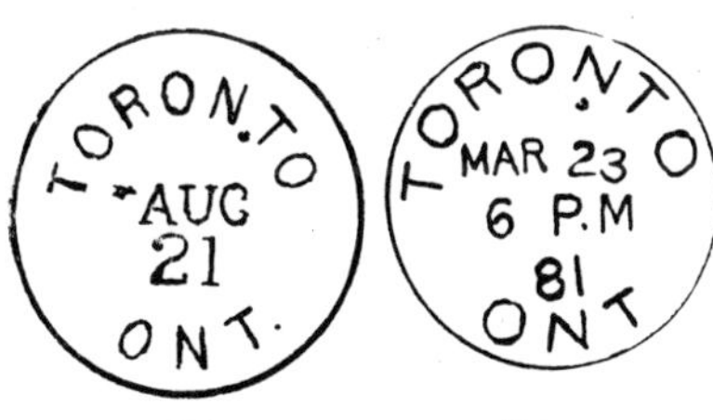

310 311

312

314

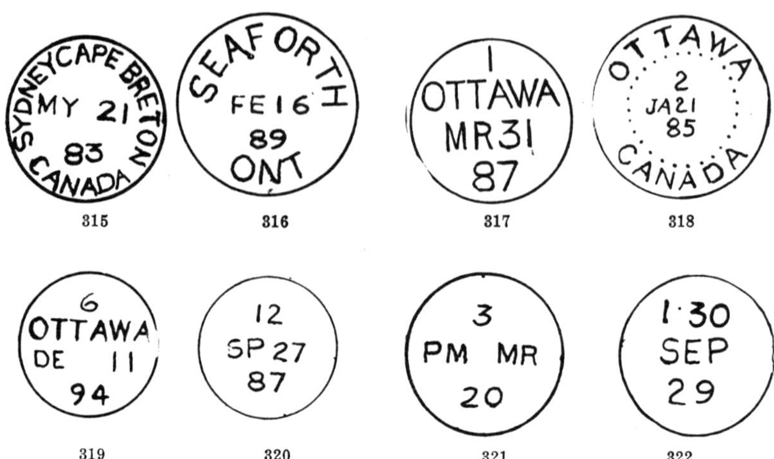

315 316 317 318

319 320 321 322

Type	Noted on	Value
310	Black. Aug. 1874.	
	1874 3c.	.30

Type	Noted on	Value
311	Black. Mar. 1881.	
	1881 3c.	.15
	8c. Registered...	
312	Black. Apr. 1899.	
	General use...........	

EUGENIA
2 JY
1890

313

313	Black. July 1890.	
	1890 1c. Yellow......	.30
	2c.	
	3c.	.35
	2c. Registered...	
314	Black. Oct. 1881.	
	1c. Yellow......	
	2c.	
	3c.	
	5c.	
	6c.	
314	1881 10c.	
	15c.	
	5c. (Small)......	

Type	Found on	Value
	1897 ½c. 4-Leaf......	
	1c.	
	2c.	
	3c.	
	5c.	
	1897 ½c. Jubilee......	
	1c. "	
	2c. "	
	3c. "	
	5c. "	
	1897 1c. Q.V. Numeral	
	2c.	
	3c.	
	5c.	
	Purple. Oct. 1905.	
	Winnipeg.	
	1897 $1 Jubilee......	$3.50
	$2 "	3.00
	$3 "	9.00
	$4 "	9.00
	$5	9.00
315	Black. May 1883.	
	1883 1c. Yellow......	.05
	3c.	.10
316	Black. General use.	
	1889 3c.	.05
	Carmine. Seaforth	
	1889 1c. Yellow......	.10
	2c.	.15
	3c.	.20
	5c.	.50
317	Ottawa, July 1876.	
	Black.	
	1876 1c. Yellow......	$ .10

Type	Noted on	Value
	2c.	.20
	3c.	.10
	5c.	.20
318	Ottawa, Jan. 1885.	
	Black.	
	1885 1c. Yellow......	.10
	2c.	.20
	3c.	.10
	5c.	.20
	10c. Magenta	
319	Ottawa, Feb. 8, 1873.	
	Black.	
	1873 1c. Yellow......	.10
	2c.	.20
	3c.	.10
	1875 5c.	.20
	1893 20c.	.60
	Daters or Date Stamps.	
320	Black. General use as backstamp.	
	1887 1c.	.10
	2c.	.15
	3c.	.10
	5c.	.20
321	Black. (Several variations.)	
	1890 1c.	.10
	3c.	.15
	5c.	.20
322	Ottawa, Sept. 1875.	
	Black.	
	1875 1c.	.10
	3c.	.15
	5c.	.20
a.	Through cloth.	
	Toronto Sept. 1875.	
	Black.	
	1875 3c.	.25

322x

322x	Newfoundland	1.00
	1894 5c. Bright Blue..	

St. John. N*B*
August, 18, 1804

323

Type	Found on	Value
323	Stampless Cover.	
	St. John, N. B., Aug. 1804.	
	Black.	
	Rate stamped or written	$6.00

WINDSOR.C.W.
6 MAR 1844

324

324	Stampless Cover.	
	Windsor, Mar. 1844.	
	Red.	
	Rate stamped or written	5.00

QUEBEC
3. SEP1802

325

325	Stampless Cover.	
	Quebec, Sept. 1802.	
	Black.	
	Rate stamped or written	5.00

Great Britain
Ireland

326

326 **Vancouver Island.**
The Postmaster affixed 2½d. stamps on envelopes to make up the rate to Great Britain and Ireland, and cancelled them with Type 326, keeping a supply available to be sold as needed. The stamps also received the regular cancellation of the office in most cases, at time of mailing. Black or Blue.
1860 2½d. Br. Col. and V.I ....
1869 5c. Perf. 14 Br. Col.......

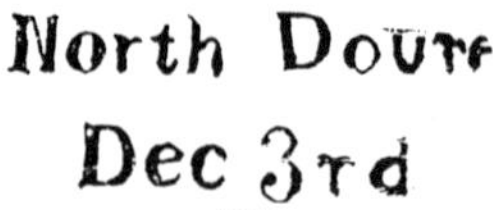

North Douro
Dec 3rd

327

Type		Value
327	North Douro, Dec. 3, 1863.	
	Stampless Cover.	
	Brown, J. '64	$2.25
	Black. (Cancellation.)	
	1863 5c. Beaver	2.50
	10c.	4.00

EUGENIA

328	Black.	
	1859 5c. Beaver	$1.50
	10c.	
	12½c.	
	1868 3c.	2.50
	1870 3c.	1.75
	1876 1c. Yellow	
	3c.	

Harwich

329

329	Black.	
	1859 5c. Beaver	1.50
	10c.	
	12½c.	
	1868 3c.	2.50
	1870 3c.	1.50
a.	Upper Case Letters. Violet.	

M. Stoutenburg

329x

329x	1878 3c.	.75
	Black. Ja. '75.	
	1875 2c.	1.75
	3c.	1.75

Berlin

330

Type		Value
330	Green. (Berlin, Ont., Kitchener since 1915).	
	1890 1c.	.75
	3c.	.75

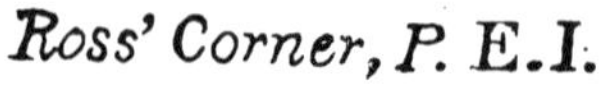

Ross' Corner, P. E. I.

331

331	Black.	
	1897 1c. Jubilee	1.00

Halifax

332

332	Black.	
	1880 1c.	.40
	3c.	.40
	1893 8c.	
	10c.	
	1880 15c.	
a.	Larger.	

ACTON

333

333	Black.	
	1880 3c.	$ .50
	2c. Carmine Regtrd.	.75

QUVOI

334

334	Quyon (Y sometimes appears as V).	
	Black.	
	1880 3c.	.60

KING

334x

Type		Value
334x	**King, Ont.**, Fe., '87.	
	1887 1c.	1.50
	3c.	1.75

INVE

335

335	Inverness, P.E.I., Sept. 1892.	
	Black.	
	1892 1c. Yellow......	

NCH

336

336	**Fenchurch** (?) London, England.	
	Black.	
	1851 1s. Nova Scotia .	

MILTON.

336x

336x	**Milton West, Ont.**, Mr. '91.	
	1891 3c.	.25

HALIFAX

337

337	Used by Stratford, Jy. 1887; Montreal, May, 1890; Quebec, May, 1890; Fredericton, Ju., 1891.	
	Black.	
	1887 1c.	$ .20
	3c.	.20
	10c.	
	1893 8c.	.40
	Toronto.	
	Black.	
	1897 3c. Jubilee......	.30

TORONTO

338

Type		Value
338	Barrie; Belleville, Oc., 1893; Brantford, Fe., 1894; Brampton, De., 1893; Charlottetown; Halifax, Mr., 1879; Kingston (3 sizes), De., 1882; London ; Montreal ; Ottawa, Ju., 1891; Quebec; Renfrew, De., 1893; Stratford; St. John; Sherbrooke, Ap., 1893; Toronto, Mr. 1879; Three Rivers; Vancouver; Victoria; Winnipeg.	
	Black.	
	Toronto.	
	1879 3c.	$ .35
338	1897 3c. 4-Leaf......	$ .25

19
APL 2
01

339

339	Used as duplex with bar cancellation, Type 367x, Toronto, April to October, 1901.	
	1897 3c. 4-Leaf......	$ .10
	½c. Q.V. Numeral........	.05
	1c.	.05
	2c. Purple......	.05
	3c.	.05
	5c.	
	6c.	
	8c.	
	10c.	
	20c.	

CARRIER Nº 1 ZOC 29 NORTH·DIST

340

CARRIERS·STAMP 1 APL 9 HEAD·OFFICE·

341

340	**Montreal.**	
	Black. 1880.........	
341	**Montreal.**	
	Black. 1877.........	

342

343

Type	Found on	Value
342	1893 3c.	.40
343	**Nova Scotia**	
	Green.	
	1877 3c.	1.00

OVAL TYPES

344

Type	Found on	Value
344	**Vancouver Island.**	
	STAMPLESS COVER.	
	Used as a Frank.	

345

Type	Found on	Value
345	**Vancouver Island.**	
	STAMPLESS COVER.	
	Used as a Frank.	
	Blue.	
	Cancellation.	
	1865 5c. V.I. Perf. . . .	
	1867 2c. B.C.	

347

Type	Found on	Value
347	**Vancouver Island.**	
	Stampless Cover.	
	Used as a Frank.	
	Blue.	
	Red	
	Used as Cancellation.	
	Red.	
	1860 2½d. Br. Col.	

FRANKS

On Vancouver Island four varieties of handstamps were used to frank letters before and after stamps were introduced. Some of the postmarks used for the Colony of British Columbia were used as franks before and after the introduction of stamps.

348

Type	Noted on	Value
348	Noted on cover to New York prepaid with 3d. Blue, via San Francisco.	
	Blue........	

349

349	Stampless Cover.	
	Used as a Frank.	
	Blue........	
	Used as a Cancellation.	
	Blue.	
	1865 5c. V.I. Perf.	
	1860 2½d. Br. Col......	
	Black.	
	3d. B.C.........	$7.50

350

Type	Found on	Value
350	**British Columbia,** Jan. 19, 1865. Used appearing on back of cover.	
	Black.......	
	Blue........	

351

351	Stampless Cover.	
	Sept. 24, 1818.	
	Rate stamped or written.	$4.00

352

352	Black.	
	1868 3c. Canada.....	2.25
	12½c. Canada.....	
	1872 15c.	
	(An oval type cancellation has been noted in blue on the Prince Edward Island "cents" stamps, reading "Summerside Bank Summerside" with date in three lines in center "Jun. 18, 1873.")	

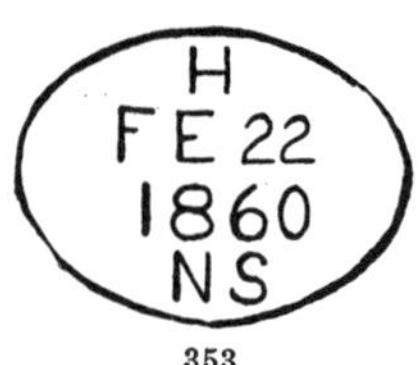

353

Type		Value
353	Backstamp used at Halifax. Black.......	

354

354	Parcel Post. Black.	
	1895 8c.	1.50
	15c.	3.50

355

355	Black.	
	1872 3c. Rose........	1.00
	1880 1c. Yellow......	.20
	3c.	.25
	15c.	

356

Type		Value
356	Black. 1903.	
	1303 2c. Purple, Q.V. Num......	$0.10
	2c. Carm. Q. V. Num......	.10
	1c. Edward.....	.10
	2c. Edward.....	.10
	5c. Edward.....	.20
	10c. Edward.....	.30

357

357	Black.	
	Purple. July, 1894.	
	1894 1c. Yellow......	.15
	3c.	.15

358

358 Oct., 1888.

Toronto and Sub Offices. Letters A to W.
Black.

1888 1c. Yellow......	$0.30
3c.	.30

St. John, N.B.
Black.......

Fredericton, N. B., without letter in center.
Black.......

Oshawa.
Black.......

a. Larger................

359

Type		Value
359	**Montreal** or **Quebec.**	
	Black.	
	1890 1c. Yellow......	.15
	3c.	.15
a.	Double size, single line, stars at ends. Violet	
	1893 8c. Grey........	.35

360

360	Black. April, 1880.	
	1880 1c. Yellow......	.50
	3c.	.50

361

361	Black.	
	1890 3c.	.50
a.	Bars straight, letters 6½ mm. high...........	

362 363

362 **Kingston** or **Halifax.** Oct., 1881. Black.

Type		Value
	1881 1c.	.15
	3c.	.25
	1883 15c.	
	1887 3c. Carmine Rose	1.00
363	Black.	
	1880 1c.	$0.25
	3c.	.35

364 365

364	Black.	
	1880 1c	.25
	3c.	.25
	10c.	
365	Used by Kingston, Aug. 1880; Aylmer, Dec., 1880; Toronto North, Toronto East, Toronto West, Dec., 1880; St. Catharines (bars heavier), Ap., 1880; Montreal and Quebec.	
	Black.	
	1880 1c. Yellow......	$0.25
	3c.	.25

366 367

366	May, 1887.	
	Black.	
	1887 1c.	$0.25
	3c.	.30
	3c. Carmine Rose	.90
a.	All bars complete, May, 1880.	
	1880 1c.	.25
	3c.	.30
367	Black.	
	1880 3c.	.40

367x

Type			Value
367x	Apr., 1901 to Oct., 1901, duplex with Type 339.		
	1901	Stamps of issue	

368

369

Type			Value
368-9	Roller, in general use, for parcel cancellation. Numbers have no philatelic significance.		
	Black.		
	1880	1c.	$0.10
		3c.	.10
		5c.	.15
		10c.	
		15c.	
	1891	15c.	
	1893	8c.	
		20c.	.60
		50c.	.60
	All succeeding issues, incl. Jubilee high values, are found with Types 368-9.		

370

Type			Value
370	Black.		
	1887	3c.	.15
		3c. Carmine Rose	.50
		5c.	.25
		6c.	
	1893	8c.	
		10c.	
		15c.	

371

372

Type			Value
371	Black.		
	1881	1c.	$0.10
		2c.	.15
		3c.	.10
		5c.	.20
		6c.	1.00
		10c.	
371	Blue.		
	1881	3c.	$0.35
		5c.	.45
372	Black.		
	1891	1c.	.10
		2c.	.15
		3c.	.10
		5c.	.20
		6c.	
		10c.	
		15c.	
	Blue		
	1893	3c.	.50
	Violet.		
	1894	3c.	.40

373

Type		Value
373	General use. Sept., 1893. Black.	
	1893 1c.	.10
	3c.	.10
	5c.	.20
	6c.	
	8c.	
	10c.	
	15c.	
	20c.	
	50c.	

374

374 General use. May, 1892.
Black.
All values.

375

375 General use. July, 1891.
Black.
All values.

376

Type
376 Used by Hamilton Toronto, London.
Black.
All values incl. 15c.

377

377 Black. 1906.
All values.

378

378 Black. 1907.
All values.

COMMERCIAL AND BANK CANCELLATIONS

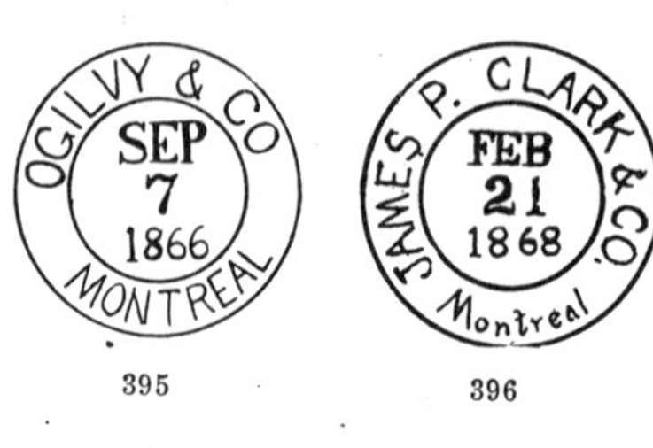

395 396

Type 395, 396 — Some of the larger offices, often bank offices, stamped mail upon receipt and in some instances portions of the marking fell upon the stamp. Black or Blue.

397

Type		Value
397	Black.	
	1868 3c.	$1.25

BRITISH COLUMBIA EXPRESS COMPANY MARKINGS

400

Type		Values
400	Black.	
	Adds to value of cover.	$5.00
	Red.	
	Adds to value.........	6.50

401

Type		Value
401	Blue.	
	1860 2½d.	5.00
	Adds to value of cover.	
a.	"Barnard's British Columbia Express" with thinner letters.	
	Blue........	

402

402	Black.	
	Stampless Cover......	25.00
	Adds to value of cover.	5.00

403

Type
403 Black.......

404

404 Black.
Adds to value of cover.
Red.
Adds to value of cover.

405

405 Green. Nov., 1885.
Used on Wells Fargo special envelope printed in Black.

"PAID, Wells Fargo & Co., over our California & Coast Routes, Victoria, Vancouver Island."

1885	3c.	$2.50
	3c. On cover....	10.00
1877	6c. Yel. Brown..	3.50
	15c.	6.00
Adds to value of cover.		2.50

405a. Similar type, date type set in center for San Francisco.
Blue.
5c. V. I. Perf.......
2½d. B.C.........

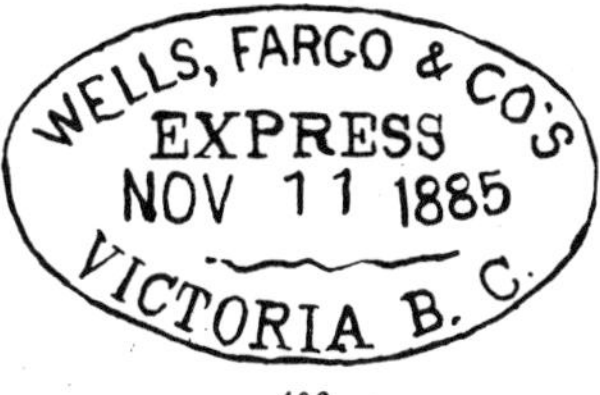

406

406 Violet. Nov. 11, 1885.
Used on special envelope, printed in Black, "PAID, Wells Fargo & Co's Express, over our lines in the United States, Victoria, Vancouver Island."

1885	3c. off cover....	$2.50
	3c. on cover.....	10.00
Adds to value of cover.		2.50

SHIP, STEAMBOAT AND PACKET POSTMARKS

Mail carried by ship was distinguished from other mail by a special marking, such as "Ship," "Ship Letter," etc. The purely Canadian markings are those on letters from Quebec to Montreal, via the St. Lawrence River, or from Montreal to Kingston, York, Queenston, etc., via the St. Lawrence and Lake Ontario. Letters between Halifax, St. John, Boston, etc., bore ship markings.

The earliest types are the straight-line "Ship Letter" markings, which have been noted as early as 1803.

Ship letter.

425

Type
New Brunswick. 1803.
425 Stampless Cover.
Black.
Rate stamped or written................ $2.50

STEAM BOAT

426

Three Rivers, L. C. 1817.
426 Stampless Cover.
Black.
Rate stamped or written................ 2.50

STEAM BOAT

427

427 **Kingston,** Aug., 1840.
Stampless Cover.
Red.
Rate stamped or written 2.50

STEAM·BOAT

428

New Brunswick.
428 Stampless Cover, 1851
Black.
Rate stamped or written 2.00
Cancellation.
1851 3d.
and 6d. ....

STEAMBOAT

429

429 Stampless Cover.
Black.
Rate stamped or written $1.00
Cancelling Stamps. Black.
1859 5c. Beaver...... $4.50
1855 3d. Beaver...... 12.00
12d. ....

STEAM BOAT

430

430 **Niagara,** U. C. to New York.
Aug. 8, 1854.
Red.
Adds to value of cover. 5.00

SHIP SHIP

431 432

Type		Value
431	Black.	
	Adds to value of cover.	$1.00
1870	2c.	1.75
432	Black.	
	New Brunswick, 1859.	
	Adds to value of cover.	1.00
	Cancelling Stamps.	
	1870 1c. Orange......	2.75

BY-CANADIAN
PACKET

433

433 Black. 1859.
Adds to value of cover. $1.00

GLASGOW PACKET
PAID
OC 23
1866

434

434 Black. Oct., 1866 to May, 1876.
Adds to value of cover. 1.50
1859 12½c. 5.00
a. Reading "COL. PAID"

SHIP LETTER
MA AT SEA
MY 24 1864

435

435 Backstamp on mail received at Halifax, N. S., May. 1864.
Black.......

SHIP-LETTER
DUE ______ CTS

436

436 Black. March, 1879.
Adds to value of cover. 1.00

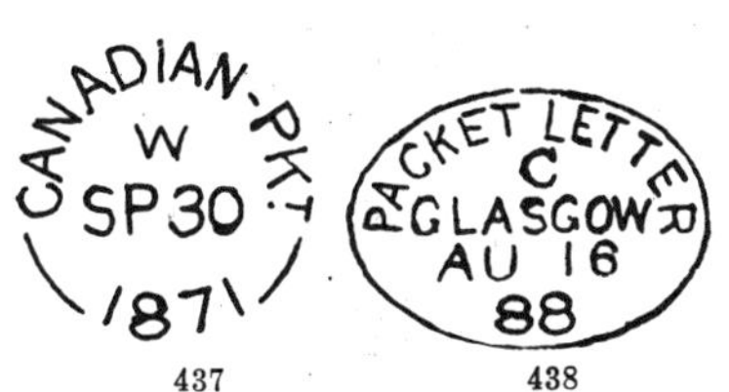

437 438

Type	Found on	Value
437	Black. 1868.	
	1868 6c.	5.00
	Adds to value of cover	1.00
438	Black. August, 1888.	
	Adds to value of cover.	1.00

439

439 Black. 1840.
Stampless Cover.
Rate stamped or written $5.00

440

440 Stampless Cover. 1840.
Rate stamped or written.

Black.......	5.00
Red........	6.00

441

Type		Value
441	Stampless Cover. 1842.	
	Rate stamped or written.	
	Black.......	5.00

442

442 Stampless Cover. Ju., '49.
Rate stamped or written.
Black.

Kingston (Numeral 1, 3 or 4)	$3.00
Quebec (Numeral 3 or 8)	2.50
Montreal (Numeral 3)	2.50
Toronto (Numeral 5 or 6)	3.00
(Majority are without numeral).	
Red.	
Kingston............	4.00
On stamped covers.	
Adds to value. Black.	2.50
Red........	4.00

As cancellation.

Black.
Montreal.

1852 3d. Beaver......	12.00
12d.	

443

443 Stampless Cover. (Sp. 5, 1855)
Rate stamped or written.

Black.......	3.00
Brown-Red..	6.00

Type		Value
	On Stamped Cover.	
	Adds to value, Black . .	3.00
	Brown-Red . .	4.00
a.	No numeral "5"	

444

444 Stampless Cover. May, 1852, Quebec or Montreal.

Rate stamped or written.

Black 2.50

On Stamped Cover.

Adds to value 2.50

a. With numeral "6" or "8" (Oc., 1853).

445

445 Stampless Cover. Ju., 1854. Rate stamped or written date usually written in. Noted on letters from Niagara, Oakville, Toronto, etc., to Montreal or points East of Kingston.

Black $3.25

On Stamped Cover.

Adds to value 3.25

446

Type		Value
446	On Stamped Cover. Red.	
	Adds to value	1.00
	1857 $7\frac{1}{2}$d.	
	10d.	

1860 $12\frac{1}{2}$c. **Nova Scotia**

447

447 Black.

Adds to value of cover . $0.50

448

448 The boat carrying mail from the mainland to Prince Edward Island was equipped with a special department for mail, which was sorted on the way, and loose letters postmarked. "Winter Mail" was carried on icebreakers, the first being the Northern Light. The cancellation above was used on later boats, the Stanley, the Minto and the Earl Grey.

The latter two were sold to Russia during the war for use out of Archangel. Winter mail is now carried on the Canadian Government Steamer Prince Edward, but mails are not sorted on board, as the mail is conveyed across in mailcars on board. The earlier boats did not have facilities for carrying cars.

March, 1912. Red.

1913	1c. Green.......	$0.15
	2c. Carmine....	.15
	5c. Blue........	.25
	7c. Olive bistre..	.25
Adds to value of cover.		.50

448x

449

448x Black. Ju., 1888.
Adds to value of cover. .25

449 Black.
Adds to value of cover. .25

450

450 Backstamped on cover New Westminster to Sumox, Fraser River, Jan. 18, 1881, prepaid with pair 3c.
Violet.
Adds to value of cover. 5.00

451

Type		Value
451	Black.	
	Adds to value of cover.	$5.00
	As cancellation.	
	1896 3c.	5.00
a.	"Steamer" in small type, "SAGUENAY" in large type, June 30, 1892.	
	Blue.	
	Adds to value of cover.	5.00
	As cancellation.	
	1892 5c. Olive Grey..	5.00
b.	"Steamer Regina" in straight lines, Aug. 31, 1899.	
	Blue.	
	Adds to value of cover.	5.00
	As cancellation.	
	1899 3c. Carmine....	5.00

452

452	Rubber stamp.	
	Violet.	
	Adds to value of cover.	$3.75
	As cancellation.	
	1901 2c. Q. V. Numeral........	3.75

453
(Incomplete)

Type		Value
453	Rubber stamp. (The "Princess Louise" plies between Vancouver and Victoria, B. C.)	
	Violet.	
	Adds to value of cover .	3.75
	As cancellation.	
	1897 2c. Carmine Q.V. Num.	3.75

454

454	The Flagship of the German High Seas Fleet visiting Halifax Harbor, used above distinctive cancellation usually on envelopes of the "Nova Scotia Provincial Exhibition, Halifax" with flag printed in Blue and Yellow in corner.	
	Black.	
	Adds to value of cover .	$5.00
	As cancellation.	
	1903 1c. King Edward	5.00
	½c. 4-Leaf	5.00
	½c. Q. V. Numeral	5.00

455

Type		Value
455	Violet. 1917. Canadian Pacific Ocean Services.	
	Adds to value of cover .	1.75

456

457

456 457	Mail posted at sea on a ship discharging mail at Halifax received Type 456; if mail taken off at Liverpool, it would receive Type 457. Belfast, St. John, N.B., and Quebec, used this marking. April, 1903 to 1927.	
	Black.	
	1903 1c. King Edward	$1.00
	2c. King Edward	1.00
	1912 1c. Green, George	.90
	2c. Carmine, George. . . .	.90

458

459

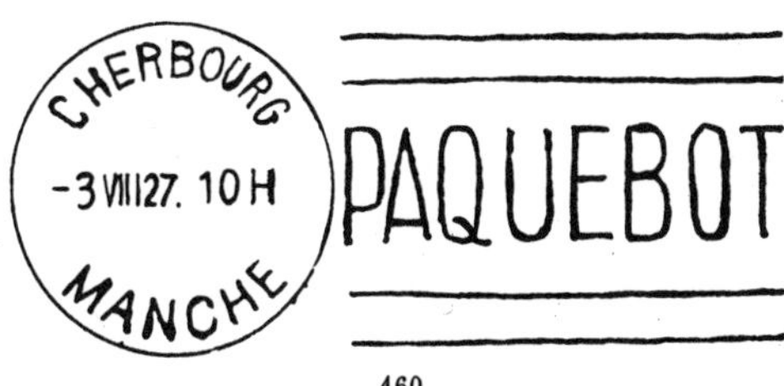

460

Type		Value
658	Black. Jan., 1923.	
	Adds to value of cover.	$0.50
459	Black. June, 1927.	
	Adds to value of cover.	.40
460	Black. June, 1927.	
	Adds to value of cover.	.40

MILITARY CANCELLATIONS

470

Type		Value
470	On covers from Canadian soldiers, usually accompanied by British postmark "Field P.O. British Army, S. Africa" in circle with date, in Black Used as a Frank	
	Pale Red	
	Cover................	$10.00

471

Type		Value
471	Used as a Frank Black Cover.	5.00
471	As cancellation Black.	
	1914 1c. Green, George. . . .	$1.00
	2c. Carmine, George. . . .	1.00
	1915 1c. War Tax. . . .	1.25
	2c. War Tax. . . .	1.25
	1916	
	2c. & 1c. Carmine.	1.00
	2c. & 1c. Brown	1.00
a.	Used as a Frank with British Field Post Office cancellation in Black and triangular Censor's mark in Pink	$2.50
b.	Used as a Frank with British Field Post Office cancellation in Black.	1.50

ROYAL REVIEW
EXHIBITION PARK CAMP
OCT 11 1901
TORONTO
ARMY POST OFFICE.

472

Type		Value
472	Rubber handstamp. Purple.	
	1901 1c. Q. V. Numeral.	1.25
	2c. Q. V. Numeral.	1.25

BRIGADE CAMP.
JU 16
86
MIL. DIST. No 4.

473

473	Black. Adds to value of cover .	$0.35

474

474	Black. Adds to value of cover .	.35
a.	Aldershot Camp, N.S., Jy., 1914.	

475

475	Black. Adds to value of cover .	.35

On Mail to British Isles from Canada, usually in Red.

485 486

Type	
485 486	These markings indicated rate fully prepaid.

487 488

489 490

Type		
487	Red.	
	1860 12½c. **Nova Scotia**	
488	Red. July, 1858.	
	Adds to value of cover	$0.25

Type		Value
	As cancellation.	
	1859 12½c.	3.75
	17c.	
	1868 3c.	2.00
	6c.	
	12½c.	
	15c.	
	1870 3c.	2.00
	1875 5c. (large)	
	1860, 12½c., N.S.	
489	Red. 1859.	
	Adds to value of cover	.25
	As cancellation.	
	1859 12½c.	3.75
	17c.	
	1868 3c.	2.00
	6c.	
	12½c.	
	15c.	
	1870 3c.	2.00
	1875 5c. (large)	
	1863 12½c. **Nova Scotia**	
	1867 25c., B.C., Perf. 14	
a.	Similar type noted as late as 1900. Brown.	
490	Red. 1859.	
	Adds to value of cover	$0.25
	As cancellation.	
	1859 10c.	.375
	12½c.	.375
	17c.	
	1868 3c.	2.00
	6c.	
	1875 8c. Regist	12.00
	1861 12½c. **Nova Scotia**	

"CANADA" AND "UNITED STATES" MARKINGS

An extract from the first postal convention between Canada and the United States signed May 25, 1851, reads: "Offices designated for the despatch and receipt of U. S. mails on the side of Canada will stamp "CANADA" upon all letters sent into the United States for delivery . . ."

Letters from the United States to Canada were stamped "United States," etc.

The rates were usually embodied in these markings. Letters to the United States were marked "PAID 10 Cts" and letters to Canada from the United States were marked "PAID 6d."

495

495x

496

Type — Value

On Stampless or Stamped Cover.

495 or 495x — June, 1851.
Black.
Adds to value of cover . $0.25
Red.
Adds to value of cover . .35
Brown, Red-Brown.
Adds to value of cover . .45

On Stamps. Black.
1855 3d. 8.00
6d. . . . .
1859 1c. . . . .
5c. 2.00
10c. . . . .
1868 2c. . . . .
3c. 2.50
1870 3c. 1.75
Red.
1855 6d. . . . .
Blue.
1859 5c. 2.50
10c. . . . .

496 — On Stamped Cover, June, 1851.
Black.

Type — Value

Adds to value of cover . $0.25
Red.
Adds to value of cover . .35
Blue.
Adds to value of cover . .35

On Stamps.
Black.
1855 3d. 8.00
6d. . . . .
1859 1c. . . . .
5c. 2.00
10c. . . . .
1868 2c. . . . .
3c. 2.50
1870 3c. 1.75
Red.
1855 6d. . . . .
Blue.
1859 5c. 2.50
10c. . . . .

CANADA·10·Cts

497

497 — On Stamped Cover, 1858.
From Montreal to Portland, Maine. Black.
Adds to value of cover . .25

498

498 — On Stamped Cover. June, 1857.
Black.

Type Value

Adds to value of cover . .50
Red.
Adds to value of cover . .75

CANADA
PAID 10 Cts

499

499 On Stamped Cover, Ja. 1856.
Adds to value of cover . $0.40
Red. .60
1856 6d. In Red......

PAID
CANADA-10-CENTS

500

500 On Stamped Cover, Fe., 1865.
(From Hamilton).
Adds to value of cover . .40
Red.
Adds to value of cover . .60

CANADA
PAID 10 Cts

501

501 On Stamped Cover.
Oct., 1853 to Mar., 1860.
General use.
Adds to value of cover . $0.40
Red. Brown-Red.
Adds to value of cover . .60

CANADA 10 Cts

502

On Stamped Cover. May, 1856.
502 Adds to value of cover . .40
Red.
Adds to value of cover . .60

CANADA. 10 Cts.

502x

Type Value

502x On Stamped Cover $1.50

CANADA-10-CENTS

503

503 On Stamped Cover, to end, 1859.
Adds to value of cover . .40
Red.
Adds to value of cover . .60
Green.
Adds to value of cover . 1.00
With Green "PAID" and no stamp, rate written............. 3.00
a. Reads "CANADA PAID-10-CENTS"
b. Reads "CANADA 10 CENTS" (No hyphens).

U.STATES.

504

504 Black. New York, Nov. 1864.
Adds to value of cover . $0.25

U. STATES

505

505 Black. Oswego, N.Y., Jan., 1852.
Adds to value of cover . .25
Red.
Adds to value of cover . .40
a. Letters have seriphs, Buffalo, N.Y., Oct., 1851.
Green.
Adds to value of cover . .75

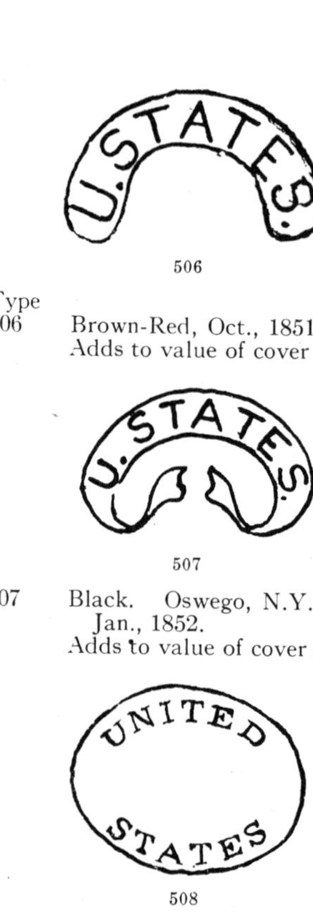

506

Type		Value
506	Brown-Red, Oct., 1851. Adds to value of cover .	.25

507

507	Black. Oswego, N.Y., Jan., 1852. Adds to value of cover .	.35

508

508	Black. San Francisco. Adds to value of cover .	.25

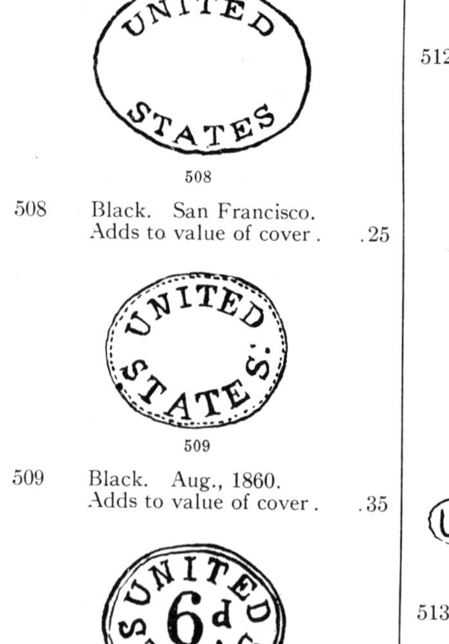

509

509	Black. Aug., 1860. Adds to value of cover .	.35

510

Type		Value
510	Red. On letters to Nova Scotia. Adds to value of cover .	$0.25

511

511	Black. Adds to value of cover .	$0.25

512

512	Red. New York, Aug., 1853. Adds to value of cover .	.60

513

514

515

516

513	Black. San Francisco. On British Columbia and Vancouver Island covers. Adds to value of cover .	$0.50
	Red, adds to value....	.75

Type		Value
514	Red. San Francisco, Oct., 1862.	
	On British Columbia and Vancouver Island covers.	
	Adds to value of cover .	.50
515	Black.	
516	Black.	
	Adds to value of cover .	.50

517

517	Black.	
	Adds to value of cover .	.35

518

518	Black. Rochester, N. Y., Jy., 1858.	
	Adds to value of cover .	.55

519

Type		Value
519	Brown-Red. October, 1864.	
	Adds to value of cover .	$0.50
	(Error — should have been made to read "6d.")	

520

520	Brown-Red. July, 1858.	
	Adds to value of cover .	.30
a.	Vertical 6d., July, 1853. Blue.	
	Adds to value of cover .	.40

521

521	Black. U.S. mail received at Halifax, Apr. 11, 1851 to Sept. 30, 1853.	
	Adds to value of cover .	.25
a.	"America-Liverpool-Jy. 14-1846"	.25

"PAID" WITH TOWN

525

Type		Value
525	Quebec, Feb., 1845, used to Frank Government and Soldiers' Mail.	
	On Stampless Cover.	
	Red. Soldier's Letter.	$15.00
	Official corres.	2.00
	With Red "3"	2.50
	With Red "6"	3.00
	With Red "9"	3.50

526

526x

526xx

527

Type		Value
526 526x	Used to frank mail from Legislative Buildings, Apr., 1855.	
526xx	On Stampless Cover.	
	Red	1.75
	With Blue "Legislative Assembly"	3.50
527	Red	1.50
	With Blue "Legislative Assembly"	3.00

528

529

528	Oct., 1853 to Apr., 1858. Stampless Cover.	
	Red	$1.50
529	Oct., 1853 to Apr., 1858. Stampless Cover.	
	Red	1.50
a.	"1" has no seriph.	

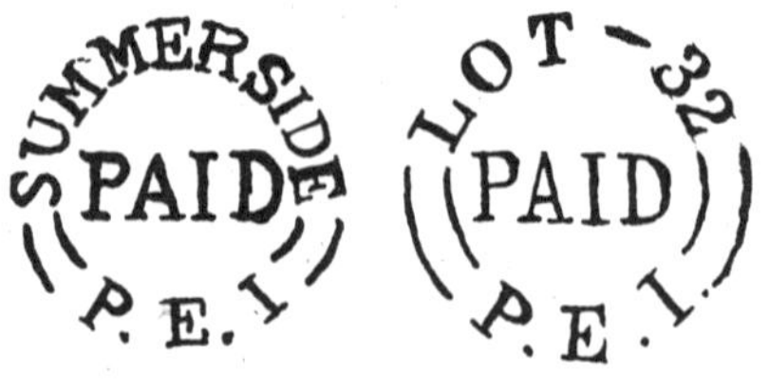

530 530a

Type		Value
530	First noted prior to 1861. Also used by Tignish.	
	Black. Stampless Cover	2.50
	1861 2d. Perf. 9, TIGNISH.....	15.00
530a	Black.	
	9d. P. E. I.	6.00

346

346 **Vancouver Island.**
STAMPLESS COVER.
Used as a Frank.
Black.......
Blue........
Green.......
Used as Cancellation.
Black.
1865 5c. Rose V.I. Perf.
Blue.................
1865 5c. Rose V.I. Perf.
10c. V.I. Imperf..
10c. V.I. Perf....
1867 2c. B.C.........
1865 10c. Blue, Van. Is.
10c. Blue, Perf. 14

VICTORIA
PAID
V. I.

531

531 **Victoria, Vancouver Island.**
Used as a Frank.
Blue........

532

532 Noted on cover with "Montreal Paid" and date in five lines, and PAID, with "3" pen-written. An offset impression from the same type of PAID marking in the same position on another cover is noted on back of cover examined, indicating that several letters of this class were stamped at the same time. It appears that the Society's mail was stamped with Type 532 at their offices for identification at the Post Office, where an account was kept and rendered to the Society at intervals.

"PAID"
Center blank.
Rate or date written in or stamped.

535 536 537

"PAID" WITH TOWN, AND RATE STAMPED IN CENTER

538 540 541

542 543 544

"PAID" WITH TOWN AND DATE TYPESET

545 546 551

553 554 555 556

Type		Value
535	Noted May, 1817. Black. Stampless Cover	$4.50
536	General use in New Brunswick. Earliest use July 25, 1843. Stampless Cover. Black	1.75
	With figure showing rate	2.00
537	Stampless Cover. General use in N.S. and N.B. from 1843. Black	1.50
538	Stampless Cover.	
	New Brunswick. Brown. Nov., 1856 (Rate usually written in.)	1.50

EDMUNDSTON N.B. PAID

539

Type		Value
539	Stampless Cover. General use Mar., 1851. Black	1.50
	With figure showing rate	1.75
540	**Salisbury, N.B.,** Nov., 1852. Stampless Cover. Black	$2.00
	Stampless Covers.	
541	**St. Stephens, N.B.,** Aug., 1852 to Sp., 1853. Red or Brown	2.00
	Richibucto, N.B., Ap., 1852. Red	2.00
	Gagetown, Jan., 1853 to Sp., 1857. Red	2.00
	Woodstock, July, 1854 to Aug., 1858. Brown	2.00

Type		Value
542	**Gagetown N.B.,** General use from 1843. Black, Stampless Cover	$2.00
543	Stampless Covers.	
	Gagetown, N.B. Dec., 1855. Black or Red	2.00
	Fredericton, N. B., 1843. Brown	2.00
	St. Stephen, N. B., 1844. Red	2.00
	Sussex Vale, N. B., 1843. Red	2.00
544	Stampless Covers. (From Sp., '55). Red	$1.00
	Black	1.50
	As Cancellation. 1855 3d. Beaver, Black	7.00
a.	Year date omitted.	
545	Stampless Covers. Ap., '63 (Impression usually lighter). Red	1.00
	To Foreign P.O.	5.00
546	Stampless Covers. Jan. '62. Red	1.00

HALIFAX
PAID
APR 23
1859
NOVASCOTIA

547

Type		Value
547	Stampless Covers. Brown, Apr., 1847	$3.00
	Red, Aug., 1856	3.00

MONTREAL
PAID
JU22
1861
CANADA

548

Type		Value
548	Red, 1845-1848........	2.00
	Black.......	2.00
	Orange......	2.50
	Any color, with PAID 3 Red..............	2.50
	Any color with Red CANADA..........	2.75
	With Mss. 3, (1873)...	2.00

AMERICA
PAID
NO 12
T54
LIVERPOOL

549

549	Stampless Cover. Oct., 1854.	
	Black. Rate written in	$0.50
	Red........	.25
	On Stamped Cover.	
	Adds to value of cover....	50
	Black.......	.50
	Red........	.35

CHARLOTTE-TOWN
MY 12
1862
PAID
P. E. I.

550

550	**Prince Edward Island.** Noted as early as 1855. Stampless Cover.	
	Brick Red, Mr., 1865, Ja., '67............	2.50
551	**San Francisco,** on cover Victoria, B.C., to Philadelphia.	
	Pink........	

552

Type		Value
552	Stampless Cover.	
	Brick-Red. Dec., 1855 to Apr., 1860. With rate written or stamped.................	1.00
	As Cancellation. Black.	
	1855 3d. Beaver......	7.00
553	Stampless Cover.	
	Red........	.50
	Black.......	.75
	Cancelling Stamp.	
	Black.	
	1851 3d. Beaver (Laid)	
554	Stampless Covers. From July, 1843.	
	Red.	
	Oromocto, N. B., Apr. 16, 1861............	.50
	Woodstock, N.B., Sept. 4, 1860............	.50
	St. John, N.B., Apr. 9, 1855...............	.50
	Fredericton, N.B., Nov., 1859...............	.50
	Dorchester, N.B., Apr., 1872...............	.50
	Red-Brown.	
	Fredericton, N.B., Nov., 1859.	
	Black.	
	Towns as above.......	$ .75
	St. John, N.B., with "3" to left..........	1.00
	As Cancellation, in Black.	
	1860 5c. N.B. Green..	
a.	Date written in.......	.75
555	Stampless Cover. General use from Oc., '53.	
	Red........	$0.40
	Deep Rose, Oct., 1853.	.60
	With "PAID 3".......	1.00
	Black.......	.60
	With "3" or "PAID 3" etc.................	1.00
a.	"Paid" at bottom.	

Type		Value
b.	Center blank or date written in.	
	Cancelling stamp.	
	Quebec.	
	Black.	
	1854 3d. Beaver......	7.00
556	Stampless Cover (from Sp., '53).	
	Red........	.75
	With Red PAID 3.....	1.75
	Black.......	1.00
	With Black PAID 3...	1.75

557 558

557	Stampless Cover.	
	Red........	.75
	Black.......	1.00
	With PAID 5.........	1.75
558	Stampless Cover.	
	Red........	$0.50
	Black.......	.75

"PAID" MARKINGS

565 566

Type		Value
565	Nova Scotia covers, Sept., 1790.	
	Black, with town, and rate written in......	6.50
566	Black, July, 1833.	
	Adds to value of cover.	.75
567	**St. John, N.B.,** Jan., 1797.	
	Adds to value of cover.	
	Black.......	.75
	Red........	.60

567x

567xx

Type		Value
567x	Stampless Cover (Great Western Rwy.)	
	Hamilton, May, 1855, Black, with Red "PAID" in addition.	5.00
	(Number 140 also noted.)	
567xx	Stampless Cover (Great Western Rwy.)	
	Black. Hamilton, May, 1857, with Red "PAID" in addition.	5.00

568 569

568	Black. Probably U.S.	
569	Black or Red. Au., '33.	
	Adds to value of cover.	.50
570	U.S. marking on mail entering via Buffalo, Oct., 1851.	
	Green.......	
	Adds to value of cover.	.50

Paid	P-A-I-D	PAID	PAID
567	570	574	575
PAID	PAID	PAID·	PAID
576	577	578	579
PAID	PAID	PAID	PAID
580	580x	581	582
PAID	PAID	PAID	Paid
583	584	584x	584xx
PAID	PAID	PAID	PAID
585	586	587	588

588x	589	590	591

PAID	PAID	PAID
592x	593	593x

PAID ALL

595

PAID

571

Type		Value
571	Black.	
	1880 3c. Canada	$0.75

PAID

572

PAID

573

Type		Value
572	**British Columbia.**	
	Black.	
	1865 5c. Vancouver I., Perf.	
	1860 2½d. B. C	
	Blue	
	1865 5c. V.I. Perf	
573	Black.	
	1860 2½d. B. C.	
574	**New Brunswick.**	
	Black or Red.	
	Adds to value of cover .	$0.25
	Red.	
	1851 6d. N. B	100.00
	3d. N.B	
	1s. N.B	
	Black.	
	1851 3d. N.B	
	6d. N.B	
	1s. N.B	
575	Black.	
	1868 3c.	1.75
	Adds to value of cover .	.25
	Blue	.35
576	Black or Red.	
	Adds to value of cover .	.25
	(Hamilton, May, 1857).	
577	Black or Red. Apr., 1843.	
	Adds to value of cover .	.25
	1868 3c. Canada	1.75
578	Black.	
	1851 6d. N.B	100.00
	Adds to value of cover .	.25
579	Black or Red. July, 1846.	
	Adds to value of cover .	.25
	Black.	
	1870 1c. Orange	1.75
580	Red. Stoufville, U. C. Au., '48	.25
580x	Black or Red. 1802.	
	Adds to value of cover .	$0.25
581	Adds to value of cover.	
	Black	.25
	Red	.35
	Brown	.50
582	Black or Red.	
	Adds to value of cover .	.25
583	**British Columbia.**	
	Blue.	
	Adds to value of cover .	.50
	1860 2½d. Br. Col	
	1865 5c. Vancouver I .	
	Also noted in Black.	
584	Black or Red.	
	Adds to value ot cover . .	.25
584x	Blue. Quebec, Au., '54	.50
584xx	Blue. Euphrasia, Fe., '52	.50

PAID

584xxx

Type		Value
584xxx	**Howard, U.C.,** De., '48. Brown.	
	Adds to value of cover .	$0.50
585	Black or Red.	
	Adds to value of cover .	.25

Paid

585x

Type		Value
585x	**Galt, U. C.,** Jy., '59, Red	1.50
586	Black or Red.	
	Adds to value of cover .	$0.25
587	Stampless Cover. 1850.	
	Adds to value of cover.	
	Black	.25
	Red	.25
	Nassagaweya, U. C., Fe., '71.	
	Green	.75
	Black.	
	1859 17c. Canada	
588	Black, Blue or Red.	
	Adds to value of cover .	.25

Type		Value
	1868 3c.	1.75
	12½c.	3.50
588x	**Sandwich, U. C.,** Fe., '48.	
	Red	.35
589	Black or Red. Jan., 1858.	
	Adds to value of cover	.25
	Stampless Cover.	
	Black. With "3" or "5"	1.25
	1875 3c.	.75
590	Black or Red. 1857.	
	Adds to value of cover	.25
	As Cancellation. Black.	
	1857 3d.	7.00
	1859 5c.	1.75
	10c.	
	12½c.	
	1868 3c.	1.50
	6c.	
591	Stampless Covers. Genl. use.	
	Adds to val., Black	.25
	Red	.35
	Blue	.45
	Green	.60
	As cancellation. Black.	
	1859 5c.	1.75
	1868 3c.	1.50
	6c.	
	1880 3c.	1.50

POSTAGE PAID

592

592	Black. 1875.	
	1875 3c.	$1.50
592x	Stampless Covers. Red or Black.	
	Rate penwritten	.25
	Rate stamped "3," etc.	.50
	With "Registered"	.60
	With "TOO LATE"	1.00
593x	Stampless Covers. Adds to value of cover.	
	Black	.25
	Blue	.40
593	Black or Red. Feb., 1874.	
	Adds to value of cover	.50

PAID
D McKENDRICK

593xx

Type		Value
593xx	Red. Kincardine, No., '57.	
	Adds to value of cover	.75

PAID

594

594	Black.	
	1871 15c.	5.00

ATTORNEY GENERAL'S DEPARTMENT
Paid

594x

PAID
R. G. O.
CANADA.

595x

594x	Blue. Ja., '75.	
	Stampless Cover	$0.75
595	Red. **New Brunswick.** Nov., 1866.	
	1866 10c. Red	3.00
	1868 3c. Canada	3.00
	6c. Canada	5.00
	1875 3c. Canada	3.00
595x	Red (Receiver General's Office.)	
	Stampless Cover	.75
	With Red "PAID 3"	1.50

FIGURES DENOTING AMOUNTS DUE OR PAID

When postage was prepaid in cash, the amount was written in the upper right corner or stamped with the amount in black.

The P.M.G. recommended that where stamps were readily procurable prepayment in that form be insisted on, and the principle of prepayment enforced by imposing an additional charge on letters which were posted unpaid. An Act subsequently passed carried out these recommendations.

If unpaid, the marking was supposed to be in red, but this rule was not always followed.

Instructions to Postmasters relative to letters to the United States read: "....when stamps are affixed representing less than the amount of postage to which the letter is liable, the stamps are to be cancelled and the letter rated with the full rate of postage as unpaid."

(Postmasters did not take kindly to the use of adhesive stamps which had to be cut from the sheet, sold to the customer, and then defaced with a cancelling instrument. They claimed a commission on stamps sold, and not receiving it they preferred to collect the rate in cash and stamp the letter "PAID" opposite the amount of the postage. This meant less bookkeeping for the postmaster. Even with the above range of "PAID" types, collectors will find new varieties, as these were cut as ordered, and all varied slightly.)

600  600a  600b

Type		Value
	Stampless Covers, Price Lists, Circulars.	
600	Black. Toronto, Fe., '55	$1.00
600a.	Black. Toronto, My., '52	1.00
600b.	Black. Montreal, Jy., '52	1.00
	Black. Quebec, Ju., '54	1.00

600c  600d

600c.	Black. Montreal, Fe., '53	1.00
	Black. Toronto, Ja., '53	1.00
	(Buffalo, N.Y., Mr., '58)	
600d.	Black	1.25

600e

600e.	Black. Toronto, Oc., '53	1.50

601 601a 601b

Type		Value
601	Stampless Cover. Sp. '54. Black.......	$0.50
	As cancellation: 1859 1c.	1.25
601a.	Stampless Cover, Black	.50
601aa.	1d. in circle...........	.60
	As cancellation: 1868 3c.	1.75
601b.	Stampless Cover, Montreal, Fe., '53; Buffalo, N.Y., Mr., '58 on price lists to Canada via Buffalo & Seneca, C.W........	.50

602 602a

602	Stampless Cover, Montreal, Ju., '63.......	$0.50
Adds to value stamped cover..............	.30
602a.	Stampless Cover......	.40
Adds to value stamped cover..............	.20

602b 602c

Type		Value
602b.	Stampless Cover......	1.00
	Adds to value stamped cover..............	.50
602c.	Stampless Cover, Au., '59................	.75
	Adds to value stamped cover..............	.40

603 603a 603b

603	**Vernonville, U.C.,** Ju., '57.
Stampless Cover, Red..$	1.00
603a.	**Nassagaweya, U. C.,** Fe., '71.
Stampless Cover, Green	1.25
603b.	**Gagetown, N. B.,** Oc., '51.
Adds to value of cover .	.50

603c 603d 603e

603c.	**Delaware, U. C.,** Oc., '54.
Stampless Cover, Black	1.00
Red...	1.50
603d.	**Bobcaygeon, U. C.,** Oc., '57.
Stampless Cover, Green	1.50
603e.	**Georgetown, U. C.,** De., '53.
Stampless Cover......	1.00

LARGER "3" TYPES

604  604a

Type		Value
604	**Halifax, N.S.,** Sp., '56	$1.00
604a.	**Indiana, U.C.,** Jy., '54.	
	Stampless Cover......	1.25
aa.	Heavier impression, Au., '61................	

604b  604c

604b.	**York, U.C.,** Ap., '58.	
	Stampless Cover......	1.00
604c.	General use, Jy., '52 to My., '80.	
	Stampless Cover, Black	.50
	Red .	.75
	As cancellation:	
	1852 3d.	7.00
	1859 1c.	2.75
	1880 3c.	2.50
	Red.	
	1859 1c.	3.25

604d  604e

Type		Value
604d.	Bytown, 1852. (General use.)	
	Stampless Cover, Black	.50
	Red . .	.75
	Blue . .	1.25
604e.	General use, 1852.	
	Black.......	.50
	Red.........	.75
	Brown......	1.00
	Blue........	1.25

605  605a

604f  605b

605c  605d

604f.	**Oakridges, C. W.,** Mr., '55................	1.25
605	**Norwood, U.C.,** Ja., '56.	
	Stampless Cover, Red..	$1.25
605a.	**Warsaw, U. C.,** Mr., '59.	
	Stampless Cover, Red..	1.50
605b.	General use, 1852.	
	Stampless Cover, Black	.75
	Red . .	.90
	Chatham, N. B., Jy., '52.	
	Green.......	1.25

Type		Value
605.c	**New Brunswick,** Gen-al use.	
	Stampless Cover......	$ .75

Type		Value
605d.	General use, Ju., '51.	
	Stampless Cover, Black	.40
	Red..	.75
	Blue..	1.25

PAID "3" TYPES

606

Type		Value
606	**New Brunswick.**	
	Stampless Cover, Black	$0.50

606a  606b

606a.	**Gananoque,** Oc., '51.	
	Stampless Cover, Black	1.75
	Red..	2.00
aa.	Dotted line under PAID extending side to side, Jy., '53.............	1.75
606b.	**Gananoque,** My., '53.	
	Stampless Cover, Black	1.75

606c  606d

606c.	**Lonsdale, U. C., Ju., '54.**	
	Stampless Cover, Red..	1.50
606d.	General use, Jy., '51.	

Type		Value
	Stampless Cover, Black	.50
	Red..	.60
	Brown	.70
	Brown-Orange	.75
	Blue..	.80
	"D" of 3d missing.	
	Sandwich, Mr., '73.	
	In Brown....	1.00
	Diam. 18 mm. on 2c., 4th issue Bill Stamp.	

606e  606f  606g

606e.	....	
606f.	General use.	
	Stampless Cover, Black	$0.50
	Red..	.60
	Brown	.75
	Blue..	.85
	As cancellation:	
	1856 3d.	8.00
606g.	**New Brunswick.**	
	General use from De., '55.	
	Stampless Cover, Black	.50
	Red..	.60

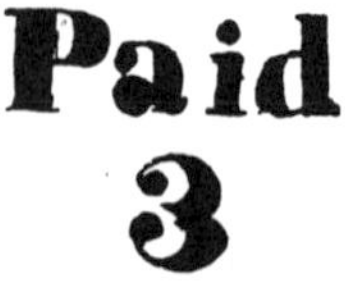

606h

PAID 3

606i

606k

PAID 3

606l

PAID 3

606m

PAID 3

606n

PAID 3

606o

PAID 3c

606p

PAID 3

606q

Type		Value
606h.	**Nelson, C. W.,** Ja., '58.	
	Stampless Cover, Brown	1.75
606i.	Stampless Cover, Black	
606k.	General use, Sp., '57.	
	Stampless Cover, Black	.80
	Red . .	.70
	Claremont, My., '56, in deep Cherry Red.	1.00
606l.	General use, Ja., '75.	
	Stampless Cover, Black	1.25
	Red . .	.75
606m.	General use, Oc., '51.	
	Stampless Cover, Black	1.00
	Red . .	.75
	Kincardine, No., '57.	
	Brown	1.25
	Any town, cancelled with Types 1-4 Black	2.00
	Hamilton, De., '53, in Red cancelled with Type 1 in Blue	2.50
	"PAID" falling on stamp:	
	1854 3d.	8.00
	½d.	
	1859 1c. In Red	4.00
	5c.	2.00
	1868 3c.	2.00
606n.	General use, Ja., '56.	
	Stampless Cover, Black	1.25
	Red . .	.75
	Kingston, Ap., '66.	
	Brown	.75
	Above cancelled "18" Type 103x and marked FREE	2.50
	Marmora, Ont., Ja., '73.	
	Orange	1.75
	As cancellation:	
	1868 3c.	1.50
	1870 3c.	1.25
606o.	**Vankleek Hill, Ont.,** Mr., '71.	
	Stampless Cover.	
	Red-Brown . .	1.50

Type		Value
606p.	**Berkeley, U. C.,** Au., '72. Stampless Cover	$1.50
606q.	**McGillivray, C. W.,** Au., '75. Stampless Cover, Red..	1.50

607 608

607	Black (in the 70's). Adds to value of cover .	$0.15
608	May, 1876. Adds to value of cover .	.40

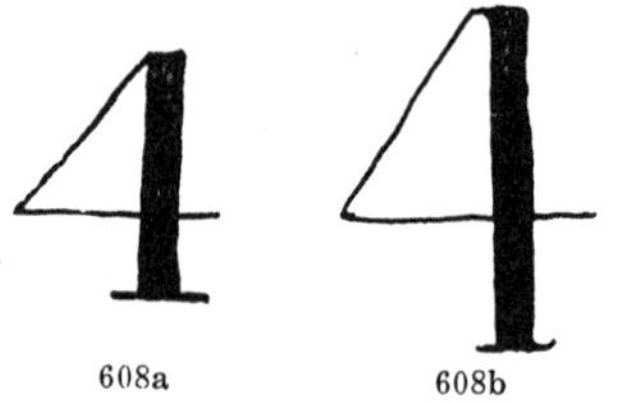

608a 608b

Type		Value
608a.	Feb., 1895. Adds to value of cover .	.40
608b.	May, 1876. Adds to value of cover .	.40

609

609	**Chatham, N. B.,** Mr., '59. Adds to value of cover .	.30
	As cancellation: 1859 3d. N.B.........	

610 (i to vii)

610a 610b 610c 610d 610e 610f 610g

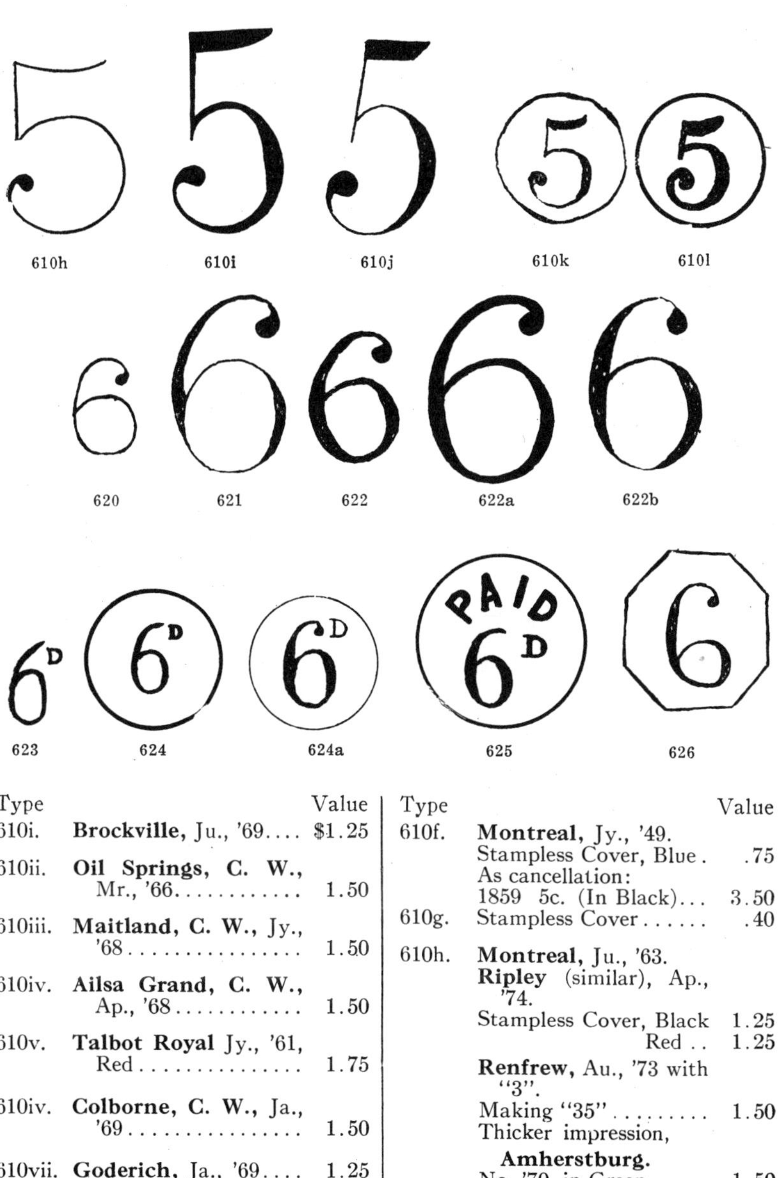

Type		Value
610i.	**Brockville,** Ju., '69....	$1.25
610ii.	**Oil Springs, C. W.,** Mr., '66...........	1.50
610iii.	**Maitland, C. W.,** Jy., '68...............	1.50
610iv.	**Ailsa Grand, C. W.,** Ap., '68...........	1.50
610v.	**Talbot Royal** Jy., '61, Red...............	1.75
610iv.	**Colborne, C. W.,** Ja., '69...............	1.50
610vii.	**Goderich,** Ja., '69....	1.25
610a.	....	
610b.	....	
610c.	....	
610d.	....	
610e.	**Nova Scotia.**	
	Adds to value of cover.	.15

Type		Value
610f.	**Montreal,** Jy., '49.	
	Stampless Cover, Blue.	.75
	As cancellation:	
	1859 5c. (In Black)...	3.50
610g.	Stampless Cover......	.40
610h.	**Montreal,** Ju., '63.	
	Ripley (similar), Ap., '74.	
	Stampless Cover, Black	1.25
	Red..	1.25
	Renfrew, Au., '73 with "3".	
	Making "35".........	1.50
	Thicker impression,	
	Amherstburg.	
	No. '70, in Green......	1.50
	Listowel.	
	Ap., '75, Black........	1.00
	As cancellation:	
	1868 3c.	1.75
	1870 3c.	1.75
610i.	Stampless Cover, Black	1.00
	Red..	.90

Type		Value
	Belleville, Ja., '69, in Green, with PAID...	1.50
610j.	**Kingston,** etc., Jy., '69. Stampless Cover, Black	1.00
	Red ..	.90
610k.	**Toronto,** Oc., '70 to De., '75. Stampless Cover, Black	1.00
	Red ..	.90
610l.	**Toronto,** Jy., '69. Stampless Cover, Black	1.00
	Red ..	.90

"5" INSTEAD OF 5c. STAMP

Between Jan. 1875 and Dec. 1875 the need for a 5c. stamp became pressing. A cover stamped "5" only in black may mean an unpaid 3c. letter with 2c. fine (see P.O. Act 1867). "Paid 5", in black, may mean the same. "5" or "Paid 5" in red, however, (red color indicating that the postage was prepaid) may be classed as a provisional, it being impossible to prepay the 5c. letter with a 5c. stamp between those dates.

Type		Value
	"5" or "Paid 5" in Red on cover dated between Jan., 1875 and Oct., 1875...........	$5.00
	"5" in Red, cover as above, with stamp prepaying postage and numeral 5 denoting registration fee paid.............	5.00

611

612

Type		Value
611	**Baddeck, N. S.,** My., '65.	
	Adds to value of cover .	$3.00
	As cancellation:	
	1865 5c.	2.75
612	This type, along with Type 639b. was cut from wood and used by Postmaster Robert Elmsley, Baddeck, N. S. They were not used to surcharge the 3d. stamps to 5c. or the 6d. stamp to 10c. as was at first thought but are postmarks or cancellations only. In 1854 a treaty was arranged with the U. S. by which it was agreed the rate should be 3d. per ½ oz. and that all prepaid letters from Nova Scotia to the United States should be stamped on the face "Paid 5 Cents" or "Paid 10 Cents."	
	Adds to value of cover .	1.00
	As cancellation:	
	1855 3d. N. S........	12.00

613

Type		Value
613	**Halifax N.S.,** Mr., '65. Stampless Cover, Red..	1.00

614 614a

614b 614c

Type — Value

614 St. John, Newcastle, Hopewell, New Brunswick, No., '60.
Stampless Cover, Black $1.00
Red .. 1.25
As cancellation:
1851 3d. N. B........
6d. N. B........
5c. Green, N. B..
In Red.
1851 3d. N. B........
6d. N. B........

614a. **New Brunswick.**
Stampless Cover...... 1.00

614b. **New Brunswick.**
Stampless Cover...... 1.00

614c. **New Brunswick.**
Stampless Cover .. 1.00

614d

614e 614f

614d. **New Brunswick,** Oc., '62.
Stampless Cover 1.00

614e. **New Brunswick.**
Stampless Cover...... 1.00

Type — Value

614f. **New Brunswick.**
Stampless Cover, Black 1.00
Red .. 1.25

615

615 **Nissouri, U. C.,** Oc., '62.
Stampless Cover, Brown Red.............. 2.50

616

616 **Craigleith,** Ja., '62.
Stampless Cover, Brown 3.00

617

618

Type		Value
617	**London, Toronto,** etc., De., '59.	
	Stampless Cover, Black	1.00
	Red ..	.90
	With "Toronto Paid", Red	2.50
	With "Montreal Paid," 5-line	2.50
	As cancellation:	
	1859 5c. (5 only).....	1.75
618	General use.	
	Stampless Cover, Black	$1.00
	Red ..	1.00
	Green, Wroxeter, U. C., Ju., '62.............	2.50
	Green, Norwich, Ap., '60	2.50
	As cancellation:	
	1859 5c.	1.75
618b.	1859	
	Stampless Cover, Red..	1.00
	Eugenie, Mr., '74, Bronze Brown	1.50
	Brougham, Mr., '67, Green..............	1.50
	As cancellation:	
	1859 5c. (5 only).....	1.75
618c.	1859	
	Stampless Cover, Black	1.00
	Red ..	1.25
	Cancellation:	
	1859 5c. (5 only).....	1.75
618d.	1859 to My., '73.	
	Stampless Cover, Black	1.00
	Red ..	1.00
	As cancellation:	
	1859 5c. (5 only).....	1.75
618e.	Dec., 1859.	
	Stampless Cover, Black	1.00
	Red ..	1.00
	As cancellation:	
	1859 5c. (5 only).....	1.75
618f.	Stampless Cover	1.00
618g.	" "	1.00
618h.	" "	1.00
	Newmarket, U. C., Oc. '59, used a "PAID 5" on Stampless Cover, Dark Brown	1.00
	As cancellation:	
	1868 1c. Orange-Yel. (5 only)...	4.00

618b

618c

618d

618e

618f

618g

618h

619

Type		Value
619	(See "Unpaid 7" notes.) General use, Au., '59. Adds to value of cover	$1.00
620	1870	
	Stampless Cover	1.00
621	General use, 1852 to 1880.	
	Stampless Cover	1.00
	Stamped Cover, add	.20
622	General use, July, 1852 to 1880.	
	Stampless Cover	1.00
	Stamped Cover, add	.20
	St. Andrews, N. B., Blue, Ap., '53	.30
	As cancellation:	
	1859 5c.	1.50
	1880 3c.	1.50
622a.	May, 1856.	
	Stampless Cover	1.00
	Add, stamped cover	.20
622b.	Dec., 1855, General use.	
	Stampless Cover	1.00
623	Stampless Cover	$1.00
624	Nov., 1853.	
	Stampless Cover, Black	1.00
	Blue	1.25
	As cancellation:	
	1859 5c.	1.50
624a.	July, 1852, general use.	
	Stampless Cover, Black	1.00
	Red	1.25

Type		Value
625	Stampless Cover, Black	1.00
	Red	.90
	Blue	1.10
	Sandwich, No., '54, Bronze-Brown	1.10
626	**Gananoque,** June, 1851.	
	Stampless Cover	1.50

627

627a

Type		Value
627	Sept., 1857.	
	Stampless Cover, Black	$1.25
	Red	1.00
	"6" as cancellation:	
	1857 3d.	7.00
	1859 5c.	1.75
627a.	Stampless Cover	1.25

"UNPAID 7"

Clause 4 of the Act to Amend the Post Office Laws assented to May 6, 1859, stated in part: "To promote simplicity and economy in the business of the Post Office all letters posted in Canada for any place within the Province and not prepaid shall be charged seven instead of five cents per half ounce on delivery."

A letter addressed to a Government Department, such as the Crown Lands Department, was free of postage, but the receiving postmaster sometimes in error stamped it "7" or "unpaid 7" in black (5c. postage plus 2c. fine) to be collected on delivery. The error being discovered by the postmaster or at forwarding office or destination the "7" or "UNPAID 7" was cancelled and the letter stamped "FREE."

628 629 630 630a 631 631a

632  632a  633  635

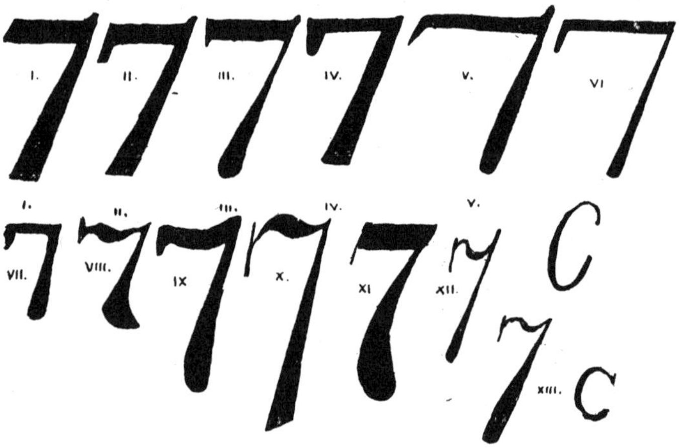

634

Type		Value
628	1858.	
	Stampless Cover	$1.00
	As cancellation:	
	1858 3d. Perf	
	1860 12½c. Nova Scotia	3.50
629	**Nova Scotia.**	
	Stampless Cover	.75
630	**Quebec.**	
	Stampless Cover	1.00
630a.	?	
631	Stampless unpaid cover, 1859	.75
631a.	1859.	
	Stampless unpaid cover	.75
632	1859	
	Stampless unpaid cover	.75
632a.	**Sarnia**, Sp., '60.	
	Stampless unpaid cover	.75
633	1859.	
	Stampless unpaid cover	.75

Type		Value
634i.	**Clarenceville, L. C.,** Sp., '61	.75
634ii.	**Paisley, U. C.,** Sp., '60	.75
634iii.	**Ottawa, C. W.,** Fe., '68	.75
634iv.	**Warsaw, U. C.,** De., '63	1.00
634v.	**Osgoode, C. W.,** Ja., '60	1.00
634vi.	**Mount Forest, Ont.,** Sp., '62	$1.00
634vii.	**Gorrie, U. C.,** Mr., '61	$1.25
634viii.	**Chatham, U. C.,** Jy., '59	1.00
634ix.	**Quebec,** Oc., '65	1.00
634x.	**Norwood, C. W.,** Mr., '65	1.00

Type		Value
634xi.	**Collingwood Harbor,** Ja., '62	1.25
634xii.	**Woodstock, C. W.,** Ja., '68	1.00
634xiii.	**Whitby, C. W.,** Ju., '69	1.00
635	1859. General use. Stampless Cover	$1.00
	Port Hope, Mr., '65, Blue	1.50
	As cancellation: 1865 12½ N. S	6.00

636

636	**New Brunswick.** Stampless Cover	1.00

636a

636a.	**New Brunswick,** Mr., '62. Stampless Cover	1.00
aa.	No bar above "7"	

637

637a

637b

637c

637d

637e

637f

637g

637h

637i

Type		Value
637 to 637i.	General use from Au., '59.	
	Stampless unpaid cover	$1.00
	Cancelled	1.50
	Cancelled and marked FREE	2.50
	Cancelled with Hamilton, 16 in. bars, Ap., '62	3.00

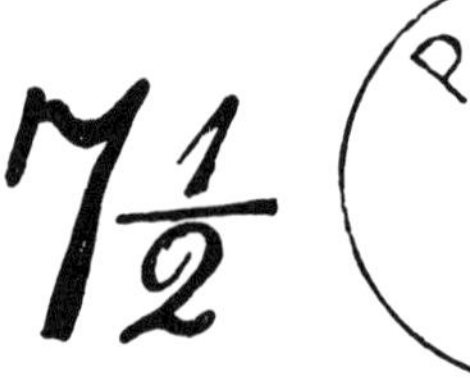

638

638x

638	**Nova Scotia,** Mr., '59.	
	Stampless Cover	$1.00
638x	Oct., 1858.	
	Unstamped cover, Black	1.25
	Red	1.00
	Green	1.50

639 639a 639b

639c 639d 639e

639f 639g

639h 639i

639j 639k

639l 640

640a 641

642 642a 642aa

642b 642c 642d

642e 642f

Type		Value
639	**Nova Scotia.** Cancellation.	
	1851 3d.	
639a.	1868.	
	Stampless Cover	$1.00
639b.	**Nova Scotia** (See 612).	
	1851 6d. N. S........	
	3d. N. B........	
639c.	**Fort William,** Fe., '65.	
	Stampless Cover	1.00
639d.	**Morrisburg, U. C.,** Sp., '64	1.00
639e.	**Quebec,** 1859.........	1.00
639f.	U.S. Marking, 1857.	
	As cancellation on:	
	1857 3d.	7.00
639g.	Feb., 1870.	
	Stampless Cover	1.00
639h.	Dec., 1869.	
	Stampless Cover	1.00
639i.	**Toronto,** June, 1874.	
	Stampless unpaid cover	1.00
639j.	Stampless unpaid cover	1.00
639k.	**St. Catharines, U. C.,** Oc., '68.	
	Stampless Cover	1.00
	Adds to value stamped cover	.30
	As cancellation:	
	1859 5c.	1.50
	1868 3c.	1.50
639l.	Feb., 1869.	
	Unstamped cover......	1.00
640 to 642e.	No information	
642f.	**Kingston**	

643 644

Type		Value
643	U. S. Marking on mail to Canada.	
	Oct., 1851, Brown-Red, add................	$0.40
	Au., '54 (Buffalo), Black add................	.30
	Buffalo, Au., '51, Blue add................	.60
644	**New Brunswick.**	
	Stampless Cover, Red..	1.50
aa.	"Paid 15"	1.75

645

645	**Kingston,** Ju., '67.	
	Stampless Cover	1.75
aa.	10 of Type 639f. with PAID..............	1.75
	Above cancelled and marked FREE......	2.50

646 647

647a 647b

Type		Value
646	**Wellington, U. C.,** Au., '46. Stampless Cover, Blue .	$1.50
647	**Toronto.** Adds to value of cover .	.35
647a.	Feb., 1859 to 1870. Stampless Cover, Red . .	1.50
	Brown	1.50
647b.	Feb., 1876. Add to value of cover. .	.25
aa.	In circle, 1873.	

648 648a

648b 648c

648	Aug., 1867. Add to value of cover. .	.25
aa.	**Goderich,** Au., '65, smaller.	
648a.	Sept., 1861. Add to value of cover. .	.25
648b.	**London, C. W.,** Fe., '68. Add to value of cover. .	.40
648c.	Aug., 1864 (Guelph, No., '67). Add to value of cover. .	.25

649 649a

649b 649c 649d

649e 649f

649g 649i

649h

Type		Value
649	Add to value of cover:	
	Black.	$0.25
	Red	.40
aa.	**Ottawa,** De., '73 (larger).	

NOTE—Goderich used "21," 1½" high, My., '67, thick block type.

649a. to 649g. No information. . . . .

Type		Value
649h.	**Kingston**............	
649i.		

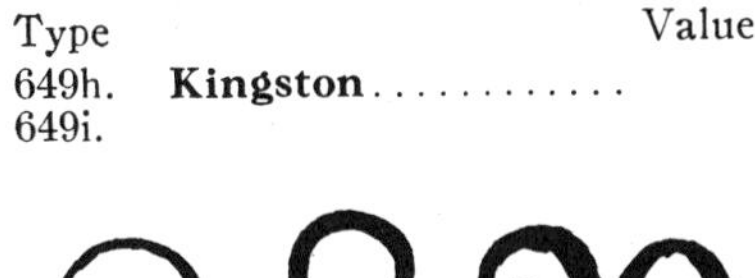

649j 650

649j. ?

650 **Sarnia,** Sept., 1860.
Add to value of cover.. $0.35

MARKINGS ON UNPAID AND INSUFFICIENTLY PREPAID LETTERS

700

700 Black. Nov., 1871.
Stampless Cover...... $1.00

701

701 **British Columbia.**
Blue........

702

702 Blue.
"Cunard' Packet Boat and Steamships,"

Type		Value
	Forbes & Lownsborough, Agents, 30 King E., Toronto, June, 1873.	
	Stampless Cover......	$1.00
	With Red, PAID 3....	1.25

MORE to PAY

MORE-TO-PAY

712 and 713

MORE-TO-PAY.

714

MORE-TO-PAY

715

MORE-TO-PAY

716

MORE TO PAY

717

DUE 10

717x 717xx

DUE·

Due

718 719

UNPAID

719x

If the receiving Postmaster found that a letter had been underrated he was instructed to mark the additional postage with the words "MORE TO PAY" and to initial the letter. The marking "DUE" was also used.

Type		Value
712	Used from 1843 in Lower Canada and Maritimes. Black.	
	Adds to value of cover .	.75
a.	45 mm. long, Caps 5 mm. high, used by Nova Scotia	
713	Black. Sept., 1855. . . .	
	Adds to value of cover .	.75
714	Black. May, 1843	
	Adds to value of cover .	.90
715	Black. Apr., 1876	
	Adds to value of cover .	.40
716	**Hamilton**, Dec., 1880.	
	Violet.	.40
	Black.	.30
	Cancelling stamp.	
	1880 3c. In Violet	1.00
	Black.	.50
a.	Light-line letters	
717	Black.	
	Adds to value of cover .	.60
717x	U.S. Markings	
717xx	Appearing on Canada Covers	
718	Black.	
	Adds to value of cover .	$0.25
719	Black, 1868. .	
	Adds to value of cover .	.25
719x	Black. U.C., My., '71	
	Adds to value of cover .	1.00

CANADA UNPAID

720

SHORT
HALF

721

RETURNED-FOR
POSTAGE

722

INSUFFICIENTLY
PREPAID

723

Type		Value
720	Black, 1864. .	
	Adds to value of cover .	.75
a.	With "10" after UNPAID.	.85
aa.	Type 720a. cancelled FREE	1.25
721	Black, 1868. .	
	Adds to value of cover .	.20
	As cancellation.	
	1868 6c.	3.50
722	Black, March, 1886. . . .	
	Adds to value of cover .	$0.25
a.	1/3 smaller	
b.	"Returned For Postage" (3 lines), Ja., '79. . . .	.25
c.	"Returned for Deficient Postage" (2 lines), Ja., '79	
723	Black, March, 1877. . . .	
	Adds to value of cover.	.25
a.	Smaller size, Nov., 1865	.25

Insufficiently Prepaid

724

724	Black, St. John, N.B., May, 1860.	
	Adds to value of cover .	$0.50

OVER ½ OZ.

725

HELD·FOR·POSTAGE

727

RETURNED FOR WAR TAX

728

Type		Value
725	Black, Apr., 1876...... Adds to value of cover.	$0.20
727	Black, Mar., 1877..... Adds to value of cover.	.25
728	May, 1915. Toronto letters without 1c. War Tax in addition to 2c. postage went to D. L. O. bearing Type 728. Black.......	

729

730

729	Post Offices in nearly all countries are supplied with these markings, to be used when the sum "Due" or to be "Taxed" is an odd amount, which is written alongside. Black, 1890..	

731 732

733

RETURNED - FOR
DEFICIENT POSTAGE 3

734

Type		Value
730 731 732	Post Offices in nearly all countries are supplied with markings similar to Types 730 to 732, for amounts from 5 to 100 which are used to denote the sum charged or "taxed" against the letter. Black, 1890..	
733	**Prince Edward Island,** July, 1854. "Due" stamp, Black... Adds to value of cover.	$0.40
734	**Belleville,** May, 1889. Black....... Adds to value of cover.	$0.50
a.	"Returned for Postage" in two lines. Black....... Adds to value of cover.	.50

BRITISH POSTMARKS

Types 740 to 748 appear on covers from Canada to Great Britain or to foreign points routed via a British Post Office.

740  741  742

Type		Value
740	Black.......	
741	Black.......	
742	On cover from Nova Scotia, October, 1857. Black.......	

743

744

745  746

747

748

Type		Value
743	On cover New Brunswick to England, Apr., 1855. Red........	
744	Black or Red, Feb., 1858	$0 75
745	Black or Red.........	.75
746	Black, May, 1858.....	$0.75
	Red.................	.85
747	Black or Red, May, 1858...............	.85
748	Stampless Cover.	
	Quebec, Oct., 1854, Red	2.50
	With MONEY LETTER, Red..........	3.75

"MONEY LETTERS"

The marking "Money Letter" did not always indicate that the letter contained Money, since the marking has often been noted on covers, the contents of which were about ordinary business matters. The author has not been able to obtain any official reference to the marking.

MONEY-LETTER

750

MONEY-LETTER

751

MONEY LETTER

751x

MONEY-LETTER

752

M O N E Y

753

MONEY-LETTER

754

Money Letter

754x

Type		Value
750	Stampless Covers, Mar. 1843.	
	Add to value of cover:	
	Black	$1.00
	Red	1.25
751	Showing heavy usage Oct., 1849.	
	Black (Simcoe)	$1.00
751x	Bronze-Brown, Sandwich U.C., No., '54	1.25
752	Stampless Cover, 1843.	
	Black	$1.00
	Red, Sandwich, U. C., Fe., '48, and other offices	1.25
	Brown or Red-Brown	1.25
	Blue, Berlin, U. C., Ja., '54	1.40
753	Black	1.00
754	Black, May, 1854	$1.00
	Red	1.25
	Brown	1.25
754x	Red, Sandwich, U. C., Fe., '48	1.25

"TOO LATE"

"Too Late" was stamped on covers delivered to the Postmaster too late to be included in the mail last made up and closed for despatch. It will be noted that in those early days of forest trails and irregular lake and river navigation, mails were not frequent. When a letter missed the post the delay was often a serious one. The marking explained the lateness of arrival to the addressee. The Postmaster General's instructions were that couriers should sound a horn on approaching and leaving a Post Office, and this ruling was in effect as late as 1867, when Section 363 of "The Post Office Act" of that year read "Every Courier should carry a Post Horn and sound the same distinctly two or three times on approaching and leaving a Post Office." The P. M. sometimes wrote in the corner "TOO LATE" or "After Closing."

Too Late

760

TOO LATE

761

TOO LATE

762

TOO LATE

763

LATE

764

TOO LATE

765

TOO LATE

766

(TOO LATE)

767

Too Late

767x

Type		Value
760	July, 1840.	
	Adds to value, Black...	$1.00
	Red....	1.25
	Orange, Brick-Red, Brown.............	1.25
	Cancelling Stamps.	
	1851 3d. In Black....	7.50
	1853 3d. In Black....	$7.50
	1857 ½d. In Blue.....	
	½c. Perf in Black	
	1859 5c. In Black....	2.25
	1868 ½c. In Black....	1.75
	3c. In Black....	2.00
	In Red......	2.25
	1870 1c. Orange in: Black...	
	3c. Red....	2.25
	1880 3c. Black...	1.75
	1c. Black...	1.50
	1883 2c. Regist......	2.50
	5c. Regist......	2.50
	1898 2c. Map, Black..	2.50
761	Noted from Nov., 1839.	
	Adds to value:	
	Black...	.50
	Red....	.75
	Cancelling Stamps.	
	1851 3d. Laid........	
	1853 3d.	7.00
	1857 ½d.	
	1859 5c.	2.00
	1868 3c.	2.00
	1c. Orange......	
	3c. In Red.....	2.25
762	Stampless Cover, 1831.	
	Red (Quebec).........	
	Adds to value of cover.	$0.75
763	Stamped Cover, Nov., 1859.	
	Adds to value, Black...	.50
	Red....	.60

Type		Value
764	Stamped Cover, July, 1866. Red (Riviere du Loup). Adds to value.........	.60
765	Stamped Cover. Adds to value, Black...	.50
	Cancelling Stamp. 1870 3c. In Black....	1.50
a.	With hyphen.........	
766	Stamped Cover. Adds to value, Black...	.50
	Cancelling Stamp. 1870 3c. In Black....	1.50
767	Stamped Cover, July, 1893. Black (Yarmouth, N.S.) Adds to value.........	.60
767x	Adds to value.........	.75

SECOND-MAIL

768

Type		Value
768	Stamped Cover. Mail made up in three sections received Type 768 reading "First Mail," "Second "Mail" or "Third Mail," in Black.....	
a.	Thick letters..........	

LATE FEE

769

Type		Value
769	A contemporary ruling was in effect in the London, England, District Post Offices that letters for the night mail could be posted for an extra payment of one penny up to 6.45 p.m. and 7.30 at the chief office. This was also the practice in Canada.	
	Stamped Cover, March, 1854. Adds to value, Black..	1.50
	Cancelling Stamps. 1854 3d. In Black....	20.00
	6d. In Black....	

"WAY LETTERS"

A letter handed to a mail carrier on his way to a Post Office, where it would be posted, was stamped "WAY," before being despatched. This might later explain any inconsistencies between the time it was handed to the mail carrier and the time received by the addressee. From 1859 the marking read: "WAY LETTER" enclosed in a circle.

In Nova Scotia and New Brunswick a regulation required mail couriers on the coach roads to accept letters for mailing when offered at a distance from the nearest office and to place them in a locked pouch provided for the purpose, to be posted at the first post office, where the Postmaster stamped them "WAY."

In the United States the regulation (Act of 1852) required the Postmaster to impress WAY LETTER on such letters and to add one cent to the rate.

WAY

775

Type		Value
775	Stamped Cover, 1855. Adds to value, Black..	$1.00
	Cancelling Stamps. 1855 3d. In Black....	20.00
	6d. In Black....	
	1868 3c. In Black....	5.00
	6c.	5.00

ST JOHN NB
WAY LETTER

776

Type		Value
776	Black, 1868.	
	1868 6c. Canada.....	$5.00

777

777	Stamped Cover.	
	Adds to value, Black...	.50
	Cancelling Stamps.	
	1868 3c.	3.00
	1c. Brown.....	

Type		Value
	1875 1c.............	1.75
	1903 2c. K.E........	1.25
	1908 2c. Que.........	1.25

778 779

778	Stamped Cover.	
	Adds to value, Black...	.50
	Cancelling Stamps.	
	1870 3c.	2.00
	1875 1c.	1.50
	1903 2c. K.E........	1.00
	1908 2c. Que.........	1.00
	New Brunswick, Nov., 1866.	
779	Stamped Cover.	
	Adds to value, Black...	.75

FORWARDED

Marked on cover at any forwarding point.

FORWARDED

785

FORWARDED

786

FORWARDED

787

FORWARDED

788

FORWARDED

789

Type		Value
785	Stampless Cover.	
	Black, Sp., 1837.......	
	Adds to cat. value.....	$0.75
786	Stampless Cover.	
	Black-Red, Mr., 1857..	
	Adds to cat. value.....	.75
787	Black................	
	Adds to cat. value.....	.25
788	Black, Ap., 1843......	
	Adds to cat. value.....	.50
	Blue................	
	Adds to cat. value.....	.75
	Red................	
	Adds to cat. value.....	.85
789	Black, Mr., 1867......	
	Adds to catl. value....	.25
	Stamped Cover.	
	Adds to value.........	.50

FORWARD·TO
DESTINATION

790

Type		Value
790	Black, Sp., '80........	
	Stamped Cover.	
	Adds to value.........	

FORWARDED

791

Type		Value
791	Black, Sp., '59........	
	Stampless Cover......	.50

Markings Appearing on Letters Not Called For, Misdirected, Advertised, Sent to Dead Letter Office, Etc.

"CALL" AND "ADVERTISED"

If a letter was not delivered, or if the addressee had not called to claim it, the Postmaster stamped it in red "CALL." Periodically these uncalled for letters were advertised and if still not claimed they were stamped "ADV.", "Advertised," etc. Early Pence Issue covers have been noted with "Advertised" or "A" written in the upper left corner. No Dead Letter Office existed at that date.

CALL

795

CALL

796

Type			Value
795	First noted Feb., 1862.		
	Adds to value of cover		
		Black.......	$0.50
		Carmine....	.60
	Cancelling Stamps.		
	1868 6c. Carmine.....		10.00
	1870 3c. Black.......		5.00
796	Adds to value of cover		
		Black.......	.50

ADV

797

798

799

Type			Value
797	**New Brunswick,** Nov., 1861.		
	Adds to value of cover		
		Black.......	.60
798	**Toronto, Windsor,** etc., Ju., '64.		
	Adds to value of cover		
		Black.......	.60
		Red........	1.00
799	**Toronto,** 1853.		
	Adds to value of cover		
		Black.......	.60

ADVERTISED

800

800	**Waterloo, Ont.,** Apr., 1883.		
	Adds to value of cover		
		Black.......	$0.25
		Blue........	
	Toronto, Oct., 1884.		
	Adds to value of cover.		.30

801

Type		Value
801	**Fredericton, N. B.,** 1849. Adds to value of cover Red	$0.75

ADV^D NOT CALLED FOR

802

802	Aug., 1867, in Black. Adds to value of cover .	.60

ADVERTISED
AND
NOT-CALLED-FOR

803

ADVERTISED-&
NOT-CALLED-FOR

804

803	February, 1874, in Black. Adds to value of cover .	.50
804	Ju., '64, in Black. Adds to value of cover .	.75
	Toronto, Oct., 1884. Blue........ Adds to value of cover .	.85
	Guelph, Fe., '77. Bronze-Brown	1.00
	a. "NOT CALLED FOR," 2″ long............	

UNCLAIMED

805

UNCLAIMED

806

Type		Value
805	October, 1875 in black. Adds to value of cover.	.20
	Cancelling Stamp. 1875 3c..............	.50
806	1880 in black. Adds to value of cover.	.25
	Cancellation. 1880 3c..............	.60

NOT CALLED FOR
NOT CALLD FOR.

807 and 808

NOT·CALLED·FOR

809

NOT CALLED FOR

809x

NOT CALLED FOR

810

Not called for.

810xx

807-8	**Prince Edward Island.** Add to value of cover Black.......	$0.50
809	June, 1877 (3 sizes). Add to value of cover ..	.30
	Cancellation. 1877 3c.	.75

Type		Value
	1897 2c. Q. V. Numeral.......	.40
	a. Length 39½ mm., Nov., 1882.	
	Bradford, Fe., '73.	
809x	Black.......	.60
810	1880	
	Adds to value of cover.	.30
	Cancellation.	
	1880 3c.	.60
810xx	**Dresden, Ont.,** Ja., '87. Violet	
	Adds to value of cover.	.75

MUST BE FOUND

810x

810x	Oct., 1874, Black.	
	Adds to value of cover.	.30

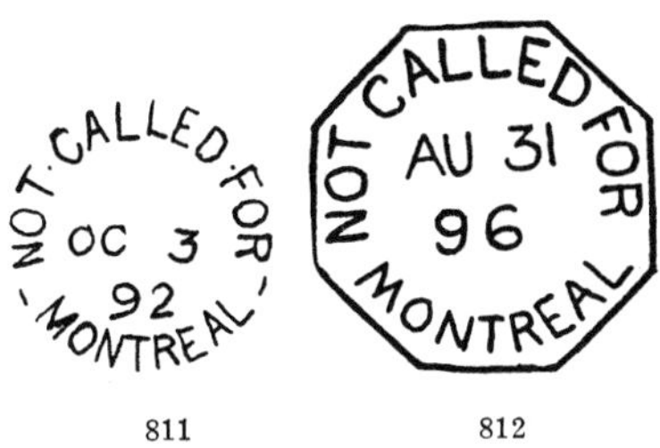

811 812

811	Oct., 1892.	
	Adds to value of cover.	.20
812	**Toronto** or **Montreal,** Aug., 1896.	
	Adds to value of cover.	.40
	a. Circle encloses date, Oct., 1879.	

"MISSENT" MARKINGS

MISSENT

813

814

MISSENT-TO

815

MIS-SENT-TO

816

Type		Value
813	1859, Black.	
	Adds to value of cover.	$0.50
814	Adds to value of cover.	.40
815	Feb., 1892.	
	Adds to value of cover.	.30
816	Nov., 1868, Black.	
	Adds to value of cover.	$0.40

MISSENT TO
VICTORIA BRITISH COLUMBIA

817

Type	Noted	Value
817	**British Columbia.**	
	Black.......	
	Adds to value of cover.	$1.00

NOT KNOWN
RETURN TO
WRITER

818x

818

Not known
Not in directory
Not called for

819

Type		Value
818x	Add to value of cover..	$0.25
	Cancellation.	
	1897 7c. Q. V. Numeral.......	.75
819	Add to value of cover..	.45
818	**Toronto,** Ju., '88. A U.S. marking copied.	
	Adds to value of cover.	.65

NOT KNOWN

820

RETURNED-TO

821

RETURNED FOR
BETTER DIRECTION

824

REFUSED

RETURNED TO

825

820	Add to value of cover..	.20
	Cancellation.	
	1897 3c. 4-Leaf......	.50
821	Jan., 1879.	
	Add to value of cover..	.35
822-3	May, 1878.	
	Add to value of cover..	.25
a.	"Returned by Carrier," Apr., 1883.	
824	1885. Black.	
	Add to value of cover..	.35
	Cancellation.	
	1885 3c..............	.75

Type		Value
a.	Light lines smaller, Feb., 1877.	
b.	2-lines, wider spacing, Oc., '69.	
825	Adds to value of cover.	.25

THE PERSON ADDRESSED
IS BELIEVED TO BE EN-
GAGED IN A BUSINESS
OF A FRAUDULENT
CHARACTER.

826

HAVE LETTERS
DIRECTED
TO STREET & NO

827

826	May, 1894.	
	Adds to value of cover.	1.25
a.	Framed "P.O. Dept. Canada. Suspected to be of a fraudulent character within the meaning of the Post Office Act." May, 1878.	
b.	"Suspected to be of a fraudulent character." 2-lines. Apr., 1890.	
827	Adds to value of cover.	.25
a.	"Please have your mail directed to street and No." 2 lines, April, 1895.	

TORONTO ONT

RECD IN DAMAGED CONDITION

828

RECEIVED
WITHOUT-CONTENTS

829

828	February, 1892.	
	Adds to value of cover.	.25
829	May, 1877.	
	Adds to value of cover.	.35

NO·STREET·OF·THE·NAME·IN·MONTREAL

FIRM·NOT·KNOWN·IN·MONTREAL

822 and 823

830

831

Type		Value
830	Dec., 1902. Adds to value of cover .	$0.35
831	June, 1876. Adds to value of cover .	.35

CLOSED AGAINST INSPECTION

831x

CLOSED AGAINST INSPECTION

831xx

831x **Parry Sound,** Feb., 1878, Black, on cover marked "No Correspondence," addressed to Crown Lands Dept., Toronto, with notation "Mr. McMurray should be written to leave Book Post fully open at the ends of the envelope." The cover bore a 1c. stamp and was taxed 10c.
Adds to value of cover . .50

831xx **Loch Winnoch,** Oct., 1881. Black.
Adds to value of cover . .50

"DEAD LETTER OFFICE"

NO-TRACE-IN D.L.O

835

NO·MONEY·ENCLOSURE WHEN·OPENED·IN·D.L.O.

836

D. L. O. Record,
No.... 23867....

837

Type		Value
835	Apr., 1886. Adds to value of cover .	$0.25
836	Mar., 1877. Adds to value of cover .	.25
837	Adds to value of cover .	$0.25
	a. Double lined.	

838

Type — Value

838 March, 1889. Numerals 1-2-3. . . . .
Adds to value of cover . .20
Cancellation.
1889. Brown. Offic. Sealed. . . . .

839 840

839 Similar, from 1859.
Adds to value of cover . .25
(Disappeared, Aug., 1878.)
Cancellation
1859 1c. 1.50
1879. Brown Offc. Sealed . . . .

840 June, 1874.
Adds to value of cover . $0.25
Cancellation.
1879. Brown Off Sealed . . . .
1878 15c. 4.00
3c. 1.00

841

841 1879.
Adds to value of cover . $0.25
Cancellation.
1879. Brown Offc. Sealed . . . .

Type — Value

1886 3c. 1.00
1897 3c. Jub. 60
a. "Rec'd at Dead Letter Branch, Canada" numerals 1 to 6 replacing AM PM (Dec., 1893.)
b. Period between words.

842

842 Aug., 1892. Numbers 1 to 6.
Adds to value of cover . .20
Cancellation.
1892. Brown Offc. Sealed . . . .
1892 3c. 60
a. "D.L.O. Canada," etc.
Cancellation.
1879. Brown Offc. Sealed . . . .
1905. Black Offc. Sealed . . . .
b. "Branch" instead of "Office."

843

843 1892.
Cancellation.
1892 3c. $0.60

845

Type — Value

From 1851 the rate on circulars and price lists was ½d. per ounce.

845 — 1851 covers. Black.
Adds to value of cover . $0.25

PREPAID
BY
PUBLISHER

846

PREPAID BY
PUBLISHER

847

PREPAID
BY PUBLISHER

848

Type			Value
846	1890. Black.		
	1890 15c.	. . . .	$6.00
	Adds to value of cover .		.35
847	1868. Black.		
	Adds to value of cover .		.35
	1868 2c.	. . . .	3.50
	6c.	. . . .	4.50
848	1880. Black.		
	Adds to value of cover .		.35
	1880 1c. Yellow	. . . . . .	1.00
	3c.	. . . .	1.25

5th CLASS

849

849 — 1885 1c. Yellow 40

CROWNS

In 1858 a cancellation was introduced which commemorated the 20th Anniversary of Queen Victoria's ascension to the throne. It usually appears (Type 850) as a rather indistinct circular blur. On close examination the collector fortunate enough to possess one may trace the outlines of the date. Distinct impressions are quite rare.

Various offices were supplied with brass seals for sealing letters and packets to the P. O. Dept. When impressed in sealing wax these produced an embossed crown with the name of the office in circular form around it, but when used as a cancellation the result was a smudge outlining a very indistinct crown, and the letters spelling the name of the office could only be deciphered with difficulty.

850x

	Black.		
850x	1857 ½d.	. . . .	
	3d.	. . . .	$15.00
	6d.	. . . .	
	1859 1c.	. . . .	
	5c.	. . . .	6.00

850

851

Type		Value
850	Black	
	Adds to value of cover .	$5.00

Type		Value
851	Black.	
	(Kingston or London).	
	1858 3d.	15.00
	6d.	
	(Little Current).	
	1898 2c. Map........	3.00
	1885 3c.	1.50
	1897 3c. Jub.........	1.50
	(Port Royal, U. C.)	
	1890 1c.	1.50
	3c.	1.50
	Town (?)	
	1897 3c. Jub.........	.75
	(Main....Newfoundland).	
	1c. Green wrapper.....	

852

853

852	**Ottawa,** Feb., 1880. Black.	
	1880 3c.	$2.50
853	**Ottawa,** Apr., 1880. Black.	
	1868 ½c.	
	12½c.	
	15c.	5.00
	1870 1c. Orange......	
	2c.	2.50
	3c.	2.50
	1880 1c. Yellow......	1.75
	2c.	2.50
	3c.	2.00
	15c.	
	1882 15c. Thick Paper.	25.00
	½c.	1.50
	8c.	2.25
	10c.	2.50
	1893 20c.	3.00
	50c.	3.00
	2c. Regist......	1.75
	5c. Regist......	1.75
	1898 2c. Map........	3.50
	1897 3c. 4-Leaf......	1.50
	3c. Jub.........	1.50
	15c. Jub.........	
	50c. Jub.........	
	2c. King Edward	1.50
	(On all values, 4-Leaf and O.V. Numeral issue.)	

854

Type		Value
854	In general use in Post Office at Victoria, British Columbia and not specifically for Legislature or Esquimalt Naval Station as sometimes stated, Sept., 1880. Black.	
	1868 15c.	$7.00
	1875 1c. Yellow......	2.50
	3c.	3.25
	1880 3c.	3.25
	5c.	
	6c.	
	10c.	
	15c.	
	1882 15c. Thick Paper.	$30.00
	1893 50c. Blue........	5.00
	2c. Regist......	2.25
	5c. Regist......	2.25
	1908 2c. King Edward	2.00
	2c. Quebec......	2.25

855 856

855	1880 3c.	2.50
856	Black. 1870.	
	1870 3c.	3.50

857 858 859

Type		Value
857	Black. 1880.	
	1880 3c.	1.50
	2c. Regist......	1.50
858	1875 3c.	1.50
859	Tudor Crown. 1880. Black.	
	1880 3c.	1.50

"LEAF" TYPES

865

866

867

868

869

870

871

872

873

874

875

876

877

878

879

880

881

882

Type		Value
865	Black.	
	1859 10c.	$5.00
	1868 1c. Yellow.	
	2c.	
	3c.	5.00
	6c.	
	Orangeville used similar type, Aug., 1870.	
	Orillia, in Pale Green, Ju., '70.	
	1870 1c. Orange.	2.25
	3c.	5.00
	15c.	
866	**Montreal.** Black.	
	1868 2c.	
	3c.	5.00
866	Lindsay used a similar type about 1870 and Oshawa, June, 1872; Glenallen, Ap., '73. . .	
a.	Corners rounded, Dec., 1869.	
867	Black.	
	1870 1c. Orange.	$5.00
	Bala, Jy., '73. Purple.	
	1873 3c.	5.00
868	Black.	
	1868 2c.	5.00
	3c.	5.00
	6c.	5.00
869	1868 3c.	3.75
	6c.	3.75
870	1873 3c.	3.75
871	1868 3c.	3.75
	6c.	3.75

Type		Value
872	1895 3c.	2.00
	Belfast, P. E. I. and Souris East, P. E. I.	
873	1903 2c. King Edward	1.00
	1c. King Edward	1.00
	3c. Brown George	1.00
	1908 2c. Quebec.	1.00
874	Black.	
	1859 5c. Beaver.	$4.00
	12½c.	10.00
	1870 3c.	2.00
875	1890 3c.	1.50
876	1890 3c.	1.50
877	1885 3c.	.75
878	1868 6c.	4.00
	1872 3c.	1.00
879	**Newfoundland. 1879.** Black.	
	1879 3c. Rouletted . . .	2.00
880	**St. John, N. B.** Black.	
	1880 3c.	.75
	5c.	.75
881	1885. (Several variations).	
	Purple.	
	1885 3c.	.75
882	**Victoria Road, Ont.** Oct., 1877. Violet.	
	1877 1c.	.75
	3c.	.75

883 884

Type		Value
883	**Toronto,** Sept., 1869. Black.	
	1868 1c. Brown......	
	3c.	5.00
884	**Toronto.** Black.	
	1868 1c. Brown......	
	3c.	5.00

885 886

Type		Value
885	**Otterville.** Purple.	
	1885 3c.	.75
886	**Hagersville,** Apr., 1880.	
886	Black.	
	1880 1c. Yellow......	$0.30
	3c.	.30
a.	5 sections to a side.	

"FLOWER" TYPES, ETC.

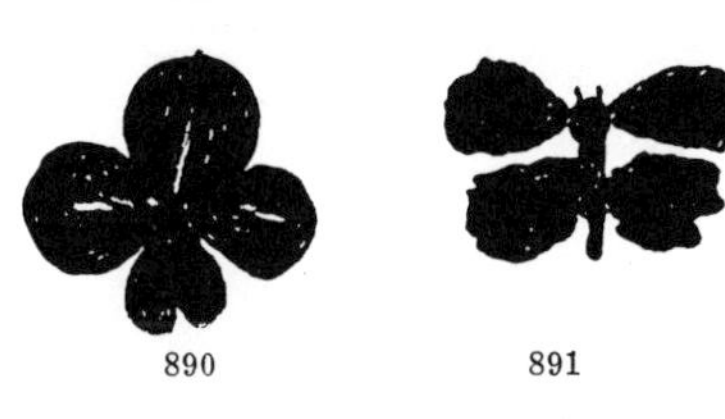

890 891

892 895

Type		Value
890	**Gravenhurst, Ont.,** Mar., 1880. Black.	
	1880 1c. Yellow......	.40
	2c.	.50
	3c.	.40

Type		Value
891	Butterfly used by Toronto.	
	1890 1c. Yellow......	.30
	3c.	.30
892	1873 15c.	2.75
895	**Toronto,** 1870.	
	1870 3c. Rose........	1.00

893 894

893	**Ottawa,** Apr., 1880. Black.	
	1880 1c. Yellow......	.20
	2c.	.30
	3c.	.30
894	**St. John's, Newfoundland,** June 24th, 1865. Black.	
	1865 6½d. Rose........	

900  901

Type		Value
	Black.	
900	1859 1c.	
	5c.	$0.60
	1868 3c.	.75
901	1859 1c.	
	5c.	.60
	1868 3c.	.75
	Blue.	
	1859 5c.	.70

902  903

Type		Value
902	1859 to Aug., 1865.	
	Black.	
	1859 5c.	.70
	1868 3c.	.80
	Blue.	
	1859 5c.	.85
	1868 3c.	.95
	a. "9 Bars" Toronto, Sept., 1861.	
903	**Toronto,** Dec., 1857.	
	Black.	
	1857 3d.	5.00
	½d.	.60
	1858 3d. Ribbed	
	1859 1c.	
	5c.	.60
	10c.	
	12½c.	
	5c. Stamped Envelope	6.50
	1868 1c. Brown	
	3c.	1.00
	Blue.	
	a. Thinner Bars.	
	1859 5c.	.75

903xy  903xyz

903y 903yx

903x  903yxz

904  905

Type		Value
904	Black.	
	1859 5c.	$1.00
	1868 3c.	.75
	Blue.	
	1859 5c.	1.15
	Red.	
	1859 5c.	1.50
905	**Ottawa.** 1880.	
	Black.	
	1890 3c.	.25

906

Type		Value
906	1890 3c.	.35

907 908

Type		Value
907	**Gypsum Mines, Ont.** July, 1894.	
	Black.	
	1894 1c.	.15
	3c.	.20
908	**McKellar, Ont.,** Feb., 1879.	
	Black.	
	1879 1c.	.15
	3c.	.20

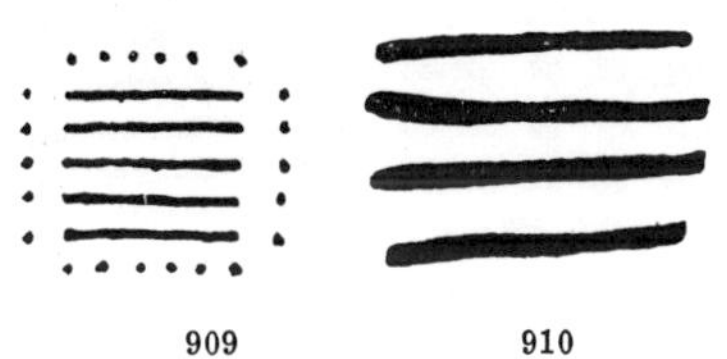

909 910

Type		Value
909	May, 1868.	
	Black.	
	1868 ½c.	
	2c.	
	3c.	1.50
	6c.	
	12½c.	
	1c. Brown	
910	**McKellar, Ont.,** July, 1876.	
	Black.	
	1876 1c.	.15
	3c.	.20

911 917

Type		Value
911	**St. John, N. B.,** Apr., 1868.	
	Black.	
	1868 ½c.	
	1c. Brown	
	2c.	
	3c.	.75
	6c.	
	12½c.	
	1870 3c.	.75
	1880 15c.	2.00
917	General use in **New Brunswick.**	
	Black.	
	1868 2c.	
	3c.	.85
	1870 3c.	
	1880 3c.	
	Blue.	
	1868 3c.	1.50
	1870 3c.	1.25
	1880 3c.	.50
	Red.	
	1868 2c.	
	3c.	1.60
	1870 3c.	1.50
	1880 3c.	.75
	Green.	
	1868 3c.	2.00
	1870 3c.	1.50
	1880 3c.	1.00
a.	10 Bars—**London, Ont.**	
b.	11 Bars — **Hamilton, Ont.**	

912

Type		Value
912	**Invermay, U. C.,** Mar., 1866.	
	Black.	
	1866 1c.	

913  914

915  916

Type		Value
913	**Ottawa,** May and June, 1872.	
	Black.	
	1872 1c.	
	3c.	.75
914	**Ottawa,** Jan., 1871.	
	Black.	
	1871 3c.	$0.75
a.	With 3 cuts dividing cork into 6 sections.	
	1870 15c. In Blue	3.50
915	**Ottawa,** Mar., 1872.	
	Black.	
	1872 3c.	.75
916	**Hamilton** and **Toronto,** 1868.	
	Black.	
	1868 1c. Brown	
	2c.	
	3c.	$0.85
	1870 3c.	.85
	1880 3c.	.10
	Blue.	
	1868 3c.	1.50
	1870 3c.	1.25
	1880 3c.	.25
	Red.	
	1868 3c.	1.60
	1870 3c.	1.50
	1880 3c.	1.25
	Green.	
	1868 3c.	2.00
	1870 3c.	1.75
	1880 3c.	1.50

918  919

Type		Value
918	**Sackville, N. B.,** 1868.	
	Black.	
	1868 3c.	.85
	1870 3c.	.85
	1880 3c.	.25
918	Blue.	
	1868 3c.	$1.50
	Red.	
	1868 3c.	1.60
	Green.	
	1868 3c.	2.00
	Purple.	
	1868 3c.	1.60
919	**Douglaston, New Brunswick.** 1851.	
	Black.	
	1851 6d.	

920x  920

Type		Value
920x	**Toronto,** Sp., '72.	
	Black.	
	1872 3c.	.40
	1c.	.25
920	General use, Feb., 1866.	
	Black.	
	1866 5c.	
	12½c.	3.25
	1868 3c.	.60
	6c.	
	2c.	
	12½c.	
	1870 15c.	3.00
	3c.	1.00

Type		Value
	Blue.	
	1868 1c.	
	2c.	
	3c.	.75
	6c.	
	1870 3c.	1.25
	Red.	
	1868 1c.	
	3c.	1.50
	6c.	
	1870 3c.	
	Green.	
	1868 3c.	1.75
	6c.	
	1870 3c.	

920a

a. 9 Bars—Montreal, Ju., '88; Woodstock, Oc., '89; Peter St. Toronto, My., '89; Bathurst St. Toronto, My., '89; Three Rivers, Ja., '89; Quebec, De., '88.
b. 10 Bars—Mitchell, Ont., Ja., '89; Carlton St. Toronto, Sp., '88.

QUEBEC FE 23 66 C.E

920xx

Type		Value
920xx	Black.	
	1866 5c.	1.00

921

Type		Value
921	General use from 1859.	
	Black.	
	1859 1c.	
	5c.	.50
	12½c.	
	17c.	
	1868 1c. Brown......	
	1c. Yellow......	
	1c. Orange......	
	2c.	
	3c.	.60
	6c.	
	12½c.	
	15c.	
	1875 5c. (Large).....	
	5c. (Small).....	
921	1880. (All values)....	
	1890. (All values)....	
	1897. (All values).....	
	(Used until after 1900).	
	Blue.	
	1865 10c.	
	5c.	
	1868 3c.	.75
	2c.	
	1870 3c.	.75
	1897 3c. 4-Leaf......	
	(Point Edward used 921 in Blue, June, 1872).	
	Violet.	
	1870 3c.	.75
	1897 3c. 4-Leaf......	.75
	Red.	
	1868 3c.	1.00
	1870 3c.	1.00
	1859 1c.	
	12½c.	
	1880 6c.	
	Green.	
	1870 3c.	1.25
	1868 3c.	1.75
	(Used up to and after 1900 in various colors.)	
a.	Section 4 mm. wide removed from center.	
	1870 3c. In Black....	.75

922

923

Type		Value
922	Blue.	
	1860 10c.	
	Black.	
	1868 1c. Brown	
	2c.	
	3c.	.75
	6c.	
	12½c.	
	15c.	
	Green.	
	1868 3c.	
	6c.	
	(Toronto was using type 922 (11 bars), Feb., 1881.)	
923	1870 3c. In Green	$0.75
	1890 3c. In Purple	.20
	14 Bars In Blue	.20

924

Type		Value
924	Duplex, supplied to 22 offices only, including Montreal, Hamilton, London, Guelph, etc. In Ju., '82, this type was supplied Winnipeg; to St. John in Ap.,'82; St. Hyacinthe, No., '89.	
	Black.	
	1859 1c.	
	5c.	.50
	10c.	
	12½c.	
	17c.	
	1864 2c.	
	1868 1c. Brown	
	1c. Yellow	
	1c. Orange	
	2c.	
	3c.	.75
	6c.	
	12½c.	
	15c.	
	1875 5c. (Large)	
	5c. (Small)	
	1870 1c. Orange	
	2c.	
	3c.	
	1872 6c.	
	Blue.	
	1859 1c.	
	5c.	.85
	10c.	
	1868 1c. Brown	
	1c. Yellow	
	1c. Orange	
	3c.	.90
	6c.	
	Red.	
	1859 5c.	1.00
	10c.	
	12½c.	
	1868 3c.	1.10
	Green.	
	1859 5c.	1.50
	10c.	
	1868 3c.	1.50
a.	15 Bars—London, No., '88.	

925

Type		Value
925	**Quebec,** 12 bars, diam. 25 mm.	
	St. John, No., '88.	
	Black.	
	1868 3c.	$0.75
	1c. Brown	
	1c. Yellow	
	2c.	
	6c.	
	12½c.	
	15c.	
	1870 1c. Orange	
	2c.	
	3c.	.70
	1872 6c.	
	1875 5c. (Large)	
	5c. (Small)	
	(Continued in use for some years).	
	Blue.	
	1868 3c.	.90
	1c. Brown	
	2c.	
	6c.	
	12½c.	
	15c.	
	1870 1c. Orange	

Type		Value
	2c.	
	3c.	.90
	1872 6c.	
	1875 5c. (Large)	
	5c. (Small)......	
	Purple.	
	1870 1c.	
	3c.	.90
	Red.	
	1868 3c.	1.25
	1870 3c.	1.25
	Green.	
	1868 1c. Brown	
	1c. Yellow......	
	3c.	1.50
	6c.	
	1870 1c.	
	3c.	1.50

926

926	13 Bars. General use from May, 1860. 13-bar types were supplied St. Catharines, Sp., '81; Hamilton, My., '81; Montreal, Fe., '82; Sarnia, Fe., '82; Belleville, Au., '81; Union Ry. Stn., Toronto, Ja., '82.	
	Black.	
	1868 1c. Brown	
	1c. Yellow......	
	1c. Orange......	
	2c.	
	3c.	.75
	6c.	
	12½c.	
	15c.	
	1870 1c.	
	2c.	
	3c.	
	1872 6c.	
	1875 5c. (Small)......	
	5c. (Large)	
	10c.	
	Blue.	
	1868 1c. Yellow......	
	2c.	
	3c.	.90

Type		Value
	6c.	
	12½c.	
	15c.	
	1870 1c.	
	3c.	.90
	1872 6c.	
	1875 5c. (Large)	
	5c. (Small)	
	10c.	
	Windsor, U.C., used Blue Aug. 13, to Dec. 3, 1879.	
	Purple.	
	1870 3c.	.80
	Red.	
	1868 3c.	1.00
	6c.	
	1870 3c.	1.00
	1872 6c.	
	Green.	
	1868 3c.	1.50
	6c.	
	1870 3c.	1.50
	1872 6c.	
926a.	**Port Hope, C. W.,** Ja., '70. Center cut out and cork cut in 8 segments inserted.	
	1870 3c. In Black	.75

927

927	**Prince Edward Island,** Black.......	

928

928	Black.	
	1859 5c.	1.00
	1868 3c.	1.00

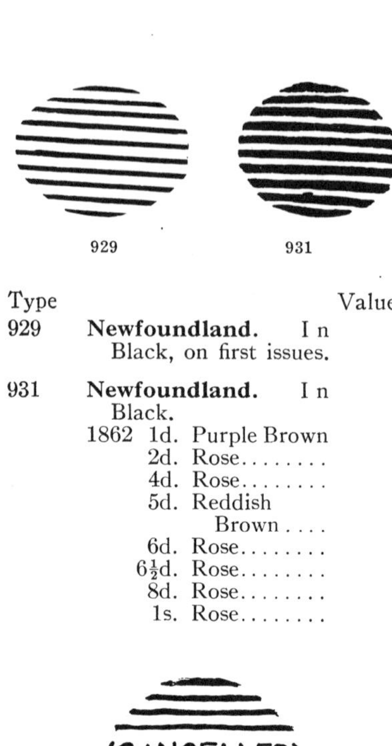

929 931

Type		Value
929	**Newfoundland.** In Black, on first issues.	
931	**Newfoundland.** In Black.	
	1862 1d. Purple Brown	
	2d. Rose........	
	4d. Rose........	
	5d. Reddish Brown....	
	6d. Rose........	
	6½d. Rose........	
	8d. Rose........	
	1s. Rose........	

930

Type		Value
930	**Newfoundland.** In Black.	
	1860 1s.	

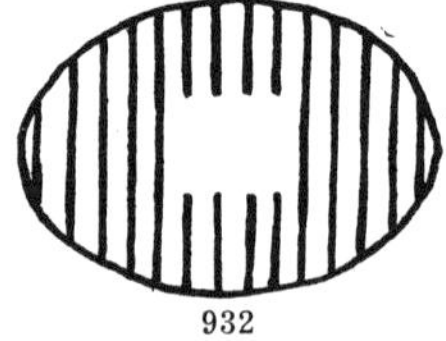

932

Type		Value
932	**New Brunswick.** Space left for inserting numeral, but numerals never used. For numeral type see, "Numeral Cancellations."	
	Black.	
	1851 3d. N. B........	
	6d. N. B........	
	1s. N. B........	
	1860 1c.	
	1863 2c.	
	1860 5c.	
	10c.	
	12½c.	
	17c.	
	Canada.	
	1868 1c. Brown......	
	1c. Yellow......	
	2c.	
	3c.	.90
932	1868 6c.	
	12½c.	
	1870 3c.	
	1875 5c. (Small)......	
	Red. (Salmon Creek, N. B., Dec., 1894).	
	1894 8c. Grey.......	1.25

933

Type		Value
933	**Nova Scotia.** Space left for inserting numeral, but numerals never used. For numeral type, see "Numeral Cancellations."	
	1868 3c. In Black....	1.00

934

Type		Value
934	Black.	
	1890 1c. Yellow......	.25
	3c.	.35

935

Type				Value
935	**Nova Scotia.** From 1851.			
	Black.			
	1851	1d.	N. S........	
		3d.	....	
		6d.	....	
		1s.	....	
	1863	1c.	....	
		2c.	....	
		5c.	....	
		8½c.	....	
		10c.	....	
		12½c.	....	
	1851	3d.	N. B........	
	1868	½c.	Canada.....	
		1c.	Brown, etc...	
		2c.	....	
		3c.	....	1.25
		6c.	....	
		12½c.	....	
	1875	5c.	(Large).....	
	1870	1c.	....	
		3c.	....	.40
	Blue.			
	1851	3d.	N. S........	
	1868	2c.	Canada.....	
		6c.	Canada.....	
		12½c.	Canada.....	
	1870	3c.	Canada.....	.60
	Red.			
	1851	3d.	N. B........	

936

Type				Value
936	**Nova Scotia.**			
	Black.			
	1851	3d.	....	
	1863	2c.	....	
		5c.	....	2.00
	1868	3c.	Canada.....	1.00
		6c.	Canada.....	

937

937	**Nova Scotia.**			
	Black.			
	1863	5c.	....	3.50

PRINCE EDWARD ISLAND BAR TYPES

The first issue of Prince Edward Island and later issues to a less extent, are noted with cancellation in blue pencil or pen strokes, often in the form of an "X" or an initial. Such cancellations are on letters from country and "Way" offices, and were often supplemented with another and more official cancellation applied at the receiving post office.

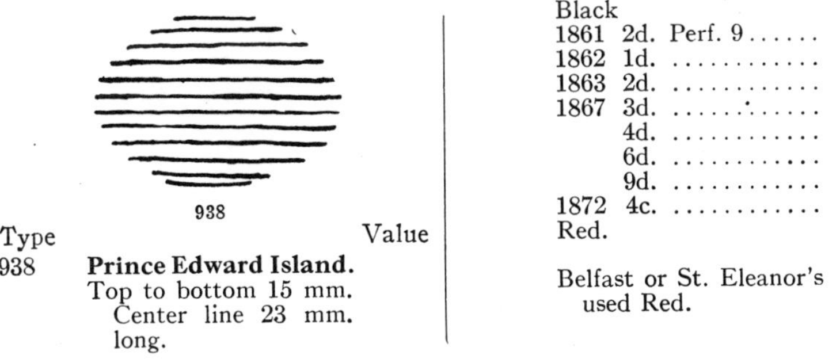

938

Type				Value
938	**Prince Edward Island.** Top to bottom 15 mm. Center line 23 mm. long.			
	Black			
	1861	2d.	Perf. 9......	
	1862	1d.	....	
	1863	2d.	....	
	1867	3d.	....	
		4d.	....	
		6d.	....	
		9d.	....	
	1872	4c.	....	
	Red.			

Belfast or St. Eleanor's used Red.

939

Type		Value
939	**Prince Edward Island.** Georgetown, Mar., 1865. Charlottetown, July, 72.	
	Black.	
939	1867 3d.	
	4d.	
	6d.	
	9d.	
	1872 1c.	
	2c.	
	3c.	
	4c.	
	6c.	
	12c.	

940

940	**Prince Edward Island.**	
	Black.	
	1865 2d.	
	1867 3d.	

941 942

941	**Prince Edward Island.**	
	Black.	
	1861 3d. Perf. 9......	
	1867 3d.	
942	**Prince Edward Island.**	
	Black.	
	1861 3d. Perf. 9......	
	1867 3d.	

943

Type		Value
943	**Prince Edward Island.**	
	Black. April, 1869.	
	1869 3d.	
	1872 1c.	

944 945

944	**Prince Edward Island.**	
	Black.	
	(Dots in early impressions are diamond shaped.)	
	1863 2d.	
	1867 3d.	
945	**Prince Edward Island.**	
	Black.	
	1863 2d.	

BARS CROSSED

946

946	Black.	
	1857 3d. Beaver......	$5.00

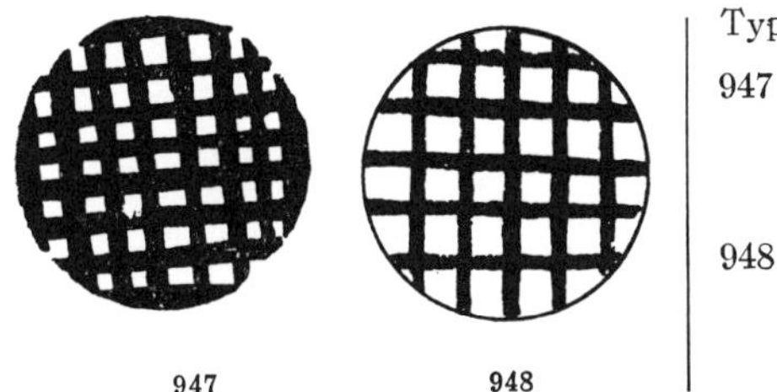

947 948

Type		Value
947	**Wallace Bridge, N. S.**	
	Black. Feb., 1900.	
	1900 1c. Q. V. Num..	.20
	2c. K. Edward..	.20
948	Black.	
	1857 3d. Beaver......	5.00
	1859 5c. Beaver......	1.25

STAR TYPES

960  961  963  964

965  962  966  967

968  969  970  971  981

972  973  980  974

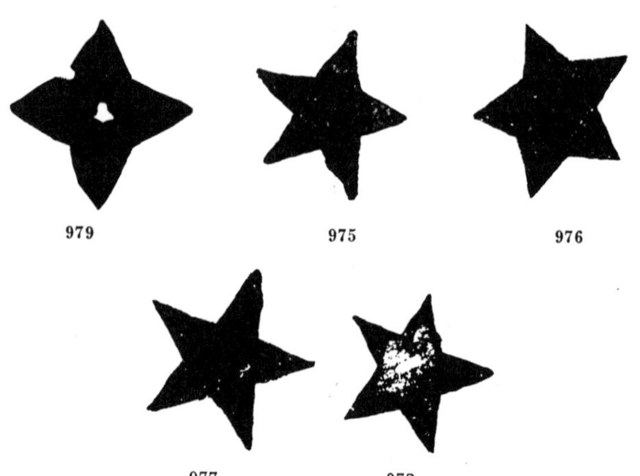
979 975 976 977 978

Type		Value
960	Used by Polly Bog, Alton, and other Nova Scotia offices, Ap., 1880; Stellarton and Enfield, C.W., Aug., 1871; Forks Road, Ont., Feb., 1895; St. Catharines, Apr., 1882.	
	Black.	
	1882 3c.	.65
	5c.	.65
	2c. Verm. Regist.	.75
	5c. Green, Regist.	.75
	(On Q.V. Numerals 4-Leaf Issues.)	
	1908 2c. Quebec......	.65
961	Black.	
	1886 3c.	.65
	2c. Verm. Regist.	.75
	1897 3c. 4-Leaf......	.50
962	Used by Collingwood, Aug. to Oct., 1871.	
	Black.	
	1871 3c.	1.25
	1c. Orange......	
	2c. Verm. Regist.	.50
963	Black. Apr., 1880.	
	1880 1c.	
	3c.	1.00
	2c. Verm. Regist.	.75
a.	No inner star.	
	1894. **Bealton, Ont.** (Feb.)	
	2c. Green.......	.75

Type		Value
964	Black.	
	1880 1c. Yellow......	$0.65
	3c.	1.00
	2c. Verm. Regist.	.65
965	Black.	
	1880 1c. Yellow......	.75
	3c.	1.10
	2c. Or. Regist...	.75
966	Black.	
	1880 1c.	$0.65
	3c.	1.00
	2c. Or. Regist...	.65
967	Blk.	
	1880 1c.	.65
	3c.	.90
	2c. Verm. Regist.	.65
968	Black.	
	1885 3c.	1.00
969	**Collingwood,** in Black.	
	1870 3c.	1.00
970	**Prince Edward Island.**	
	Black.	
	1876 15c.	2.00
	1875 1c. Yellow......	.75
971	**Collingwood.**	
	Nov., 1871, to June, 1872.	
	1871 1c.	.75
	3c.	1.10
972	Black.	
	1868 6c.	$2.50
	1870 3c.	1.25

Type		Value
973	**Cookstown, Ont.**	
	June, 1870.	
	Black.	
	1868 2c.	2.50
	3c.	1.75
	1870 3c.	1.50
974	Black.	
	1880 3c.	.50
975	**Charlottetown, P.E.I.**	
	Jan., 1873.	
	Black.	
	1873 3c. P.E.I........	
	12c. P.E.I........	
976	Black.	
	1868 2c.	2.00
	3c.	1.00
977	**Stellarton, N.S.**	
	Dec., 1888.	
	Similar type Durham, Ont., Ap., 1873.	
	Black.	
	1873 3c.	.75
	1888 1c.	.50
	3c.	.50
	3c. Carmine.....	1.00
978	Black.	
	1890 3c.	.50
	Violet.	
	1890 3c.	.65
	Toronto.	
979	Black.	
	1868 2c.	$2.50
	3c.	1.25
	1870 1c. Orange......	
	3c.	1.25
	1880 6c.	
980	Port Perry, Ont., Jan., 1872 ; Cookstown, Ont., June, 1870 ; Durham, Ont., May 10th to Dec. 26th, 1871.	
	Black.	
	1868 ½c.	1.50
	1c. Yellow......	
	3c.	1.75
	6c.	
	12½c.	
	1870 3c.	1.75
981	Black.	
	1870 3c.	1.50
	a. Hollow Center.	

982

983

Type		Value
982	**Prince Edward Island.**	
	Black.	
	Bisecteds of 2nd issue.	
983	**Prince Edward Island.**	
	1871-2.	
	Black.	
	1872 3c. Rose........	2.75
	a. Larger, Oct., 1872.	
	Black.	
	1872 4c. Green.......	5.00

LETTERS, REPRESENTING INITIALS OF POSTMASTERS POST OFFICES, ETC.

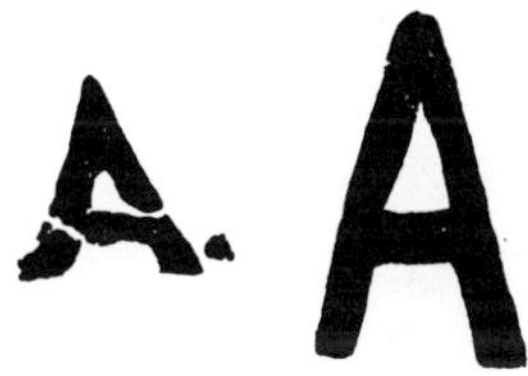
991 991

990	Blue.	
	1859 1c.	$1.75
991	Black.	
	1890 3c.	.50

992

Type		Value
992	**Prince Edward Island.**
	Black.
	1872 1c. P.E.I.......
	3c. P.E.I.......

994

994 Black.
1868 12½c............. 3.00

996 995 997

995	Black.	
	1868 1c. Yellow......	
	2c.	
	3c.	2.00
	12½c.	3.25
996	Black.	
	1887 3c. Carmine.....	$1.25
997	Green.	
	1880 3c.	.75
	Violet. -	
	1880 3c.	.50

998 998a 999

998	....	
998a.	**Bridgewater, C. W.**	
	Black. Oct., 1876 to Feb., 1879.	
	1876 1c.	.60
	3c.	.75
999	Black.	
	1890 3c.	.75

1000 1001

Type		Value
1000	Black. **Barrie, Ont.**	
	1880 3c.	.60
1001	Black. **Barrie, Ont.**	
	1880 3c.	.60

1002

1003

1002	Black.	
	1885 2c. Regist......	.75
1003	Black., in two types.	
	1878 3c.	.75

1004

1005

1004	Black.	
	1870 3c.	1.25
1005	**Port Carling** (BHJ), **Ont.,** Oc., 1875.	
	Black.	
	1875 1c.	1.75
	3c.	2.00

1006

Type		Value
1006	Black.	
	1868 2c.	
	3c.	1.50
	12½c.	
	15c.	

1007

1007	Barnard's X Ranch (or Route) used in British Columbia. Black.	
	1866 2½d. Br. Columbia	
	1868 3c. Canada.....	5.00
	1870 3c. Canada.....	5.00

1008

1008x

1008	**Lambton Mills.**	
	Sp., '82.	
	1882 1c.	$0.60
	On Cover............	1.50
1008x	Black.	
	1859 5c. Beaver......	2.00
	1868 3c.	1.50

1009 1010

1009	Black.	
	1868 3c.	1.60
1010	Black.	
	1880 1c. Yellow......	.50
	3c.	.60

1011

1012

Type		Value
1011	Black.	
	1880 1c. Yellow......	.30
	3c.	.40
1012	**Ottawa,** May, 1892.	
	Black.	
	1892 3c.	.40
	10c.	1.50
	15c.	2.00
	1898 2c. Purple Numeral.......	.30
	2c. Carm. Numeral.......	.25

1013

1015x

1013	Black.	
	1890 3c.	$0.15
1015x	Black.	
	1880 3c.	.50

1014

1015

1014	1876 1c.	$0.15
	3c.	.25
a.	No circle............	
1015	Toronto, Montreal, and other cities used Type	

Type | Value

1015 with various letters designating Postal Stations, from Dec., 1906. . . . .

1016

1016 1880 3c. In Black $0.75
a. "D" in circle.
Black.
1880 3c. 75

1017 1018

1017 Black.
1880 3c. 60
1018 Black.
1880 1c. 75
3c. 85

1019 1020

1019 Black.
1875 3c. 65
1020 Black.
1880 3c. $0.50

1021 1022

Type | Value

1021 Black.
1890 3c. 40
1022 Black.
1890 3c. 60

1023 1023x

Georgetown, U. C.
Nov., 1875 (Impression sometimes heavier).
1023 Black.
1875 3c. $0.75

Grand Narrows, N.S.,
June, 1897.
1023x Black.
5c. . . . .
3c. 1.00
1897 1c. . . . .
2c. . . . .

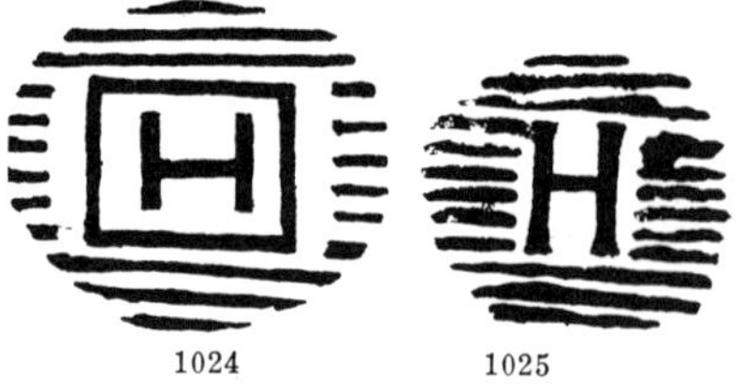

1024 1025

Halifax, N. S.
1024 Black.
1876 3c. 75

Horton's Landing, N. S.
1025 Black.
1890 3c. 75

1026

Type		Value
	Nova Scotia "H" for Halifax, used May, 1861	
1026	Black.	
	1861 1c. N. S........	
	2c. N. S........	
	5c. N. S........	1.75
	8½c. N. S........	
	10c. N. S........	
	12½c. N. S........	
	1872 4c. P. E. I......	

1027

Type		Value
1027	**Nova Scotia** "H" for Halifax, December, 1863.	
	Black.	
	1863 1c. N. S........	
	2c. N. S........	
	5c. N. S........	
	8½c. N. S........	
	10c. N. S........	
	12½c. N. S........	

1029 1028 1030

Type		Value
1028	**Nova Scotia** "H" for Halifax used as duplex Oct., 1867, until after 1876.	
	Black.	
	1867 1c. N. S........	
	2c. N. S........	
	5c. N. S........	
	8½c. N. S........	
	10c. N. S........	
	12½c. N. S........	
	1868 ½c.	
	1c. Yellow, Canada.......	
	1c. Brown, Canada.......	
	2c.	
	3c.	.90
	6c.	
	12½c.	
	15c.	
	1870 1c. Orange, Canada.......	
	3c.	1.00
	1875 5c. (Large).....	
	1876 15c.	
1029	"H" 7 mm. high enclosed by eleven thick horiz. bars as Type 1028, appearing about 1870.	
	Black.	
	1868 3c.	$1.00
	12½c.	
	1870 1c.	
	3c.	1.00
1030	"H" 8 mm. high enclosed by eleven thick horiz. bars as Type 1028, appearing about 1873.	
	1873 1c.	
	3c.	.75
	1875 5c. (Large).....	

1031

Type		Value
1031	**Harrington E., Que.,** Nov., 1881.	
	Black.	
	1881 3c.	$0.35

1032 1032x

Type — Value

1032 **Andover, N. B.,** Oct., 1881.
Black.
1881 3c. 1.00

1032x **Stratford,** Mr., '79.
Black.
1879 3c. .... .40

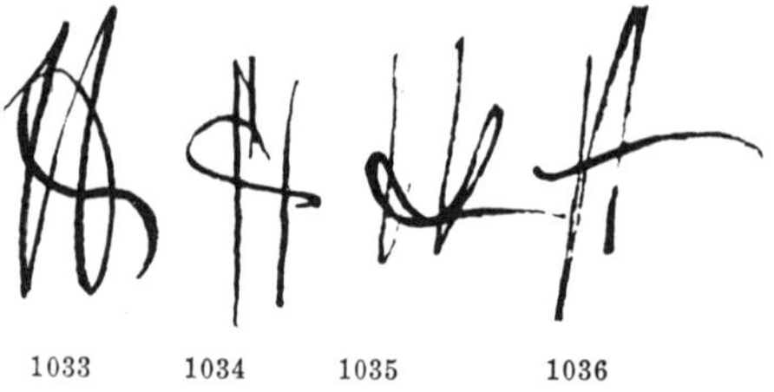

1033 1034 1035 1036

1033 Black.
1875 3c. $0.25
1868 3c. .... .75

1034-5 **Vittoria, C.W.,** Apr., 1853.
Black.
1853 3d. 4.50
1859 5c. .... .75
1868 3c. .... .90

1036 **Otterville,** Mar. 4, 1863.
Black.
1863 5c. .... .75
1868 3c. .... .75

1036 1870 3c. .... $ .90

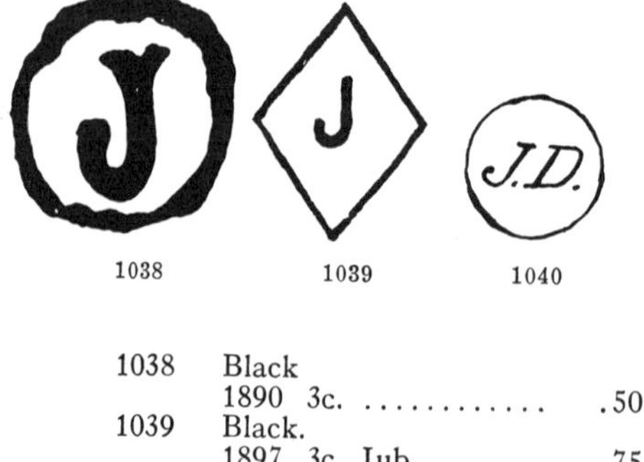

1038 1039 1040

1038 Black
1890 3c. .... .50

1039 Black.
1897 3c. Jub......... .75

1040 Black.
1890 3c. .... .75

1041 1042 1043

Type — Value

1041 Black.
1897 2c. Purple 4-Leaf .25
3c. 4-Leaf...... .25
2c. Purple Num. .25

1042 Black.
Harrington, P.Q. in two slightly different types.
1890 3c. .... .60

a. **Weymouth Bridge, N.S.** July, 1882, double size.

1043 Black.
1870 3c. 1.50

1044

1044x 1044xx

1044 Black.
1880 3c. .... .50

1044x

1044xx **Toronto.** 1879. (Blue) .50
1879 3c. ....
6c. 1.25

1045

1045 Black.
1880 3c. .... .35

1046

1047

1048

Type		Value
1046	Black.	
	1890 3c.	.50
1047	Black.	
	1872 3c.	.60
	10c.	
1048	**Elora.** Feb. 25, '71.	
	Black.	
	1871 3c.	1.00

1049

1050

Type		Value
1049	**Moncton, N.B.** Oct., 1881.	
	Black.	
	1881 1c.	
	2c.	
	3c.	.75
	5c.	
	6c.	
	8c.	
	10c.	
1050	**Fort Garry.** Apr., 1873 "M" for Manitoba.	
	Black.	
	1868 6c.	5.00
	1870 3c.	5.00
	1873 3c.	4.00

1050x 1051

Type		Value
1050x	**Port Carling.** Ju., '74.	
	1874 1c.	.75
	2c.	.75
	3c.	.75
1051	Black.	
	1880 3c.	1.00

1052

1053

Type		Value
1052	Black.	
	1880 3c.	.75
	(Port Carling used an "M.S." similar to 1005 Type, Apr. 21, 1874).	
1053	Black.	
	1885 3c.	.75

1054

1055

Type		Value
1054	**New Westminster, B.C.** July, 1881.	
	Black.	
	1881 3c.	.75
1055	Black.	
	1879 3c.	.45

1056

1057

Type		Value
1056	Black.	
	1879 3c.	.60
1057	**Ottawa.** June, 1872.	
	Black.	
	1872 1c.	.50
	3c.	.75

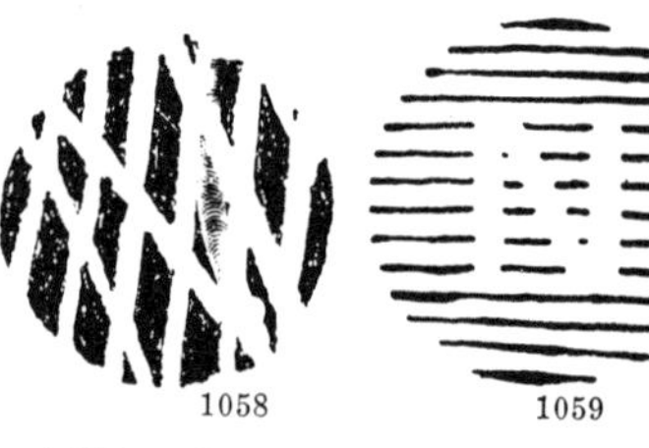

1058 1059

1058	**Ottawa.** March, 1877.	
	Black.	
	1877 3c.	.50
1059	**Toronto.** 1881.	
	Black.	
	1881 3c.	.60

1060

1061

1060	Black.	
	1880 3c.	.50
1061	Black.	
	1880 3c.	.50

1062

Type		Value
1062	Black.	
	1880 3c.	.50

O.K.
F.T.E.

1063

1063	Violet.	
	1890 3c.	.75

OK OK

1064 1065

1064	**Black Rock, N.B.,** 1880.	
	Black.	
	1880 3c., 1c.	1.00
1065	**Black Rock, N.B.** Mar., 1894.	
	1894 3c.	1.00

PV PM

1066 1067

1066	**Piedmont Valley, N.S.** 1890.	
	Black.	
	1890 3c.	1.25
1067	Black.	
	1880 3c.	1.25

1068

Type | Value

1068 **Prince Edward Island.**
Black. (About 1865).

1069

1069 Black.
1859 5c. Beaver...... 3.50

1070 1071 1072

1070 Black.
1880 3c. .... .75
1071 Black.
1876 3c. .... .25
1072 Black.
1876 3c. .... .25

1073

1073 Black.
1880 3c. 1.00
10c. 3.00
a. Smaller.

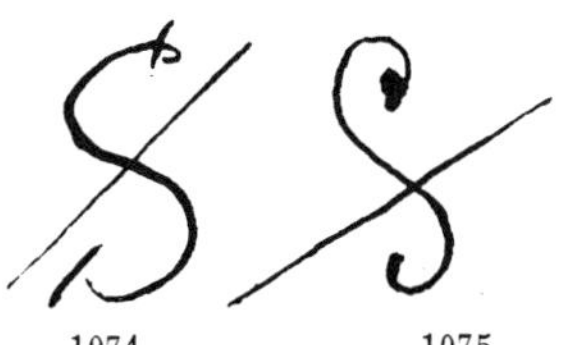

1074 1075

Type | Value

1074-5 **Prince Edward Island,**
Apr., 1865. Black.
1865 2d. Perf. 9......
3d. Perf. 9......
6d. Perf. 9......
1d. Yellow......
2d. Rose........
3d. Blue........

1076 1077

1076 Black.
1880 1c. .... .40
3c. .... .60
1077 Black.
1890 1c. .... .40
3c. .... .60
1078 "SW" surrounded by 6 bars within circle. London, England, in black, appearing.
1866 12½c. Green.... 4.00

1079 1080 1081

1079 Black.
1880 1c. .... .30
3c. .... .50
1080 Black.
1868 1c. Yellow...... 5.00
1c. Brown...... 5.00
3c. 5.00

Type		Value
1081	Black.	
	1890 1c.	.40
	3c.	.50

1082x 1083

1082x	**Lambton Mills,** Dec., '83.	
	1883 1c.	.60
	On Cover....	1.50
1083	Black.	
	1880 1c.	.75
	3c.	.85
	6c.	1.25

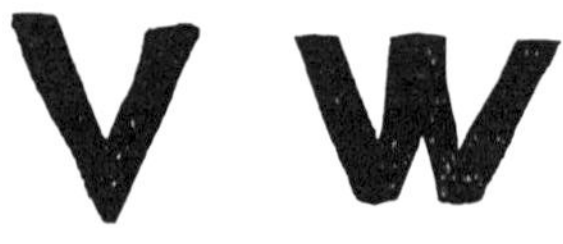

1082 1084

1082	Black.	
	1890 3c.	.60
1084	Black.	
	1890 3c.	.60

1085 1086

1085	**Wakefield, Que.** Feb., 1878.	
	Black.	
	1878 3c.	.40
1086	Black, about 1876, complete circle seldom showing.	

1087

Type		Value
1087	Violet, from rubber stamp.	
	1890 3c.	1.00

Y.K.

1088 1089

1088	Black.	
	1890 3c.	.40
1089	Purple.	
	1880 3c.	.75

Crosses, (Sometimes called "Crossroads") and Maltese Crosses.

1125x 1125 1125xx

1125	**Collingwood.** Jan., 1872.	
	Black.	
	1872 3c.	.75
1125x	Black.	
	1868 ½c.	1.75
	6c.	2.50
1125xx	Black.	
	1868 1c.	3.50

1126 1127

Type		Value
1126	**Collingwood**	
	Black.	
	1875 3c.	.70
1127	Black.	
	1872 15c.	2.50

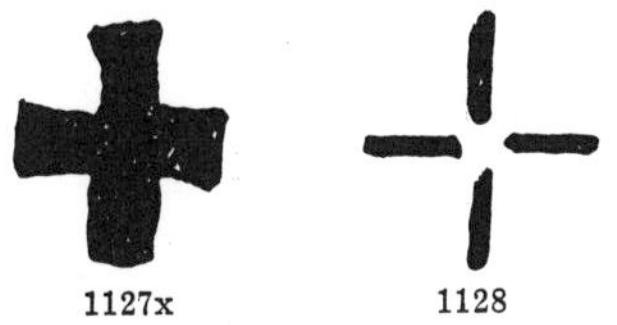
1127x 1128

1127x	1880 3c.	.25
1128	Black.	
	1875 3c.	.60

1129 1130 1131

1129	**Arcadia, N.S.** Feb., 1878.	
	Black.	
	1878 3c.	.35
1130	**St. Catharines.** July, 1878.	
	(This type used by many offices).	
	Black.	
	1868 ½c.	1.25
	1878 1c.	.15
	3c.	.20
1131	Black.	
	1859 5c.	.75
	1868 3c.	.85

Type		Value
	Owen Sound. Oct., 1882.	
	Blue.	
	1882 1c.	.15
	3c.	.25
	2c. Regist.......	.35

1132 1133

1132	**Huntsville.** Oc., 1877. Pop., 500.	
	Black.	
	1877 1c.	.50
	3c.	.75
1133	Violet.	
	1890 3c.	1.00

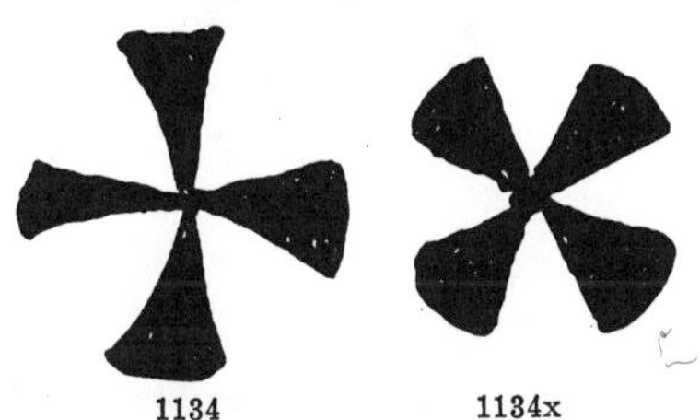
1134 1134x

1134	Black.	
	1875 3c.	.30
	Carmine.	
	1875 3c.	.40
	Green.	
	1875 5c. (large)......	
1134x	Black.	
	1880 3c.	.30

1135

Type		Value
1135	**St. Catharines.** Oct., 1882. Black.	
	1882 1c.	.50
	3c.	.75

1136

1137

1136	Black.	
	1868 1c. Brown......	
	2c.	
	3c.	1.25
1137	(Showing late stage of 936 with sections missing).	

1138

1138	**Kingston.** Jan., 1874. Black.	
	1874 3c.	1.25
	(Impression illustrated is for June, 1874 — earlier impressions show more open spaces in ornaments at top bottom and sides.)	

FACES, BOGEY HEADS, Etc.

1140

1141

Type		Value
1140	Black.	
	1895 3c.	1.50
1141	Black.	
	1890 3c.	1.50

1142

1143

1142	Black.	
	1895 3c.	1.75
1143	Black.	
	1897 3c. Jub.........	1.00

COGWHEEL TYPES

1144

1146

1151

1159

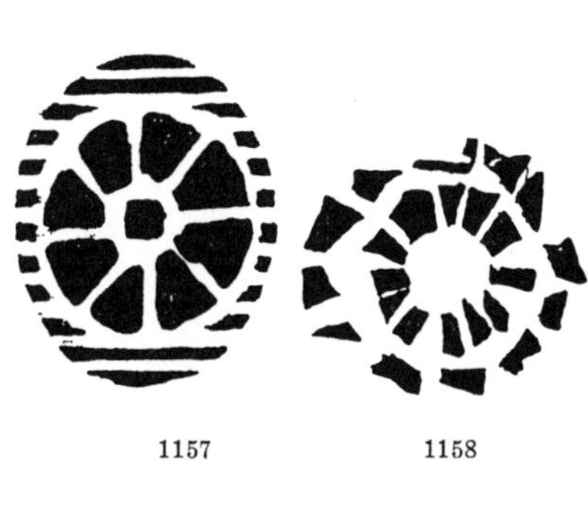

1150 1156 1157 1158

1147 1152 1149 1162

1148 1154 1155 1153

1160 1145 1161

Type		Value
1144	Black	
	1859 5c.	$ .85
a.	Similar design.	
	1890 3c.	.25
b.	With 10 Cogs.	
	1875 3c.	.35
c.	With 14 Cogs, smaller.	
	1870 3c.	.75
1145	Black.	
	1875 3c.	.40
1146	Black.	
	1890 3c.	.40
1147	Black.	
	1890 3c.	.45
1148	**Toronto.** Nov., 1870. Black.	
1148	1870 3c.	$1.00
	1880 15c.	
	1885 3c.	.35
	2c. Regist.......	.35
1149	Black.	
	1890 3c.	.45
1150	Black.	
	1880 3c.	.50
1151	Purple.	
	1880 3c.	.75
1152	Black.	
	1885 3c.	.50
1153	Black.	
	1880 3c.	.40
1154	**Charlottetown, P.E.I.** Aug., 1875. Black.	
	1875 1c.	.40
	3c.	.50
1155	Black.	
	1880 3c.	.50
1156	**Halifax, N.S.** Mar., 1881. Black.	
	1881 1c.	.35
	2c.	.45
	3c.	.40
	5c.	.50
a.	In circle, 1883.	
1157	**Halifax, N.S.** Mar., 1881. Type 1156 inserted in Type 1128.	
	1881 1c.	.50
	3c.	.60
	(Type 1157 is known with four bars replacing cork cog-wheel, Mar., 1881).	

Type		Value
1158	Black.	
	1890 3c.	.30
1159	**San Francsico, U.S.A.** on covers from British Columbia and Vancouver Island, portions falling on stamps. Used with 309x. Black.	
	1865 5c. B.C. Perf..14	
1160	**Guelph.** Aug., 1871. Black.	
	1868 2c.	2.50
	3c.	1.25
	1871 3c.	1.25
1161	(Later impressions of Type 1160).	
1162	Black.	
	1868 3c.	1.50
	1872 1c.	.75
	3c.	1.00

1165

Masonic Emblems

1165	**Beechville, Ont.,** Chas. Mason, P.M. from 1850 to 1880. Used about 1872. A smaller size was used later. Black.	
	1872 3c.	1.75
	Woodstock, Ont., Aug. 1872.	
	1872 3c.	1.75

1166 1167

Type		Value
1166	Black.	
	1890 3c.	1.25
	Purple.	
	1890 3c.	1.25
a.	**Simcoe.** Dec., '75. Smaller type.	
	Black.	
	1875 1c.	.50
	3c.	.75
1167	Black.	
	1870 1c. Orange......	2.50
	3c.	1.75

Geometrical and other Unclassified Types

1170 1171

Type		Value
1170	**Kingston, Ont.** Feb., 1872.	
	Black.	
	1872 3c.	.75
1171	**Charlottetown, P.E.I.**	
	Black.	
	1872 3c. P.E.I........	

1172 1173

Type		Value
1172	**Prince Edward Island**	
	Black.	
	1872 3c. P.E.I........	
1173	**Prince Edward Island**	
	Black.	
	1872 3c. P.E.I........	

1174 1177

Type		Value
1174	**Prince Edward Island**	
	Black.	
	1872 3c. P.E.I........	
1177	**Mount Albert, Ont.** Oct., 1879.	
	Blue.	
	1879 3c.	.75

1175 1176

Type		Value
1175	Black.	
	1880 3c.	.60
1176	Black. (Later impression Type 1175?)	
	1880 3c.	.60

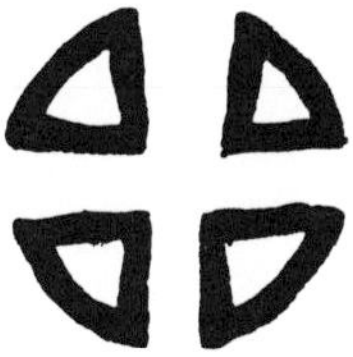

1178 1179

Type		Value
1178	A Canadian cork cancellation but similar type also used by New York 1870-76 on outgoing foreign mail.	
	Black.	
	1870 1c. Orange......	1.25
	3c.	1.00
1179	**Toronto.** Oct., 1874.	
	Black.	
	1874 3c	1.00

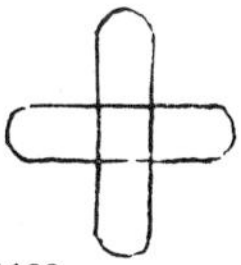

1180 1182

Type		Value
1180	**Owen Sound.** Nov., 1878.	
	Black.	
	1878 3c.	.60

Type		Value
a.	**Hanover.** Apr., 1894.
	Black.
	1894 3c.	.50
	1898 3c. M.L.	.30
b.	Right angle design.
	Black.
	1868 12½c. . . . .
	1870 3c.	.60
	1875 1c.	.40
	3c.	.50
	5c. (small)	.50
1182	**New Brunswick.**
	Black.
	1860 5c. N.B.	.90
	10c. N.B.	2.25

1181

1181	Black.	
	1880 3c.	.60

1183 1184

1183	Black.	
	1880 3c.	.35
1184	Black.	
	1880 3c.	.35

1185 1186x

1185	Black.	
	1880 3c.	.35
1186x	1876 3c.	.50

1186

1187

Type		Value
1186	**McKellar, Ont.** Nov., '75.
	1875 3c.	.40
1187	Black.
	1875 3c.	.50

1188 1189

1188	Black.	
	1890 3c.	.25
1189	Black.	
	1898 1c. Q.V. Num. . .	.15
	1c. 4-Leaf	.20

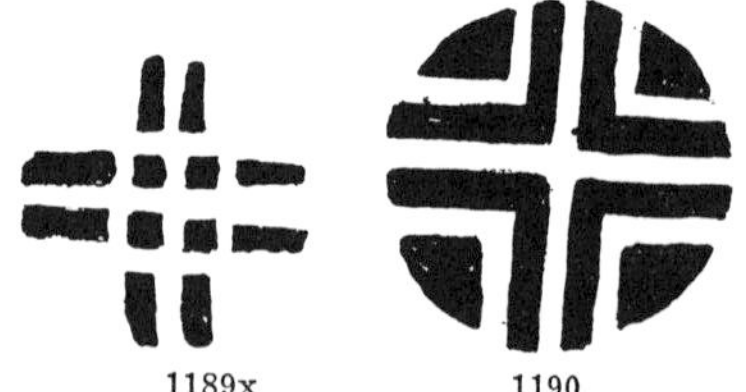

1189x 1190

1189x	Black.	
	1898 1c. 4-Leaf	.25
	8c. 4-Leaf	.90
1190	Black.	
	1868 3c.	1.00

1191 1192

Type		Value
1191	Black.	
	1885 3c.	.40
1192	Black.	
	1868 2c.	2.00
	3c.	.85
	6c.	2.25
	1870 3c.	.85

1193 1194

Type		Value
1193	Black.	
	1868 2c.	2.00
	3c.	1.00
	(New York P.O. used type 1193 on outgoing foreign mail, 1870-76.)	
1194	**Ottawa.** May, June, 1872.	
	Black.	
	1872 3c.	1.00
	15c.	2.50

1195

1196

1196x

1197

1198

1199

1200

1201

1201x

1202

1203

1203x

1204 1205

Type		Value
1195	Black. Early impression.	
	1868 2c.	
	3c.	1.50
	6c.	
1196	Late impression Type 1195.	
	1868 2c.	
	3c.	1.25
	6c.	
1196x	Black.	
	1868 3c.	1.50
1197	Made by Sub-Postmaster Baird.	
	Winnipeg, Dec., 1927. Black.	
	1927 3c. Confed......	.25
1198	Black.	
	1880 1c. Yellow......	.35
	3c.	.40
1199	Black.	
	1868 2c.	2.25
	3c.	1.00
	6c.	2.25
	1870 3c.	1.00
1200	Black.	
	1870 3c.	1.00
	15c.	
1201	1868 3c.	1.50
1201x	Black.	

Type		Value
	1870 1c.	2.00
	3c.	1.25
1202	**Toronto.** Black.	
	1868 1c. Yellow......	
	3c.	1.25
a.	Black centre.	
	1868 3c.	1.00
	12½c.	3.00
1203	**Toronto.** Ja., '70. Black.	
	1868 3c.	1.25
	6c.	
	Stampless cover, "5" struck in error cancelled will Type 1203 and marked PAID, Toronto, Ja., '70.....	2.00
1203x	**Toronto,** Feb., '72. Black.	
	1872 3c.	1.00
1204	Black.	
	1868 1c. Yellow......	
	3c.	1.25
1205	Black.	
	1868 3c.	1.25

1206

1208

1209

1212

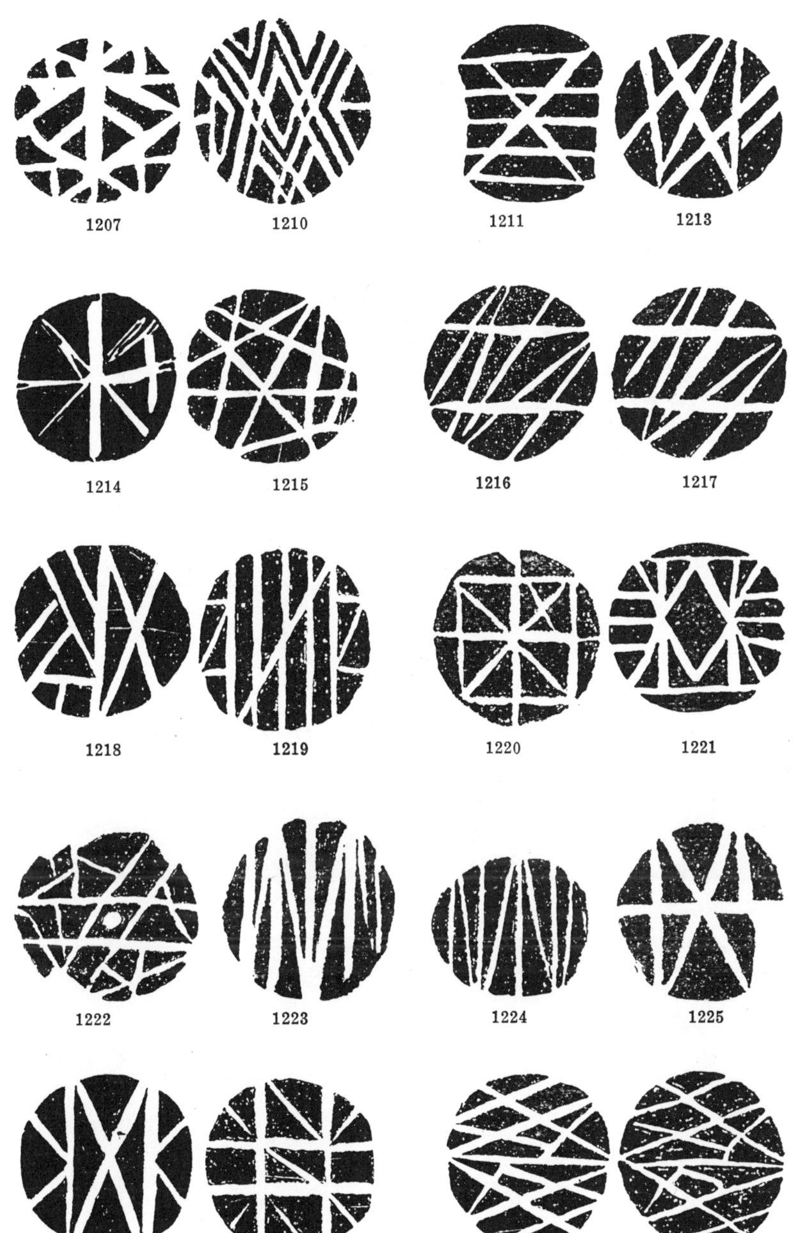

1207 1210 1211 1213

1214 1215 1216 1217

1218 1219 1220 1221

1222 1223 1224 1225

1226 1227 1228 1229

1230 1231

1232

1233

1234

1235

1236

Type		Value
1206	**North Winchester** Mar., 1873.	
	Black.	
	1873 3c.	1.00
1207	**Ottawa.** May, 1872.	
	Black.	
	1872 1c.	.35
	3c.	1.00
1208	**Bowmanville.** Mar., 1870.	
	Black.	
	1868 1c. Yellow......	
	3c.	1.00
1208	1870 1c.	
	3c.	1.00
1209	Black.	
	1880 1c. Yellow......	.20
	3c.	.30
1210	**Ottawa.** June, 1872.	
	Black.	
	1872 1c.	.35
	3c.	1.00
	15c.	2.25
1211	**Ottawa.** Aug., 1878.	
	Black.	
	1878 1c.	.20
	3c.	.25
1212	**Ottawa.** Jan., 1875.	
	Black.	
	1875 1c.	.20
	3c.	.25

Type		Value
1212a	Similar, eight sections, squared, Kleinberg, Mar., '83. See 1404-5-6.	
	1883 1c.	.15
	3c.	.15
	2c. Reg.........	.20
1213	**Ottawa.** Oct., 1877.	
	Black.	
	1877 1c.	.20
	3c.	.25
1214	**St. Johns, Newfoundland.** July, 1865.	
	Black.	
	1862 1d Nfld.........	
	3d Nfld.........	
	5d Nfld.........	
1215	**Ottawa.** May, 1877.	
	Black.	
	1877 1c.	.20
	3c.	.25
1216	**Ottawa.** Aug., 1878.	
	Black.	
	1878 1c.	.20
	3c.	.25
1217	**Ottawa.** Aug., Sept., 1878.	
	Black.	
	1878 1c.	.20
	3c.	.25

Type		Value
1218	**Ottawa.** Mar., 1878. Black.	
	1878 1c.	.20
	3c.	.25
1219	**Ottawa.** Jan., Feb., 1880. Black.	
	1880 1c.	.20
	3c.	.25
a.	Similar, Feb., 22, 1873.	
1220	**Ottawa.** July, 1876. Black.	
	1876 1c.	.25
	3c.	.30
a.	Inner sections quartered Grenville, N.S., Aug., 1882.	
1221	**Ottawa.** Feb. to Mar., 1872. Black.	
	1872 1c.	.35
	3c.	.75
1222	**Ottawa.** May, 1872. Black.	
	1872 1c.	.35
	....	.75
1223-4-5	**Ottawa.** Jan., 1875, Feb. to Oct., 1875 and Sept. to Oct., 1875 respectively. Black.	
	1875 1c.	.30
	3c.	.35

1226 to 1236 inclusive used by Ottawa. 1226 Sept., 1876; 1227 Jan., 1877; 1228-9 May, 1877; 1230 June, 1877; 1231 Jan., 1878; 1232 Feb., 1878; 1233 Apr., May, 1878; 1234 Jan., Feb., 1880; 1235 Mar., 1880; 1236 Apr., 1880.

Cork Dots

These may be described as small, medium, large; square, round, oblong, diamond, fancy, etc.

1299 1300

Type		Value
1299	Black	
	Black.	
1300	1857 ½d.	20.00

1300x 1301

	Riviere du Loup, P.Q.	
1300x	1870 3c.	1.00
	1890 3c.	.30
	Green.	
	1870 3c.	1.75
1301	**Newfoundland.** Black.	
	1876 2c. Rouletted...	3.50

1302

Used as Duplex with Toronto Town Type, Oc. '63.

1302	Black.	
	1863 5c.	1.50

1302x 1303

1302x	Black.	
	1859 5c. Beaver......	1.50
	1868 3c.	.85
	1880 3c.	.20

Type		Value
1302xa	Small round dots, smaller diam.	
	1857 ½d.	20.00
1303	Black.	
	1868 ½c.	
	2c.	
	3c.	1.00
	1875 3c.	.50
	15c.	
a.	Larger square dots.	
	1868 3c.	1.00
	12½c.	

1304 1304x

Type		Value
1304	**New Brunswick.**	
	Black.	
	1851 3d. N.B.	
	6d. N.B.	
	1s. N.B.	
1304x	Canada Black	

1305 1306

Type		Value
1305	**Toronto.** Oct., 1866.	
	Black.	
	1866 1c.	1.50
	5c.	1.25
	1868 3c.	1.00
	1870 3c.	1.00

1307 1308

Type		Value
1306	**Pickering, U.C.** June, 1863.	
	Black.	
	1863 5c.	$2.00
	10c.	
1307	Black.	
	1855 3d.	5.00
	6d.	
	1859 5c.	2.00
	10c.	
a.	Oblong dots or short bars Hamilton, March 1855.	
	1855 3d.	5.00
	6d.	
	1859 5c.	2.00
	10c.	
1308	Black.	
	1868 2c.	2.50
	15c.	2.75
	3c.	1.00
	6c.	
	1875 5c. (small)	.40

1309 1310

Type		Value
1309	Black.	
	1871 15c.	2.00
	1868 2c.	
a.	Larger with extra square each way.	
	1868 2c.	
1310	**Prince Edward Island (Charlottetown)** Sept., 1870. Rectangles often more clearly defined.	
	Black.	
	1870 1d. Yellow PEI.	
	2d. Rose PEI.	

1311 1312 1313

Type		Value
1311	**Newfoundland.**	
	Black.	
	1876 5c. Rouletted...	
1312	**Prince Edward Island**	
	Black.	
	1867 9d.	
1313	**Leskard.** Ap., 1872.	
	Black.	
	1872 3c.	1.00

1314

1315

1314	Blue.	
	1868 3c.	1.50
1315	**Toronto.** Oct., 1866. (Port Perry used similar type).	
	Black.	
	1866 5c.	1.00
	10c.	
	1868 3c.	.90

1315x

1316

1315x	**Ottawa.** Ap., '75.	
	Black.	
	1875 1c.	.20
	3c.	.30
1316	Purple.	
	1880 3c.	1.50

1317

1318

Type		Value
1317	**Ottawa.** Sept., 1877.	
	Black.	
	1877 1c.	.20
	3c.	.30
1318	**Ottawa.** June, 1878.	
	Black.	
	1878 1c.	.20
	3c.	.30
a.	Similar type on	
	1891 15c.	2.00

1319

1320

1319	**Cap-Sante, Que.** Ap., 1895.	
	Black.	
	1895 1c.	.10
	3c.	.25
1320	Black.	
	1890 15c.	.35

1321

1321	**Ottawa.** Apr., 1875.	
	Black.	
	1875 1c.	.20
	3c.	.30
a.	8 oblong dots vertically.	

1322
1323
1324
1325
1326
1327
1328
1329
1330
1331
1332
1333
1334
1335
1336

Type — Value

1322 **Ottawa.** July, 1878.
Black.
1878 1c. .... .15
3c. .... .20

1323 **Toronto.** May, 1872.
Black.
1872 1c. .... .20
3c. .... .30

1324 **Ottawa.** Oct., 1875
Black.
1875 1c. .... .15
3c. .... .20
5c. (large)......

1325 Black.
1859 5c. Beaver...... 1.00
1868 3c. 1.00
1870 3c. 1.00
15c. ....
a. Larger dots wider spacing.
1868 3c. 1.00
6c. ....

1326 **Ottawa.** July, 1877.
Black.
1877 1c. .... .15
3c. .... .20
a. Similar, ealier date, different towns Black.
1868 3c. 1.00
2c. ....
1870 3c. 1.00

1327 **Ottawa.** April, 1877 and similar type for July, 1878.
Black.
1868 ½c. ....
1877 1c. .... .15
3c. .... .20

1328 **Ottawa.** Jan., 1877.
Black.
1877 1c. .... .15
3c. .... .20
a. Smaller diamonds.
1868 12½c. ....

1329 **Ottawa.** July, Aug., 1875.
Black.
1875 1c. .... .15
3c. .... .20

Type — Value

1330 **Ottawa.** May, 1877 and similar type for June, 1879.
Black.
1877 1c. .... .15
3c. .... .20

1331 **Ottawa.** Apr., 1879.
Black.
1879 1c. .... .15
3c. .... .20

1332 **Ottawa.** 1869.
Black.
1868 1c. Yellow......
1c. Orange......
1c. Brown......
2c. ....
3c. 1.00
6c. ....
1870 3c. 1.00
15c. ....
a. Larger diamonds 4 wide.
b. Small diamonds 9 wide.

1333 **Ottawa.** Oct., Nov., 1878.
Black.
1878 1c. .... .15
3c. .... .20

1334 **Ottawa.**
Black.
1880 1c. .... .15
3c. .... .20

1335 **Ottawa.** Jan., 1880.
Black.
1880 1c. .... .20
3c. .... .30

1336 Blue.
1871 3c. 1.25

1336x

1336x **Dundas.** Oct., '76.
Black.
1876 .... .35

Corks Quartered

It is a conservative estimate to state that a thousand postmasters satified their artistics desire and everyday requirements in the matter of cancellations by using a cork. The cork, of course, came from the neck of a bottle, and it seems to have been a cork of a diameter to suggest the neck of a bottle that did not contain perfume. Many of these corks were carved into effective cancelling instruments before they were "pulled" but a little study of the cork cancellations of that wonderful period of Canadian history satisfies us that most of them were carved after the cork had been taken from the bottle and the contents transferred to better premises.

The usual procedure was to cut one groove across the cork and another at right angles to it, resulting in the "quartered cork." A few cut notches in the base of each of the four segments, giving the cancellation the appearance of four crude arrows pointing to a common center.

Corks were also cut into six or seven segments, sometimes notched, and into eight nine or more segments, these then assuming the form of a "sunburst."

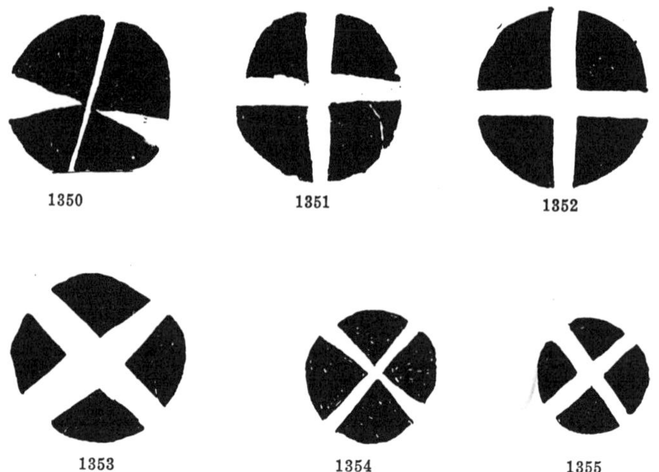

1350 1351 1352

1353 1354 1355

Quartered and Notched to form Arrowheads, Hearts, Conventional Flowers, etc.

1356 1357 1358

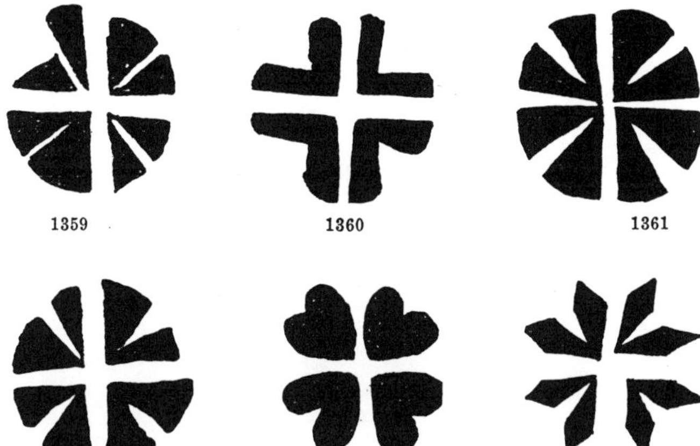

1359 1360 1361

1362 1363 1364

Type		Value
1350	**Toronto.** Sept., 1876.	
	Black.	
	1876 3c.	.15
1351	**Nanaimo.** Aug., 1884.	
	Black.	
	1884 3c.	.15
	Newmarket. 1880.	
	1880 3c.	.15
	Bellevile. 1879.	
	St. John, N.B. Mar., 1881. (Diam. 19 mm.)	
	Napanee. Dec., 1875.	
	1868 3c.	.85
	12½c.	
	1875 1c..............	.10
	3c.	.15
	1882 15c.	
	Blue. 1880.	
	1880 3c.	.30
	Purple or Violet.	
	1880 3c.	.25
	Green.	
	1880 3c.	.40
1352	**Prince Edward Island**	
	Black.	
	1868 6d. Blue Green P.E.I......	
	Similar on	
	1888 3c. Carmine Rose	.75
1353	**Newfoundland.**	
	Black.	
	1862 1d. brown.......	
	1s. rose.........	

Type		Value
1354	**Newfoundland.**	
	Black.	
	1866 2c. Green.......	
1355	Black.	
	1890 3c.	.20
	Purple.	
	1890 3c.	.30
1356	Purple.	
	1890 3c.	.40
1357	**Emberson, Ont.** Sept., 1876. A common type found, with many variations, on the stamps listed.	
	Black.	
	1868 3c.	.85
	1870 3c.	.85
	15c.	
	1876 3c.	.25
	Blue.	
	1876 3c.	.45
1358	**Port Hope.** Ju., 1879.	
	Black.	
	1879 3c.	.35
1359	**Ottawa,** early 1868.	
	Black.	
	1868 3c.	.85
1360	Black.	
	1870 3c.	1.00
	1872 3c.	1.00
1361	**Providence Bay, Ont.** May, 1878.	
	Blue.	
	1878 3c.	1.00

Type		Value
1362	**Prince Edward Island** Black. 1872 6c. P.E.I........	
1363	**New Westminster, B.C.** Ja., '76. Black. 1876 3c.	.75
1364	**Seaforth, Ont.** Aug., '75. Black. 1875 3c.	.75

1365 1377

Type		Value
1365	**Lindsay, Ont.** July, '76. Black. 1876 3c.	.85

In Six, Seven, or Eight Segments

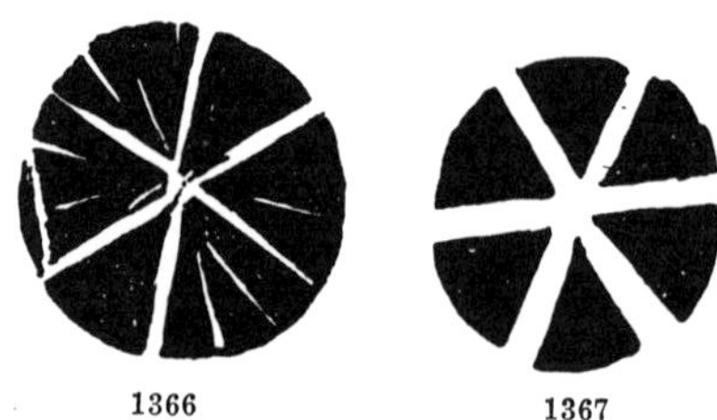

1366 1367

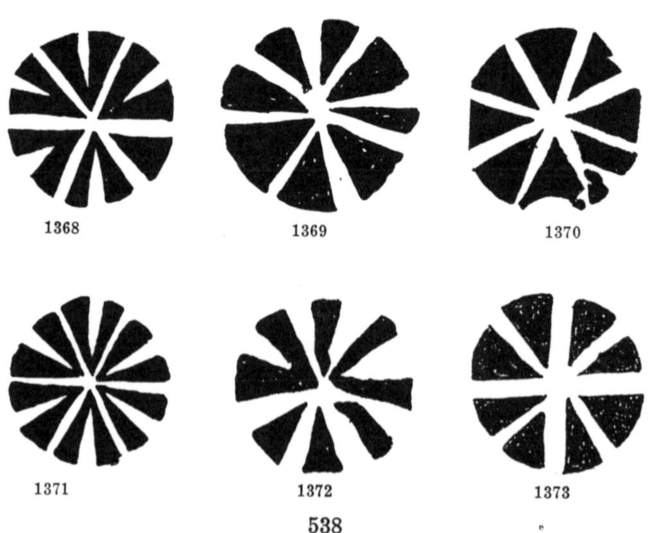

1368 1369 1370

1371 1372 1373

1374

1375

1376

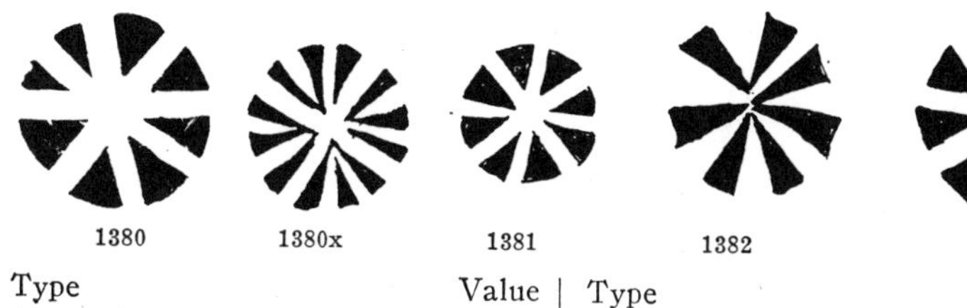

1380 1380x 1381 1382 1383

Type		Value
1366	**Toronto.** Oct., '69.	
	Black.	
	1868 3c.	.75
1367	Black.	
	1880 3c.	.20
	Violet.	
	1880 3c.	.35
1368	Black.	
	1868 3c.	.85
	1870 3c.	1.00
	1880 3c.	.25
	Violet.	
	1880 3c.	.40
1369	**Toronto.** July, '72.	
	Black.	
	1872 3c.	.85
	1875 3c.	.25
	Blue.	
	1875 3c.	.40
	Green.	
	1875 3c.	.50
1370	**New Brunwsick.**	
	Black.	
	1866 10c. N.B.	
1371	Black.	
	1868 3c.	.85
	6c.	
	1880 15c.	
1372	**Bothwell.** July, '83.	
	Black.	
	1883 3c.	.35
1373	**Ottawa.** Jan., to Feb., '72.	
	Black.	
	1868 2c.	
	3c.	.85

Type		Value
	1870 3c.	1.00
	1872 3c.	1.00
	1c.	.50
	15c. 12½c.	
a.	Similar designs.	
	(**Providence Bay, Ont.** April, '75.)	
	Black.	
	1875 2c. Regist.	
	5c. Regist.	
	8c. Regist.	
	(Appears through to 4-Leaf Issue.)	
	Blue.	
	1875 3c.	.40
	Violet.	
	1875 3c.	.40
	Brown.	
	1875 3c.	.50
	Green.	
	1875 3c.	.75
1374	**Ottawa.** Aug., Sept., '76, again appears April, '80. **Bothwell, Ont.,** used July, '83.	
	Black.	
	1876 1c.	.15
	3c.	.20
1375	**Ottawa.** June to Nov., '84.	
	Black.	
	1884 3c.	.20
1376	**Ottawa.** Oct., '75.	
	Black.	
	1875 3c.	.25

Type		Value
1377	**Parry Sound.** Dec., '75	
	Black.	
	1875 3c.	.50
a.	Eight segments, notched, as Type 1377, also used by Lochlin, April 1900 (22mm. diam.) and New York (20-mm. diam.) both thin and thick lines, on outgoing foreing mail 1870-76.	

1378

1379

Type		Value
1378	**Bracebridge.** May, '76	
	Black.	
	1876 3c.	.60
a.	No circle.	
	1868 6c.	

Type		Value
1379	Black.	
	1868 ½c.	2.00
1380	Black.	
	1880 3c.	.30
1380x	Black.	
	1880 3c.	.50
1381	Black.	
	1880 3c.	.50
1382	**Chatham, N.B.** Feb., '86.	
	Black.	
	1886 3c.	.50
1383	Black.	
	1876 3c.	.60

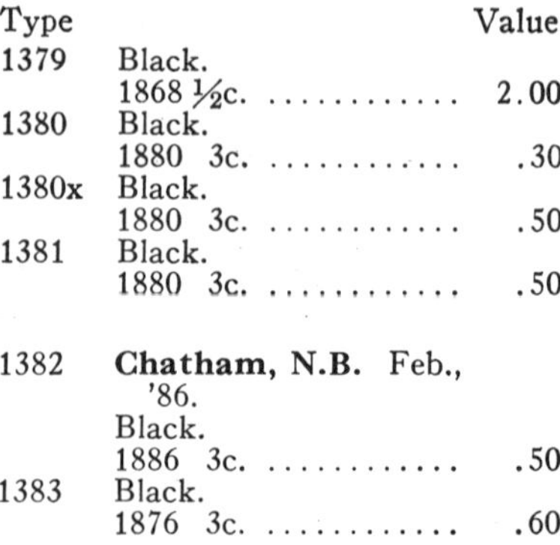

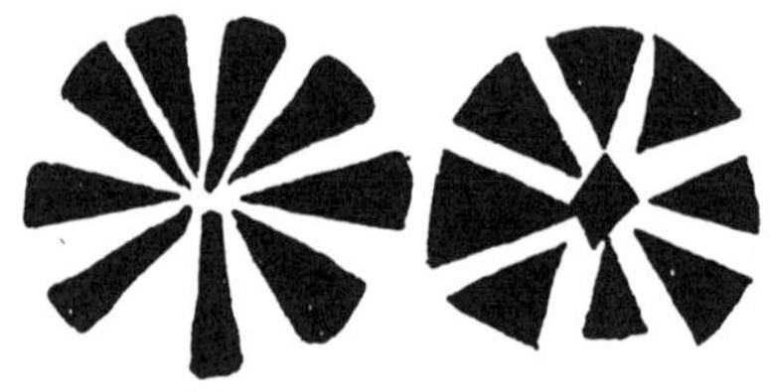

1384 1385

1386 1387 1388

1389 1390 1391

1392 1393 1394

1395

1396

1397

1398 1400 1402 1403

Type		Value
384	Black.	
	1868 1c. Yellow......	
	2c.	
	3c.	1.00
	6c.	
	1870 3c.	1.00
	1875 5c. (small)......	.40
1385	Black.	
	1868 2c.	
	3c.	1.00
1386	Purple.	
	1880 3c.	.75
1387	**Toronto.** Aug., '71.	
	Black.	
	1871 3c.	1.00
a.	Similar, Waterloo, Jan., '72.	
	1872 1c.	.50
	3c.	1.00
1388	Black.	
	1859 5c. Beaver......	1.25
	1868 3c.	1.00
a.	Sixteen Rays.	
	1898 3c. 4-Leaf......	.25
	5c. 4-Leaf......	.50
	8c. 10c.........	
1389	**Owen Sound.** Sept. to Nov., '71.	
	Black. 15 Rays.	
	1871 1c.	.50
	3c.	1.00
a.	Aylmer, Que. 17 Rays Dec., '76.	

Type		Value
b.	Dunville, Ont. 34 Rays, 28mm. diam. Mar., '74.	
	Black.	
	1868 2c.	
	3c.	1.00
c.	Enniskillen, C. W. Mar., '76.	
1390	Black.	
	1868 3c.	1.00
1391	Black.	
	1897 1c. 4-Leaf......	.25
	3c. Q.V. Numeral	.25
1392	**Ottawa.** April, '72.	
	Black.	
	1872 3c.	1.00
a.	Similar in Red on	
	1868 6c.	3.25
1393	**Ottawa.** Aug. to Oct., '71.	
	Black.	
	1868 6c.	
	1871 3c.	1.00
a.	Similar for Pendleton, C.W. May, '75.	
	Black.	
	1875 3c.	.30
	5c. (small)......	.40
b.	Similar in Black on	
	1897 3c. 4-Leaf......	.20

Type		Value
1394	**Ottawa.** 1869.	
	Black.	
	1859 12½c.	
	1868 3c.	1.25
	1870 3c.	1.25
1395	**Ottawa.** June, '70.	
	Black.	
	1870 3c.	1.25
a.	Dunnville Mar., '75, 8 sections each with 4 or more "rays."	
	1875 15c.	2.25
1396	Black.	
	1868 3c.	1.50
1397	Black.	
	1868 6c.	
1398	Black.	
	1868 2c.	
	3c.	1.25
a.	Similar, on	
	1897 2c. 3c.	.25

1399 1401

Type		Value
1399	**Hunterstown, L.C.** July, 1869 and Aug., 1871.	
	Blue.	
	1869 3c.	1.75
	1870 3c.	1.50
1400	Black.	
	1870 3c.	1.50
1401	Black.	
	1880 3c.	.75
1402	Black usually indistinct.	
	1868 3c.	1.00
1403	Black.	
	1870 3c.	1.00
	15c.	2.25
	1874 15c.	2.25

1404 1405

Type		Value
1404	**Kleinberg, Ont.** (See 1212).	
	1859 5c. Beaver.	1.25
	1868 3c.	1.00
	1883 1c.	.15
	3c.	.20
	2c Regist.	.25
1405	Black.	
	1859 5c. Beaver.	1.25
	10c.	
	1868 3c.	1.00

1406

Type		Value
1406	**Owen Sound, Ont.** April, '83.	
	Blue.	
	1883 1c.	.20
	3c.	.40

FLAG TYPES

(Special cancellations, Types 1430 and 1431, were prepared for the Jubilee issue, applied in Ottawa and Montreal, with the first electric cancelling machines used in Canada, June, 1897. Other flag types followed, but it will be noted that these appear on stamps issued prior to 1897. In due course Toronto made use of an electric cancelling machine and introduced the first advertising cancellation, Types 1432-1433, in connection with the Canadian National Exhibition.)

1425
(Enlarged ⅓)

Type		Value
1425	An interesting cancellation is illustrated by Type 1425. It consists of a coat-of-arms design with draped flags extending from right and left sides of a triangle in which is contained a tree, an Indian head or sphinx, and other figures. Crossed cannon are pendant from the base of the triangle. From the shade of the stamps on which it is seen the date may be fixed at late 90's.	
	Bluish-black.	
	189? 3c.	2.50

1426

1426	Black.	
	1890 3c.	.60

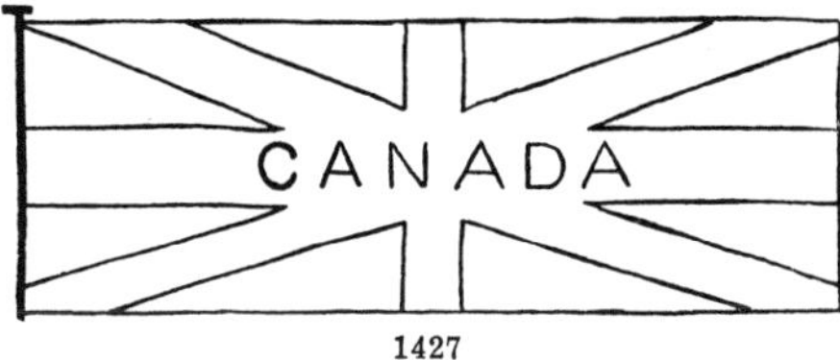

1427

1428

1429

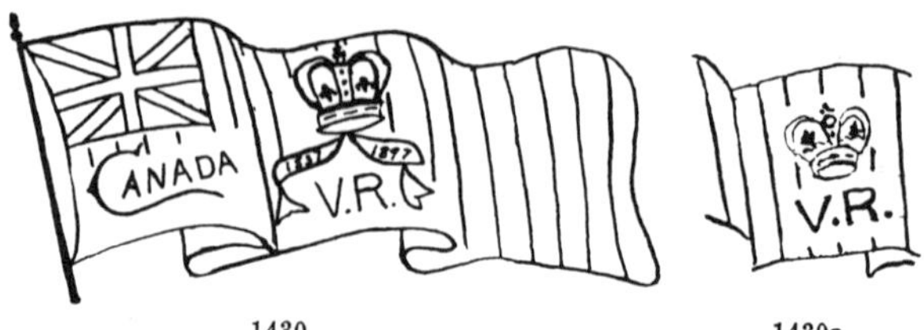

1430 1430a

1431

1432

Type		Value
1427	Black.	
	1896 3c.	.15
	1897 3c. Jub.........	.15
	(Appears on all Jubilee stamps except $ values).	
1428	**Toronto,** for Postal Stations A, B, C, D, E, F.	
	1896 3c.	.15
	1897 3c. Jub.........	.15
	(Appears on all Jubilee stamps except $ values).	
a.	One vertical bar between flagstaff and let er "C" designating station.	
1429	Black.	
	1896 3c.	.15
	1897 Jubilee as above.	
a.	Letters "A", "B", etc., under Union Jack; two parallel horiz. bars above and below CANADA.	

Type		Value
	1898 3c. Q.V. Num...	.10
	All values.	
b.	Flag with rounded corners, lines not connected.	
	1926 2c. George......	.15
1430	Black.	
	1896 3c.	.25
	1897 1c. Jub.........	.25
	2c. Jub.........	.30
	3c. Jub.........	.25
	(Appears on all Jubilee except $ values).	
a.	V.R. under Crown no dates, Canada omitted	
1431	Black.	
	1896 3c.	.30
	1897 3c. Jub.........	.30
	1c. Jub.........	.30
	2c. Jub.........	.25
	(Appears on all Jubilee except $ values.)	

1433

1434

Type		Value
1432	Black.	
	1897 3c. 4-Leaf......	.25
1433	Black.	
	1897 3c. 4-Leaf......	.25
1434	Black. June, 1927.	
	1927 All values Georgian.)	

Slogan Cancellations

It has been found impossible to include these in this volume, already growing to expensive proportions, but the list of Newfoundland "Slogans" being complete we give them below. The electric cancelling machines were in use in St. Johns and St. Johns East since 1914.

1. Food will win the war, don't waste.
2. Have you contributed to the War Memorial.
3. Buy Made in Newfoundland Goods.
4. Address Mail to Street or Number.
5. British Empire Exhibition 1924.
6. British Empire Exhibition 1925.
7. Wear a Poppy Remembrance Day.
8. Newfoundland for your Vacation.

"Kicking Mule"

This popular U.S. cancellation (dangerously counterfeited of late) appears on Canada 3c. 1890 in purple.

BUY WAR SAVINGS
STAMPS AND HELP
RECONSTRUCTION

1440

1440 This is a type of electric machine cancellation used in a great many post offices, the list of slogans and other advertising reminders being added to at a rate which necessitates a complete listing in a separate volume The war period, 1914-1918, produced a number of these, the post-war period further increased the list, until today they are likely to be met with from every town holding a Fall Fair. Those used to advertise and commemorate Stamp Exhibitions are of more than ordinary interest, and are illustrated below.

1440	Black on entire cover cancelling stamp, common variety.....	.10
	Scarcer varieties, to....	1.00

1441

1442

1443

1444

Type		Value
1441	Black on entire cover cancelling stamp.....	.50
1442	Black on entire cover cancelling stamp.....	.50
1443	Black on entire cover cancelling stamp.....	.50

Type		Value
1444	Black on entire cover cancelling stamp....	.50
a.	THIRD instead SECOND Apr., 13-14, 1928, same type as 1344.	
	Black on entire cover..	.50

1445

1445 Rubber stamp impression, usually accompanied by INDUSTRIAL EXHIBITION
Violet or Purple.

1903	1c.	Q.V. Num...	.25
	2c.	Q.V. Num...	.25

1446

1446 Metered mail, in various colors, usually red or green. The House of Assembly, Toronto, used green, License No. 4102, from Dec., 1926. The use of the meter has grown steadily until used in thousands of business offices.

On entire cover....... .15

1447 (Not illustrated) Letter dated June 21, 1926, from A. Jacques, Assistant Postmaster, Montreal: "Your communication dated the 18th inst. has been referred to us and in reply you are informed that the use of the rubber stamp reading:

250 {eme Anniversaire
{th Anniversary
LACHINE, P.Q.
4-5-6 September 1926

was authorized by the Post Office Department and the cancellation appearing on the cover of mail matter mailed at Lachine is made by post office employees either at Lachine or Montreal.

Black cancelling stamp, on entire cover...... .50

Registered Mail Markings

An agreement was made with the Post Office Department of the United States in October 1856 whereby letters passing between the two countries could be registered for the additional fee of 3d, and if desired, a continuous record be obtained from point of mailing to destination. A similar system was used for strictly Canadian mail as early as December 1854.

REGISTERED

1450

Type		Value
1450	General use Dec., 1854 Stampless Covers.	
	Adds to value, black...	.25
	red.....	.40
	blue....	.50
a.	Error RERISTERED Brantford Fe., '56.	
b.	Type 1450 4mm. high.	
c.	Type 1450 4mm. high framed. (Add to value of stamped cover as above.)	
	Appearing on stamps, Black.	
	1854 3d. Beaver......	4.50
	10d.	
	1859 5c. Beaver......	1.00
	1c.	
	1868 1c. Orange......	
	3c.	.90
	1870 1c.	
	2c.	
	3c.	1.00
	Red.	
	1870 3c.	1.10
	Blue.	
	1870 3c.	1.25
	Green.	
	1870 3c.	1.50

RECISTERED

1451

Type		Value
1451	General use Dec., 1854. Stampless Cover.	
	Adds to value, black...	.25
	red.....	.40
	blue....	.50
	Bronze-brown Eugenia, C.W., Mr., '74......	.75
1451	Appearing on stamps.	
	Black.	
	1854 3d. Beaver......	4.00
	10d.	
	1859 1c.	
	5c. Beaver......	1.00
	1868 1c. Orange......	
	3c.	.90
	1870 1c.	
	3c.	1.00
	Red.	
	1870 3c.	1.10
	Blue.	
	1870 3c.	1.25
	Green.	
	1870 3c.	1.50
	Purple.	
	1890 8c. Grey........	.50
a.	4mm. high.	
	Black.	

Type		Value
	1868 3c.	.75
	1875 8c. Registered. . .	
	Red.	
	Adds to value of stamped cover.	.50
b.	5mm. high.	
	Black.	
	1859 5c. Beaver.	1.00
	1868 3c.	.75
	1875 8c. Registered. . .	
	Red.	
	1868 3c.	1.00
	Blue.	
	1868 3c.	1.10
	Green.	
	1868 3c.	1.50

REGISTERED

1452

1452	General use April, 1860. On Stampless Covers.	
	Adds to value, black. . .	.25
	red.	.40
	blue. . . .	.50
	Appearing on stamps,	
	Black.	
	1859 5c. Beaver.	1.00
	1868 2c.	
	3c.	.90
	Blue.	
	1859 5c. Beaver.	1.25

REGISTERED

1453

1453	General use Sp., '64.	
	Black.	
	1878 3c.	.15
	2c. Registered. . .	.20
	Blue.	
	1878 3c.	.25
	2c. Registered. . .	.35
	Violet.	
	1878 3c.	.25
a.	4mm. x 34mm. Sept., 1869.	

REGISTERED

1453x

1453x	**Morrisburg.** Ja., '57.	
	Black.	.25

REGISTERED

1454

Type		Value
1454	Stampless Covers.	
	Adds to value, Black. . .	.25
	Red. . . .	.40

REGISTERED

1455

1455	Black.	
	1878 3c.	.20
	2c. Registered. . .	.25
	1880 8c.	.50

REGISTERED
PAID

1456

1456	**Brockville,** Ju., '58.	
	Black.	
	Stampless Cover, add. .	.75
a.	Same size with PAID omitted.	
	1875 3c.	.25

REGISTERED

1457

1457	**Ottawa.** May, 1898, Senate.	
	Black.	
	1898 3c. 4-Leaf.	.20
	Violet.	
	1898 3c. 4-Leaf.	.30

REGISTERED

1458

1459

Type		Value
1458	Black.	
	1880 3c.	1.50
	2c. Regist.	1.75
1459	Black.	
	1890 3c.	1.25
	2c. Regist.	1.25

1459x

1459x	Red Nov., '67 with FREE initialed by M.P.	2.50

1459xx

1459xx	Red Mar., '59 with Type 1518 initialed by M.P.	5.00
	Add to value	2.00

REGISTERED AT THE

HOUSE OF ASSEMBLY

ONTARIO

1460

1460	(Parliament Bldgs., Toronto).	
	Black.	
	1880 3c.	2.50
	2c. Regist.	4.00
	Red.	
	Cover.	1.50

REGISTERED
AT THE
LEGISLATIVE COUNCIL
OF
CANADA

1461

Type		Value
1461	Green, March, 1859. Adds to value of stamped or stampless cover	2.50

1462

1462	Black. Sept., 1873.	
	Stampless Cover.	.50
	With Initials or Signature of M.P.	.75

1463

1463	General use Jan., 1880.	
	Black.	
	1880 3c.	.20
a.	"No. " instead of date. November, 1875.	

1464

Type		Value
1464	**Newfoundland.** 1891 Black.	

1465

1466

Type		Value
1465	Black. 1894.	
	1894 3c.	.20
1466	London, Eng.	
	Red.	
	1859 12½c.	3.00
	17c	
	1868 3c	1.25
	6c	
	12½c	
	1870 3c	1.15
	1875 5c. (large)	
	5c. (small)	.50

1467

1468

1469

Type		Value
1467	Black. May, 1872.	
	1872 3c.	.15
	2c. Regist.	.20
	Blue.	
	1872 3c.	.25
	2c. Regist.	.30
	(Adds to value of cover as above).	
1468	Rubber stamp impression. July 3, 1891	
	Violet.	
	1891 3c.	.50
a.	Reading "No. A. . . ."	
1469	October, 1870.	
	Black.	
	1870 3c.	1.00
	1875 2c. Reg.	1.00
	Red.	
	1870 3c.	1.25
	(Adds to val. of cover, black, .75; red, 1.50).	

1470

Type		Value
1470	Black.	
	Adds to val. of cover. . .	.30

1471

Type		Value
1471	**Halifax.** Ja., '83. Black.	
a.	Circle for Toronto My '83.	

1472

1472	Black. Sp., 1870.	
	1868 3c.	1.00

1473

1473	Black. My., '69.	
	1868 3c.	1.00

1475

1475	Black. 1890.	
	1890 3c.	.25
	8c.	.50
	1897 3c. 4-Leaf	.15
	2c. 4-Leaf	.15

1474 1476

Type		Value
1474	Black or Purple, 1892.	
	1892 3c.	.10
1476	Black. 1890.	
	1890 3c.	.10
	2c. Regist.	.15
	8c. Regist.	
	(The letter "R" comes in many sizes and variations).	

"Registered" Markings Used by Railways

1477

1477.	Black. Sp., '75.	
	1875 3c.	1.00
a.	"Muskoka Branch" Ap. '76.	
b.	"T.G. & B." Au., '75.	

1478

1478.	Jy., '78.	
	1878 3c.	1.00
	Black.	

1479

1479. Jy., '78.
1878 3c.............. 1.00
Black.

REGISTERED
P. D. & L. H

1480

REGISTERED
H & L. E. R.

1481

REGISTERED
C. S. R.

1482

REGISTERED
WELLAND-R.

1483

REGISTERED
G.W.R. EXPR.

1484

REGISTERED
ST CLAIR BRANCH

1485

REGISTERED
WEST. EXT

1486

REGISTERED
G.W.R. ACCOM.

1487

REGISTERED
G. W. R.

1488

REGISTERED
B. & L. H. R.

1489

REGISTERED
G.T.R.S.B.

1490

Type		Value
1480	Port Dover & Lake Huron. Apr. 12, 1876. Black.	
	1876 3c.	1.00
	2c. Regist.......	1.00
1481	Huron & Lake Erie Rwy. Fe., '75 to Ap., 78. Black.	
	1875 3c.	1.00
	2c. Regist.......	-1.00
1482	Black. Au., '78.	
	1878 3c.	1.00
1483	Black. Ja., '75.	
	1875 3c.	1.00
	2c. Regist.......	1.00
	Great Western Rwy.	
1484	Black. Ap., '78.	
	1878 3c.	1.00
	2c. Regist.......	1.00

Type		Value
1485	Black. Au., '78.	
	1878 3c.	1.00
	2c.	1.00
1486	On cover from Wroxeter, Ont. May, 1878 to Toronto. Black.	
1487	Great Western Rwy. Accommodation.	
	Black. Ap., '78.	
	1878 3c.	1.00
	2c. Regist.......	1.00
1488	Great Western Rwy.	
	Black. Ap., '78.	
	1878 3c.	1.00
	2c. Regist.......	1.00
1489	Grand Trunk Rwy. Sarnia Branch.	
	Black.	
	Also used by:	
	F.W.PT.P.L. & V. RYS. (No. '78).	
	GRAND JUNCTION RWY. (Fe., '82).	
	H. & T. R.	
	H. & N.W.R. (Mr., '79).	
	L.H. & B. Ry. (Mr., '81).	
	P. DOVER & L H.R.	
	P.D. & L.H.R. (Fe., '79).	
	P.D. & L.H. Ry. (Mr., '81).	
	SOUTHERN EXT.	
	T. & S.	
	W. PT. P.L. & W. RYS. (No. '78).	
	WEST. EXT.	
	W. G. & B.	
1490	Black.	

1491

1491 Black. Jy., '78.

Franks

Government and official correspondence enjoyed franking privileges. "FREE" was the usual marking or Frank, the earliest noted being 1840, although possibly used earlier.

The fee for Registration had to be paid, however, and we therefore have franked covers with stamps affixed to the amount of the registration fee.

FREE FREE FREE FREE

1500 1501 1502 1503

Type		Value
1500	Black 1840, 20mm. x 4½mm.	
	Stampless Cover.......	.25
	With initials or signature of M.P. or official	.50
	North Douro. Ja., '64.	
	Brown..............	.35
1501	Black. April, 1843.	
	Stampless Cover......	.25
	With initials or signature of M.P. or official.................	.50
	Blue.................	.75
	On Stamps; in Black.	
	1851 12d............	
1502	Black 1857.	
	Stampless Cover......	.25
	With initials or signature of M.P. or official.................	.50
	Appearing on Stamps.	
	185? ½d.	
	1868 1c. Brown......	5.00
	3c.	3.50
a.	Slightly Smaller Newbury, U.C. Mr., '69.	
	Green................	1.00
1503	Black Au., '67 with heavier impression for late dates.	
	Stampless Cover.......	.25

Type		Value
	Initials or signature of M.P. or official stamped or written........	.50
	With Railway Marking "Ottawa & Prescott"	5.25
	Blue slightly heavier type. Pembroke My., '67................	.35
	Appearing on Stamps.	
	1880 2c.	1.00
	3c.	1.00
a.	Slightly Smaller.......	.25
	Black Au., '60 Toronto.	

1504 1505

1504	**Sandwich, U.C.** Ja., '59.	
	Black.	
	Stampless Cover......	.45
	With REGISTERED..	.85
1505	**Toronto.** Ap., '60.	
	Black.	
	Stampless Cover......	.30
	With initials or signa- of M.P. or official....	.60
	With Legislative Assembly frank, red.......	2.75
	Red.................	.40
	With Legislative Assembly frank, red.......	3.00

FREE FREE

1505x 1505xy

1505x	Black values as above..	.75
	Ultramarine Frankford Mr., '67............	.90
	Deep Chocolate Kingston Ap., '66........	.75
1505xy	Black................	1.50

1505xx

Type		Value
1505xx	**Ottawa.**	
	Adds to val. of cover..	.75

1506

1506	Black Ap., '80.	
	Stampless Cover......	.35
	Appearing on Stamps.	
	1880 3c.	1.00

1507

1507	Red Admiralty Office Halifax.	
	Stampless Cover......	6.00

1508

1508a

Type		Value
1508	Quebec Oc., '61. Toronto Fe., '59.	
	Stampless Cover, black.	.75
	red...	1.00
	blue..	1.00
1508a	Ap. 2, '58............	

1509

1509	Black.	
	Stampless Cover......	.25

1511

1511	Black.	
	Stampless Cover......	.50

1512

1513

1512	Red or Dull Red No. '67	
	Stampless Cover......	1.00

Type		Value
	With FREE and initials or signature of M.P. or official...........	1.75
1513	**Ottawa.** Ap., '74.	
	Blue.	
	Stampless Cover......	.75
	With black FREE....	1.00
	With black REGISTERED...........	1.00
	With initials or signature of M.P. or official add............	.25
	Red.	
	As above.	
a.	"Ottawa" instead "Canada".	
b.	In two rings with FREE outside "Ottawa" My., '78. in blue.	

1512x

1512x	Ap., '72.	
	Blue, with FREE and Member's Initials....	1.75

1510xx

1510xx	Red with FREE, M.P. Initials.............	2.00

1510

Type		Value
1510	**Toronto.** Ap., '53. Blue.	
	Stampless Cover......	2.00
	With black or red FREE	2.25
	With blue...........	3.00
a.	Size one third smaller..	2.00

1510x

1510x Blue Ap., '58, Stampless Cover.
Adds to value of cover. 1.00

1514

1514	**Toronto and Quebec.** Jy., '51.	
	Blue.	
	Stampless Cover......	1.50
	With red PAID 3......	2.25
	With red "Quebec Paid"	3.00
	With red "1d Paid at Quebec"...........	3.00
	Green.	

Type		Value
	Stampless Cover......	2.00
	Varieties as above, plus .50.	

1515

1515	Black or Red, Au., '63	
	Stampless Cover......	.75

1515x

1515x As above.

1516

1516	Black.	
	Stampless Cover......	.75
	Green.	
	Stampless Cover......	.75
a.	Circle instead oval. Black.	
	1886 3c.	1.00

1516x

1522

1516xx

Type		Value
	Both the 1881 and the 1906 types of "House of Assembly" Crown were coupled with the 9-bar cancellation and used as a duplex.	
1516x	Blue.	
	1881 1c.	.80
	3c.	.90
	5c.	1.25
1516xx	Purple.	
	1881 1c.	.80
	3c.	.90
	Black 1906.	
	(On Georgian and later issues).	
1522	Stampless Cover, black.	.25
	red...	1.00

1517

1517	Brick red Fe., '68, Deep Pink De., '69.	
	Stampless Cover......	.75
	With red "PAID 3"...	1.75
	Blue Fe., '75.	
	Stampless Cover......	.60
	As Cancellation.	
	Blue.	
	1875 3c.	1.00

1518

Type		Value
1518	Red or Blue, Mr., '59.	
	Stampless Cover......	2.50
	With black FREE.....	2.75
	With red FREE.......	3.00
	With initials or signature of M.P. or official add .25.	
	With Railway marking.	5.00

1518x

1518x "House of Commons". Prices as above.

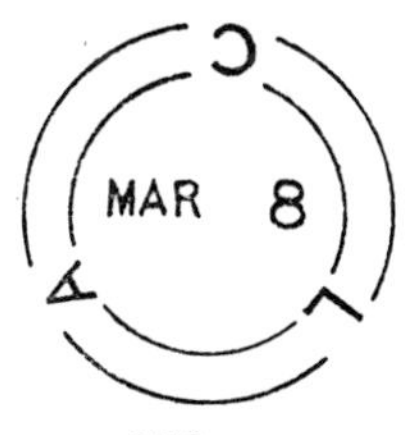

1518xx

1518xx Legislative Assembly of Canada.

1519

Type		Value
1519	Black.	
	Stampless Cover......	.75
a.	"Ontario"............	
	Mauve, Fe., '72.	
	Stampless Cover......	.75

1520

1520	Black.	
	Stampless Cover......	.60

1521

1521	Blue.	
	Stampless Cover......	1.00
	With initials or signature of M.P. or official................	1.25
a.	Without FREE at bottom...............	

1523

Type		Value
1523	Black.	
	Stampless Cover......	.50
	Initialed or signed by M.P. or official......	.75
a.	Larger from Sp., '91. Black or blue.	

1525 1525x

1525	Red brown. Fe., '83.	
	Stampless Cover......	.75
	Initialed by Senator or official.............	1.00
	Pink. Jy., '85.	
	Stampless Cover......	.75
	Initialed by Senator or official.............	1.00
a.	Lettering heavier, crown higher Nov., '93.	
1525x	Crown narrower 1897.	

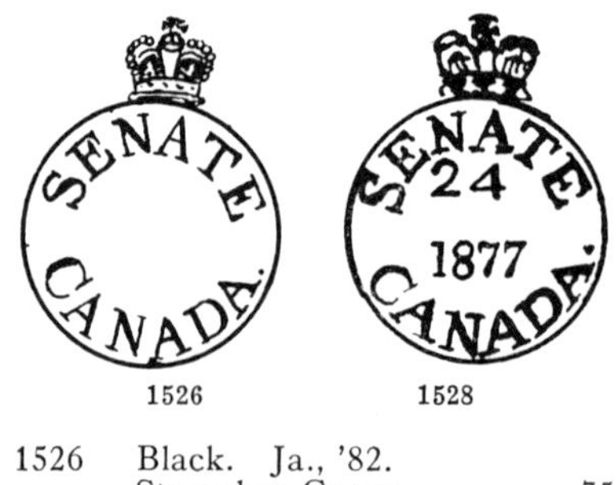

1526 1528

1526	Black. Ja., '82.	
	Stampless Cover......	.75
	Initialed by Senator or official.............	1.00

Type		Value
1528	My., '70 to My., '98. Black Red or Purple.	
	Stampless Cover......	.75
	Initialled by Senator or official.............	1.00

1527

1527	Magenta. Fe., '75.	
	Stampless Cover......	1.75
	Initialed by Senator or official.............	2.00

1529

1529	Black.	
	Stampless Cover......	.25
	Blue, May, 1902.	
	Stampless Cover......	.50
	Initialed or signed by M.P. or official......	.75

1532

Type		Value
1532	Black bi-lingual 1926.	
	Stampless cover.......	.25

1530

1531 1533

1530	Black. Ja., '27.	
	Stampless Cover......	.25
1531	Black. June, 1900.	
	Stampless Cover......	.25
a.	Circle complete, FREE unframed outside (1899).	
b.	Montreal instead Ottawa (Dec., 1907) with A.M. or P.M...	.25
1533	Black.	
	Stampless Cover......	.25
a.	Circle completed, used to Dec., 1926.......	

Departmental Franks

1534

1534	**(Ottawa).** Mr., '65. Blue.	
	Stampless Cover......	.50

1535

Type		Value
1535	(**Ottawa**). Fe., '92. Black.	
	Stampless Cover......	.50
	With black FREE.....	.75
a.	Similar for Senate.....	
b.	Similar for Indian Affairs.............	

1536

1536 Black. My., '65.
Stampless Cover...... .75

1536x

1536x Blue, Adds to val. of cover.............. 1.00

1536xx

Type		Value
1536xx	Pink, with FREE and Minister's Sig.......	1.50

1537

1537 Black, probably British, G.D. for Government Department...

1538

1538	Black. Au., '77.	
	Stampless Cover......	.75
	With black FREE.....	.75
a.	"F. Braune" above CANADA, My., '62.	.75
b.	Railways and Canals, My., '80...........	

1539

1539 Black (Crown Lands Dept.)
Stampless Cover...... .75

MARINE & FISHERIES

1540

1541

1541xx

Type		Value
1540	Black. Oc., '67. Stampless Cover......	.75
1541	Black. Stampless Cover......	.75
1541xx	Red, Mr., '72.........	1.25
	With signature of Minister or Dept. Official (Green, Mr., '71)....	1.50

1541x

1541x	Stampless Cover......	1.25

1542

Type		Value
1542	Black used by Connell, P.M.G. of New Brunswick. Stampless Cover......	.75

RECEIVER GENERAL

FREE

CANADA

1543

1543	Black. No., '69. Stampless Cover......	.75

1544

1544	Blue. Stampless Cover......	.75

1545

1545	Black backstamp of receiving P.M.........	

1546

Type		Value
1546	Blue. Ja., '68. Stampless Cover......	.75

1547

Type		Value
1547	Blue. Stampless Cover or Postal Card........	.50
a.	"Post Office Department Canada" Fe., '83................	

THE RAILWAY POST OFFICE—"POSTE AMBULANTE"

Its inception in the then "Province of Canada" and its early development.

By S. Tanner Green

What is the Railway Post Office?

In a few words, it is a travelling Post Office—a specially appropriated apartment or part of a Railway car, or a whole coach, now specially constructed and designed for the purpose, in or attached to a train operated on regular schedule between given points on a Railway.

Its beginning was decidely crude, merely comprising a space partitioned off in a passenger or baggage coach, fitted with a number of small squares, commonly called pigeonholes, in which to separate letters—larger ones for newspapers and a rack or hooks along the side walls to hang the mail bags.

Now a standard has been adopted in Canada for Postal cars divided into 30 ft. space, or half a car, and whole cars the recognized length of which is 60 ft.

There is a regular scale of rates of remuneration paid by the Post Office Department, fixed, according to space afforded, at so much per train mile (distance travelled).

In the early days, the price varied and seems to have been more or less the outcome of separate agreements between the Governments of the day and the Railway owners.

A special class or grade of Postal employees—called Railway Mail Clerks—man these Post Offices on wheels. In the early days they travelled singly, but with the enormous expansion of mail communication the group or crew of a Railway Post Office (R.P.O. is the Official abbreviation) is at present frequently much more numerous—each member having his specifically allotted task for the trip—such as handling the Registered matter—assorting the ordinary letters or newspapers, etc., as the case may be.

On the longer Trunk lines of Railway, the Railway Mail Clerk crews operate in sections as it would be a physical impossibility for individuals to work from end to end. Such sections are called "Runs" and each run has its particular date-stamp or postmark—in which the Railway number of the train, apart from name and date is shown. Thus on the Canadian National (formerly Intercolonial Railway) there are four separate and distinct runs between Montreal and Halifax, i.e.:—

"Montreal and Levis"	163 miles
"Levis and Campbellton"	304 miles
"Campbellton and Moncton"	187 miles
"Moncton and Halifax"	189 miles
	843 miles

These are the through trains only, which are supplemented by numerous "Locals" on many of which there are likewise R. P. O's.

The following information is gleaned from such meager records as the writer has been able to discover combined with the recollections of the very few surviving Postal employees of the early seventies and his own connection of over forty years with the Postal Service of the Dominion.

Great Bitain (England) was in this, as so many other things, the pioneer—because that Island Kingdom had one or more travelling Post Office in 1838. There is some possibility that Spain had an "ambulante" Postal Service some time previous, but of this there is not any positively reliable record.

Postmaster-General James Morris, in his annual report to Earl of Elgin and Kincardine, Governor-General of British North America, dated 12th August, 1853, says, in part:

"This officer will also be charged with the duty of enquiring into the management of the Railway travelling Post Office attached to the trains carrying the mails in England, as the approaching completion of some important lines of railroad in this country will probably render a similar arrangement advisable for such portion of our Mail Service as may be covered by these roads."

Then, in the report, dated 10th November, 1854, of his successor Malcolm Cameron (who died ere the report was fyled) it is related:

"The great accession of labour caused in the western section of the Province, more especially by the transfer of mail conveyance to the Great Western and other Railways recently opened, requiring the entire reorganization of all depending and connecting Mail Routes, and the most unremitting vigilance to correct the irregularities constantly arising upon such extensive alterations in the service.

Further on, in the same report:—

"The travel of the mails on the line of route between the Niagara River and Hamilton, London and Windsor, was transferred to the Great Western Railway, as the different sections of the road went into operation and the mails have passed over the whole route between the Niagara and Detroit frontiers, 229 miles, since the 25th January, 1854. Two mails a day are conveyed each way, and the transit of the mails between the two extreme points connected by this road is now effected in from eight to ten hours, instead of four days, the time ordinarily occupied by stage."

Also:—

"Under the provisions of the Act of November, 1852, the United States Post Office has, since the completion of the Great Western Railway, been permitted to forward a closed mail over that line between the Detroit and Niagara frontiers, without Postage charge:—affording a like privilege to this Department of the transmission of mails between Montreal and Canada West over the "Ogdensburg road."

Before the inauguration of the carrying of the mails by the Great Western Railroad they were carried, in 1852-3, by the then "St. Lawrence and Atlantic" R.R. between Richmond and Sherbrooke, Que., a distance of only 25 miles, however!

Thus we see that though the mails went over the rails in closed bags like baggage or freight as early as 1852 the travelling post office wherein the regular assorting of mail matter was done did not appear until two years later, i.e., 1855, inasmuch as Postmaster-General Robert Spence in his annual report, dated 15th February, 1856, writes:—

"Moreover, on all railway lines of importance, the proper management and distribution of the mails indispensably necessitates the employment of Post Office Clerks or Conductors, to travel with the mails in a railway car or portion of a car, appropriated as a Post Office, and attend to the duties required to be performed whilst the mails are in transit.

"Very important facilities are unquestionably secured in this way to correspondence, but at the same time another expensive feature is created by this peculiar requirement of the Railway Mail Service."

The records show that the mails were carried in 1854 by rail between:—

1. Barrie and Toronto (Canada West)
2. Montreal and Ogdensburg (N.Y.), U.S.A.
3. Montreal and Plattsburg (N.Y.), U.S.A.
4. Montreal, St. John's and Rouse's Point (N.Y.)
5. Richmond and Sherbrooke (Canada East)
6. Windsor and Suspension Bridge (Niagara Falls)

in charge of contractors who accompanied the closed bags or by those placed in charge by the railroad themselves. In 1855, the number of railway routes had more than doubled by the addition of:—

Burlington and Rouse's Point (U.S.)
Bytown (now Ottawa) and Prescott
Chippawa and Niagara
Cobourg and Peterboro
Industry (now St. Paul d'Industrie) and Montcalm
Lewiston and Toronto
Montreal and Quebec
Ogdensburg and Rouse's Point

1855 is therefore the advent of the Railway Post Office—and its necessary corollary the Railway Mail Clerk—7 years ahead, it seems, of their equivalent in the United States of America. The Railway Mail Conductors were few in number, 32 permanent with 12 temporaries. Prior to 1855, there were Railway Conductors or Guards who accompanied the overseas mails between Toronto and Boston and New York, but no sorting was done on the way.

Their new contemporary was the Money Order system in the Province of Canada (Canada East and Canada West); because Confederation was consummated only 11 years later. Their combined salaries and allowances amounted to £837 5s 8d currency—about $433.00 each, which was considered good pay in those days.

It is obvious that the change from stage to steam was an immense advance in Postal communication, and in his report of 12th February, 1857, Postmaster General Robert Spence declares:—

"The sections of the Grand Trunk Railway lying between Brockville and Toronto became available for mail transport in October, 1856 and thus by uniting at Toronto with the Great Western, completed the line of communication by railway between Quebec in the east and Windsor in the extreme west.

"This therefore, appears to be an appropriate time to draw attention to the effect of this change in the mode of transport, in the acceleration of the mails, especially in the winter season—and the following comparative statement will show what the time occupied in the conveyance of a letter was in winter only four years since, between Quebec and some of the principal cities and towns to the Westward and the present course of Post by Railway Mail:—

	In 1853	In 1857
Quebec to Windsor	10½ days	49 hours
Quebec to London	9 days	45 hours
Quebec to Hamilton	8 days	42 hours
Quebec to Niagara	8 days	50 hours
Quebec to Owen Sound	10 days	3½ days
Quebec to Guelph	9 days	51 hours
Quebec to Toronto	7 days	40 hours
Quebec to Cobourg	6 days	36 hours
Quebec to Bellville	5 days	34 hours
Quebec to Kingston	4 days	31 hours
Quebec to Brockville	3 days	29 hours
Quebec to Ottawa	3 days	34 hours

"The advantage thus gained between the more distant points, applies also to the reduction of the time occupied in conveyance between intermediate places and will be shared, in a greater or lesser degree, by nine-tenths of the whole correspondence of the Province, for at least that proportion of the letters conveyed by mail partake in the benefit of Railway transport. Besides this gain in speed, further important advantages are reaped in the comparative immunity of Railway Mail conveyance from the irregularities; the damages from exposure to the weather, and other causes of injury unavoidably incidental to the transport of heavy mails by stage or waggon over the ordinary roads of the country, and above all, in the greater security from robbery or loss whilst 'en route'."

On the 30th of September, 1857, the staff of Railway Mail Clerks had increased to 59 which shows how rapidly that mode of handling mail was progressing. In that year also, the perforated postage stamp was introduced in Canada, when the ½d, 3d and 6d were issued in that form. It also was the end of pence currency as the issue from 1859 was in cents, including the 1c, 2c, 5c, 10c, 12½c and 17c.

At the present time there are 221 Railway Post Offices on 169 routes in the Dominion of Canada which embraces the former Provinces of New Brunswick, Nova Scotia, Prince Edward Island, British Columbia and the then great unknown lands which are now the flourishing Provinces of Alberta, Manitoba, Saskatchewan, the Yukon territory as well as all the lone Northland extending to the Arctic circle.

In addition, supplementing these, there are 534 Baggage Car Services (closed mails without R.P.O. or distinguishing marks).

RAILWAY CANCELLATIONS AND POSTAL MARKINGS

There are known, 475 varieties, Maritime Provinces; 1401, Quebec; 1298, Ontario; and 424 Western Provinces a total of 3,598. This list may be increased by possibly 250 additional postmarks.

In the inscription, where "North", "UP", "E", etc., is given it will be understood that the cancellation or marking also exists with the opposite direction indicated, as "South", "Down", etc.

The letters A, B, C, D, etc., were intended to designate the stamper or mail clerk, but the use of any cancelling or making iron was not always restricted to any one person.

Under this heading are included all markings of a postal nature which were n any way identified with a railway. These were rarely used as cancellations. Their main purpose was to assist those responsible for the mail to follow the course of a letter from sender to receiver. These markings take on a newer and fuller meaning if the student will but study the early railway history of Canada.

It will be discovered, for example, that British Columbia's entry into the Dominion was contingent on the C.P.R. being built to the Coast at the earliest possible date.

The following is an interesting comment from "Truth" of London, England, in 1885, regarding this railway and the Provinces it was to serve:

"The C.P.R. will run, if ever finished, through a country frost-bound for eight months of the year, and one about as forbidding as anything on the face of the earth. British Columbia is barren, cold, mountainous—not worth keeping. Fifty railways would not galvanize it into prosperity. Canadians know that the road will never yield a single red cent of the money sunk into it People cannot stand the cold of Manitoba. Men and cattle are frozen to death in astonishing numbers. Manitoba's street nuisances kill the people with malaria, or drive them mad with plagues of insects. It is through a death-dealing land of this kind that the railway is to run. Canada is one of the most over-rated Colonies we have." (No comment needed. Ed.).

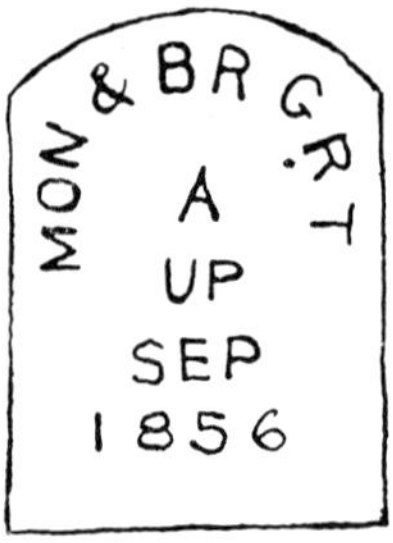

MON & BR G.R.T A UP SEP 1856

1600

Type		Value
1600	(Drawn from description). Black. Sep., '56. 1856 3d.	12.00

ST. LAWRENCE & ATLANTIC-RAILROAD JU 23 1855

1601

1601	Black. Ju., '55. On cover prepaid by 3d	15.00

INTERCOLONIAL-RAILWAY WEST AP 25 1874 S.T. ST. JOHN & AMERST

1602

Type		Value
1602	Black. Ap., '74. 1874 3c.	1.75

O. S. & H. R. R. 14 AU POST OFFICE

1603

1603	**Ontario, Simcoe and Huron.** Black. Au., '56. Cover, prepaid by 3d...	15.00

ONTARIO-SIMCOE & HURON-RAILROAD APR 4

1604

Type		Value
1604	Black. Fe., '60.	
	1859 5c. Beaver......	2.50
	Cover, prepaid by 5c...	7.50

1605

1605	Black. Ap., '60.	
	Adds to val. of cover...	1.50
	Cancellation.	
	1860 5c. Beaver......	2.00
	1868 3c.	1.75
	1870 1c.	2.00
	3c.	1.85

1606x

1606

1607

1606x	....	1.25
1606	Black Ja., '60 to Jy., '63.	
	Adds to val. of cover...	1.25
	Cancellation.	
	1860 5c.	2.00
	1868 3c.	1.75
	1870 3c.	1.75
1607	Black Au., '63 to Au., '75	
	Adds to val. of cover...	1.00
	Cancellation.	
	1863 5c.	2.00
	1868 3c.	1.75
	1870 1c.	2.00
	2c.	2.00
	3c.	1.75
a.	With Numeral under Year...............	
b.	"Ry" instead "R" (My., '84)..........	

1608

Type		Value
1608	Black. Ju., '73.	
	Adds to val. of cover...	1.25
	Cancellation.	
	1873 1c.	1.00
	3c.	1.00

1609

1610

1609	Black Jy., '78 (No. 1-2-3)	
	Adds to val. of cover...	1.25
	Cancellation.	
	1878 1c.	1.00
	3c.	1.00
1610	Black Jy., '78 (No. 1-2-3)	
	Adds to val. of cover...	1.25
	Cancellation.	
	1878 1c.	1.00
	3c.	1.00

1611

1611	Black. Ja., '69.	
	1869 3c.	1.75
	1870 1c.	2.00
	3c.	1.75
	Adds to val. of cover...	1.25

1612

1613

Type		Value
1612	Black. Ja., '77.	
	Adds to val. of cover...	1.50
1613	Black. Ja., '77.	
	Adds to val. of cover...	1.50

1614

1614 Prince Edward Island Rwy. The Postmaster at O'Leary Road P.O. was Station Agent also, and used the railway ticket dating stamp as a post office cancelling instrument.

	Green.	
	1875 1c.	3.50
	Adds to val. of cover...	2.50

1615

1616

Type		Value
1615	**New Brunswick.**	
	Black.	
	1851 6d.	
	Adds to val. of cover...	5.00
1616	**New Brunswick.**	
	Black.	
	1851 6d.	
	Red.	
	1851 3d.	
	Adds to val. of cover,	
	Black..............	5.00
	Red...............	6.00

1617

1617	Black 1858.	
	1858 3d. Ribbed......	
	Adds to val. of cover...	5.00

1618

Type		Value
1618	Black. Sp., '57.	
	1857 3d.	10.00
	Adds to val. of cover...	6.00
a.	"Toronto & Sarnia Railroad C.W. No. 1 Down Nov. 18, 1859"	
	1859 5c. Beaver......	
b.	"Mon. & Kings, Gd. Trk. R.W. Post Office No. 2 C Down Feb. 22, 1860"...........	

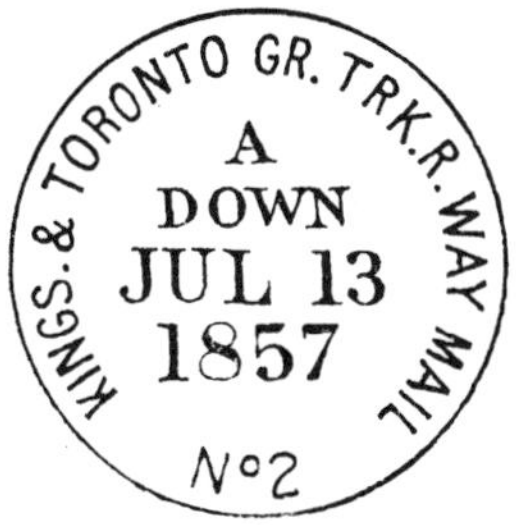

1618x

1618x	Black.	
	Adds to val. of cover...	6.00

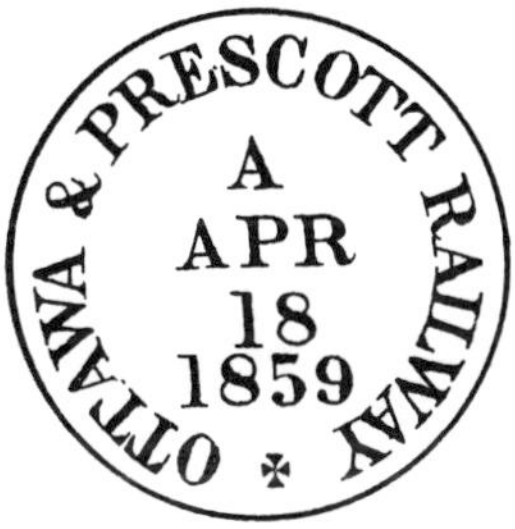

1618xx

1618xx	Ottawa and Prescott Black..............	6.00

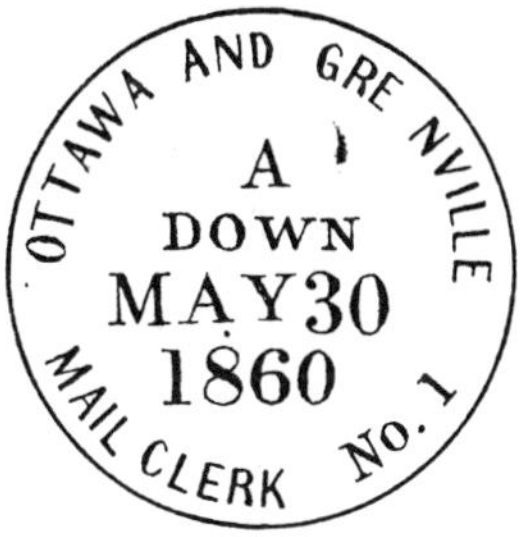

1618xxx

Type		Value
1618xxx	Adds to val. of cover..	6.00
a.	"Greenville" in error...	
b.	"Ottawa and Grenville Mail Clerk No. 1" Clockwise, and "A Down May 21, 1859"	
	1859 5c.	4.00
	1868 3c.	2.00
	1872 3c.	1.75

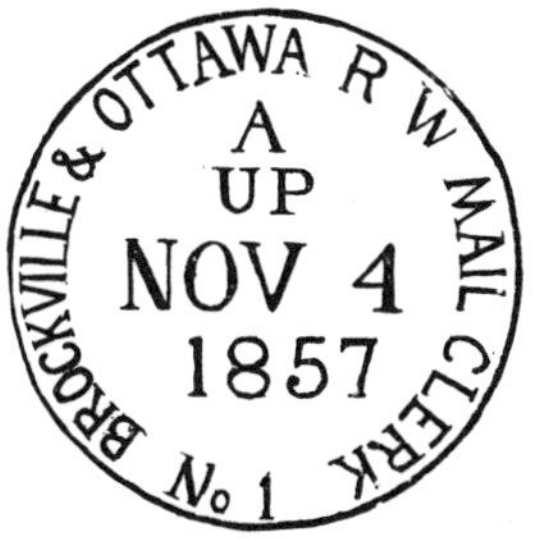

1619

1619	Black, No., '57.	
	1859 5c.	4.00
	Adds to val. of cover...	
	5c. On cover....	7.00

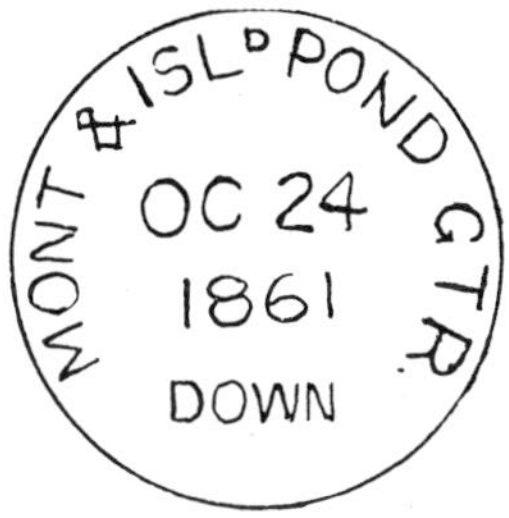

1624

1624	Black, Oc., '61.	
	1861 5c.	6.00
	Adds to val. of cover...	7.00

Inner Circle Added.

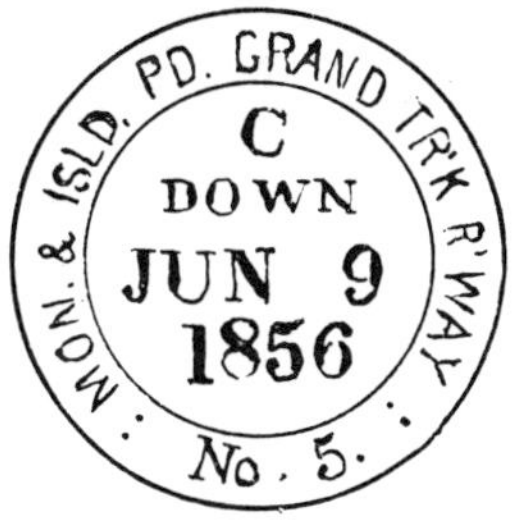

1620

Type		Value
1620	Black, Ju., '56.	
	1856 3d.	8.00
	1859 5c.	5.00
	1868 3c.	2.00
	1870 3c.	2.00
a.	"Brockville & Ottawa R.W. Mail Clerk No. 1 A Up Nov. 4, 1861"	
	1861 5c.	3.50

1620x

1620x	Black, Ju. 21, '59.	
	Adds to val. of cover...	6.00
a.	"Greenville" in error...	

1621

1621	Black, Fe., '55.	
	Nos. 1-2-3-4-5-6-7.	
	1855 3d.	7.50
	1859 5c.	5.00
	1868 3c.	2.00
	1870 3c.	2.00

1622

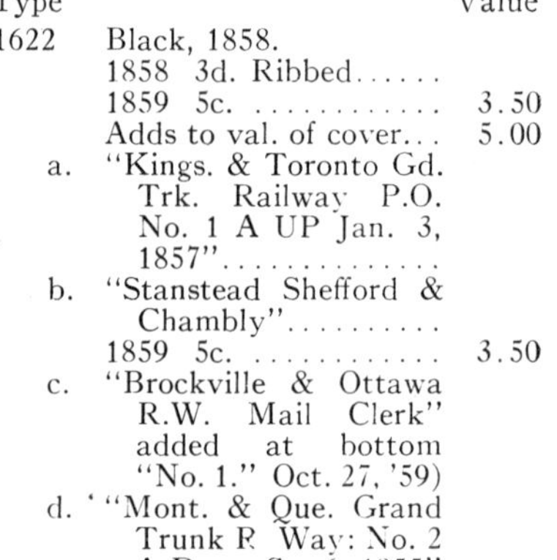

Type		Value
1622	Black, 1858.	
	1858 3d. Ribbed......	
	1859 5c.	3.50
	Adds to val. of cover...	5.00
a.	"Kings. & Toronto Gd. Trk. Railway P.O. No. 1 A UP Jan. 3, 1857"............	
b.	"Stanstead Shefford & Chambly"..........	
	1859 5c.	3.50
c.	"Brockville & Ottawa R.W. Mail Clerk" added at bottom "No. 1." Oct. 27, '59)	
d.	"Mont. & Que. Grand Trunk R Way: No. 2 A Down Sp. 6, 1855"	

1622x

1622x	Black.	
	Adds to val. of cover...	9.00

1623

Type		Value
1623	Black, No., '55.	
	1855 3d.	7.50
	1859 5c.	5.00
	1868 3c.	2.00
	1870 3c.	2.00
	On face of cover adds to val..................	5.00
a.	"Mon. & Kings. Grd. Trk. R. Way P.O. No. 1"............	
b.	"Montreal & Kingston G.T.R. Way P.O. No. 3 B UP Nov. 26, 1858"..............	
c.	Mont. & Kings. G.T.R. Night Mail No.1 A Down Mar. 9, 1860"	
d.	Montreal & Kingston G.T.R. Way P.O. No. 3, B. Down Apr. 10, 1860............	

1625

1625	Black, Oc., '72.	
	1872 3c.	2.00
	Adds to val. of cover...	5.00

1626

Type		Value
1626	Black, Oc., '66.	
	1867 5c.	5.00
	Adds to val. of cover...	6.00
a.	"P.M." instead of "NORTH". Sp., '67.	

1627

1627	Black, 1855.	
	1855 3d.	7.50
	1859 5c.	5.00
	1868 3c.	2.00
	1870 3c.	2.00

1628

1628	Black. From No., '64 or earlier.	
	1864 5c.	5.00
	1868 3c.	3.50
	1870 3c.	3.50

1629

Type		Value
1629	Black, Oc., '70.	
	1870 3c.	2.00
a.	Reads "Grenville & Ottawa".	

1630

1630	Black, 1863.	
	1863 5c.	8.50
	Adds to val. of cover. . .	7.00
a.	"Feb., 26" solid "1864" double letters, "No. 1" at bottom, double.	

Double Outer Circle.

1630x

1630x	Black.	
	Adds to value of Cover.	7.00

Double Outer Circle and Single Inner Circle

1631

1631	Black, Oc. 22, '61.	
	Adds to val. of cover. . .	8.00

1631x

1631x	Black, Ja., '61.	
	1863 5c.	7.50
	Adds to val. of cover. . .	8.00

1632

1632	Black, My., '67, Nos. 1-2-3.	
	1867 5c.	5.05
	1868 3c.	2.50
	1870 3c.	2.50
	Adds to val. of cover. . .	5.00
a.	"G.T.R." added and outer circles closer, Mr., '63.	

1632x

Type		Value
1632x	Black.	
	Adds to value of cover.	5.00

1632xx

1632xx	Black.	
	Adds to Value of Cover.	5.00

1633

1633	Black, Ju., '64.	
	1864 5c.	5.00
	Adds to val. of cover...	6.00

Type		Value
a.	"Stanstead Shefford & Chambly No. 1" Mr., '64.	
	1859 5c.	5.00
b.	"Arthabaska & Three Rivers G.T.R. No. 1 South Jy. 26, 1866"	
	1872 10c.	5.00

1634

1634	Black, No., '63 Nos. 1 to 8.	
	1863 5c.	5.00
	Adds to val. of cover...	6.00
	1864 2c.	10.00

Thick Outer Circle,

Thin Inner Circle.

1634x

1634x	Black.	
	On face of cover adds to val.	7.50

Types 1640 to 1663 are noted on the 3c and other values of the "Small Cents" issue. In some cases they may be found on later issues. The values for the 3c stamp vary from 50c to $2.00 depending on color, shade or variety of stamp, scarcity of type, etc.

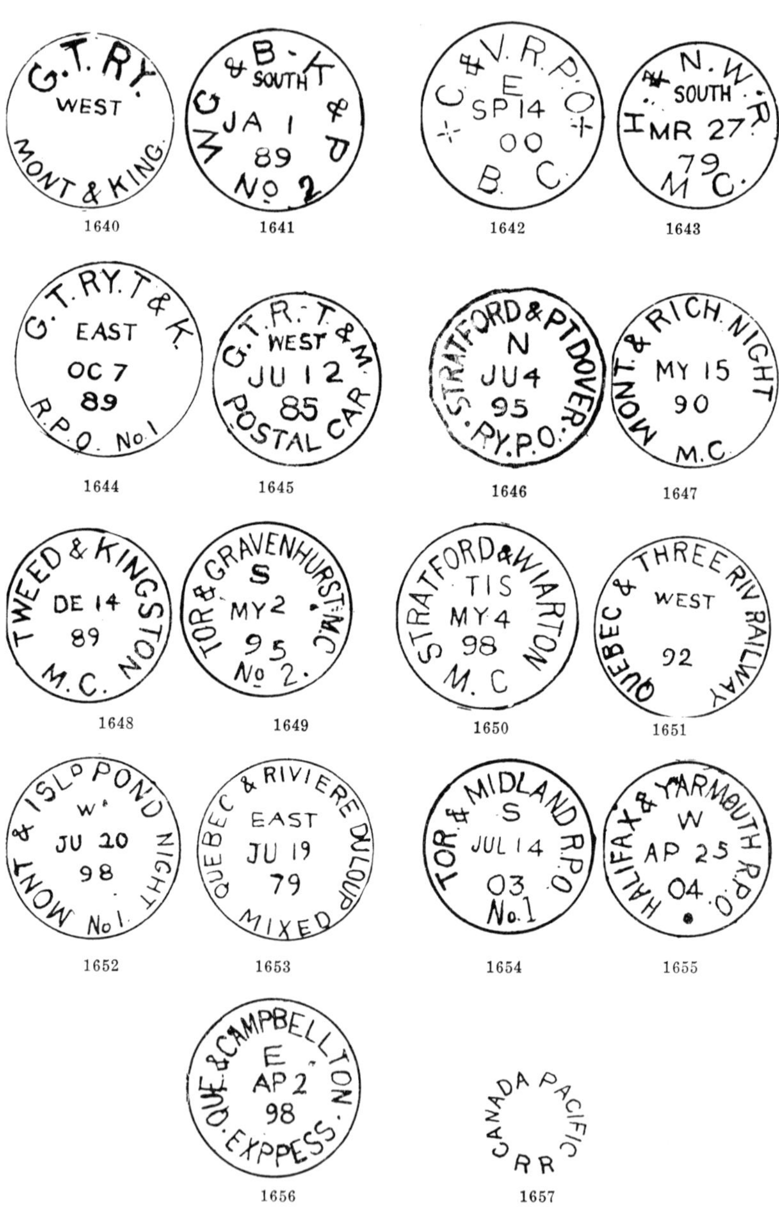

1646 Noted without ring, smaller.
1657 Noted for Ja '82. Rare. Not known as cancellation.

1658  1659  1660

1658-1659-1660 Types 1658-1659-1660 were soldered to side or bottom of regulation stamper by mail clerk.

1658	1880	3c.	.60
1659	1880	3c.	.50
1660	1897	3c.	.50
		3c. 4-Leaf	.40
		1c.-2c. 4-Leaf	
		3c. Q.V. Num.	.40
		1c.-2c.	

1661 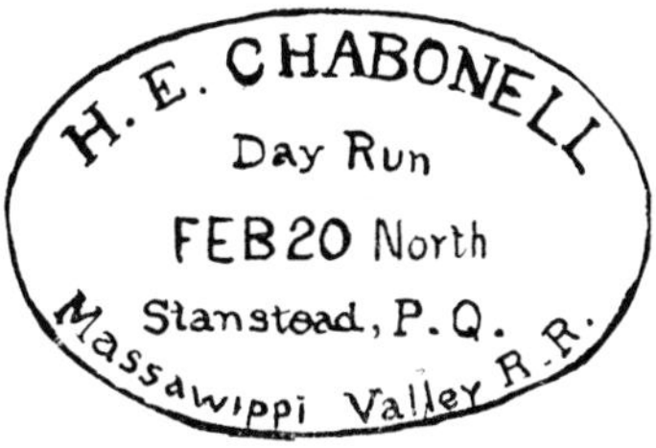 1662

1661 Violet rubber stamp used by Mail Clerk A. Stafford (?) May, 1890.
1890 3c. .... .75
1662 Carmine, 1885.
1885 3c. .... .75
a. "1889" instead "Day Run" and "Mail Clerk" instead "Stanstead".
1889 3c. Carm. Rose 1.50
Types 1661-1662 were retained by the individual Mail Clerk.

1663

1663 Black.
1894 3c. .... .85
a. Similar to Type for "Que & Camp"

GODERICH & BRANTFORD

1664

GODERICH & STRATFORD

1665

Type Value

ANNAP. & YARM.
ARTH & THREE RIVERS.
ALL. & BEETON.
ALL. & PENETANG.
BARRIE & MEAF.
BELL. & MADOC.
BELL. & PET.
BL'K & MID.
BRANTFORD & FORT ERIE Ju 94.
CHARL'TN. & TIGNISH.
CH'TOWN & GEORGE-TOWN Au 93.
CH'TOWN & SOURIS EAST Au 93.
CANADA ATLANTIC Fe 92.
1664 CAN. NORTHERN RAILWAY.
1898 1c. Q.V. Num... .40
GALT & ELMIRA Ap 93.
GRAV. & N. BAY Ja 94.
GODERICH & BRANTFORD.
1665 GODERICH & STRATFORD (Ap '95).
1895 3c. .... .90
1897 3c. 4-Leaf...... .90
HALIFAX & MONCTON. I.C.R.
HALIFAX & ANNAP.
HALIFAX & MONCTON. C.P.R.
HALIFAX & AMHERST.
HAM & COLL.
KING. & SHER. LAKE.
KING. & TWEED.
KING. & TOR.
NIGHT EAST.
a. Day East.
b. Night East.
c. Night West.
LONDON HAMILTON & TORONTO RY Jy 93.
LONDON ST. MARYS & TORONTO RY Jy 93.
LONDON & WINGHAM Jy 94.
LON. & CANFIELD.
LON. & SAR.
LIN. & HAL.
LON. & NIAG. FALLS Ap 91.
EXPRESS.
MONT. & WATERLOO Oc 91
MONT. & OTT. M.C. Ja 93.
MONT. & THREE RIVERS.
MONT. & KING.
DAY EAST.
a. Day West.
b. Night East.
c. Night West.
MONT. & RICH.
NIGHT EAST.
a. Night West.
MONT. & I. POND.
DAY EAST.
a. Day West.
b. Night East.
c. Night West.
MONT. & DUNDEE.
MONT. & SHER.
MONT. & MANS.
MONT. & CALUMET.
MONT. & ST. ARMAND.
MONC. & CAMP.
NEW GLAS & PT. HAWK.
NICOLET & ST. HYACINTHE Mr 94.
NAP. & TAM.
ONTARIO & WESTERN.
OTT. & BROCK Fe 92.
OTT. & CALUMET Fe 92.
OTT. & TORONTO Fe 92.
OTT. & PRESCOTT Fe 92.
OTT. & PT. ARTHUR Fe 92.
OTT. & MANIWAKI My 93.
OTT. & FT. COULONGE Fe 92.
OTT. & PARRY SOUND Fe 94.
OTT. & PEM.
OTT. & MONT. C.P.R.
OTT. COT. & MONT. C.A.R.
OTT. & ARDEN.
OTT. & TOR.
ORANGE & TEES No. 1 Fe 93
PORT HOPE & MIDLAND Jy 90.
PT. C. & PT. D.

PERTH & MONTREAL.
QUE. & R. DU LOUP.
EXPRESS.
a. Local.
QUE. & RICH.
QUE. & THREE RIVERS.
QUE. & CHAMBORD.
R. DU LOUP & CAMP.
RENF. & SHAR. LAKE.
ST. JOHN & MONC.
ST. JOHN & VANCE.
DAY.
a. Night.
ST. JOHN & AMH.
ST. J. & WATERLOO.
ST. THOS. & FT. ERIE.
ST. THOS. & WINDSOR.
SALISB'Y & H. BANK.
S'SIDE & PT. DU CHENE.
SHER & LEVIS.
STRAT. & WIARTON No 90.
SMITH'S FALLS & MONT.
M.C. Ja 93.
SHER. & AGNES.
SOREL. & SUTT.
SHER. & STANSTEAD.
SUD. & S.S.M.
STREETS. & ELORA.
TOR. & GRAV.
TOR. & OWEN SOUND
My 94.
TOR. & O. SOUND Ju 90.
TOR. & HAM. Ju 90.
TOR. & SAR. Ju 90.
TOR. & ST. THOS. Ju 90.
TOR. & PT. HOPE Ju 90.
TRENT. & COE. HILL.
TRENT. & PICTON.
TRURO & PICTOU.
VANCE & ANDOVER.
WHIT. & MAN. Ju 90.
WALKERVILLE & LEAMINGTON Ju 90.

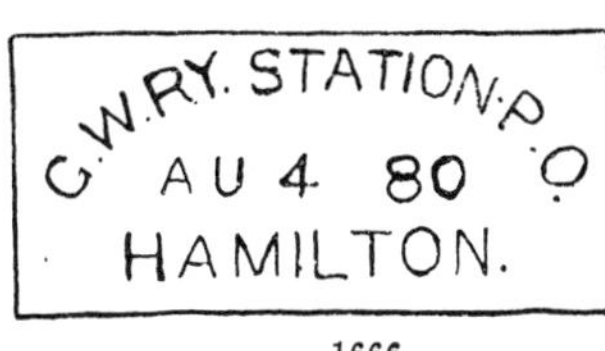

1666

1667 1668

Railway Station Post Offices

1666 G. W. Ry. Station P.O. Au '80 Hamilton.
C.P.Ry. Mail Room Winnipeg (AM PM) Sp 86.
G.T.Ry. Stn. Hamilton Can. (AM PM) Ja 91.
G.T.R. Station Hamilton (AM PM) Ap 97.
G.T.Ry. Stn. London Can. (AM PM) Ju 95.
Gd. Tk. Ry. Stn. London Canada (AM PM) No 92.
Gt. Western Rwy Statn London Canada (AM PM) Au 82.
a. Hamilton Ap '81.
London Ry. P.O. No. 1.
Medora Station Man Ap 97.
River du Loup Station Fe 95.
Raily Stn. Hamilton.
Richmond Station Que. Ju 95.
St. Dominique Station Que (Violet Sp 94).
Strath Clair Station Man Mr 97.
Ste. Thecle Station De 94.
Union Rwy. Station Toronto Canada Au 79.
1667 Union Rwy. Sta. Toronto Ja. 82.

CITY SUB-STATION POST OFFICES

No attempt has been made to list Sub-station Offices which came into existence after 1900.

Inscription

Toronto: Bathurst St. De 86.
Bleecker St. De 86.
Bleecker AMPM No 93.
Bloor St. No 90.
Broadview Ave. No 93.
Clinton St. No 93.
Carlton St. De 86.
Dundas St. De 86.
Elm St.
Gerrard St. Fe 92.
Parliament St. Jy 91.
Parliament St. Oc 93.
Queen St. East De 86.
Riverside B'ch.
Peter Street My 89.
Rusholme Road No 90.
Spadina Ave. Ju 90.
Spadina Ave. De 86.
St. Joseph St. Fe 93.
Strachan Ave. De 91.
York Street AMPM Au 92.

Montreal: Charboille Square De 96.
Ontario Street AMPM No 88.
St. Catharines St. Centre AMPM No 93.
Notre Dame St. West Ap 95.
St. Cath. St. W. L.C.D. Ju 93.
Ste. Cath. St. West AMPM No 88.

Hamilton: Pearl St. AMPM Ap 91.
Stevens St. Ap 91.
James Street Au 87.

Halifax: Gottingen Street Fe 94.
Morris Street 1 & 2 No 95.

List of Railway Cancellations.

Type	Particulars
	A.N. & N.W. Ry.
	Annapolis & Yarmouth M.C.E. (or EAST) No. '79.
	Albert Railway.
	Alta A. & Coal Co. M.C. No. 1 Oc 98.
	All. & Penetang N. Mr. 91.
	All. & Mea. Bch. Ry. M.C. S. My 90.
	(In violet Ap 92).
	Arthabaska & Three Rivers GTR Jy 16 1866 South No. 1.
	Arth. & Three Rivers M.C. North Ju 83.
	B. & L.H.R.R. East DE 70.
	B. & L.H. West.
1607	B. & L.H.R. East AU 63.
	B. & L.H.R. East Ap 79.
	B. & O.R.R. 2N De 80.
	Barrie & Meaford M.C. G.T.Rwy. North My 94 (June, in violet).
	Beeton & Collingwood M.C. North Oc 92.
	Beeton Branch H. & N.W.Ry 1 & 2 Au 81.

Type	Particulars
	Beechus Falls & Dudswell Jc.
	Belleville & Madoc Rwy M.C. (AM or PM) Ja 83.
	Belleville & Peterboro M.C. E De 89.
	Blackwater Jct. & Midland.
	Blenheim & Leamington.
	Blenheim & Sarnia Ry. P.O. N. Ju 87.
	Blen & Sar.
	Blyth & Kincardine.
	Blackwater & Mid. M.C. No. 1 or 2 N Sp 89.
	Blackwater & Mid. N Au 89.
	Brantford & Fort Erie M.C. Ju 94.
	Brantford & Goderich Ry P.O. E. Mr 25 02.
	Brandon & Estevan.
	Bridgeburg & Goderich.
	Bridgeburg & St. Thomas.
	Brockville & Montreal.
	Brockville & Westport M.C. E. Ju 96.
	Brockville & Carleton Place M.C. CPRy E No 86.
	a. North Au '86.
1617	Bytown & Prescott R.R. Jul 9.
1691	Brockville & Ottawa R.W. Mail Clerk A UP Nov. 4 1861 No. 1.
	C.P.Ry. M.C. British Columbia E Ja 93.
	C.P.R. British Columbia.
	C.P.Ry. M.C. Brit. Col. Au 86.
	C.P.R.W.Y. M.C. B.C. Mr 90.
	a. E or W Mr 90.
	C.P. Ry. Mail Rooms Winnipeg Sp 86.
	C.P.Ry. Mont. & Sher. Fe 89.
	C.P.R. Winnipeg & Glenboro Jan 87.
	C.P.Ry. West of Winnipeg E 1-2-3 Ja 82.
	C.P.R. West of Winnipeg E A-B-C-D Au 83.
	C.P.Ry. M.C. W'Peg & Brandon E My 97.
	C.P.Ry. West of Winnipeg.
	C.P.R. West of Winnipeg Local 1-2-3 Ju 93.
	C.P.Ry. Pt. Arthur & W'Peg E (1 to 7) No 86.
	C.P.Ry. Ott. & Brock. M.C. N Ju 90.
	C.P.Ry. Ottawa & Montebello M.C. E Mr 90.
	C.P.Ry. B. & O. Div. M.C. No 80.
	C.P.Ry. Ottawa & Pembroke North Ju 82.
	C.P.Ry. Ott. & Pt. Arthur E Sp 96.
	C.P.Rwy. Pembroke & Ottawa North Au 82.
	C.P.Ry. Ottawa & Brockville North Ja 82.
	C.P.Ry. Ottawa & Pembroke North De 81.
	C.P.Ry. Ott. & Pt. Arthur M.C. E (1 to 11) Oc 89.
	C.P.Ry., N.B. Div. Mr 91.
	C.P.R. Winnipeg & Deloraine E (1-2-3-) Ja 87.
	C.P.R. Winnipeg & Gretna N (1-2) Ap 94.
	Canadian Pacific R.R. Ja 82.
	Canada Atlantic M.C.
	Canada Atlantic Ry M.C. East Mr 87.
	Canada Atlantic Ry. Sp 83.
	Canada Atlantic M.C. E Fe 94.
	Can. Atlantic Ry. M.C. East Ap 79.
	Can. Centl. Rwy. North No 76.
	Canada Southern.
	Ca. Southern R. East Ja 23 '77.
	Campbelltown & Levis.
	Canfield Dundas & St. Thomas.
	Central Ont. Ry. MC N Au 86.

Type	Particulars
	Ch'town & Georgetown MC E Au 93.
	Ch'town & Souris MC Au 93.
	Chatham & Walkerville.
	Clifton & Windsor M.C. My 83.
	Clifton & London M.C. My 83.
	Charlottetown & Tignish M.C.
	Columbia & Kootenay.
	C. & V.R.P.O.,—B.C.—E. Sp 14-00.
	Connors & R. du Loup.
	Collingwood Branch H. & N.W.Ry. Oc 79.
	Credit Valley Rwy. Main Line East Au 82.
	Credit Valley Rwy. Elora Br. North Au 82.
	Can. Atl. Rwy. M.C. Ju 86.
	a. M.C. added.
	Calgary & Edmonton M.C. No. 1 N Ap 94.
	C. & V.R.P.O. E Sp 14 00 B.C. (Chilliwack & Vernon).
	Drummondville & Sutton.
	E. & N.A.R. East Sp 73.
	E. & N. Rwy. B.C. N. Sp 86.
	F. W. Pt. P. L. & V. Rys. (No '78).
	G.T.R. & T.S. Postal Car East Au 82.
	G.W.Ry. Express (AM or PM) (Duplex with 180) Ja 84.
	G.B. & L.E. Ry. N. (1 to 4) No 90.
	G.B. & L.E. Ry. North M.C. No. 82.
	G. Bay & L.E. Ry. M.C. (AM or PM) Jy 82.
	G.T.R.T. & K.E. (1-2-3) Ju 80.
	G.T.R. T & S West 20 Feb 68.
	G.T.Ry. T & K. No. 1 E Jy 90.
	G.T.Ry. Mont. & King. East My 80.
	G.W.R. (Express or Accom.) East Ap 79.
1605	G.W.R. Sarnia Branch East Fe 13, 61.
1606	G.W.R. East Ja 2 '60.
	G.W.Ry. Sarnia Branch East My 81.
	G.W. & B. Ry. N (1-2-3) Ju 89.
	Galt & Waterloo M. C. (AM or PM) Fe 92.
	Galt & Elmira M.C. Ap 93.
	Goderich & Brantford M.C. E Ju 94.
	Goderich & Ft. Erie Ry P.O. E My 87.
	Grand Junction Rwy. (Fe '82).
	Gravenhurst & Nth Bay Au 94.
	G.T.Ry. T. & K. RPO (No. 1-2-3-4-5) East Au 83.
1625	H. & A.R. East Oc 16 1872 N.S.
1611	H. & P.R. East N.S. Ja '69.
1610	H. & T.R. No. 2 West Ju '81.
	H. & N.W.R. M.C. North Mr 79.
	Huron & Erie Rwy. M.C. AM Ja 84.
	Halifax & Amherst E Ja 77.
	a. M.C. EAST Ju 86.
	Halifax & Amherst P.O. Car East Ja 77.
	Halifax & Annapolis M.C. East or E Mr 83.
	Halifax & Annapolis Ry. M.C. East Fe 81.
	Halifax & Campbellton.
	Halifax & Camp.
	Halifax & Moncton M.C. E (or East) Au 82.
	Halifax & Moncton C.P.Ry. E De 89.
	Halifax N.S. & Sack. N.B. R.R. Car E Au 80.

Type	Particulars
	Halifax & Sydney R.P.O. W. Ap 93.
	Halifax & St. John W. 1897.
	Halifax & St. Jn.
	Halifax & Yarmouth E De 97 or 3c Jul 2-371
	Halifax & Yarmouth R.P.O. W Ap 04.
	Hamilton & Allandale M.C. North Oc 92.
	Hamilton & Alliston.
	Hamilton & Blackwater Jct.
	Hamilton & Bolton.
	Hamilton & London.
	Hamilton & Lake Erie.
1613	Ham. & Lake Erie R. North Ja '77.
	Ham. & Lake Erie R. North.
	Hamilton & Meaford.
1608	Hamilton & Nor. Wstn. R.R. North Ju '73.
	Hamilton & Port Dover Ry. P.O. N Ju 87.
	Harrisburg & Southampton M.C. N 1-2 Sp 93.
	Intercolonial Ry. U.S.A.P.S. Car De 94.
	Intercol. R.R. Amhers & Halifax East Au 74.
1661	International Railway, Aug. 16, 1890 Shefford, P.O.
1602	Intercolonial Railway St. John & Amherst West Ap 25, 1874.
	King & Sh Lake M.C. N Oc 88.
	Kingston & Tweed.
	Kingston & Pembroke Ry M.C. AM No 79.
	L.H. & B. Ry M.C. North Mr 81.
	Lake Megantic & Tring N Feb 98.
	Levis & Kennebec Railway North Ju 79.
	Levis & Deschaillons.
	Levis & Lake Megantic.
	Levis & Mont.
	Levis & Richmond.
	Levis & Sherbrooke.
	Levis & St. Francois Beauce.
	Levis & I. Pond.
	Levis & R. du Loup.
	Levis & Riviere du Loup.
	Lindsay & Haliburton M.C. N De 94.
	Lindsay & Hamilton.
	Lindsay & Midland.
	London Hamilton & Toronto M.C. My 93.
	a. E added De 95.
	London & Niagara Falls M.C. AM Ap 92.
	Lon. Ham. & Tor. M.C. E.
	Lon. St. Mary's & Tor. M.C. East Ja 93.
	London & Sarnia Ry P.O. E My 87.
	London & Windsor Ry P.O. E My 87.
	London & Hamilton.
	London & Niagara Falls Ry P.O. T15W etc. Ju 87.
	London & Niagara Falls Ry P.O. (1 to 7) Ju 87 45c.
	London & Canfield Ry. P.O. M.C.
	London & Canfield Jun Ry P.O. E Ju 87.
	London & Kincardine Ry P.O. T15N Ju 87.
	London, Paris & Tor.
	London, Port Hope & Midland.
	London St. Mary's & Tor. M.C. E. No 95.
	London & Wingham M.C. T1N T1S T2N T2S Ju 94.

Type	Particulars
	Man. & N.W. Rly. East (or E).
	Man. & N.W. M.C. Jy 87.
	Man. & Nor. WSTn R.N.
	Man. & N.S. RWy. M.C. E MC 1-2 Jy 94.
	Massiwippi Valley Ry M.C. E Au 86.
	Mattapedia & Pastebiac W. Aug. 95.
	Mattapedia & Gaspe.
	McAdam & Andover P.C. N Oc 87.
	Medicine Hat & Nelson.
	Megantic & Montreal.
	Mid. R'Wy No. 2 North Ap 83.
	Midland Rwy. M.C. N. Oc 87.
	Michigan Central.
	Moncton & Camp. P.C. Day Jy 90.
	Moncton & Campbellton I.C.R. North Ja 81.
	a. No. circle.
	Moncton & Campbellton M.C. North Ja 81.
	a. No circle.
	Moncton & Campbellton P.C. My 88.
	Moncton & Camp. P.C. N. No 99 Day.
	Monc. & Camp. M.C. De 94.
	Moncton & Campbellton R.P.O. (Centre blank.)
	Moncton & Campbellton M.C. North De 90.
	a. With Day or Night De 93.
	Moncton & Quebec.
1600	Mon. & Br Grt A Up Sep 1856.
	Mon. & Champ. Jc. Rly.
	Mon. & Isl. Pond.
	Mon. & Dundee Rwy. De 86.
	Mont. I. Pond & Portland.
	Mont. Is. Pond & Portland.
	Mont. & I. Pond Ry. M.C. E Ap 91.
	Montreal & Is. Pond.
	Montreal & I. Pond Rly.
1652	Mont. & Isld. Pond Night No. 1 W Ju 20 '98.
	(This is the old Grand Trunk line to Portland. The western part of the line was from Montreal to Island Pond, Vermont, originally called the St. Lawrence & Atlantic, while the eastern branch from Island Pond to Portland was called the Atlantic & St. Lawrence. Elliott Perry writes "I have found the Atlantic and St. Lawrence postmark on U.S. covers and wonder if the earliest form used on the route west of Island Pond was "St. Lawrence and Atlantic". I have looked for it in vain."
1621	Montreal & Island Pond G.T.R. Way A Feb 17 1855 No. 2.
	Montreal & Calumet E Jy 96.
	Montreal & Dundee M.C. N Oc 93.
	Montreal & Eastrey.
1620	Mon. & Isld. Pd. Grand Trk. R'way E Down Jun. 9, 1856 No. 5.
1631	Same, but B Down Jan. 14, 1861. No. 7.
	Mont. & King. E Day GTRy Ap 90.
	Mont. & King. M.C. Au 89.
1623	Mon. & Kings. Grd. Trk. R.W. Post Office No. 2. D Down Nov. 1, 1855.
	Montreal & Malone.
	Montreal & Mt. Laurier.
	Montreal & Mansonville Ap 95.
	Mont. & Mans. Ry M.C. North Ap 80.
1624	Mont. & Isld. Pond G.T.R. Oc 24, 1861 Down.
	a. Ry omitted Jy 93.
	Montreal & Massena N Sp 96.

Type Particulars

Mont. & Picton.
Montreal & Richmond.
Montreal & St. Jerome.
Montreal & Toronto C.P.Ry E Ja 91.
Montreal & Waterloo M.C. E De 91.
Montreal & Campbellton M.C. Night Dec 93.
Montreal & Ottawa M.C. No 91.
Montreal N.R.H. Mr. 31 82.
Montreal E.R.H.
Mont. & Sher. C.P.Ry. M.C. Fe 89.
1633 Mont. Shefford & Chambly Railroad 23 Ju 1864 West.
Mont. & Sherbrooke C.P.R. Ap 95.
Mont. & Rich Day M.C. Au 89.
Mont. & St. John N.B. C.P.R. E Sp 91.
Mont. & Three Riv. Ry. M.C. East Fe 80.
Mont. & Three Riv. M.C. C.P.R. E Oc 94 (Sp 94, in violet).
Mont. & Tor. G.T.Ry. NW4W DWNE 1 to 12 De 90.
Mont. & Tor. C.P.R. E 1-2.
Montreal & St. John M.C. W Jan. 97.
1622 Mont. & Toronto G.T.B. Way Mail B up Jul 17 1859 No. 1.
1627 Montreal & Kingston G.T.R. Way No. 3 D Down Mar 29 1859.
1610 Musk. Br. South Oc 82 No. 1.

Nanaimo & Esquimalt 97.
Napanee & Tamworth Ry. M.C.
Napinka & W'pg.
Napinka & Winnipeg M.C. East 1-2 Ja 94.
New Glasgow & Point Tupper M.C. W My 93.
Nicolet Sorel & Montreal.
Nicolet & Montreal.
Nicolet & St. Hyacinthe M.C. E Ju 93.
N.O.R. Railway S.
Nor. Pac. Rwy. E. Au 90.
Nor. Pac. Rwy. M.C. W'PEG & Brandon No. 1 E No 91.
1608 Nor. Railway North 1-2 Ja 78.
North Bay & Ft. William.
North Bay & S. Ste. Marie E 1-2 My 96.
N. Bay & S. Ste. Marie.
North Bay & S.S.Marie.
North Shore Ry. De 86.
Nor. & P. Jn Rwy. M.C. N. Ja 87.
North Battleford &............
North Simcoe Branch RWY M.C. Sp 79.

1603 O.S. & H.R.R. Post Office 14 Au.
1604 Ontario-Simcoe & Huron Huron Railroad Apr 4.
Orangeville & Teeswater M.C. No. 1 Ju 94.
Ott. & Brockville M.C. N No 95.
Ott. & Brock. P.C. N No 95.
Ott. & Calumet M.C. E Sp 94.
Ott. & Ft. Colounge M.C. E Ap 93.
Ott. & Depot Harbour.
Ott. & Pt. Arthur.
Ott. & Port Arthur Oc 93.
Ott. & Man.
Ott. & Parry Sound M.C. E Fe 94.
Ott. & Montebello M.C.
Ott. & Waltham.
Ott. & Toronto M.C. No. 1 Jy 93.
Ott. & Pt. Arthur M.C. No 3 Jy 93.

Type	Particulars
	Ott. & Port Arthur C.P.R. No. 8 No 91.
	Ottawa & Montebello M.C.
	Ottawa & Grenville Up Oc 9 '74.
1629	Ottawa & Grenville No 1 Up Jy 16, 1872.
	Ottawa & Pt. Arthur M.C. Ju 86.
	Ottawa & North Bay M.C. C.P.Ry. E Jy 86.
	Ottawa & Prescott M.C. N No 92.
1626	Ottawa & Prescott Railway Au. 31, 1867 North.
1630	Ottawa & Prescott Railway A Sep 21, 1865.
	Ottawa & Pembroke M.C. Mr 88.
	Ottawa & North Bay M.C. C.P.Ry Jy 86.
	Ottawa & Toronto M.C. E 1-2 No 91.
	Oxford & Picton M.C.
	Oxford & Picton M.C. E De 95.
1614	P. E. I. Railway O'Leary Road Aug 1875.
	P.D. & L.H.R. North No 77.
	P.D. & L.H.Ry. MC Mr 81.
	P. & P. Jn Rwy M.C. E Au 88.
	P. E. I. Mail Car No 89.
	P. E. Island Ry. M.C. Ja 81.
	P. Dover & L. Huron R.R. Ap 76.
	Penticton & Okanagon Landing.
	Palmerston & Kincardine M.C. E Ja 95.
	Perth & Montreal M.C. E Sp 94.
	Pembroke & Renfrew.
	Point Tupper & Sydney M.C. E De 91.
	Port Arthur & W'Peg.
	P. Dover & L.H.R.
	Port Hope & Midland M.C. N 1-2 Au 90.
	Port Colbourne & Port Dalhousie M.C. North Jy 92.
	Port Colbourne & Pt. Dalhousie.
	Port Hope & Tor.
	Portage la Prairie & Winnipeg.
	Prince Edward Island Railway (in green).
	Q.R.R.
	Q.M. & O. RWY East My 78.
	Q.M. & O. RWY East Mont. & Cal. My 78.
	Q. & Riv. du Lp. M.C. E Through or Local De 89.
	a. Thro Express or Local Express De 89.
	Q. & Lake St. John M.C. N De 89.
	Que. & Campbellton Express E2 or W2 My 91.
	a. 'E' or 'W'. b. Accommodation.
	Que. & Campbellton M.C. Local or Express E1-2-3-4-5My 91.
	Que. & Camp.
	Que. & Camp. M.C. Local N20 Sp 94.
	Que. & Richd. M.C. E De 89.
	Que. & Richmond M.C. E My 91.
	Que. & Lake St. John Ry M.C. N Oc 89 (or North).
	Que. Drum & Montreal.
	Que. Roberval & Chicoutimi.
	Quebec & Riviere du Loup Express or Mixed East Ju 79.
1632	Quebec & Riviere du Loup No. 3 My. 2, 1867 Down.
	Quebec & Campbellton Express E Ap 00.
	Quebec & Richmond Railway East Ju 79.
1634	Quebec & Richmond G.T.R. Way No. 2 A UP Nov. 14, 1863.
	Quebec & Roberval.
	Quebec & Richd. M.C. Through Express De 89.
	a. Local Express.

Type	Particulars
	Quebec & Lk. St. John N De 95.
	Quebec & Lake St. John M.C. N My 91.
	Quebec & Three Rivers C.P.R. M.C. E Oc 80.
	Quebec & Three Rivers Railway East Ju 79.
	Quebec Centreal M.C. N No 82.
	Quebec Centreal Ry (East) Ju 92.
	Quebec & Montreal.
	Quebec & St. John M.C. E Au 93.
	Quebec and Richmond G.T.RWAY A UP Jy 71.
	Regina & Colonsay No 90.
	Renfrew & Sharbot Lk N M.C. Sept 97.
	Reston & Wolseley.
	Rich. & I. Pond M.C. E No 90.
	Rich. & T. Pond M.C. Au 89.
	Ridgetown &........
	Riv. du Lp. & Camp. M.C. Through Express Oc 89.
	Riv. du Lp. & Camp. M.C. De 89.
	Riv. du Lp. & Campbellton M.C. Jy 87.
	Riviere du Loup & Campbellton Ry East Ju 79.
	Riviere a Pierre & Garneau Jc.
	S. & O. RWY. M.C. B.C. N Jy 94.
	St. Clair Branch C.S. Railway Oc 78.
	S.S. Marie & Meaford.
	St. George & Beauce.
	St. Armand & Montreal.
	St. John & Amherst M.C. Mr 92.
	St. John & Amherst Inter. Col. Rwy. East Jy 76.
	St. John & Amherst I.C.R. East Oc 77.
	St. John & Amherst E.
	St. John & Amherst Ry. East Dec 85.
	St. John & Moncton M.C. E Ja 95.
	St. John & Moncton Ry. EAST Night April 85.
	St. John & Moncton Nighr My 90.
	St. John & Amherst M.C. AME PME AMW or PMW Mr 92.
	St. John & Vanceboro M.C. Day Oc 92.
	St. John & Vanceboro Ry East Day Ja 82.
	St. John & Vanceboro Ry Day Ja 82.
1601	St. Lawrence & Atlantic Railroad Ju 23, 1855.
	St. Thomas & Courtright Ry. P.O. E Ju 87.
	St. Thomas & Fort Erie Ry P.O. E My 87.
	St. Thomas & Vanceboro.
	St Thomas & Windsor Ry P.O. E My 87.
	St. Marys & Tor.
	St. Sabine & Beauce.
	St. L. & O. Ry. M.C. North Fe 81.
1611	St. L. & O. R.R. South Oc. 13, 75. No. 1.
	St. Vincent & Winnipeg M.C. North Au 83.
	St. Vin. & Winnipeg M.C.
	Sarnia Stratford R.P.O. East Au 83.
	Salisbury & Harvey M.C. N Jy 94.
	Sarnia & Brantford R.P.O. E No 89.
	Sherbrooke & Lake Megantic.
	Sherbrooke & Lake Megan. M.C. No 91.
	Sherb. & L. Megan. M.C. No 91.
	Sherbrooke & Levis M.C.
	Sherbrooke & Stanstead M.C. Oc 92.
	Sicamous & Okanagan Landing.
	Sharbot Lake & Renfrew.

Type	Particulars
	Shefford Ry. M.C. Au 89.
	Smiths Falls & Mont. M.C. Ja 93.
	Sorel & Sutton Ap 95.
	Sorel & Sutton Ry. M.C. N or North Ap 80.
	a. Ry omitted Mch 96.
	Souris & Winnipeg M.C. E or East 1-2 Sp 93.
	Souris (C.P.R.) Section M.C. E Au 92.
	Stanstead Shefford & Chambly Railway No. 1 East My 64.
	Stratford & Wiarton.
	Stratford & Wiarton S No. 1 Oc 94.
	Stratford & Wiarton M.C. My 98 TIS or TIN.
	Stratford & Pt. Dover Ry. P.O. N Ju 87.
	Streets & Elora M.C. My 90.
	Sud. & S S.M. No. 1 or 2 E My 89.
	Sud. & Sault Ste. Marie M.C. E No 2 Oc 95.
	Swift Current & Pasque.
	T.G. & B. Ry. M. C. S No 90.
	T.G. & B. Ex. Ry. E. Jy 88.
	T.G. & B.C.P.Ry. E. No. 1 My 86.
	Temiscouata Ry. M.C. N Sp 92.
	Three Riv. & Que. C.P.Ry. M.C. E Ap 91.
	Three Rivers & Que. C.P.Ry. M.C. Ap 91.
	Three Riv. & Grand Piles.
	3 Rivers & Grand Mere.
	Trent & Picton M.C. Oc 88.
	Trent & Coe Hill M.C. Oc 88.
	Tring & LK Megantic.
	Truro & New Glasgow M.C. E My 93.
	a. "E" or "W" omitted May 93.
	Truro & Pictou Ry. M.C. E (East) Fe 80.
	a. "EAST" or "WEST" Nov. 92.
	Truro & Point Tupper M.C. E Ja 93.
1648	Tweed & Kingston M.C. De 89.
	Truro & Port Hawkesbury Ry M.C. Fe 81.
	Truro & Amherst.
	Truro & New Glasgow.
	Truro & Point Tupper.
	Truro & Port Hawkesbury M.C. East Jy 81.
	Tor. & St. Thos. M.C. E 1-2-3 My 90.
	Tor. Ham. & London.
	Tor. St. Mary & Lond.
	Tor. Gravenhurst M.C. G.T.R. N Ap 92.
	Tor. & Hamilton R.P. Car.
	Tor. & Ham. P.O. Car (1-2-3-4-5) E Oc 89.
	Tor. & Gravenhurst M.C. (1-2) N My 95.
	Tor. & Gravenhurst R.P.O. No. 1 N Ap 04.
	Tor. & Lorne M.C. N 1-2- De 94.
	Tor. & Lorn. M.C. E Ju 90.
	Tor. & Lon M.C. E (1-2-3) Sp 94.
	Tor. & Kingston P.O. Car East Ap 80.
	Tor. & King. P.O. Car East My 81.
1654	Tor. & Midland R.P.O. No. 1 S Jy '03.
	Tor. M. & I. South.
	Tor. & Mont. G.T.Ry. (1 to 12) De 90.
	Tor. & Mont. G. T. Ry NE SE DE NW (1 to 12) De 90.
	Tor. & Pt. H.E. (1-2) Au 89.
	Tor. & R.I.Ry.
	TOR. & NIP. R. South Ju 18 79 No. 2.
	Tor. & Nip. R.P.O. N 1 or 2 Oc 86.

Type Particulars

Tor. & Nipissing P.O. Car North (1-2) Ap 82.
Tor. & Sar. M.C. No. 1 (2-3) Au 93.
Tor. & Sr. E.
Tor. & Sar. P.O. Car E (1-2-3) No 89.
Tor & Sar. S & S Railway West Ju 79.
Tor. & Sar. M.C. E (1-2) Ja 95.
Tor. & Ottawa C.P.R. E (1-2-3-4) Ja 91.
Tor. & Ottawa M.C. E (1-2-3-4) Mch 96.
Tor. & Ott. M.C. E (1-2-3-4) Mch 96.
Tor. & Smith Falls.
Tor. & St. Thomas M.C. E July 94.
Tor. & St. Thomas M.C. (1-2-3) My 90.
Tor. & Mont. G.T.Ry. (1-2)My 95.
Toronto & Niagara Falls M.C. E Ap 93.
Toronto & North Bay M.C. G.T.R. N (1-2-3) Mr 95.
1618 Toronto & Sarnia R.W. Post Office C Down Sept. 17, 1857. No. 1.
Tor. & Pt. Hope.

Vanceboro & Andover N Sp 93.
a. "P.C." Sp 95.
Victoria Railway R.P.O. North Au 83.
Victoria & Wellington.

W.G. & B.K. & P. No. 1 or 2 North Ja 88.
W.G. & B.K. & P. M.C. (1-2) N Sp 94.
W.G. & B.K. & P. East My 75.
W.G. & B.K. & P. No. 1 or 2 North Ja 88.
W.G. & B.K. & P. N. Au 89.
W. Mac. P.O. Car De 89.
W. Ont. Ry.
W. Pt. P.L. & W. No 80.
With "RYS" added (No. '78).
Walkerville & Leamington M.C. North Ju 90.
Welland Rail Road Up No 64.
1628 Welland Rail Road Au. 3, 1875 UP.
Welland Railway M.C. North Fe 81.
Welland Railway P.O. Ap 76.
West Br. Railway St. John & Vanceboro East Ja 81.
Winnipeg & Moose Jaw.
Winnipeg & Gretna N 1 or 2 De 88.
Winnipeg & Amherst Rly.
Winnipeg & Manitoba Ry.
Winnipeg & Glenboro M.C. Jy 87.
Winnipeg & Deloraine M.C. Jy 87

PRECANCEL CATALOGUE

1923 Type

In 1888 Ottawa and St. John postmasters precancelled sheets of stamps with the regular cancellations of their offices, Toronto precancelled complete sheets of the 1c, 2c, 3c values by ruling with pen and ink lines across each set row of stamps. These were never authorized. These early precancels can be distinguished only if in pairs or blocks with the cancellation repeated without the date stamps, or on covers from firms known to have used the precancel privilege, when the cancellation on the stamp will not touch the envelope at either side.

Stamps in sheets, precancelled, were sold to the purchaser for use on mail of a certain class, to be taken to the post office in bulk, when it was allowed to pass without further cancellation. This expedited deliveries and saved labor.

The earliest type is the "roller 21" from Montreal, found on stamps identified as belonging to 1889 by their shades. This cancellation was used for the Pence Issue in 1858 the first "cents" issue of 1859, and rarely in the case of the 1868 issue. When the demand for precancelled sheets of stamps arose in 1888 this cancelling instrument, being on a roller or wheel, offered the easiest solution to the labor involved, and it was again brought into use.

Following the various types down to Type H, came a cancellation which showed the town and province. These were printed in sheets from plates.

In 1903 a type was introduced consisting of the town name and name of the Province separated by two horizontal bars. These were authorized for use only by firms sending out a minimum of 25,000 pieces of a particular class of mail matter. Few firms were qualified to use these. They were sold under conditions which precluded the possibility of the stamps being used again for the prepayment of postage. This type of cancellation quite superseded the other types, in fact the use of the first types, applied with a roller or wheel (AA to H) was strictly forbidden. At a later date the use of precancels was permitted for mailings consisting of a minimum 10,000 pieces at a time. At present precancelled stamps may be purchased by any reputable firm for use on even limited mailings.

Since precancels cover quite an extensive field, no attempt is made herein to list the various town types. To date no catalogue has been published which was not out-of-date almost as soon as it reached the collectors, who have by their own efforts been able to keep in touch with the new varieties as they appeared.

Some forty Town types are recognized, differing in the type used and in the style of the bars. These are found double, triple, inverted, misplaced, with broken letters, etc., and there are therefore innumerable sub-varieties. For example, the 1c King Edward "Montreal" is frequently found with the letters of the city name mutilated so that it reads "Muniklal."

Precancels are known from more than forty-four cities and towns in the Dominion.

Good copies of the older issues are not by any means easy to find. Used, as they were, principally on advertising matter, the bulk of them promptly found its way to the waste basket.

I am indebted to Professor R. De L. French of McGill University for the following excellent suggestion for:—

PLATING PRECANCELS

A B C	D B E
F G H	I G J
K L M	N L O
A B C	D B E

The best one can do with the early issues is to assemble the stamps in strips of three, one normal stamp in the centre, flanked by stamps from the right and the left edges of the sheet showing the termination of the precancelling design, which at the edges extends only part ways across the stamp. All the Georgian issues may be plated. The edge stamps are called "terminals."

The charts above shows how a "condensed sheet" of the Georgian issues may be built up. The rules indicate straight edges, where the original sheet of 400 stamps was cut apart into panes of a hundred before being issued to the post-masters. The bottom line is added solely for the sake of symmetry.

A.—Left terminal, perf. all round.
B.—Normal, perf. all round.
C.—Right terminal, right straight edge.
D.—Left terminal, left straight edge.
E.—Right terminal, perf. all round.
F.—Left terminal, bottom straight edge.
G.—Normal, bottom straight edge.
H.—Right terminal, right and bottom straight edges.
I.—Left terminal, left and bottom straight edges.
J.—Right terminal, bottom straight edge.
K.—Left terminal, top straight edge.
L.—Normal, top straight edge.
M.—Right terminal, top and right straight edges.
N.—Left terminal, top and left straight edges.
O.—Right terminal, top straight edge.

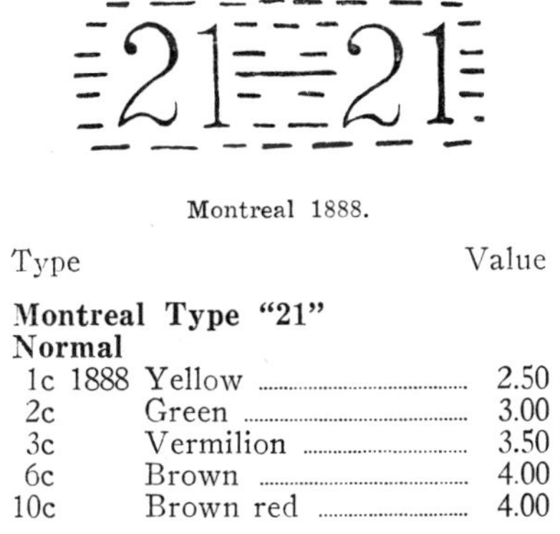

Montreal 1888.

Type		Value
Montreal Type "21"		
Normal		
1c 1888	Yellow	2.50
2c	Green	3.00
3c	Vermilion	3.50
6c	Brown	4.00
10c	Brown red	4.00

Type		Value
Inverted		
1c 1888	Yellow	2.50
2c	Green	3.00
6c	Brown	4.00
Vertical		
1c 1888	Yellow	2.50

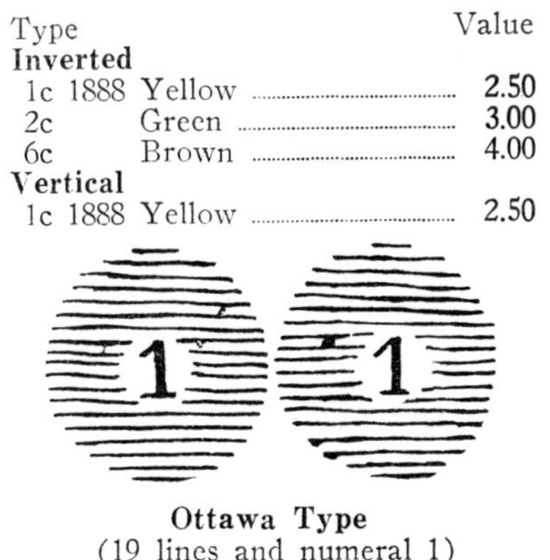

Ottawa Type
(19 lines and numeral 1)

Type			Value
Normal			
1c	1888	Yellow, pair	5.00
2c		Green, pair	5.00
3c		Vermilion, pair	5.00
5c		Grey, pair	5.00

St. John N.B., Type
(14 lines and numeral 1)

1c	1888	Yellow, pair	5.00

A

Type A

Normal			
1c	1889	Yellow	.50
10c		Brown red	1.50
Vertical			
1c	1889	Yellow	.50

A2

Type A2

Bars 2 mm. wide.

Normal			
1c	1889	Yellow	.50
2c		Green	.75
Vertical			
1c	1889	Yellow	.50
10c		Brown red	2.00

A3

Type			Value
Type A3			
Normal			
1c	1889	Yellow	.75
Double one vert.			
1c	1889	Yellow	1.00
Type A4 (Four bars)			
Normal			
½c	1889	Grey	1.25
		Grey (Violet overprint)	1.50
1c		Yellow	.20
3c		Vermilion	1.25
Vertical			
½c	1889	Grey	1.25
1c		Yellow	.40
Double one vert.			
On ½c	1889	Grey	1.50
1c		Yellow	.50
Double one vert. Type A3			
1c	1889	Yellow	.50
Double both vert.			
½c	1889	Grey	1.50
Double			
½c	1889	Grey	1.50
1c		Yellow	.50
Double one vert. Type A5			
1c	1889	Yellow	.60
Triple			
1c	1889	Yellow	.75
Triple two vert.			
1c	1889	Yellow	.75

A5

Type	Value
Type A5	
Normal	
1c 1889 Yellow	.20
Double	
1c 1889 Yellow	.60
Double one vert.	
1c 1889 Yellow	.60
1c Yellow (Violet overprint)	1.50
Double one vert. Type A3	
1c 1889 Yellow	.75
Double one vert. Type A4	
1c 1889 Yellow	.75
1c Yellow (Violet overprint)	1.50
Triple two vert. Type A4	
1c 1889 Yellow	.75

Type	Value
Vertical	
1c 1889 Yellow	.60
Double vertical	
1c 1889 Yellow	.60
Type A6	
(6 Bars.)	
Normal	
1c 1889 Yellow	.40
Double	
1c 1889 Yellow	.75
Double one vert. Type A4	
1c 1889 Yellow	.75

B6

Type	Value
Type B6	
Normal	
1c 1889 Yellow	.30
5c Slate green	1.50
Double	
1c 1889 Yellow	.30

Type	Value
Vertical	
½c 1889 Grey	**1.00**
1c Yellow	.30
Double vertical	
1c 1889 Yellow	.60
Type B7	
Normal	
½c 1889 Grey	1.00
1c Yellow	.50
5c Grey	1.00
Vertical	
1c 1889 Yellow	.60
5c Grey	1.25
Double vertical	
1c 1889 Yellow	.75
2c Green	1.50
Type B8	
Normal	
½c 1868	5.00
½c 1889 Grey	2.00
1c Yellow	.75
3c Vermilion	1.25
15c	10.00
Vertical	
1c 1889 Yellow	1.00
2c Green	1.25
Double vertical	
1c 1889 Yellow	1.00
Type B9	
Normal	
1c 1889 Yellow	1.00
2c Green	1.00
10c Brown red	2.00
Vertical	
1c 1889 Yellow	1.00
2c Green	1.25
1c	.30
Type B10	
Vertical or Horizontal	
2c 1889 Green	1.25
8c Grey	1.25

C2—Two single lines.
C3—Three single lines.
C4—Four single lines.
C5—Five single lines.

Type			Value
Type C2			
1c	1891	Yellow	.40
Double			
1c	1891	Yellow	.50
Vertical			
1c	1891	Yellow	.60
Type C3			
Normal			
1c	1891	Yellow	.30
Double			
1c	1891	Yellow	.40
Triple			
1c	1891	Yellow	.50
Quadruple			
1c	1891	Yellow	.75
Vertical			
1c	1891	Yellow	.50
3c		Vermilion	1.00
Double vertical			
1c	1891	Yellow	.60
Type C4			
Normal			
1c	1891	Yellow	.20
3c		Vermilion	1.00
Double			
1c	1891	Yellow	.30
Triple			
1c	1891	Yellow	.50
Double vertical			
1c	1891	Yellow	.40
Type C5			
Normal			
1c	1891	Yellow	.60
Vertical			
1c	1891	Yellow	.75

D3—Three double lines.
D4—Four double lines.

Type			Value
Type D3			
Normal			
1c	1891	Yellow	.30
Type D4			
Normal			
1c	1891	Yellow	.25
Vertical			
1c	1891	Yellow	.60

E.

Type			Value
Type E			
Normal			
½c	1892	Grey	.75
1c		Yellow	.04
2c		Green	.75
3c		Vermilion	.60
5c		Grey	1.00
6c	1889	Yellow brown	1.50
6c	1892	Red brown	1.25
8c			1.50
10c		Pink	1.50
10c	1889	Magenta	1.50
10c	1892	Brown red	1.25
20c	1893	Vermilion	1.75
Double			
1c	1892	Yellow	.20
2c		Green	.75
3c		Vermilion	.75
6c	1889	Yellow brown	2.00
Double one vert.			
½c	1892	Grey	1.50
Triple			
1c	1892	Yellow	.60
2c		Green	1.00
3c		Vermilion	1.00
Vertical			
½c	1894		1.00
1c	1892	Yellow	.30
2c		Green	1.00
3c		Vermilion	1.00
5c		Grey	1.25
6c		Red brown	1.75
10c		Brown red	1.50
10c	1889	Magenta	2.00
10c		Pink	2.00
20c	1893	Vermilion	2.00

Type			Value
Double vertical			
1c	1892	Yellow	.50
Quadruple two vert.			
1c	1892	Yellow	.75
Pair one Type F			
6c	1892	Brown red	2.00

F.

Type			Value
Type F			
Normal			
½c	1894	Grey	1.00
1c		Yellow	.05
2c		Green	.75
3c		Vermilion	.75
5c		Grey	1.25
5c	1889	Grey	1.75
6c	1892	Red brown	1.00
10c	1894	Brown red	1.25
10c		Dull rose	1.25
20c	1893	Vermilion	1.50
Double			
1c	1894	Yellow	.25
2c		Green	1.00
3c		Vermilion	1.00
6c		Red brown	1.00
20c	1893	Vermilion	2.00
Double one vert.			
1c	1894	Yellow	.75
Triple			
1c	1894	Yellow	.75
Vertical			
1c	1894	Yellow	.40
2c		Green	1.00
3c		Vermilion	1.00
5c		Grey	1.50
10c		Dull rose	1.50
Double vertical			
1c	1894	Green	.60

G.

Type			Value
Type G			
Normal			
½c	1894	Grey	1.00
1c		Yellow	.06
2c		Green	.75
3c		Vermilion	.60
5c		Grey	1.25
6c		Red brown	1.50
8c		Grey	1.50
10c		Brown red	1.25
10c		Pink	1.50
10c		Dull rose	1.50
15c	18.....	Lilac	6.00
½c	1897	Grey	.75
1c		Green	.04
2c		Purple	.30
3c		Carmine	.40
3c		Surcharged	.75
5c		Blue	.50
6c		Brown	1.25
8c		Yellow	1.50
10c		Brown violet	1.75
1c	1897	Jubilee	.50
2c			1.25
3c			.50
5c			1.75
8c			1.50
10c			1.75
15c			1.75
20c			2.00
$2			3.00
2c	1898	Map	2.00
½c	1898	Numerals	.25
1c			.02
2c		Purple	.25
2c		Carmine	.03
3c		Carmine	.10
3c		Surcharged	.75
5c			.25
6c			1.50
7c			.60
8c			.75
10c			.75
20c			2.00
1c	1903	Edward	.04
2c			.30
5c			.25
7c			.25
10c			1.00
Double			
1c	1894	Yellow	.30
2c		Green	1.00
3c		Vermilion	.85
5c		Grey	1.50
6c		Red brown	1.75
15c	18.....	Lilac	7.00
½c	1897	Leaves	1.25

Type			Value
1c			.30
2c			.50
3c			.75
8c			2.00
10c			2.00
1c	1897	Jubilee	1.00
3c			1.00
15c			2.00
20c			2.00
½c	1898	Numerals	.60
1c			.12
2c		Purple	.75
2c		Carmine	.50
3c		Carmine	.40
5c			.60
7c			1.00
8c			1.50
10c			1.00
1c	1903	Edward	.40
2c			.75
5c			.60
7c			.60

Vertical

Type			Value
1c	1894	Yellow	.20
2c		Green	1.25
3c		Vermilion	1.00
20c	1893		2.00
15c	18.....	Lilac	6.00
1c	1897	Leaves	.05
3c		Surcharged	1.00
5c			1.00
2c			1.00
1c	1897	Jubilee	1.25
2c			1.75
2c	1898	Map, Lavender	2.50
		Blue	2.50
½c	1898	Numerals	.60
1c			.30
2c		Purple	1.00
2c		Carmine	.50
3c		Carmine	.40
3c		Surcharged	1.00
5c			.50
6c			1.50
10c			1.25
1c	1903	Edward	.50
2c			1.00

Double vertical

Type			Value
1c	1894	Yellow	.60
2c		Green	1.25
5c		Grey	1.50
6c		Brown	1.75
15c	18.....	Lilac	7.00
1c	1897	Leaves	.50
1c	1897	Jubilee	1.50
3c			1.50
1c	1898	Numeral	.40
2c		Purple	.75
2c		Carmine	.50
3c		Carmine	.75
5c			.60
6c			1.75
10c			1.50
2c	1903	Edward	1.25

Double one vertical

Type			Value
1c	1897	Leaves	.60
1c	1898	Numerals	.60
7c	1903	Edward	1.25

H.

Type H

Normal

Type			Value
½c	1895		1.00
1c		Yellow	.03
2c		Green	1.00
50c		Blue	2.00
½c	1897	Leaves	1.00
1c			.75
½c	1898	Numerals	.25
1c			.02
3c			.75
3c		Surcharged	.75
8c			1.50
10c			1.50
1c	1903	Edward	1.00
2c			1.00
5c			1.25

Double

Type			Value
½c	1895		1.25
1c		Yellow	.06
50c		Blue	2.00
1c	1897	Jubilee	1.25
3c			1.25
2c	1898	Numerals, Carmine	.50
3c		Carmine	.75
10c		Brown purple	2.00
1c	1903	Edward	.40
2c			1.00

Triple

Type			Value
1c	1895	Yellow	.40
1c	1898	Numerals	.03
2c		Carmine	.60
3c		Carmine	.75

Type	Value
Vertical	
½c 1895	.75
1c Yellow	.05
2c Green	.75
3c Vermilion	1.50
5c Grey	1.75
6c Brown	1.75
50c Blue	2.00
½c 1897 Leaves	.60
1c	.03
2c	.75
3c	.75
5c	1.25
1c 1897 Jubilee	1.00
3c	1.25
15c	1.75
0c	1.75
50c	1.75
2c 1898 Map, Lavender	2.00
Blue	2.00
1c 1898 Numerals	.03
2c Purple	.75
2c Carmine	.04
3c Carmine	.75
5c	.60
10c	1.50
1c 1903 Edward	.12
2c	.60
5c	.75

Type	Value
Double Vertical	
1c 1895 Yellow	.30
2c Green	1.25
5c Grey	2.00
50c Blue	2.00
½c 1897 Leaves	1.00
1c	.30
2c	1.50
1c 1897 Jubilee	1.25
3c	1.50
2c 1898 Map (Blue)	2.50
½c	.60
1c	.30
2c Carmine	.40
3c Carmine	.75
5c	.60
10c	1.75
1c 1903 Edward	.40
2c	.75

Type	Value
Double one vert.	
1c 1895 Yellow	.60
1c 1898 Numerals	.50

Type	Value
Triple vertical	
1c 1895 Yellow	.40
1c 1898 Numerals	.50

MONTREAL

QUEBEC

11

Type	Value
Type 11. Montreal (1903)	
Normal	
On 1895 50c	1.00
Double	
On 1895 50c	1.50
Inverted	
On 1895 50c	1.75
Type 11. Toronto (1903)	
Normal	
On 1895 50c	1.00
Double	
On 1895 50c	2.00
Triple	
On 1895 50c	2.25
Inverted	
On 1895 50c	1.50
Double inverted	
On 1895 50c	2.00
Double, one inverted	
On 1895 50c	1.75
Triple, one inverted	
On 1895 50c	2.25
Triple, Two Inverted	
On 1895 50c	2.25
Quadruple, one inverted	
On 1895 50c	2.25
Quadruple, two inverted	
On 1895 50c	2.25